Appreciative Management and Leadership

The Power of Positive Thought and Action in Organizations

Revised Edition

Inspire to find your greatest strength within ourselves.

Dr. Karen Norum
Gonzaga University
Spokane, WA 99258-2505

Williams Custom Publishing
Euclid, Ohio   •   1999

Copyright 1999 by Williams Custom Publishing
All rights reserved
No part of this work may be reproduced in any form,
or by any means, without the permission of the publisher.

Published by: *Williams Custom Publishing*, Div.
Lakeshore Communications
24100 Lakeshore Blvd.
Euclid, OH 44123
(216) 731-0234

Appreciative Management
and Leadership, Revised Edition

Printed in the United States of America

B C D E F G

ISBN 1-893435-05-9

This publication is designed to provide accurate and authoritative information with regard to the subject matter involved. It is sold with the understanding that the publisher is not engaged in rendering legal, accounting or other professional advice. If legal advice or other expert assistance is required, the services of a qualified professional person should be sought.
-From: **A Declaration of Principles**, jointly adopted by a Committee of the American Bar Association and a Committee of Publishers and Associations.

Visit our home page at: http://www.willese-press.com

Appreciative Management
and Leadership

*Suresh Srivastva,
David L. Cooperrider,
and Associates*

Contents

Preface   xiii

The Authors   xxi

1. Introduction: The Call for Executive Appreciation   1
   Suresh Srivastva, Ronald E. Fry, David L. Cooperrider

   Part One: Foundations of Appreciative Knowing   35

2. Shifting Context for Executive Behavior: Signs of Change and Revaluation   37
   Willis W. Harman

3. Merging of Executive Heart and Mind in Crisis Management   55
   Philip H. Mirvis

4. Positive Image, Positive Action: The Affirmative Basis of Organizing   91
   David L. Cooperrider

5. Appreciating Diversity and Modifying
   Organizational Cultures: Men and Women at
   Work   126
   Barbara Benedict Bunker

   **Part Two: Processes of
   Appreciative Interchange**   **151**

6. Affect and Organization in Postmodern Society   153
   Kenneth J. Gergen

7. Appreciative Interchange: The Force That
   Makes Cooperation Possible   175
   John D. Aram

8. The Role of Executive Appreciation in Creating
   Transorganizational Alliances   205
   Thomas G. Cummings

9. The Quest for Altruism in Organizations   228
   Rabindra N. Kanungo, Jay A. Conger

10. The Logical and Appreciative Dimensions of
    Accountability   257
    Larry L. Cummings, Ronald J. Anton

    Part Three: Processes of Appreciative Action   **287**

11. Appreciating Executive Action   289
    Peter J. Frost, Carolyn P. Egri

12. Executive Development as Spiritual
    Development   323
    Peter B. Vaill

13. The Illusion and Disillusion of Appreciative
    Management   353
    Max Pagès

Contents   xi

14. Appreciative Organizing: Implications for
    Executive Functioning   381
    Suresh Srivastva, Frank J. Barrett

15. Appreciative Inquiry In
    Organizational Life   401
    David L. Cooperrider, Suresh Srivastva

16. The Emergence of the
    Egalitarian Organization   443
    Suresh Srivastva, David L. Cooperrider

    References   485

    Index   523

Preface

Appreciative Management and Leadership is about how executives develop, nurture, and introduce high human values into organizational life. It explores modes of thought and processes of leadership that result in the most important kind of cooperation of all — the conscious cocreation of a valued future. The book rests on our belief that an *appreciative reperception* of the world will be our greatest aid in meeting the organizational and societal challenges of the twenty-first century. One of humanity's greatest gifts is that in times of profound crisis, new perspectives are forged. Such moments are *historical moments* — times when new possibilities for humanity can be established and new eras born. The search in this book is ultimately for those executive processes of thought and action by which groups and organizations develop the positive values that can guide their lives.

Background

We first became intrigued by the theme of executive appreciation in our research on professional organizations that were expressly postbureaucratic or egalitarian (Srivastva and Cooperrider, 1986). In that work — with hospitals, accounting partnerships, research and development groups, engineering departments, and even military outfits made up of computer and systems specialists—we were continually struck by how important a role positive affect, positive cognition, and processes of affirmative interaction play in organizing. At the time we did not have a definition or even a word for the appreciative processes involved. But one thing repeatedly asserted itself: the import of the *positive*. For example, just as affirmative affective states like optimism have been shown to be associated with the mental and physical well-being of individuals, the processes of appreciative management, we observed, were intimately implicated in social system health: high organizational morale, capacity for cooperation, confidence in the future, interpersonal responsiveness and caring, creative achievements, and the like.

And yet we had *no language of the positive*. To see and speak about organizational life in positive terms ran counter to our training acculturation as scientists, as organization development consultants, as critical theorists, *and* as members of the cynical society at large. Our early and clumsy attempts to speak about the affirmative sides of organizing were met with head shaking, disbelief, and sometimes even anger. Friendships were destroyed. It was almost as if by talking about organizations in terms of the true, the good, or the beautiful, one had broken a rule or committed an unforgivable heresy. And perhaps one had. From the perspective of modern science, words like *positive* and *good* are sentimental valuations that have no place in value-free research. In the critical or theoretical perspective, the positive is categorically denied. And from a problem solving perspective, the positive is utter nonsense; every good manager and organizational consultant "knows" that organizations *are* problems to be solved, continuously in need of diagnosis, problem analysis, and prioritized treatments. Even among the public at large we were confronted time and again by the harsh lesson that it was entirely unfashionable to speak about organizations, much less the executives that lead them, in positive terms. The times of naïveté, we were implicitly told, are gone. No one would be fooled by our idealistic absurdities. Both in workshops with managers and in the classroom with students, especially early on, people would look at us as if we were just peddling another empty-headed "principle of hope," or one more manipulative attempt to lure them into the chase after unattainable ideals.

Preface

In all of this we began to feel the weight of Peter Sloterdijk's vivid description of postmodern society, in which he argues that our culture is cynically disposed to a degree that scarcely any previous culture in history has been: "The late twentieth century rides on a wave of negative futurism. 'The worst is always expected,' it just has 'not yet' happened" (Sloterdijk, 1987, p. 12). Although this is not the place for a full discussion of the historical circumstances surrounding this outlook, it is clear that the pervasive sense of disillusionment that has followed in the wake of the 1960s, and the apocalyptic consciousness that comes from continual meditation on the bomb and our many ecological disasters, have become two of the most dangerous symptoms of the malaise of our times. The boom in disaster prophecies has created a pervasive numbness and sense of caution toward any hopeful perspective. No one believes anymore that today's action solves tomorrow's problems; it is almost certain that it causes them. The future, for many, will be scarcely anything more than a vaster replication of the worst in the past. Nothing can keep pace with the problematic, and because everything is problematic, it is also somehow a matter of indifference. This minimal hope in the face of maximal catastrophe, as defensive as it is, at least precludes cheap optimism. But the discontent in our culture, argues Sloterdijk, has assumed a new quality. It appears as a universal, diffuse cynicism. It has become the collective, realistic way of seeing and knowing. In a way it has become *chic* to join in the derisive laughter — every form of foolish idealism will receive its due.

This volume is the culmination of a symposium held at Case Western Reserve University in October 1988. The symposium was organized in the belief that the time was ripe for the discipline of organizational behavior to venture outside its own culture of pessimism and to help initiate a broadening of the forms of inquiry and interpretation permitted to shape postmodern society. In a world in which almost everything is under assault, it was felt that there was a need for a new vocabulary and grammar of understanding that was no longer imprisoned by the cynical, intimidated by the positive, or distorted into vacuousness by the overly wishful. Our call was for a *scholarship of the positive*.

More specifically, our hope for the symposium, "The Functioning of Executive Appreciation," was to open interdisciplinary exploration into the life-generating social and organizational forces of positive affect, cognition, and interaction. The aim, which we conveyed when inviting leading scholars from throughout the world to participate, was to stimulate inquiry into the affirmative and esthetic, the caring and altruistic, the empathic and intimate, as well as the passionate and purposeful sides of leadership and organization. For example, it was asked, To what extent is organizing a creative work? Are organizations, as cooperative systems, really caring systems, owing their existence to the altruistic intention to act in a manner that takes into consideration the interests of others as persons? To what extent do positive cognitions—perceptions and thoughts of truth, goodness, and beauty—actually focus attention and generate their own reality-producing actions? What is the role of the appreciative eye in the executive capability for constructing compelling belief systems, values, and visions? Is there a relationship between the democratic capacity for self-organization and an organization's appreciative system? Is it possible that organizational learning and innovation depend more on positive than on negative self-monitoring, and that the key to diffusion of innovation is a capacity for appreciative interchange? Perhaps organizations are arenas of human interaction whose purpose is some kind of esthetic interweaving of differences and diversities, arenas where people come together to learn how to share, to care, to cooperate, to dream, and to coproduce? Finally, is it not possible that organizations are heliotropic in character, constantly searching for and moving toward those affirmative projections or images of possibility that are the brightest and boldest, the most illuminating and inspiring?

Amidst the discourse at the symposium, it became abundantly clear that the theme of appreciation represents a fertile area for concept development. It constitutes an interdisciplinary crossroads for diverse fields of knowledge and research. For example, the literature on healing systems, athletic performance, placebo effect, hypnosis, and cognitive psychotherapy all points to the possibility that the power of positive cognition is far greater than normally assumed. Similarly, the vast movement in the area of social constructionism and interpretive sociology continues to shed light on the complex relationship between social perception and beliefs. It has shown how thoughts and beliefs govern what we look for and what we perceive, as well as how we interpret what we see through the use of traditions and conventional structures passed along to us by the groups and sociohistorical contexts to which we belong. The reality perceived — whether critically or appreciatively — is often a consequence of the reality believed, a situation that leads to self-fulfilling expectations within groups, organizations, or even whole societies. On a more fundamental level, philosophers of knowledge have argued that tacit knowing precedes all explicit thought and that appreciation is at the core of such knowing. Broadly speaking, it becomes clear that there is an appreciative component in all human knowing, being, and interrelating.

Others in the areas of management and administration have argued that the key to understanding social processes lies in an understanding of the dynamics of valuing; it is the "appreciative system" that is the source of both morals and the guiding values of cultural evolution. Of interest here as well is the solid and scholarly work on organizational culture, as well as the more speculative literature on organizational transformation. All of this seems to reveal a powerful rationale for introducing appreciative leadership. The premise of this volume is that executive appreciation is what makes for good organizing.

Brief Overview of the Contents

Appreciative Management and Leadership begins with Chapter One, which builds a contextual "showcase" for the parts and chapters that follow. This chapter presents a highly detailed overview of the book's contents. The balance of the book is divided into three parts: Part One, "Foundations of Appreciative Knowing"; Part Two, "Processes of Appreciative Interchange"; and Part Three, "Processes of Appreciative Action."

Part One focuses on appreciative knowing as a distinct experience and cognitive process by answering three questions: (1) What is appreciative knowing, and how is it distinct? (2) What are the philosophical or metatheoretical grounds of appreciative knowing? (3) Why is appreciative learning a powerful vehicle for executive ability to create?

Chapter Two submits that executive appreciation is an agent in the "global mind change" that represents a "second Copernican revolution" in Western thought. Chapter Three elaborates on the thesis of Chapter Two by analyzing a dramatic corporate takeover. In Chapter Four, the author carries the logic of appreciative knowing further by examining the assumption of impermanence. What does it mean that all social-organizational action is open to revision? The author of Chapter five examines our understanding of appreciative processes for recognizing intercultural diversities: How do people from different cultures and backgrounds come together and create a workplace where their differences are a positive, rather than a negative, factor?

Part Two focuses on postmodern society's generation of new integrative languages, processes, and methods for rediscovering our common humanity to broaden our concepts of relatedness and transorganizational action.

Chapter Six argues that executive appreciation is not a "thing" waiting to be discovered but, instead, a "language of understanding." This chapter reframes the task of social theory. In Chapter Seven, the author shows that appreciative interchange has been an underrated "way of being" in Western society. He examines how cooperation has played only a supporting role in American society and presents a metaphor of organizational life, the "prisoner's dilemma." Chapter Eight carries Chapter Seven's argument forward with respect to the challenge of interinstitutional cooperation. This author defines a relatively new field of executive endeavor called *transorganizational systems*. Chapter Nine examines altruism as the core of what we are calling appreciative interchange, and Chapter Ten focuses on the classic managerial theme of accountability and the dilemmas of responsibility toward others.

Part Three, which includes Chapters Eleven through Fourteen, discusses ways to improve our cooperative capacities. In Chapter Eleven, the authors define *appreciative action* and argue that appreciative action is not merely desirable but is a necessary condition for executives operating in a postmodern world. Chapter Twelve focuses on value systems and the organizational rediscovery and development of moral purpose and mission. The author of Chapter Thirteen sounds a note of caution, warning that theories of appreciation might become tools for human control through ideologization processes leading to lies and manipulation. Finally, in Chapter Fourteen, the authors outline emerging principles of organizing from an appreciative stance.

Audience

Appreciative Management and Leadership should appeal to both academics and executives. For educators it provides some of the most innovative thinking in the field, and taken together with the earlier volumes by Suresh Srivastva and Associates in this series — *The Executive Mind, Executive Power,* and *Executive Integrity* — it provides a state-of-the-art portrait of the human side of the executive task. For executives the book is an invitation to revisit conventional assumptions, and it provides compelling new insights into a continuing enigma: Ultimately, what exactly is leadership in the postmodern world?

Finally, this volume should appeal to researchers. It is a veritable storehouse of new hypotheses and propositions. But perhaps most important, it is an invitation to members of the discipline of organizational behavior. In the past the preponderance of organizational behavior research has called attention to the entropic forces of organizational life, the naturally fragmenting and deteriorating processes that must be offset to guarantee the survival of the system. Many of our studies have emphasized the problematic and untenable features of collective existence at the expense of the admittedly more difficult-to-study "life-giving" factors. Researchers have had a tendency to sketch a half-empty perspective, which raises the question, Have we painted a picture of organizational life that has left out a whole palette of possible colors? We hope that this look at executive appreciation will become a standard reference for all those who wish to bring more holistic understanding to the study of management.

Acknowledgments

This book has benefited greatly from the goodwill and unreserved support of friends and colleagues and from an environment favorable to appreciative inquiry. We were supported most ably by all our faculty colleagues in the Department of Organizational Behavior in the Weatherhead School of Management at Case Western Reserve University. Our faculty colleagues included Frank Barrett, Barbara Bird, Richard Boyatzis, Ronald Fry, Harry Jonas, David Kolb, Michael Manning, Susan Taft, William Pasmore, and Donald Wolfe. Splendid support was provided by a group of graduate students in our integrative seminar, which included Christine Dreyfus, Kathy Gurley, Pamela Johnson, Cecilia McMillen, Robert Niemi, Asbjörn Osland, Mary Ann Sharp, Louise Simone, Ram Tenkasi, Tojo Thachankery, Xiaoping Tian, and Shirley Wilson. These students acted as "shadow" scholars to invited authors and created a community for exciting learning opportunities. Two of our colleagues, Harry Jonas and Pamela Johnson, carried out the major task of managing the conference, and their thoughtful diligence and personal commitment was at the core of our success. Dean Scott Cowen of the Weatherhead School of Management provided personal encouragement as well as much of the financial support. We are grateful to all—and to many others who remain unmentioned.

Warren Bennis, Richard O. Mason, and Ian I. Mitroff, who are the consulting editors for the Jossey-Bass Management Series, have been continually thoughtful, supportive, and generous with their ideas and time. William Hicks of Jossey-Bass has been a true friend and guide during this whole process, and his courage and encouragement to launch new approaches in management thinking will certainly assist us in preparation for the twenty-first century. And, of course, our administrative staff—Cass Ricker, Bonnie Reynolds, and most of all Retta Holdorf—deserve special thanks for their help in preparing this manuscript.

Cleveland, Ohio Suresh Srivastva
June 1990 David L. Cooperrider

The Authors

Ronald J. Anton, S.J., is a Jesuit priest and an assistant professor of management at the Sellinger School of Management, Loyola College, in Maryland. He holds M.S. and Ph.D. degrees in organizational behavior from the J. L. Kellogg Graduate School of Management, Northwestern University, as well as an M.Ed. degree from Johns Hopkins University. Father Anton has also earned a Th.M. degree in social ethics and an M.Div. degree from the Western School of Theology (Cambridge, Massachusetts); earlier he did graduate work at Gonzaga University (Spokane, Washington) and Ohio University in philosophy and public relations, respectively.

John D. Aram studied economics at Yale University and received his Ph.D. degree (1968) from the Sloan School of Management at MIT with a specialization in organizational studies. He is professor of management policy at the Weatherhead School of Management at Case Western Reserve University and chair of the Department of Marketing and Policy Studies, and since 1984 he has been associate dean for M.B.A. Programs at the Weatherhead School.

Frank J. Barrett received his Ph.D. degree (1980) in organizational behavior from Case Western Reserve University.

xxi

He received both his B.A. degree (1975) in government and international relations and his M.A. degree (1977) in English from the University of Notre Dame. He is also an active jazz pianist. He has worked with the Cleveland Foundation, Cleveland Clinic, University Hospitals of Cleveland, General Electric, and municipal and county government agencies. His current research interests include the role of language, metaphor, and myth in group processes and the creative management of conflict.

Barbara Benedict Bunker received her Ph.D. degree in social psychology from Columbia University. She is associate professor and director of graduate studies in the Psychology Department at the State University of New York, Buffalo. She teaches social and organizational psychology and, in her role as organizational consultant, supervises the training of doctoral students who wish to become organizational consultants and trainers. Her writing and research interests are diverse but focus on the general areas of social change and organizational effectiveness. She is the author of three books and numerous articles. Recent research and writing interests include organization dynamics in periods of decline, theory of practice in experiential learning structures, commuting couples' life-style patterns, male and female patterns of competition, and the structure of organizational development in business organizations. In 1984 Bunker was a Fulbright lecturer at Keio University Graduate School of Business Administration in Japan. She is currently Fulbright lecturer at the University of Kobe in Japan.

Jay A. Conger received his B.A. degree in anthropology (1974) from Dartmouth College, his M.B.A. degree (1977) from the University of Virginia, and, after a stint as an international marketing manager, his doctorate of business administration (1985) from the Harvard Business School. Conger is assistant professor of organizational behavior at the Faculty of Management, McGill University, Montreal. Conger's research centers on charisma, executive leadership, and the management of organizational change. He is particularly interested in the role that leaders play in revitalizing troubled organizations and in entrepreneurial leadership. His work on these subjects has been published as articles in the *Academy of Management Review* and as chapters in various books. He is the coauthor of *Charismatic Leadership: The Elusive Factor in Organizational Effectiveness* (1988, with R. N. Kanungo and Associates). Conger is an active consultant to industry and the public sector.

David L. Cooperrider received his B.A. degree (1976) from Augustana College in psychology, his M.S. degree (1982) from George Williams College in organizational behavior, and his Ph.D. degree (1985) from Case Western Reserve University in organizational behavior. Cooperrider is assistant professor of organizational behavior at the Weatherhead School of Management, Case Western Reserve University. Recently he has been engaged in research on the relationship between an organization's guiding image of the future and its current actions or behavior.

Cooperrider is co-chairperson (along with William A. Pasmore) of a ten-year research study looking at global social change organizations — transnational organizations that have emerged to manage the most complex, persistent global issues of our time. Cooperrider's writings include "Appreciative Inquiry in Organizational Life" (1987, with S. Srivastva) and "The Emergence of the Egalitarian Organization" (1986, with S. Srivastva). He is currently coediting a special issue for *Human Relations* on social innovations in global management.

Larry L. Cummings is the Carlson Professor of Strategic Management and Organization at the University of Minnesota. Formerly, he served as the J. L. Kellogg Professor of Organizational Behavior at Northwestern University and as the Slichter Research Professor, an H. I. Romnes Faculty Fellow, and director of the Center for the Study of Organizational Performance in the Graduate School of Business, University of Wisconsin, Madison. He has also served as associate dean of the graduate school there. He teaches and does research in the areas of organizational behavior, organizational theory, personnel, and management.

Thomas G. Cummings received B.A. and M.B.A. degrees from Cornell University and a Ph.D. degree in sociotechnical systems from the University of California, Los Angeles. Cummings is professor of management and organization at the Graduate School of Business Administration, University of Southern California. He was previously on the faculty at Case Western Reserve University. He has authored several books, written numerous scholarly articles, and given several invited papers at national and international conferences. He is associate editor of the *Journal of Occupational Behavior,* past chairman of the Organizational Development Division of the Academy of Management, and past president of the Western Academy of Management.

Carolyn P. Egri has been trained in organizational behavior and industrial relations management and is currently completing the requirements for a Ph.D. degree in organizational behavior at the University of British Columbia. She brings to the study of organizational behavior extensive experience as a human resource management professional. Her areas of applied expertise include personnel planning, performance appraisal, employee counseling, and personnel administration.

Peter J. Frost was trained in chemistry, and later in psychology and personnel and organizational behavior. He received his Ph.D. degree (1973) from the University of Minnesota. He is the Edgar F. Kaiser, Jr., Professor of Organizational Behavior in the Faculty of Commerce and Business Administration at the University of British Columbia and also has experience in management and consulting. Frost is on the board of governors of the Academy of Management and is currently executive director of the Organizational Behavior Teaching Society. He has served on the editorial board of the *Academy of Management Review,* the *Journal of Management,* the *OB Teaching Review,* and the *Canadian Journal of Administrative Sciences.* He has also served as a special issues editor for the *Journal of Management* (on organizational symbolism).

The Authors

Ronald E. Fry joined the faculty of the Department of Organizational Behavior, Weatherhead School of Management, Case Western Reserve University, in 1978. Previously he was a research associate at the Alfred P. Sloan School of Management at MIT, where he received his Ph.D. degree in organizational psychology (1978). At Case Western Reserve University he has served as director of the Master of Science in Organization Development and Analysis (MSODA) Program. Fry's interests center on the study of management development and education.

Kenneth J. Gergen received his B.A. degree at Yale University and his Ph.D. degree at Duke University. After teaching for four years at Harvard University, he became chairman of the Department of Psychology at Swarthmore College. Since that time he has been the recipient of a Guggenheim Fellowship, a Fulbright Research Fellowship, and several grants from the National Science Foundation. He has also held visiting positions at the Sorbonne, Kyoto University, and Heidelberg University.

Gergen is professor of psychology at Swarthmore College. Among his present interests are the social construction of knowledge, the structure and function of psychological discourse, narratives of the self, and the development of relational theory. He is a fellow of Divisions 8, 9, 10, 24, and 26 and has just completed a term as president of Divisions 10 and 24 of the American Psychological Association.

Willis W. Harman is president of the Institute of Noetic Sciences, Sausalito, California, a nonprofit research and educational organization founded in 1973. The institute's purpose is to expand knowledge of the nature and potential of the mind and to apply that knowledge to the advancement of health and well-being for humankind and the planet. Harman is also emeritus professor of engineering–economic systems at Stanford University and is a member of the board of regents of the University of California.

Rabindra N. Kanungo is professor of psychology and management at McGill University, Montreal, Quebec. He received his B.A. degree in philosophy, with honors (1953), from Utkal University, India; his M.A. degree in psychology (1955) from Patna University, India; and his Ph.D. degree in psychology (1962) from McGill University. His work experience as a university professor, researcher, and consultant spans both East (India) and West (Canada and the United States). His academic and professional honors include a Commonwealth Fellowship, a Seagram Fellowship, and a Fellowship of the Canadian Psychological Association. Kanungo has published widely in both the basic and applied areas of psychology and management. His publications include more than seventy professional articles in such journals as *Experimental Psychology, Social Psychology, Organizational Behavior and Human Performance,* and *Psychology Bulletin.*

Philip H. Mirvis is an author and private consultant. He received his B.A. degree (1973) in administrative science from Yale University and his Ph.D. degree in psychology (1980) from The University of Michigan. His areas of study concern social and organizational change with a particular emphasis on the changing characteristics of the workforce and workplace. He consults with organizations in the areas of mergers and acquisitions, large-scale change programs, quality-of-work-life surveys, and the implementation of social and technological innovations. He is the author of many articles on these subjects and two edited books on organizational assessment and change.

Max Pagès has trained in psychology at the Sorbonne in Paris and received his doctorat de psychologie (1964) and doctorat ès lettres (1968) there. He also studied at Case Western Reserve University and at the University of Chicago with Carl Rogers. He was trained at the National Training Laboratories in Bethel, Maine, and later had a working relationship with them. Pagès is now professor of clinical social psychology at the University of Paris VII and is responsible for doctoral studies in clinical psychology for the Universities of Paris VII and XIII and the University of Amiens. Previously he taught at the University of Rennes, the Sorbonne, and Paris Dauphine. He began his career working for CEGOS, a European consulting firm. Pagès has made numerous trips to North and South America. He is the author of several books and many articles.

Suresh Srivastva is professor of organizational behavior in the Department of Organizational Behavior at the Weatherhead School of Management, Case Western Reserve University, and served as chairman of the department from 1970 to 1984. He received his Ph.D. degree (1960) from the University of Michigan in social psychology. Besides working as a consultant for industrial enterprises and health care systems in the field of organizational development, he is the author of numerous articles in the area of psychology and management problems. His major books include *Behavioral Sciences in Management* (1967), *Human Factors in Industry* (1970), *Anatomy of a Strike* (1972, with I. Dayal and T. Alfred), *Job Satisfaction and Productivity* (1975, with others), *Management of Work* (1981, with T. Cummings), *The Executive Mind* (1983, with others), *Executive Power* (1986, with others), and *Executive Integrity* (1988, with others).

Peter B. Vaill is professor of human systems at the School of Government and Business Administration, George Washington University, and former dean of the school. He has also served on the faculties of the University of California, Los Angeles, Graduate School of Management; the University of Connecticut School of Business Administration; and the Stanford Graduate School of Business. He holds a B.A. degree (1958) in psychology from the University of Minnesota and M.B.A. (1960) and D.B.A. (1964) degrees from the Harvard Business School. His research and writing have chiefly been in the fields of organizational excellence, strategic management, organizational development, and the philosophy of social science. He has been a consultant to corporations, government agencies, health systems, and educational institutions. He is the author of many books, including a book of essays on management, *Managing as a Performing Art* (1989).

Appreciative Management
and Leadership

1

Introduction: The Call for Executive Appreciation

Suresh Srivastva
Ronald E. Fry
David L. Cooperrider

This book is an invitation to an imaginative and fresh perception of organizations. Its scholarship is deliberately constructive. Its "metacognitive" stance is choicefully affirmative. And its central thesis—as an extension of the Lewinian premise that human action is critically dependent on the world as perceived rather than the world as it is—is substantively hopeful. Putting the matter directly, this work argues that executive appreciation is a powerful reality-producing perspective and that when seen collectively with new eyes, our organizations can be vitally transformed in ways that eclipse anything the modernist world has yet known. Organizing, in a word, is the triumph of the dynamic patterning in perspective—perhaps *even* choiceful ones.

The call for executive appreciation cannot be understood in isolation from the global context of change in which we all play a part. As is widely agreed, the age of modernism is rapidly waning. Almost every person living in the twentieth century has witnessed more world-shaping change than anyone since the Copernican revolution, and probably since the fall of ancient Rome. A whole diverse set of intellectual titans like the German social philosopher Oswald Spengler (1926), the English historian Arnold Toynbee (1972), and the Russian-American sociologist Pitirim Sorokin (1963) all believe that the massive changes we are witnessing in ethics, the arts, the sciences, philosophical thought, and other aspects of culture signify a grand tidal transformation that involves the decline and ultimate disappearance of our present civilization. In a declining civilization, observed all three historians, the leaders have lost their way while most others experience a passive if not cynical sense of drift as if experiencing their lives to be out of control. Toynbee (1972), for example, in his early travels through Europe, observed that society was already sinking into spiritual atrophy. Great advances in technology and material well-being were simply not enough and, in fact, he said, they served only to temporarily stave off the breakdown: modernist civilization, Toynbee forecast, would corrupt the world and then likely self-destruct in a terrible collapse. But after years of careful study, he still refused to declare this apocalyptic conclusion as foregone. The agony of a dying culture, he hoped, might well force people to open their eyes to the life-negating hollowness of their values. While an avowed agnostic during the time of his writing, Toynbee nonetheless urged modern people to search their souls "in a humble spirit" and to adopt a renewing stance, akin to what the great Albert Schweitzer called "a reverence for life." Only then would a vital awakening occur.

Appreciative Management and Leadership: The Power of Positive Thought and Action in Organizations is a book that champions the fullest development of our executive powers, including that special athleticism of soul known as leadership. It is an honest and penetrating search for these human processes of knowing, relating, and acting by which the highest standards of groups and organizations are generated and appropriately used to nourish the social bond. As has been said many times, the meaning of everything is under assault in this chaotic world. Many organizations have literally lost their way, and for this reason, virtually all are now in some kind of a process of deep search for a renewed sense of purpose—or soon will be. The modernist world is experiencing no temporary upset. When viewed from the eye of the postmodern hurricane, where the shared sen-

Introduction: The Call for Executive Appreciation

timents and affective ties between people have been tossed apart in an upheaval of the greatest historic magnitude, there is little question that the concerns raised by the authors of this book are among the most important in all of management thought. Every organization today, in one way or another, is affected by trends, dynamics, and occurrences for which there are no apparent "fixes" or proven tools of analysis, or even agreed-on protocols for inquiry. Let us now look just a bit further at some of the more important and unprecedented challenges that beset executives and organizations everywhere.

Enter Postmodernism

In spite of their diverse backgrounds and the fact that they worked on their essays mostly apart from one another, a remarkable number of authors of this book share in the consensus that postmodernism signifies an era of "business not as usual." Five contextual themes that run throughout this volume are crucial, then, for understanding why bringing the appreciative perspective to a new level of world discourse is one of the primary tasks of this effort.

1. Planetization and the Ecology of Interconnection. All of the authors are convinced that the postmodern organization will be a virtual seedbed for diversities of all kinds as a result of the crystallization of planetary interconnectedness. The sheer intensity of human interconnectedness is rising at staggering rates by the moment. In the less than 5,000 days between now and the end of the century, the world population will break the six billion person barrier, a number that will likely double in forty years, given current rates of growth. Such increases will be felt most in the cities where most of our organizations will be physically squeezed. Just as an example, demographics have shown that the number of people living in cities has grown from 600 million in 1950 to over 2 billion in 1986. And *megacities* are growing fastest of all. By the end of the decade, the United Nations projects over seventy-eight cities of four million or more and twenty-two megacities of over ten million. The extraordinary aspect of all of this is that it comes at a time when physical distance between people the world over has been eclipsed through the marvels of telepower. Encircling the globe, the new telepower—telecommunications, computers, robotics, and artificial intelligence—has redefined the concept of national boundaries. Three billion people, together, witnessed the opening celebration at the last Olympics. Similarly, the 1987 Wall Street crash sent instant shockwaves through the unstable global economies in every corner of the world. And since the last World War, some 20,000 new transnational organizations have emerged, many of which span at least three different countries; it is a time, too, where international trade is growing at twice the rate of domestic trade. Yet overlaying all of this is what the French have called the world *problématique,* that myriad of interpenetrating worldwide eco-economic problems that know no boundaries and tie the planet and its people into a tightening web of common fate. In its postmodern metamorphosis, the word *interconnection* has taken on a whole new meaning, the implications of which most can barely fathom, much less successfully enact.

2. *Partners in Multiplicity and Rise of the Feminine.* As the authors of this volume submit, if there is one single theme that most characterizes postmodernism, it is the theme of *multiplicity in perspectives.* Building again on the notion of primacy of perspective in guiding human action and recognizing the difficulties in valorizing one perspective over another, the postmodernist context is calling for a cooperative stance that recognizes that there are multiple ways of knowing, each of them valid when judged according to their own purposes, assumptions, or localized settings.

It is with this in mind that one must consider what management in the future will look like, especially in human terms. Futurists have forecast that the workplace of the twenty-first century is going to represent a virtual kaleidoscopic array of cultural grouping, each with their own values, aspirations, and experiences of reality. Some have argued that such melting of diversities will make us "partners in chaos"—each group believing that their world is *the* world. In one complex organization, where the authors recently gave a speech, the human resources secretariat concluded that there were more than 100 diverse cultures

Introduction: The Call for Executive Appreciation

and ethnic groupings represented in their workforce, in this one organization alone. The globalization of the workplace does not just mean operating overseas.

Clearly one of the most significant demographic factors affecting the future of the corporation will be the mass entry of women into the workforce. In sheer numbers, women are rapidly approaching men in parity. Increasingly organizations are recognizing the dysfunctional consequences of exercising double standard labor strategies whereby different sets of rules are used for different groups. The most progressive organizations are embracing the opportunity to make women full partners with men in the domain of the corporate agenda. Leaving behind the culture-annihilating theory of the "melting pot," many are now learning what it means to create settings where diverse perspectives are valued and used to expand the range of potential scenarios. In this spirit the widely expected "clash of cultures" becomes instead an adventure in learning, raising one of the most perplexing questions of all: What constitutes the nature of the "androgynous" organization where both women and men are empowered to realize their potential beyond that currently experienced as a result of management theory and practice derived primarily from male-dominated institutions?

3. *Organizing in the Midst of a Global Mind Change.* Much has been written in recent times about the dawning of postmodernism within the world of science and specifically within social theory (Harman, 1988; Gergen and Gergen, 1988; Sloterdijk, 1987; Lawson, 1985). While the voices sometimes clash and the arguments reel in complexity, there is one powerful consensus that reverberates throughout: The scientific materialism that so confidently dominated the postindustrial era and so thoroughly insinuated itself into virtually every aspect of institutional life is now a dying orthodoxy. While there is little agreement as to exactly what we are moving toward, there is no question that the shift now taking place in society's dominant metaphysic—Who are we? What kind of universe are we in? What is ultimately important?—will have a transforming effect on all our institutions.

The most important implication for our purposes is that

the whole realm of values that will rise to the forefront of inquiry. Discourse, everywhere, will be thrown open to the free play among all new and emerging value systems. We now understand, with clear and sharpened hindsight, that however successful materialist science was in providing us with the power to predict and control the universe, it had serious negative influence on our understanding and even development of higher values. More than that, it actively suppressed them by systematically transforming questions of value or ideology into technical concerns, thus working so uncritically in the service of short-term pseudovalues such as material progress, accumulation of wealth, efficiency, and the like. So if the basics of this argument are correct—that the deepest assumptions of society and science are shifting at the same fundamental level that they did at the time of the scientific revolution in the seventeenth century—then as the authors of this book submit, the postmodern twenty-first century will likely be as different from modern society as the modern was from medieval times. But since no new metaphysic will necessarily be locked in place, and since no preceding ones will be altogether negated, the questioning of value systems will surge to the fore: Value dynamics will be thrust center stage as the prime unit of relational exchange governing the creation or obliteration of social existence. Organizing, one might foretell, will no longer be confined to the metaphor of machine, but will instead be seen as *a living value system*—a multiperspective colloquy of valuing.

4. *The Future as Opportunity, Not Destiny.* The upshot of the postmodern turn in social theory is more than a gloomy epitaph for a strictly objectivist science. When closely considered, the postmodern turn begins to offer the social and organizational sciences exciting new ways of conceptualizing its primary task and its potentials. At its core, the postmodern movement revolves around the idea that organizations and societies are made and imagined and are human artifacts rather than mere expressions of some predestined natural order. As Roberto Unger (1987), in particular, has so well summed up, in all domains we are being challenged to break loose from a style of social understanding that allows us to explain ourselves only as helpless

Introduction: The Call for Executive Appreciation 7

puppets of the systems we inhabit or of the lawlike forces that have supposedly brought such worlds into being.

Recognizing that "the contextual quality of all thought is a brute fact" (Unger, 1987), the postmodern stance invites a generative conception of theory that seeks to maximize the context-revising freedom of human beings everywhere. The task of social theory, in this sense, is not only to provide a critique of debilitating assumptions and practices but to open the world to new and untold intellectual possibilities. Beginning with the powerful premise that the future is opportunity, not destiny, the postmodern thinker is invited to discover the *affirmative task of social theory* and to engage in forms of knowing that serve to make collective reality comprehensible from the perspective of human possibility. Rather than "telling it like it is," the challenge for the postmodern scholar is to "tell it as it may become." Needed are scholars willing to be courageous, to break the barriers of common sense by offering new forms of theory, of interpretation, of intelligibility.

5. *The Goodness and Decency of Human Beings and Their Institutional Creations Goes Almost Unproclaimed in Our Cynical Age.* And hence our continuing predicament (Eccles, 1984). A good example, perhaps most telling of all, comes from actual experiences at the symposium that resulted in this volume. Somewhere toward the concluding point, after hours of intensive deliberations at our three-day conference, one of the scholars confessed to a challenging group of doctoral students:

> Writing about the phenomenon of appreciation was one of the most enervating and gut wrenching tasks of my entire professional career. Every argument sounded so hopelessly naive that before it could ripen to maturity, it was consumed and shredded by literally dozens of pathetic, hopeless, and incredibly articulate critical voices, internal voices you know. At one high point of exhaustion I was convinced that all I was capable of writing was a scathing critique of any attempt to see or speak about organizations in our society in positive terms. Ridiculous. Out of

order. Dangerous. My blood boiled. My mind was literally aflame with a whole bonfire of brilliantly articulated cynicisms. But I was intrigued. I allowed myself to follow where the topic took me, which was further beyond my competence than was safe to dare. But I learned as I wrote, and what I learned was mostly about me.

As mentioned in our preface, our age is cynically disposed like no other in history. If for no other reason than this there seems to be ample justification for this work. It will be especially justified, however, if it stimulates a younger generation of scholars to expand the positive forms of intelligibility permitted to exist in organizational studies and if it challenges people to reconsider the intimate relation between theory and practice; if human society is largely a social construction, and if social theorists are indeed members of this society, then what role do social and organizational theorists play in the "scientific construction of reality"? Is it not true that alterations in conceptual practices, in ways of symbolizing the world, hold tremendous potential for guiding changes in social practice? (We must remember that at one point in the not-so-distant past there was no such thing as a "Theory Y" manager, nor a whole cadre of management consultants attempting to cultivate him or her.) Perhaps there is something self-fulfilling about our work.

What we have tried to do with this chapter so far is to build a contextual showcase for the gems to follow. Planetization, the crystallization of interconnection, partners in multiplicity, the rise of the feminine, global mind change, and recognition of the future as opportunity, not destiny — all of these form the backdrop for the call to appreciative action. Rich evidence all around us shows us that all our once trusted maps and road signs are no longer sufficient. The world requires leadership with a qualitative change in perspective. It is calling for, argue the authors of this book, a stance of executive appreciation, which by combining the pivotal ideas throughout this work can be defined something like this:

Introduction: The Call for Executive Appreciation

Executive appreciation represents a towering capacity to cognitively dissociate all seeming impossibilities, deficiencies, and imperfections in a given situation and to see holistically and compassionately into an organization as a totality and especially into that which has fundamental value. The appreciative stance awakens the desire to discover and envision new social-organizational possibilities and draws one to inquire beyond superficial appearances to the deeper life-enhancing essentials and potentials of collective existence. In all of this it creates a language and climate of interaction that embraces differences, accepts polarities, and helps create new cultures where diverse values are heard and honored. If taken deeply enough, appreciative processes of knowing and interaction enlarge our sense of solidarity with others, overcome the arrogance of prejudice and cultural blindness, and allow for the cooperative evolution of the shared values, accountabilities, and meanings that shape the collective good.

Detailed Overview of the Contents

The remaining thirteen chapters making up this book were originally written as a source of dialogue among management scholars and professionals. Their character is vibrant—intellectually alive, expansive, gutsy, and heartfelt. There is no holding back. It is all there, from the most systematically worked out concept to the most privately held speculation. All of the authors were carefully chosen not only because of their continuing intellectual leadership in the fields of management and social theory but because of their generous lifelong *commitment* to the vocation of human learning, scholarship in ideas, and contribution to the well-being of organizations and all of society. The authors were invited, therefore, in the context of discovery: ". . . to open new doors to understanding and action . . ., to view this event as a forum for sharing nascent ideas in collegial dialogue, to accept Toynbee's well known challenge 'to dare in scholarship,' and to generate systematic propositions and hypotheses for continuing explorations into the functioning of executive appreciation."

The chapters are organized into three parts: (1) "Foundations of Appreciative Knowing"; (2) "Processes of Appreciative Interchange"; and (3) "Processes of Appreciative Action." Each chapter builds on the others through complementary contrasts in level of analysis, abstraction, and metatheoretical underpinnings. As an example, vivifying case study material is juxtaposed with the more abstract renderings of a theme (for instance, Philip H. Mirvis following Willis Harman; Barbara Benedict Bunker in contrast with David L. Cooperrider). Also, where possible, major points of controversy are placed together for purposes of modeling the appreciative stance: Our task in this inquiry is not to diminish opposing views, but to include them in a holistic learning process that affirms the core that each offers to the larger theoretical structure (for example, the reader is urged to discover the larger pattern that connects Peter B. Vaill and Max Pagès). As we now turn to a brief overview of each of the contributions, we hope to show that, taken together, this group of thinkers have succeeded, even if only in some small way, in opening the boundaries of our field to those underappreciated aspects of our organizational world.

Part One: Foundations of Appreciative Knowing. The chapters by Willis W. Harman, Philip H. Mirvis, David L. Cooperrider, and Barbara Benedict Bunker form a natural unity in their conviction that appreciative knowing is a distinctive experience and cognitive process that simultaneously appreciates, values, and constructs that which has fundamental meaning. Each author, in his or her own way, deals with elements of three basic questions: (1) What is appreciative knowing, and how is it distinct from a critical, deficiency-oriented comprehension and/or a detached objectivism inherent in conceptions of logical empiricist science? (2) What are the more philosophical or metatheoretical grounds of appreciative knowing and how do we conceive of appreciative knowing in relation to today's global mind

Introduction: The Call for Executive Appreciation 11

change? (3) Why is appreciative apprehension a powerful vehicle for executive knowing and creating? Is it really a "towering capacity" that leads to "systemic wisdom" with far-reaching implications?

The importance of the topic of executive appreciation, submits Willis W. Harman in Chapter Two, is that it *is* an agent in the "global mind change" emerging in virtually every quarter, spreading around the world, changing everything. Significant recent changes in our images of the executive and our metaphors of organizing do not occur in isolation; they are part of a larger pattern in society, and it is to this pattern — signs of change in society's prevailing picture of reality — that this scholar so clearly addresses himself. Modern industrial society, like every society in history, has rested on a set of largely tacit assumptions about who we are, what kind of universe we live in, and what is ultimately important. The core of the global mind change we are in, proposes Harman, is a transformation from a social knowledge system that views the basic stuff of the universe as matter-energy to one that recognizes, especially in the sociobehavioral area, the macrodeterministic primacy of mind. The scientific materialism that so confidently dominated modernist society, argues Harman, is a dying orthodoxy. We are in the midst of a "second Copernican revolution" in that no such change has occurred in Western thought for four centuries.

There is no need to dwell here on the details of Harman's thesis. The mountain of literature from which he draws is there for all to see: Kuhn's analysis that "progress" in knowledge proves, on closer inspection, to be socially constructed shifts in ways of seeing; Sperry's "scientific heresy" involving recent developments in mind-brain research that clear the way for a macrodeterminist concept of mind and values; relevant lessons from hypnosis and exceptional capacities research, and more. It is all solid work. Yet the full story is not told, and this is what Harman's vocation is about. In the midst of the ruins of our former value systems, we need processes of knowing that allow for a scientific restructuring of the world, a *revaluation* that brings questions of values from subsidiary to focal concern. We must recognize, Harman challenges, that the whole pattern, the whole underlying premise of Western science, has masked questions of human value and has led inexorably to the kinds of problems and dilemmas we now face: *It is impossible to create a well-working society on a knowledge base that is fundamentally inadequate, seriously incomplete, and mistaken in its basic assumptions.*

For Harman, executive appreciation bespeaks a form of knowing that is capable of shaping possible new worlds. Embedded in a broader mosaic of "participatory science," appreciation is described as a knowing process that recognizes the power of mind and the importance of *compassionate consciousness* in allowing for the cooperative evolution of the shared meanings and values that guide our lives. The restructuring of the world that is occurring today, concludes Harman, has implications that are so far reaching that one can easily imagine all our institutions being profoundly affected.

Philip H. Mirvis, in Chapter Three, provides a vivifying account of Harman's thesis in a case analysis involving a dramatic corporate takeover. Disbelief, uncertainty, anxiety—these are typical first reactions of executives faced with corporate takeover. And for good reason, says Mirvis. Studies have found that seven out of ten mergers and acquisitions are failures. Half of all executives in target companies are dismissed or depart in less than one year. Win-lose dynamics creep into every exchange. The language of acquisition is replete with negative images of "war," "rapists," and "raiders." During such periods, crisis perception is narrowed and distorted. Self-interest is paramount as managers find themselves vying for the top spots. Similarly, in the face of the overwhelming impact of organizational *cultural differences*, let alone the affective tides of fear and anger, executives themselves (in the midst of it all) begin to question the futility of such "rational" efforts. In a word, one is placed squarely in the eye of the postmodern hurricane of multiple realities, overwhelming change, clash of cultures, and the like.

There is something deep at stake here, argues Mirvis. For him the topic of appreciative management is not just another soft-hearted human relations approach used to make people feel good. Recognizing that finely formed, high-minded ideas about executive appreciation might well be met with head shaking and

Introduction: The Call for Executive Appreciation

disquiet, and might be presumed nice but not necessary for getting the job done, Mirvis demonstrates that such prejudgment is naively mistaken. Executive appreciation, concludes Mirvis, is the process of knowing that which uniquely gives rise to the "systemic wisdom" that has the force of "correcting the world" even during moments of crisis management. After a detailed account of the myriad of factors that contend against the appreciative mindset, Mirvis usefully provides a set of insights into the values and cognitive processes of two executives who discovered creative ways of building a whole new enterprise by drawing on an appreciative analysis of the strengths of each company: "All notions of takeover, of victor and vanquished, were dismissed," declared one of the executives.

If he had left the matter here, Mirvis's storyline might appear nothing more than an exercise in optimism, a rhetoric of hope. But the case study contains another lesson about the executive epistemologies underlying the appreciative modes of knowing. Paralleling Harman's argument for a participatory scientific metatheory, Mirvis outlines the holistic worldview that appeared to guide the executives' appreciations—that is, how they perceived the world around them and their acts of appraisal and valuation. Most important, illustrates Mirvis, it is a worldview that forms the basis for a synergistic view of organizing, for example, "like strings on a harp." The appreciative executive, concludes the author, is a leader who, even under severe crisis conditions, is able to create "mind-expanding," "heartrending" settings that empower people to an enlarged view of the organization which transcends and encompasses the new whole.

David L. Cooperrider, in Chapter Four, carries the logic of appreciative knowing an important step further. His is an empassioned, provocative call for a process of knowing that propels the postmodern social constructionist and mentalist paradigms "to the hilt." At the heart of such thought is the assumption of impermanence: No matter what the durability to date, virtually any pattern of social-organizational action is open to revision. There are no iron laws. Viewed as the product of broad social agreement, whether tacit or implicit, patterns of organizational action are not fixed by history or nature in any automatic physical, economic, technological, or environmental way. Cooperrider is emphatic in his conviction that social thought needs to give a larger role to human beings' context-revising freedom. Thus, he explores the thesis that the artful creation of positive imagery on a collective basis may well be the most prolific activity that individuals and organizations can engage in if their aim is to help bring to fruition a positive and humanly significant future.

Appreciative ways of knowing are powerful, submits Cooperrider, precisely because organizations are, to a much larger extent than normally assumed, *affirmative systems* — they are guided in their actions by anticipatory "forestructures" of positive knowledge that, like a movie projection on a screen, project a horizon of confident expectation which energizes, intensifies, and provokes action in the present. The forestructures or guiding images of the future are not the property of individuals but cohere within patterns of relatedness in the form of dialogue. Appreciation is thus the source of positive guiding images that have "heliotropic potential." In this view appreciative inquiry refers to a process of knowing that draws one to inquire beyond superficial appearances to the deeper life-enhancing essentials and potentials of organizational existence (like Harman's compassionate consciousness). A key point here is that appreciation is not merely a synonym for admiration: It represents the creation of new values and new ways of seeing the world through the very act of valuing. As Nietzsche once put it, "Valuing is creating: hear it ye creating ones! Valuation is itself the treasure and jewel of valued things" (in Rader, 1973). Appreciative knowing, concludes Cooperrider, is the mental capacity that allows a leader to peer into the life-giving present only to find the future brilliantly interwoven into the texture of the actual.

In Chapter Five, Barbara Benedict Bunker treats all of us to one of those rare and moving essays that come alive through personal experience and undeniable contemporary relevance. "We are at the edge of knowledge," she concludes, when it comes to our understanding of appreciative processes of knowing intercultural diversities. Futurists have forecast that the workplace of the twenty-first century is going to represent a kaleidoscopic

Introduction: The Call for Executive Appreciation 15

array of cultural and ethnic groupings — each with their own values, worldviews, aspirations, and experiences of reality. Some have argued that such a meeting of diversities will make us "partners-in-chaos" — each group believing that their world is *the* world.

So how, asks Bunker, do people from different cultures and backgrounds come together and create a workplace where their differences are embraced rather than becoming a source of dominance and conformity pressure? One thing here *is* certain: We will be dealing with feelings, attitudes, unconscious assumptions, and perspectives that are difficult to understand, much less change. This, says the author, suggests that whatever process is used, it has to be deep; it must deal with affect, and people must change themselves before they will be able to make informed decisions that create new models of organizational functioning.

Appreciative knowing, proposes Bunker, is a deep and powerful way of helping members of different cultures understand and value their differences and create a new culture where diverse values are understood and honored. It means affirming the whole of another culture, including those aspects that may seem less desirable. Appreciation is, in this sense, an antidote to both arrogance and ignorance; it fights the tendency to "see our way as superior." All of this is illustrated in an innovative case study of a large chemical company attempting to create a system for the purpose of apprehending the gender-related differences of the male and female cultures. By looking at American social construction of gender, and the gender-related aspects of social construction, the organization expanded its cocreative capacity to construct a valued future. The power of appreciation, Bunker concludes, is that it allows for a reperception of cultural diversity: Diversity is no longer that which divides us, it is that which unites us. There it is in a nutshell. These words cannot be taken lightly, since it will be impossible to both fear diversity and enter a cocreative postmodern future at the same time.

Part Two: Processes of Appreciative Interchange. Not only does postmodern society signal the revisiting and probable reconstruing of many of our traditional value systems, it also brings with it unprecedented increases in heterogeneity and diversity, including all the corresponding challenges of parochialism, ethnocentricism, single-value fanaticism, economic and cultural imperialism, and sheer confusion based on innocent cultural blindness. Operating in a dynamic arena of multiple values, temporary relationships, and multi-interactive consequences — and where complexity is feeding on itself and growing exponentially — the postmodern organization is understandably fraught with schisms of all kinds. There is, as many in this section point out, considerable confusion about the nature of integration.

A core challenge of the present era, submit the authors in Part Two, is the generation of new integrative languages, processes, and methods for rediscovering our common humanity and postures that help us break through our historical refusal to accept the human condition of plurality. Like it or not, argue the authors here, we have all been socialized into a world of theoretical individualism that has buried a sense of community, that has made a mockery out of basic notions such as altruism, and that had led to widespread "tragedy of the commons." The effort in Part Two is to be applauded, because it represents a beginning of a broad expansion in the forms of relatedness permitted to prosper in organizational life. Confirming our basic proposition that appreciative processes are among today's most promising discoveries, this section covers, for example, how appreciative interchange makes transorganizational action possible; it looks at how appreciation can become the broadest integrating capacity that allows people to discover that common interests lie above interests of any particular group or above personal interest; and it suggests that there may be an isomorphic relation between the emergence of postbureaucratic egalitarian forms and the human capacity for appreciative interchange. Perhaps most important, the authors throughout this section serve to expand our *social vocabularies* of understanding that revive the capacity for identification with the life of "the commons" — and awaken it anew from its condition of dormancy in the parochial frame of Western society.

Kenneth J. Gergen opens the intellectual drama of Part

Introduction: The Call for Executive Appreciation 17

Two with a bold assertion in Chapter Six: There is no such "thing" as executive appreciation. We have little idea — unless we have given long thought and study to the issue of empiricist and postempiricist metatheory — how important and far reaching this assertion really is. To read Gergen, therefore, one is treated to one of the most articulate renderings of the topic, especially in his perspective on the postmodern turn in social constructionism. While it would be misleading to say that this broad movement is also a new one, as its roots are properly traced to earlier eras, Gergen takes a look at its current metamorphosis in postmodern thought and envisions that the time has now come to fashion a social-organizational science of vital significance to society.

Executive appreciation, he takes as an example, is not a thing, something "out there" in the external world waiting to be discovered and documented. No, argues Gergen, "it" is a *language of understanding* that appears today to have broad potential for becoming a significant reality-producing perspective. Its generative potential can be traced to a number of sources: The language of appreciation appears to have great potential for enhancing our social vocabulary of understanding; it is distinct enough from contemporary renderings in management thought to stimulate reconsideration of that which is "taken for granted"; and it is bold enough to compel us to furnish new alternatives for an enriched relational view of life.

This chapter provides a profound reframing of the task of social theory. An essential calling of this volume and all of social-organizational theory in general, says Gergen, is to generate theoretical languages that have rhetorical power — the power to enliven, compel, delight, and transform. In this view, the primary task of the theory is not to reflect accurately on what is the so-called case; our future does not lie in the enterprise of holding mirrors to nature. Rather, social-organizational discourse is a cultural resource for the world of reality-in-the-making. "To renew, refresh, and enrich this discourse is to make not an insignificant contribution to cultural life," states Gergen.

Why are we so compelled, asks the author, by a topic like executive appreciation? Is it true, as others have said, that because we have been living in such a competitive, abrasive, and insecure world, where relationships are impersonal and easily fractured, that we are developing a "hidden hunger" to be loved a little bit? Gergen points out that such issues of affect have somehow been left out of most accounts of organizational functioning. The language of appreciation is crucially important, then, because it reminds us that organizations are arenas of human interchange, replete with the interplay between the cognitive, conative, and affective realms so well described by William James. *Appreciation does not exist apart from the relational dance in which two or more persons participate.* Even further, proposes Gergen, the language of appreciation also helps to transform our conventional notions of the "self" beyond the confines of the skin-encapsulated ego and to view it as a dynamic property of the socius. Most important (and building on the self-as-relationship metaphor), the language of appreciation does not valorize one perspective over another; its call is for a kind of epistemological humility never known to the hegemonic character of thought in the modern world. In all of this, one thing shines through in this chapter: The number one agenda of the twenty-first century is to learn the art of "serious play" amidst the cacophony of voices in a multicultural, postmodern life.

In Chapter Seven, John D. Aram shows that appreciative interchange has been a conspicuously underappreciated way of being in Western society, particularly in America. Suggested in Aram's work is the proposition that appreciative interchange is the force that makes cooperation possible; yet "cooperation is the short suit in the cultural deck of cards we have been dealt." Historically, cooperation has played only a supporting role in the cast of values structuring American society. In fact, one wonders—as Aram has—how processes of appreciation and regard for others can be fully experienced both inside organizations and between institutions without a larger wholesale revision of our broader social philosophies.

Drawing on the metaphor of organizational life as a "prisoner's dilemma," Aram fashions a theory of executive appreciation as the broadest integrating capacity that allows people to discover that common interests lie above the interests of

Introduction: The Call for Executive Appreciation

any particular group or above personal interests. The integrative process, in any organization, can be increased, suggests the author, to the extent that individuals representing opposing values redefine their assumptions, not at the loss to others, but in *addition* to their success. In essence, appreciative interchange functions as a "yes/and" rather than "either/or" form of interaction. The prisoner's dilemma is a powerful metaphor, argues Aram, because it (1) calls for an awareness of the dynamic character of interdependence in relationships; (2) teaches that collective existence is a set of possibilities that will become what we as individuals concretely contribute; (3) demonstrates that vulnerability is a fact of mutual dependence, hence the importance of trust; and (4) experientially demonstrates that reality is largely an experience created by our assumptions about self and others.

So what do we do? The author admits that the massive force of American business ideology (excesses of individualism, zero-sum competitors, laissez faire capitalism, individual property rights, and so on) creates a steep incline for the traveler of appreciative systems. And yet, intensive interdependence is now a fact of life and is challenging executives to create new, complementary relationships at the institutional level, such as cooperatives, networks, research consortia, associated industries, and global partnerships. Thus, in designing more cooperative institutional relationships, Aram models how executives can make sense of large systems in ways that generate possibilities for collaboration (in this case the win-win option). The concepts and tools for enhancing appreciative interchange are unmistakably at hand. The key question Aram submits is, Will we choose to use them?

In Chapter Eight Thomas G. Cummings carries Aram's argument forward with respect to the challenge of interinstitutional cooperation. He draws our attention to the transcendent capacity of appreciative interchange by labeling and defining a relatively new field of executive endeavor: *transorganizational systems*. The transorganizational system, says Cummings, is a hybrid mechanism whereby single organizations join together for common purposes such as sharing information, carrying out joint research, coordinating services, understanding complex projects beyond the capacity of any one organization alone, joining R&D forces, and solving communal problems. The 1980s witnessed rapid proliferation in the area of transorganizational systems and most of these represent radical departures from the values and assumptions underlying bureaucratic modes of collective action. Needless to say, there are many differences in the transorganizational form, but most of these systems are postbureaucratic in the sense that they operate under more egalitarian principles of consensual decision making and shared governance. There is no hierarchical authority in the sense of one organization having chain-of-command authority over another, subordinate organization. The intriguing proposition to emerge from Cummings's discussion is that appreciative interchange might well be the foundational concept for explaining the creation and development of successful egalitarian transorganizational systems. Complex, egalitarian systems could not exist or even be understood without an understanding of the (socially constructive) appreciative process required to make transorganizational action possible.

Building on Vickers's work the author explores how executive appreciation involves the art of merging reality judgments with judgments of value. In the transorganizational arena appreciative interchange involves (1) the discovery of the possibility of collaboration, (2) the establishment of positive vision and recognition of the actualities of shared fate, (3) the building of an experience-based trust, (4) the creation of a deliberately supportive environment for the mobilization of a fragile consensus, and (5) the establishment of a cooperative structure of shared governance. The challenges of transorganizational leadership are among the most difficult in executive life. Integrative visions, values, and structures must be created and enacted in a nonauthoritarian relationship among institutional equals. Differences must be embraced. They need to be more synthetic than analytic. Uncertainties and complexities abound. And consensual decision making—value-intensive decision making—must be fearlessly approached in often brief time frames inviting representative persons in temporary face-to-face

Introduction: The Call for Executive Appreciation

settings. Indeed, concludes Cummings, appreciative competence is a complex, social, political, and analytical skill that is rarely taught; yet it is crucial for managing nonhierarchical arrangements involving lateral relations across organizational boundaries. This then raises the obvious unanswered question: Is it possible to consciously and programmatically develop, nurture, or educate for executive appreciation? If so, then how?

In Chapter Nine, Rabindra N. Kanungo and Jay A. Conger enact Gergen's earlier conviction that one of the most important tasks of the present-day organizational theorist is to generate illuminating social vocabularies of understanding. Thus, Kanungo and Conger begin with the observation that the organizational sciences have been severely limited through a continuing romance with the ideology of "self-contained individualism"—the belief that each of us is an entity separate from every other with a sharp boundary that ends at one's skin. Their case in point is a powerful one: Not one major textbook in the field of organizational behavior shows reference in the subject index to the word *altruism*. Does this mean that altruism is nonexistent in organizational life? Obviously, the question is a rhetorical one.

For Kanungo and Conger, altruism is at the core of what we are calling appreciative interchange. Altruism, they suggest, represents a selflessness that manifests itself in voluntary acts intended to help or benefit other people, regardless of the beneficial effects such behavior has on the benefactor. The voluntary and altruistic act is a ubiquitous phenomenon, they contend, and is an expression of our essential relatedness with one another ecologically, socially, and spiritually. The authors hasten to acknowledge that altruism is everywhere around us, even in organizations, if we only care to look. The real dilemma, they suggest, is that the inherent propensity toward altruism goes almost unproclaimed in the overwhelming cacophony of individualist ideology permeating Western organizational theory. Describing it as a "virtue that is alien to capitalistic economics," Kanungo and Conger provide an incisive analysis of the anti-altruistic values of laissez faire capitalism, Darwinian notions of survival of the fittest, and the theory of self-contained individualism traced all the way back to Europe in the beginning of the second millennium A.D. Just like all theories in social sciences, theoretical individualism is not some neutral conception exploring the workings of some external world "out there" waiting to be objectively recorded. According to Kanungo and Conger, the theoretical individualism that permeates most of our management thought and education has contributed to the tragedy of our world commons and to a widespread self-fulfilling perception in the public mind that executives are self-centered, egotistical, and devoid of moral obligation toward the interests of others (according to recent surveys). The major task of the current time, conclude the authors, is to cultivate concern for the larger community rather than our present indifference.

From this point of view, Kanungo and Conger's medium is also a message for researchers. We each have a choice of what to spend our careers studying and writing about. Through research we take part in either cultivating or destroying concern for the larger community merely by bringing attention to some topics while obscuring others (for example, the conspicuous absence of the subject of altruism from organizational behavior texts). The choice of what to study, how to study it, and what to report implies some degree of responsibility. Because the conduct of organizational inquiry cannot be separated from the everyday negotiation of reality, such research is, therefore, a continuing moral concern, a concern of social reconstruction and direction. The act of topic choice really is the message.

Our final entry in this section on appreciative interchange is a conceptual refiguration of the classic managerial theme of accountability. The dilemmas of responsibility toward others, argue Larry L. Cummings and Ron Anton in Chapter Ten, lie at the center of our understandings of organizational coordination and integration; accountability is the locus of a web of expectation, the predictability and endurance of which are part of the social bond, an important force holding organizations together. Accountable behavior is entirely a social concept, so that this chapter—like the other chapters in this section—emphasizes the social context of humans in organizations.

Introduction: The Call for Executive Appreciation 23

Any claim, submit the authors, to an adequate understanding of executive behavior must include considerations of who holds whom accountable, for what, and in what manner.

Building on the work of Robert Bellah (1985) in the popular study *Habits of the Heart*, Cummings and Anton develop the "appreciative dimension of accountability" in a radically different fashion from conventional models that see accountability primarily as a control mechanism for monitoring. They propose that when (1) work is seen as a vocation that demands that we utilize our unique gifts for service to others, and when (2) parties involved in an accountability exchange value each other as unique human beings worthy of the dignity and respect of persons, the accountability process is qualitatively transformed from monitoring to mentoring. Accountability, in this reframing, can become an energizing force in the enactment of growth promoting mentoring relationships whose consequences include more shared responsibility and action, deeper bonds of collaborative interest and sense of mutuality, and joint meaning making (versus verbal justifications or rationalizations). Because of its broad implications, the model proposed here certainly deserves further research. It is an invitation, conclude Cummings and Anton, to place relational issues of affect — in this case positive affect — at the forefront of organizational behavior scholarship.

Part Three: Processes of Appreciative Action. Sir Geoffrey Vickers was fond of telling anecdotes to make his complex ideas come alive in the hearts and minds of people everywhere. One such story, "The End of the Free Fall," is especially apropos as an introduction to Part Three. Briefly, it is the story of the man who fell from the top of the Empire State Building; in his descent he was heard to say to himself, as he whistled past the second floor, "Well, I'm all right so far."

This story, submits Vickers, caricatures two absurdities into which we often fall. One is the absurd speed with which we come to accept as normal almost any outrageous condition, once we have actually lived with it, even if only briefly. The other is the absurd slowness with which we come to accept as real any impending change that has not yet happened, however near and certain. Both tendencies exist. Perhaps, says the realist, they evolved for our protection. But they do become absurd when they come to threaten everything and all that we value—as may be happening today. We are living in a time of "free fall."

The call to appreciative action that the authors voice in this section comes as we stand at the threshold of the last decade of the twentieth century. It is a time when the recognition is growing that we are, as yet, still infants when it comes to our cooperative capacity for building a global community congenial to the life of the planet and responsive to the human spirit. For many people throughout the world the possibility of appreciative life is anathema: The image of the future engenders a sense of fear, defeatism, and despair. Repeatedly we are warned about the consequences of nuclear winter, mass starvation and poverty in the midst of plenty, the impending collapse of our ecosystems and species, and unprecedented numbers living in states of human degradation and misery. Yesterday's optimism has been all but extinguished; it grows clearer everyday that the time of free fall is coming to an end.

In this section, Peter J. Frost and Carolyn P. Egri, Peter B. Vaill, and Max Pagès argue that it is precisely during an Age of Endarkenment that we need perspectives that offer positive pathways for dealing with our dilemmas and that can move us to inspired (spiritual) action; that there *is* a need for perspectives large enough to embrace the fact that we are living, valuing beings—and to place that value-centric fact at the core of our studying of the leadership equation. Taken together, a new model of appreciative action is presented that (1) refers to the degree to which executives act on values that transcend sheer material conditions of the world, (2) is guided by the constructive intent to produce enduring change for the betterment of self and others, (3) achieves the creative integration of traditional polarities, and (4) results in new vision and practice for the collective good. However, there is one important voice of caution. As the end of this free fall approaches, the hypermodern world falls prey to any number of insidious defense mechanisms intended to distort reality and bury all conflict in utopian fantasy and empty promise. When used pathologically for the exploitation of persons, appreciative action might well be transformed into a defensive and aggressive means by which individuals and social systems use ideals and the promise of positive values to indirectly perpetuate unresolved conflict. Yes, it is true that we need certain paranoia as regards executive appreciation. But more than qualified hope, we need greater understanding; we must learn to distinguish between the creative and destructive uses of the appreciative process. We need, contend the authors of Part Three, a tough-minded call to appreciative action if we are to make a genuine contribution.

The promise of a constructive and creative new paradigm is intoxicating — so begins Chapter Eleven, coauthored by Peter J. Frost and Carolyn P. Egri. In a most comprehensive treatment of the theme of executive appreciation, Frost and Egri challenge scholars and leaders everywhere to recognize that appreciative action is not merely desirable but is a necessary condition for executives operating in a postmodern world. The journey toward appreciative action, they insist, is worthy of our deepest commitment. But what exactly is meant by the term *appreciative action*?

To answer this complex question, Frost and Egri artfully compose a set of definitions, a script, and a new metaphor reframing the executive role. In this working conceptualization, appreciative action has four essential dimensions: (1) It is action that is guided by the positive intent to produce enduring change for the betterment of self and others; (2) it is inspired by the art of seeing the invisible; (3) it is guided by, and contributes to, new vision and practice for the collective good of the organization and society; and (4) it empowers others to reach toward their highest potential. Such action is scripted, propose the authors, in response to the three fundamentally unanswerable questions of "What is right?" "What is right to do now?" and "Who is doing things right?" Of particular interest to Frost and Egri are the realistic visionaries in contemporary society (like Lech Walesa) who appear as magicians to those locked into old modalities. Leaders like Walesa are magical, state the authors, not only because they have an appreciative eye for seeing creative linkages where others have not (seeing the invisible), but because they are masters at transcending dichotomies of all kinds. The magician, in this sense, respects the validity and merit of opposing sets of values; he or she thinks with a "both/and" mentality. The magician works and moves with differences instead of trying to overpower them. The chapter ends on a pragmatic note, recognizing that the admittedly ideal conceptualization will be challenged by both a roadblock and a hazard. The roadblock: Modern industrial society was built on models that are essentially hierarchical and authoritarian; it was built around premises of men's power of domination and control over nature and others. The hazard: At this moment, all people on earth are confronted daily with imminent and growing threats of universal catastrophe in nuclear war and unimaginable environmental destruction. In a world where such issues are now responded to in terms of probabilities rather than possibilities, the authors pose an important query that all of us must share: Whether such a future is inevitable or whether fundamental change in society, its organizations and its leadership, can be effected to avert such an outcome.

We are now positioned for the passionate critique and the very important suggestions put forward by Peter B. Vaill in Chapter Twelve, "Executive Development as Spiritual Development." In a superbly original piece of writing that champions the fullest development of our executive powers, Vaill's words have potential for shocking our discipline out of its complacency: "The problems I am talking about . . . are the most important contemporary problems in management"; "It is a scandal that there should be so little discussion of them in the mainstream of management education and development"; "I am genuinely embarrassed for myself and my colleagues that we should, by and large, be leaving these deep questions of executive character unaddressed."

For Vaill, the centerpiece or superordinate datum and concern of the disciple of organizational behavior should be the full spectrum of human values, their workings, and their vital development. Especially in this period in history when so many organizations have lost their way, when values continue chronically to be in doubt, and when executives (mostly privately) anguish over the haunting choices handed them in an era of turbulence,

Introduction: The Call for Executive Appreciation 27

change, paradox, and contradiction—it is here, in the momentary present, that the discipline of organizational behavior can hopefully rediscover its own small sense of moral purpose and mission. For Vaill, organizations are "living value systems." The executives and others who comprise them are therefore living value systems. And to be sure, as used here, this phrase is not meant to be yet another interesting but empty metaphor. Social existence *is* fundamentally structured by human values. *Organizing is the interplay among living value systems.*

If one accepts this premise, the import of this author's effort to "develop a new vocabulary and grammar of spirituality" is easy to grasp. Striking out against views that have so thoroughly technicalized and intellectualized the job of the organizational leader, Vaill defines the spiritual not as a private holiness but as the feeling people have about the fundamental meaning of who they are, of what they are doing, and of the contributions they are making. Appreciative action *is* inspired action. In this context the spiritual refers to the degree to which executives act on values that transcend sheer material conditions and events of the world. The best leaders, in Vaill's observation, are able to reach deeply into themselves for inspiration, for courage, for spirit, and if we are not talking about these qualities, then we are not talking about leadership.

This means that questions must be raised about modern higher education, especially business management, which is primarily oriented to technique rather than values and toward competency acquisition instead of the liberalization of the mind. According to Vaill's logic, if an executive college were to be created and were to be worthy of its name, it would be one whose whole curriculum and pedagogy would be designed to strengthen that special quality of soul that creates leadership. It would be a program that seeks to develop (1) multivalued thinking that emphasizes "as-if" possibilities over "either-or" judgments, (2) inquiry processes that include the power of empathy and passionate reason, (3) methods of spiritual development that would be group based and shared with others, (4) capacities for valuing and experiencing the spirit of others (a prerequisite to multicultural understanding), and (5) a new spiritual vocabulary of understanding. The main point, concludes Vaill, is that it makes little sense to talk about leaders inspiring others if the leaders' own spiritual condition is not also considered. One wonders what our MBA programs might look like if they substituted, for example, the word *spirit* for *profit*. A more difficult question is, Can such sources of appreciative action be taught?

In Chapter Thirteen, Max Pagès begins in complete and utter protest against the theme of appreciation, including its fantastic hopes and basic trust in human possibility. Just as Karl Marx spoofed the idealizations of the early utopian socialists, Pagès sounds a postMarxian cry and provides a sobering note of advice. For, according to Pagès's studied analysis, we have now entered a hypermodern era, an Orwellian period whose basic concern is the control and elimination of conflict. The real danger, warns Pagès, is that theories of appreciation might well become strategic tools for human control — "I fear it may be used to create an illusion so distinct from reality that one could view it as a defense mechanism rather than a visioning process grounded in reality."

The caution Pagès articulates is an important one. It is precisely because human beings are valuers that they are vulnerable to processes that illuminate compelling ideals. The risk of appreciation, argues Pagès, is that when used as a tool for exploitation it can result in ideologization processes leading to lies and manipulation as a form of living. The hypermodern organization, explains Pagès, is one that controls individuals, not through the authoritarian coercions of classical capitalism, but because it has a grip on individuals' own ideals and meanings promised but never fulfilled. In the hypermodern world of "double discourse" the unpleasant takes on a pleasant look, oppression is beclouded in the name of freedom, and questions of genuine integrity are increasingly replaced by a public relations industry whose sole purpose is to manage people's consciousness and beliefs. In a word, the hypermodern society is masterful at ideological and psychological *seduction*. Pagès concludes, however, that ideals are a central and essential part of organized existence. Thus, in an interesting turn, he proposes the following: The very weapons used by the hypermodern or-

Introduction: The Call for Executive Appreciation 29

ganization to limit individual and group autonomy can also be used to enlarge it. Yet there must be caution: Utopia too often drowns in its own discontent. Illusion makes one vulnerable to disillusion. All this is summed up in the author's concern about the call to appreciative action: Perhaps we should find out the exact amount of paranoia we should maintain in regard to executive appreciation.

Finally, in Chapter Fourteen, Suresh Srivastva and Frank J. Barrett expand the concept to one more metalevel of inquiry: appreciative organizing. Taking to heart the premise that appreciative leadership has important potential in shaping postmodern organizations, they set out to outline emerging principles of organizing from an appreciative stance. The exciting message in their work here is that examples already exist. Readers will no doubt be able to find examples of appreciative organizations—or parts of them—in their own experience once they see those of the authors. Beyond showing that the effects of executive appreciation are "real," the authors help us expand our lenses or perceptual frames and provide a road map for what to focus on in building or making the transition to an appreciative system. Among their frame-breaking propositions for appreciative organizations are the concepts of "generative distinctions" and "expansive promises" as ways of defining work; continuous creativity and "openness to breakthrough" as an antidote to planning; "responsibility for the whole" as the source of member identity; and "commitment to valuing" and "committed listeners" as procedural mechanisms to empower people to push the boundaries of their own potential. As the capstone piece to this volume, the authors fulfill the promise in this introduction to break our current frames for viewing and understanding organizations in a way that is exciting, invitational to future inquiry, and generative in that it adds to our ideas without rejecting our experience to this point.

Implications for Executive Functioning

It is clear from the richness and breadth of the scholarly works just described that the theme of appreciation represents a fertile arena for concept development. We and our colleagues in this inquiry are passionately convinced that appreciative leadership can have a powerful role in the real world—that there is or should be an appreciative component in all human knowing, human relating, and human being. This is particularly relevant to the study of executive functioning because executives' primary tasks set the tone, shape, and texture of how knowledge is acquired and how members relate in the enterprise. As "meaning makers" (Jonas, Fry, and Srivastva, 1989), executives construe the world around them in ways that make collective action possible. In doing so they focus on three core tasks: to envision the future for the organization based on knowledge from their experience, to lead a collective sense-making process about how the organization works and can work toward a vision, and to enact steps and processes to transform the organization based on collective views of what is required (Srivastva and Associates, 1983). Executive appreciation is a particular stance toward these three core tasks: a way of knowing and perceiving the present that generates visions of the possible; a way of relating with others in making sense of shared experiences so that collective action is desirable; and a way of acting or being that, in itself, enables the executive to provide a life-giving force to the continuity of everyday organizational reality. As a starting point for the detailed inquiry and consideration of the works that follow, we suggest the following propositions or premises as the bases for understanding executive appreciation.

An Appreciative Stance Toward Knowing: Executive appreciation embodies the discovery and utilization of social science knowledge that heightens the "generative potential" of social systems in a postindustrial society. To the extent that all social-organizational theorizing—on which visions are formed—is an intervention into the ongoing social construction of reality, we must seriously grapple with an important question of responsibility: Isn't it possible that through our assumptions, choice of topics, frame of reference, and methodological approaches, we largely create (envision) the world that we later discover? In this context, appreciation is a selective perceptual process that apprehends "what is" rather than "what isn't." It represents

Introduction: The Call for Executive Appreciation 31

in the executive the capacity to be selectively attentive to the lasting, the essential, or the enlivening qualities of a living human system. Appreciative management is thus a process of valuing that requires in the executive a rigorous ability to dissociate all seeming imperfections from that which has fundamental value.

Appreciation reflects a transcendent function, one that accepts polarities, synthesizes differences, and lies in the sphere between an untransformed world and a transforming vision. Executive appreciation operates to both construe and create a climate where people can picture and debate the polar opposite of what has been declared in order to keep alive the possibilities suggested by new ideas and innovations. Thus the appreciative executive models and leads a process of inquiry into people's experiences of the organization by embracing relational dynamics, simultaneity, holism, requisite variety, the causal impact of consciousness, and shared meaning as "real" phenomena.

An Appreciative Stance Toward Relating: Executive appreciation includes the active process of valuing and affirming the worth of others via interaction and dialogue. Caring for growth-promoting relationships as the core foundation of any social system is fundamental to this stance we are describing. Such an executive exhibits more than the simple sentiment of liking or agreeing. Care is a state in which something does matter; it is the opposite of benevolence, tolerance, or apathy. Heidegger ([1927] 1962) thinks of care as the basic constitutive phenomenon of human existence. The effect of appreciation and care is ontological to organizational action: People initiate because they care, they organize because someone or something matters.

Appreciative executives, therefore, seek in daily interchanges with others to deliberately create supportive contexts where exploration, experimentation, and self-generated development are made possible. They make verbal accounts, search for meaning, direct, and probe from a sense of themselves as beings in the organization—not mere roles—and intentionally interact with the expectation that something new will result from the exchange.

An Appreciative Stance Toward Action: Executive appreciation is embodied through acts of dialogue, shared decision making, and celebration of others. It is through such acts that people feel a sufficient degree of essentiality required for the maintenance of commitment, a sense of identity with the whole, and a spirit of volunteerism. Appreciation, as a conscious act, calls executives to shift to a more positive perception and articulation of the world around them; this is no less realistic than other assumptions but is far more likely to lead to a constructive response. In other words, the executive leads from a core belief that organizing is not so much a problem-to-be-solved as it is a solution-to-be-embraced.

Talk is key to the executive's work (Jonas, Fry, and Srivastva, 1989), and the language of positive affect, affirmation, and appreciation is both subtle and often metaphorical. Because complex communication is frequently difficult in the workplace, the language of appreciation is often enacted through indirect mechanisms like sagas and myths, metaphors, and verbal imagery. The appreciative executive must, therefore, be able to see and describe the tacit realms of human interaction and cultural experience.

Our final proposition or premise for exploring executive appreciation is that, in sum, it is this stance toward knowing, relating, and acting by the executive that results in good organizing. The good executive is appreciative and can create an appreciation organization. The role of appreciative cognition, interchange, and affect is far more important to the life of social-organizational systems than is ordinarily assumed. Executive appreciation is powerfully related to an organization's capacity for managing novelty (genesis, innovation, surprise), for managing continuity (consensus, cooperation, community), and for managing transformation (envisioned, planned change).

Throughout these notions about executive appreciation is the intent to be generative, in ways of knowing what our experience tell us, in ways of relating with others to achieve common sense, and in ways of being oneself in a social-organizational system. The use of language to shape new possibilities, reframe old perspectives, and excite new commitments is the

Introduction: The Call for Executive Appreciation 33

common tool of the appreciative executive. His or her work becomes talk that embodies the invitational, caring, inclusive, transcendent, reciprocal, cooperative, courageous, and spiritual characteristics of leadership expressed in the works contributed to this volume. The appreciative executive becomes a scholar, colleague, and sculptor of conversations that seek to give new voice to the mystery, not mastery, and wonder, not problems, of organizational life.

PART ONE

Foundations of Appreciative Knowing

2

Shifting Context for Executive Behavior: Signs of Change and Revaluation

Willis W. Harman

This paper examines the changing context within which a topic like executive appreciation is viewed.

Particulalry in business, we have recently seen significant changes in the image of the executive. The metaphor of the corporation as an organism is frequently heard: It is made up of more or less autonomous smaller organisms, and exists in and interacts with a larger whole, and executives play a far more organic role than in the past. Management was once defined as the direction of resources (including human resources) to accomplish a predetermined task; it is coming to have more to do with enabling individuals to respond creatively to a changing situation. Management was the wielding of power; it is more and more *giving away* power. Intuition is increasingly honored in management; alignment around a shared vision and purpose is a recognized characteristic of the creative organization. Executives are finding that for corporations to attract and hold the most creative people (and hence to compete in the national and global markets) they have to become cooperative and caring systems, in which appreciative relationships are based on shared meaningful activity.

Such changes as these do not occur in isolation; they are part of a larger pattern in society. It is that pattern that we seek to understand here. This volume is focused on the study of executive behavior through appreciative inquiry. It aims at opening an interdisciplinary exploration into the life-giving, generative forces of positive affect, cognition, and interaction in organizations—at stimulating inquiry into the affirmative and esthetic, the caring and altruistic, the empathic and the intimate, as well as the passionate and willful sides of executive leadership and organization. The context of such an endeavor will have much to say about the success of the endeavor and the interpretation of the outcomes. In this contribution I will be exploring indications of profound change in that context.

Conflicting Pictures of Reality in Modern Society

Every society throughout history has guided itself by some tacit answers to the great questions, Who are we? What kind of universe are we in? What is ultimately important? The accepted answers to these questions amount to an assumed set of underlying metaphysical assumptions. Whatever this prevailing picture of reality is, it affects all of our thinking about such topics as human development, organizations, and the values guiding organizations. There are contemporary indications that the prevailing picture of reality may be changing, that is the context within which we need to view executive appreciation. It is a context within which we can explore not only how executive appreciation influences management toward the old goals, but influences reassessment of the organizational goals as well—a context within which we completely reassess what we might mean by making management "better."

Modern society is distinguished by turning to empirical science for its answers to these fundamental questions. There is considerable justification for this. The scientific view has been, in its way, outstandingly successful—yielding both technological and predictive successes—and hence has gained tremendous prestige. It is increasingly accepted as the nearest we can come to a "true" picture of the universe. On the other hand, the cosmos described by modern science is devoid of meaning and lends no support to the profound spiritual insight of thousands of years of human experience.

Sir Geoffrey Vickers, who made significant contributions toward a sociology of management, was one of the earliest to use the term *appreciative system* for the source in society of morals and values and cultural evolution. He wrote of the important contribution of the scientific attitude, saying of it that "It is a morality which at its best is one of the noblest elements in the appreciative system of the West . . . It is precious in every field and every level of inquiry" (1968, p. 167). At the same time he argues that the worldview of modern science is biased, inadequate, and misleading when used as a guide to social action.

Most people guide their lives on the basis of some (unscientific) concept of the human spirit, some sense of essence that goes beyond the material. For a majority, probably, there is some real sense of contacting the numinous and of at least secretly giving it an important role in their lives. But at the level of society and its institutions, and certainly at the planetary level, there is no consensus. There is no agreement as to whether or not we live in a spiritual universe, and if so which version of the spiritual picture should be accepted—Christian, Hindu, Islamic, shamanistic, Theosophical, or any other.

The modern society has been attempting the impossible. We have been trying to manage our own lives, our societies, and our planet on the basis of two mutually contradictory views of reality, the scientific-materialist and the spiritual. But both of these views are limited. Within the spiritual view there is no evident consensus after one gets past the most general propositions. And the adequacy of the scientific view is basically questionable because of its systematic neglect of those deep inner experiences from which all societies have, throughout history, obtained their sense of ultimate meaning and guiding values.

Generations have puzzled over this contradiction between the scientific and the spiritual descriptions of the cosmos. Surely two such discrepant pictures of reality could not both be right! Yet there seemed no satisfactory way to choose one and discard the other. The differences in individual and social implications were too important to ignore. It did not suffice, as some urged, to simply pass off the conflict as "two complementary images, like the wave and particle nature of light"; the confrontation was too direct.

The Historic Peculiarity of Western Science

The materialist, behavioral science predilection of Western science had, by the middle of the twentieth century, become dominant—particularly in the United States. Nevertheless, there remained a suspicion on the part of many scientists as well as nonscientists that something was wrong with the scientific picture since it seemed unable to deal adequately with

- Complex "instinctual" behaviors of organisms that appear to require a teleological explanation
- Behaviors of humans and other organisms that imply a choosing "self"—volition, intention, paying attention, comprehension, and so on
- The realm of social organization and social action, and the meaning underlying systems of social groupings and societies
- Self-awareness, conscious awareness
- Creativity, intuition, and other experiences that imply an unconscious "self" or component of the "self," or perhaps a "higher self"
- Reported phenomena involving mind or consciousness that "do not fit"—for example, paranormal phenomena such as clairvoyant "remote viewing" and psychokinesis

Since the discovery of unconscious mental processes, it has been apparent that Western science, like the belief system of any other society, *could* be fundamentally mistaken. For what has been discovered, through experimental work in hypnosis and a great variety of other areas, is our inescapable tendency to see and experience the "reality" we are unconsciously programmed to see and experience. The most obvious demonstration of this is in the area of hypnosis. Through hypnotic suggestion, I can be led to perceive what is not there, or to fail to perceive what is there (according to other observers, at least). Because of the suggestions, I may experience limits that are not there, or transcend limits that all my previous experience had led me to believe were there. But enculturation works exactly like hypnosis. Persons who grow up in any society are "culturally hypnotized" to perceive reality the way that culture experiences it. Furthermore, the tests that are applied in a given culture prove out, consistently revealing that reality indeed is the way everybody believes it is. Science, then, does not offer such a uniquely true picture of reality as we may have thought. In its present form it is a cultural artifact of Western society, and it could in certain respects be quite misleading. The fact that science does so well at prediction and control is somewhat less significant than it may have appeared to be at the peak of our scientistic self-confidence.

The scientific development in Western Europe in the seventeenth and eighteenth centuries early became characterized by the following three assumptions:

- The *objectivist* assumption, that there is an objective universe, more or less separate from and independent of the observer, which can be explored by the external probes of scientific inquiry, and which can be approximated, progressively more precisely, by analytical models
- The *positivist* assumption, that what is scientifically "real" must take as its basic data only that which is physically observable
- The *reductionist* assumption, that scientific explanation consists in explaining higher-order phenomena in terms of more elemental events (for example, gas temperature in terms of the motions of the molecules; human behavior in terms of stimulus and response)

These characteristics have seemed so integral to the scientific method that it was hard to imagine they would ever be replaced.

Yet many scientists today—probably most—would admit that science has moved away from the strict behaviorist, determinist, positivist, reductionist dogma that prevailed at mid-twentieth century. What is not at all clear is what we are moving *toward*.

Characteristics of a Restructured Science. As I implied earlier, the realization has been spreading recently that somehow science seems to miss important aspects of human experience. Although the quiet rebellion takes some cultish and bizarre forms, the growing interest in such areas as Eastern religious philosophies, yoga and meditation, channeling, near-death experiences, imagery approaches to healing and education, paranormal phenomena, and so on has made clear the public's dissatisfaction with the scientists' exclusive claim to valid truth seeking. In the area of executive development, a host of new forms of workshops and seminars are teaching techniques and concepts (such as the power of inner imagery and affirmations, of vision and purpose) that simply do not fit into the still-influential reductionistic worldview.

In the historical development of science there were good reasons for an initial limiting of the scope of the new inquiry—to the aspects of reality that are physically measurable, and to explanations that are nonteleological and reductionistic. One of the consequences, however, has been the necessity to deny the validity of a host of phenomena that do not fit within those limits. As a result, a tremendous amount of effort has gone into defending the barricades against, or explaining away, these outcasts, including miraculous healings and psychic phenomena, but also more ordinary experiences such as volition, intention, conscious awareness, selective attention, and the hunger for social meanings.

How to deal scientifically with the mystical, the paranormal, and the miraculous has long been a most perplexing puzzle. The more rigorously the methodologies of science were applied, the more the claimed phenomena appeared to disappear; and yet under other nonlaboratory conditions the reports persisted. The idea that the presence or absence of the phenomena might have something to do with the state of mind of the observer met with less than enthusiastic response on the part of most scientists.

A challenge to the adequacy of present science comprises an integral part of the outlook of recent New Age movements in North America and Europe, although it is not always clearly articulated as such. It amounts to, simply and brashly, a proposal that science be reformulated. The proposed basis for the reformulation is the "redefinition of the possible." Instead of starting with a limiting bias and having to defend against the anomalous, let us start with the assumption that *any class of inner experiences that have been reported, or of phenomena that have been observed, down through the ages and across cultures, apparently in some sense exist and have a face validity that cannot be denied.* The need then is for a science to accommodate all that exists. (There are a lot of subtleties involved, of course. Whole societies can perceive things that observers from other societies do not, so one has to be very cautious about claiming that some class of experiences is universal, even in potential.)

What would be the nature of such a reformulated science? Three aspects stand out as probably essential.

1. *From Objectivism to Participation.* The first of these has been described by Henryk Skolimowski (1988) as complementing the Western "yoga of objectivity" with a "yoga of participation." The method of scientific objectivity, he observes, amounts to a training of the mind to see the world in a selective way—a way that is detached, objective, analytical, coldly clinical. Becoming a scientist involves many years of training in this "yoga of objectivity." The untrained person, for example, is not able to see through a microscope what an experienced microbiologist would see. The naive person does not sense, as the trained scientist does, general laws underlying diverse physical phenomena.

As the shortcomings of "objective," atomistic science have become more apparent, the need has been increasingly expressed for a more holistic science—one that can deal better with wholes, such as a whole ecological system or a whole human organism. Wholeness implies that all parts belong together and partake of each other. Each is a part of the whole; each participates in the whole. Thus *participation* is an implicit aspect of wholeness. In participatory research (in contrast to objective research, where the observer tries as far as possible to separate himself or herself from that which is being observed) one gains knowledge by *identifying with* the observed. Rather than objective consciousness, participatory research involves *compassionate* consciousness. This involves training, but of a very different sort from the training of objective consciousness. Just as the yoga of objectivity prepares the ground for objective research, so a yoga of participation is necessary to prepare one for participatory research. (Something like a yoga of participation is currently involved in the education of psychotherapists and cultural anthropologists; it used to be part of the training for systematic biology, where connoisseurship is so essential. In most areas of modern science, however, the yoga of objectivity comprises essentially the entire training.)

Nobel Laureate Barbara McClintock is one of the rare scientists who has stated publicly what others confess secretly — that participatory methodology, identifying with what is being observed, was an important aspect of her research. She has described how in her research with chromosomes in corn cells, "I found that the more I worked with them, the bigger and bigger [the chromosomes] got, and when I was really working with them I wasn't outside, I was down there. I was part of the system . . . It surprised me because I actually felt as if I was right down there and these were my friends. . . . As you look at these things, they become part of you" (in Keller, 1985, p. 165).

This kind of intuitive approach is not antithetical to that of objective science; rather, it is complementary. The rational/analytical and the intuitive/compassionate are, in a sense, aspects of each other. Morris Berman (1981) makes a strong case that an adequate science cannot be based on attempting to know Nature from the outside, through controlled experiments in which phenomena are examined in abstraction from their context. With participatory research we understand that Nature is revealed only in our relations with it, and phenomena can be known only in context (that is, through participant observation).

Strict interpretations of objectivity and of reliability through replication are inappropriate in participatory research. But if they are, there must be other criteria something like these that *are* appropriate. Perhaps as the tradition of participatory research matures, something like the Buddhist ideal of "nonattachment" will replace the concept of strict objectivity, which, as is well known, no longer seems to fit even the relatively dependable area of the physical sciences. And something like "trustworthiness" (perhaps established on the basis of multiple imperfect tests) may replace strict reliability through replicability of controlled experiments.

The method of "appreciative inquiry" (Cooperrider, 1986; Cooperrider and Srivastva, 1987) would appear to be an example of participatory research adapted to the task of guiding social action.

2. From Reductionism to Holism. Few would gainsay the accomplishments of reductionistic science. For the purpose toward which it evolved—prediction, manipulation and control of the physical environment—it is superb. The issue is whether it needs to be complemented by another kind of science that can deal more adequately with wholes, with living organisms, and particularly with human consciousness.

Holistic science departs from the reductionist faith that the whole can be explained from knowledge of the component parts. Living organisms have emergent properties that are not predictable from their physics and chemistry (for example, tropisms of plants, or instincts of animals). Similarly, science dealing with human consciousness involves concepts beyond those needed to describe nonsentient organisms. Thus there is a natural hierarchical relationship among the sciences, higher levels of organization involving more holistic concepts.

Nobel Laureate Karl Popper (Popper and Eccles, 1981) has suggested one form that such an arrangement could take (see Figure 2.1). Imagine a bookshelf with four shelves, the bottom one labeled "Physical Sciences." In the books on this shelf nature is deterministic, explanations are reductionistic, reality is physically measurable: This is "hard science." In the books on the second shelf, labeled "Life Sciences," we find concepts like "organism" and "survival instinct" and "system function" that are more holistic, often teleological, and do not reduce at all to concepts that would fit on the bottom shelf. The third shelf up is labeled "Human Sciences" and includes the social sciences. Here are found still more holistic concepts, such as "consciousness" and "volition" and "culture." I will discuss a possible fourth shelf labeled "Spiritual Sciences" shortly.

Note that the biological phenomena described in the books on the second shelf are not completely reducible to the phenomena of the physical sciences. Similarly, the experiences of humans, described in the books on the third shelf, are not completely reducible to phenomena found in the life sciences. Each level contains concepts that are *emergent* in that system level and not pertinent to the levels below. Living organisms have emergent properties not predictable from their physics and chemistry (for instance, tropisms of plants, or instincts of animals), and so on.

Statements made at these different levels tend to be *complementary* in their relationship to one another. For example a description of the process of digestion (biological level) complements the descriptions of the enzyme-food interactions and the pumping action of the stomach (physical sciences level). The evidence that attitude and stress (psychosociology level) can seriously interfere with the digestive process is not contradicted by the apparent physical determinism of the physical sciences level.

It is worth noting that acceptance of this hierarchical idea implies that the universe is *not* deterministic. It is not possible, in principle, to predict the state at the level of biology, for example, through knowledge of the state at a lower level, no matter how complete.

3. From Positivism to Consciousness as Causal Reality. In the positivistic faith, consciousness is epiphenomenal; that is, it is derivative from the physical and chemical processes going on in the brain and need not be separately understood. In our everyday life experience, consciousness is primary; it is through

Figure 2.1. The Bookshelf of Knowledge.

Downward Causation ↓	Spiritual Sciences
	Human Sciences
	Life Sciences
	Physcial Sciences

Upward Causation ↑

conscious awareness that we understand anything at all. Nobel Laureate Roger Sperry has been more forceful than most in insisting that science cannot be adequate until it recognizes "inner conscious awareness as a causal reality" (Sperry, 1981).

In a recent paper Sperry (1987) urges inclusion of what he terms "downward causation," according to which "things are controlled not only from below upward by atomic and molecular action but also from above downward by mental, social, political, and other macro properties. [Furthermore,] primacy is given to the higher level controls rather than the lowest." Up to now, scientific explanations have largely involved an attempt to understand the higher level in terms of the lower. But as Sperry points out, to reap the full benefits of the scientific mode of inquiry (especially to derive from it value and ethical implications), it will be necessary to give scientific validity to the complementary explanations—of the lower level in terms of the higher.

The combination of these latter two ideas (hierarchical structuring and downward causation) has been described by Popper as leading to a "new view of evolution and a different view of the world," and has been hailed by Sperry as a "consciousness revolution in science." But it is only in the context of the "redefinition of the possible" identified earlier that its revolutionary significance becomes fully apparent.

Further Characteristics of the Emerging Science. These three aspects combine to give us a potential restructuring of science that allows the outgrowing of a number of generations-old problems (such as "free will versus determinism"). Some of the phenomena and experiences reported at the higher hierarchical levels have in the past received rather harsh reception by scientists. One class of these in particular, which come under the heading of spiritual and religious, have played a very significant role in history and in the shaping of our social institutions— yet science has in the past tended to be rather unaccepting of these matters, insisting that the phenomena could not happen or the experiences have no meaning.

The three characteristics just discussed do not entirely define the new science. It is worth remarking on several others.

In addition to what has already been said about the role of the observer in participatory research, one other important point should be noted—the fact that in such research the experience of observing brings about sensitization and other changes in the observer. *A willingness to be transformed is an essential characteristic of the participatory scientist.* Anthropologists who would see other cultures clearly must allow that experience to change them so that the new cultures are seen through new eyes, not eyes conditioned by the scientists' own culture. Psychotherapists who would see clients clearly must have worked through their own neuroses, which would otherwise warp perception. Social scientists who would use the method of appreciative inquiry to understand and guide organizational arrangements and processes will almost certainly be changed through their involvement with the "miracle of organizing." Scientists who would study in the area I have termed "spiritual science" have to be willing to go through the deep changes that will make them competent observers.

In the past, scientists have tended to insist that teleological and value-focused questions are not appropriate to science. (Of course, some such questions have always been asked, for example in the area of health sciences. A question about the function of some part of the body's regulatory system is teleological, and certainly a question about what leads toward health is value-focused.) The argument has arisen because of confusion about levels in the hierarchy. Teleological questions have no place at the level of reductionistic science of physical reality. At the next level, however, it *is* appropriate to ask about the function of elaborate instinctive patterns in animal behavior. At the level of the human sciences, volition may be acceptable as a causal factor and personality is a meaningful construct. At the suprapersonal level, questions about "other kinds of consciousness" achieved in meditative states, and guidance of choices by some kind of deep intuition, may be meaningful.

It seems clear that the new science will in some way have to deal with subjective reports of deep inner experience. When this proposal has been put forward in the past (for example, in introspectionism, phenomenology, gestalt psychology) the idea was rejected by the main body of scientists. Perhaps it will come forward now in more sophisticated form. At the level of "physical reality" admissible data are primarily in the form of quantifiable physical observation. At the organism level somewhat more holistic kinds of observations (requiring subjective judgment) become important—for instance, instinctive behavior patterns, or the functioning of the digestive system. Self-reports of inner, subjective experience become relevant at the personal level, and essentially comprise the sole source of data at the suprapersonal level.

The Significance of the Scientific Restructuring

It is easy to miss how radical a shift all this really amounts to, and how pervasive its effects will be on social institutions. We are not merely speaking of a proposed reformulation of science; we are examining the possibility of a fundamental shift in the metaphysical foundations of modern society.

What and Where Is Consciousness? Biologist George Wald, another Nobel Laureate, describes how toward the end of his life as a scientist he had come to a startling conclusion: "A few years ago it occurred to me that . . . I had always thought of consciousness, or mind, as something that required a particularly complex central nervous system and was present only in the highest organisms. The thought now was that mind had been there all the time, and the reason this is a life-breeding universe is that the pervasive, constant presence of mind had guided the universe that way. . . . Our growing scientific knowledge . . . points unmistakably to the idea of a pervasive mind intertwined with and inseparable from the material universe. This thought may sound pretty crazy, but such thinking is not only millennia old in the Eastern philosophies but arose again and again among the monumental generation of physicists [Eddington, Schrödinger, and Pauli, among others] in the first half of this century" (personal communication, 1988).

It has been part of the arrogance of Western science to ignore the findings of those research laboratories that have existed for thousands of years and turned their attention particularly to the depths of human inner experience—namely the monasteries of both Eastern and Western religous groups. The idea that underlying the world's spiritual traditions might be a substrate of potentially universal human experience was introduced in the West by a number of Indian scholars, including Swami Vivekananda and Sarvepalli Radhakrishnan, and popularized in the West by Aldous Huxley in his little volume *The Perennial Philosophy* (1945).

The key finding of such searches for the common core in ancient traditions and contemporary insight might be expressed as follows:

1. In each of the world's major spiritual traditions there tends to be one or more *exoteric* or public forms, which are characterized by certain beliefs, rituals, traditions, and so on. There is also to be found in each case an *esoteric* or inner-circle understanding of the tradition. This latter tends to centrally involve some sort of spiritual discipline, meditative practice, yoga, and so forth, and to emphasize inner experience over outer belief and ritual.
2. In general, the exoteric forms of religion in the various traditions tend to be very different, one from the other. However, the esoteric forms are remarkably similar, varying mainly in emphasis. The core of this universal esoteric religion, found in each of the world's spiritual traditions, has sometimes been termed the *perennial wisdom* because of its tendency to recur across cultures and down through centuries.
3. Furthermore, this esoteric knowledge is more *outside* the present form of science than directly in opposition to it. The confrontations of science with religion have been mainly with specific doctrines of the exoteric forms.

Thus the possibility seems greater than ever in history that a common, potentially universal human experience would come to be recognized as underlying all religions, and that there could be essential agreement about the nature of the spiritual reality so experienced. (No doubt the world will always contain a diversity of religious efflorescence, just as there are a diversity of colorful flowers. But at the level of metaphysical assumptions there must be common ground, or else no one can claim to have an adequate representation of reality.)

We thus see the possibility of a potential restructuring of science that permits the resolution of some generations-old problems. One of the most important of these is the reconciliation of the human experience of spirituality with the material world picture presented to us by the investigations of science.

The Possible Transfiguration of Modern Society. Let us put this development more clearly in a historical context. The seventeenth century in Western Europe can reasonably be taken as the birthdate and birthplace of modern society. That century saw the scientific revolution, the capitalist revolution, the first of the modern liberal-democratic revolutions (in England), and the "invention" of the nation-state. By the end of the century the defining characteristics of modern Western society were in place — centrality of the economic and technology-centered institutions, rising demand for democracy and equity, unbridled national sovereignty, and "reality" defined by science. These characteristics account for the astounding successes of modern society; they are also the source of the global dilemmas we now face.

Underlying these characteristics is a prevailing image of reality, and it is that which most fundamentally distinguishes modern from medieval society. For a person living in the medieval world, the earth as the center of the cosmos is the seat of change, decay, and Christian redemption. Above it circle the planets and the stars, themselves pure and unchanging, moved by divine spirits and signaling and influencing human events by their locations and aspects. The universe is alive and imbued with purpose; all creatures are part of a Great Chain of Being, with human beings ranked between the angels and the lower animals. The working of enchantments, the occurrence of miracles, the presence of witches and other beings with supernatural powers are, if not commonplace, assumed to be quite real and consequential. The kinds of dichotomies that come so naturally to the modern mind — human beings versus nature, facts versus values, science versus religion—simply do not exist (Berman, 1981).

This image of reality was displaced by the scientific revolution—one of the great watershed epochs in history. The world perceived by the educated person in Western Europe in 1500 was still the world of the Middle Ages. By 1700 "scientific heresy" had become so widely accepted that the informed person literally perceived a different reality, much more like today's. He or she saw essentially a dead universe, constructed and set in motion by the Creator, with subsequent events accounted for by mechanical forces and lawful behaviors. In this picture human beings are separate from, and potentially controlling of, nature.

As the hypnotized person may see things that are not there or fail to see things that are, so when the "cultural hypnosis" shifts, "reality" is transformed. It was not just that people now believed that the earth went around the sun, or even that the web of meaning had been displaced. The change was far more fundamental. It essentially consisted of a different perceived universe, and a different basis on which truth was to be decided—a shift from the ecclesiastical authority system of the Middle Ages to the new authority system of empirical science. As we now know, when the picture of reality changed, everything changed. The spread of the "scientific heresy" affected not just scientists, but everyone.

By the latter part of the twentieth century it was becoming apparent that, however successful science might be in providing the power to predict and control in the physical world, it had a serious negative influence on our understanding of values. Its effect was to undermine the common religious base of values and to replace it with a sort of moral relativism. Into the vacuum came, as a kind of pseudovalues, economic and technical attributes—material progress, efficiency, productivity, and so on. Decisions that would affect the lives of people around the globe, and generations to come, were made on the basis of short-term economic considerations. The "technological imperative" to develop and apply any technology that could turn a profit or destroy an enemy came to endanger both the life-support systems of the planet and human civilization.

Shifting Context for Executive Behavior

Thus in recent years we have seen the rise of a "new heresy." Like the "scientific heresy" of several centuries ago, it essentially amounts to a widening group of people discovering that their experienced reality is not like what the established authorities have been telling them. Both in the broader society (in interest in various meditative disciplines, mind-body approaches to health care, arcane studies, and religious philosophies) and in the scientific community, there are indications of a reexamination of the long-accepted tacit metaphysical assumptions of modern society.

The prevailing metaphysical assumption of modern science has been that the basic stuff of the universe is matter-energy. Whatever consciousness is, it emerged out of matter at the end of a long evolutionary process. Whatever can be learned about consciousness must ultimately be reconciled with the kind of knowledge we get from studying the physical processes of the brain.

The metaphysical assumption implied in the "perennial wisdom," which could well become that of the reformulated science, finds the ultimate stuff of the universe to be consciousness. Mind or consciousness is primary, and matter-energy arises out of universal mind. Individual human minds are not separated (although individual brains appear to be); they connect at some level not accessible to ordinary conscious awareness. The physical world is to the greater mind as a dream image is to the individual mind. Ultimately, reality is contacted, not through the physical senses, but through the deep intuition. Consciousness is not the end product of material evolution; rather, consciousness was here first!

We cannot say at this point that these *will* be the new assumptions; we can say it is quite likely that they will be. If things turn out that way, the impact on all institutions of society, and on the course of history, will be as great as have been the effects of the scientific revolution.

Regardless of whether the new metaphysic can be clearly identified, there will almost certainly be some fundamental transformation of modern society. The demonstrated inadequacy of the present scientific worldview has produced an imperative:

It is impossible to create a well-working society on a knowledge base that is fundamentally inadequate, seriously incomplete, and mistaken in its basic assumptions. Yet that is precisely what the modern world has been trying to do.

If these surmises are correct and the metaphysical assumptions underlying modern society are shifting at the same deep level that they did at the time of the scientific revolution, the "transmodern" society of the twenty-first century is likely to be as different from modern society as that is from medieval times. The task of anticipating the form of management and executive leadership in "transmodern" society is analogous to forecasting the shape of the modern business organization from the mid-seventeenth century.

And yet we can be aware of the transition in a way that our seventeenth-century European counterparts could not. We can examine the forerunner changes that are already observable in the business world, and can anticipate the kind of social transformation that would result if those values and outlooks came to prevail. Perhaps in transmodern society it will really be true that organizations are essentially arenas of interaction where people come together in order to learn how to care, to nurture, to cooperate, and to love.

3

Merging of Executive Heart and Mind in Crisis Management

Philip H. Mirvis

Disbelief. How could this have happened? Uncertainty. What does it mean for me and my company? Anxiety. Can I cope with what might happen? These are the first reactions of executives faced with a corporate takeover—followed by rage, self-doubt, and insecurity as new ownership takes charge. The emotional pattern tracks the stages of shock and grief experienced by those who face death or suffer tragic loss: First there is denial, then anger, then vulnerable executives "bargain" with their families and co-workers, with their old bosses and new ones, in a desperate attempt to clarify their future and sort things out. Finally, there is a stage of resolution, where losses are acknowledged, career decisions are made, and executives get on with their working lives. Studies show that a great many choose to leave their firms. Lamilie Associates found that nearly 50 percent of top managers in target companies voluntarily depart within one year. Another 25 percent plan to leave within three years.

However, there are executives who stay with their companies, who openly defend traditional ways of operating, and who proactively develop the terms of the combination with new ownership. Lester Richardson, former CEO of the DC Corporation—a 1,000-person manufacturing firm—stayed this course. Richardson was a "wounded leader" following his firm's acquisition by GrandCo in the late 1970s. DC had been hit by an unfriendly takeover attempt by a well-known raider and was then purchased by GrandCo, a conglomerate thirty times its size, in a "white knight" acquisition. Richardson was a vigorous, task-oriented leader right after the takeover bid, and, according to peers, "the leader we like him to be" in making the deal with GrandCo. Then he went through weeks of depression, suffering from the loss of personal authority, the break up of his board of directors, and constant challenges to his company's independent way of doing things. One morning his wife called a DC confidant and fitfully reported that "Les just doesn't want to get up today."

Richardson and his top team knew that they had to come to grips with the situation, regain the confidence of wary managers, and reassure worried employees. They also had to learn to work effectively with new "superiors" at GrandCo. This would require soul searching and the mourning of loss. The group would then have to respond to the threatening situation with purpose and determination.

The emotional set of executives on the other side of a takeover is quite another story. Winners savor, for a time, the thrill of conquest. Martin Burlingame oozed confidence and self-satisfaction the day after his company, Alpha, an industrial giant, launched a successful bid to purchase Omega, another Fortune 100 company, in 1986. Burlingame had spent months plotting the takeover attempt and had a clear vision of how the combined company would succeed in the marketplace. Remember: DC and Richardson had been "hit by a truck" as a takeover target. Burlingame, by comparison, was in the driver's seat—and his company was poised to run over Omega.

Harry Levinson (1970) reports that conquering companies are impelled to consolidate their gains after a successful bid, for they fear a subsidiary will turn on them. Alpha had won the takeover battle and many of its top executives were relishing the prospects of what one termed "raping and pillaging." But Burlingame was preaching a different message—promising there would be a partnership between the two companies. He wanted to create a new company, with a new identity, to be staffed by a new team that drew from the best of both organizations. One of Alpha's executives lamented, "Martin spends all his time with

Merging of Heart and Mind in Crisis Management 57

Omega and is bending over backwards courting their executives." Many others felt betrayed.

Still Burlingame had nights of sleeplessness. Top Omega exeutives had generous "golden parachutes" and could leave, profitably, at any time. His own executives began to lobby for decisions that would grant them new powers and more sway. Could he get people to work together? Burlingame would have to "psych out" key executives, some of whom in Omega were suffering through loss and some of whom in Alpha were already denigrating their counterparts.

There were also organizational challenges: putting functions together, making divestitures and staff reductions, and satisfying customers nervous over future product line, upgrades, and service. Vacations were canceled; work days were lengthened; executives from both companies were organized into a crisis management mode. Top people understood that they were on trial and that the next few months would make or break their careers in the new company. Meanwhile, rumors flew through both companies, misinformation was in good currency, and the thrill of victory gave way to a protracted period of nerve-racking tension and mind-numbing work.

Executive Conduct in Crises

Richardson and Burlingame were each facing crises: one struggling to preserve his company's and his own integrity and the other trying to combine his firm with another to create a new and more effective enterprise. There are conventional myths, such as "when the going gets tough, the tough get going," that inform conmonsense prescriptions for executives facing personal and organizational crises. Be tough, logical, crisp, decisive, and so on go recommendations for personal conduct, and cover-all-the-bases, leave-nothing-to-chance, and hold-feet-to-the-fire goes the received wisdom for analyzing problems and making decisions.

These recommendations appeal to the cognitive capabilities and behavioral skills of top executives who have themselves presumably risen to the top because of their intellectual prowess and political savvy. They also validate "masculine" definitions of heroism under fire and affirm the leaderly self-image. They are, however, insufficient for managing the challenges posed by corporate combinations where emotions are raw and uncertainty reigns.

Statistical evidence shows that seven out of ten mergers and acquisitions are failures. It can be argued that this failure rate is in part testament to the inability of chief executives and their teams to manage the crises of combining successfully. The challenges posed require leaders to rally doubters and credibly communicate the larger purpose behind an otherwise financial transaction. They need to create a crisis management process that gives rise to creative thinking and to operate in a way that builds commitment to a common direction. Finally, they have to care for and counsel those who are overwhelmed or undersupported, some of whom will inevitably be "casualties," and open themselves to the emotional highs and lows experienced by those they lead, if only to lead by example.

There is an emerging vocabulary that describes these kinds of heroic figures as, for example, "transformational leaders," and scholarly studies attribute their success to charisma, androgyny, or zen-like ways. This volume aspires to define and describe such capabilities and their operations under the rubric of *executive appreciation*. The term, as used here, refers to how leaders perceive the world around them, including people and situations, and to their acts of appraisal and valuation.

The Appreciative Capability

This chapter describes the leadership of Burlingame and Richardson as they sought, in one case, to develop a new culture and, in the other, to maintain an existing one in the case of a merger and acquisition respectively. It focuses on the ways that the two executives attended to, appraised, and evaluated the circumstances around them — the key facets of executive appreciation as defined by Geoffrey Vickers (1972) — as they led their companies through months of combination-related crises.

Appreciative leadership, as described here, begins with the way that leaders perceive and conceptualize the world around

Merging of Heart and Mind in Crisis Management 59

them. The way they see things, in turn, activates processes of *attention* that bring particular issues, ideas, and values into focus in their organizations. In this chapter we will see how Burlingame and Richardson each defined the requirements and opportunities posed by their unique situations and directed people, through front- and backstage leadership, to a common vision and course.

The next facet of appreciation concerns the ways leaders relate to and come to understand the world around them. Here, again, leadership stimulates processes of *appraisal* that influence the way executives experience particular events and go about solving problems and making decisions. In this chapter, we will examine how groups of top managers in the companies under study gained a more informed understanding of their problems and responsibly resolved conflicts with their counterparts and among themselves.

Finally, appreciation involves judgment, for executives must ultimately act based on their perceptions and analyses and, in turn, stimulate others to action. The decision to act is foreshadowed by processes of *evaluation*—how executives come to conclusions about particular courses of action and gain (or fail to gain) the commitment of those who will implement decisions. Here we will see how Burlingame and Richardson applied their beliefs and values to decisions affecting the re-creation and preservation of their respective company cultures.

Of course, perception, analysis, and judgment are found in many acts of leadership, and skilled leaders need not be "appreciative" in approach or style to focus people's attention, solve problems, and have decisions implemented. To understand the appreciative character of leadership, then, we need to look beyond executive conduct and into its roots in leaders' beliefs and values. Here we will see that appreciative executives have an uncanny ability to see deeply into situations and people, can analyze, simultaneously, on rational and emotional levels, and can exercise control in ways that liberate, rather than constrain, people's creativity and empower them to make voluntary commitments to action.

What leaders choose to attend to, for example, is to some degree a function of their worldviews and the assumptions they hold about human nature. The appreciative executive, it will be argued, has an enlarged view of what an organization can be and emboldens people to imagine and bring to life a more effective mode of operation. This is perception—but infused with insight and imagination. In turn, the appreciative executive needs an enriched view of human nature to see perceptively into people, gain their confidence, and rally them to a risky undertaking. This requires the capacity to empathize with people—to see and experience their feelings—and to be self-aware.

How leaders go about appraising a situation is related to their fundamental orientations to experience. Of course, hardheaded realism and cold calculation are part of any business decision. But here it will be argued that appreciative leaders also exercise and stimulate curiosity, innovative thinking, and purposeful problem solving. This involves analysis—but of the type informed by both facts and feelings.

Finally, there is judgment—the precursor to action. A so-called "bias for action" is found among many in leadership positions. What distinguishes the appreciative executive is his or her ability to infuse action with larger meaning and to orchestrate it with a deft, as opposed to a heavy-handed, touch. In this way people internalize their responsibilities and make action commitments freely. All of this is in keeping with an executive orientation to action based on trust between the leader and the led and a willingness to reperceive and reanalyze new situations as they develop.

Studying Executive Appreciation

This chapter will describe how Burlingame and Richardson exercised such leadership to unify people, to guide their executive teams through fact-finding, problem solving, and conflict resolution, and to set them on a new course of action. The data reported come from the researcher's direct observation of meetings and events or from interviews of Burlingame, Richardson, and other executives about these meetings and events. Inferences drawn about the worldviews and orientations of the two executives are my own.

This study does not purport to show a direct, linear, causal relationship between processes of attention, appraisal, and valuation observed in the organizations under study and the beliefs and values of the two executives in charge. Obviously there is some linkage, but it is confounded by the complexity of the situations and the idiosyncrasies of the many people involved. Moreover, it may not be possible to formally model and measure such linkages. Appreciative action is informed by situational and personal attributes in qualitative and nonconscious ways. Furthermore, to trace precise linkages between events and beliefs understates the often tacit and reciprocal aspects of human information processing (Polanyi, 1958) and what has been called the social construction of reality (Berger and Luckmann, 1967).

Cooperrider and Srivastva (1987) have devised principles for "appreciative inquiry" that place it firmly in the sociorational tradition of research—where theory, data, and interpretation emerge through the act of research and reflection and are recognized to be personally and situationally determined. My own translation of these principles has led me into the roles of an active agent in corporate combinations and researcher-as-storyteller. This fits what I have characterized as the "art" of assessment where close interaction between the researcher and material (people) under study, mutual probing and influence, and care about process and conclusions lead to the creation of an "artful" product—whether that be a new form of organization or a new way of understanding the phenomena (Mirvis, 1980). To my view this kind of inquiry fits the study of appreciative phenomena. Appreciation is, after all, most often associated with the arts, where both the creative act and its study are not reducible to logical-empirical formulation.

Executive Appreciation in Context

Vickers (1965) makes it plain that executive action shapes the larger action setting in an organization. Hence the appreciative executive shapes what Vickers calls the appreciative setting in the enterprise. In this instance, Richardson and Burlingame worked to create a setting that would enable their teams to see new possibilities in the combination. They also tried to develop an empowering milieu where managers could explore and develop new ways of organizing themselves in response to novel circumstances. And, finally, they sought to validate their people in their quests through ritual, ceremony, and other acts of affirmation.

The creation of such mind-expanding and heartrending settings is well documented in social and behavioral science research, particularly in the case of laboratory education programs, but also in on-line management situations (see Bennis and Slater, 1968; Sarason, 1972; Torbert, 1976). Many executives draw on such appreciative techniques as environmental scanning, value clarification, and introspection in defining problems and how they are looked at; make use of group brainstorming, synergistic conflict resolution, and their own intuition in fact-finding and decision making; and gravitate to the role of visionaries and keepers of the culture.

There are, in turn, protocols for leadership in turbulent times that envelop the artful practice of individual executives in systemic models of organizational conduct, many of which have appeared in this series on executive affairs. The theoretical requirements for designing "learning systems" have been critically formulated (Michael, 1973), and many have studied what makes for effective and ineffective learning in organizations (Argyris, 1982; Argyris and Schön, 1974). Vickers (1965, 1967) anticipated this line of thinking and, to my knowledge, introduced the concepts of appreciation and the appreciative setting into the managerial vocabulary.

The problem here, as in other highly charged crisis situations, is that forces contend against the appreciative mindset and creation of an appreciative setting. Perception is narrowed and distorted, critical faculties are biased and inefficient, and judgments are often flawed and self-serving. Hence preferences for systemic learning give way to a bias for action. In this milieu, finely formed, high-minded ideas about appreciation are met with head shaking and disquiet, and are presumed nice, but not necessary, for getting the job done. All of this is to say that, in my experience, executives in crises are driven above all by the exigencies of the task and are less oriented to the longer-term prospects of learning.

Yet they can, and do, in their own ways create settings that merge mind and heart and that, in turn, stimulate fresh

Merging of Heart and Mind in Crisis Management 63

thinking and restore personal worth. Burlingame and Richardson, while not "textbook" examples (should any exist), operated in a way emblematic of executive appreciation and created, in their fashion, appreciative settings. A colleague, Mitchell Marks, and I worked with Burlingame beginning the day after Alpha made its bid for Omega. I worked with Richardson starting six months after his company was acquired by GrandCo. Richardson preserved, for the most part, DC's independence and way of life through pain and passion during his tenure while heading a "subsidiary." Burlingame united Alpha and Omega, forming Unico, through vision and vigor. Both were under stress and surrounded by stressed-out executives. Both faced repeated crises in combining companies. The events reported here concern their efforts to create a setting through which executives could gain a broader and more fully informed perspective on the combination and events surrounding it, could actively and critically participate in decisions that defined the new company, and could help to create a new culture that would affirm their efforts.

The Usual Focus of Attention in Takeovers

Acquisitions, mergers, and takeovers are crisis-inducing events for people in organizations. In such situations, the uncertainty and likelihood of change, whether favorable or not, becomes a focal point of attention for the people involved and ultimately affects their first impressions of a combination, how they perceive people in their own and the other company, and how they go about sizing up and responding to their situation. Stress is manifest in people's personal preoccupation with the change, in their vigilance to rumors, whatever the source, and in their hyperattentiveness to signs and signals of what it might mean for themselves and their work areas (Fink, Beak, and Taddeo, 1971).

Corporate combinations introduce some unique stressors in working lives that have a bearing on sum, substance, and symbolism of executive information processing. First, executives involved in putting the companies together simply have more information to attend to and less time to do it in. Of course, all organizational changes are complicated, but combinations involve a thoroughgoing consideration of the implications for company structures, systems, products, processes, and people. The set of independent and interdependent decisions facing executives in a combination are far more complex and ambiguous than those encountered in normal change situations, and the time pressures are more demanding.

Second, these decisions are being made in a complex and generally inhospitable context. In the business and social environment of today, for example, mergers and acquisitions are viewed with distrust and cynicism and horror stories are the stock-in-trade of newspapers and business periodicals. People expect the worst from a combination and know of neighbors, friends, or family who have been seriously harmed by a deal. This context informs executives' going-in assumption about a combination and delimits, consciously or not, their perceptual sets. Moreover, executives are surrounded by would-be advisers who are anxiety-ridden and self-interested and are likely to selectively distort information.

Finally, combinations produce what might be regarded as a more primal constraint on executives' abilities to see a situation clearly. Hirsch and Andrews (1983) note that the language used to describe combinations, replete with imagery of war and marriage, conveys the emotional undercurrent of a seemingly rational business deal. In the case of DC, for instance, Grand-Co was anthropomorphized as a "wolf" slavering over its profits and as an "amoeba" trying to absorb the company. In turn, Burlingame was characterized as a "raider" for leading a takeover attempt and Alpha was personified as a "rapist" for "breaking down the door and forcing its way into the bed" of Omega.

Research on crisis-induced stress shows that it produces emotional disequilibria and often results in "fight or flight" reactions to decisions, tasks, and interpersonal relationships (see Quick and Quick, 1984). People are edgy and cranky; they suffer from sleeplessness, impotence, infections, illnesses, and other somatic and psychosomatic symptoms of distress; and their cognitive processes tend to be jumbled and disorganized. These personal reactions to a combination, commonplace among executives, further undermine their capacities to openly and fully attend to the complex, contextually rich, and often deeply disturbing range of stimuli in their environment, not to mention their capacities to delve fully into the emotions they are experiencing. All of the foregoing means it is incumbent on transformational leaders to proactively manage how people see the combination and come to grips with the emotional upset, and thus to create an appreciative setting.

The Omega/Alpha Partnership

Right after the announcement of the bid for Omega, Burlingame issued a pamphlet entitled "The Omega/Alpha Partnership." The juxtaposition of the lead and target company names and the characterization of the hostile takeover as a partnership signaled his intentions to make this a "friendly" combination. The text, drafted in evocative language, announced that "Great companies are built by people willing to make bold moves, who take events into their own hands and dare to act of their vision. . . . We are in the vanguard of a movement that is sure to redirect the course of the . . . industry." This was intended to be more than "PR" and something other than self-aggrandizement: It invited people from the two companies to venture forth on a new course.

From the outset, Burlingame was "purposing" the combination (see Vaill, 1982). Industry analysts had characterized the merger as "two male dinosaurs attempting to mate." Burlingame emphasized that keeping two separate product lines (the dinosaurs' equipment) would reassure customers and that combining the companies would give them more product options and better services. This also sent a message to the technical and sales communities in both companies that they would have many more opportunities in a larger and stronger company.

Burlingame set out on a worldwide tour of former Omega plants, sales offices, and user groups shortly after the sale was completed. A video of him "speechifying" about the future of the new company was seen by thousands of Omega employees. Public speaking was one of Burlingame's strong suits and a key element in what he regarded as a successful "merger personality."

His speeches were followed by question-and-answer sessions where he "told the truth" about impending layoffs and staff reductions and emphasized that no one yet had the "answers" about individual jobs or functions.

In a sense, Burlingame was "telling it like it is." This distinguishes him from many top company communicators who issue bland promises that "nothing will change" or who try to finesse or smooth over issues that are troubling and promise disruption. At the same time, he was telling it "like it ought to be." Tichy and Devanna (1983) note that a statement of vision spells out an idealized image of the future. It does more, however, than stimulate hope; it also sets out a blueprint that makes the future concrete and seemingly attainable. Burlingame described this as "the ability to think several steps ahead, to be able to visualize the process of creating. . . . " He noted, "I think I was able to visualize that process. I don't know exactly how to get from here to there, but I visualized that process from the beginning . . . not just as a series of steps, but as a series of steps leading to some desired result."

All of this amply illustrates Burlingame's powers of imagination, as well as persuasion, as a front-stage leader. He was, importantly, also creating a setting in which people would be focused on the prospects, rather than the problems, of the partnership and defining the steps that would be taken to bring the combination into being. Backstage, meanwhile, Burlingame was meeting with fretful executives about "human fears and foibles." "People really get scared in this situation, maybe they shouldn't but they do, they're anxious," he said, adding, "You have to be able to relate to that and you have to be able to say to yourself 'I have to be tolerant of that and I have to assuage it, and channel it constructively. . . . '"

Mitchell Marks and I conducted seminars on the "merger syndrome" for executives from both Alpha and Omega in the first months after the sale to help them to understand emotional reactions to a takeover. The aim was to help them collectively cope with the ambiguity and insecurity, in part by seeing they were "all in this together." These seminars were not intended to eliminate the stresses and strains experienced by executives.

Merging of Heart and Mind in Crisis Management 67

On the contrary, the point was made that stress reactions were "normal" and "to be expected." We worked with executives, individually and in groups, to examine how their feelings were impinging on their views of the combination and affecting relationships with their peers, subordinates, and superiors. This kind of self-knowledge, it was reasoned, would be crucial to their effectiveness and well-being when they faced complex, emotionally charged analyses and decisions.

Beyond opening eyes and reaching into hearts, Burlingame also sought to infuse his purposes with principle. He defined guiding precepts for putting the two companies together that included meritocracy (Choose the "Best Organization"/Appoint the "Best Person") and unity (Create a New Company/Develop a New Culture). These principles would govern the combination whereby design functions would be merged and people would be out of work. They promised, however, that managers would build the new enterprise by drawing on the strengths of each company and by choosing the most able people. The meaning to top executives, as one observer put it, was that "all notions of takeover, of victor and vanquished, were dismissed." The broader implication was that the "old" Alpha and "old" Omega would die and a new company would be born.

Retaining DC's Values

A sense of shock permeated DC's top executives after they agreed to be acquired by GrandCo. Feelings of injustice and anger marked many high-level conversations. Accordingly, Richardson, working with a consulting psychologist, proposed that they hold a "grieving meeting" to mourn their losses and "come to grips" with the situation. He recalled, "So few people understand what the trauma is all about. I could hardly bear to talk with them. . . . They (say) you're crying all the way to the bank. So few people understood our mission, our community, our value system. . . . You can't just dismiss that and say, well, here today and gone tomorrow." It was this deep insight into his company, his team, and himself that led Richardson into his grief.

The grieving meeting began with each member of top management sharing his personal losses and guilt at not being able to prevent the takeover attempt. One by one, they shared their fears, disappointment, and frustrations and collectively examined their anger at the "shithead" who had tried to take them over and forced them to be acquired by a "White Knight."

Suddenly the tone and character of the meeting shifted. DC had been "bought" — management had not "sold out." Richardson was credited with making a "hell of a deal" and was really a hero to the company. GrandCo executives were "honorable people" who wanted to join forces with DC. Perhaps DC could even become a "guiding light" for the GrandCo organization. In one sense, DCers were working through their sense of loss and anger and were preparing to "bargain" with GrandCo over the terms of the combination. In another way, however, they too were creating a new setting for themselves. At once they were reperceiving their situation and giving themselves a new purpose.

GrandCo, it was agreed, had "no script" for the combination and could be managed with a "good first show of strength." This focused executives' attentions on the herculean tasks ahead. One urged the group to "avoid technocratic steering." Richardson redefined their aim as "holding onto what we value." The meeting concluded with the executives burning in effigy a figure of the "shithead" that had forced their acquisition and resolving to maintain their "identity" in the months ahead.

This sacrificial rite marked a change in Richardson and his top team. To this point, they were overwhelmed by the prospects of combining with GrandCo and by their own grief over the loss of their company. "Herds of accountants" had already visited and initial contacts were marked by conflict and putdowns. The grieving meet focused them on a new mission. They set about the task of formulating a bargaining strategy by systematically listing a roster of twenty-five values "to be retained" in their company's combination with GrandCo. Central were values having to do with their management process, specifically, their desires to make decisions based on the "authority of knowledge" and through "consensus-style participation." This was to be their version of an appreciative setting.

Managers and supervisors were thereafter gathered together for meetings where key values were discussed and strategies were developed for working with GrandCo executives. Their charge was to act politely and cooperatively while looking at the merits of integration decisions in light of DC's values. One manager, describing early conflicts with GrandCo, noted that the "enemy is us," not one of their "fat cats." Conflicts, he proposed, could be managed as long as people could understand their emotions and respond to initiatives by "walking in the other guy's shoes." His urgings were translated into DC's version of combination principles.

DCers planned to work with their counterparts to arrive at a "mutual understanding" of each company's policies and practices and to look at the "advantages and disadvantages" of particular integration decisions. They favored establishing task groups of executives from the two companies to study these decisions and come to mutually agreeable recommendations. However, GrandCo's leadership never viewed this combination as a partnership, nor did they subscribe to the notion of applying meritocracy to combination decisions. Rather they had "rules" for integrating subsidiaries and "procedures" for ensuring financial control over their operations. "One (financial type) brought in a big book of rules and regulations and thrust it at me," Richardson recalled, "in effect saying, 'this will bring you to heel.'" "We just had to do it the way they wanted it done, period. No ifs, ands, or buts. It was done thoughtlessly, territorially. . . . "

This illustrates one of the complications of constructing an appreciative setting in a complex situation, specifically what Vickers terms the conflict engendered by "rival appreciative systems." GrandCo and DC executives had distinct and conflicting perceptions of the combination. Each team, in turn, focused on different aspects of the situation, read it in different ways, and applied different standards to specific combination decisions. Jemison and Sitkin (1986) note that large parent companies create combination problems when the integration is "handed off" to varied functional heads. All are inclined to consolidate the combination in the best interests of their function. This speaks to the requirement of combination leaders to not only focus people's attention on the possibilities of a new situation but also to regulate the processes by which they find problems and develop solutions to them.

Problem Finding and Problem Solving

In the typical organizational crises, a top body of executives emerge to "take charge" of the situation. Authority is centralized in this body, however formally constituted, information flows to it, and decisions emanate from it. Research shows that organizations tend to fragment in the first stages of a crisis (Hermann, 1963). Executives and functions go their own way in analyzing the situation and responding to it; there are high levels of interpersonal and intergroup tension; and turf protection and self-promotion are commonplace. The creation of a crisis management structure is aimed therefore at pulling executives together and focusing their "brain power" on the problems at hand (Smart and Vertinsky, 1977).

Decision making in crisis management bodies can be crisp and authoritative. Executives describe their work as stressful yet exhilarating, and many involved in company combinations have likened themselves to battlefield generals and commanders. In crisis management forums, executives, in concert with able and trusted associates, are able to sort through information, map strategy, and review contingencies in a focused and task-oriented fashion. Moreover, they are able to bond together with their colleagues, gain moral and emotional support, and at least attain the illusion of control of the situation.

Certainly there are risks in relying on high-level decision-making groups in any organizational crisis. The centralization of authority in such a body, for example, can insulate its members from relevant information and isolate them from dissent. High-level decision-making bodies often have less insight into specific organizational issues and are prone to "groupthink" in their analysis and decision making. There are, moreover, special problems posed by the creation of a crisis management structure in corporate combinations.

By their very structure, corporate combinations produce "we" versus "they" relationships between companies that lead

Merging of Heart and Mind in Crisis Management 71

to win/lose conflicts. Differences in the two companies' relative size and power, as well as the structure of the combination—whether for example a horizontal merger or conglomerate acquisition—to some extent determine what conflicts arise and how they are likely to be resolved. Still, there are many ways to combine companies, and the postcombination period is marked by negotiation over these terms (Mirvis, 1985).

Each company in a combination has its own definition of the situation and its needs, its preferred methods for analyzing problems and adjudicating disputes, and distinct interests to satisfy in formulating solutions. In the present case, the notion of getting lots of people together to revew options and make participative decisions about the best form of integration was alien to GrandCo. It seemed a needless waste of time and energy in a routine situation where GrandCo had a "plan" for integrating subsidiaries, where the "authority of power" was to be taken for granted, and where, as a matter of course, the parent company implemented standard procedures and strictures. DC's complaints about these givens smacked of ingratitude and disrespect.

In the case of Alpha and Omega, Alpha executives came in with a "fix it" mentality, "looking for problems," according to one observer, where they could "fix us." Burlingame and Richardson, each facing distinct challenges, had to create and manage a setting in which their executives could size up one another, study the situation, and devise plans and strategies for, in the one case, creating a new company, and, in the other, retaining some form of "independent identification."

Creating Newco

To concretize his vision of a new company, Burlingame created a Merger Coordination Council, staffed by top executives from Omega and Alpha, and formed task forces to prepare studies and recommendations on the desired organization of all functions in the new company. The coordinative council was the focal point for senior-level review and deliberation of task force recommendations. It issued cost bogeys and policy guidelines for each task force. These were the only givens in the situation.

Burlingame pointedly emphasized that although cost guidelines were sacrosanct, executives had free reign in formulating recommendations so long as they yielded the "best organization." In this respect, he was opening himself and his team up to new possibilities, as long as they could pass critical assessment.

The task forces, cochaired by executives from each company, met continuously for six months after the sale and reported their findings over the course of several high-level review meetings. Burlingame had clear reasons for using this kind of transition structure: "First of all, we had to be substantively sure, say how you put together the field service organization, that you get the best thinking into it. Second, you want to begin to identify the best people to run things, which comes out through this process. And, third, you want people to have ownership, so that both sides feel they've had fair input . . . and are both architects. It wasn't just a Burlingame thing. We didn't want to make unilateral decisions."

Burlingame was the orchestrator of this crisis management structure, constantly appraising the situation and people and exercising appropriate direction. On the matter of task force leadership, for example, he consulted with key executives from both companies and personally selected the task force heads. In so doing, he quizzed each candidate to find people with "breadth, good analytic capability, and objectivity" and who were, crucially, "team players." There was also a risk that he would prematurely signal his preferences about the organization and drive out creative thinking. On this matter, Burlingame noted, "it was evident where the relative strengths and weaknesses [of the two companies were]. . . . Nobody goes into this with a blank mind . . . but I really wanted participation. . . . I always took a posture, well, for example, we could set up a Line-of-Business organization or we might not. . . . You guys look at it, there are pluses and minuses."

Having created this transition structure, Burlingame recognized the need to infuse it with a sense of purpose. Many transition structures are conceived of as temporary bodies where problems are studied, solutions developed, and all concerned then return to business as usual. In this instance, by comparison,

Merging of Heart and Mind in Crisis Management 73

Burlingame had hopes that the processes and norms developed in the transition body would be carried back to the new organization. As a result, the transition structure was conceived of as the seedbed of a new company culture. Early on executives began to refer to themselves as part of "Newco," meaning new company, and within this microcosm of the new company began to develop new working relationships.

In turn, Burlingame vowed to personally put his imprint on this executive body: "I have a view and therefore a style of how I think a company ought to be run and how decisions ought to be made at the top. . . . You try to be open and honest and let it all hang out with your colleagues and try to have a sort of team consensus type of thing. . . . I tried to do that (as head of the Merger Coordination Council) with occasional lapses into arbitrariness."

During one meeting, for example, he reviewed his career with his colleagues, telling stories of his upbringing and of how an experience of lying to his mother convinced him of the importance of always telling the truth. At another, he recounted his experiences in government and large private industry to illustrate why he abhorred bureaucracy and petty politics. The implications for the executives were clear: They had better be "straight" in their functional reviews and had better not get caught up in turf battles or brinkmanship.

Burlingame also introduced symbols of the new value system: He passed out red baseball caps, bearing the Omega and Alpha logos, at one executive review. Whenever one or the other organization was being criticized and a "we/they" mentality was emerging, executives would have to put on their hats and think like "one company."

By encouraging participation, suspending judgments, setting norms, and regulating the work of Newco, Burlingame was managing the setting through which top managers could "appreciate" problems and develop solutions to them. The agenda of each task force was open ended. Members could ask, Why is each company organized in particular ways? How does this contribute to our goals? And they could explore new possibilities: What is the best way to be organized? How might a new company be organized to meet future needs? The process was governed by regulations (meet targets and find the best organization), norms (meet your counterparts with an "open kimono" and tell the truth), and values (we are one company and striving for unity), all developed in situ and personified in Burlingame's leadership of Newco.

At the same time, Burlingame had to contend with executives from each company vying for top posts. He held countless private meetings with managers from Alpha and Omega to gain their counsel and discuss their careers. In each case, he would be a "pocket psychologist" working from hunches and impressions and drawing on his counseling and persuasive skills. This is the behind-the-scenes work of the appreciative executive. Every executive in Newco had his or her own preferred image of the new organization, and each had a stake in looking good and securing a top post. Burlingame's response to individual managers varied from case to case. In the case of two competitors for a top job, for example, he used "persuasion and money." "I appealed to their self-interest," he recalled. "I made it financially worth their while and I said there is absolutely no reason why you should not emerge from it as a key player. And the beauty of that was I really meant it."

The task of bringing people through this trying period was central on Burlingame's agenda. He recalled, "People are important for reasons of substance and for reasons of perception. It was very important in the beginning to have a merger where the key people were perceived and seen by everybody to be working together as a team. I worked extremely hard to bring that about."

The Cambridge Meeting

By comparison, the people side of the GrandCo and DC combination deteriorated that first year after the sale. A GrandCo group vice president was assigned responsibility for running DC—without the consultation or assent of DCers. He was, in their eyes, a "nuts-and-bolts" type, with high needs for control and scant interest in DC's managerial style or values. Richardson recalled, "it was like imposing a jail sentence on me." Then there were cross-company conflicts as executives from the two sides fought over budgeting and control systems, human resource requirements, and lines of authority and discretion. Finally, there was a financial review where GrandCo "picked and picked" at DC's projections and questioned in agonizing detail the prudence of its operational plan.

For a time, DC executives were "obsessed" with the combination. They met frequently, however, with a consulting psychologist to sort through their emotional reactions to particular events and review new strategies. At one meeting, Richardson was challenged for being an "impediment" to better relationships with GrandCo people. To this point, he saw himself as a "buffer" between his company and the parent organization and was trying to "insulate" his team from needless interference. After a heavy and heartfelt session, Richardson acknowledged the "need to recognize and accept the fact that changes are and will continue to be necessary. . . . " It was the first time he publicly stated that DC was truly a "subsidiary" of GrandCo.

Thereafter, management agreed "to work on major differences which develop by confronting them directly, having open discussion, and selecting an appropriate approach to resolution." The group also recognized that their obsession with GrandCo was having an impact on managers and other employees. At a meeting of managers and supervisors, then, they discussed their need to be "more visible" and to stop "emphasizing GrandCo."

Richardson and his team were, in their own fashion, operating in an appreciative setting through which they analyzed, gauged, and regulated their relationship with GrandCo. In many respects, there was greater depth to their inquiry than found in the case of Alpha and Omega. DC's top managers were comfortable with disclosing and analyzing their emotions and accustomed to considering feelings, alongside facts, in their deliberations. In other respects, however, it was a closed learning system, because GrandCo was never a partner in studying the integration effort.

Indeed, the whole idea of studying the integration process was seen as "kooky" by GrandCo, and DCers' efforts to explain how self-study and openness were important elements in effective management were heard as "Swahili." Thus, I worked only with DC's leadership to help them to study their integration with GrandCo. This involved interviewing each executive periodically, scanning memos and meetings notes, and preparing a summary document for collective review. The Cambridge meeting was our first annual review. It began with one manager likening himself to Robert E. Lee, who "knew the South was going to lose the war" but felt honor-bound to defend it.

The meeting went on with a review of all the "wars" and culminated in Richardson's query, "Why fight a battle that you're never going to win . . . just to preserve your own sense of pride and integrity and self-righteousness?" From this emerged a discussion of factors over which DC had "minimal or no control." These would have to be managed "skillfully and well." With that, top management could "focus time and energy and creativity" on areas where they had "degrees of freedom." This redefined "honor" in DC. To this point, DC had looked at every conflict with GrandCo from a "self-righteous perspective." "Without detachment from that," Richardson noted, DC would always "fight GrandCo tooth and nail."

Several strategies emerged from the Cambridge meeting. It was agreed that attaining good results was "mandatory" and that DC had to develop "boundary" managers to cultivate more and better relationships with GrandCo executives. The norm had been to "not fraternize with the enemy"; now it was to seek "acceptance and encouragement." The key was to relate to their counterparts without "overdramatizing differences" and by building one-to-one relationships. The group agreed to "experiment" with new ways of working with GrandCo and among themselves.

Thenceforth, DC executives agreed not to "present too radical a model" when discussing issues with their counterparts and to show more "sensitivity" to the prerogatives and values of GrandCo. Richardson and his team learned, in turn, how to "wow" their superiors at budgeting meetings with slick graphic presentations and detailed analysis. At the same time, they continued to meet among themselves to ensure that they were not conning themselves and becoming like "Jekyll and Hyde." This required a "self-conscious examination of how things are going in the relationship."

Clash of Cultures

Much has been written about how differences between two companies' operating philosophies and management styles, as well as their distinct approaches to production, marketing, and innovation, can sabotage a seemingly sound combination (Kitching, 1967; Marks and Mirvis, 1986). To an extent this is a by-product of the cultural learning process that occurs whenever cross-cultural contact is initiated.

People learn about their own culture through contact with other ones. In meeting counterparts in a corporate combination and learning how they do business, executives become clear about how their own company operates and what makes it work. Many aspects of company life, such as a firm's relative emphasis on finance versus products or sales versus service, become more salient. Distinctive appetites for detail versus the big picture or for control versus autonomy, as well as differing attitudes about authority, methods of problem solving, and orientations to human relations—all heretofore taken for granted—become visible and valuable. Managers in a combination identify with their own culture and strive to protect it.

Naturally, there is a tendency for people in each company to see their ways as superior and to denigrate the practices and philosophy of the other firm. It would be mistaken to conclude, however, that combinations of companies with different cultures are doomed to failure. The key is to sensitize executives on both sides to the differences and take account of them when making combination decisions and implementing them.

This is not simply a matter of cultivating so-called objectivity or eliminating cultural bias. Rather, it requires executives to appreciate how culture informs differing perceptions, appraisals, and valuations and thus to find ways of synthesizing cultural differences or devising new options that bespeak transcendent cultural values. Such values are often expressed symbolically in rites and rituals (Beyer and Trice, 1984). Finding new cultural rites was the challenge facing Alpha and Omega leaders.

In the case of DC, the challenge was to avoid "inauthenticity." Small companies going through a combination are often assimilated into the larger culture. Moreover, as these companies are assimilated by their parent organization, whether in substance, say the loss of valued autonomy, or in symbol, perhaps the imposition of a new name or logo, their culture is at risk (Sales and Mirvis, 1984). Hence Richardson and his team tried first to defend their culture and then to redefine it in light of changed circumstances. To do so required them to find culturally appropriate symbols: poetry and song.

United Company — Unico

In the case of Alpha and Omega, Burlingame had aspirations of creating a new company identity and culture. This was begun with fanfare: Employees were invited to "name the new company." Over 10,000 entries were submitted and the winning entry proposed that the company be called Unico — representing united company.

Mitchell Marks and I were called on to highlight cultural similarities and differences between the two companies and identify potential cultural conflicts. As an example, Alpha was very "bottom line" oriented, achieved through product rationalization and centralized control, whereas Omega was marked by autonomy and customized development, which yielded the company less margin but produced greater market penetration. Alpha's executives viewed Omega managers as profligate and undisciplined spenders. Those in Omega saw their counterparts as narrowminded and neanderthal. To our eyes, these reflected cultural differences, and the resulting conflicts threatened the integration of business systems.

To separate symbolic from substantive conflicts, the task forces divided their analyses into three "bit buckets." First, there were "no brainers" where one company or the other had a better system and there were no deep value differences between the companies over a preferred way of doing business. Second, there were "traps" where decisions were unimportant but differences between the companies were marked. These conflicts led to "religious wars" where the battle was over turf and symbol—as substance was insignificant. It was agreed that such traps were to be avoided. Finally, there were "hot ones" where decisions were important and differences between the companies were sharp.

In these decision areas, time was set aside to study why each company had followed a particular path. Veteran employees were called in to explain the reasoning behind past decisions, and an effort was made to make the "best case possible" for continuing to follow one company's model or the other's. Ultimately it was left to the leadership of the task forces to resolve differences and come to final recommendations.

Plainly this made values an integral part of decision making. In some instances, however, neither company's values or systems offered the "best solution." On the matter of distribution systems, for example, Burlingame argued that merging two "half-assed" systems would make a "complete ass" out of everyone. Accordingly, the task force was charged with developing a new system from scratch. This exemplified Burlingame's leadership: He consistently spoke out in favor of meritocracy and excellence and against empire building and flank protection. Those who could not abide by these ground rules were eliminated from the exercise and, ultimately, the company.

A final ceremony illustrates Burlingame's sensitivity to the clash of cultures between the two companies and the requirements for building a new culture. A CAO (chief anthropological officer) drew on the work histories of executives to tell the story of Alpha and Omega's history. Then several executives contributed mementos from their careers to the archives of the new company—just named Unico. The ceremony ended by their signing of a log signifying their presence at the day of its creation.

Today Burlingame has a new team of executives reporting to him. "We don't have a president/chief operating officer. We have instead a management board. . . . " "The reason for that is I'm closer to retirement and wanted a group of younger people who could work together as a team." Culture building is only partly symbolic. New people, committed to new values, also contribute to creating a new culture.

"Or Else We Wither Up and Become Businesspeople"

The two years of culture change at DC were defined by one manager's prophesy: "Unless we fight this thing, we will wither up and become businesspeople." Accordingly, their self-study of their relationship with GrandCo and changes in their own company was guided by some culture-specific, decidedly "unbusinesslike" features and rituals.

The symbolic burning in effigy of the raider that sought to take them over was only one example of this—DC's executives also regularly prepared songs and poetry to mark their progress and plights. One poem, "The Miserable, Wretched, Sorry Saga of Rubber Margins," about a meeting at GrandCo, read in part:

> And some said this and some said that
> And the punts went here and forth and back
> The questions put were full penetrating
> And the answers said with pain and aching.
>
> And "shit" I said in wisdom wise
> I kinda like and respect these guys
> And to admit the truth entire
> We needed our feet held to the fire.
>
> Glad to know you, glad you came
> Thanks for guidance and wisdom
> And much pleasure with the pain
> But Holy Christ, please never again.

This poetry, often put to song, helped DCers to live their culture even as they struggled to retain it. When Richardson first took charge of DC, he and his team envisioned themselves as a special band, truly knights in Camelot, as they conceived of themselves. It was a romantic image and helped to congeal them into a group committed to consensus-style decision making. I used this im-

Merging of Heart and Mind in Crisis Management 81

agery in my own work with DC, once preparing a poem about the princess in Camelot who was saved by a "White Knight" and then threatened by him. It concluded,

> KINGDOMS COME AND KINGDOMS GO, princesses marry and marriage means change. Beasts do battle and nobles count money, but battles do end and more than gold makes a reign. The days of Camelot are passing, what call ye the next days? Will harvests still flourish? Will the princess still shine? With the old spark gone, will a new one arise?
>
> Scholars can ponder and knights dream of glory. But the answer awaits the princess's story. . . .

After two years the story's conclusion was that DC had retained its valued aim of "independent identification." There was change: Areas where DC had no control were given over to GrandCo influence. But DC had also retained key maneuvering room, and most of the critical values — as identified shortly after the company's acquisition — were alive and well in the eyes of top managers and, importantly, in the eyes of employees, as a survey showed.

It is hard to determine to what extent Richardson's leadership of his team through their crisis — and how they appraised their situation and responded to their counterparts — led to an easing of tensions and a more congenial relationship with GrandCo. In the same way, I cannot say that Burlingame's model of leadership and the crisis management structure he devised and infused with values led to the successful integration of Alpha and Omega. What is clear is that both adopted a leadership style that drew on appreciative faculties and that both sought to create an appreciative system through which to manage and regulate the crises of combining. As I have suggested, this leadership model is based on certain underlying philosophies about the material and human world and is expressed in a type of action not generally associated with conventional crisis management. To conclude the story, then, requires a closer look at these assumptions and actions and at why the concept of appreciation helps in describing and understanding the work of these two leaders.

Executive Appreciation and Crisis Management

Current interest in the concept of appreciation stems in part from a paradigmatic shift in the ways scholars understand organization life and how they go about researching it (see Gergen, 1982; Cooperrider and Srivastva, 1987; Berg and Smith, 1988). This critique is paralleled in challenges to conventional assumptions about managerial conduct and clarion calls for a new model of management (Berlew, 1974; Leavitt, 1975a, 1975b). In the same way, conventional assumptions about and models of crisis management can be so critiqued.

The conventional wisdom about crisis management, with its emphasis on tough-minded, rational analysis and top-level, centralized control, derives from and sustains certain assumptions about human beings, nature, and their interaction in organizations. Associated with these beliefs are preferred ways of knowing the world and of acting in it. The many contributors to this volume have their own ways of characterizing these assumptions and beliefs and join a long list of influential thinkers in dividing them, for the sake of convenience, into competing systemic models—the traditional model and the alternative. In this instance, Figure 3.1 summarizes these competing orientations and how both were appreciated in crisis management applications in the two cases.

View of an Organization. One outlook on crisis management rests on the belief that the world is composed of discrete objects and events, interacting in sequences that can be understood as chains of causes and effect. As such, elements of a crisis situation can be studied and managed one by one, then in aggregate, building to a whole. This is a linear view of reality, where the object of attention can be abstracted from its context. This view implies that there is an objective reality "out there" awaiting analytic understanding and skillful management.

Neither Burlingame nor Richardson subscribed fully to this mechanical worldview. Burlingame, for instance, viewed

Merging of Heart and Mind in Crisis Management

organizations as "social structures with a continuing life and soul of their own." He characterized himself as an organizational architect; hence his emphasis was on drafting a vision of the future that would bespeak partnership and embody a new way of operating. As an effective communicator, he breathed life into this vision, acknowledging the realities of problems and pains, all the while promising a brighter future ahead. He was, in this sense, guiding people's construction of reality in both Alpha and

Figure 3.1. Competing Worldviews and Their Merging in Action.

Competing Perspectives in Theory (Choose one or the other)		*Merged Perspectives in Action* (Appreciate the need for both)	
Conventional Perspective	Alternative Perspective	Creating a Culture	Defending a Culture
View of an Organization			
Mechanical: linear relations between variables "Parts of a machine"	Holistic: dialectic interrelationships "Strings on a harp"	Social structure with soul and life: envision a new company "Partnership"	Value system to live by: affirm what is important "Independence"
View of Human Beings at Work			
Rational and calculative: driven by habits and routines	Emotional and intuitive: driven by values and relationships	Fears and foibles/ a flag to rally: meritocracy and unity	Grief-stricken/ purposeless: mourning and commitment
Orientation to Experience			
Abstract and logical: focus on facts and quantities "Concrete"	Experiential and symbolic: focus on feelings and qualities "Imaginative"	Objective and relativistic: focus on facts but "when in doubt, do it now"	Subjective and value laden: focus on feeling but do not "shoot yourself in the foot"
Orientation to Action			
External control: plans, measurements, and incentives	Internal control: orientation, feedback, and validation	Coordination and acculturation: clan gatherings, ceremonies, and peer review	Self-regulation and acceptance: study group, poetry and song, reality testing

Omega—recognizing that whatever it was to be would come from the hearts and minds of employees, as well as investors, industry analysts, customers, and other constituencies.

Richardson saw an organization as essentially a value system. Hence he and his team focused their inquiry on values to be retained in the combination with GrandCo. Also a self-described architect, he led his team in formulating a "game plan" that would allow them to retain DC's values and make it "fun" to continue leading a symbolically "independent" company.

For the sake of simplicity, I depict these two leader's worldviews as holistic—a complex and enlarged view of reality where mutual and reciprocal causation governs relationships between systemic elements. Rather than seeing organizations as comprised of "parts of a machine," those who hold to this perspective see elements "like strings on a harp." This worldview forms the basis for a synergistic view of organization—where the whole is more than a sum of the parts—and allows people to imagine new possibilities for themselves and their companies.

Leaders who have this worldview recognize that systems pose emergent problems (or opportunities) that are not fully defined or wholly constrained by what precedes them. As such, new situations truly are created and are amenable to social architecture. Burlingame designed a complex transition structure to accomplish the merger, while Richardson and his team banded together, like King Arthur and his knights, to carry on traditions in a new context.

View of Human Beings. A machinelike image of the world is easily transposed into a view of human nature in which people are defined as rational and calculative, governed by instrumentality and organizational routines. Taken together, these views of the material and human world imply that it is feasible to make discrete changes in organization attributes whose consequences are predictable and under control.

Such an orientation was antithetical to Richardson's and DC's value systems. Richardson was deeply committed to human development and believed that a company should help people to "reduce the gap between their performance and their poten-

Merging of Heart and Mind in Crisis Management 85

tial." These convictions made it especially difficult for him personally to work with a group vice president who "toyed" with people and made his executives behave like "dancing bears." In a sense, his conflicts with a new boss exemplified the clash of cultures between the two companies.

Accordingly, Richardson and his team sought ways to, first, mourn their loss and expunge their anger over their circumstances. The grieving meeting, replete with ceremony, allowed them to vent their anguish and come to collective resolve on a new course of action. Still, the group often found themselves powerless in the face of GrandCo's prerogatives. Again, through a collective examination of their relations with the "parent" company, DCers came to see how they were acting like "ungrateful little brothers and sisters." This helped them to redefine the relationship—respecting requirements for change without "losing our integrity or sense of purpose."

Burlingame was, by comparison, more of a "player." Certainly he was willing to use "money and persuasion" to hold on to some key executives. Yet he also spoke about people's desires to "rally behind a flag" and "have something to believe in larger than their own self-interest." Acting on these assumptions, Burlingame defined principles and devised the framework for the construction of Unico. He also empowered his executives, for reasons of substance and perception, to participate in defining the "new."

These two leaders acknowledged the emotional and intuitive aspects of human nature and combination principles and processes that respected values and human relationships. Burlingame personally referred to his managers as "colleagues" and was sensitive to their emotional welfare and concerns throughout the combination period. He regularly counseled executives, talking to them about their spouses and families, careers and future prospects, their hopes and worries. All of this bears witness to a degree of empathy and fellow feeling. At the same time, he was intolerant of gamesmen and simply replaced them with "team players."

The point to make is that both leaders recognized the human trauma and trial wrought by a combination. Richardson, by training and tradition, delved deeply into his emotional life and worked with colleagues to collectively define for themselves a state of equilibrium and acceptance. Burlingame, more paternal and matter of fact, nonetheless acknowledged "fear and foibles" and tried to "help people overcome that." Both also celebrated the more impassioned aspects of organization life in song and ceremony and poetry and pageantry.

Orientation to Experience. Subscribers to a mechanistic view of human nature and the material world show a preference for detached and dispassionate analysis, for objective measurement and verifiable documentation, and base their decisions on rigorous and rationally derived conclusions—all of which conform to conventional canons of scientific methodology. This is presumed to minimize, if not eliminate, bias, error, and subjectivity, and to yield valid, value-free conclusions. Much of what is known as management science rests on conventional scientific epistemology, optimistically transposed from the laboratory, where variables can be abstracted and isolated and turbulent systems tend to self-destruct or go to equilibrium. Plainly this did not match the orientation to experience of Burlingame and Richardson.

Richardson's and DC's executives' reaction to their experience was certainly subjective and value-laden. To an extent, they were blind to certain "facts": a powerful new owner could, as desired, impose its will on them. Yet in-depth self-scrutiny helped them to clarify how the company's relationship with GrandCo was personified in Richardson's unhappy experiences reporting to a "technocratic" superior, also dubbed a "turkey." Only when he was confronted with the consequences—more intrusiveness by GrandCo—could he "let go" of his personal feelings and adapt to the "new realities." The dual watchwords became: "do not be inauthentic" but "do not shoot yourself in the foot."

The problem finding and problem solving in Newco was, by appearances, dominated by objectivity and logic. The "unwritten merger principle," as noted by participants, was "meet your bogey." Yet the recommendations that came from this study proved sensitive to cultural differences between the two companies and led to a synergistic model of organization—neither anticipated nor predictable from the characteristics of the two companies. To an extent, this was a by-product of Burlingame's willingness to give executives free reign in making design recommendations, so long as cost projections were met. More than this, it was a result of heightened cross-cultural awareness and adherence to an unwritten principle, "when in doubt, do it now." This encouraged executives to take risks and recommend something bold and new that transcended either of the former company cultures.

Orientation to Action. In the conventional model, managers resolve crises through high-control aspirations that suppress nonrationality, emotionality, and expressiveness in favor of logic, impersonality, and instrumentality. As such, they are oriented to "things" rather than people and exercise overt rather than subtle forms of control. In the crisis situation, especially, control is to be in the hands of the decision makers who gather inputs and calls the shots. And then events are turned over to line managers who execute the plans and calibrate by measurement and are rewarded or punished for getting the job done.

The participative process created at Newco depended for its success on executives' abilities to coordinate their analyses and to arrive at complementary recommendations. It was simply impossible to plan all contingencies. Hence Burlingame sought to orchestrate periodic gatherings and peer reviews. On three occasions, task forces reported their findings as to organizational structure and direction to peers for review and critique. A cadre of coordinators arranged cross-functional meetings and ensured that key information was disseminated to other relevant task force leaders. In a sense, the organization was building its own internal control and coordination mechanism for ensuring things would turn out right.

Harrison (1983) uses the terms *alignment* and *attunement* to describe these internal regulating processes. On the one hand, Burlingame was setting a direction and Newco functioned to align executives behind that. On the other, the participative and coordinative work had executives attuning themselves to one another. Symbols and ceremonies, ranging from the red hats at an early gathering of the clan to a culture-building ceremony at the birth of Unico, affirmed purpose and bore witness to the pleasure of "making bold moves."

This model of control is sympathetic to self-management and dependent on guidance, feedback, and affirmation for its success. Self-regulation was a longstanding norm at DC and was kept alive throughout the combination period. That GrandCo could never become a full contributor to this meant that feedback was necessarily distorted and that the benefits of self-study were thereby limited. DCers could only "guess at where we stood." Still, I tried to represent how GrandCo might be viewing the combination and tried, as well, to help DCers gain a deeper appreciation of their effectiveness and ineffectiveness in the combination period. This stimulated self-inquiry into my own effectiveness as an adviser to them (Mirvis and Louis, 1985) and made me very much a part of their own learning system.

Merging Mind and Heart in Crisis

The validity of the conventional crisis management assumptions about organizations and human nature, about how one analyzes and responds to crisis situations, and about appropriate models of control rests on their continuing success. Plainly many executives and companies succeed at surmounting crises by following the received wisdom. To my mind, however, these assumptions are often limiting and constraining—antithetical to the kind of creativity and caring needed in coping with combination crises. In addition, I believe the traditional models of analysis and methods of control that follow from them leave people unprepared to understand deep value and cultural differences and unable to respond flexibly to unanticipated and undesirable consequences (Michael and Mirvis, 1977).

Still, there is a natural tendency for people to revert to previously learned successful behavior in a crisis, which means that there is a natural inclination for executives to embrace tough-minded rationalism and adopt a high-control posture in

Merging of Heart and Mind in Crisis Management 89

the case of corporate combinations. That Richardson and Burlingame could also adopt a more holistic view of reality, could promote vision, support emotionalism, and sustain values alongside analyses, and could lead through participation and by example rather than solely by pronouncement and fiat, is testimony to the effectiveness of another model of crisis management — one where executive appreciaion is at work.

The worldview and assumptions about human nature of top executives shape what people see in a new situation and see in themselves. These influence how organization members interpret their circumstances, and how they act when called on to contribute to a combination. Burlingame said it simply: "It's not only what you do, it's how you do it." Transition processes follow a dynamic, no matter how they are appreciated, but the crucial point to recognize, as Polanyi (1966) reminds us, is that transition processes are important because we live in them. This chapter has made the claim that an appreciative setting is both more livable and workable than one that is solely informed by and consistent with conventional images of crisis management. Such settings give rise to new ways of looking at life and new ways of living. They are hospitable to what Bateson (1972) calls "systemic wisdom." That is to say that they allow a dynamic to unfold wherein appreciative observation and creation have the force of "correcting" the world.

Regrettably, there is a tendency to draw artificial distinctions between conventional executive conduct and that of the holistic, intuitive, expressive type — as though people can only operate out of one mindset and in one mode. This misses the point of how the appreciative capacity works. Certainly, human and thus managerial character is marked by particular tendencies, as Jung (1923) and Maccoby (1976) point out. But appreciative executives have the capability of drawing on diverse, sometimes polar, but often complementary faculties as the situation dictates.

In other words, an appreciative capability is not defined by one's ability to see the world holistically rather than piece by piece, nor by being able to empathize with people rather than relating to them logically. On the contrary, executive appreciation connotes the capacity to observe a situation fully and to respond appropriately to its requirements. That way the full faculties of perception, appraisal, and valuation are exercised. Torbert (1983, p. 322) has termed this the capacity of the *executive mind* and quotes Barnard (1938) as saying that it requires "'attaining proportion between speed and caution, between broad outlines and fineness of detail, between solidity and flexibility. . . . '" To penetrate the executive mind, Torbert (1983, p. 7) emphasizes, "it is necessary to destroy the sense of antagonism between science and art. . . . "

Thus this chapter has not focused on artful management per se. It has concerned the minds and hearts of executives and their merging in an appreciative setting. Richardson and Burlingame were, at times, tough-minded, decisive, dispassionate, and product oriented, the conventional requirements of crisis managers. But they were also tenderhearted, tentative, impassioned, and deeply committed to principle — in proportion and as they appreciated the need.

4

Positive Image, Positive Action: The Affirmative Basis of Organizing

David L. Cooperrider

> Be not afraid of life. Believe that life is worth living, and your belief will help you create the fact.
> — *William James*

> We can easily forgive a child who is afraid of the dark. The real tragedy of life is when men are afraid of the light.
> — *Plato*

Modern management thought was born proclaiming that organizations are the triumph of the human imagination. As made and imagined, organizations are products of human interaction and mind rather than some blind expression of an underlying natural order (McGregor, 1960; Berger and Luckmann, 1967; Pfeffer, 1981; Gergen, 1982; Srivastva and Associates, 1983; Schein, 1985; Unger, 1987). Deceptively simple yet so entirely radical in implication, this insight is still shattering many beliefs—one of which is the longstanding conviction that bureaucracy, oligarchy, and other forms of hierarchical domination are inevitable. Today we know that this simply is not true.

Recognizing the symbolic and socially constructed nature of the human universe, we now find new legitimacy for the mounting wave of sociocognitive and sociocultural research, all of which is converging around one essential and empowering thesis: that there is little about collective action or organization development that is preprogrammed, unilaterally determined, or stimulus bound in any direct physical or material way. Seemingly immutable ideas about people and organizations are being directly challenged and transformed on an unprecedented scale. Indeed, as we move into a postmodern global society we are breaking out of our parochial perspectives and are recognizing that organizations in all societies exist in a wide array of types and species and function within a dynamic spectrum of beliefs and lifestyles. And according to the social constructionist viewpoint, the possibilities are infinite.

Interestingly, there is an important parallel to this whole area of thought that has grown out of the neurosciences and studies of cognition and mind-brain interaction. The "consciousness revolution" of the 1970s is well documented and represents, argues Nobel Laureate Roger Sperry (1988), more than a mere Zeitgeist phenomenon; it represents a profound conceptual shift to a different form of causal determinism. According to the mentalist paradigm, mind can no longer be considered the opposite of matter. Mental phenomena, this paradigm contends, must be recognized as being at the top of the brain's "causal control hierarchy" whereby, after millenniums of evolution, the mind has been given primacy over bioevolutionary (Darwinian) controls that determine what human systems are and can become. In direct contradiction to materialist and behaviorist doctrine, where everything is supposed to be governed from below upward through microdeterminist stimuli and physiochemical forces, the new mentalist view gives subjective mental phenomena a causal role in brain processing and thereby a new legitimacy in science as an autonomous explanatory construct. Future reality, in this view, is permeable, emergent, and open to the mind's causal influence; that is, reality is conditioned, reconstructed, and often profoundly created through our anticipatory images, values, plans, intentions, beliefs, and the like. Macrodeterminism or the theory of downward causation is a scheme, asserts Sperry, that idealizes ideas and ideals over chemical interactions, nerve impulse traffic, and DNA. It is a brain model in which conscious, mental, and psychic forces are recognized as the crowning achievement of some 500 million years or more of evolution.

The impetus for the present contribution grows from the exciting challenge that is implicitly if not explicitly posed by the social constructionist and mentalist paradigms: that to a far greater extent than is normally acknowledged, we human beings create our own realities through symbolic and mental processes and that because of this, conscious evolution of the future is a human option. Taking this challenge—that of a future-creating mental activism—one step further, the thesis explored in this paper is that the artful creation of positive imagery on a collective basis may well be the most prolific activity that individuals and organizations can engage in if their aim is to help bring to fruition a positive and humanly significant future. Stated more boldly, a *New York Times* headline recently apprised the public that "Research Affirms Power of Positive Thinking" (Goleman, 1987, p. 15). Implied in the popular news release and the scholarly research that we will soon sample is the intriguing suggestion that human systems are largely *heliotropic* in character, meaning that they exhibit an observable and largely automatic tendency to evolve in the direction of positive anticipatory images of the future. What I will argue is that just as plants of many varieties exhibit a tendency to grow in the direction of sunlight (symbolized by the Greek god Helios), there is an analogous process going on in all human systems.

As a whole this essay is intended to serve as an invitation to broadly consider a number of questions: What is the relationship between positive imagery and positive action? More specifically, what are the common processes, pathways, or global patterns whereby mental phenomena attract or even cause those actions that bring about movement toward an ideal? Where do positive images of some unknown and neutral future come from in the first place? Could it be that organizations are in fact affirmative systems, governed and maintained by positive projections about what the organization is, how it will function, and what it might become? If so, what are the implications for management? Is it true that the central executive task in a post-bureaucratic society is to nourish the *appreciative* soil from which affirmative projections grow, branch off, evolve, and become collective projections?

To set the stage for our discourse, the first section will begin with a general introduction to the concept of imagery. The second will look specifically at the relationship between positive imagery and positive action by reviewing recent works from diverse areas of study — medicine, cognitive psychology, cultural sociology, and athletics. While I am careful not to suggest that the studies sampled make anything close to an exhaustive case, I do submit, nevertheless, that the convergence of insight, across disciplines, represents an exciting step forward in our understandings of the intricate pathways that link mind and practice. Finally, in the third section, I will discuss how such knowledge from diverse quarters holds a thread of continuity that has broad relevance for understanding organizations. In particular, I will offer a set of eight propositions about the *affirmative basis of organizing*. These propositions are provided for discussion, elaboration, and active experimentation and converge around three basic conclusions: (1) Organizations are products of the affirmative mind; (2) when beset with repetitive difficulties or problems, organizations need less fixing, less problem solving, and more reaffirmation — or more precisely, more *appreciation;* (3) the primary executive vocation in a post-bureaucratic era is to nourish the appreciative soil from which new and better guiding images grow on a collective and dynamic basis.

Imagery: An Introduction

Throughout the ages and from a diversity of perspectives, the image has been considered a powerful agent in the guidance and determination of action:

> A vivid imagination compels the whole body to obey it.
> —*Aristotle* (in Sheikh, 1984, p. 5)

Positive Image, Positive Action

> One of the basic theorems of the theory of image is that it is the image which in fact determines what might be called the current behavior of any organism or organization. The image acts as a field. The behavior consists in gravitating toward the most highly valued part of the world.
> —*Kenneth Boulding* (1966, p. 115)

> Mental anticipation now pulls the future into the present and reverses the direction of causality.
> —*Erich Jantsch* (1980, p. 14)

> Man is a being who, being in the world, is ever ahead of himself, caught up in bringing things alive with his projection. . . . Whatever comes to light owes its presence to the fact that man has provided the overall imaginative sunlight for viewing. . . .
> —*Edward Murray* (1986, p. 64)

> To the empowering principle that people can withhold legitimacy, and thus change the world, we now add another. By deliberately changing the internal image of reality, people can change the world.
> —*Willis Harman* (1988, p. 1)

> Imagination is more important than knowledge.
> —*Albert Einstein* (in Sheikh, 1984, p. 5)

It is clear that images are operative virtually everywhere: Soviet and U.S. diplomats create strategies on the basis of images; Theory X managers construct management structures that reflect the picture they hold of subordinates; days or minutes before a public speech we all feel the tension or anxiety that accompanies our anticipatory viewing of the audience; we all hold self-images, images of our race, profession, nation, and cultural belief systems; and we have images of our own potential as well as the potential of others. Fundamentally, too, it can be argued that every organization, product, or innovative service first started as a wild but not idle dream and that *anticipatory realities* are what make collectivities click. (This is why we still experience a thrill on hearing transforming speeches like Martin Luther King, Jr.'s "I Have a Dream" and sometimes find ourselves enlivened through the images associated with the mere mention of such figures as John F. Kennedy, Gandhi, Winston Churchill, Buddha, or Christ.)

Given the central and pervasive role of the image in relation to action, it is not surprising that research on the workings of the image has risen to be "one of the hottest topics in cognitive science" (Block, 1981, p. 1). Theorists disagree over definitions and argue whether images are direct encoding of perceptual experience (Pavid, 1971), are an artifact of the propositional structuring of reality (Pylyshyn, 1973), represent the sensory system par excellence that undergirds and constitutes virtually every area of cognitive processing, are primarily eidetic or visual (Ashen, 1977), or represent constructive or reconstructive process (Kosslyn, 1980). But in spite of the largely technical differences, Richardson (1969, pp. 2-3) seems to have provided adequate synthesis of a number of competing views in his often-quoted definition of the image as quasi-sensory, stimulus-independent representative experience: "Mental imagery refers to (1) all those quasi-sensory or quasi-perceptual experiences of which (2) we are self consciously aware and which (3) exist for us in the absence of those stimulus conditions that are known to reproduce their sensory or perceptual counterparts, and which (4) may be expected to have different consequences."

In subsequent work, Richardson (1983) retracts the fourth criterion; between 1969 and 1983 there was simply too much new evidence showing that self-initiated imagery can and often does have consequences, many of them physiological, that are indistinguishable from their genuine sensory counterparts. Merely an anticipatory image, for example, of a hostile encounter can raise one's blood pressure as much as the encounter itself. Similarly, numerous new studies now show that consciously constructed images can lead directly to such things as blood glucose increases, increased gastric acid secretion, blister formation, and changes in skin temperature and pupillary size. In an example closer to home, Richardson (1983, p. 15) suggests that "it suffices to remind the reader of what every schoolboy (or girl) knows. Clear and unmistakable physiological consequences follow from absorption in a favorite sexual fantasy." Mind and body are indeed a unified interdependent system.

Perhaps most important, as the above begins to make clear, it is the time dimension of the future—what Harry Stack Sullivan (1947) referred to as "anticipatory reality"—that acts as a prepotent force in the dynamic of all images (for a decision theory counterpart to this view, see Mitchell, Rediker, and Beach, 1986; Polak, 1973). The recognition that every social action somehow involves anticipation of the future, in the sense that it involves a reflexive looking-forward-to and backward-from, has been analyzed by Alfred Schultz (1967) and Karl Weick (1976). Similarly, in Heidegger's brilliant formulation it is our nature not only to be thrown into existence (*Geworfenheit*) but to always be ahead of ourselves in the world, to be engaged in the unfolding of projected realities; all action, according to Heidegger, has the nature of a project (Heidegger refers to this as *Entwurf*, the continuous projecting ahead of a design or a blueprint). Much like a movie projection on a screen, human systems are forever projecting ahead of themselves a horizon of expectation that brings the future powerfully into the present as a causal agent.

Recent Works on the Positive Image– Positive Action Relationship

What all this suggests, of course, is that the power of positive imagery is not just some popular illusion or wish but is arguably a key factor in every action. To illustrate the heliotropic propensity in human systems at several levels of functioning I will now turn to six areas of research as examples—placebo, Pygmalion, positive emotion, internal dialogue, cultural vitality, and metacognitive competence.

Positive Imagery, Medicine, and the Placebo. The placebo response is a fascinating and complex process in which projected images, as reflected in positive belief in the efficacy of a remedy, ignite a healing response that can be every bit as powerful as conventional therapy. Though the placebo phenomenon has been controversial for some twenty years, most of the medical profession now accepts, as genuine, the fact that anywhere from one-third to two-thirds of all patients will show marked physiological and emotional improvement in symptoms simply by believing they are given an effective treatment, even when that treatment is just a sugar pill or some other inert substance (Beecher, 1955; White, Tursky, and Schwartz, 1985).

Numerous carefully controlled studies indicate that the placebo can provide relief of symptoms in postoperative-wound pain, seasickness, headaches, angina, asthma, obesity, blood pressure, ulcers, and many other problems. In fact, researchers are now convinced that no system of the body is exempt from the placebo effect and that it is operative in virtually every healing encounter. Even more intriguing, the placebo is sometimes even more potent than typically expected drug effects: "Consider a series of experiments with a woman suffering from severe nausea and vomiting. Nothing the doctors gave her seemed to help. Objective measurement of her gastric contractions showed a disrupted pattern consistent with the severe nausea she reported. The doctors then offered her a 'new extremely powerful wonder drug' which would, they said, unquestionably cure her nausea. Within twenty minutes of taking this new drug, her nausea disappeared, and the same objective gastric tests now read normal. The drug which was given was not, of course, a new drug designed to relieve nausea. It was syrup of ipecac, which is generally used to *induce* vomiting. In this case, the placebo effect associated with the suggestion that the drug would relieve vomiting was powerful enough to counteract and direct an opposite pharmacological action of the drug itself" (Ornstein and Sobel, 1987, p. 79).

According to Norman Cousins, now a faculty member at the UCLA School of Medicine, an understanding of the way the placebo works may be one of the most significant developments in medicine in the twentieth century. Writing in *Human Options* (1981), Cousins suggests that beyond the central nervous system, the hormonal system, and the immune system, there are two other systems that have conventionally been overlooked but that need to be recognized as essential to the proper functioning of the human being: the healing system and the belief system. Cousins (1983, p. 205) argues that the two work together: "The healing system is the way the body mobilizes all its resources to combat disease. The belief system is often the activator of the healing system."

Using himself as a living laboratory, Cousins (1983, p. 44) has movingly described how the management of his own anticipatory reality allowed him to overcome a life-threatening illness that specialists did not believe to be reversible and then, some years later, to again apply the same mental processes in his recovery from an acute heart attack: "What were the basic ideas involved in that recovery? The newspaper accounts had made it appear that I had laughed my way out of a serious illness. Careful readers of my book, however, knew that laughter was just a metaphor. . . . Hope, faith, love, will to live, cheerfulness, humor, creativity, playfulness, confidence, *great expectations*—all these, I believed, had therapeutic value."

In the end, argues Cousins, the greatest value of the placebo is that it tells us that indeed positive imagery can and often does awaken the body to its own self-healing powers. Research in many areas now confirms this view and shows that placebo responses are neither mystical nor inconsequential and that ultimately mental and psychophysiological responses may be mediated through more than fifty different neuropeptide molecular messengers linking the endocrine, autonomic, and central nervous systems (White, Tursky, and Schwartz, 1985). While the complex mind-body pathways are far from being resolved, there is one area of clear agreement: Positive changes in anticipatory reality through suggestion and belief play a central role in all placebo responses. As Jaffe and Bresler (1980, pp. 260-261) note, the placebo "illustrates another important therapeutic use of imagery, namely, the use of positive future images to activate positive physical changes. Imagining a positive future outcome is an important technique for countering initial negative images, beliefs, and expectations a patient may have. In essence it transforms a negative placebo effect into a positive one. . . . The power of positive suggestion plants a seed which redirects the mind—and through the mind, the body—toward a positive goal."

Before moving on, there is one other perhaps surprising factor that adds significantly to the patient's placebo response—the expectancy or anticipatory reality of the physician. Placebo effects are strongest, it appears, when belief in the efficacy of the treatment is shared among a group (O'Regan, 1983). This then raises a whole new set of questions concerning not only the individual but the interpersonal nature of the positive image–positive action relationship.

Pygmalion and the Positive Construction of the Other. In effect, the positive image may well be the sine qua non of human development, as we now explore in the Pygmalion dynamic. As a special case of the self-fulfilling prophesy, Pygmalion reminds us that from the moment of birth we each exist within a complex and dynamic field of images and expectations, a vast share of which are projected onto us through an omnipresent environment of others.

In the classic Pygmalion study, teachers are led to believe on the basis of "credible" information that some of their students possess exceptionally high potential while others do not. In other words, the teachers are led, on the basis of some expert opinion, to hold a positive image (PI) or expectancy of some students and a negative image (NI) or expectancy of others. Unknown to the teachers, however, is the fact that the so-called high-potential students were selected at random; in objective terms, all student groupings were equivalent in potential and are merely dubbed as high, regular, or low potential. Then, as the experiment unfolds, differences quickly emerge, not on the basis of any innate intelligence factor or some other predisposition but solely on the basis of the manipulated expectancy of the teacher. Over time, subtle changes among students evolve into clear differences as the high-PI students begin to significantly overshadow all others in actual achievement. Over the last twenty years there have been literally hundreds of empirical studies conducted on this phenomenon, attesting both to its continuing theoretical and to its practical importance (Jussim, 1986; see Rosenthal and Rubin, 1978, for an analysis of over 300 studies).

One of the remarkable things about Pygmalion is that it shows us how essentially modifiable the human self is in relation to the mental projections of others. Indeed, not only do performance levels change, but so do more deeply rooted "stable" self-conceptions (Parsons and others, 1982). Furthermore, significant Pygmalion effects have been experimentally generated in as little time as fifteen minutes (King, 1971) and have the apparent capacity to transform the course of a lifetime (Cooper and Good, 1983). (I wonder how many researchers on this subject would volunteer their own children to be part of a negatively induced expectancy grouping?) Specific to the classroom, the correlation between teacher expectation and student achievement is higher than almost any predictive IQ or achievement measure, ranging in numerous studies from correlations of .5 all the way to an almost perfect .9 (Brophy and Good, 1974; Crano and Mellon, 1978; Humphreys and Stubbs, 1977). Likewise, in one of the earliest organizational examinations of this phenomenon, Eden and Shani (1982) reported that some 75 percent of the variance in achievement among military trainees could be explained completely on the basis of induced positive expectation on the part of those in positions of authority.

Obviously the promise of Pygmalion as a source of human development depends more on the enactment of positive rather than negative interpersonal expectancy. But how does the positive dynamic work and why?

A summary of the three stages of the positive Pygmalion dynamic is presented in Figure 4.1. In the first phase of the model, positive images of the other are formed through any number of means—for example, stereotypes, reputation, hearsay, objective measures, early performances, and naive prediction processes. As interactions occur over time, positive images begin to take shape and consist not only of *prophesies* but also tend to become elaborated by one's sense of its other *possibilities* as well as one's sense of "what should be," or *normative valuations*. Taken together the prophesies, possibilities, and normative valuations combine to create a broad brushstroke picture of interpersonal expectancy that has its pervasive effect through two primary mediators—expectancy-consistent cognition and expectancy-consistent treatment.

Considerable evidence, for example, indicates that a positive image of another serves as a powerful cognitive tuning device that appears to trigger in the perceiver an increased capacity to (1) perceive the successes of another (Deaux and Emswiller, 1974), (2) access from memory the positive rather than negative aspects of the other (Hastie and Kumar, 1979), and (3) perceive ambiguous situations for their positive rather than negative possibilities (Darley and Gross, 1983).

While often spoken about in pejorative ways as cognitive bias or distortion ("vital lies," to use Goleman's popular term), it is quite possible that this affirmative capacity to cognitively tune into the most positive aspects of another human being is in fact a remarkable human gift; it is not merely an aberration distorting some "given" reality but is a creative agent in

Figure 4.1. The Positive Pygmalion Dynamic (adapted from Jussim, 1986).

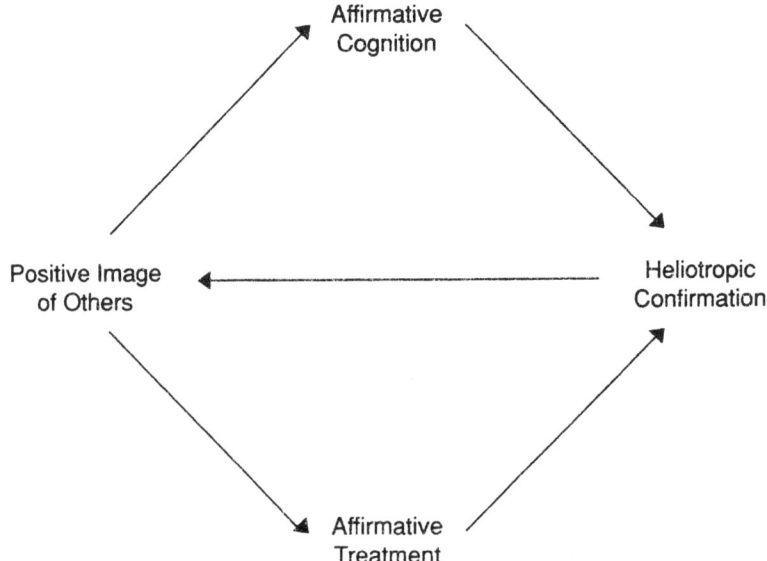

Positive Image, Positive Action

the construction of reality. We see what our images make us capable of seeing. And affirmative cognition, as we will later highlight in our discussion of positive self-monitoring, is a unique and powerful competency that owes its existence to the dynamic workings of the positive image.

The key point is that all of our cognitive capacities — perception, memory, learning — are cued and shaped by the images projected through our expectancies. We see what our imaginative horizon allows us to see. And because "seeing is believing," our acts often take on a whole new tone and character depending on the strength, vitality, and force of a given image. The second consequence of the positive image of the other, therefore, is that it supports differential behavioral treatment in a number of systematic ways.

For example, it has been shown, both in the field and the laboratory, that teachers who hold extremely positive images of their students tend to provide those students with (1) increased emotional support in comparison to others (Rist, 1970; Rubovitz and Maehr, 1973), (2) clearer, more immediate, and more positive feedback around effect and performance (Weinstein, 1976; Cooper, 1979); and (3) better opportunities to perform and learn more challenging materials (Brophy and Good, 1974; Swann and Snyder, 1980).

Finally, in the third stage of the model, people begin to respond to the positive images that others have of them. When mediated by cognitive, affective, and motivational factors, according to Jussim (1986), heliotropic acts are initiated on the basis of increased effort, persistence, attention, participation, and cooperation, so that ultimately, high PIs often perform at levels superior to those projected with low-expectancy images. Research also shows that such effects tend to be long lasting, especially when the Pygmalion dynamic becomes institutionalized. High-PI students, for example, when assigned to the higher academic tracks, are virtually never moved to a lower track (the same is also true for negative-expectancy students, according to Brophy and Good's 1974 review of the "near permanence" of tracking).

The greatest value of the Pygmalion research is that it begins to provide empirical understanding of the relational pathways of the positive image–positive action dynamic and of the transactional basis of the human self. To understand the self as a symbolic social creation is to recognize — as George Herbert Mead, John Dewey, George Simmel, Lev Vygotsky, Martin Buber, and many others have argued — that human beings are essentially modifiable, are open to new development, and are products of the human imagination and mind. We are each made and imagined in the eyes of one another. There is an utter inseparability of the individual from the social context and history of the projective process. And positive interpersonal imagery, the research now shows, accomplishes its work very concretely. Like the placebo response discussed earlier, it appears that the positive image plants a seed that redirects the mind of the perceiver to think about and see the other with affirmative eyes.

Positive Affect and Learned Helpfulness. While often talked about in cognitive terms, one of the core features of imagery is that it integrates cognition and affect and becomes a catalytic force through its sentiment-evoking quality. In many therapies, for example, it is well established that focusing on images often elicits strong emotional reactions; whereas verbal mental processes are linear, the image provides simultaneous representation, making it possible to vicariously experience that which is held in the imagination (Sheikh and Panagiotou, 1975).

So what about the relation between positive emotion — delight, compassion, joy, love, happiness, passion, and so on — and positive action? To what extent is it the affective side of the positive image that generates and sustains heliotropic movement so often seen in human systems? While still in the formative stages, early results on this issue are making clear that there is indeed a unique psychophysiology of positive emotion (as Norman Cousins has argued) and that individually as well as collectively, positive emotion may well be *the* pivotal factor determining the heliotropic potential of images of the future.

This line of research is partly predicated on knowledge growing out of studies of negative affectivity. In one of the most hotly pursued lines of research of the last decade, investigators are now convinced of the reciprocal connections between high negative affectivity and (1) experiences of life stress; (2) deficiency

Positive Image, Positive Action 105

cognition; (3) the phenomenon of "learned helplessness"; (4) the development of depression; (5) the breakdown of social bonds; and (6) the triggering of possible physiological responses like the depletion of brain catecholamine, the release of corticosteroids, the suppression of immune functioning, and ultimately the development of disease (Watson and Clark, 1984; Seligman, 1975; Brewin, 1985; Peterson and Seligman, 1984; Beck, 1967; Schultz, 1984; Ley and Freeman, 1984). Table 4.1, for example, illustrates the linkage between negative affect and disease. In spite of diversity of subjects, methods, and measures, a salient pattern emerges: A host of diseases, especially various forms of

Table 4.1. The Relationship Between Negative Affect and Disease: Conclusions from 28 Papers on Affect and Disease (adapted from Ley and Freeman, 1984, p. 57).

Disease	*Affective State*
Cancer	Depression
Cancer	Loss of hope
Leukemia	Depression, anxiety
Leukemia	Loss of significant other
Neoplasm	Hopelessness, despair
Cancer	Self-directed aggression
Cancer	Depression
Cancer	Hopelessness
Cancer	Depression, hostility
Lung cancer	Rigidity, repression, hostility, despair
Cancer	Decreased depression
Cancer	Lethargy, depression
Cancer	Affective disorder
Cancer	Affective disorder
Cancer	Affective disorder
Cancer	Repression of anger
"Physical illness"	Depression
Pernicious anemia	Depression
Hay fever	Helplessness
Asthma	Helplessness
Tuberculosis	Poor coping with stress
Coronary heart disease	High and frustrated aspiration
Coronary bypass, mortality	Hopelessness, depression
Psychosomatic illness	Hostility, depression, frustration, anxiety, helplessness
Various illnesses	Helplessness, hopelessness

cancer, are associated with chronic and persistent negative images, expressed and embodied in feelings of helplessness and hopelessness. As one physician from Yale concludes, "cancer is despair experienced at the cellular level" (Siegel, 1986).

Probably the one finding that emerges most conclusively on the other side of the ledger is that while negative affectivity is notably linked to the phenomenon of learned helplessness, positive affect is intimately connected with *social helpfulness*. Somehow positive affect draws us out of ourselves, pulls us away from self-oriented preoccupation, enlarges our focus on the potential good in the world, increases feelings of solidarity with others, and propels us to act in more altruistic and prosocial ways (see Brief and Motowildo, 1986, for a review of altruism and its implications for management).

According to the work of Alice Isen and her colleagues, mood, cognition, and action form an inseparable triad and tend to create feedback loops of amplifying intensity. Positive affect, the evidence indicates, generates superior recall or access to pleasant memories (Isen, Shalker, Clark, and Karp, 1978); helps create a heightened sense of optimism toward the future (Isen and Shalker, 1982); cues a person to think about positive things (Rosenhan, Salovey, and Hargis, 1981); and, as a result, predisposes people toward acts that would likely support continued positive affect, like the prosocial action of helping others (Cunningham, Steinberg, and Grev, 1980; Isen and Levin, 1972; Isen, Shalker, Clark, and Karp, 1978). In addition, positive affect has been associated with (1) increased capacity for creative problems solving (Isen, 1984); (2) more effective decision making and judgment (Isen and Means, 1983); (3) optimism and increased learning capacity — in particular, a sharpened capacity for perceiving and understanding mood-congruent or positive things (Bower, 1981; Clark and Isen, 1982).

In perhaps the most intriguing extension of this line of thought, Harvard's David McClelland has hypothesized a reinforcing set of dynamics between positive imagery, positive affect, prosocial action, and improved immune functioning. McClelland has even gone so far as to argue that merely watching an altruistic act would be good for the observer. He may be right.

For example, in one of McClelland's experiments, students were shown a film of Mother Teresa, a Nobel Peace Prize recipient, attending to the sick and dying poor in Calcutta. During the film, measures were taken of the student's immune functioning as defined by increases in salivary immunogobulin A (IgA—a measure of defense against respiratory infection and viral disease). In all cases, it was found that IgA concentrations immediately increased during the film and for some observers remained elevated for a period of up to one hour afterward.

It should be emphasized that these findings are controversial and that we are clearly in our infancy when it comes to really understanding the role of positive emotion as it relates to individual and collective well-being. The most important fact, however, is that studies like these are even being done at all. They represent a vital shift in research attention across a whole series of disciplines and reflect a change in the mood and spirit of our times. For example, as Brendan O'Regan (1983, p. 3) observes in relation to the field of psychoneuroimmunology, "We will no longer be focused on only the reduction of symptoms or the removal of something negative, and instead begin to understand health and well-being as the presence of something positive. It [the focus on the psychophysiology of positive emotion] may well be the first step in the development of what might be called an affirmative science . . . a science for humankind."

The Off-Balance Internal Dialogue. One of the more fascinating refinements of the notion of positive imagery comes from Robert Schwartz's development of a cognitive ethology: the study within human systems of the content, function, and structure of the internal dialogue. Here the image is conceptualized as self-talk. Traced back to Plato and Socrates, cognition is seen as discourse that the mind carries on with itself. As in James's stream of consciousness, it is argued that all human systems exhibit a continuing "cinematographic-show of visual imagery" (Ryle, 1949) or an ongoing "inner newsreal" (Becker, 1971) that is best understood in the notion of inner dialogue.

The inner dialogue of any system—individual, group, organization, society—can be understood, argues Schwartz

(1986), by categorizing its contents at the highest level of abstraction with respect to its functional role in achieving a specified aim. It is illustrated, for example, from a study of a stressful medical procedure, that people may have thoughts that either impede the aim of the clinical intervention ("the catheter might break and stick in my heart" — negative image) or conversely may facilitate the goals of the care ("this procedure may save my life" — positive image). Hence, the inner dialogue functions as an inner dialectic between positive and negative adaptive statements, and one's guiding imagery is presumably an outcome of such an inner dialectic.

A whole series of recent studies have looked at this process, and results suggest a clear and definitive pattern of difference in the cognitive ecology of "functional" (healthy) versus "dysfunctional" (unhealthy) groups.

Table 3.2 presents data showing the ratios of positive to negative image statements for functional and dysfunctional groups across a series of seven independent studies. In all cases, there is a definite *imbalance* in the direction of positive imagery for those identified as more psychologically or socially functional. As can be seen, the functional groups are characterized by approximately a 1.7:1 ratio of positive to negative images. Mildly dysfunctional groups ("high" dysfunction was not studied) demonstrate equal frequencies, a balanced 1:1 internal dialogue.

Obviously, the sheer quantification of cognition has certain weaknesses. For one thing, it is clear that just one idea or image can transform the entire gestalt of a thousand others. But the findings do have meaning, especially when linked to other studies showing that images of hope or hopelessness can affect the body's innate healing system, its immune functioning, and other neurochemical processes. Especially disturbing are reports indicating that many of our children today are growing up in family settings where as much as 90 percent of the home's internal dialogue is negative, that is, what not to do, how bad things are, what was done wrong, who is to blame (Fritz, 1984).

But it is not just our children. In his powerful *Critique of Cynical Reason*, Peter Sloterdijk (1987) observes that the whole of postmodern society is living within an internal dialogue or

Table 3.2. Ratios of Positive and Negative Thoughts for Functional and Dysfunctional Groups Across Seven Independent Studies (Reported in Schwartz, 1986).

Focus of Study	Cognitive assessment	Functional M			Dysfunctional M		
		Positive	Negative	Ratio	Positive	Negative	Ratio
Assertiveness							
1. High vs. low assertive	Inventory/ASST[a]	57.0	33.0	1.7:1	48.0	51.0	1:1.1
2. High vs. low assertive	Inventory/ASST	59.0	35.0	1.7:1	48.0	51.0	1:1.1
3. High vs. low assertive	Inventory/ASST-R[b]	41.8	23.8	1.8:1	38.0	33.2	1.1:1
Social anxiety							
4. High vs. low socially anxious Sample 2: Females and males combined	Inventory/SISST[c]	54.9	33.0	1.7:1	42.7	47.3	1:1.1
5. High vs. low socially anxious	Production/thought listing[d]	1.6	1.2	1.3:1	1.5	2.0	1:1.3
Test anxiety							
6. High vs. low test-anxious	Production/talking aloud	67.3	32.0	2.1:1	45.0	61.3	1:1.4
Self-esteem							
7. High vs. low self-esteem	Production/thought sampling	2.4	1.5	1.6:1	2.3	2.0	1.2:1
	Mean ratio			1.70:1			1:1.14

[a] Assertiveness Self-Statement Test.
[b] ASST-Revised generalizes to a broader range of assertion situations.
[c] Social Interaction Self-Statement Test.
[d] Scores averaged across high and low anonymity conditions.

cognitive environment of a universal, diffuse cynicism. As a predominant mindset of the post-1960s era, Sloterdijk takes the cynic not as an exception but rather as the average social character. It is argued that at both the personal and institutional levels, throughout our society there is widespread disturbance of vitality, a bleakening of the life feeling, a farewell to defeated idealisms, and a sense of paralyzing resentment. Sociologically, Sloterdijk contends, today's cynicism is bureaucratic and it has become the predominant way of seeing things; psychologically, the modernist character is said to be a borderline melancholic, one who is able to keep the symptoms of depression under control and keep up appearances at both home and work. Our internal dialogue, as a society, Sloterdijk laments, has become more and more morose, and nowhere, he argues (1987, p. 12), is this better exemplified than in the halls of academia: "The scenery of the critical intelligensia is . . . populated by aggressive and depressive moralists, problematists, 'problemholics,' and soft rigorists whose existential stimulus is no."

Whether one agrees with Sloterdijk or not, it is important to recognize that all human systems are conditioned by their internal dialogue. Our minds are bathed within any number of cognitive environments—family, school, church, play, and even the environments created by our research methods and problem-solving technologies—that provide cues to the ways we perceive, experience, and imagine reality.

So the question must therefore be asked, What kinds of cognitive environments maximize the "human possible"? What kinds of cognitive ecologies are we generating, and why? Can cognitive ecologies be developed, transformed, or enhanced? And what kinds of cognitive ecologies do we want?

The Positive Image as a Dynamic Force in Culture . As various scholars (for instance, Markley, 1976; Morgan, 1987) have noted, the underlying images held by a civilization or culture have an enormous influence on its fate. Ethical values such as "good" or "bad" have little force, except on an abstract level, but if those values emerge in the form of an image (for example, good = St. George, or bad = the Dragon), they suddenly become a power shaping the consciousness of masses of

Positive Image, Positive Action

people (Broms and Gahmberg, 1983). Behind every culture there is a nucleus of images—the "Golden Age," "child of God," "Enlightenment," "Thousand-Year Reign of Christ," or "New Zion"—and this nucleus is able to produce countless variations around the same theme.

In his sweeping study of Western civilization, the Dutch sociologist Fred Polak (1973) argues essentially the same point concerning the heliotropic propensity of the positive image. For him (1973, p. 19), the positive image of the future is *the* single most important dynamic and explanatory variable for understanding cultural evolution: "Any student of the rise and fall of cultures cannot fail to be impressed by the role played in this historical succession of the future. *The rise and fall of images of the future precedes or accompanies the rise and fall of cultures.* As long as a society's image is positive and flourishing, the flower of culture is in full bloom. Once the image begins to decay and lose its vitality, however, the culture does not long survive."

For Polak, the primary question then is not how to explain the growth and decay of cultures, but how to explain the successful emergence or decay of positive images. Furthermore, he asks, how do the successive waves of optimism and pessimism or cynicism and trust regarding the images fit into the cultural framework and its accompanying dynamics? His conclusions, among others, include:

1. Positive images emerge in contexts of "influence-optimism" (belief in an open and influenceable future) and an atmosphere that values creative imagination mixed with philosophical questioning, a rich emotional life, and freedom of speech and fantasy.
2. The force that drives the image is only part cognitive or intellectual; a much greater part is emotional, esthetic, and spiritual.
3. The potential strength of a culture could actually be measured by the intensity, energy, and belief in its images of the future.
4. The image of the future not only acts as a barometer but actively promotes cognition and choice and in effect becomes self-fulfilling because it is self-propelling.

5. When a culture's utopian aspirations die out, the culture dies: "where there is no vision, the people perish" (Proverbs 29:18). Of special note here, anthropologists have shown that certain tribes have actually given up and allowed themselves to die when their images of the future have become too bleak. Ernest Becker (1971) notes the depopulation of Melanasia earlier in this century as well as the loss of interest by the Marquesan Islanders in having children. In the second case it appears that the islanders simply gave up when, in the face of inroads from white traders and missionaries, everything that gave them hope and a sense of value was eroded.

On this final point, Polak was intrigued with the following conclusion: Almost without exception, everything society has considered a social advance has been prefigured first in some utopian writing. For example Plato's *Politeia* opened the way, shows Polak, for a series of projections that then, via Thomas More's *Utopia*, had an impact on England's domestic and foreign policy. Similarly, Harrington's *Oceana* had immediate impact on France through the work of Abbé Sieyès, who used Harrington's model as a framework for his *Constitution de l'An VIII* (about 1789). Later, these themes were "eagerly absorbed" by John Adams and Thomas Jefferson and emerged in a variety of American political institutions, not to mention the Declaration of Independence. While the word *utopia* has, in our society, often been a derogatory term, the historical analysis shows utopia to be, in Polak's words (1973, p. 138) "a powerhouse": "Scientific management, full employment, and social security were all once figments of a utopia-writer's imagination. So were parliamentary democracy, universal suffrage, planning, and the trade union movement. The tremendous concern for child-rearing and universal education, for eugenics, and for garden cities all emanated from the utopia. The utopia stood for the emancipation of women long before the existence of the feminist movement. All the concepts concerning labor, from the length of the work week to profit-sharing (and sociotechnical systems design and QWL), are found in utopia. Thanks to the utopists, the twentieth century did not catch humanity totally unprepared."

Positive Image, Positive Action

Metacognition and Conscious Evolution of Positive Images. To the extent that the heliotropic hypothesis has some validity — that human systems have an observable tendency to macrodeterministically evolve in the direction of those "positve" images that are the brightest and boldest, most illuminating and promising — questions of volition and free agency come to the fore. Is it possible to create our own future-determining imagery? Is it possible to develop our metacognitive capacity and thereby choose between positive and negative ways of construing the world? If so, with what result? Is the quest for affirmative competence — the capacity to project and affirm an ideal image as if it is already so — a realistic aim or merely a romantic distraction? More important, is it possible to develop the affirmative competence of large collectivities, that is, of groups, organizations, or whole societies affirming a positive future together?

With the exception of the last question (there just has not been enough research here), most of the available evidence suggests quite clearly that affirmative competence can be learned, developed, and honed through experience, disciplined practice, and formal training.

Reviews on this topic, for example, are available in the areas of athletics and imagery, psychotherapy and imagery, imagery and healing, hypnosis and imagery, imagery and sexual functioning, and others related to overall metacognitive capacity (see Sheikh, 1983, for ten excellent reviews on these subjects).

In the case of athletics, as just one example, imagery techniques are fast becoming an important part of all successful training. In *Superlearning,* Ostrander (1979) discusses the mental methods used by Soviet and Eastern European athletes who have had such success in the Olympics in recent decades. Similarly, Jack Nicklaus's book *Golf My Way* (1974) offers a compendium of mental exercises to sharpen the affirmative function. For Nicklaus there is an important distinction to be made between a negative affirmation (for example, an image that says "don't hit it into the trees") and a positive affirmation (for instance, "I'm going to hit it right down the middle of the fairway"). Here again we find that the whole body, just like a whole culture, responds to what the mind imagines as possible. The important lesson, according to Nicklaus, is that affirmative competence can be acquired through discipline and practice and that such competence may be every bit as important to one's game as sheer physical capability.

Recent experimental evidence confirms this view and suggests something more: It is quite possible that the best athletes are as successful as they are because of a highly developed metacognitive capacity of differential self-monitoring. In brief, this involves being able to systematically observe and analyze successful performances (positive self-monitoring) or unsuccessful performances (negative self-monitoring) and to be able to choose between the two cognitive processes when desired. Paradoxically, while most in our culture seem to operate on the assumption that elimination of failures (negative self-monitoring) will improve performance, exactly the opposite appears to hold true, at least when it comes to learning new tasks. In one experiment, for example, Kirschenbaum (1984) compared a set of bowlers who received lessons on the components of effective bowling to those who did not receive the lessons (controls) and to groups who followed the lessons with several weeks of positive self-monitoring or negative self-monitoring (that is, they videotaped performances, edited out the positive or negative, and then selectively reviewed the corresponding tapes with the appropriate groups). As predicted, the positive self-monitors improved significantly more than all the others, and the unskilled bowlers (average of 123 pins) who practiced positive self-monitoring improved substantially (more than 100 percent) more than *all* other groups. Since then, these results have been replicated with other athletic activities such as golf, and evidence repeatedly indicates that positive self-monitoring significantly enhances learning on any task and is especially potent in the context of novel or poorly mastered tasks.

Some Implications for Management: Toward a Theory of the Affirmative Organization

> We are some time truly going to see our life as positive, not negative, as made up of continuous willing, not of constraints and prohibition.
> — Mary Parker Follett

That was a judgment of one of the great management prophets of the early 1940s who, in moving out of step with her time, prefigured virtually every new development in organizational thought and practice. Today, her ideas do not seem quite as strange as they once must have been. As we have seen in our overview of the placebo effect, Pygmalion dynamic, positive emotion, imbalanced inner dialogue, and positive self-monitoring, as well as of the role of utopian imagery in the rise and fall of cultures, scholars are recognizing that the power of positive imagery is not just some popular illusion or wish but an expression of the mind's capacity for shaping reality. A theory of affirmation *is* emerging from many quarters. Admittedly its findings are still limited; unifying frameworks are lacking, and generalization across levels of analysis and disciplines makes for unintelligible and often confusing logic. Nevertheless that knowledge—limited though it is—has important practical implications for organizations and management. In the rest of this discussion, I hope to push the current perspective onward by offering an exploratory set of propositions concerning what might be called the *affirmative basis* of organizing. When translated from the various disciplines into organizationally relevant terms, the emerging "theory of affirmation" looks something like this:

1. *Organizations as made and imagined are artifacts of the affirmative mind. An understanding of organizational life requires an understanding of the dynamic of the positive image as well as of the processes through which isolated images become interlocked images and of how nascent affirmations become guiding affirmations.* The starting point for a theory of affirmation is simply this: When it comes to understanding organizational existence from the perspective of human action, there is no better clue to a system's overall well-being than its guiding image of the future. In the last analysis, organizations exist because stakeholders who govern and maintain them carry in their minds some sort of shared positive projection about what the organization is, how it will function, and what it might become. Although positive imagery (in the form of positive thinking, utopian visions, affirmation, and the like) has not been paraded as a central concept in organizational and management thought, it can be usefully argued that virtually every organizational act is based on some positive projection on the part of the individual or group. Organizational birth itself, to take just one example, is impossible in the absence of some affirmative projection. But positive or negative, enabling or limiting, conscious or unconscious — all action is conditioned by the fact that we live in an anticipatory world of images. These guiding images are not detailed objectives but are paintings created with a larger brush stroke. They encompass many aspects of organizational life that mission statements, corporate strategies, or plans alone do not reveal. Just as it has been observed that the rise and fall of images of the future precede or accompany the rise and fall of societies, it can be argued that as long as an organization's image is positive and flourishing, the flower of organizational life will be in full bloom.

2. No matter what its previous history is, virtually any pattern of organizational action is open to alteration and reconfiguration. Patterns of organizational action are not automatically fixed by nature in any blind microdeterminist way — whether biological, behavioral, technological, or environmental. There is no such thing as an inevitable form of organization. There are no "iron laws." While affected by microdeterminist factors, existing regularities that are perceived are controlled by mentalist or "macro" factors exerting downward control. Just as in the Pygmalion dynamic reviewed earlier, organizations are genetically constituted socially in and through the images born in transaction among all participants. In this sense, existing regularities that are observed depend not on some dictate of nature but on the historically and contextually embedded continuities in what we might call (1) the prophetic image — expectancies and beliefs about the future; (2) the poetic image — imagined possibilities or alternatives of what might be; and (3) the normative image — ideological or value-based images of what should be. When organizations continue to hold the same expectations and beliefs; when they continue to envision the same possibilities or alternatives; or when they continue to project the same conventional values, norms, or ideologies — it is under these macrodeterminist conditions that continuities in structures and practices will in fact be found.

3. To the extent that organizations' imaginative projections are the key to their current conduct, organizations are free to seek transformations

Positive Image, Positive Action

in conventional practice by replacing conventional images with images of a new and better future. To a far greater extent than is normally assumed, organizational evolution is isomorphic with the mental evolution of images. In many respects, it can usefully be argued that organizations are limited primarily or even only by (1) their affirmative capacities of mind, imagination, and reason, and (2) their collective or *coaffirmative capacity* for developing a commanding set of shared projections among a critical segment of stakeholders.

In regard to the latter point, it can be argued further that the guiding image of the future exists deep within the internal dialogue of the organization. The image is not, therefore, either a person-centered or a position-centered phenomenon; it is a situational and interactional tapestry that is a public "property" of the whole rather than of any single element or part. While such things as executive vision and charismatic leadership may be understood as parallels to what I am talking about, their emphasis on the "Great Man" leads them to seriously understate and miscast the complex cooperative aspect of an organization's guiding image of the future. When it comes to collective entities like groups, organizations, or even whole societies, we must emphatically argue that the guiding image of the future does not, even metaphorically, exist within some individual or collective mass of brain. It exists in a very observable and tangible way in the living dialogue that flows through every institution, expressing itself anew at every moment.

4. *Organizations are heliotropic in character in the sense that organizational actions have an observable and largely automatic tendency to evolve in the direction of positive imagery. Positive imagery and hence heliotropic movement is endemic to organizational life, which means that organizations create their own realities to a far greater extent than is normally assumed.* As we have seen in the placebo, Pygmalion, and self-monitoring studies, the positive image carries out its heliotropic task by generating and provoking image-consistent affirmative cognition, image-consistent emotion, and self-validating action. Hence, it can be argued that positive images of the future generate in organizations (1) an affirmative cognitive ecology that strengthens peoples' readiness and capacity to recall the positive aspects of the past, to selectively see the positive in the present, and to envision new potentials in the future; (2) it catalyzes an affirmative emotional climate, for example, of heightened optimism, hope, care, joy, altruism, and passion; and (3) it provokes confident and energized action (see Weick, 1983, on this third point).

Another aspect of the heliotropic hypothesis is that it predicts the following: When presented with the option, organizations will move more rapidly and effectively in the direction of affirmative imagery (moving toward light) than in the opposite direction of negative imagery (moving against light or toward "overpowering darkness"). Existing in a dynamic field of images, it can be argued that organizations move along the path of least resistance (Fritz, 1984) toward those images that are judged to represent the organizations' highest possibilities — those images that are the brightest, most purposeful, or most highly valued. Positive images whose prophetic, poetic, and normative aspects are congruent will show the greatest self-fulfilling potential.

5. Conscious evolution of positive imagery is a viable option for organized systems as large as global society or as small as the dyad or group. Also, the more an organization experiments with the conscious evolution of positive imagery the better it will become; there is an observable self-reinforcing, educative effect of affirmation. Affirmative competence is the key to the self-organizing system. Through both formal and informal learning processes, organizations, like individuals, can develop their metacognitive competence — the capacity to rise above the present and assess their own imaginative processes as they are operating. This enhances their ability to distinguish between affirmative and negative ways of construing the world. The healthiest organizations will exhibit a 2:1 or better ratio of positive-to-negative imagery (as measured through inner dialogue), while less healthy systems will tend toward a 1:1 balanced ratio. Similarly, it can usefully be argued that positively *biased* organizational monitoring (with selective monitoring and feedback of the positive) will contribute more to heliotropic movement than either neutral (characterized by inattention) or negative organizational monitoring (with a focus on problems or deficiencies). This effect, we would expect based on studies in athletics, will be more pronounced in situations where the affirmative projection is of a novel or complex future and where the tasks or actions required to enact the images are not yet fully tested or mastered.

The more an organization experiments with the affirmative mode, the more its affirmative and heliotropic competence will grow. This is why, in many organizations that have experimented with it, people have come to believe that organizationwide affirmation of the positive future is the single most important act that a system can engage in if its real aim is to bring to fruition a new and better future. An image that asserts that the future is worth living for will, as William James ([1895] 1956) argued, provoke those actions that help create the fact. While not every future can be created as locally envisioned, there is always a margin within which the future can be affected by positive affirmation. The size of this margin can never be known a priori. Put another way, an organization will rarely rise above the dominant images of its members and stakeholders; or as Willis Harman (1988, p. 1) hypothesizes, "perhaps the only limits to the human mind are those we believe in."

6. *To understand organizations in affirmative terms is also to understand that the greatest obstacle in the way of group and organizational well-being is the positive image, the affirmative projection that guides the group or the organization.* Theorist Henry Wieman (1926, p. 268) gave a clear description of the seeming paradox involved here many years ago in his comparative analysis of *Religious Experience and Scientific Method:* "We are very sure that the greatest obstacle in the way of individual growth and social progress is the ideal [affirmative projection] which dominates the individual or group. The greatest instrument of achievement and improvement is the ideal, and therefore our constant failures, miseries, and wickedness are precisely due to the inadequacy of our highest ideals. Our ideals have in them all the error, all the impracticability, all the perversity and confusion that human beings that themselves erring, impractical, perverse and confused, can put into them. Our ideals are no doubt the best we have in the way of our constructions. But the best we have is pitifully inadequate.

Our hope and full assurance . . . [are] that we can improve our ideals. If we could not be saved from our ideals, we would be lost indeed."

One of the ironies of affirmation is that it partially cripples itself in order to function. By definition, to affirm means to "hold firm." As we have seen, it is precisely the strength of affirmation, the degree of belief or faith invested, that allows the image to carry out its heliotropic task. So when our institutions are confronted with repetitive failure and amplifying cycles of distress; when time and energies are expended on such issues as compliance, discipline, obedience, motivation, and the like; or when almost every "new" surefire problem-solving technique does little but add a plethora of new problems—in every one of these cases the system is being given a clear signal of the inadequacy of its "firm" affirmative projections. To repeat, our positive images are no doubt the best we have, but the best is often not responsive to changing needs and opportunities. The real challenge, therefore, is to discover the processes through which a system's best affirmations can be left behind and better ones developed. For if we could not be saved from our best affirmative projections, "we would be lost indeed."

7. *Organizations do not need to be fixed. They need constant reaffirmation. More precisely, organizations as heliotropic systems need to be appreciated. Every new affirmative projection of the future is a consequence of an appreciative understanding of the past or the present.* Up to this point we have examined the nature of the positive image–positive action relationship but have said nothing about the mental artistry by which guiding images—prophesies, possibilities, and normative values—are in fact generated. We seem to have become preoccupied with the question of "how to translate intention into reality and sustain it" (see for example Bennis and Nanus, 1985) and have ignored what is perhaps the more essential question.

An earlier set of writings (Cooperrider and Srivastva, 1987; Cooperrider, 1986) described a process of knowing that was preeminently suited to the task of providing both the data and the mental inspiration through which human systems can fashion new affirmative projections on a dynamic and continuous basis. It was argued that appreciative inquiry is based on a "reverence for life" and is essentially biocentric in character: It is an inquiry process that tries to apprehend the factors that give life to a living system and seeks to articulate those possibilities that can lead to a better future. More than a method or technique, the appreciative mode of inquiry was described as a means of living with, being with, and directly participating in the life of a human system in a way that compels one to inquire into the deeper life-generating essentials and potentials of organizational existence.

As this concept relates specifically to leadership, an important clue to the meaning of executive appreciation is found in Isaiah Berlin's (1980, pp. 14–15) account of Winston Churchill's leadership during England's darkest hour:

> In 1940 he [Churchill] assumed an indomitable stoutness, an unsurrendering quality on the part of his people. . . . He idealized them with such intensity that in the end they approached his ideal and began to see themselves as he saw them: "the buoyant and inperturbable temper of Britain which I had the honour to express"—it was indeed, but he had the lion's share in creating it. So hypnotic was the force of his words, so strong his faith, that by the sheer intensity of his eloquence he bound his spell upon them until it seemed to them that he was indeed speaking what was in their hearts and minds. Doubtless it was there; but largely dormant until he had awoken it within them.
>
> After he had spoken to them in the summer of 1940 as no one else has ever before or since, they conceived a new idea of themselves. . . . They went forward into battle transformed by his words. . . . He created a heroic mood and turned the fortunes of the Battle of Britain not by catching the [life-diminishing] mood of his surroundings but by being impervious to

it, as he had been to so many of the passing shades and tones of which the life around him had been composed.

Churchill's impact and the guiding images he helped create were the result of his towering ability to cognitively dissociate all seeming impossibilities, deficiencies, and imperfections from a given situation and to see in his people and country that which had fundamental value and strength. His optimism, even in Britain's darkest moment, came not from a Pollyanna-like sense that "everything is just fine" but from a conviction that was born from what he, like few others, could actually see in his country: "Doubtless it was there; but largely dormant until he had awoken it."

In almost every respect the cognitive and perceptual process employed by Churchill, like many great executives, was that of the artist. The appreciative eye we are beginning to understand apprehends "what is" rather than "what is not" and in this represents a rigorous cognitive ability to bracket out all seeming imperfections from that which has fundamental value. For as the poet Shelley suggests, appreciation "makes immortal all that is best and most beautiful in the world. . . . It exalts the beauty of that which is most beautiful. . . . It strips the veil of familiarity from the world, and lays bare and naked sleeping beauty, which is in the spirit of its forms" (in Cooperrider and Srivastva, 1987, p. 164).

But this is only part of the story: Appreciation not only draws our eye toward life, but stirs our feelings, excites our curiosity, and provides inspiration to the envisioning mind. In this sense, the ultimate generative power for the construction of new values and images is the apprehension of that which has value. Nietzsche once asked of appreciation, "Does it not praise? Does it not glorify? Does it not select? Does it not bring [that which is appreciated] to prominence? In all this, does it not strengthen or weaken certain valuations?" (in Rader, 1973, p. 12).

No one has expressed this more effectively than the artist Vincent van Gogh, who, in a letter to his brother (in Rader, 1973, p. 10), spelled out what could actually be an entire leadership course on the relationship between appreciation and the emergence of new values:

> I should like to paint a portrait of an artist friend, a man who dreams great dreams, who works as the nightingale sings, because it is in his nature. He'll be a fine man. I want to put into my picture of appreciation, the love I have for him. So I paint him as he is, as faithfully as I can. But the picture is not finished yet. To finish it, I am now the arbitrary colorist. I exaggerate the fairness of the hair; I come even to use orange tones, chromes, and pale lemon-yellow. Behind the head, instead of painting the ordinary wall of the mean room, I paint infinity, a plain background of the richest, intensest blue that I can contrive—and by this simple combination of the bright head against the rich blue background, I get a mysterious effect, like a star in the depths of an azure sky.

Like Churchill, van Gogh began with a stance of appreciative cognition. He viewed his friend through a loving and caring lens and focused on those qualities that "excited his preference" and kindled his imagination. The key point is that van Gogh did not merely articulate admiration for his friend: He created new values and new ways of seeing the world through the very act of valuing. And again, as Nietzsche (in Rader, 1973, p. 12) has elaborated: "valuing is creating: hear it, ye creating ones! Valuation is itself the treasure and jewel of valued things."

In contrast to the affirmative projection that seeks certainty and control over events, the appreciative eye actually seeks uncertainty as it is thrown into the elusive and emergent nature of organizational life itself. Appreciation is creative rather than conservative precisely because it allows itself to be energized and inspired by the voice of mystery. As an active process of valuing the factors that give rise to the life-enhancing organization, appreciation has room for the vital uncertainty, the indeterminacy that is the trademark of something alive. In this sense, too, it differs from affirmation in that it is not instrumental.

It does not have the capability of shaping the world closer to preexisting wants because it tends, in the end, to transform those wants into something very different from that which was originally affirmed. Executive appreciation, then, represents the capacity to rediscover in organizations what Bruner refers to as the "immensity of the commonplace" or what James Joyce terms the "epiphanies of the ordinary" (see Bruner, 1986, p. 198). Appreciation, as Churchill must have understood, is the mental strength that allows a leader to consciously peer into the life-giving present, only to find the future brilliantly interwoven into the texture of the actual.

8. *The executive vocation in a postbureaucratic society is to nourish the appreciative soil from which affirmative projections grow, branch off, evolve, and become collective projections. Creating the conditions for organizationwide appreciation is the single most important measure that can be taken to ensure the conscious evolution of a valued and positive future.* The "how" of appreciative inquiry is beyond the scope of this discussion. But a number of final thoughts can be offered on the organizational prerequisites of appreciation. These comments stem from experiences with a number of systems that have actually experimented with appreciative inquiry on a collective and organizationwide basis.

First, it is clear that the appreciative process has been most spontaneous and genuine in relatively egalitarian systems — organizations committed to an ideology of inclusion, consent, and coevolution (Srivastva and Cooperrider, 1986). Put more strongly, experience suggests that the creative power of appreciation will never be realized in a world that continues to place arbitrary restrictions or constraints on speech and action. It is the realm of action, not mind, that is the preeminent basis of those creative images that have the power to guide us into a positive future.

Second, experience indicates that if pursued deeply enough, appreciative inquiry arrives at a dynamic interpersonal ideal. It arrives at knowledge that enlarges our sense of solidarity with other human beings and provides an ever-expanding universe of examples and images concerning the possibilities for a more egalitarian future.

We are infants when it comes to our understanding of

appreciative processes of knowing and social construction. Yet we are beginning to see that the power of appreciation rests with its self-reinforcing and self-generative capacity. Through appreciation of organizational life, members of an organization learn to value not only the life-enhancing organization but also learn to affirm themselves. As new potentials for inquiry are revealed and experienced within the "student," new insights are made available and shared with others in the organization. As sharing occurs, the inquiry becomes a joint process of knowing—others are invited to explore and question their own ideals or affirmative projections. Through dialogue, new knowledge and new images of possibility are constantly being made available. And while such knowledge is always felt as an interruption in the status quo, it is valued and turned into a heliotropic project because it represents a joint creation of a world that corresponds to the jointly imagined projection of human and social possibility.

5

Appreciating Diversity and Modifying Organizational Cultures: Men and Women at Work

Barbara Benedict Bunker

Differences between cultures are sometimes blatant and sometimes subtle. Readers of Garreau's *Nine Nations of North America* (1981) find their traditional view of the fifty states of the United States reframed into a proposal that there are really nine culturally diverse regions that better describe our differences.

This chapter proposes that understanding and knowing how to include persons of different cultures in the traditionally homogeneous culture of American business is the key to changing organizational cultures to support innovation, collaboration, and productivity. The working relationships of men and women are the case example on which this chapter will focus. There are, of course, many other examples.

Before cultures can be changed, we have to be aware that they exist. Perhaps the easiest way to discuss how cultural awareness is raised is to describe the process of crossing cultural boundaries, for example, by spending time in a country very different from your own.

A few years ago, I spent a year in Japan teaching and trying to understand a new culture. I chose a non-Western culture quite purposefully since part of my motivation was to acquire a broader perspective. I wanted to become more aware of some of the assumptions that underlie my own culture. When you enter a new culture, the assumptions of your own culture are apt to move from background into more prominence. Awareness of the new culture's assumptions sharpens understanding of your own culture, in other words.

Entering a culture that is very different from your own is a challenging process, more so if you do not know the language. Acts that are meaningful in the familiar culture cannot be taken for granted in a new one, because the inferred meanings are shared within cultures. The world of social interaction becomes much less under control and much less predictable. The way things are done changes while you have to learn a whole new set of procedures in daily life.

One product of my first few months in Japan was a minitheory of the stages of entry and adjustment in a different culture that was based on my own experience. I have described these ideas to several groups of scholars who have had overseas experience. Their appreciative responses make me willing to describe them here.

Stages in Cultural Appreciation

When you first arrive in a new culture, there is a period of *confusion* that comes from the situation just described as well as from a lack of information. It leaves you quite dependent and in need of help in the form of information and advice. The second stage begins as you start to interact with the new culture. It is called the stage of *small victories*. Each new encounter with the culture—for example, opening a bank account, riding the bus or subway, going to the local market, or attending a faculty reception—is fraught with peril. It is preceded by anxiety and information collection and rehearsal. Then the event occurs and you return home either triumphant or defeated. When successful, the feelings really are very much as though a major victory has been won. A heightened roller coaster of affect is particularly characteristic of this stage. The support needed is emotional support, people who appreciate what you are going through and who can cheer you onward.

It often happens that once some of the fundamentals of

life are mastered, there is time to explore and discover the new culture. This is the *honeymoon* stage of wonder and infatuation. In it there is heightened appreciation for the new, the different, the esthetic. Depending on the degree of cultural immersion and exploration, it may continue for a considerable period of time. During this time there is no interest in attending to the less attractive downsides of the culture.

After a while, a self-correction takes place. No honeymoon can last forever. *Irritation* and *anger* begin to be experienced. Why in the world would anyone do it that way? Can't these people get their act together? Now the deficits seem glaringly apparent. For some people, they overwhelm the positive characteristics and become predominant.

Finally, if you are lucky enough to chart a course through these stages and not get stuck (and people do get stuck in stages), there is a rebalance and *reality*. There is the capacity to understand and enjoy the new culture without ignoring those features that are less desirable.

This cultural entry and engagement process is both cognitive and affective. New information is acquired and remembered; old schemas and perceptions are revised and qualified. An active learning process occurs. At the same time anxiety arises in reaction to uncertainty and the challenges of the learning processes. It must be managed, as must the extremes of feeling that occur in this labile period. Thus, I am describing a learning process that results in valuing and affirming the best in the culture while at the same time seeing it in its completeness, seeing it whole. The capacity to affirm the whole—including those aspects that are less desirable yet are part of the whole—is critically important. As Williams (1983, p. 5) says in *The Velveteen Rabbit,* "Once you are real you can't be ugly, except to people who don't understand."

When fully experienced—that is, when all the stages are traversed and you arrive at reality—could it be said that you now most fully appreciate another culture? I raise this question early in this exploration because I want to view the changing gender composition of the workplace and the problems that are being raised by this shift from a culture-change perspective. An appreciative process, "appreciative inquiry," is proposed as a way of helping members of different cultures recognize and value their differences and create a new culture where diverse values are understood and honored. Executives—those who must lead these culture-change projects—need to understand that equal employment opportunity, affirmative action, and sexual harassment policies as viewed and implemented in American organizations are problem-oriented change strategies. They focus on correcting what is wrong rather than creating a valued future. Executives themselves will need to inquire appreciatively into cultures that are not known to them before they are equipped to lead cultural change in their own organizations. I have selected gender as a case example because it is not immediately clear to all that gender issues require an awareness of two cultures.

In the next sections of this paper there will be a discussion of the cultures of men and women as well as of the processes that need to occur if the world of work is to fully utilize the gender diversity of the workforce. Although this paper is about gender, I believe that the same processes are involved in the appreciative inquiry into any other cultures, such as those involving race, ethnic group, or sexual preference.

Culture and the World of Work

The notion of organizational culture has become popular in recent years (Schein, 1985; Deal and Kennedy, 1985). Enthusiastic programs are being mounted to shape, revitalize, and change organizational cultures. The more serious among those who offer these services agree with Schein (1985) that culture is a complex and deep process that is not easily susceptible to change. They talk about programs of from three to five years of intensive commitment that involve political, structural, symbolic, and personal frameworks and processes (Nadler, 1987; Bolman and Deal, 1984).

The formation of an organization's culture begins with the executive who founded the company and who is a key actor in the establishment of company practices and values. Subsequent executives play important roles in extending, maintaining, or altering that culture. Systems tend to mirror the values and orientation of those in authority. In the business world of the United States, entrepreneurs and their successors have been men, predominantly white men, often with a Christian religious background. It should therefore come as no surprise that the culture of the world of work in America reflects the culture and the norms of the all-male group.

What does this mean? What is the typical culture of the world of work? Aries's research (1976, 1982, 1987) is very helpful in clarifying key issues. Aries used Bales's (1970) interaction coding scheme to examine behavior in all-male, all-female, and mixed-sex groups. These groups met serially in sessions for discussion. Aries examined what they chose to talk about, the climate of the group, the dominance order, and the interpersonal interaction patterns. She examined these issues for all three types of groups. It is instructive to consider what she found.

Male Group Culture. The all-male group had discussions about a series of topics. Men talked about their work, sports, money, cars, political life, current events, women, and many other topics. Of equal importance is the way they talked about topics. There was a friendly, good-humored, but nonetheless competitive atmosphere in the all-male group. When the men told jokes, a "Can you top this?" atmosphere developed. They vied with each other to tell the best story as one joke followed the next. This characteristically male process also occurs when men tell war stories about work. They talk about events that have happened to them in their business roles and how they coped with them. In these stories heroes emerge, and often they are the men telling the stories—who manage to do just the right thing in the nick of time. Sometimes they are funny stories in which the teller does not cope well; then the moral of the tale is to make others feel empathic . . . with so many things going against him, his survival is a miracle! Another familiar competition is to tell the best story about difficult situations. We should not overlook the fact that a great deal of information about roles and how they are enacted and what others are doing in their jobs is exchanged in the telling of war stories. Reputa-

Appreciating Diversity

tions are also enhanced in this process, as I show you how competent I am by describing in this socially acceptable ritual deft feats in the face of adversity.

Competition is more friendly than vicious in the all-male club. "Zinging" or "zapping" are labels used to describe one game that is played. It is a competition to score points on the other by teasing or ridiculing some personal weak spot. Nonverbal acknowledgments are usual so that the flow of conversation is not interrupted by this sidebar. A man may lick his index finger and write a nonverbal "1" as a sign that the other has scored a point. Another may enact the slow removal of a knife from the chest if a barb has been particularly telling, usually to the glee of others present. It is always understood to mean that I now "owe you one"; and the one on whom the point was scored will be looking for ways to redress the zing, "get" the other person, and even out the score.

It is important to emphasize that this competition is good-natured; it has the feeling of gamesmanship. It is not to be taken too seriously. The attitude is that you win some and you lose some! It is all in good fun. In this culture, both winning and losing are expected and commonly experienced. For those who possess the skills to take part in these games, they provide warm relationships that have energy and wit and exchange a great deal of information.

The all-male culture to a greater or lesser degree is the culture of business organizations today. Therefore, it is important to understand both the values and the downsides of this culture. If we look at it from an appreciative framework (Cooperrider and Srivastva, 1987), we can see that it has a number of very valuable attributes. On the other hand, there are also obvious drawbacks.

Any strong culture absorbs into it those opposing elements that would threaten to change it. This is especially true of the culture of competition. Students of conflict and its resolution (Deutsch, 1973) have pointed out that competition tends to be dominant over other "softer" cultural forms such as collaboration. It is, for example, both difficult and potentially self-destructive to behave collaboratively toward someone who is fiercely competitive toward you. Consequently, a person may get stuck in competitive interactions even when wishing for another form of interaction. I will never forget a dinner with three male colleagues during which they told war stories and generally paraded their competence for several hours. It appeared to me that they were all enjoying themselves thoroughly until I asked one of them after the event how he felt about it. I was shocked and delighted to discover that he had found it just as tiresome and lacking in depth as I. That experience has given me courage to try to change the course and culture of social interactions when I experience them as unproductive or unpleasant, or at least to raise the question of whether we are enjoying the culture we have created.

At the individual level, the person with the greatest range of behaviors becomes most valuable in group life because he or she can do things the group needs. The greater the person's behavioral repertoire, the greater the capacity of that person as a group member to contribute. If all I can do is ask questions, I can make only limited contributions; if I can also be supportive, add knowledge, make proposals and defend them, and deal openly with conflict, I will be more helpful and more influential in the group.

Might we not say something similar about groups and organizations? If the only modality in which an organization operates is competition, its effectiveness is limited. Would it not be more effective if it could shift to other modalities such as collaboration or individual initiative when the circumstances warrant? Such a transition is not without difficulties. Conflict resolution researchers have invested considerable time and energy trying to specify the conditions that enable a competitive situation to change to collaboration. Because the parties may be afraid of being vulnerable if they collaborate when others are still competitive, mutual agreements and signals are essential and possible. Organizations need to be able to shift into appropriate modalities in order to be maximally effective.

Before proceeding further, I do need to acknowledge that my choosing to do this analysis at the level of culture should not be understood as disparaging the usefulness of other levels

Appreciating Diversity

of analysis. Social reality is complex and individual, and interpersonal process analysis will enrich our total understanding. My colleague John Carter (personal communication, 1988), for example, points out that the bonding in the all-male executive club is a product of many shared experiences in which men get to know each other very well. Through this process in which they make decisions that are more or less risky, successful, or ethical, they become vulnerable to each other. That is, they know things about each other that could be used in harmful ways. The "trust" that they have for each other is a mutual agreement not to use this information to hurt each other. When a stranger comes into the group, especially if that person is different in gender, race, or ethnicity, the majority will not be certain that they either know how or are willing to "play by the rules." Because they are different, an unknown quantity, they are avoided, though these processes may be subconscious. Thus, both the intrapsychic and the interpersonal levels of analysis add to our understanding of the all-male group.

Female Group Culture. Turning now to the all-female group, we find that when women are together different cultural norms and behaviors are likely to be present. In Aries's research (1976), the topics that women discussed included some of the same topics that men talked about. They also discussed more issues relating to family and home as well as dress, diets, and men. What distinguished women's discussions was not so much the differences in topics as the level at which they talked with each other. Women tended to be more personally disclosing about their feelings about the events in their lives. This was particularly true of issues affecting their own self-esteem and competence. They were more "personal" with each other.

The climate of the all-female group was (probably as a result) much more collaborative. Women have as a value egalitarian relationships. Their group structure reflects this value. Therefore, when we look at dominance order or patterns of who spoke and how much, we find that the rank order of who spoke most to least changed in women's groups from one session to the next. In observing the groups it was almost as if these women kept track of how much time they were taking and when they ran over their "quota," they instinctively turned to others and drew them into participation to correct the balance.

Other more informal evidence of this egalitarian norm in all-female groups comes from noticing how women organize when they form their own organizations. Many women's organizations of the 1970s did not survive in part because there was an insistence on equal status. Thus it was not possible to select someone for special functions, such as chairperson, since that implied different and probably higher status. The failure to differentiate functions in order to maintain equal status made some of these organizations unable to transact business with the outside world and they died. More recently, groups that have tried to be less hierarchical have created alternative forms of governance to try to overcome these problems without adopting a hierarchical organizational form.

The resistance to differentiation in all-female groups is true of issues of competence as well as structure and status (because they are all related). All-female teacher groups to which I have consulted steadfastly resist acknowledging that there may be different levels of teaching competence in their ranks. "We are all equally good teachers here; after all, none of us have been fired!" In a very interesting discussion of women in medicine, Klass (1988) discusses how women behave and the culture they create when they have the power to do so. Although there are now many women being trained as doctors, surgery is still largely a male domain. When women surgeons are running an operating room, several respondents agreed that there was a difference. Men emphasize control and power differences while women "don't usually command quite as fiercely. . . . You get camaraderie with the other staff members . . . treating the nurses like intelligent people, talking to them . . . not the big ruler" (Klass, 1988, p. 46). Said one woman surgeon, "The boys need high mass, incense, and altarboys. They need boosting up. The women are much lower church" (Klass, 1988, p. 48). This perceived difference in managing authority creates a different working culture. It is also manifest in interpersonal behavior between doctor and patient. Women doctors who exhibit the feminine characteristic

Appreciating Diversity 135

of empathy and concern for relationships (Eagley, 1987) are apt to draw patients out, spending more time talking with them and teaching them than their male counterparts (Klass, 1988).

In the discussion up to this point, I have been purposefully portraying the differences between masculine and feminine cultures using research as the database. How clearly are these cultures defined in the world outside the laboratory? Are men and women aware of them?

Members of "the establishment" are usually surrounded by others in similar roles. They are often unaware that they have a "culture" and simply believe that their world is *the* world. Outgroups that must deal with the establishment are an excellent source of information about it. They must study it and understand its norms and rules in order to survive. Notice, for example, the number of books written by women about how to play the game and succeed in the business world. Thoughtful executive men may be aware of their culture, especially at points when it is threatened by the entrance of women. Those willing to examine the sense of resistance and feelings of loss will realize that there is indeed "something" to which they are clinging.

Is there a women's culture? If so, are women aware of it? There is substantial research that indicates that women and men differ in some value orientations and subsequent behavior (Eagley, 1987). One of the strongest is women's concern with interpersonal relationships while men are more achievement oriented. Speaking to a meeting of the Eastern Psychological Association in April 1988, Eleanor Maccoby spent time talking about differences in behavior of boys and girls at the youngest ages, under three years old, again raising the subject of whether differences that are observed are a product of nature or of socialization.

Research on gender differences has only become acceptable in the last ten to fifteen years. In the mid-1960s, we used to run mostly male subjects in laboratory studies of "human" behavior and generalize their behavior to everyone. We did this because "men took the set we gave them"; they could be counted on to respond to the experimental induction. Women's data often went off in other directions, and we described these irritating subjects as "unpredictable." Rather than find their data interesting and worthy of study, we found it contributed to high variances and thus needed to be excluded from the data we were collecting. At worst, gender differences were seen as messing up otherwise good data, and at best, they were uninteresting.

With the arrival of the 1970s and the women's movement, women began in consciousness raising groups and in other all-female gatherings to consider and develop a way of being together than can certainly be described as a culture. After years of dinner parties where women listened to men talk and focused on their interests, I recall several where after dinner women clustered together to talk with such energy and excitement that the men present felt excluded and miffed. Women who experienced that transition from ignoring other women and seeing them as less desirable to be with than men to discovering how interesting and enlivening the company of other women can be, have had a learning experience that is indelibly part of them.

The same is not true for many women born to the fruits of the 1970s but not old enough then to have lived through that experience. These younger women came into a different world, one of more opportunity and apparent equality. If there is subtle sexism, it is difficult to pinpoint. If there is discrimination, it occurs at the highest organizational levels, where for the most part there are few women. For these women the idea of a female culture gets very mixed reviews . . . since it can be seen to threaten by differentiating on the basis of gender when they wish to be treated without regard to gender. "I am just doing my job, and I do it just the way the men who work here do it; and I am judged in the same way they are."

Despite the different levels of belief and awareness among both women and men, I propose that it is very useful to entertain the notion that men and women in same-sex groups and organizations create predictably different environments.

Mixed-Sex Group Culture. These accounts of different cultures and orientation lead us to the next very important question. What happens when women with their orientation and culture enter the culture of the world of work, the culture of

Appreciating Diversity

the all-male group? What happens when women go to work? Aries's data on mixed-sex groups was collected in 1973. She did another study in 1982 to see if there had been changes in the way men and women relate to each other when cultures are joined.

When men and women are together, "male themes of aggression, competition, victimization, and practical joking were no longer frequent. These gave way to talk by males of themselves and their feelings. . . . We may conclude that the presence of women changes the all-male style of interacting, causing males to develop a more personal interaction, greater self revelation, and a decrease in the aggressive, competitive aspects of the encounter" (Aries, 1976, p. 14). A much less dramatic change was noted for women. They talked less about home and family but were no less personal. Thus mixed-group interaction appears to enable men to talk more about themselves and their feelings than they are able to do in all-male groups. In work settings this may be important when group agendas include analyzing how the work process is going or how individuals are contributing, when nonrational aspects of problems or planning need to be discussed, or when consensus-building discussion is the agenda.

In 1982 when Aries again looked at mixed-sex interaction, she was interested in whether the patterns of the early 1970s — in which men talked more than women in groups — had been changed by the cultural revolution in the West. In fact, though she predicted equality, she found that the women in the group of very bright young men and women who participated in her study talked more than men, a reversal of the previous trend. However, she also found that interaction styles remained traditional, with men engaging in more task-oriented behavior and women in more socioemotional behavior, despite predictions that that too would be equal. Further, nonverbal dominance behavior measured by body posture remained traditional, with men assuming more dominant nonverbal postures and women less dominant ones even when women were talking more and men less. It appears that women no longer hang back and wait for men to take the lead in verbal interaction, but that some deeper traditional behavior is still evident.

When I first became aware of the different cultures embodied in single-sex groups, women were just moving in larger numbers into the workplace. I became intrigued with the kinds of behaviors women would need to survive and succeed in a work world that was characteristically mostly male and quite competitive (Bunker and Bender, 1980). Men gain the skills of middle-range competition during adolescent socialization when they are members of sports teams, gangs, and clubs. Until recently, women have not participated in team sports to the same degree. Women's adolescent socialization is not primarily in groups but in one-to-one friendships. For many, competition is discouraged as "not nice." Women are encouraged to be concerned for others, collaborative, and supportive.

When women find themselves in the midst of the all-male culture, do they have the skills to compete if they want to? This interesting question was pursued in a program of training workshops and then in research. My graduate students and I created a series of workshops to explore this issue. We asked women to compete so that we could know more about their attitudes and skills. Our first major discovery was that women (these were middle managers in business) are absolute geniuses at taking a potentially very competitive situation and converting it into a collaborative one. We planned three workshops before we created a design that was able to block this collaborative urge and channel their energy into competition. They did compete, but many reported considerable discomfort and stress. They also were noticeably without a competitive overall strategy, even though the tasks presented choices that could have been strategic. Then we asked them to participate in some training exercises that would prepare them to interact in the competitive all-male situation. We called these skill practice exercises, "Boast, Roast, and Toast." In boast, they had to tell stories about their work competence so that they came off looking good. In roast, they had to play a game in which they were zinging each other. In toast, they had to say nice things about others and leave them feeling good about the one who gave the compliment. They did wonderfully at toast, awkwardly at boast, and miserably at roast. In fact, we almost had a rebellion around this last exercise be-

Appreciating Diversity

cause it was so distasteful to them. Since these workshops were all-female, they provided anecdotal evidence of how women react in the presence of other women. What would they do when there were men to compete with?

We designed a research study that created a competitive situation for dyads of women, men, and a mixed-sex pair. We found that men and women in same-sex groups were equally competitive, but in mixed-sex groups competition was significantly reduced. We are still in a data analysis process of trying to understand the nature of the difference in the mixed-sex dyad.

Women's concern that they not simply adjust to the dominant culture raises a fundamental question that needs to be addressed. Should women join the dominant male culture and "do it their way"? Or should they try to change the culture toward more collaboration, which may enable women to use their own skills more readily? These are difficult questions. There is evidence that when numbers of the non-majority group are small, the culture represented by the majority holds sway and is not easily influenced (Kanter, 1977).

An appreciative framework would look for those aspects of each culture that are valuable and contribute to work and relationship quality. It would help skill-deficient members of either gender to participate in training to acquire skills. It would not set up one culture or set of skills as the one right way. Rather what is needed now is an exploration of when competition is functional and helpful in work settings and when collaboration has more merit.

Executive Appreciation as a Process for Melting the Glass Ceiling

The *Wall Street Journal*'s special section on "The Glass Ceiling" (March 24, 1986) made prominent the question of why so few women are at the top of U.S. corporations. Is there some kind of invisible barrier that keeps women from rising above a certain level? The hypothesis is that there is a "glass ceiling" around the general-manager level that prevents women from going further.

Since the glass ceiling hypothesis has achieved currency, speculation about the causes of this phenomenon has grown. Recently, Morrison, White, Van Velsor, and Center for Creative Leadership (1987) have published an extensive research study that tries to ascertain causes. In it they not only talk to 76 women in Fortune 100 companies who have "broken the glass ceiling"; they also asked senior management at some of the same companies to describe the characteristics of women who had succeeded and those who derailed or plateaued. The latter were women who were expected to be promoted into the highest levels but did not achieve the promotion.

When these authors talk about breaking the glass ceiling, they mean shattering the invisible barrier and getting promoted to the highest levels of power in the organization. They also acknowledge that just getting the job is only the first step. Real acceptance into the senior level of executive management is acceptance into the power elite. To be effective, both are necessary. Since senior management in virtually all Fortune 500 companies is white male, this means acceptance into the all-male group. Thus, when women succeed in the power elite we need a metaphor that creates a positive image of the process—not simply a barrier-breaking one.

What happens when a woman becomes a member of an all-male group? There are several possibilities. One is that she behaves like one of the boys and they treat her as an exceptional woman who has the capacity to play their game and live by their rules. When this happens the group changes very little. Another possibility is that her very presence makes the group a mixed-sex group. This means different norms and ways of doing things, and giving up some of the behavior of the all-male club. When this happens the established group of men may feel uncomfortable. They must deal with their feelings of loss and anger at being asked to give up their comfortable and familiar culture. A third possibility is that the woman gets promoted but not accepted. In this case she is walled off or isolated; she is psychologically treated as if she is not there (Wolman and Frank, 1975). When this happens there is a high probability of job failure, since she will be isolated from the information flow and influence channels that are necessary to function effectively.

Appreciating Diversity

What are the characteristics of today's executive women? The research of Morrison, White, Van Velsor, and Center for Creative Leadership (1987, p. 50) helps us to understand what may be happening when women do succeed in management. Successful senior executive women were studied and compared with male executives at the same level. They found that "executive women are more like executive men than they are different in terms of their goals, motives, personalities, and behavior." This was true for dozens of measures. Lack of significant gender differences is also reported by other researchers working at middle-management and executive levels (Catalyst, 1986; Harlan and Weiss, 1981; Personnel Decisions, Inc., 1987).

There were five differences that did appear in the Morrison, White, Van Velsor, and Center for Creative Leadership (1987) data. Two of them can be said to reflect male comfort with their surroundings. Executive men were (1) more in tune with their surroundings (they perceived things the way their peers did), and (2) more comfortable in the climate of achievement via conformity than women. That is, conformity to intellectual authority was seen as desirable and they agreed. The criteria for excellence were clearly spelled out, and they were comfortable with them.

Executive women, on the other hand, were (3) more likely to move in new and original directions and (4) more likely to behave as individuals and to personalize their experiences. Remembering that most of these women are in pioneering roles, this is not surprising. Executive men were (5) more apt to feel equal to the demands for time and energy in their daily lives. Given the double roles that most working women fill, this also is not surprising.

Despite the many demonstrated similarities, people in organizations evaluating what it takes for men and women to achieve the executive level described some overlapping and some unique requirements for men and women. "Women often have to meet the demanding performance standards set for executive men while being seen as outdoing the men in areas where women are traditionally perceived as weak (e.g. commitment, toughness, career risks)" (Morrison, White, Van Velsor, and Center for Creative Leadership, 1987, p. 48). Almost twice as many success

142 Appreciative Management and Leadership

factors were listed for women as for men by the sixteen male corporate executives and the six female executives that were the panel of observers. This provides some support for the notion that women have to work harder to get to the same place as male colleagues.

Perhaps the most interesting issue raised by their data is that the latitude for acceptable behavior for women executives appears to be very narrow (see Figure 5.1) On the one hand, women must be able to perform job-related masculine-type behaviors without becoming "too masculine," lest they be stereotyped and rejected. Examples of behaviors that are too masculine — depending somewhat on the culture of the organization — might be swearing, telling dirty jokes, smoking cigars, or politicking. On the other hand, women must be feminine but not objectionably so. This means that behaviors associated with traditional nonprofessional women are not acceptable. The result is that executive women must walk a very difficult tightrope, selecting from a rather limited set of acceptable behaviors that must be intuited from the normative messages that that particular cultures gives off.

Because women in work environments are enacting a role that has traditionally been valued for males only (Broverman and

Figure 5.1. The Scope of Acceptable Behavior for Women Executives.

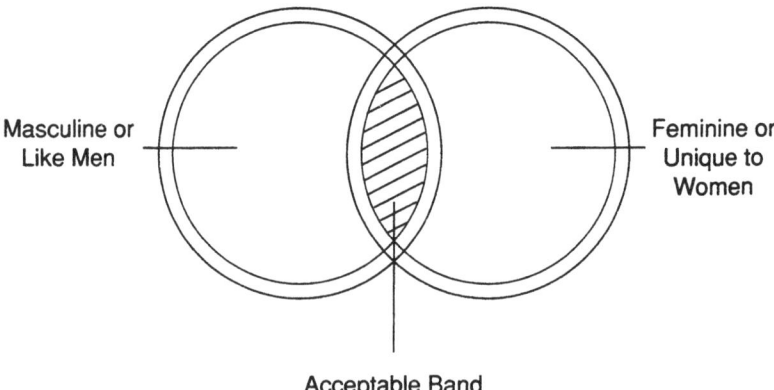

(*Source:* Morrison, White, Van Velsor, and Center for Creative Leadership, 1987.)

others, 1970), the expectations with which women have to deal are far more complex than for their male counterparts. They are in fact coping with very different environments. Men are dealing with the world and the expectations of the all-male group. Certainly there are some men whose socialization was different from the majority or who do not like the all-male culture. They may have difficulties, but in general, it is a familiar world. Women, however, enter a new world with expectations that they carry both masculine and feminine roles, but not too much or too far. Certainly there are some women who were raised in settings where they learned to compete and love it. But as adults they still must judge how far they can go without being seen as unacceptable.

Thus, we are beginning to have some good descriptions of the issues that are being created by the movement of more and more women into the workplace. Are women adjusting to masculine culture or modifying it? Do they feel they have much choice? What we do not have are many alternatives or even proposals for new models of a work culture that would embrace and allow differences. Furthermore, gender is only one of the issues of differing cultures that confront the contemporary workplace. Futurists looking at the workforce in the year 2000 are predicting that it will be radically different in composition, with more ethnic diversity and non-English speaking people in large numbers. I believe that executive appreciation provides one beginning way to think about next steps to deal with these challenges.

How do people from different cultures and backgrounds come together and create a workplace where their differences are embraced rather than becoming a source of dominance and conformity pressures? This question is recognized as urgent at the lower levels of organizations because there the numbers are beginning to change and problems are emerging. I want to suggest that the most urgent part of the organization for this work is at the executive level. We know that what happens at the top is reflected back down into the organization. Only if the executive group is diverse and finds ways to appreciate and utilize that diversity will the rest of the organization have a model and motivation for their own work. That means the modification of the current dominant culture, the culture of the all-male group.

How do such modifications come about? As Schein (1985) has pointed out, we are dealing with feelings, attitudes, and unconscious assumptions that are difficult to understand, much less change. This suggests that the process has to be deep, that it must deal with affect, that people must change themselves before they will be able to make informed decisions that create a new model of organizational functioning. We should be talking about melting the glass ceiling rather than breaking it.

We are now at the edge of our knowledge. Here I can only cite examples of current projects that I believe may lead to a better capacity to create new models.

Executive Appreciation: A Case in Progress. How does an organization that has the culture and traditions of the male establishment change its culture and traditions so that women, blacks, and people from many cultures can work together in a culture that supports who they are and permits their full contribution? Consultant Janice Eddy has been working with the senior vice president of one of the divisions of a widely diversified chemical company on this issue. The program that is emerging in her work with the top-management group of that division and with colleague Richard Orange is not labeled "executive appreciation," but I believe it fits this understanding.

The goal of Eddy's work is to help management create a culture where diversity is understood and valued. To do this the members of the top-management group committed to a year of study with representative and diverse others in the company in order to prepare themselves to lead an analysis of the organization's norms, policies, and procedures. The study was conducted in an appreciative framework. The group involved is composed of five executives (men) and five women and black organizational members. All meet with the consultants once a month for a day. For the first six months they studied race, specifically black culture in America; for the second six months they studied gender.

Of crucial interest is the study experience itself. What happens to people in it? As described by the consultants, it is a process of providing stimulating information and events that the group share and discuss. Initially, the consultants distributed

Appreciating Diversity

articles to read and recommended books, movies, and plays. While each session had some special preparation that everyone shared, members were encouraged to bring in articles, other literature, and information about national and world events that they had reacted to and wanted to discuss. As the discussions deepened, people found themselves reading books they would not otherwise have read, going to the theater in settings where otherwise they might not have ventured, and expressing reactions, concerns, and personal feelings that they might not otherwise have disclosed. The structure was flexible and emergent at meetings. The group always shared two meals during the day. There was a time for one-to-one conversations that helped members develop more personal relationships within the group. Between sessions, members were asked to have one conversation with someone that would stretch them (they might not have ventured it under normal circumstances) and to come back and talk about it.

The consultants, both knowledgeable about issues of race and gender and themselves representing white and black, male and female, provided the structures, the initial materials, and the skilled consultation to the group about their process and the group's development.

Group members were encouraged to involve wives, husbands, children, and significant others as much as possible in their learning but without oppressing them. They attended events together and had discussions in their own homes and social groups. They were urged to let closely related others proceed at their own speed, but to share their experience when they could.

What was the impact? In the first six months the discussions were about black culture, so that understandably the impact was different for white and black persons. White members of the group began to see and experience a part of the world that had not been available to them before. For many it was a kind of awakening, like a first visit to another country, exciting, anxiety producing, yet energizing. Yet these were not tourists, since this learning occurred with others who were black and was a product of discussions, explorations of the sources of different reactions in the group, and shared feelings and experiences. It was also like awakening to the obvious. All of this learning had been nearby and available but untapped.

As white members grew in their appreciation and understanding, they had to learn to manage their frustration and appalled reactions to other members of the white establishment with whom they worked or lived. They also began to initiate meaningful actions at work and in their local communities. One man, for example, offered himself as a resource to a local black youth program by asking the center to suggest ways that he could be useful to them. Another called a high-placed colleague when racial troubles erupted at a nearby university and offered advice from his own new perspective. Their new understanding helped them to act in ways that were constructive and supportive.

Black members of the group also changed. The experience of really being heard, so rare for many minorities, caused them to feel much more empowered. A new sense of hope and belief emerged that the organization was really serious about change and that significant changes could occur. There was a sense of not being alone anymore, but of being supported. At the same time, black persons had to wrestle with their own hesitancy to trust if this was to become an empowering experience for them.

The work on gender is currently under way. From this work will come a new definition of what it means to be a leader in this kind of organizational change process. The goal is to create organizational leadership that develops a vision of what the organization can become and provides the sustained leadership for that process over time. This will include the analysis of organizational norms, policies, and procedures mentioned earlier.

Implicit in this change strategy is the notion that people have to experience affectively as well as conceptually how others feel, think, and move in the world if they are to create human relationships that energize and empower each other. In other words, they have to appreciate and thus value the other. When this happens, the foundation for organizational action is laid. Without this experience, creating a vision or goals and making decisions cannot be meaningful. In order to create a new future, people must have some glimmer of what that future can be. The appreciative inquiry process creates a ground from which to move into that future.

Appreciating Diversity

Men and Women as Colleagues

One difficulty that many men and women describe is not having a positive or clear image of what an excellent working relationship between a man and a woman would look like. Obviously, personalities will vary and relationships will reflect these differences. Given these natural variances, are there characteristics that are desirable?

The work of creating a positive model of colleagueship is just beginning. The appreciative inquiry process suggests that we search our past and identify excellent experiences of working with a person of the other gender from which to learn and draw ideas. My experience in working with several groups that have been asked to do this task has produced a set of relationship characteristics that can be used as a basis for describing a model of colleagueship between men and women.

Four characteristics were present in both men's and women's descriptions of their best working relationship with a person of the other gender. First, these were relationships that involved the *whole person* interacting with each other. The old maxim that one should separate business and pleasure—the idea that one only brings part of oneself to work—was clearly rejected. These relationships were about work but they did not ignore the personal. In fact, they were valued precisely because they included and acknowledged the personal. They knew about and were concerned about the other person's family, interests, hopes, and struggles. They experienced a broad range of emotions with each other, warmth, sadness, anger, joy. The descriptions were very close to what many would call very meaningful friendships. They worked together and in the course of work they had fun and enjoyed each other. Their relationship enlivened the work and the work enlivened the relationship.

Second, excellent working relationships develop a *sense of shared history* over time. Like other successful relationships, these people had been through good times and bad with each other. They had weathered crises and come out on the other side. Usually they had learned how to talk about the relationship when they needed to. They also said that they learned a great deal from each other.

The third characteristic of these relationships was that they were collaborative rather than competitive. As someone has said, intimacy is nonstrategic interaction. Thus, status differences were acknowledged and seen as a strength of the working partnership. Each partner had certain strengths that could be counted on and well-known weaknesses that had to be taken into account in his or her work.

Finally, there was a very strong sense of valuing and affirming the partner. They were each other's supporters and admirers. This affective bond was universally acknowledged and viewed as a source of energy in the relationship.

We should note, however, that the boundary between liking and sexual attraction is often a changing one. Those who acknowledged that there was sexual attraction in their relationship said that it had been very important to bring that issue into discussion and clarify the agreements about it early in the relationship. This observation is important for managing between the partners. Others' perceptions on this issue may also affect the relationship. When others think there is sexual intimacy between two colleagues, there are apt to be a variety of reactions. Carter's (personal communication, 1988) interesting notion is that sexual relationships will only be seen as problematic (that is, disturbing to me) if they are perceived as changing the power relations in the work setting (that is, if there is an increase in others' power or a decrease in mine).

This set of characteristics was generated from a small sample and needs to be more rigorously researched. The people who generated these data were professional people in consulting and staff roles. Perhaps there are organization-specific characteristics having to do with the particular work of that organization or its norms. In organizations, the process of talking about positive models of colleagueship may be as beneficial as the model itself.

Next Steps. The challenge that is confronting American business is to make a shift from a work culture in which we work comfortably because we share a culture with our fellow workers to a work culture that embraces and manages differences. A

Appreciating Diversity

change of this magnitude—some call it *organizational transformation* (Kilmann, Covin, and Associates, 1987) and appropriately contrast it with incremental change (Nadler, 1987)—cannot be mandated even though policies and structures will help to bring it about. Change in an organization's culture must be led at the executive level by men and women who are seeking to embody the organization's vision. This means that individual executives must understand and be able to appreciate differences. To do this usually requires "a change in the hearts and minds of men." In other words, it requires change in people's attitudes and values as well as their behavior.

Executive appreciation and its corollary process, appreciative inquiry, hold promise for facilitating this level of change. As such, they have an important contribution to make to the healthy development of organizations in the 1990s and beyond.

PART TWO

Processes of Appreciative Interchange

6

Affect and Organization in Postmodern Society

Kenneth J. Gergen

In recent times scholars have come to take an increasing interest in the process of appreciation or caring within organizational life. They are concerned that issues of affect have somehow been left out of most accounts of organizational functioning. They feel that the expression of certain kinds of sentiments within the organization would not only enhance the quality of life, but would operate as an actualizing force in the personal development of the participants. Yet, at the same time, many believe this colloquy is just a rearguard action. It is a residual discussion left for the tenderhearted, once the real business of business is given solid foundation. For organizations owe their viability to a satisfactory bottom line. And the achievement of such outcomes is linked not to sentimental expressions but to the concerted application of reason combined with astute attention to the realities of production, market, and the like. Thus, whether people actually like what they do, each other, or themselves is rather secondary.

In reply to cautions about economic reality, the "tender hearts" are inclined to point out that the engendering of appreciation in the organization is favorable to the bottom line. Organizations in which people care for each other, empathize, help, enjoy positive group spirit, and so on are successful organizations. Executive appreciation is "bottom line–friendly." Yet this voice must be raised with caution. For, once appreciation is treated as a tool for greater production, the nature of caring is altered.

Note: I am indebted to Pamela Johnson for her insightful critique of an earlier draft of this manuscript.

When appreciation, altruism, and other positive sentiments are used as a means to profit, rather than as ends in themselves, they cease to be significant as positive sentiments. They are transformed into mere strategies or manipulations. We confront, then, the possibility of an impasse.

Yet let us remove ourselves a step from this interchange between the bleeding hearts and the economic realists. For debates such as this, if they are intelligible, must proceed on a set of understandings. There must be a conversational forestructure already in place—agreements concerning what there is in the world, how it functions as it does, what is valuable, and why. And, if we probe this unarticulated forestructure—this preliminary context from which the debate arises—we may locate new ways of treating the problem of appreciation in organizations. We may locate unquestioned assumptions, problems of incommensurability, points of potential agreement, or possibly new modes of integration.

It will be my attempt in what follows first to locate sociohistorically the discursive forestructure for the two protagonists in this case. I will try to show how the case for executive appreciation has its major roots in nineteenth-century Romanticism. In contrast, economic realists owe the rhetorical power of their arguments primarily to modernist thought of the twentieth century. After reflecting on these issues, I will shift concern to the present. For, it seems, we are entering a new and challenging era, that of postmodernism. The grounds for considering executive appreciation are shifting in important directions, and such considerations form an important new dimension to our dialogue.

On the Social Construction of the Person

To understand the present enterprise more fully, additional background is useful. The forestructure for the present remarks essentially derives from a social constructionist standpoint (Gergen, 1985). Constructionism is basically concerned with people's shared understandings of the world, as they now exist, have existed, and might exist in the future. It is concerned as well with the processes by which constructions are generated, stabilized, and changed, along with their social, ethical, and political consequences. Fundamentally constructionism takes the position that the words or categories we use to describe and explain the world are not derived from the nature of the world itself. There is no means by which whatever there is can necessarily determine or constrain discourse about the world. In this sense, words (including the words of scientists) are not pictures or maps of an independent reality. Rather, our accounts of what is the case are derived from discursive interchange. Our vocabularies of understanding grow and change through social interaction, through processes of negotiation, conflict, improvisation, and the like. (The interested reader may consult Gergen and Davis, 1985; Coulter, 1979; Averill, 1982.) Or, extending Wittgenstein (1963), our vocabularies of understanding gain their meaning through their use, and this use is preeminently social.

The force and implications of this position become clarified when we turn more specifically to the science of human behavior. For here it is proposed that our conceptions of the person are not derived from the actual nature of human beings, but rather from our discursive practices. In this sense, constructionists are sympathetic to the anthropologists' many demonstrations that our Western view of the human being is a parochial one. For example, our view of the human being as having a psyche or mind that directs his or her actions across time and situation is not widely shared across cultures. And there are many people for whom our common distinction between reason and emotion is unintelligible. Such terms simply have no place in their lexicon of understanding. Further, the constructionist is sensitized to the historical context of various conceptions of the person. Historical accounts demonstrating that what is taken for granted about the nature of human nature changes with time and circumstance are all useful and supportive to the constructionist view. Here one may wish to consult such accounts as Badinter (1980) on the recent emergence of "mother love" and Luhmann (1986) on changing conceptions of passionate love.

In both the cultural and the historical domains, the constructionist is also concerned with the political or ideological impact of these varying conceptions of the person, and with the way in which such concepts have altered (or sustained) various social practices. To view deviant behavior as "the work of the devil" has far different implications than viewing it as "intentional," an expression of "mental illness," or a product of a "defective economic structure." In effect, our modes of constructing the world are not so important in terms of their truth or falsity. Rather, their importance lies in their implicit logics for action. And a consideration of these uses will necessarily force us to consider our values and goals. Because our discursive practices are used to sustain certain patterns of conduct, and often destroy or oppress others, our constructions of the world are inherently political.

It should finally be noted that the constructionist orientation shares much with organizational theory stressing the creation of reality in organizational culture, and with various attempts to carry such thinking into the realm of scientific metatheory and practice (Bhagat, 1983; Moch, 1982; Morgan, 1987; Cooperrider and Srivastva, 1987).

Romanticism and the Roots of Appreciation

With this brief précis in mind, we are now positioned to consider the historical roots of our contemporary vocabularies of the person. Most particularly, we must attend to the manner in which our present concerns with executive appreciation gained their power. Or, to be more self-conscious, why is it that we are so compelled by a topic like executive appreciation in the first place? (Why are we not, in contrast, focusing on the spatial aptitude of the executive?) Why do we believe people need or want the caring of others? (Why do we not believe that their esthetic needs are more powerful?) What is it about such terms as *altruism, empathy, positive regard,* and *intimacy* that they have such powerful rhetorical force? (To praise an executive for his or her meditative capacity would hardly carry the same weight.)

I propose that the importance of these various terms—*caring, empathy, intimacy,* and the like—can be traced to an earlier period of Western history, and primarily to what is often called the age of Romanticism (with its peak occurring in the mid-nineteenth century). The nineteenth century began with two vocabularies of mind in broad prominence. Rationalist thinkers—primarily of the seventeenth century—had carved out a central place for a vocabulary of reason. For philosophers such as Descartes, it was the individual's "powers of reason" that enabled him (and begrudgingly her) to acquire knowledge, to surmise the good, and to select successful courses of action. Empiricists—in the seventeenth but primarily eighteenth century—had made an equally strong case for "powers of observation." As philosophers such as Locke, Berkeley, and Hume made clear, it is when the individual's consciousness is sensitive to the nature of the surrounding world that knowledge is obtained. By the nineteenth century, the concepts of "reason" and "experience" (and their cognates) were commonplace. Those possessing such characterics were praised; those failing to demonstrate their use were subject to disapproval.

It is in this context that one must marvel at the works of nineteenth-century poets and novelists, philosophers, artists, and composers. For in their works they managed to create what was virtually a "new reality of the person." In particular, their works generated a strong sense that what was most essential about human makeup existed at a level beneath or beyond reason and the conscious experience of the world. Reason and experience were but superficial overlays on a "deep interior." And, within this deep interior one might find such phenomena as love, spirit, passion, despair, imagination, and genius. It was these denizens of the deep interior that also furnished a *raison d'être*, a justification for one's course of life. For poets such as Keats, Shelley, Byron, and Schiller, love, passion, and imagination were placed at the center of the motivational sphere. For Goethe, lost love was reason for suicide. For composers such as Beethoven and Brahms, music was not a practice in rationality, but a means for expressing the human depths. For Romantic and symbolist artists, what was given to the eyeball was banal. The problem was to depict what lay beyond and within.

Let us center our attention on the concept of love, since it is this concept that is most relevant to our present dialogue. Several characteristics of this emotion may be distilled. At the outset, to love fully was considered a *summum bonum;* one could scarcely find a higher calling. For example, as Shelley (in Enscoe, 1967, p. 62) said of love, it is "that powerful attraction towards all that we conceive, or fear, or hope beyond ourselves, when we find within our own thoughts the chasm of an insufficient void, and seek to awaken in all things that are, a community with what we experience within ourselves." Second, because friendship was an expression of love, it too was considered a cherished ideal. As Keats (in Enscoe, 1967, p. 104) wrote, "... the chief intensity: the crown ... is made of love and friendship, and sits high upon the forehead of humanity; friendship ... issues a steady splendour." Third, relations of love and friendship were essentially ones in which the domains of the deep interior were conjoined between two persons. In Keats's phrase (in Enscoe, 1967, p. 113), love is an "interknitting of souls." In effect, love and friendship were bonds of the deepest and most valuable kind.

In my view it is largely to this nineteenth-century form of discourse that the contemporary emphasis on executive appreciation owes its strong appeal. As a culture, we still carry with us these forms of discourse—albeit muted and rephrased in terms such as *appreciation* and *caring*. (Sympathy is closely related, as it suggests one's resonance with the deep interior of another; altruism is positive behavior toward another that is essentially beyond rational appraisal, and is thus a reflection of more fundamental caring.) We still believe that love and friendship are matters of the greatest importance in life. (Public opinion surveys suggest that they are among the most important values in American culture.) And, it follows, when one spends the greater part of his or her waking life in an environment where expressions of such utmost significance are lacking, this environment is seriously deficient.

The discourse of Romanticism becomes reified in the twentieth century in various scientific accounts of human behavior. For many, Freud and Jung firmly fixed the importance of the deep interior for this century. The profession of psychiatry may be credited for keeping a belief in the deep interior fully alive. The Romantic reality is also carried into the present in various theories of organizational life. The human relations movement, from Mayo and Roethlisburger to the present, is strongly Romantic in its emphasis on the fundamental capacity of the individual for positive growth, the need for relatedness, and the expression of the emotions and creative impulses. Mitroff's use of Jungian theory in *Stakeholders of the Organizational Mind: Toward a New View of Organizational Policy Making* (1983) is also an expression of Romanticism. And when scholars such as Leavitt (1986) argue for a style of leadership that deemphasizes rational problem solving and celebrates instinct, imagination, and wisdom, he is also recapitulating Romantic discouse.

Of particular concern for our debate, Adler's (1926) concept of "social interest," with its emphasis on the deep roots of our desire to identify and empathize with others, gave twentieth-century expression to the social implications of Romantic thought. However, it was not until Carl Rogers' (1961) explorations of positive regard that the scientific community began to admit the possible importance of positive sentiments in human life. For various reasons, psychological science had been — and continues to be — reluctant to place high value on the sentimental side of life. And even now, the name of love is variously abused by reinterpreting it as the "labeling of arousal" (Berscheid and Walster, 1969), feelings of "profit" from an exchange of behaviors (Homans, 1974), "need of compatibility" (Kerckhoff and Davis, 1962), and "interpersonal similarity" (Byrne, 1961). Among recent feminist accounts the concept is slowly regaining some of its Romantic character. For example, Carol Gilligan's (1982) view of love as a close, relational bonding restores it to the center of the human arena, and replaces rationality as the basis for decision making about relationships.

Modernism and the Search for Fundamentals

The rise of the modernist worldview, beginning late in the last century and continuing for the greater part of the present century, can largely be traced to industrialization, world war, and major advances in technology. In particular, the natural sciences were generating what seemed to be fundamental progress in understanding. As it appeared, human beings were beginning to master the fundamental order of the universe—including the behavior of human organisms. With such mastery, one could truly begin to conceive of utopia on earth. Within the intellectual world, and here I would also include psychology, such developments were largely expressed in the concern for foundations. Empiricist philosophers of science were the most articulate. In this case the attempt was to generate the rules of procedure by which the various scientific advances had been accomplished. The belief was that if these rules of method were made available to the culture, progress of the sort demonstrated in the natural sciences could be achieved across the cultural spectrum. The good life was to be the scientific life.

This concern with foundations was hardly confined to the sciences. Certainly there are parallels, for example, between the empiricist climate within the sciences and developments in both modern architecture and modern art. Modern architecture was largely preoccupied with reducing form to function (consider especially the work of the Bauhaus School). Modern art was abandoning the decorative while searching for essentials of form and color (consider Albers, Kandinsky, and Klee). In effect, both art and architecture shared in the seach for enduring fundamentals. And, it might be speculated, it was largely the search for underlying fundamentals that enabled composers to cast aside popular conventions of musical expression, that invited choreographers to abandon ballet in search of elemental movements (now termed modern dance), and that challenged literary theorists to discover basic rules of literary criticism (consider the "New Criticism"). So the heady and optimistic belief in foundations appears central in the modernist worldview.

Although psychologists hardly spoke in a single voice during the modernist age, there is one conception of human selves that became central. Institutions of science, technology, and industry were making impressive achievements by treating their subject matter as machinelike. It is this conception of the person as machine that largely dominated the field of psychology in the modernist period. Let us briefly consider three components of the mechanical self.

1. *Environmental Products.* Just as machines are products of inputs (electricity, gasoline, and the like), modernist psychology viewed people largely as products of environmental forces. These forces were variously seen in terms of environmental associations, reward and punishment, drive reducers, situational demands, social pressures, social stimuli, or models. The message in all cases was roughly the same: People are fundamentally products of the environment in which they live. On the level of daily life it is precisely this kind of rationale that supported the youth training programs so popular at the time. Schools, religious training, youth groups, vocational programs, and the like all were to help in the shaping of the individual. All these institutions served as the great factories of the age, producing personal dispositions like so many sewing machines.

2. *Fundamental Dispositions: The Individualist Presumption.* Machines operate to produce finished products according to a standard. In the same way, according to the mechanistic view of modernist psychology, proper socialization should produce mature, fully developed, well-balanced, and emotionally well-adjusted individuals. With proper socialization people should come to possess an enduring character, personality traits, or fundamental dispositions that guide or direct them for the remainder of their life. That is, properly socialized persons should operate in virtual independence of their environment. They should act on the basis of the inner traits or dispositions acquired through socialization. Properly socialized individuals are, in effect, the center of their own actions.

3. *Persons as Predictable.* The products of proper machines should perform in predictable ways. One should be able to rely on the quality of a Ford car or a General Electric washing machine. In similar fashion, the ideal human being in modernist psychology was one whose actions are reliable: knowable and predictable according to scientific method. Once individuals have been fashioned by universal processes of heredity and environment, their actions should be reliable and stable across situations. This set of assumptions is now responsible for virtually an entire industry devoted to personality testing and measurement. It is this confluence of assumptions that has also been

largely responsible for the creation of organizational management as a discipline of study. "Taylorism" in the industrial setting was an initial beneficiary of this line of thinking. However, the modernist tradition remains robust in virtually all theories and organizational investigations where systematic antecedents of human behavior are posited. Theories of scientific management, early cybernetic or information systems theory, and political theories of organizational life are largely compatible with a modernist view (see also Kanungo and Conger's contribution to the present volume).

Of course the modernist-mechanical view of selves began to pose major challenges to the Romantic conception. For the Romantic the important aspects of the self were deeply buried, mysterious, and often chaotic, and were active forces of good or evil. For the modernist the self was close to the surface, knowable by observation—a reliable and controllable product of conditions. Consider, for example, the difference between common conceptions of love in the two periods. In the Romantic period love could be all-consuming; it was a reason to live (or to die), it was unpredictable, and for its sake one might pledge a lifetime of commitment. Contrast this view with the modernist attempt to develop a technology of proper mate selection. Love by thunderbolt was replaced by questionnaire compatibility.

Romanticism, Modernism, and Executive Appreciation

The preceding analysis helps to sensitize us to the historical contexts in which our contemporary views of the individual have been nurtured. It is useful to pause at this juncture to consider more explicitly several implications of the foregoing for our present dialogue on executive appreciation. How are we now to understand such issues and their outcomes? Let us focus on three significant implications of the preceding:

1. *The Deconstruction of "The Problem."* At the outset, there is a strongly entrenched tendency (a modernist legacy) to view issues in executive appreciation as ontologically grounded. That is, we tend to assume that terms such as *appreciation, altruism, empathy,* and *need for approval* stand in a systematic, referential

Affect and Organization in Postmodern Society 163

relationship to events in an independent world. On this account, we might mount research to determine whether participants in organizations truly need or require appreciation for their sense of well-being, whether they are more highly motivated in the workplace as a result, and whether managers can be tested for their capacities to give such appreciation. In light of such research, again following the modernist orientation, we might finally "get to the bottom" of the problem — and determine empirically, once and for all, the components of the healthy organization.

However, as the present analysis suggests, the grounds for such investigations are shaky indeed. Our vocabulary of understanding persons does not grow from the soil of observation but from discursive relations among people. Terms such as *appreciation, self-esteem, empathy,* and the like do not thus stand in a definitive relationship to a world of objective particulars, but represent an interpretive forestructure through which events are indexed. In effect, such terms are constituents of meaning systems used by groups to codify the world. They are akin to lenses through which the world is seen — or more explicitly, interpretively shaped. On this account, empirical research cannot tell us how human relationships "really work"; rather the linguistic forestructure will determine the limits of what the research can tell us. From the present standpoint, then, we are not likely to make substantial progress in understanding if we treat issues in executive appreciation as "reality-based problems." To do so will succeed only in allowing us to exercise our interpretive forestructure — to elaborate in the name of reality what is already implicit in our contemporary language conventions.

2. Beyond Individualistic Paradigms: Self as Relationship. If we shift our attention from the problem in itself to discourse about the problem, there are significant implications for our forms of scholarly activity. To elaborate, let us consider the Romantic and modernist conceptions of self as paradigms of understanding. We might reasonably locate a modal ontology of the person for each of these historical periods, a set of generally acceptable propositions about the nature of human beings, and a set of attendant values. For the Romantic, it is proposed, the paradigm of understanding placed the deep interior at the center of human functioning. One's capacities to express positive sentiments, to give deeply, to achieve a unity of understanding with others were all supremely valued. For the modernist, however, this deep and mysterious core is virtually nonexistent. Rather, it is replaced by the immediately accessible processes of reason and conscious experience. It is the use of these facilities that is now prized, and it is presumed that such functioning is (and should be) systematic and reliable rather than buffeted by sentiment.

From this standpoint, we can view much of our scholarly debate in terms of a competition of linguistic paradigms. And, to borrow from debates in the history of science, one might view the Romantic and the modernist views as "incommensurable" paradigms. They cannot be compared as to empirical adequacy; they in fact presuppose different formulations of the basic subject matter (for example, the person). This is to say that there is no convincing a hardheaded economic realist about the importance of executive appreciation, since such concerns are by definition relegated to peripheral status. The Romantic cannot be convinced of the propriety of bottom-line thinking and nononsense decision making, because such an orientation is by its very nature suspect. The concept of altruism is a good case in point. While the Romantic can speak at length about the benefits of selfless contributions to others, for the modernist altruism simply does not exist. Altruistic acts are, by definition, carried out for a reason. They have a "payoff" for the altruist (Piliavin, Piliavin, and Rodin, 1975) — which for the Romantic is not altruism at all.

It seems to me that if we wish to press beyond the competition of competing paradigms, a particular form of scholarly activity is required to make sense of executive appreciation within the modernist conception of the organization. The scholarly challenge is to press toward new forms of discourse. In particular, we must search for metaphors that may enable us to utilize and combine elements of both preceding paradigms in new and more fruitful ways. Required from the scholar, then, are new forms of intelligibility.

Affect and Organization in Postmodern Society 165

I cannot propose at this juncture a fully developed alternative — a compelling new metaphor that will solve all remaining problems. However, in preparation for our final discussion of postmodern discourse, I do wish to outline an alternative that I find especially intriguing. It is inviting in large measure because it allows us to escape from the prison of individualistic language. Both the Romantic and the modern views identify the individual person as the critical element of culture. To understand human conduct one searches the interior of the person (for example, emotions, cognitions, motives). Yet this individualized orientation simultaneously informs the culture that each of us is fundamentally alone, isolated, and self-contained. In addition to the alienation and suspicion generated by such views, they also blind us to the possibility and potential of interdependence. It is useful, then, to press toward a metaphor of "self as relationship." By this I mean that we reconsider all that was previously attributed to single individuals as possessions of persons in relationship. We take matters of rationality, experience, self-esteem, desire for appreciation, and the like out of the heads of individuals, and we view them as properties of relational process.

Preliminary moves in such a direction would include Mary Douglas's (1987) thoughts of rationality in organizations, along with the work of John Shotter (1988) and others on the social organization of memory. For Douglas, it is not the individual executive who carries out the process of rational decision making. Rather, individuals in organizations each contribute resources to the organizational whole, and these contributions may collectively be said to be rational. In the same way, Shotter proposes that memory is not the possession of single individuals, but that what we call memory is a product of negotiated settlements among persons. Parents teach their children what it is to perform in a way that, for cultural purposes, "displays memory." People negotiate "what actually happened," and it is this negotiated outcome that must be reported by the member of a relationship if he or she can properly be said to remember.

Mary Gergen and I have attempted to reconceptualize emotions as constituents of relational forms (see Gergen and

Gergen, 1988). Rather than viewing emotions as the private possessions of single individuals, the attempt has been to view emotional expressions as integral parts of broader rituals of interchange. Working with what we call *emotional scenarios,* we have tried to show how emotional expressions are only appropriate to certain kinds of situations. Feelings of anger or depression can only be announced within a suitable context. Further, once such expressions have occurred, there is only a limited range of responses that are appropriate. (If someone announces his or her depression, you cannot blithely begin to speak of last Saturday's frivolities without risking your claim to being completely human. Yet, if you make the appropriate move in the unfolding interaction, and the person follows your move with one that is similarly appropriate, and so on, there will be a point at which the scenario will be complete. At that point, you may begin to speak without trepidation of the weekend's festivities.)

Now, you may well ask, how does the metaphor of self as relationship help us in the case of executive appreciation? First, the elaboration of this form of intelligibility enables us to escape the previous forms of question. We need not ask, for example, whether members of organizatoins *really* need appreciation, nor whether empathy and altruism are compatible with bottom-line decision making. Such terms, as they have traditionally been used to refer to status or characteristics of individuals, have essentially been deconstructed (de-ontologized) by the previous analysis. Although we can continue to use such terms as *appreciation* and *rationality,* the context of usage has now changed. Their meanings and implications have been altered by their placement in the new metaphor. Executive appreciation is no longer a leadership style that one can simply learn and apply on an autonomous basis (as argued by Bennis and Nanus, 1985, for example). What we call executive appreciation is embedded within relational forms that require mutual participation. It does not exist independently of a relational dance in which two or more persons participate. For a "Romantic" manager to "give appreciation" to a "modernist" colleague is to fail in the generation of meaningful action. It is to call a step that the others cannot perform. Similarly, the modernist manager who evaluates the rationality of all his or her subordinates' actions when subordinates still cling to a Romantic heritage is to fail in the kinds of collaborative interchanges that make for successful organizations. I will expand on these issues at the close of the chapter.

3. *The Conduct of Organizations.* As we find, our constructionist approach removes the putative object of discussion — executive appreciation — and replaces it with issues in discourse. Yet to make this argument is not to shift our attention entirely toward the scholarly effort of generating new forms of intelligibility. We must also ask about ongoing activities in organizations. If the problem is relocated in the domain of discourse, what are the implications for life in the organization itself? I wish to open a discussion here, the conclusion of which will be set aside for an excursion into postmodernism.

Participants in organizations are no less participants in the culture. As a result, they have typically incorporated the existing forms of cultural intelligibility. People bring with them into organizations the languages of both the Romantic and the modernist. Further, both the Romantic and the modernist intelligibilities are also embedded within more extended cultural practices. We not only speak of executive appreciation, but in uttering such words as "I appreciate very much what you have done . . . " we employ a certain tone of voice, a posture, a manner of gazing, and so on that are appropriate. (Failing to embed the words in the appropriate practices is indeed to negate their significance. The words seem insincere, superficial, or even sarcastic.)

In this vein we see that the problem in organizations is largely one of conflicting modes of comportment. Romantics will thrive on certain forms of practice and modernists on others. Or, because individuals are not simply one or the other, most will primarily adopt a modernist orientation, while occasionally worrying about the residual status of their ability to care, sacrifice, or empathize. On these grounds it could be contended that the task is to avoid conflict among these competing modes, whether intrapersonal or interpersonal. Various training procedures or modes of restructuring might also be carried out to effect such reductions in conflict. However, I do not wish to follow this path toward conflict reduction at this juncture. The reasons will become apparent as we explore the postmodern turn.

The Postmodern Turn

As many believe, the age of modernism is rapidly waning. The evidence is all around us. It is most apparent in the phalanx of new and related scholarly and esthetic ventures. In the academy, there has been widespread discontent with the foundationalist ventures of the modernist period. As is widely agreed, the positivist-empiricist conception of knowledge is unworkable, and we are now in a state of *postempiricist* philosophy. In architecture the modernist vision of the Bauhaus has been replaced by a cacophony of competing styles, now called *postmodern architecture*. The modernist attempt to capture fundamentals of color and form has now been pushed aside in favor of a freewheeling adventure into a multiplicity of mixed forms, now called *postmodern art*. And we have a plethora of volumes—see Lyotard (1984), Lawson (1985), Hudson and van Reijen (1986), and Sloterdijk (1987)—dealing with one or another aspect of what is commonly viewed as a "postmodern turn" in thought and sensibilities.

What is common to these broad cultural changes, and how are they to be contrasted with the age of modernism? Again, space limitations require reduction to just a single theme. The modernist era was characterized as foundationalist in its emphasis. The general concern was with fundamental truths, essences, building blocks, methods, and the like. In contrast, if there is one single theme that runs the gamut of postmodernism, it is a *multiplicity of perspectives*. One might say that in the modernist search for foundations there were many voices, each with its own account of what is basic or essential. And, as the competition among voices ensued, no means could be found to adjudicate among the voices—save yet another voice. In effect, a pluralism of positions or orientations could be located, none of which could justify its "truth" in the face of competitors.

Thus, in the philosophy of science one began to speak of "nonjustificationist" philosophy (or philosophical positions without foundations), in the history of science of multiple and incommensurable paradigms, in symbolic anthropology of "local knowledge," in literary criticism of "interpretive communities" (as determining the meaning of texts), in hermeneutics of historically located "forestructures of understanding," in psychology of "cognitive sets" or "schemata" (that determine what is learned and remembered), in cybernetics of self-organizing processes that obliterate the distinction between subject and object, in Foucault's (1966) writings of culturally embedded epistemes that guide forms of thought in various cultural eras, in Derrida's (1976) writings of the "free play of signifiers" (deconstructing any attempt at transcendent meaning), and so on. In each case, the emphasis moves from "things in themselves" (that is, what there is to be known) to perspectives that determine what we take to be the case. The shift is from the object to be known to the primacy of *perspective* in guiding human activity, and the problematics of valorizing any single perspective over another. In the organizational arena, summary volumes by Gareth Morgan (1986) and by Bolman and Deal (1984) pick up the postmodern rhythm in removing organizational theory from hypotheticodeductive evaluation and asking the reader to view such theories as metaphorical "images" and reality-producing "perspectives." And, as should be evident, the directions of this work are quite congenial to the social constructionist orientation underlying my earlier analysis.

Judging from the ways in which both Romanticism and modernism influenced the Western construction of the person, we should also anticipate an infusion of the postmodern perspective into our daily modes of understanding and relating. In my view, this infusion is already well underway. Romantic and modernist views of the person are slowly giving way to a postmodern vision of human functioning. Slowly waning is the traditional view that people possess fundamental essences— whether in terms of basic selves, deep character, obdurate identities, or personality traits. And, as these fundamental essences are disappearing as realities, we are developing a new discourse of the person. The new discourse views the individuals not as *actual* but as *virtual*. The person is not a fixed entity, but forever a possibility in motion—actualized as perspectives are adopted and realized in action. And this actualization in situations is often seen to depend on the complicity of others. Realizing the identity of the moment requires coordinating efforts among persons, gaining information, consent, affirmation, and so on.

One detects this *discourse of the virtual self* emerging in a variety of domains. The popular press features numerous accounts of how presidential identities are "fashioned" for public appeal, popular performers must develop "interesting lives" to remain in the public eye, and leaders of social movements opt for media coverage as opposed to unadulterated expressions in their beliefs. The media have made it increasingly clear that a person's public life (as a minister, politician, school teacher, and so on) may be at strong variance with his or her private life, and that there may be multiple private lives at dislocating variance with each other. Young people are increasingly aware that a résumé is less an accurate reflection of their "true personalities" than the tactics they have used to garner the relevant line items. In the academic sphere the virtual self is further objectified and legitimated. In the social sciences we find detailed treatments of "situated identity," "protean man," "Machiavellianism," "the dramaturgical self," "multiple identity," "androgyny," "self-monitoring," and "possible selves." Each account further elaborates a discourse of the virtual, of possible transformations in the self. And almost all such accounts place a strong value on those who remain in motion.

As can be seen, such a discourse threatens the reality of both the Romantic and the modern views of the person. The individual is no longer "deep," "intense," or "inspired," as the Romantic would have it, or "reliable," "knowable," and "self-directed," as the modernist maintains. Rather, the individual is potentially all of these (or more), depending on unfolding of social process. In a world of virtuality the fixed identity is indeed a liability.

Executive Appreciation in the Postmodern Era

Thus far we have seen how Romantic discourse becomes embodied in the quest for executive appreciation, and how modernist discourse of the person represents an oppositional force within organizations (including the organization of scholarship). We have outlined one possible means of transcending such disputes within the scholarly domain, and we have postponed the problem of pragmatic implications following a discussion of the postmodern shift. In light of the postmodern shift, what now is to be said of organizational life? And how are scholarly pursuits to be fashioned? To answer these questions it is first essential to consider the implications of postmodern discourse for the preceding conceptions of the person. As we have already seen, Romantic discourse discredited the rationalist view of the person. In turn, modernist discourse stood in sharp opposition to the Romantic conception of the person. Does it follow that postmodernist conceptions will bring an end to both Romantic and modernist views? Will issues of executive appreciation and rational calculation simply pass on to become quaint relics of earlier modes of talking — similar, let us say, to the concepts of "melancholy," "nervous breakdown," and "inferiority complex"?

To this question I believe the answer is negative. For, unlike predecessor discourses, postmodernism does not valorize any particular ontology over another. That is, postmodern discourse does not specify the nature of human beings, such that competing accounts are discredited. It does not say that the individual is basically rational, thereby reducing the emotions to a secondary status, nor vice versa. Postmodernism offers no perspective on the person, such that previous discourses must be abandoned. To be sure, the ontological supports are removed from previous perspectives; no longer can one claim them to be objectively true. However, they are not thereby removed from the field of human interchange. Such perspectives retain importance as constituents of meaning systems and associated patterns of interaction.

This conceptual agnosticism of the postmodernist turn has a number of important implications for our present colloquy.

First, the domain of discourse is thrown open to a free play among all previous assertions. That is, since no new ontology is locked in place, and since no preceding forms are negated, then all previous forms are legitimated as sense-making devices. The Romantic may speak freely about needs for self-esteem, empathy, personal commitment, and the like, while the modernist can continue unabashedly to speak of bottom-line logic. And we may on this account envision the entry of still other forms of discourse into the organizational setting. For example, women are now importing new forms of intelligibility into the workplace, intelligibilities placing an emphasis on relationships, interdependence, nurturance, and symbiosis. Many struck by the success of Japanese business organizations are beginning to speak of the organization as a family. Nor should one rule out the entry of still further forms of discourse from the past. Spiritualism, for example, is ripe for a return to the marketplace. (Given the robust growth of organizations such as Amway, one might say that it has acquired a decided presence.) In effect, postmodernism opens the organization to the entry of a multiplicity of discourses.

The second point is that with the advent of postmodern sensibility, none of these discourses—Romantic, modernist, feminist, Japanese, spiritualist, and the like—can be viewed as ultimately true. That is, postmodernism stands in the way of accepting such discourses as linguistic representations of an independent reality, as accurate pictures of human beings, their needs, inclinations, actions, and the like. This is not at all to trivialize these various forms of discourse and the patterns of action of which they are a part. For, regardless of their truth value, these intelligibilities are embedded within our life forms. Musical genres offer a convenient comparison. We have at our disposal Baroque, classic, Romantic, and modernist music, along with jazz, rock, Country and Western, New Age, and a variety of other forms. To none of these do we ascribe truth; they are not pictures of the world. And in this sense, we do not take them seriously—as matters to believe in, truths for all time. They are not guides to life; they are life itself.

This argument prepares us for a third point. Within the postmodern era we may anticipate the emergence of what may be called *serious play*. That is, the individual will find that while the number of discursive possibilities continue to mount, there is no ultimate justification for any single one. One is invited to join, much as in a game or a dance, but no game or dance is ultimate, final, or true. Thus, the individual may join in the vocabularies (and their associated patterns of action), not because they are true or final, but because they are available and possibly attractive. They may be taken seriously, but in the same sense that a game or a dance would periodically grasp one's total attention. One may be wholly absorbed in a game, and while engaged there is virtually no other reality extant. However, in the end, though exhausted, one may look back and say, "it was only a game."

And so it may be with cases of friendship, bonding, empathy, praise, and appreciation within organizations. These are available forms of relationship. For many they have a strong appeal; they serve well under many circumstances. Like games and dances, they are exciting, enjoyable, dramatic, and quickening. As postmodernist discourse is elaborated and extended, so may these forms come to have increasing appeal. As discourses (and related behaviors) they may be acquired and increasingly honed. And, because they are not ultimately true or false, one need be less concerned with whether one is basically mushy, soft, or sickly sentimental while indulging in its expression. They are valid within themselves, as valid as all competitors. Thus, they may be played with vigor and enthusiasm, after which one is free to absent the field.

In the final analysis, the postmodern orientation of serious play may be linked to the earlier metaphor of relational forms, since, as is readily apparent, each vocabulary of the person is embedded within certain forms of interchange. In the same way that expressions of anger or depression can only be made under certain conditions, and require certain kinds of responses and not others, so it is the case with the vocabulary of the Romantics and the modernists. I cannot appreciate the fruits of your labors unless we can negotiate a reality in which there are "labors" and resulting "fruits." And once I have praised you for your work, you are not free simply to speak of your next vacation, or to attack me for my shortcomings. Appreciation, then, takes place within particular scenarios for which at least two persons must know their parts.

When viewed in this way, we can begin to see the organization as composed of a wide range of relational scenarios. Each interchange between or among persons has at its disposal a certain range of scenarios from which it can draw. To employ such scenarios is to make sense; to be lacking in such skills is to absent oneself from relationship. More important, the greater the number of available scenarios, the greater the viability of the organization. Or, to put it another way, the broader the range of scenarios in which organizational members can successfully participate, the greater their ability to confront the vicissitudes of daily life in a complex and ever-changing society. Thus participants who are skilled in carrying out only the scenarios of modernism have only a limited way of dealing with variations in work quality, innovation, personal loss, and the like. To add the scenarios of the Romantic legacy is to add a broad new latitude of relationship under such circumstances. It is to enrich the possibilities of organizational life, and thereby enhance the capacities of the organization to endure within a complex and ever-changing environment. And, by the same token, as new scenarios are added, those of nurturance, interdependence, spirituality, and the like, the potentials of organizations to withstand the buffeting of an unpredictable environment are thereby increased.

In Quinn's (1988) sense, the problem is not to discover a "rational" course of action, a fixed form of management, but to expand the alternatives for action in a world of ever-changing and unpredictable demands. From the postmodernist perspective, appreciation scenarios add significantly to the texture of organizational life. Even though largely a holdover from the Romantic period, they are invaluable additions to the quality and potentials of organizational life. They should be fostered as forms of relationships, not as fixed and final endprints but as active and contributing participants within the organizational mix. Their revitalization is much to be welcomed. However, this revitalization must be viewed only as a beginning of a broad expansion in the forms of relatedness permitted and prospering within the organization.

7

Appreciative Interchange: The Force That Makes Cooperation Possible

John D. Aram

Historically, cooperation has played only a supporting role in the value structure of American society. Individual struggle against nature and the life-threatening frontier are dominant American images, and human relationships are primarily utilitarian. People join together for instrumental reasons, such as their common defense. An unwritten motto in the United States is "live and let live." Americans can be immensely tolerant without being particularly caring.

In this context it is not surprising that executive appreciation would be the topic for a volume like this. Cooperation is the short suit in the cultural deck of cards we have been dealt, and relatively less attention has been given to exploring the importance and contributions of this "soft" value. Books pertaining to individuality, autonomy, and independence today would be more concerned with how to preserve these assumed values than how to define and highlight their significance.

Observers frequently point to the management of interdependencies as a critical requirement for our society to function in today's world. Independencies are pervasive. Mutual dependencies increasingly challenge our ability to manage relations between economies, between institutions, between races and classes, between labor and management, between industry and environment. The speed of technological advance, the accessibility of information and rapidity of communication, the strength of demands for human and social rights, and the sophistication of political action are a few of the factors that simultaneously dignify the individual and call for a more comprehensive, integrative means to identify and solve problems. Mutual appreciation, cooperation, and a collective perspective are precious, and limited, qualities in this complex world.

I am sure that all of us cherish those wonderful occasions of uninhibited caring in our lives where moments and personal relationships are filled with deep, full, and unqualified appreciation. But the challenge to appreciative values lies beyond the dyad and the small group. The issue for society arises in moving from strictly personal relationships to institutional contexts. Our greatest challenges lie in the management of large-scale organizational and social relationships where the capacity to appreciate or to cooperate is more difficult but no less vital.

This chapter takes a broad perspective in addressing the topic of executive appreciation. The viewpoint attempts to appraise realistically our society's ways of structuring institutional relationships. Assumptions about organizing are influenced by traditional economic and political ideas that misdirect our thinking about dealing with current institutional realities. Managers often use models of cooperation derived from market processes when models of institutional cooperation are needed to manage the challenge of organizing under conditions of interdependence.

I propose that the prisoner's dilemma game is a more appropriate model than conventional economic ideologies for today's managers. The prisoner's dilemma more closely reflects the challenge of managing large-scale organizational relationships, and it conveys a better understanding of a needed managerial perspective. Guidelines for managers and for management educators are developed.

This approach is broadly social, somewhat historical, and definitely institutional. It asserts the existence of dilemmas and paradoxes in organizing. It arrives at a hopeful path for action.

Traditional Employer-Employee Relations in the United States

The judicial doctrine of "liberty of contract," articulated by the Supreme Court for about forty years in the late nineteenth and early twentieth centuries, exemplifies the historical values of our economic system. In the wake of advancing industrialization in the late nineteenth century, questions about the status of employees vis-à-vis employers naturally arose. Could state or national governments legally establish minimum wage and salary levels? Could they determine health and safety conditions of work? Did employees have the right to bargain collectively?

The "freedom of contract" doctrine answered these questions in the negative. At the turn of this century, the State of New York passed a law limiting bakers' work to ten hours a day or sixty hours a week. In spite of a substantial increase of respiratory disease and shortened life span among bakers, in 1905 the Court found this law infringed on the ability of the parties to purchase or sell labor (*Lochner v. New York*). Moreover, the Court's decision was justified in terms of the laborer's interests. " . . . [T]he acts of the legislature," reasoned the Court, "might seriously cripple the ability of the laborer to support himself and his family." Supposedly, each worker's ability to gain and weigh information about the long-term health risks of working more was equivalent to that person's information about the economic benefits of working additional hours.

Similarly, states were prevented from passing laws that kept employers from conditioning employment on the prospective employee's promise not to join a union. Restricting the individual's choice to negotiate in his own interest was deemed unconstitutional. Ignoring differences in bargaining power between individual and employer, in 1915 the Court found that freedom to bargain was "as essential to the laborer as to the capitalist, to the poor as to the rich" (*Coppage v. Kansas*).

In 1918 the Court struck down a national law that prohibited the shipment of goods produced by factories that employed children under fourteen years of age or employed children between fourteen and sixteen years for more than eight hours a day (*Hammer v. Dagenhart*). This law would have equalized competition between states with child labor laws and states without such laws. The Court, however, disagreed with this reasoning. Taking from one state and giving to another was deemed as great an interference with freedom as the national government's taking from one individual and giving to another. What was the value placed on child development in this discussion?

More completely, the doctrine of economic due process was a coherent and defensible body of thought having direct ties to Voltaire, Locke, and Montesquieu (Siegan, 1980). Property rights played a key role in the philosophy of governance presented by Madison and Hamilton in *The Federalist* (Wright, 1961). Natural rights, private property, and democracy were inextricably linked in the founding of this country. There is little wonder, then, that cooperation and appreciation do not leap to mind to describe employee-employer relations in the late eighteenth and early twentieth centuries of American economic history. Economic freedom and property rights resided closer to the heartbeat of American business ideology than did community, cooperation, or appreciation. Social Darwinism was an intellectual influence consistent with the assumptions of economic liberty underlying this country's industrial development.

Although the "freedom of contract" doctrine was anchored in an important, formative stage in U.S. business history, this doctrine is not now an active basis of protecting the employee-employer relationship from state intervention. History shows that after Franklin Roosevelt changed the composition of the Court in the late 1930s, the principle of "freedom of contract" was rapidly subordinated to a Constitutional interpretation more hospitable to state protection and more accommodating of perceived public interests. A different balance between economic and social values was struck as the principle of public regulation of business became a consistent feature of our social landscape.

Judicial abdication of judging the reasonableness of public regulation is not inherently more appreciative, however. Siegan (1980) advocates the cause, for example, of Nancy Dukes, the owner of a pushcart business selling hot dogs, drinks, confections, and novelties in the French Quarter of New Orleans. A city ordinance that prohibited all but two long-standing pushcart businesses in this district was challenged by Dukes as an interference with her economic rights. The Supreme Court sustained the authority of the city government to regulate the individual's economic affairs, continuing a view since the late 1930s in which apparently any governmental body can override an individual's economic freedom at any time for any reason whatsoever. In other words, no governmental purpose or reason need be explicit. Siegan and others (see, for example, Epstein, 1985) decry the recent Court's tendency to respect social and personal freedoms of speech and the press, but to subordinate economic freedom.

Economic and social freedom comprise two faces of individualism in American society. Deriving from the same historical roots, these values have come to represent distinct ideological and political positions and compete with each other rather than recognize their shared origins. Neither addresses the fact of interdependence of parties in modern society nor places cooperation or appreciation very high in their value hierarchies.

Individualism is also embedded in the assumptions of social science. Social science has invented a convenient and descriptive term—groupthink—to describe excessive social cohesion in organizational settings, but social science seems to lack comparable interest in the excesses of individualism. The view that altruistic or charitable behavior is incapable of regenerating itself across generations can be traced to Darwin's theory of survival. Population growth will be determined by the progenitive instinct, wrote Darwin, since nature will dictate that the variety "homocontracipiens" would, by natural selection, become extinct. This argument has not been lost by social philosophers in appraising the general development of conscience in a science: "The argument . . . applies equally well to any instance in which society appeals to an individual exploiting a commons to restrain himself for the general good—by means of his conscience. To make such an appeal is to set up a selective system [assuming conscience is hereditary or is conveyed by a process of social osmosis] that works toward the elimination of conscience from the human race" (Hardin, 1968, p. 1246).

Philosopher Hannah Arendt (1963) observed the tendency for societies to develop ideological polarities, such as our competing legal doctrines about the relative primacy of economic and social freedoms. This tendency derives, in Arendt's view, from two contradictory and irreconcilable aspirations of revolutionary political change. On the one hand, founders of the American Revolution sought to devise a stable and durable political structure. On the other hand, the founders were bound to have "the exhilarating awareness of the human capacity of beginning" and to value change and newness. Thus, stability and change are two competing values structured into the fabric of our political and social life. Arendt (1963, p. 225) writes:

> Perhaps the very fact that these two elements, the concern with stability and the spirit of the new, have become opposites in political thought and terminology—the one being identified as conservative and the other being claimed as the monopoly of progressive liberalism—must be recognized to be among the symptoms of our loss. Nothing, after all, compromises the understanding of political issues and their meaningful debate today more seriously than the automatic thought-reactions conditioned by the beaten paths of ideologies which all were born in the wake and aftermath of revolution . . . In other words, to the extent that our political terminology is modern at all, it is revolutionary in origin. And the chief characteristic of this modern, revolutionary vocabulary seems to be that it always talks in pairs of opposites—the right and the left, reactionary and progressive, conservatism and liberalism, to mention a few at random.

Two major beliefs compete for dominance in American social ideology. Given the dominant role of the firm in the structure of our economy, conservative and liberal ideologies differ in their assignments of social power to corporations and to individuals. Economic individualism reveres the integrity of the corporate entity and preserves managerial freedom of action against state action. Individual interests may need to stand aside for economic freedoms to be exercised and for the market system to allocate resources efficiently. Management students commonly think and write in this framework. Recently, an M.B.A. student concluded that national legislation is needed to reform the product liability system in the United States: " . . . Federal legislation would stop the current system from placing businesses at the mercy of compassionate juries and fee-obsessed lawyers." There is not much appreciation for the interests of injured parties in that statement.

In contrast, social rights doctrine seeks to empower individuals—the employee, the consumer, the user of the environment—in the name of "fundamental" human liberties or in the name of the public or community interest. Prescriptions from this vantage point restrict the discretion of managers and lack an appreciation for the ability of the firm to expand the size of the pie for all. What is the level of understanding of the firm as a creator of economic value, for example, in the concept of treble punitive damages?

These ideologies share a common definition of their situation: Interests are independent and reconciliation is political. The two ideologies prefer different resolutions of the individual's relationship with the organization; they share, however, assumptions about the terms of the contest. Appreciation would not be high on the list of either.

Several lessons can be extracted for employee-employer relationships from this abbreviated review of economic and legal history. First, this history makes transparent the provisional character of our assumptions about organizational relationships. Our current understandings about the economic and social rights of individuals are value-laden perceptions, available ways to interpret our current circumstances. While persons inevitably experience their beliefs as permanent and as "right," in the long run beliefs are vulnerable to redefinition and change.

Second, each of the dominant belief systems in this society accepts a fundamental distinction between individual and organizational interests. Individuals and organizations are believed to have separate, distinct, and often conflicting interests. Differing interests are not assumed to merge or to meld easily, and reconciliation of distinct individual and organizational interests is achieved by organizational, political, and legal conflict. We create opposing interests and balance them grudgingly.

While these belief systems are most clearly identifiable in the political sphere, they also underlie different managerial assumptions. Beliefs surrounding employee dismissal represent a case in point. An organizational perspective says that managers need freedom to dismiss employees and that employees should carry the burden of proof to show that a discharge was unjust. Employees, on the other hand, may argue that organizational members have a right to secure employment and the firm should carry the burden of proof to show that an individual has not performed on the job. While these respective positions differ, both assume the separability of individual and organizational interests, rely on judgment-based methods of conflict resolution (arbitration, litigation) and grant little appreciation for the validity of the other's position. Such conflicts seek all-or-nothing solutions. Individuals and organizations too often engage in a cat-and-mouse game, the outcomes of which are determined by relative social power. Quality-of-life improvements too frequently are viewed by managers as concessions. Disregard or perhaps indifference might be better attitudes to characterize institutional relations in American economic history. Integrative solutions are defined away by assumptions and driven away by zero-sum processes.

An Alternative Paradigm: The Prisoner's Dilemma

An altogether different comprehension of the relationship between individual and organization arises from research on the prisoner's dilemma, perhaps the most widely studied phenomenon in the behavioral sciences. This simple game mocks the strict demarcation between self and other that dominates social ideologies guiding organizational relations. One cannot maximize points in this game without taking the interests of the other party into account. Attempting to maximize my immediate gain leads me to a "defect" strategy, but the fact of my interdependence in the game with another usually makes that strategy self-defeating. Similarly, consistent selection of the "cooperate" choice puts me at the mercy of the other and is likely to yield both a relative and an absolute loss for me.

Appreciative Interchange

The basic prisoner's dilemma is a two-person non-zero-sum game based on the idea that two individuals are apprehended and charged with committing a crime. The state only has circumstantial evidence, however, and must rely on confessions to develop a successful case. The two prisoners are interrogated separately. They both know that if neither confesses, the state's evidence will be insufficient and they will each receive sentences of only three years for a lesser offense. However, each is offered the possibility of being released without prosecution for turning state's evidence, even though the other individual will receive a maximum sentence of ten years. If both confess, each gets a mitigated sentence of five years. Thus, interdependence exists—whatever decision is best for each person is contingent on their anticipation of the decision of the other. The dilemma is that if each tries to maximize individual gain and confesses, both do worse than if they had cooperated by not confessing.

The game illustrates a nontangible entity, a joint or collective interest, that transcends the individual parties' interests. Personal interests do not diminish, but they are certainly complicated by the fact of interdependence. My future interest is equivalent to my respect for the current interest of the other party, and my appreciation for the other is a means to affirm my future interest. In this framework, pursuit of my interests incorporates an appreciation of others' immediate and long-term interests. Successful outcomes are achieved through "yes/and" rather than "either/or" thinking.

The problem is not whether the individual or the organization predominates as dictated by conventional ideals. Existing ideologies or beliefs about how to organize social relations are woefully inadequate to address common situations of interdependence. Discussion becomes focused on whether or not, for example, to pass legislation requiring notification of plant closings. Political positions on this issue are highly predictable. Perhaps a more productive focus would be the question of how communities and firms can achieve their interdependent interests of stable employment and profitable operations.

Ideologies are similarly predictable on the issue of employee freedom of speech. While great energy is expended in struggling with this issue, larger and more important common interests of employees and employers are slighted, if not ignored. Our natural inclination is to define problems in ideological terms. However, this inclination rarely leads us to generate anything other than either/or solutions, and these solutions fail to correspond to the realities of interdependence in institutional life.

Traditional political/managerial ideologies also represent static views of the world. Advocates of each ideology struggle to have their value systems predominate. However, the effects of our current interaction on our succeeding interactions are rarely taken into account. My "winning" today simply may induce more sophisticated and intense counterstrategies by the other party that diminish my ability to achieve my goals tomorrow. Viewing issues in ideological terms, we fail to ask Garrett Hardin's (1985) valuable ecological question, "And then what?" Neither of our dominant ideologies explores secondary and tertiary consequences.

The prisoner's dilemma game, on the other hand, calls for awareness of the dynamic character of interdependent relationships. The choices I will face tomorrow will be a consequence, in part, of my actions today. Present actions should be influenced by the desire to create a desired state of affairs in the future. A sense of historical process is a valuable diagnostic aid that may illuminate how my past choices influence my present circumstances.

The provisional character of assumptions about "reality" is also highlighted by the prisoner's dilemma game. The game may be cooperative or competitive. It may be positive or destructive. The game itself is simply a situation. It is a set of possibilities; it becomes, concretely, what individuals bring to it. Players create their own outcomes.

Finally, this game bears witness to the existential nature of human experience. Players do face a dilemma: Will the other cooperate in the face of my defection? Will the other defect or cooperate as I cooperate? Inherent uncertainty and lack of knowing necessitate choice. "Right" and "wrong" dissolve in the face of the uncertainty of humanness. While the individual influences the future, its outcomes cannot be fully specified. Vulnerability is a fact of the human condition.

Appreciative Interchange

The prisoner's dilemma game offers an alternative to conventional ideological influence on perceiving and experiencing organizational relations. This alternative holds that individual and group (organization and society) are not separable and distinct, that the future needs to be accounted for in the present, and that reality is an experience created by the assumptions of interdependent parties. The game also illustrates the inherent uncertainty of human experience. Ideologies are born of the certitude of "right." Appreciation respects the indeterminate and uniquely human character of experience.

The "Yes/And" Perspective Generalized

I am endorsing what might be called an "integrationist" perspective on organizations. The manager's task is to create conditions for achieving individual and organizational goals. Group leaders need to manage stability and change. Organizations need to be loose and tight simultaneously. Effective leaders combine a concern for people and a concern for tasks. Some advantages come from centralization, other advantages come from decentralization. The task is to capture the benefits of seemingly opposing elements.

In short, multiple and often-conflicting criteria for action exist in all human organizations. Rarely is a manager's life uncomplicated by seemingly incompatible expectations between subordinates and supervisors, between a desire to be fair to all employees and a wish to accommodate the special needs of a few, between an instinct for advancing one's own interests and an obligation to respect the good of the firm, or between a sense of what should be done and a belief about what powerful others want to occur.

Large, hierarchical organizations seeking to accomplish complex tasks have conflicting interests, functions, and values built into their very character. Surely, particular criteria can dominate an organization for a period of time, but long-term success requires a full appreciation for counter or opposing values, interests, and functions. Paradox and dilemma are central features of organizational life. How can opposing characteristics be simultaneously satisfied? Why do successful outcomes often contain the seeds of their own deterioration? How can a world of egoists identify and act on the common good?

Managerial ideas and tools are often ill-suited to address the complex character of large organizations. We have theories and practices of innovation and concepts and policies of control; rarely do we seek conceptually or practically to integrate innovation and control. Many extol the virtues of change. Why isn't comparable emphasis placed on the benefits of stability, and why not address ourselves more to the important challenge of balancing stability and development? Some persons seek to make our organizations more efficient. Others want to make them more humane. Doesn't the key lie in making organizations both more efficient and more humane? A "yes/and" perspective is a valid and valuable approach to addressing the theory and practice of management.

If organizations are inherently complex entities, unbelievable complications are introduced when you put people into them. People—what do we know about people? First, we know they strive for consistency and persistence in perception and attitude. Even though a physical stimulus may be ambiguous and complex, people simplify it and make it definitive.

Social psychologists also tell us that in general people are prone to self-justification. Rather than admit an error we throw good money after bad, we rationalize decisions after the fact, and we tend to escalate behavior in the name of lost causes simply because we are personally identified ourselves with the cause. We are susceptible, in Barbara Tuchman's (1984) terms, to woodenheadedness. How often do we find two persons or two groups in the prisoner's dilemma game engaged in mutual defection?

Psychologists inform us of several other interesting things about human behavior. Projection and introjection—the putting of one's own feelings and experiences onto the outer world and the wholesale incorporation of external symbols and events as internal realities—are common psychological processes. Thus, we perceive different aspects of our self-images, aspirations, anxieties, roles, accomplishments, and felt responsibilities to be a "real" part of our environment irrespective of what may be out there. Also, we often accept external beliefs and ideologies as "reality" without breaking them down and deciding which to digest. We may frequently be unaware of our confusion between self and environment.

What does this mean for organizations? It means that the innate challenges of organizing are multiplied many times by psychological processes at work. Different crosscurrents of values and interests inherent in organizing are "adopted" by different organizational participants and become imbued with all the righteousness at these individuals' disposal. Subtleties are easily lost. In all our frailties, our work and our organizations become part and parcel of our internal struggles. The integrative requirements for organizing easily get lost in the "either/or" world of human interaction. It is little wonder that simply maintaining goal-oriented organizations absorbs tremendous human energies.

Managerial Implications of Institutional Life

I have argued that organizations are perhaps more notable for their lack of appreciation than for a high level of mutual regard among members. The inherent complexities of organizing large-scale human activity are even more complicated by human tendencies toward simplification and self-justification and by psychological processes of projection and introjection. While individuals obviously differ in the degree to which we enact these psychological processes, we rarely seem to be entirely free of them and they certainly characterize a great deal of organizational life.

Managing organizational relations is a task of integrating divergent forces through people who often perceive in absolutes, define their interests parochially, justify their actions as right, and confuse themselves with elements of their environments. There is little wonder that "either/or" cultures prevail in organizations and that practicing managers indicate organizational relations are the most important job skills for both entry-level and advanced managers.

I am also advancing the thesis that social history in the

United States complements this analysis of the relative absence of appreciation in organizational dynamics. Our individualistic culture has defined employee-employer relations primarily in adversative terms where advancing the interests of one party is seen and experienced as a concession of the other. Under the duress of international competition, considerable progress has been made to discover forms of workplace cooperation; yet examples are often isolated, less than comprehensive, and infrequently institutionalized. The massive force of American business ideology creates a steep incline for the traveler of appreciative systems. In fact, how can the processes of appreciation and regard be fully experienced within organizations without a wholesale revision of our broader social philosophies?

Solutions from a Theory of Cooperation. The prisoner's dilemma game represents, for me, the clearest and most general statement of the need for appreciative processes in organized relations. Our understanding of the dilemmas and dynamics of interdependent relations is greatly aided by this game, which has so many parallels and manifestations in the real world. Consequently, a discussion of the managerial implications of organizational life begins with a return to the game and specifically to the work of Robert Axelrod, who has devoted attention to the question of how to promote cooperation (Axelrod, 1984).

Axelrod proposes five strategies for improving the level of cooperation between people in a social system based on his studies of prisoner's dilemma tournaments between computer programs written by a variety of social and decision scientists. First, Axelrod observes that individuals often misperceive or misinterpret the actions of others. We may wrongly assume distrustful intentions of the other or improperly impute decency. Little chance of mutual cooperation is possible if the other's efforts to cooperate are not accurately perceived when they are present. Thus, a step to cooperation begins with reducing some of the perceptual distortion brought to the situation by the individuals involved.

Two of Axelrod's other proposals—teach caring and teach reciprocity—go to the heart of appreciative behavior. Cooperation and regard may simply be skills or competencies capable of being learned and utilized in organizational settings. In a sense, a thrust of the human potential movement is to obtain greater interpersonal competency and to reduce the behavioral "noise" created by dysfunctional processes of projection and introjection. No doubt these interventions can be successful in individual change. However, their advocates inevitably face institutional settings where the interventions have shown less potency as mechanisms of reform. Moreover, if social ideologies and values play the role I am attributing to them, efforts to change individuals' appreciative behavior will last little more than will castles of sand in the way of an oncoming tide.

Axelrod proposes two other measures to promote cooperation. One is to change the payoffs that people experience. In employment organizations consideration of payoff matrices primarily directs our attention to recognition, reward, and compensation systems. The prisoner's dilemma may offer the field of human resource management a conceptual paradigm for achieving greater imagination in developing personnel systems and for making greater contribution to the management of organizations.

Analysis of payoff structures may also be useful in exploring principal-agent issues embedded in the conundrum of stockholder-director-manager relationships. For example, each spring the business press has a field day analyzing executive salaries, a required disclosure with the annual proxy statements. The spring of 1988 provided a good example of how the executive compensation system works (Bennett, 1988). One study reported that in 1987 executive salaries and bonuses grew by 11.5 percent while salaries of all other white collar personnel rose only 5.5 percent. A ten year study of executive salary increases showed this to be a highly consistent pattern. From 1977 to 1987 chief executive salaries and bonuses increased 12.2 percent annually, compared to an average annual increase of 6.1 percent for hourly workers, a yearly average inflation rate of 6.5 percent, and an annual average profit increase of 0.75 percent.

It is less the absolute level of salaries that shocks many than it is the apparent ability of executives to gain a greater share when other parties—employees and shareholders, for example—are taking lesser shares. Why should senior officers of Bethlehem Steel receive guaranteed pensions when the pensions of middle managers taking early retirement may be vulnerable in case of a bankruptcy? Why should the CEO of J. P. Morgan Bank receive a $600,000 cash bonus when the bank's earnings for 1987 dropped over 90 percent (Bailey and Guenther, 1988)? Attempts to explain these facts as efficient outcomes of the market for executive services or as necessary "agency costs" miss the point. Society will hold its institutions to fairness as well as efficiency.

Do U.S. company executives receive 40 percent greater salaries on the average than their Japanese counterparts because the American managers have outperformed the Japanese so well in domestic and international markets? What justification is there for this differential? We need to know more about incentive structures and payoff matrices that underlie such differences, and we need to explore their consequences better.

Finally, Axelrod entreats managers to increase the frequency and durability of interaction among persons or groups whose cooperation or appreciation is needed for system development. Defection and cooperation strategies are inevitably dictated by the players' anticipation of the end of the game—a highly interactive relationship with an indefinite point of termination magnifies players' interdependence and places a premium on their cooperation. Infrequent or uncertain patterns of interaction and short-term relationships reduce incentives to cooperate. The power of different Japanese practices, such as long-term employment, the Japanese system of decision making, and high levels of business-government cooperation are illustrated by this dimension of cooperation theory. These ideas reinforce the search for models of organizational design, planning systems, and managerial processes that call for high and sustained interaction by interdependent parts of an organization. The ideas also call for more frequent and durable relationships between organizations and their external constituencies.

Axelrod's work leads to the conclusion that the dilemma of individual and collectivity is not insurmountable, that specific conditions and processes aggravate or mitigate the conflict between self and other. The individual inclined to cooperation can be greatly aided by wise design of interaction patterns, payoff structures, and personal development processes. Management counts. Moreover, this point of view is based on a rational choice theory of individual behavior. Our individual-group problems and prospects for solutions depend on no notions of altruism. Individuals may endorse such noble motives, but these sentiments are not required to understand and respond to the dilemmas and paradoxes of organizing.

The prisoner's dilemma is a two-party game in which a pattern of complete or partial defection implies that the parties fail to create a mutual benefit. The failure to create a common benefit may also be true for multiparty situations, such as large organizations and societies. In this case, individuals have to choose whether to contribute their fair shares in order to create the common good or whether to "let George do it."

Mancur Olson (1965, 1982) has pointed out that under conditions of nondivisibility of the goods created, there is an incentive for the individual to be a free rider on the efforts of others. The time, effort, and expense to the individual to help create nondivisible public goods are far greater than the individual's share of the benefit, unless contributing individuals can selectively obtain monetary or nonmonetary benefits. This effect is especially true in large, heterogeneous groups; individuals in smaller and more homogeneous groups have both a more favorable incentive structure for participation and an easier time arriving at consensus about the group's interest.

Olson's analysis puts the individual-collectivity paradox in a broad social context. He helps explain such social phenomena as low voting turnout in the United States, the presence of numerous loopholes for the wealthy within a progressive taxation system, and frequent means of special recognition for charitable contributions. A number of associations also give opportunities to members to receive a variety of reduced fares and rates. Olson argues that this logic of collective action makes possible the disproportionate influence of small, zealous groups on public policy and to an institutional inflexibility that causes economic decline.

Developing cooperation between many, heterogeneous

parties is a particularly vexing challenge. Limitations on information availability and communication inhibit individual actions, which all may agree are in their interests. Olson argues that three mechanisms gain participation toward desired public goods. First, selective incentives, consisting of monetary and nonmonetary benefits, can be used widely. Positive selective incentives surely are consistent with pay for performance and with employee participation and recognition. Second, a large group of people organized into more numerous small groups will be more likely to contribute to a common good than will fewer large groups of the same numbers of people. Thus, a thousand groups of ten may be more likely to generate involvement than ten groups of a thousand persons each. Finally, Olson's analysis leads to support for "peak associations," whose function is to span many different groups, to reconcile differences, and to forge policy in the development of a common interest. In a world of seeming growth in numbers, diversity, and interdependence, we may be well advised to develop greater understanding and competency in an alternative logic of collective action than what we commonly experience in organizations and society.

Inclusive Over Exclusive Decision Making. In the 1770s Americans were asked to choose between two distinct political philosophies. Making the geographically small states the primary political units appealed to many individuals. To them, smaller political units would minimize oppression by allowing like-minded persons to control their own affairs.

Federalists, such as James Madison, argued to the contrary. Strengthen the national political unit, said the Federalists, and take into account greater social and economic diversity. Conflicting interests will balance each other and protect against an oppressive minority. A larger number of persons in a political unit bring difference and diversity, which act as safeguards against collusion and control by a few.

Managers of large organizations might take a lesson from this historical experiment in governance. While the American political system may often be painfully slow to forge solutions to problems, it is eminently capable of integrating differences

Appreciative Interchange 193

and resolving conflict among competing groups. Multiple forums are available to address any particular issue. Decisions are continually open to renegotiation, and they are responsive to shifting coalitions among interested parties. The openness of the system earns the parties' commitment to its preservation.

Examples of efforts to rule exclusively are common in recent human affairs. The intensity and brutality of conflict are often quite visible and may be inescapable. After the Second World War, South Africa officially declared African Blacks an alien race. Members of that country today struggle with the results of that ill-fated decision of exclusivity. As journalist Suzanne Garment (1985, p. 18) observes, "the unnatural acts committed by [earlier] generations will be visited upon their children for generations to come."

Between 1973 and 1989 Pinochet's government in Chile placed a higher value on the freedom of some persons over others as the government has sought to remake society in its own exclusive vision. Granted, this Chilean government was faced with a society deeply divided about social and political values. But were steps taken to depoliticize institutions and create a free society for all, or were institutions viewed as a means to transmit the government's particular values? What are the long-term consequences for the stability of society of continuing institutional politicization? Seeking to restrict privileges and rights for those who think or look like themselves, officials create conditions for continuing disintegrative conflict and moral contradiction.

What does this have to do with the management of the firm? Large organizations are interdependent systems. They have multiple objectives. Differing parties have competing stakes in their decisions. Various internal and external actors represent opposing criteria for decision and advocate differing allocations of effort and rewards. In Phillip Selznick's (1969) words, large corporations are essentially "private governments."

Management, likewise, can govern inclusively or exclusively. Officials can seek to remake institutions in their own images and according to their values. Leaders may endow themselves with power to make tradeoffs about the interests of others with no direct or meaningful accountability for those decisions.

Garrett Hardin (1985, p. 94) points out, for example, the absurdity in Hitler's self-justification that "I was responsible for the fate of the German people, and thereby I became the supreme judge of the German people." Social or organizational leaders may find comfort in the opportunity to surround themselves with persons and systems that diminish rather than heighten accountability. Greed, status seeking, and ego enhancement also may aggravate some persons' tendency to put personal interests above institutional responsibilities.

Exclusive attitudes among managers destroy the ability of organizations to integrate opposing values and forces. Symptoms of deficient institutional integration are seen in workforce alienation, failure to respond to market and technological change, and inability to be cost competitive in an international context. These signs mean that one or another organizational quality has gone neglected too long in the decision-making process. One or another group whose interests are inherently interdependent with the success of the firm has treated its own interest as separate and distinct from the entity as a whole, or it has been so treated by the management process. Suppressed values will surface in corporations over time if the dilemmas of organizational life have not been respected. When decisions err on the side of exclusivity, the price of weak integration requires payment.

Corporations are economic institutions, one might respond. Their function is not to integrate the differing interests of society; that is the role of political institutions. Businesses need to develop and produce goods and services efficiently. Corporations cannot afford to delay until everyone agrees to act. Managers cannot yield power to every party that lays claim to an interest in the firm. To do so undercuts the managers' ability to act.

Corporations in today's society are both economic and political institutions. Of course, their primary function is economic; managers must know the worlds of efficiency and rationality. They do not, however, have the luxury of ignoring the existence of interest politics. Tomorrow's managers must also be comfortable in managing claims of fairness, justice, and equity.

The role of managers is to govern, not solely to issue commands. Managers are required to broaden the definition of interests, to show the relationship among values, to think in a longer time horizon, to merge individual and collective interests.

In short, a premium is placed on the ability to recognize the value of building commitment to the enterprise through inclusive decision making. This does not mean that managers need to cave in to each and every demand. It means that differing interests are given the benefit of credibility and that each interest is asked to accept its responsibility for the welfare of the whole. Appreciation as a two-way street is the key to working through the dilemmas of organizational life.

A recent example of achieving higher integration among workers and managers in Britain was reported in the business press. In 1985 Japan's Sumitomo Rubber Industries purchased the tire operations of nearly bankrupt Dunlop Holdings, which had annual losses of about $37 million (Hemp, 1988). By 1987 this company already made a slight profit, turning out 50 percent more tires with 30 percent fewer workers. The following are some of the reported changes:

- Supervisors have started to hold regular meetings about production and financial results.
- Management's parking lot was removed, and executives are now encouraged to spend more time on the shop floor.
- Managers lost their private toilets and executive canteen, and they are asked to wear the same "team" jackets as the production workers.
- Blue collar workers have been asked to take on more tasks without increases in pay.
- Rather than taking a work break when machinery is down, employees now shift production to another machine. They also shift work when waiting for components.
- Unskilled workers make machine adjustments previously performed only by production engineers.

An integrative management philosophy and set of practices have often been able to revolutionize the productivity and satisfaction of a business operation. How often need such stories be told before the point gets through? Contrast the Sumitomo example with the following description by an M.B.A. student (personal communication, 1988) of his work environment: "As a CPA in a corporation with a weak MIS department, I continually raise questions about various controls and the efficiency of different procedures. I have made suggestions which, when formalized in a cost-benefit analysis, show they would increase operating earnings. Yet my approaches to improving the company's earnings are repeatedly turned down. Accounting and computer systems are viewed as overhead costs. The typical reply is 'Your idea has merit. But it requires that people would have to work harder.' Yet we all agree that implementation, even given its costs, would increase profit! I wonder how many of the analyses turned down by top management would have been desired by the stockholders." How many more situations are mired in zero-sum processes when simple and effective management practices are readily available? What is the incredible loss of energy and effectiveness in our consistent inability to establish integrative relationships with employees, customers, stockholders, and communities?

The amazing thing about our organizations is that the two-way street of appreciation is as available as the debilitating mutual disregard common to many of our experiences. Sumitomo proceeded with a very simple and direct idea: to make employees feel that what is good for Sumitomo is good for them. What monumental achievements inclusive management processes can create.

The Social Construction of Organizational Reality

Douglas McGregor (1960) first pointed out how different assumptions, perceptions, and beliefs create conditions for different organizational outcomes. More recently, socioratonalists argue that virtually all aspects of organizational life— innovation and change, policy and strategy, culture and norms— are influenced by social processes. If this is a valid perspective, we should not lose the point in exploring how the dilemmas of organizing can be aggravated or mitigated. The integrative capability of an organization is increased to the extent that individuals representing opposing values and interests redefine their assumptions and perceptions about achieving their goals, not at the expense of others but in addition to their success.

Several years ago a group of M.B.A. students developed analyses of social leaders who had dramatically altered the assumptions of a large group of people so that the things the people believed about themselves and their realities were substantially changed. In a way, these papers were devoted to the personal heroes of the class members. Important national political figures were selected—Cromwell in England, Hamilton in the United States, Ataturk in Turkey, Mossadegh in Iran. Others selected religious and social leaders—Nanak, founder of Sikhism, Betty Friedan of the women's movement. Current or recent political (Ed Koch) or business (Mark McCormack, John Johnson) leaders were also discussed. The students examined the personal and situational characteristics involved in each case.

Several provisional observations can be tendered from these examples of political leaders. First, each noted political leader lived in a time of social fragmentation and conflict. Tension might be between the King of England and the gentry-based parliament in the seventeenth century, between sectional interests in trade and agriculture in the new American Republic, between the populist Islamic movement and a corrupt royal regime in Iran in the 1950s, or between vested economic, racial, and social groups in a teetering New York City in the early 1980s. Confusion and the threat of social disintegration were present in each of these situations.

In each case the leader exerted a unifying force that raised the pride, sense of nationalism, and morale of the people involved. A new vision or realization of who they were was shaped and became widely shared. The leader's effect was to create a broader identity or image. Rather than clutching narrow and more parochial definitions of their realities, people saw their interests tied to a more general entity.

Toughness and integrity were personal characteristics considered to be common to these individuals. Strong actions needed to be taken and oppressive, possessive interests were removed, occasionally by force. Several of these individuals became virtual dictators, if not simply strong administrators. Personal integrity—living one's allegiance to a purpose or ideal—seemed common to most. Of course, oratory and the power of brilliant communication often played a role as well.

The point is that order has often been brought out of fragmentation and chaos. Political leadership has often laid the foundation for the growth of modern nations or the rebirth of contemporary cities. Leaders frequently have acted outside the existing premises of most persons' realities and have effected an important reversal in the redefinition and the integration of social and economic interests.

Can the actions of these political reformers be reconciled with the above prescriptions for inclusive decision making? Did not these political leaders actively exclude or severely restrict the role played by certain interests—for example, the King of England or the royal family of Iran? These examples show that the reformer directed higher allegiance to the development and welfare of the nation (or whatever entity) than to the importance of any one group or party. It is one thing to administer possessively, excluding legitimate interests. It is another to allow one interest to dominate the whole for its own, limited wellbeing. Special groups with particular claims on a public good may not yield easily. Forcefulness may be a necessary characteristic of the administrator. This is not to say, however, that that individual should fall into the trap of woodenheadedness and govern exclusively and narrowmindedly. "A summit in the art of govern[ance]," is reached, writes Barbara Tuchman (1984, p. 32), "if the mind is open enough to perceive that a given policy is harming rather than serving self-interest, and self-confident enough to acknowledge it, and wise enough to reverse it. . . ." A credible perception appears vital to the reformer's ability to transform the assumptions and perceptions of others. This perception is that common interests lie above the interests of any particular group or above the personal interests of the reformer himself or herself.

Markets, Institutions, and Management Education

Our society organizes relations among varied interests in two primary ways. Market exchange is a brilliant method of structuring interactions efficiently among large numbers of persons and organizations. Markets are mechanisms for integrating differing values, preferences, abilities, and income levels. Efficient market functioning is vital to our ability to function as a society. "The free market," writes economist Albert Sommers (1977, p. 11), "offers no priorities, no values, no end, no purpose; it makes do with man as it found him." Markets are appreciative by fostering the autonomy and independence of the individual. They represent the ultimate in large-scale cooperative systems. Individual and collectivity destinies are mutually bound; as one advances, the other is enhanced. Aggregate cooperation, though, is driven by individual incentive and reward, antiegalitarianism, and individual dominance.

Large, enduring organizations — institutions — are also a common feature of our postindustrial society. Institutions are, or need to be, cooperative systems. However, the same patterns and norms of competitive interaction and dominance that successfully produce aggregate cooperation in markets often damage institutions. Most of us try to play the prisoner's dilemma games of organizational life, which call for institutional-type cooperation, with a strategy more appropriate to market-type cooperation. The Lochner era of labor relations in the United States tried to make institutional relations conform to market models that were affecting the country so profoundly in the economic sphere. Sumitomo has shown the power of an institutional-cooperative model in the British tire industry over the market-cooperative model that had been misapplied previously.

The point here is not to downgrade the market system. In its function, the market does a superior job to any other system. But let's not confuse the type of cooperation needed at the organizational level with that of the market, and let's not try to make the market process do the job — namely, institutional integration — that it is ill-prepared to do. Managers and other interested parties need to learn and to use the skills of institutional cooperation in institutional settings. Marketplace ideologies and behaviors are inappropriate in working through the dilemmas and paradoxes of organizational life. They give wrong signals for behavior and induce unproductive results. Market-oriented behavior in organizations in place of institutional-cooperative behavior induces institutional fragmentation.

Transaction cost or information economics demonstrates how arguable conclusions for internal corporate management derive from valid external ideas. The idea that economic relations can be organized hierarchically or in terms of market transactions traces from the influential insights of economist Ronald Coase (1937). Oliver Williamson (1975, 1985) developed and applied this idea in a variety of contexts, such as antitrust policy and enforcement, the organization of work, the organization of labor, and corporate governance. Following this line of thinking, financial theorists find it convenient to view the firm simply as a "nexus of contracts," including contracts with employees, suppliers, stock- and bondholders, and so forth (Jensen and Meckling, 1976).

Alchian and Demsetz (1975) make a significant contribution to organization theory from an information cost perspective. In this view, when productivity is enhanced by a team effort, production relations are organized within the firm, as opposed to interfirm transactions. Although input activities can often be identified separately, outcomes are not separable into the contributions of individual parties. In this sense, the concept of an organization as numerous interdependent relations is similar to viewing organizational relations in terms of the prisoner's dilemma structure—individual contributions are needed for all for the joint benefit to be created.

Alchian and Demsetz (1975) recognize that the availability of the defection option, such as leisure or relaxation, for team members detracts from the team effort. These authors term this behavior *shirking*. The full cost of shirking to the group is not represented in the individual's cost structure, and according to rational decision analysis individuals will contribute less to the group than they otherwise could have. The authors view monitoring of individual input behavior by managers as the primary way organizations can influence individual actions. However, monitoring is not costless, and behavior will only be monitored to the point that its marginal gains equal its marginal costs. The cost of monitoring acts as a tax on the work rewards of group members.

These authors have married microeconomic analysis — the staple framework for explaining the investment, production, and pricing decisions of the firm — with information cost assumptions and with an awareness of the interdependencies of work. While their observations touch on the dilemmas and paradoxes of organizing, the framework carries its own biases. Why, for example, are control and surveillance the only perceived solutions to the dilemma of individual and group relationships? Cannot the marginal benefits of individual effort be altered by changing the context for rational individual decisions, as in changing the payoff structures? Cannot the duration of the individual's relationship to the group become a more salient factor in people's calculations about the marginal benefits of their contributions? Are we to be content that our organizations cannot achieve any greater performance than that determined by the equilibrium of the marginal costs and benefits of employee surveillance?

In other words, there is no inherent reason why the search for solutions to the individual-group relationship should stop with an analysis of the information costs of monitoring. The problem is deeper and it has broader ramifications. Information cost analysis leads us to underappreciate the significance of this problem and its potential resolutions. Concepts that may help us understand efficient market structures may be harmful in the development of managerial capabilities that improve the performance of our institutions.

Our educational systems need to teach both market-based and institutional-based cooperative dynamics. I believe, based on some familiarity with professional-level management educational practices, that we are a long way from meeting this need. The philosophical positions of faculty often place students in an either/or posture with respect to the two types of cooperative behavior. It is more common for adherents of one to teach possessively, to be deeply suspicious of the merits of the other system and yet to feel quite familiar with its limitations. Students are, at best, confused about the differences and the implications of the differences for their roles as managers. At worst, students are simply unaware of the multiple responsibilities required of them as managers. Moreover, students most likely will fall into the pattern of applying inappropriately the assumptions of the conventional business ideology and frameworks of efficient markets to problems of organizational and institutional integration.

Conclusion

The management of institutional interdependence is critical to the effective functioning of today's society. Increasingly, we face the task of organizing relationships between large organizations that perceive their immediate interests to conflict. Interactions are often fraught with dilemma and paradox, and our organizing abilities are complicated by the limitations of human psychology.

I have argued that our predominant thought patterns are inadequate to deal successfully with the demands of institutional relationships. Mostly we use conventional political-economic ideologies to explain our situations and to advocate courses of action. Resulting ideological prescriptions fail to correspond to the realities of interdependence and yield inappropriate managerial policies.

Furthermore, confusion among managers, educators, and students of management often exists between market concepts of cooperation and concepts of cooperation within and across institutions. The dynamics of institutional cooperation need to be emphasized in management thought and education on a par with knowledge about cooperation through market transactions. The prisoner's dilemma paradigm offers, for me, a valuable initial statement of the former. Relations among the two processes need much more thorough evaluation.

Certainly, these ideals are consistent with an "integrationist" perspective in management thought that traces its roots at least back to Mary Parker Follett (1949). My analysis observes processes at institutional and social levels similar to ones that organization theorists have discussed within the firm. These processes appear to qualify as "appreciative." Whatever they are called, however, they seem to me to be critically important.

In one sense, the current analysis provides an interpretation of why concepts of interdependence and integration have made limited inroads into management practice. Our prevailing assumptions and perceptions about societal relationships have been inhospitable to effective management of interdependence. Not only are such premises ingrained in our mental structures, but they are formalized in legal doctrine as well. I have argued that the predominant political-legal paradigm in the United States casts the issues in wrong terms. And yet the debate goes on. A predictable outcome of the conceptual terms of our thinking is the inability to resolve issues.

I have tried to demonstrate the logic of several alternatives to conventional ways of thinking in this country about institutional relations. The prisoner's dilemma has been the focus of productive theory development in game theory and has constituted a valuable model and experiential learning device for interpersonal and group behavior. In my view, Robert Axelrod has placed the prisoner's dilemma in another rightful context of institutional relationships. Rich implications for addressing the management of interdependence flow from his work. Axelrod's analysis of policy tools, such as increasing the frequency and durability of interaction, changing payoff structures, and teaching reciprocity and caring, is an important point of departure for management practice and education.

Another handle for managing institutional interdependencies can be found in political theory. We might learn valuable lessons from our experiences with resolution of conflicting political interests. Often, practice appears tilted toward exclusive decision making processes when inclusive decision making seems more appropriate to the problems many institutions face. This perspective is, of course, consistent with an "integrationist" view of the world. It also presumes a different concept of the responsibilities of participating interest groups and different policies and roles for managers.

I have assigned an influential role to institutional leaders in the degree to which societies' varied interests are related. First, the ideals of leaders are expressed in the structuring of institutional relations where, for example, frequency and durability of interaction are determined. Second, policies and actions that determine the degree of inclusivity of decision making follow from leaders' grasp of institutional processes. Finally, historical experience demonstrates that assumptions are malleable and social perceptions are fluid. Definitions of interests are, to an extent, influenced by the enactment of symbolic roles and the use of social power of leaders. These factors together imply that the effectiveness of our institutions is subject to managerial action. Concepts and tools to affect our circumstances are largely at hand. The key question is, Will we choose to use them?

8

The Role of Executive Appreciation in Creating Transorganizational Alliances

Thomas G. Cummings

The 1980s have witnessed a rapid growth in new forms of organization. Faced with increasingly complex tasks, uncertain environments, and scarce resources, a growing number of business and public organizations have sought new ways of organizing to respond to these conditions. This has led to a proliferation of organizing innovations aimed at making firms more competitive, efficient, and responsive to today's environments. Many of these innovations are focused inward on the organization itself, and include attempts to make it leaner and more flexible. A smaller yet growing number of organizing innovations are aimed outward toward the organization's environment, and involve cooperative strategies for teaming up with other organizations to share information and resources and to mutually benefit from each other's competence.

This externally oriented innovation has resulted in the growing use of a significant new form of organization that transcends the boundaries of single organizations. Called *transorganizational systems* (TSs), this organizational form consists of diverse organizations that have joined together for a common purpose (Cummings, 1984). Such alliances among organizations enable members to undertake tasks and solve problems that are too complex and multifaceted for single organizations to perform. By sharing resources, information, and expertise, organizations can respond better to the complexity and uncertainty of today's environments.

This chapter addresses the development and use of TSs, with particular attention to the key role that executive appreciation plays in creating them. It starts by describing transorganizational systems, and explains how they are an effective response to the demands facing contemporary organizations. Then, the role of executive appreciation in creating TSs is described. It is argued that TSs are a radical departure from the values and assumptions underlying bureaucratic organizations, and consequently require a fundamental shift in executives' appreciations about organizing. The chapter next identifies executive functions that are necessary for developing TSs, and concludes by speculating about the skills and personal characteristics needed to perform those functions effectively.

Transorganizational Systems

Transorganizational systems refer to a diversity of collaborative arrangements where single organizations join together for a common purpose. Such systems can be more or less permanent, and can involve a variety of purposes, such as sharing information, coordinating services and exchanges, undertaking complex projects, and solving common problems. As a mechanism for allocating and controlling resources, TSs fall between markets that allocate resources through bargaining over prices and hierarchies that allocate resources through authority relations (Williamson, 1975; Chandler, 1977). TSs represent a hybrid mechanism for allocating resources through cooperative arrangements among organizations (Powell, 1987). These nonmarket, nonhierarchical arrangements can take a variety of forms, and have been variously referred to as *interorganizational systems* (Cash, 1985), *action-sets* (Aldrich and Whetten, 1981), *social action systems* (Van de Ven, 1976), *interorganizational domains* (Trist, 1983), *network organizations* (Miles and Snow, 1986), *consortia*

(Dimancescu and Botkin, 1986), *joint ventures* (Harrigan, 1986), and *business alliances* (Gerlach, 1987).

Although TSs can differ on various dimensions, such as formalization of decision making, they have a number of common features distinguishing them from other kinds of organizational collectives, such as networks and mergers. TSs are functional social systems representing a level of social systems between single organizations and societal systems. They constitute a logical type (Whitehead and Russell, 1910) higher than that of single organizations, and consequently require a shift from the egocentric focus on single organizations to the network-centric view of systems of organizations (Aldrich and Whetten, 1981). In terms of inclusive decision making, TSs are federative or coalition structures whose member organizations maintain their separate identities and disparate goals, yet employ some formal mechanism or informal collaboration for joint decision making (Warren, 1967). TSs may have a corporate identity (Aldrich and Whetten, 1981), or in some cases, a "referent organization" (Trist, 1983) that can act on behalf of the collective. TSs are embedded in a larger environment that itself can be considered a network or field of organizations (Aldrich and Whetten, 1981; Warren, 1967) whose parts are causally related (Emery and Trist, 1965).

TSs are a significant part of the contemporary organizational landscape (Powell, 1987). Their application is growing rapidly in both the public and private sectors. For example, there is a proliferation of strategic alliances among high-technology companies for carrying out joint research and development and for bidding on defense contracts (Dimancescu and Botkin, 1986). Multinationals are increasingly entering into joint ventures with foreign firms to transfer technology and to gain access to global markets (Harrigan, 1986). Government agencies are facing growing demands to coordinate their services to eliminate costly duplication and overlap of resources (Rogers and Whetten, 1982). Public and private partnerships are increasingly being created to revitalize communities and urban areas and to respond to shared problems, such as unemployment and plant closures (Fosler and Berger, 1982).

The rapid growth of TSs can be explained in terms of their responsiveness to highly competitive and turbulent conditions facing many modern organizations. Organizational environments are increasingly complex, uncertain, dynamic, and resource scarce (Miles and Snow, 1986; Galbraith and Kazanjian, 1986; Powell, 1987). Rapid shifts in technological innovation, customer preferences, patterns of foreign competition, and global capital markets are placing severe pressures on businesses to become more efficient, flexible, and responsive to changing conditions. Growing demands for streamlining government, reducing taxes, and offering better services are forcing public agencies to do more with less resources. A growing number of complex "messes" (Ackoff, 1975) or "metaproblems" (Chevalier, 1967), such as crime, pollution, and drugs, are affecting a diversity of organizations and severely stretching their coping abilities.

TSs are an effective response to these environmental conditions. They enable organizations to combine their complementary expertise, information, and resources to perform tasks and solve problems that are too complex and multisided for single organizations to undertake (Trist, 1978; McCann, 1983). TSs allow organizations to gain rapid access to new technologies and markets, and to share the economies of scale derived from joint research and production (Powell, 1987). They enable organizations to share the risks of costly research and innovation (Ouchi and Bolton, 1988) and to improve the overall health of their industries (Miles and Snow, 1986). TSs help organizations coordinate exchanges and services so they are conducted more quickly and efficiently (Aldrich and Whetten, 1981). They enable organizations to reduce environmental uncertainty by negotiating more orderly responses and interactions (Emery and Trist, 1973).

While TSs are an organizing form well suited to today's environments, several barriers need to be overcome to create them, particularly in the United States. Relatively strict antitrust laws prohibit collaboration that results in collusion or harms competition, though antitrust officials have recently loosened these restrictions if efficiency gains offset harm to competition (Harrigan, 1986). Also, in 1984, the National Collaborative

Research Act was passed; this clarifies the legal status of joint research and development among organizations and encourages its use where appropriate (Ouchi and Bolton, 1988). In addition to legal barriers, organizations may resist creating TSs because they fear a loss of autonomy and control. In the United States, for example, there is a strong emphasis on individual achievement, and organizations frequently act like "rugged individualists" when faced with resource scarcity and environmental uncertainty. Rather than collaborate with other organizations, they seek to protect their autonomy while outmaneuvering one another to gain scarce resources (Pfeffer and Salancik, 1978). Moreover, organizations may not see the need to collaborate with other organizations; they may be unaware of appropriate partners or feel that the costs of joining with others outweigh the benefits. The expense of forming a TS can be sizable, including heavy commitments of money, time, personnel, materials, and communications (Harrigan, 1986). Organizations may also have problems knowing how to create and manage TSs. They may not have the skills and expertise needed to manage nonhierarchical arrangements involving lateral relations across organizational boundaries (Galbraith and Kazanjian, 1986).

Despite growing applications of TSs, organizations are still heavily invested in bureaucratic responses to environmental conditions. Executives who are responsible for making organizing decisions often fail to appreciate the need for or the value of TSs. They have a strong tendency to make organizing decisions within an existing bureaucratic frame of reference, where responses to environment turbulence and resource scarcity are sought within existing hierarchical arrangements. The barriers just described reinforce executive appreciations for bureaucratic ways of organizing. They make it difficult for executives to appreciate alternative organizing modes, particularly those involving nonhierarchical arrangements crossing organizational boundaries. These differ widely from bureaucratic appreciations for hierarchy and autonomous organizational responses. Yet executives need to transcend these bureaucratic appreciations if they are to create TSs.

The Need for Transorganizational Appreciations

Executives are generally responsible for making strategic organizational decisions, and their appreciations about organizing can strongly affect the organizational forms chosen. By building on the work of Vickers (1965), we can see that executive appreciation involves two interrelated aspects: judgments of reality and judgments of value. Reality judgments include assessments about the facts of the situation, while value judgments relate to the significance of those facts. The latter give meaning to the former. When applied to organizing modes, executive appreciation involves reality and value judgments about effective ways of organizing in specific situations. These appreciations are largely implicit, and consequently are rarely examined or questioned (Cummings, 1981). They become imperatives for organizing, focusing attention on certain organizing modes while neglecting others.

As discussed previously, there are significant barriers to creating TSs, and those impediments reinforce executives' appreciations for bureaucratic modes of organizing. These appreciations focus executives' attention on bureaucratic responses to environmental conditions, and make it extremely difficult for them to consider alternative ways of organizing, particularly those like TSs that differ widely from bureaucracies. TSs tend to be underorganized with loosely coupled relations among members, and leadership and power dispersed laterally among autonomous organizations (Cummings, 1984). Bureaucracies, on the other hand, with tight coupling among members and hierarchical authority relations. These differences strongly suggest that TSs derive from entirely different appreciations than those underlying bureaucracies.

Recent reviews of the relevant TS literature have identified key executive appreciations that are instrumental in forming collaborative partnerships among organizations (Rogers and Whetten, 1982; Cummings, 1984). Executives holding these appreciations actively seek opportunities for transorganizational collaboration. They vigorously network with others, and through the interchange of appreciations, they create the collective values and identity necessary for forming TSs. Appreciative exchange is crucial for creating TSs. Members from different organizations are likely to hold divergent views on the possibilities of transorganizational linkage. Sharing these appreciations can help them discover areas of mutual interest and can foster the trust building needed to create TSs.

Specifically, executives actively involved in forming TSs tend to share at least three interrelated appreciations: (1) appreciation for interdependence among organizations, (2) appreciation for mutual adjustment among organizations, and (3) appreciation for collaboration among organizations. These are described below, and are contrasted with bureaucratic appreciations for purposes of clarification.

Interdependence Versus Autonomy. The first transorganizational appreciation involves the notion of *interdependence* among organizations. TSs are based on at least partial interdependence among organizations, either through shared fate or goals or through task specialization. Executives who pay attention to such interdependence are sensitized to possibilities for collaboration with other organizations. For example, their appreciations for interdependence can raise opportunities to work together on a common problem — such as occurred in Jamestown, New York, where leaders from government agencies, labor organizations, and local businesses worked together to revitalize the economic base of a failing community (Trist, 1986). These executives appreciated the fact that their respective organizations were all affected by the economic health of the community, and through a series of appreciative exchanges, they came to the realization that they all needed to contribute special skills and resources for improving it. Appreciation of interdependence can also raise opportunities for organizations performing interrelated tasks to better coordinate their performances, such as occurs in "value-adding partnerships," where firms specializing in discrete stages of production join together to coordinate the flow of goods and services (Johnston and Lawrence, 1988).

Appreciation for interdependence among organizations contrasts sharply with bureaucratic appreciations that are heavily oriented to preserving organizational independence and autonomy. Executives operating from a bureaucratic perspective seek to maintain or gain organizational autonomy by reducing dependence on other organizations (Pfeffer and Salancik, 1978). Although they enter into relationships with other organizations to gain needed resources, they attempt to minimize dependence on such linkages as much as possible.

Mutual Adjustment Versus Hierarchical Control. The second transorganizational appreciation concerns the nature of control in such systems. Unlike bureaucratic organizations that are based on hierarchical authority relations, TSs are polycentric with power dispersed among member organizations. Members cannot turn to some higher authority to control behavior, but must rely on *mutual adjustment* among organizations to control interactions. Executives who appreciate mutual adjustment are oriented to managing lateral relationships with organizations that they do not control. They tend to focus on achieving a negotiated order about such issues as members' contributions, benefits, behaviors, and interactions. Galbraith and Kazanjian (1986) pointed out that TSs resemble matrix organizations, but without the ability to appeal to a higher authority to resolve conflicts. Consequently, executives of TSs need to pay special attention to managing lateral relations and to negotiating among peers to coordinate interactions and resolve disputes. Although this negotiation may produce formal planning and coordination mechanisms for the TS, considerable informal adjustment and day-to-day negotiation are still needed to address emerging issues (Ouchi and Bolton, 1988; Galbraith and Kazanjian, 1986).

Collaboration Versus Competition. The third transorganizational appreciation includes a concern for *collaboration* rather than competition among organizations. Executives who value and actively seek collaborative relationships with other organizations are more likely to create TSs than those who do not (Rogers and Glick, 1973; Rogers and Molnar, 1976). They are able to transcend bureaucratic appreciation for competition as the basis of interorganizational relations, and see other organizations as potentially valuable partners. Appreciation for collaboration rests on the belief that organizations can mutually benefit from interacting. The benefits, however, go beyond those deriving from simple exchange among organizations, such as occurs in markets, to include the synergistic effects that can accrue from combining members' information, resources, and expertise around a common purpose. These positive interaction effects are well documented in the small-group literature (Hackman, 1976; Hackman and Morris, 1975; Cummings, 1981), and Cummings (1984) has extended that research to TSs. He described the interaction processes occurring among member organizations as directly affecting the collective performances of TSs. When collaboration is characterized by healthy relations among members, it is likely to result in collective performances far more powerful than the performances of single organizations. Moreover, collaborative experiences can improve the response capability of single organizations by providing TS participants with new skills and knowledge that can be transferred to their respective organizations.

It is interesting to note that much of the research on TSs has been conducted in the public sector, and has focused on promoting collaborative linkages among agencies delivering related services (Aldrich and Whetten, 1981; Rogers and Whetten, 1982). Apparently, appreciation for collaboration is more pervasive among public agencies than among business firms. The latter are more accustomed to market conditions that promote competition among organizations as the basis for effectively allocating resources.

When taken together, the three transorganizational appreciations form a coherent set of value and reality judgments about organizing. When executives appreciate interdependence, mutual adjustment, and collaboration among organizations, they are heavily oriented toward creating partnerships with other organizations. They actively seek collaborative solutions to problems, and engage in the networking and appreciative exchange necessary to get others to join with them. Growing evidence suggests that transorganizational appreciations are well suited to conditions of resource scarcity and environmental turbulence

(Cummings, 1984; Ouchi, 1984). When translated into action, they provide organizations with the necessary flexibility, range of responses, and expertise to respond to complexity and change.

Transorganizational appreciations contrast sharply with bureaucratic appreciations that focus on autonomy, hierarchical control, and competition as the basis for organizing. Executives holding these appreciations are unlikely to seek TS solutions to problems. Rather, they attempt to reduce external dependencies, tighten hierarchical control, and compete fiercely with other organizations when faced with external demands. Such bureaucratic responses are unsuited to the highly competitive and turbulent conditions facing many organizations today. They do not provide organizations with sufficient resources, flexibility, and speed to compete successfully in complex and uncertain environments.

While transorganizational appreciations are better suited to today's organizational environments than bureaucratic appreciations, they must be translated into appropriate executive action if they are to have an impact on organizational life. Specifically, executives need to exchange TS appreciations with members of other organizations in order to arrive at a sufficiently agreed-on view of TS opportunities to permit joint planning and action. They need to identify relevant TS members, to convene them to explore collective purposes and motivations for creating a TS, and to organize their joint efforts. The following section describes these executive functions for creating TSs.

Executive Functions

Executives need to play an active role in creating TSs. The relevant literature strongly suggests that the leadership function is essential to forming and managing TSs (Rogers and Whetten, 1982; Cummings, 1984; Nathan and Cummings, 1988). This follows from the simple fact that TSs tend to be underorganized in contrast to most organizations. Generally, relationships among members are loosely coupled, leadership and power are laterally dispersed among member organizations, and commitment to the system is sporadic as membership ebbs and flows. These typical features of TSs make it extremely difficult to bound them apart from their environments, to control members' behaviors, and to sustain commitment to joint task performances. Consequently, a strong executive function is needed to bring diverse organizations together and to provide sufficient motivation and organization to create and maintain an effective TS.

Action researchers have identified specific developmental steps for creating and maintaining TSs (Trist, 1983; Gricar, 1981; McCann, 1983). Borrowing from the work of Brown (1980) on planned change in underorganized systems, Cummings (1984) integrated that action research into a general model of planned change in TSs called *transorganizational development*. He identified three stages for creating TSs: (1) identification of potential member organizations, (2) convention of members to start the linkage process, and (3) organization of the system to regularize interactions and joint performances. This general model of TS development is a useful starting point for linking executives' transorganizational appreciations to specific actions needed to create TSs.

Identifying Potential Members. The first executive function involves identifying those organizations potentially comprising the TS. Executives who are considering forming a TS must be able to identify potentially relevant members who would be amenable to collaboration. This generally requires considerable environmental scanning and networking with other organizations to discover possible recruits and to gain information about them. Because TSs frequently form along existing networks of organizations (Aldrich and Whetten, 1981; Trist, 1983; Gricar, 1981), executives should be particularly attentive to cultivating interorganizational networks. This can help to identify possible TS members and to establish initial linkages with them. Such networking facilitates the kind of appreciative interchange needed to energize and direct organizations' actions toward creating a TS. It enables executives to exchange appreciations about TS opportunities and to explore mutual benefits that might accrue from joint action.

Executives can facilitate the identification process by making criteria for membership explicit and practically meaningful. Although the choice of criteria is inherently arbitrary, at least three general kinds of criteria seem relevant: technical, political, and social. Technical criteria have to do with the purpose of the TS. TSs are formed for specific purposes, and potential members can be assessed in terms of the relevance of their expertise and resources to those purposes. For example, executives who formed a TS to deal with problems of sudden large-scale unemployment in Great River, Michigan, used their existing network connections to identify potential member organizations in terms of their skills and resources for dealing with unemployment (Taber, Walsh, and Cooke, 1979).

Political criteria for membership are concerned with the ability of organizations having vested interests in the TS to impact it, either positively or negatively. Such stakeholders can control resource flows, information, or legitimacy related to the TS. Identifying those organizations may involve examining the wider context of the TS, including organizations having indirect ties to it. Failure to consider such organizations for membership in the TS can seriously damage its subsequent viability and legitimacy (Boje, 1982; Williams, 1980). It can also foster opposition to the TS from the wider political context, such as often occurs in the public sector when key stakeholders are excluded from policy-making groups (Gricar and Brown, 1981).

Social criteria for TS membership involve assessing potential member organizations in terms of their status, performance, personnel, and compatibility with each other. In identifying possible partners, executives often consider such factors as how prestigious they are, how competent their personnel are, and how effectively they perform (Rogers and Whetten, 1982). These serve as indicators of whether organizations are likely to be competent partners. Similarly, when different organizations have compatible features, they are likely to get along with each other. For example, research has shown that common operating philosophies, goals, values, and professional ethics can facilitate cooperation among organizations, as can complementary technologies and resource needs (Hall and others, 1977; Whetten, 1977;

Benson, 1975). Executives should apply these social criteria only after making technical and political judgments about TS membership. Getting along with other organizations only seems relevant once it has been determined that they have something valuable to contribute to the TS purpose.

Convening Members. Once executives have identified potential TS members, they need to bring them together to assess whether creating a TS is feasible and desirable. This convening function typically involves considerable face-to-face interaction among potential members. It facilitates the kind of appreciative exchange necessary for members to arrive at a sufficiently agreed-on view of the TS purpose to focus and motivate joint action around it.

At this stage of creating a TS, potential members are likely to have diverse motives and views, weak if nonexistent linkages among themselves, and limited methods for resolving conflicts. These factors make it extremely difficult for members to come together and share their views about the TS purpose and reconcile their self-interests with those of the TS. Consequently, executives need to play an active role in convening members and helping them share perceptions and explore motives to join together. Such leadership provides direction for the convening activities, and facilitates members sharing perceptions and resolving differences.

An initial focus of the convening function is to help participants reach a consensus about the purpose of the TS. The purpose provides a rationale for creating the TS, and members need to reach agreement about its nature and how they can jointly contribute to achieving it. Such consensus helps to legitimize the purpose as a realistic direction for joint action. It provides a basis for assessing the costs and benefits of TS membership, and orients subsequent planning and task-performance activities.

Defining the TS purpose typically involves considerable discussion and analyses among potential members. They may hold different appreciations about what the purpose should be, and may need to exchange information and communicate with each other to discover a purpose whereby differing self-interests can be made compatible. This appreciative exchange can be the source of new collective values and identity, and can help members uncover TS opportunities that previously might not have been imagined. Members may also be uncertain about the nature of tasks or problems requiring multiorganization actions. Such tasks tend to be complex and highly uncertain, and it may require considerable joint analyses to understand and define them.

Executives can facilitate such communication and analyses. They can act as communication channels among organizations facilitating the exchange of pertinent information. Executives can bring members into face-to-face meetings where they can directly share perceptions and work through differences. For example, executives have employed "search conferences" (Emery, 1977; Williams, 1980) to help members identify common TS purposes. These conferences are highly participative and interactive, and are based on principles of group dynamics. They involve a series of joint tasks for assessing TS purposes, sharing different perceptions and values, and arriving at an acceptable definition of the TS purpose. Executives can also help members gather pertinent information about the TS purpose and its context, and analyze those data to gain a better understanding of the purpose.

Once members have agreed on a common purpose, they need to establish whether there is sufficient motivation to create a TS for accomplishing it. This involves assessing the costs and benefits of joining the TS relative to each member's goals and interests. For example, costs can accrue from a variety of sources, including loss of autonomy, resource investments, and interaction problems. Benefits can derive from such diverse motives as resource dependence, commitment to solving common problems, and legal mandates to interact. Members may have problems identifying specific costs and benefits, weighting them appropriately, and judging their value. Executives can help members identify and assess the costs and benefits of creating a TS, and arrive at a realistic appraisal of whether the benefits are likely to outweigh the costs. They can facilitate the negotiation of inducements/contributions among members, assuring that they will receive equitable benefits for the costs incurred. Such negotiation can be either formal or informal, and can help to allay members' natural fears that partners will gain at their expense and will not perform according to expectation (Powell, 1987). Executives can help members mutually confront issues of equity and reliability, and begin to establish the trust necessary to form a partnership. Although much of this initial trust building occurs interpersonally during the convening activities, members may also engage in legal contracting as a prerequisite to forming a TS, particularly in cases where heavy financial investments are involved, such as joint research and development consortia, value-adding partnerships, and operational joint ventures.

Organizing Members. Once members have identified a common purpose and gained sufficient motivation to create a TS, they need to design structures and mechanisms for regulating their joint performances. This organizing activity is geared to the task requirements of the TS purpose, and serves to coordinate members' joint behaviors toward achieving that purpose.

Because TSs tend to be underorganized, members may need considerable direction and leadership in organizing themselves. The task requirements of the TS purpose may be ambiguous, and members may have difficulties devising appropriate performance strategies, functional roles, and coordination mechanisms. They may be unaware of the kinds of organizing decisions that need to be made. Executives can facilitate the organizing process by providing necessary direction and assuring that relevant organizing tasks are accomplished. They can also help bring sufficient organization to the TS to enable it to become functionally operational.

Executives can begin the organizing process by focusing members' attention on the task requirements of the TS purpose. They can help members assess what kinds of tasks are necessary to achieve the purpose. Identification of these task contingencies reveals the kinds of interaction and information processing that are needed for joint task performances, and organizing can be oriented to satisfying those needs. For example, when TS tasks are highly structured, such as might be found in a multi-university library consortium that simply lends materials among members, interactions might be highly formalized and involve only standardized kinds of information processing to accomplish the purpose. Conversely, when TS tasks are unstructured, such as typically occurs in joint efforts at community problem solving, members may have to engage in considerable personal interaction as a means for processing large amounts of complex, ambiguous information to define the underlying causes of the problem and to devise joint actions to resolve it. Here, organizing might be more organic and aimed at facilitating heavy interpersonal contact among members.

Based on this task analysis, executives can direct members' attention to appropriate organizing mechanisms. They can help members explore alternative methods and make relevant decisions. Although there are numerous organizing possibilities, at least two key mechanisms seem essential for TS organizing: structure and leadership. Structure involves decisions about what functions members will perform and how they will coordinate them to achieve a joint outcome. In negotiating functional roles and responsibilities, members need to consider their respective competence and divide labor accordingly. A major reason for creating a TS is to take advantage of members' complementary abilities, and executives can help members identify their respective expertise and make appropriate role assignments. Coordination of member role performances can vary from personal contacts and informal norms to more impersonal, formalized rules and procedures. Research suggests that when members need to interact frequently or when heavy resource investments are involved, communication and exchanges are likely to be formalized and standardized through rules, policies, and procedures (Marrett, 1971; Van de Ven, 1976; Lawless, 1982). Informal mechanisms, such as personal contacts and meetings, are inefficient for governing such interactions. They are more appropriate for coordinating interactions occurring periodically or involving negligible resource exchanges.

Like structure, leadership can help to organize and manage TS performances. So far in this chapter, leadership has been discussed in terms of specific executive functions for creating

TSs: identifying potential members, convening them, and helping them organize the TS. Here, leadership is extended to managing and maintaining TSs over time. Executives can help members establish such leadership by focusing attention on what that role should comprise and who should perform it. The relevant literature has identified many leadership behaviors for organizing and managing TSs (Litwak and Hylton, 1962; Aldrich and Whetten, 1981; Lawless, 1982; Trist, 1983). These include regulating member interactions, promoting exchanges, adjudicating disputes, mobilizing resources, establishing environmental relations, and serving as a gatekeeper for the values and purposes of the TS. The different behaviors are heavily oriented to managing lateral relations among members, and to maintaining the integrity of the TS. They are typically performed by a particular individual, a coordinating committee, or an organization. Such leaders can emerge naturally from within the TS, usually by occupying a dominant or centralized position, or they can be appointed to perform the leadership role on behalf of the member organizations.

Skills and Characteristics of TS Executives

This chapter has argued that transorganizational systems are a radically different form of organizing than bureaucracies. They derive from an entirely different set of executive appreciations than bureaucracies, and require special executive functions to create them. This last section identifies personal skills and characteristics that contribute to performing those functions successfully. It is important to emphasize, however, that executive skills and attributes are not the only factor that affects the success of the functions. For example, the wider environment, organizational interests and motives, competitive conditions, and past history of interorganizational relations can all impact whether the executive functions are effective in creating TSs. These other conditions have been the subject of considerable research (Rogers and Whetten, 1982; Cummings, 1984; Harrigan, 1986), and it is beyond the scope of this discussion to review that extensive literature.

Although there has been little systematic research on the topic, considerable anecdotal evidence suggests that the skills and characteristics of effective TS leaders differ substantially from those traditionally ascribed to hierarchical leaders in bureaucracies (Friend, Power, and Yewlett, 1974; Sheane, 1977; Sarason and Lorentz, 1979; Gricar, 1981; Trist, 1983). If so, it is important to specify, at least in a preliminary manner, these personal skills and characteristics. This would provide a basis for identifying and reinforcing executives already having those capabilities, and perhaps more important, for developing executives needing to acquire those special skills and abilities. In today's competitive and turbulent environment, there is a growing need for executives with TS competence.

Skills. People who are actively involved in creating TSs have been referred to as *leader-coordinators* (Sarason and Lorentz, 1979), *reticulists* (Friend, Power, and Yewlett, 1974), and *networkers* (Boje, 1982). Examination of descriptions of their behaviors suggests a common set of skills relevant to identifying, convening, and organizing TS members. These skills fall into three general categories: social, political, and analytical.

Social skills include the ability to form relationships with a diversity of people, and to use those relationships to promote linkages among members from different organizations. Such networking is based heavily on personal ties among people, and TS leaders actively cultivate relationships with people from a variety of organizations. They seek to establish sufficient trust and reliability in those relationships to facilitate the flow and exchange of information about organizations' needs and capabilities. TS leaders use that information to seek areas where organizations' differing self-interests can be made compatible through joint action. They facilitate appreciative exchange among people, helping them to discover collective interests and opportunities. For example, they might introduce potential partners to each other, funnel relevant information to key stakeholders, and establish new networks to address problems that could be resolved by joint action.

Political skills have to do with managing the conflicts of

Transorganizational Alliances

interest, value dilemmas, and power dynamics inherent in transorganizational relations. Organizations typically have different interests and levels of power, and these differences can impede opportunities for collaboration. Consequently, TS leaders spend considerable time helping organizations reconcile their differences and arrive at an equitable basis for interacting. This third-party role requires a good deal of political savvy. TS leaders must know when to push for consensus, when to bargain, and when to persuade in situations varying in conflict among members. They must maintain their neutrality and resist being coopted by powerful members. They cannot rely on hierarchical authority to resolve disputes, but must be seen as legitimate and credible authorities because of their impartiality, collaborative values, and expertise in creating TSs.

Analytical skills involve the ability to assess complex situations and to discover opportunities where organizations might mutually benefit from joint action. TS leaders continually scan the environment for possible matches among organizations. They employ what has been called an *associational habit* (Sarason and Lorentz, 1979), making connections among organizations that others may not see or imagine. This frequently results in reformulating the boundaries of tasks, problems, and exchanges to account for the resources and needs of other organizations.

Personal Characteristics. TS leaders tend to possess personal characteristics that are well suited to performing the executive functions described in this chapter. Because identification of such attributes is based mainly on anecdotal accounts of TS leaders appearing in the literature, the following discussion is highly speculative and is intended mainly to spur systematic research in this area.

Although TS leaders differ considerably in terms of personality, style, and interests, they appear to share several personal characteristics. They are highly *purposeful* individuals, with clear, persuasive missions or visions of what can be accomplished when people and organizations collaboratively work together (Sheane, 1977; Sarason and Lorentz, 1979; Gricar, 1981; Dimancescu and Botkin, 1986). This visionary zeal helps them focus their energies and actions and draw others to their cause. It helps to communicate a clear rationale for why organizations can mutually benefit from joining together, and inspires others to engage in the kind of appreciative dialogue needed to discover collective interests and opportunities.

TS leaders are *action oriented,* actively engaging with others to create new possibilities for joint action (Sheane, 1977; Trist, 1983; Nathan and Cummings, 1988). They locate and resonate with other individuals having similar appreciations, and seek to create new role space for themselves. They often become change agents or activists who constructively challenge the status quo and are willing to take personal risks to improve it.

TS leaders are *novelty detectors* (Ravenswaaij, 1972) who make new appreciations of emerging environmental forces. They have a restless curiosity about things, and continually network with others and scan the environment to detect emergent forces and interconnections among them (Sarason and Lorentz, 1979).

TS leaders are *boundary spanners* who are oriented outward toward connecting with others (Rogers and Whetten, 1982; Trist, 1983). They typically work at the periphery of organizations or in the space between them, and have learned what Trist (1983) calls "the art of walking through walls."

TS leaders have a *cosmopolitan ethos* that focuses their attention on broader issues and concerns than those within single organizations (Becker, 1970; Caroff, 1977). This worldview predisposes them to joint efforts with others; it enables them to see others as valuable resources (Rogers and Whetten, 1982).

Executives possessing these characteristics as well as the skills discussed earlier are heavily oriented to making transorganizational appreciations and to enacting them through joint efforts. They actively engage in networking and appreciative exchange with others to discover areas where different organizations might mutually benefit from collaboration. Their social, political, and analytical skills facilitate the interpersonal exchange and trust building that are necessary to arrive at a collective purpose and to organize for joint performances. The skills enable executives to carry out the identifying, convening, and organizing functions successfully. The personal attributes channel executive action toward these activities while providing a strong personal basis for collaborative exchange.

It is open to question, however, to what extent executives already possess such skills and characteristics, and to what extent they can be developed in people. These are key issues for identifying and developing transorganizational competence. In many cases of TS development reported in the literature, several people having all or some of these skills and attributes emerged into leadership roles over time. This suggests that personal skills and attributes promoting TSs may be more widespread than is currently imagined. In a few cases, TS leaders explicitly helped members develop TS skills and abilities (Sarason and Lorentz, 1979; Trist, 1986). Moreover, there is a small yet growing array of training materials and programs aimed at developing transorganizational competence (Klonglan, Mulford, Warren, and Winklepleck, 1975; Fisher and Brown, 1977; Lauffer, 1978). Although these efforts need to be rigorously assessed, they are a promising direction for enhancing personal skills and characteristics necessary to create TS.

Conclusion

This chapter addresses the role of executive appreciation in creating transorganizational systems. TSs are nonmarket, nonhierarchical structures that are composed of loosely coupled organizations that have joined together for a common purpose. Such systems are particularly responsive to today's highly competitive and turbulent environments. They afford organizations the opportunity to perform tasks and solve problems that are too complex and costly for single organizations to undertake. They enable organizations to gain resources and reduce external uncertainty by jointly acting.

Creating TSs requires three interrelated factors: (1) executive appreciations for this new way of organizing, (2) executive functions that translate these appreciations into specific actions for creating TSs, and (3) personal skills and characteristics necessary to perform those functions. Figure 8.1 summarizes the key elements of each factor, and shows that they are interrelated.

TS appreciations include reality and value judgment about organizing, and emphasis interdependence, mutual adjustment, and collaboration among organizations. These views contrast sharply with many contemporary executives' organizing appreciations, which promote autonomy, hierarchical control, and competition between organizations. Executives must transcend these bureaucratic appreciations if they are to see the need for and value transorganizational forms of organizing.

Moreover, they must translate these TS appreciations into specific actions for creating TSs. These key executive functions are oriented to forming a loose collection of organizations into a system capable of joint action. They involve identifying potential member organizations, convening them to define the TS purpose and to create motivation to join together, and organizing the members for joint task performance.

Figure 8.1. TS Appreciations, Executive Functions, and Personal Skills and Characteristics.

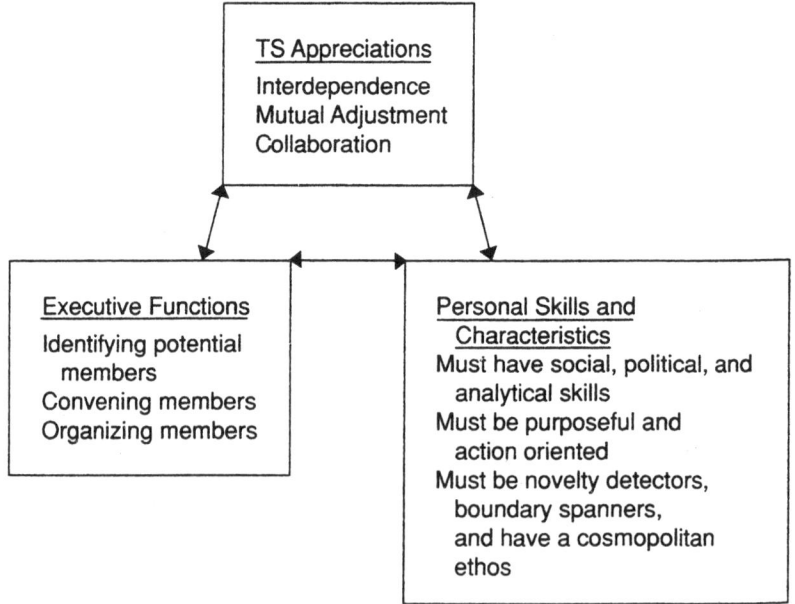

Transorganizational Alliances

In order to perform these tasks, executives need to have specific skills and personal characteristics. They must have social, political, and analytical skills aimed at detecting opportunities for joint action and facilitating appropriate linkages among organizations. Personally, TS leaders tend to be highly purposeful and action oriented. They are novelty detectors and boundary spanners, with strong cosmopolitan views. Such skills and attributes contribute to transorganizational competence.

The need for such competence in today's organizations is strong and likely to grow even stronger. The environments facing modern organizations are increasingly complex and turbulent, and are fast outstripping the response capability of single organizations acting alone. Organizations need to share information, resources, and expertise with each other, and mount collaborative responses to external demands. Hopefully, this chapter makes clearer what role executives need to play in creating greater collaboration among organizations.

9

The Quest for Altruism in Organizations

Rabindra N. Kanungo
Jay A. Conger

Recently DuPont Canada executives decided to join a group of chemical companies to find ways to preserve the earth's protective ozone layer at a cost of $8 million. This decision came in response to scientists' warning that the destruction of the ozone would lead to greater human suffering in the forms of skin cancer, eye damage, and floods and droughts.

Samuel Bronfman donated $2 million to provide improved physical facilities for business education at McGill University, and Bronfman-owned Seagram company provided faculty fellowships for business-related research in Canada.

Auto industry executives at Ford and Chrysler devised programs for the training of hard-core unemployed and instituted a buddy system for the induction of newly hired trainees.

Managers at the Ritz-Carlton Hotel held a gala banquet with five-course dinner and accompanying orchestra for chambermaids and waiters in recognition of their devotion and service to the organization.

A design engineer in an autoshop stayed over hours after his shift to help his replacement and to do chores no one else would do in the production department.

All of these are examples of unique behavior in organizational contexts. They reflect a wide spectrum of activities ranging from executive decision making at strategic levels to the day-to-day operational behavior on the workshop floor. They also reflect the responses of organizational members to both external environmental demands and to internal organizational concerns. Although heterogeneous in nature, these examples of behavior have one thing in common: They are all intended to help or benefit other people, regardless of whether the individual engaged in these behaviors benefited from them or not. Their focus on benefiting others makes these behaviors a special form of prosocial activity commonly called *altruism*.

Some twenty years ago, a *Time* magazine article entitled "The Executive as Social Activist" asserted that "The American businessman is being challenged to effect change within his own organization: to hire more of the poor, to stop the pollution that his company produces, to manufacture safer and more reliable products. Beyond that, he is being asked to reach more broadly into the community: to use his company's talent, capital, and organizational skill to repair the rattles in the nation's social machinery." In responding to such challenges, the article noted, "U.S. corporate leaders have begun articulating a new philosophy: that business is part of the total society and has an obligation to attack a broad range of social problems if need be in ways that temporarily retard profits. The new mood reflects much genuine altruism" (1970, p. 50). In spite of such observations in the popular press, behavioral scientists have ignored the existence of altruistic behavior among organizational members to a surprising extent. Consequently, the organizational behavior literature shows no systematic treatment of this issue.

In reality, altruistic behavior in our day-to-day lives is quite common. Parental behavior in nurturing children and voluntary community services offered by adults are examples of such behavior in our society. Early socialization practices in family, school, and religious contexts encourage such behaviors, considering them as the moral foundations of one's personality. For this reason, we support the activities of organizations like the Boy Scouts, YWCA, and Salvation Army. Since altruistic behaviors are a common occurrence and are considered vital to our moral development, many scholars have proposed a stable dispositional and motivational basis for such behavior. For instance, Murray (1938) and later Jackson (1967) postulated the need for nurturance as the basis of altruistic behavior. Likewise, Maslow (1967) suggested that the self-actualizing value of "goodness," when internalized, may prompt unselfish behavior.

Although altruism as a form of prosocial behavior stemming from an intrinsic motive has been investigated in both the motivational and social psychological literature (for example, see Mook, 1987; Worchel, Cooper, and Goethals, 1988), such behavior in organizational contexts has been neglected as a subject of serious scientific study. A cursory look at recent reviews of the research literature (for instance, House and Singh, 1987) and textbooks in organizational behavior (such as Schermerhorn, Hunt, and Osborn, 1988; Steers, 1988) shows no reference to altruism. Instead management research has centered primarily on achievement and power phenomena within organizations (McClelland, 1961, 1975; Mintzberg, 1983; Pfeffer, 1981; Winter, 1973) to the complete exclusion of examining altruistic motives and behaviors among organizational members.

At the same time, there is a growing sensitivity to the need for altruism. For example, public criticism of business during the 1950s and 1960s for social evils such as environmental pollution and unsafe products forced corporate leaders to pay attention to issues of corporate social responsibility. Such concerns are amply reflected in the literature on social responsibility and business ethics. Management training programs today contain courses on business ethics (Schermerhorn, Hunt, and Osborn, 1988), and during the last three decades, numerous research publications on corporate morality have appeared (Baumhart, 1968; Schmidt and Posner, 1983; Toffler, 1986). The literature on business ethics and social responsibility, however, deals only with the macrolevel issues of organizational values and their compatibility with society's moral standards. The literature does not deal directly with the more microlevel issues of the nature, causes, and consequences of altruistic motives and behaviors among organizational members. Indirectly, however, the business ethics literature strongly suggests that in order to achieve organizational compatibility with society's moral standards, there is a need for recognizing and promoting altruism among organizational members.

Part of this neglect can be traced to the absence of conceptual and analytic frameworks to identify altruistic behavior in organizational contexts. This has made it difficult for researchers and practitioners alike to notice such behavior, let alone study the phenomenon in depth. Our purpose in this chapter therefore is to address the importance of altruistic behavior in organizations, to explore the reasons for its neglect, and to offer a tentative framework for identifying, describing, and understanding the phenomenon.

Why Altruism Is Ignored in Organizational Contexts

In a study of public attitudes toward altruism or helping behavior in twenty selected occupations, Rotter and Stein (1971) found executives of large companies close to the bottom. They were only slightly better than used car salesmen and politicians. And in spite of differences in education and geography, four separate samples of respondents uniformly maintained that executives act in their own self-interest and help others only if they lose nothing by doing so. Such is the stereotype of executives in large corporations. The study also revealed that members of the clergy and physicians are high on altruism, showing concern for the good of others through personal sacrifice.

As can be seen, there is a bias in the public mind that executives are self-centered, egotistical individuals. They and their organizations are perceived as economic entities concerned primarily with gaining material advantage for themselves. Their main objective is to make themselves and their organization "winners" in the cutthroat competition of the free market. To win, executives are expected to protect their self-interest even if it requires harming their competitors. Thus managers are viewed primarily as selfish individuals devoid of moral obligations for the interests of others. This selfish nature is seen as the natural outcome of environmental demands. Just as religious and health service organizations promote altruistic behavior among clergy and physicians in the service of their clients, industrial organizations are assumed to promote competitive behavior on the part of executives to benefit themselves and their clients (shareholders, investors, and so on). These expectations have formed the social norms for executive behavior and have fostered a self-fulfilling prophecy for executives. Guided by such norms, executives themselves have been somewhat reluctant to exhibit altruistic behavior. In the public's attitude, they have found a rational justification for their lack of altruistic concern. Considering altruistic behavior and motives to be less relevant to executive functioning, organizational theorists likewise have concentrated on researching executive power and achievement and have largely ignored altruism.

The perceived irrelevance of altruistic behavior among executives was most eloquently expressed some time ago by Theodore Levitt (1958, p. 49). Levitt observed that "altruism, self-denial, charity, and similar values are vital in certain walks of life. But for the most part, those virtues are alien to competitive economics." To emphasize his point Levitt (1958, p. 48) argued that business should never indulge in altruism unless it makes economic sense: "The governing rule in industry should be that something is good only if it pays. Otherwise it is alien and impermissible. This is the rule of capitalism." In contrast to certain other professions, Levitt (1958, p. 46) commented, the executive "whose only aim is personal aggrandizement and whose tactics are a vulgar combination of compulsive demagoguery and opportunistic cynicism is less dangerous than the social evangelist who, to borrow from Nietzsche, thinks of himself as 'God's ventriloquist.' . . . There is nothing more corrupting than self-righteousness and nothing more intolerant than an ardent man who is convinced he is on the side of the angels."

Exploring these public perceptions at a deeper level, we find several important reasons why organizational theorists and the public censure altruism from the repertoire of executive behavior. Part of the problem can be attributed to the absence of an altruism construct in the literature of organizational behavior. Such a construct has simply never been utilized. So while we may find examples of altruistic behavior in the workplace, they are often not classified as such. Activities such as mentoring (Levinson, 1976), Japanese management practices (Ouchi, 1981; Pascale and Athos, 1978), empowerment behaviors (Burke,

1986; Conger and Kanungo, 1988; Kanter, 1983; Neilsen, 1986), and teambuilding (Dyer, 1977) all contain elements of altruistic behavior. They involve actions for the benefit of others. These activities, however, are identified as specific management practices rather than as a subclass of a larger category of altruism. Because they have not been categorized under this single unifying construct, their altruistic component is often overlooked by organizational theorists.

On the other hand, this is not to say that altruistic behavior is prevalent in business. In reality, it is relatively rare and infrequently rewarded. There are certain important cultural and historical reasons why it is less apparent in North American business. The sociohistorical forces of our capitalist and Protestant roots have fostered a form of individualism that precludes altruistic behavior in organizational contexts. These forces can be analyzed from both economic and psychological perspectives. From an economic perspective, organizations are considered most efficient when the classical mechanism of a laissez-faire philosophy is at work. The work of Adam Smith ([1776] 1936) and, more recently, Milton Friedman (1963) advocates the notion that a free and competitive market contributes not only to the profitability of the most efficient organization, but also to the good of society. Human selfishness in this context is considered divine providence. The Darwinian notion of "survival of the fittest" and Jeremy Bentham's hedonistic psychology and utilitarian moral philosophy emphasizing an "enlightened self-interest" are often considered ideological justifications for an economic laissez-faire philosophy. It is believed that what is true for biological organisms has to be true for economic organisms as well. Thus the concept of "economic" human being has evolved out of these intellectual traditions and has become the dogma of the American corporate world. Guided by the desirability of a competitive free market characterizing the external environment and an "economic" human being characterizing the internal environment, organizations consider it ideal to create conditions that facilitate individual autonomy and complete freedom of choice. In addition, it is acceptable to use information to one's own advantage and to compete intensely among individuals to maximize personal benefits. These conditions simply preclude the possibility of altruistic behavior.

Although organizations promote selfish and egotistical (rather than unselfish and altruistic) behaviors on the basis of these dual assumptions of free competition and "economic" human being, both assumptions have been found to be untrue. Economists such as Galbraith (1967), for instance, suggest that American corporations do not operate in an ideal free market environment. Markets do not control them. They control the markets, and consequently they are able to engage in monopoly pricing, price cutting to eliminate competition, employment and customer discrimination, deceptive advertising, environmental pollution, and so on. All of these forms of egotistical behavior at the organizational level directly produce many social "evils" rather than social "goods." They have led to public criticism of business ethics and a public demand for corporate altruism and social responsibility.

The "economic" human being assumption has also been challenged by psychologists (Maslow, 1965; McGregor, 1960; Schein, 1980). Contemporary motivation theories suggest that human nature is not limited simply to maximizing personal economic benefits. It is much more complex. It includes both social and self-actualizing tendencies, as Schein's "complex" human being concept would suggest. Thus organizational practices that promote individual competition and maximize personal benefits may not be in tune with human nature as we know it today.

In addition to the influence of the economic assumptions of free market and economic human being, a second trend that has to do with the development of a self-centered psychology in America acts against giving altruism its rightful place in organizational contexts. America has promoted a psychology of the self that Edward Sampson (1988) describes as a "self-contained" individualism. It is a conception of the self that is based on "the belief that each of us is an entity separate from every other . . . with a sharp boundary that stops at one's skin . . . " (Spence, 1985; p. 1288). It is exclusive of others. Altruistic behavior, on the other hand, requires a conception of self that is more inclusive of others. As a result, altruism is not perceived as important or as beneficial as it might be in other cultures. Instead there is a strong emphasis on individual accomplishment and material prosperity, often at the expense of others.

If we look historically, the evolution of this "self-contained" individualism can be traced back to medieval Europe (Morris, 1972) and to its crystallization in the sixteenth century (Baumeister, 1987). Before this time, conceptions of the self were of individuals who had only limited control over their environments. External forces played a more determinate role, and the notion of an individual independent of others was quite foreign. For example, in the Greek Oedipus cycle, circumstance rather than personality was central: "The personal character of Oedipus is really irrelevant to his misfortunes, which were decreed by fate irrespective of his own desires" (Morris, 1972, p. 4). In contrast, we find an emphasis on individualism and personal control by the time of Shakespeare's tragedies in the Renaissance: "The fault, dear Brutus, is not in our stars, but in ourselves" (Morris, 1972, p. 4).

These notions of self-authorship and self-contained individualism reached their zenith or most exemplary expressions in the American culture of the twentieth century. Spence (1985, p. 1287) argues that "individualism is so central to the American character and its positive aspects so taken for granted that it is difficult to conceive of any alternative kind of self-conception."

The American emphasis on individualism arose largely from the country's early ties to the Protestant work ethic and its emphasis on individual achievement (Weber, 1958). Protestantism brought a relatively radical view of humankind's relationship to God. There were no intermediaries such as a Pope. Instead a direct relationship existed between God and the individual. As a result, individuals were directly responsible to their Maker. The glorification of God became the principal aim of one's life and could only be accomplished through productive work. Work was perceived as humankind's calling, and not to work would be to risk falling from grace: " 'To lose time, through sociability, "idle talk," extravagance, even through taking more sleep than is necessary for health (six to at most eight hours), is considered worthy of total moral condemnation. Franklin's remark that "time is money" is not yet found, but the proposition is true, so to speak in a spiritual sense: it is infinitely valuable, since every hour lost is taken away from work in the service of God's glory, hence passive contemplation is also valueless, indeed in some cases actually objectionable.' " (Weber, in Runciman, 1978, pp. 141-142).

Under this system, the attainment of worldly success through hard work was interpreted as a sign of God's grace. And while strict adherence to this philosophy was perhaps limited in reality, the moral imperatives of working hard, making a success of oneself, and becoming materially prosperous survived (Spence, 1985, p. 1289). Over time these beliefs became secularized and incorporated into a national value system. In addition, they combined with a belief that success depended on a measure of individual competition. It was not enough to work hard, but to "win" in the competition against others for signs of achievement. Individualism and with it the notion of personal rights and freedom became sacred values. These beliefs and those of the philosophy of the Enlightenment ultimately guided the forrmulation of the Declaration of Independence and the Constitution. As such, both documents spell out the assumption that the individual is supreme and that government exists to serve the individual and not the other way around: "We hold these truths to be self evident, that all men are created equal, that they are endowed by their creator with certain inalienable rights" (Spence, 1985, pp. 1287-1288). These ideals derive directly from a notion of individualism where freedom is based on personal or individual expression.

These beliefs are so ingrained in our sense of self that children, at an early age, are expected to learn self-reliance and independence (Spence, 1985). For example, parents—especially the fathers of boys—encourage their children to be competitive and to win and be the best (Block, 1973). Spence (1985) also notes that in our theories of ego and moral development, the highest stage is one in which the individual reaches an autonomous level above the acceptance of and the conformity to standards of society (for example, Kohlberg, 1969; Loevinger, 1976).

Quest for Altruism in Organizations

This value system fosters an individualism that is narrowly defined in terms of self-interest. It precludes a sense of self that might be more inclusive—one that would recognize interdependence and a sense of community. It encourages, at best, only limited acts of altruism.

It is also a conception of self that is in sharp contrast with the one that predominates in other cultures. In fact, it is not the dominant psychological type for most of the world (Geertz, 1973; Morris, 1972). For example, in Japan, individuals are socialized to develop a self whose boundaries are more diffuse. The self is identified not only with the immediate family and a larger kinship group but also with the company at which one works and the nation itself. A sense of mutual obligation is cultivated in which the desires of the individual are subordinate to the needs of the larger community. Unlike in the West, where the "me" is essentially "I alone," the "me" in Japan joins the "we" (Devos, 1968; Doi, 1973; Lebra, 1984; Spence, 1985). These two distinct senses of self lead to opposite emphases on "rights versus obligations, on autonomy versus interdependence, on the pursuit of happiness versus personal sacrifice, and on the priority of the individual versus that of the group" (Spence, 1985, p. 1288).

Similar conceptions of this more inclusive self are found throughout the world. In China, for example, Confucianism depicts individuals as embedded in a larger social order with a set of obligations to define themselves in relation to others and to foster harmony in their relations (for example, Ho, 1985; Tuan, 1982). Similarly, Islamic thought portrays a self that has limited personal choice and responsibility and is dependent on a larger physical and spiritual world (Harré, 1981). In India, the Hindu way of life preaches that individuals view themselves as instruments of divine will, born to engage in performing moral duties that benefit the social order at the cost of considerable personal sacrifice (Buck, 1978).

In societies such as these, emphasis on interdependence and pressures to conform are high. Conformity may play an important role in minimizing the expression of creativity and entrepreneurial activity. For example, whereas the Japanese are adept at capitalizing on Western innovations, they often lack the creativity and originality of scientific explorations characterized by the individualistic West (Spence, 1985; Yukata and others, 1985). Entrepreneurship is also more limited in Japan. In Western societies, however, individualism has resulted in its high degree of independence and freedom for the individual. Of equal significance, Westerners are encouraged to find satisfaction in their own work and to strive for intrinsic personal goals rather than simply to meet the needs and expectations of the family or an organization. In addition, the emphasis on hard work, accomplishment, and the notion that "time is money" have led to a fast-paced competitive climate that has brought great material success and technological advancement to the West. But such freedoms and advancements have not been without a price.

Why Altruism Is Needed in Organizational Contexts

There are distinct liabilities to America's emphasis on individualism. Examples of the unhealthy search for self-interest are easily found. The recent insider trading scandals of Ivan Boesky are representative. The actions of corporate raiders whose objectives are to enrich themselves while simultaneously dismantling productive companies are further signs. In companies undergoing financial difficulties, it is not uncommon to read of senior executives raising their own pay levels while forcing pay cuts on workers. All of these represent an individualism that is driven by narrow self-interest with little sense of responsibility to a larger public good.

Even the academic world is not immune from this sense of unconcerned individual gain. In a panel discussion on the topic of growing scientific fraud, Robert Petersdorf, dean of the medical school at the University of California at San Diego, argued that science is too competitive and entrepreneurial with an emphasis on winning. He argued that measuring achievement on the quantity of an individual's publications and research grants has led to greater fraud (Spence, 1985).

Furthermore, this sense of individualism has led to the

creation of a "me generation"—Americans caught in narcissistic self-absorption. Material prosperity has brought with it a lessening dependence on others. Services are now purchased that the family or community formerly provided. Technological advances and geogrpahically dispersed career opportunities have also led to a more mobile society. As a result, a sense of aloneness and alienation has steadily grown. These forces and their outcomes stand as powerful commentaries on the price of egotism stemming from an emphasis on individual autonomy and freedom. One might reasonably argue that commitment to one's own achievements at the expense of others undermines the long-term success of the society itself. Hardin (1968) refers to such consequences of self-centeredness as the *tragedy of commons,* citing the metaphor of sharing a common pasture by a number of herdsmen.

What is needed is a greater sense of balance between this individualism and a concern for the larger community. In his book *The Duality of Human Existence* (1966) David Bakan proposed that each of us has two fundamental but opposed senses: a sense of self that is demonstrated in self-protectiveness and self-assertiveness, and a sense of selflessness that manifests itself in communion with others. He contends that both are necessary for survival. The difficulty facing individuals and societies, however, is to reconcile these two polar senses. Dawes (1975) characterizes this difficulty as the *commons dilemma,* borrowing the concept from Hardin (1968). In the West, the balance is tilted in favor of self-assertiveness; in the East, in favor of communion. There is a need to move more toward a point of balance — to cultivate a concern for the larger community rather than one of indifference. For example, Deutsch's (1973) work on competition and cooperation demonstrated the positive achievements of cooperative groups in which members sought to help an entire group in reaching its goals. Recent research on Japanese and European manufacturing strategies, where collective achievements are rewarded over individual goals, further support the notion that a more inclusive self can lead to greater effectiveness (for example, Ouchi, 1981; Schein, 1980).

In addition, studies in psychology have shown that striving for individual achievement can, at times, be self-defeating for individuals. Spence and Helmreich (1983) found that interpersonally competitive individuals were less likely to achieve than peers who were less competitive. The compulsively driven Type A individual may succeed in the short run only at the expense of their long-term health (Jenkins, Rosenman, and Zyzanski, 1974). The phenomenal economic success of Japan and other Asian countries is testimony to the role that a more inclusive self, a more altruistically driven self, can play in increasing rather than lessening business effectiveness.

The rewards of altruism may stretch significantly beyond "good business sense" to our own personal health and well-being. In the controversial study mentioned in Chapter Four, Harvard psychologist David McClelland found a surprising link between altruism and the body's immune system. He showed students a film of Mother Teresa working among the poor and sick of India. Afterward, tests showed increased levels of Immunoglobulin A, an antibody used by the body against respiratory infections. Even students who expressed a dislike for Mother Teresa showed the enhanced immune response (Growald and Luks, 1988, pp. 52–53). Perhaps the benefits of altruism may be far greater than we realize.

Organizations can no longer be viewed merely as economic machines designed for technological progress and personal benefit for those who control them. Instead they must be seen as sociotechnical systems responsive to human needs both in their external and internal environments. As human systems, organizations must develop the moral obligation to respond to the needs of consumers, minority groups, and others in their external environments. They must also respond to the social and altruistic needs of their members. As human systems, organizations must be dedicated to improving the quality of life of their members (and customers) by promoting their self-development through altruism.

Business organizations in America are in a transition (Salk, 1973), moving from an industrial to a postindustrial stage. As Lippitt (1982, p. 8) points out, our organizations are still managed "with the values, organizational structures, and leadership styles that characterized an industrial era. That era adhered strongly to the values and beliefs of the Christian work ethic, economic efficiency, and unresponsiveness to the external environment." The industrial era promoted organizational philosophies of self-centered competitive relations within a mechanistic and bureaucratic structure. It also promoted cultural values of personal achievement and independence. If we are to manage organizations believing that we are in the industrial era, and that precedents of the past guide the future, we are bound to fail. The contemporary postindustrial environment is different and more complex. In order to respond to a complex and turbulent environment, organizational and individual adaptation are necessary. Organizational philosophies must shift toward more organic forms with collaborative relations and an emphasis on improving quality of life in our society. Personal values must shift from self-centered achievement and independence to altruistic self-actualization and interdependence. It is time for a reexamination of our individualism in light of a more inclusive, altruistic self.

These value shifts are also evident in debates on technology versus humanism. Scholars are arguing more and more in favor of limiting technological and economic benefits when they are achieved at the expense of human values (Braden, 1970; Reich, 1971). As Mintzberg (1982) points out, "economic morality" cannot be promoted if it amounts to "social immorality." Such trends in the thinking of management scholars clearly attest to the need for promoting altruism in organizations.

What Is Altruism in Organizational Contexts?

A certain man went down from Jerusalem to Jericho, and fell among thieves, which stripped him of his raiment, and wounded him, and departed, leaving him half dead. And by chance there came down a certain priest that way: and when he saw him, he passed by on the other side. And likewise a Levite, when he was at the place, came and looked on him, and passed by on the other side. But a certain Samaritan, as he journeyed, came where he was: and

> when he saw him, he had compassion on him. And
> went to him, and bound up his wounds, pouring in oil
> and wine, and set him on his own beast, and brought
> him to an inn, and took care of him. And on the
> morrow when he departed, he took out two pence,
> and gave them to the host, and said unto him. Take
> care of him; and whatsoever thou spendest more,
> when I come again, I will repay thee [Luke 10:30-35].

This biblical story captures the essence of altruistic behavior. The story depicts three types of behavior: (1) the behavior of the thieves who actively harmed the traveler for their own personal gain, (2) the priest and the Levite who showed complete apathy toward the traveler to avoid incurring any personal costs from involvement, and (3) the Samaritan who helped the traveler even when such behavior may have demanded considerable self-sacrifice. Clearly the Samaritan's behavior is commonly seen as altruistic, while the other two types of behaviors are perceived as egotistical. The Samaritan is seen as being motivated by a concern for the benefit of others and a disregard for his own personal costs. The behavior of the thieves, the priest, and the Levite is perceived as motivated by a concern for their own benefits and costs and a disregard for the benefits and costs of others. It is this reference to concern for "benefiting others" versus "benefiting self" that distinguishes altruistic from egotistical behaviors.

Social psychologists define altruism in two ways. First, it is defined as an attributed dispositional intent to help others. Thus Krebs (1982, p. 55) describes altruism as a "Willingness to sacrifice one's welfare for the sake of another." Behavior is identified as altruistic only when it is intended to benefit others without the expectation of an external reward (see Macaulay and Berkowitz, 1970). Second, altruism is defined in terms of manifest behavior and its consequences without any reference to one's dispositional intentions. Thus altruism is referred to as behavior "that renders help to another person" (Worchel, Cooper, and Goethals, 1988, p. 394) regardless of the helper's intentions. The first type of definition refers to altruism as an internal state and the second type refers to it as a form of behavior with consequences. Since it is often difficult to identify the helper's dispositional intentions, researchers have preferred to define altruism as a form of overt behavior that benefits others. In this sense, altruism as a behavioral construct has a broader scope which includes many forms of prosocial behavior (cooperation, helping, charity, empowering, and so on) that benefits others regardless of whether it is, in intent, unselfish or not. Once a manifest behavior is identified as altruistic on the basis of its benefiting consequences for others, one can then explore the underlying motivational processes that energize, direct, and maintain such behavior in individuals.

Thus altruism has to be studied in two stages. First, as a form of overt behavior, it must be identified in terms of its consequences. Second, the underlying motives or reasons for such behavior have to be discovered in order to understand the conditions that trigger and maintain these behaviors.

Consistent with existing motivational theories, we maintain that all human actions are purposive in character. They are directed to achieve some purpose or goal of the individual. Altruistic acts are no exception to this rule. Such acts are directed primarily to fulfill the purpose of benefiting others. While meeting this aim, these acts do satisfy some needs of the individual. All behavior, whether directed toward benefiting self or benefiting others, is energized by some needs or inner drives without which there would be no behavior. For us, the so-called "hedonistic paradox" (that questions the existence of altruism), much like the chicken-and-egg problem, is a nonissue.

Altruistic behavior defined as benefiting others can stem from internal need states. For instance, Murray (1938) and later Jackson (1967) have postulated a "nurturance" need as being the source of altruistic behavior. Although psychologists generally view nurturance as a learned psychological need, sociobiologists argue in favor of some genetic preprogramming underlying an alruistic behavior mechanism (Wilson, 1978). It is difficult to establish the validity of a genetic basis for altruism. However, one can analyze how the need for nurturance or altruism (the urge to care for and help others) develops in human beings as a learned phenomenon.

Social psychologists have offered two major explanations

for the development of the need for altruism. The two explanations are anchored in notions of (1) a reciprocity norm and (2) a social responsibility norm. Through the socialization process, we develop these internal norms that guide our future behavior. According to Gouldner (1960), all human beings develop an internal moral code of reciprocity that dictates that individuals will help those who have helped them. Thus people help others with the expectation that others will help them in return during times of need. This norm generally applies when people are interacting with their equals or with those who possess greater resources. However, when individuals deal with others who are dependent and unable to reciprocate, an inner moral code of social responsibility may be evoked. This norm of social responsibility refers to an internalized belief that helping others without regard to future personal benefit is a moral imperative (Berkowitz, 1972; Schwartz, 1975). Such internalized beliefs regarding social and moral obligations toward others form the basis of an altruistic motive that in turn energizes altruistic behavior.

In the light of the preceding discussion, we would define altruistic behavior of organizational members as any work-relevant behavior that benefits others regardless of the advantages such behavior has for the benefactor. This definition assumes that altruistic behavior in organizational contexts must be work or organizationally relevant. It is the work life of the employees and not their private life that concerns the organizational researcher's quest for altruism. Furthermore, altruistic work-relevant behavior must exhibit a helping and not harming consequence for others. In the context of a person's work life, the reference to benefiting "others" may include a number of units at various levels. The behavior of an organizational member may benefit other organizational members (peers, superiors, subordinates, and so on) at the interpersonal level, at the group or departmental level, at the organizational level, and finally at a societal level. Such behaviors in an organizational context can also manifest themselves at the strategic decision levels and/or at the day-to-day operational levels.

Altruistic work behavior can easily be distinguished from egotistical work behavior in terms of the two bipolar dimensions as presented in Figure 9.1.

Quest for Altruism in Organizations

The two dimensions are (1) behavior reflecting (in its consequences) a concern for benefiting or harming others, and (2) behavior reflecting (in its consequences) a concern for benefiting or harming oneself. The two axes in Figure 9.1 represent these two dimensions on which work behaviors can be assessed. For example, when a behavior reflects a helping concern (or deriving benefits) for self but a harming concern for others (such as the thieves' behavior in our biblical story), it represents what we call *hedonistic egotism*. Much of the cutthroat competition in organizational contexts illustrates hedonistic egotism. Often a behavior reflects helping concern for oneself with no apparent concern for others (either actively helping or harming others). Such behavior can be termed *apathetic egotism* (as in the cases

Figure 9.1. Different Forms of Altruistic and Egotistical Behavior.

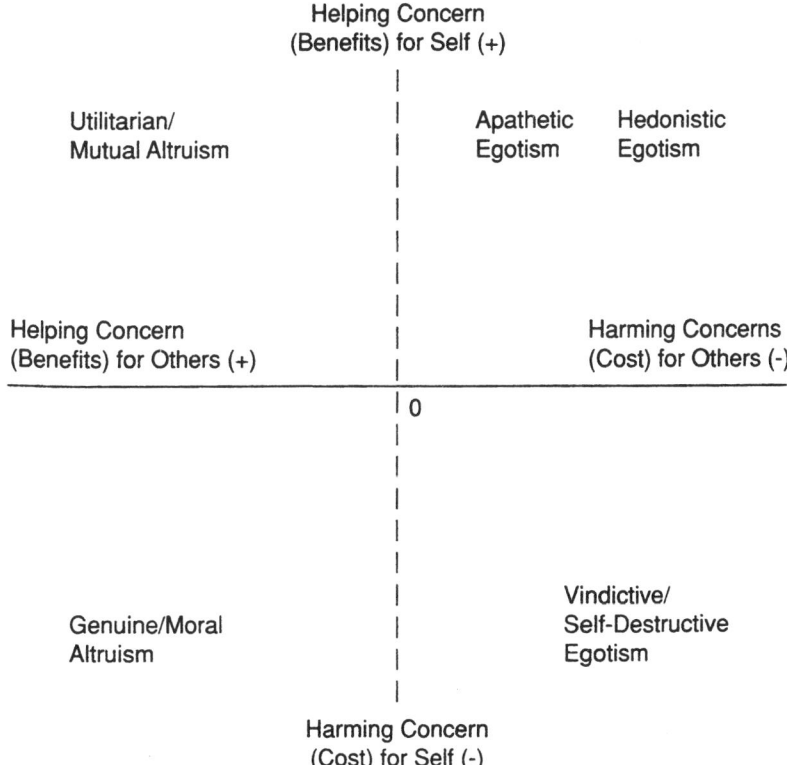

of the priest and the Levite in our biblical story). Within organizational contexts, this type of behavior is quite common. Business organizations often encourage their members to promote their own self-interest and leave the task of social responsibility to the organizations themselves (or consider the matter to be a task for other institutions such as government agencies).

Another category of behavior that reflects a harming concern for both others and one's own self can be called *vindictive* or *self-destructive egotism*. An individual who exhibits such behavior has an "I will take you down with me" attitude. In organizational contexts, occasional terrorism, sabotage operations by employees, and feuding among owners and executives would fall into this category. The recent takeover speculations in the Canadian grocery chain Steinberg's — caused by family feud — is a case in point.

In contrast to these forms of egotistical behavior, altruistic behavior always reflects a helping concern for others. When such a concern is combined with a helping concern for one's own self, the behavior can be called *utilitarian* or *mutual altruism*. (The innkeeper in our biblical story who helped the injured traveler after being assured of compensation by the Samaritan demonstrated utilitarian altruism.) When organizational members cooperate and help each other to increase productivity and thereby increase their shares of an annual profit, they exhibit altruism of the utilitarian variety. Monetary donations to charity to improve the corporate image, or managerial reward tactics to increase a manager's influence over subordinates, are examples of utilitarian altruism. Organizational members engage in utilitarian altruistic behavior primarily because of their internalized reciprocity norms. Expectations about the mutually beneficial consequences of obligatory behavior form the motivational basis of utilitarian altruism.

Finally, when work-relevant behaviors reflect a helping concern for others without any regard for self-interest or involve considerable self-sacrifice (harming self-interest), such behaviors can be categorized as *genuine* or *moral altruism* — an example being the behavior of the Samaritan in our biblical story. Work dedication, organizational commitment, empowering leadership practices, and organizational responses to the challenges of corporate morality such as antipollution investments represent this type of moral altruism in organizational contexts. Internalized social responsibility norms (or moral imperatives) are the primary motivational force behind these moral altruistic behaviors. Unfortunately, such behaviors are neither adequately recognized nor actively promoted in organizations for reasons discussed earlier.

Some might argue that many organization development (OD) theorists (Argyris, 1964; Beckhard, 1969; McGregor, 1960) have recognized the necessity for altruism in organizations in their attempts to promote organizational health and self-development of employees. The intervention strategies they have suggested for this purpose (see for instance Porras and Berg, 1978) do reflect a concern for benefiting others. But a closer look at OD literature suggests that OD specialists do not aim at developing altruistic behavior and motives. In trying to promote self-development, OD specialists have suggested organizational interventions aimed at promoting belongingness, power, and achievement-oriented behavior among organizational members (see Kolb and Boyatzis, 1974) to satisfy affiliation, power, achievement, and self-actualization (ability utilization) needs. In the approaches suggested by OD specialists, the idea of a more active orientation toward benefiting others at the risk of personal cost or of no return benefit is absent. Organizational development specialists are as ensnared in the individualistic paradigm of the West as any other. To understand altruism in its most exemplary forms, it is important to move beyond this paradigm. Organizations must create conditions for members to see themselves as fulfilling a moral obligation in which they are not relating to others only for their own benefit. For example, they may benefit others and not achieve a personal sense of belonging. Likewise, the concept of self-actualization must be redefined so that one can "actualize" by meeting the moral obligation of benefiting others rather than simply actualize through personal autonomy and ability utilization. Maslow (1967) himself suggested this in his later writings on "metamotivation."

Where to Look for Altruism in Organizations

As noted earlier, altruistic behaviors represent responses of organizational members to the needs of their social environment at four different levels: interpersonal, group or departmental, organizational, and societal. Thus utilitarian and moral forms of altruistic behavior can be identified at each of these levels of the social environment with which organizational members interact. The following list presents examples of altruistic behavior at each level:

1. *Directed to Benefit Individuals*
   Consideration of others' needs
   Technical assistance on the job
   Job orientation in new jobs
   Buddy system of induction for new employees
   Training to acquire new skills
   Empowerment practices including mentoring and modeling for others to gain competence
2. *Directed to Benefit Groups*
   Team building
   Participative group decision making
   Protecting people from sexual harassment
   Minority promotion and advancement programs
   Counseling programs
   Educational support programs
   Interdepartmental cooperation
3. *Directed to Benefit the Organization*
   Organizational commitment and loyalty
   Work dedication
   Equitable compensation programs
   Whistleblowing to maintain organizational integrity
   Protecting and conserving organizational resources
   Presenting a positive image of the organization to outsiders
   Sharing of organizational wealth through profit-sharing programs
4. *Directed to Benefit the Society*
   Contributions to social welfare and community needs in the areas of health, education, the arts, and culture

Lobbying for public interest legislation
Affirmative action programs for minorities
Training and employment for handicapped and hard-core unemployed
Environmental pollution control
Economic sanctions against oppressive social control
Assuring product safety and customer satisfaction

At the interpersonal level (one-to-one dyadic) both "consideration" and task or technical assistance provided by co-workers and superiors are examples of altruistic behavior. Such behavior may be motivated either by internalized reciprocity norms, as in the case of co-workers' assistance, or by internalized social responsibility norms, as in the case of the empowering practices of the supervisor designed to make subordinates feel more skilled and competent in handling organizational tasks on their own.

At the group level, altruistic behavior is directed at meeting the needs of specific groups operating within the organization. Such behavior might include within-group activities such as team-building efforts, participative group decision making, and between-group activities such as interdepartmental cooperation to achieve group objectives. Besides such activities, management efforts to improve the life of various groups of employees through advocating policies and practices related to sexual harassment, minority promotion and advancement, counseling and rehabilitation for absenteeism and drug abuse, educational support for self-development, and so on will fall into this category.

Another form of altruistic behavior is directed at benefiting the total organization as an entity. Examples would be behaviors reflecting organizational commitment, loyalty, and work dedication benefiting the entire organization rather than single individuals or groups with whom the member interacts. Such behaviors maximizing organizational welfare are often undertaken at a personal cost or sacrifice on the part of the members. Other activities such as equitable reward allocation practices, protection and conservation of organizational resources, whistle-blowing to maintain the integrity of the organization (Dozier and Miceli, 1985), and so forth fall into this category. Many of the altruistic behaviors that benefit the total organization are instances of "good citizenship" behavior (Bateman and Organ, 1983). The motivational basis of such behavior may lie primarily in the member's internalized social responsibility norms.

Finally, altruistic behaviors may benefit the society at large. Several broad areas of activities in this category have been identified in the literature concerned with business ethics. Activities such as affirmative action programs, training and employment of the handicapped and hard-core unemployed, protecting society against environmental pollution, assuring product safety and consumer satisfaction, and economic sanctions against oppressive social control through income restriction and capital divestment are examples of altruism that benefits the whole society. This type of altruistic behavior represents good citizenship within a societal context and stems primarily from one's internalized social responsibility norms.

The preceding scheme provides a convenient way of locating altruistic behavior in organizations. Effective organizational functioning requires that members' behavior be directed to meet the needs and demands of its constituents. Behaviors that benefit the constituents therefore need to be clearly recognized and encouraged.

How Can Altruism in Organizations Be Promoted?

In order to encourage organizational members to engage in altruistic behavior, one needs to consider both predisposing and situational conditions. Some members are more likely to engage in altruistic behavior than others because of their strong internalized moral beliefs about what is right and wrong. Likewise some situations are more likely to trigger altruistic behavior in members than other situations, because of the presence of some facilitating or reinforcing conditions.

Predisposing Conditions. Altruistic behavior often stems from a deeply held personal value system regarding social justice and personal integrity. These values are sometimes referred to as *end values* (Burns, 1978), and when internalized, they constitute the socializing and moral agency of one's personality—

the *superego* in psychoanalytic theory (Freud, 1940). Such internalized end values dictate moral imperatives of both reciprocity norms ("help others who help you") and responsibility norms ("help others in need") that cannot be negotiated or exchanged for personal gain (Kuhnert and Lewis, 1987). In fact, particularly at the lower levels, organizational members may engage in mutual altruism to achieve a sense of social justice and equity. Likewise, in order to maintain a sense of personal integrity, many members—particularly those in leadership roles—may exhibit self-sacrificing behavior for the benefit of others. Both mutual and moral altruism do require a certain level of maturity and moral development.

Theories of personality and moral behavior often identify predisposing conditions for altruism in terms of different developmental stages. For instance, using a developmental perspective, Piaget (1948) talks of the autonomous morality that develops out of a mutual respect for one another and manifests itself in terms of reciprocal rights and obligations. In an extension of the Piagetian framework, Kohlberg (1969) suggests six stages of moral development (see Kegan, 1982, for details). In the two highest stages of such development, moral acts are guided by beliefs about meeting social obligations because of a utilitarian social contract and belief in the moral righteousness of such action beyond obligatory pressures. These beliefs resemble the reciprocity and responsibility norms that form the basis of altruistic behavior.

A constructive/developmental theory of personality proposed by Kegan (1982) also describes the beliefs underlying the personality structure conducive to the manifestation of altruistic behavior. Kegan suggests that at higher levels of adult development, individuals first coordinate their needs with the needs of others in an interpersonal transactional way. But further in the development process, individuals operate purely in terms of their own internal subjective standards of meeting mutual and moral obligations.

Review of the literature on moral development suggests that the higher the moral development, the more altruistically the individual will behave (Rushton, 1980). In organizational contexts, lower-level employees in co-worker roles and managers in their supervisory, leadership, informational, and representational roles need to engage in altruistic behaviors to meet the demands of both the internal and external social environment. Thus it is necessary to promote mutual and/or moral altruism in specific roles of organizational members. Such promotion of altruism would be facilitated if individuals are selected for their roles on the basis of their nurturant, altruistic, and moral dispositions. In this context, psychological tests to assess the need for nurturance and strength of moral judgments (one's belief in reciprocity and responsibility norms) would be helpful. Development of such diagnostic tests to meet organizational needs is an important task of future research.

Situational Conditions. Beyond the predispositional needs and beliefs of organizational members, several situational conditions that facilitate the manifestation of altruistic behavior can be identified. Both overt altruistic behaviors and underlying needs and beliefs are learned through a socialization process. In family, school, and work organization contexts, individuals are exposed to social interaction situations that form the basis of their beliefs about social reciprocity and responsibility norms. Once the beliefs in these norms are developed through cognitive learning, individuals are encouraged to internalize them as a part of their self-image. Internalization of these norms is achieved through the psychological mechanisms of identification (Freud, 1940), imitation or modeling (Bandura, 1986), and reinforcement (Skinner, 1974). Once the norms are internalized, they operate as a need state or a need to maintain an internal standard of personal integrity. Altruistic behavior stems from such learned needs, and by engaging in altruistic behavior, an individual develops a sense of self-fulfillment. When such norms are completely internalized, external reinforcers may not be necessary to maintain altruistic behavior. In this case, an individual engages in altruistic behavior purely to achieve an inner sense of personal integrity and fulfillment. On the other hand, if internalization is not complete, external material and social reinforcers may be necessary to maintain altruistic behavior.

In view of the learned nature of altruism, organizations may take a number of steps to promote altruistic behavior. First, organizations must ensure that members are cognitively aware of the importance of the reciprocity and responsibility norms guiding their behavior within the organization. Such awareness can be developed, first by emphasizing the need for mutual and/or moral altruistic behaviors and by clarifying their significance or meaningfulness in given situations and/or roles. Second, the saliency of altruistic acts can be enhanced by assigning clear responsibility for altruistic behavior to specific individuals. The social psychological literature on helping behavior and social loafing (Latane and Darley, 1970; Latane, Williams, and Harkins, 1979) clearly suggests that people engage in altruistic acts when they perceive the need for such acts and accept personal responsibility for them. Feelings of responsibility for the welfare of others both within the organization and outside (customers and society at large) must be fostered among members by the organization's socialization practices. Furthermore, assigning specific responsibilities for altruistic acts involves giving precise instructions on whom to help, when to help, and how to help. Such instructions would develop competencies in helping others and, in turn, increase members' sense of personal worth and efficacy.

An organizational climate of mutual interdependency and trust tends to promote altruistic behavior. A social facilitation effect often is in evidence with regard to altruistic behavior because of the influence of reciprocity norms. Individuals tend to behave altruistically when they perceive that others are behaving in an altruistic manner. Furthermore, it has been suggested that experiencing empathic emotion facilitates altruistic behavior (Batson and others, 1983). Organizational practices that encourage empathic understanding of the problems of others (identifying with or taking other persons' perspectives) would increase altruism among members. Experiencing mutual trust, interdependence, and empathy reinforces one's beliefs about the social reciprocity and responsibility norms underlying altruistic behavior.

At the manifest behavior level, organizational reward systems could be designed to reinforce the altruistic behavior of members. Social reinforcers in the form of supervisory and co-worker recognition and praise, as well as material rewards in the form of merit raises in pay, prizes, and so on would tend to increase the occurrence of altruistic behavior among organizational members. Another important way in which altruistic behavior could be promoted among subordinates is through a leader's modeling and mentoring behavior. By their personal exemplary behavior, organizational leaders can provide opportunities for subordinates' vicarious learning of altruistic behavior.

Training in altruism can also be devised for different groups of employees in various task roles with the explicit objectives of fostering a sense of social reciprocity and social responsibility, and enhancing employee competencies in helping behavior. In such programs, techniques such as informational and cognitive learning sessions about the value of altruism, altruistic role playing to develop competencies in helping behavior, exercises on empathetic understanding, and observation of helpful models can be used.

If organizational effectiveness and employee self-development depend, at least in part, on the altruistic behavior of members, an organization must develop an explicit management philosophy that includes recognition of altruism as a key component of employee behavior. Based on such a philosophy, the organization then must set specific objectives in this regard. Behavioral objectives with respect to who should engage in altruistic behavior, in what task roles, and directed to which segment of the interacting environment need to be clearly specified. Having the objectives formulated, specific action plans can be worked out in the design of selection, training, and reward systems.

Conclusion

Our aim has been to bring to the forefront of attention the significances of altruism in organizational contexts. While the current interest in business ethics has sparked attention, it has failed to address the underlying dynamics and consequences of altruistic motives and behaviors. It has failed to see altruism at the level of the individual and, more important, has ignored its role in enhancing organizational effectiveness. This narrow and singular focus, as we have argued, reflects a more general neglect that altruism has suffered in our society and in our organizations. Our culture has promoted an individualism and competitiveness that inhibit expressions of altruism. Even on those occasions where such behavior does occur, the lack of an analytical framework has made it difficult for both researchers and practitioners to discern and interpret altruism. In addition, organizational systems and rewards have not been designed and structured to foster such behaviors. As a result, there is little encouragement to perform altruistic acts.

We have attempted to address this shortcoming in our understanding and, more important, to promote altruism in business today through the introduction of a conceptual framework. We are realistic enough to recognize that such a model alone is insufficient as a catalyst for change. Rather receptivity to altruism will depend on the realization that such behaviors are necessary to ensure more effective performance. It is conceivable that widespread concern for altruism will not arise until it makes good economic sense. This presents a paradox for Western businesses. Deeply held paradigms of organizational effectiveness dictate that self-interest is the pathway to success. To shake this belief, dissatisfaction and perhaps crisis will be needed. In reality, the world is now proving the contrary of this paradigm—that altruism does indeed make good economic sense and can lead to greater organizational effectiveness. Japan, Taiwan, and Korea are examples of community-defined societies that are succeeding economically. Today's new era of business demands more organic organizational forms. The greater complexity of the world's marketplace requires a higher degree of interdependence, more attention based on cooperation instead of competition, and greater loyalty to the organization rather than to the individual. Ultimately, such interdependence may require efforts beyond those that our organizations will be able to structure and reward. Unprompted individual acts of cooperation and unrewarded personal sacrifice must be present to ensure this transition (Saleh, 1987). Individuals must be prepared and willing to make sacrifices for the welfare of the community. This requires that certain societal values, expectations, and socialization practices be changed and that encouragement for such behavior begin in our homes and schools.

Though it is unlikely that North American society can or would wish to achieve the level of "other-dependence" so characteristic of Asian societies, we must certainly find a more balanced position than our current one of extreme individualism. Both a sense of self that is self-assertive and a sense of selflessness that is other-supportive are needed for survival (Bakan, 1966). In the West, our task is to cultivate a concern for the larger community rather than our present indifference. As a major social force in society, industry can and should play a vital role in this transition. In a recent article, Saleh (1987) describes changes that can be made to promote a greater relational emphasis in organizations. Through the four processes of managing—planning, organizing, controlling, and leading—companies can structure a more relational orientation that encourages altruistic acts. For example, in planning and decision making, collaboration can emphasize structures based on groups rather than on individuals. Responsibilities, reporting relationship, and assignments can be defined in terms of collective units. Control systems can be based more on emotional appeals to loyalty and identification with the firm than on simple performance measures. Group norms can serve as important sources of control, and in selection, greater value can be placed on attitudes rather than simply on abilities. In leading, organizational systems and rewards can encourage leaders' commitment to the shared goals of the organization rather than toward purely personal aims. In addition, the emphasis can shift from the individual to the collective. These steps, combined with our earlier suggestions, are critical to the growth of more altruistic systems in our workplaces. They are ultimately essential for organizations wishing to adapt to a world in great transition.

10

The Logical and Appreciative Dimensions of Accountability

L. L. Cummings
Ronald J. Anton

Accountability lies at the center of three important issues and processes of organizational life. It is because of this centrality that accountability is worthy of our renewed attention and emphasis as scholars of organizational behavior.

First, accountability is central to our understanding of organizational coordination and integration. Accountability is the locus of a web of expectation, the predictability and endurance of which provide an important force holding organizations together. Without accountability as a distinct binding quality of organizational life, organizations and people within them would find organizational life increasingly precarious and tentative.

Second, since organizations can be viewed as essentially social phenomena, accountability—as the mutual exchange of behavioral expectations—provides an important vision of behavior as a social concept and emphasizes the social context of humans in organizations. The social meaning of organizations is, in part, dependent on people holding one another accountable for their decisions and actions.

Note: The comments and suggestions of the following colleagues are greatly appreciated: Harold Angle, Philip Bromiley, Carolyn Egri, Peter Frost, Kathy Gurley, Cassandra Ricker, Peter Ring, Linn Van Dynne.

Third, any claim to an adequate understanding of executive behavior must include consideration of who holds whom accountable for what and in what manner. Executive behavior, in both its socially responsible and abusive forms, can best be understood and influenced by incorporating the concept of accountability generation and the consequences of accountability use and abuse.

In our analysis of accountability we first introduce a systematic model of the logical structure of accountability. The basic constructs of the model include (1) the *event* for which an individual assumes personal responsibility and for which he or she can be held accountable, and (2) *responsibility*, defined as the personal causal influence on an event. Two possible processes link responsibility with specific outcome behaviors. One, which is predominantly internal to the person, is (3) *felt responsibility*, or the cognitive and emotional acceptance of responsibility. The second, predominantly an external social process, is (4) *accountability*. Accountability is defined as the calling to give accounts (excuses or justifications) to another (or others) for deviation between the event for which one is responsible and organizational expectations or norms. (We will use the term *principal* to refer to the party who holds another accountable and *agent* for the party held accountable. We are aware that this terminology is used differently in other literature.) When necessary, accountability includes bearing the consequences for that deviation. The model further suggests a series of moderators and mediators between the constructs.

Equally important as the logical structure are matters of affect and appreciation that inform the implementation of the model. When viewed from the *perspective of the principal*, the principal's appreciation of (1) the human person, (2) the specific agent, and (3) work significantly influence the structure.

The principal's appreciation of the human person affects the model. The social justice literature contends that whether the principal treats the agent with politeness, with respect, and with dignity influences the perception and the response of the agent to the process itself.

Dimensions of Accountability 259

In addition, several bodies of literature (performance review, attitude change, trust) suggest that the principal's appreciation of the specific agent in a particular exchange also affects the process. This literature indicates that the principal allows a wider zone of indifference and more latitude of discretion to the extent that familiarity discovers similarity between the two parties.

The principal's own appreciation of work also influences the model toward either monitoring or mentoring. If work is seen as purely functional and aimed solely at productivity, then the structure of accountability becomes instrumental and the process becomes one of monitoring and control. If, however, the principal sees work as the means whereby a person creates oneself (that is, one's identify and personality) and creates community (that is, social relations) in addition to creating an external world (the product), then the accountability structure becomes one of nurturing and mentoring.

There exist several important emotional and affective dimensions of accountability when viewed from the *perspective of the agent*. We will explicate and develop three. First, the agent will respond to efforts to hold him or her accountable in accordance with the perceived motives of the principal. Is the principal perceived to have the best interests of the organization in mind? Are the consequences of the accountable act for society taken into active consideration? Alternatively, is the act of being held accountable perceived by the agent as mostly the pursuit of self-interest by the principal?

Second, the agent will evaluate the accountability exchange (both its definition and its execution) with reference to the fairness or justice of the interaction. Do openness, trust, and caring characterize the episode? Or do deception and secrecy prevail as accountability is implemented?

Third, the accountability exchange will be interpreted by the agent in the context of the history of exchanges between principal and the agent. It is likely that this history has yielded a psychological contract between the parties. This contract, in turn, will likely impact the interpretation of the substance of the accountability episode and the affective evaluation of the process of implementation as well as the perceived outcomes of the exchange.

The conclusion of the chapter suggests future empirical research based on the model and will offer a reinterpretation of the nature and practice of accountability based on its emotional and affective structure.

The Logical Structure of Accountability

The basic components of the model are shown in Figure 10.1. First we will define and discuss the basic constructs. They are (1) the event for which an individual assumes personal responsibility and for which he or she can be held accountable; (2) responsibility, defined as the personal causal influence on an event; (3) "felt responsibility" or the cognitive and/or emotional acceptance of responsibility; and (4) accountability, defined as the calling to give accounts (excuses or justifications) to another (or others) for deviation between the event for which

Figure 10.1. Model of Responsibility and Accountability.

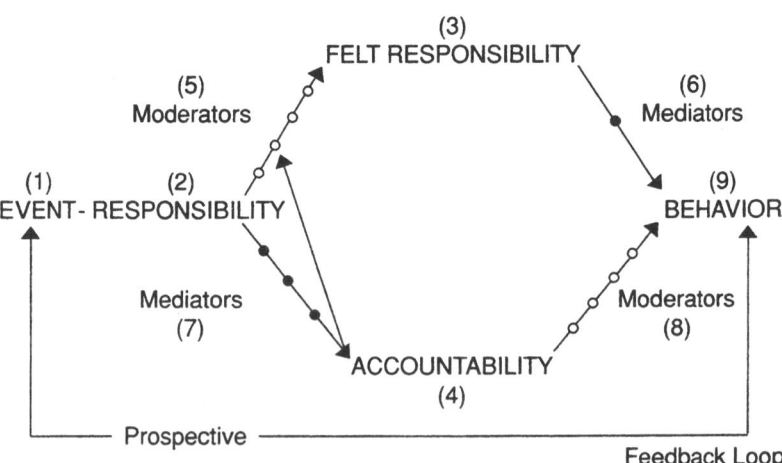

Dimensions of Accountability 261

one is responsible and the relevant expectations of norms, and, when necessary, to bear the consequences for that deviation.

In the second part, we will examine the connections between the constructs. These include (5) the moderators between responsibility and felt responsibility, (6) the mediators between felt responsibility and socially desirable behavior, (7) the mediators between responsibility and accountability, and (8) the moderators between accountability and socially desirable behavior.

Major Constructs. As mentioned, four major constructs will be discussed.

1. *The Event.* The first component is a composite construct we term the *event,* as seen in Figure 10.2. The event is someone making a decision or engaging in behavior that has an outcome and includes any directly attributable future consequences that may occur later. This topology is similar to that used in decision theory where the components include a person making a decision (to have surgery), the decision has an outcome (surgery is successful), and the outcome has consequences (the person lives without an organ) (see Behn and Vaupel, 1982).

Figure 10.2. Elements of an Event.

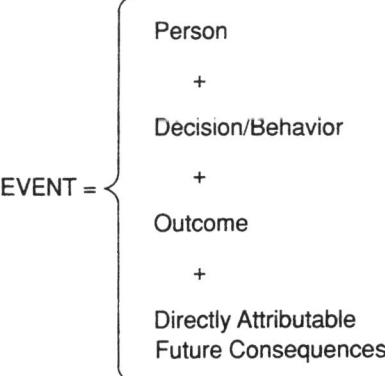

These distinct elements of the event can be seen in, and used to interpret, other literature. For example, in Caldwell and O'Reilly's (1982) study of failure and impression management, we can interpret their design in terms of the elements of an event. In that study, the subject (person) was assigned the role of administrative manager of a small growing technical company. He or she was then told to review several résumés and decide on the most appropriate candidate for the job of contract officer. Each subject reviewed the applications of three candidates and selected one (decision/behavior). That person was then hired by the company as the contract manager (outcome). The event may well have ended there had all gone well. Any future consequences of that particular selection would have gone unnoticed. But the company soon lost a major government contract due to the ineptitude of the new officer (directly attributed future consequences). These components taken together define an event.

2. *Responsibility.* The second component in our model is *responsibility* for the event. In this section we first define the concept of responsibility, and then posit the determinants of responsibility.

Responsibility can be defined as the *personal causal influence on an event.* Without a particular decision or action by the person, things would have turned out differently; things would not have happened this way. It is a basic reflective statement of "I did it."

From the perspective of a psychologist, John Shotter (1981, p. 279) reaches the same conclusion: "Thus, to be autonomous, not reliant like a child upon others to complete and give appropriate meaing to one's acts, is to be accorded . . . the right to be accorded to their author, to be taken as responsible for them." Tetlock (1985, p. 307) adds: "Attribution theorists have long noted that in everyday life people are presumed to be agents of their actions, i.e., they are responsible for what they do."

Our definition of responsibility rules out two other uses of the term. On the one hand is a more inclusive definition. According to that definition, responsibility is identical to behavior; it includes all *physically* causal action. This meaning is sometimes found in common usage of the term. For example, "Who's responsible for that hole in our yard?" "The neighbor's dog is." Or for another example, "What's responsible for the sudden changes in the weather?" "A low front in Ohio." Here responsibility is equated directly with cause.

By our definition of "*personal* causal influence" we mean more than behavior caused by simple, mechanical, linear connections between stimuli and response—that is, we mean more than automatic causality. There is a volitional act that is either direct or indirect, either proximate or distant. There is some form of human choice involved.

On the other side of our definition there is a more exclusive definition. This would equate responsibility with a feeling or *acceptance* of one's being a causal influence. Our definition of responsibility does not include that added qualifier. If acceptance were a necessary condition for responsibility, one could individually and selectively choose what one was to be responsible for by merely refusing to accept or "feel" responsibility. This state of cognitive or emotional acceptance of responsibility is a concept distinct from responsibility. We label it *felt responsibility* and will discuss it below.

The basis of the connection between an event and responsibility is choice. This is common to the organizational behavior literature. Commenting on a series of studies by Staw and associates (Fox and Staw, 1979; Staw, 1976; Staw and Fox, 1977; Staw and Ross, 1978, 1987), Caldwell and O'Reilly (1982, p. 121) state that "Staw and his co-workers manipulate responsibility in their experiments by allowing the decision maker to choose a strategy. . . . Choice is equated with personal responsibility." As seen in Figure 10.3, there are three ways by which choice determines responsibility.

The first is *direct choice*. It is personal, explicit, and unambiguous. One chooses this act rather than that act. One constantly makes choices: This product will go into production, we will charge that price, the company will not enter that market, we are not going to give a bribe no matter what the local customs are.

Once one chooses, or chooses not to choose, one is responsible for that decision and action. "It is my decision."

264 Appreciative Management and Leadership

The second way one can become responsible for an event is *group membership*. This involves a *primary personal choice to accept membership* and then secondary choices made either directly or vicariously.

When one is responsible through group membership, one chooses to be a member of a group and as long as one maintains membership in that group, one shares in the collective responsibility of that group. It is rare that one can control all the choices or all the decisions a group makes. But one's choice to be a member of a group includes accepting responsibility for choices of action that the group makes even if the particular decision or actions were not the member's direct choice.

Likewise, if one joins a group after the group has embarked on a journey or has chosen a certain path, one joins in the responsibility for that decision.

A third way to be responsible, in addition to choice and group association, is *role acceptance*. Semin and Manstead (1983, p. 133) write that "role responsibility can be seen as a special case of vicarious responsibility, in which the person is answerable for the action of others by virtue of his/her role; thus managers are . . . [responsible] for the actions of subordinates, editors are responsible for what appears in their journals, captains of ships are responsible for their passengers and so on [though in each case one does not directly engage in the action]."

Figure 10.3. Determinants of Responsibility.

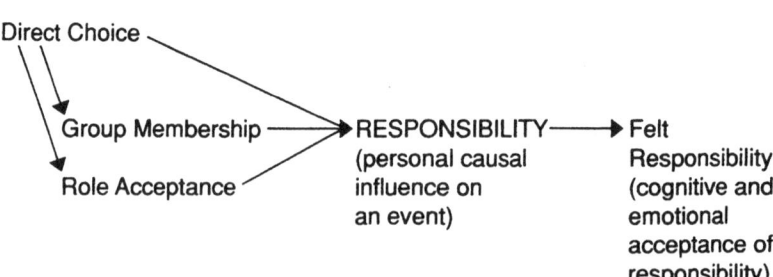

Dimensions of Accountability

In role responsibility one again *makes a primary choice to accept or take on a specific role.* Associated with that choice of a role are specific, prescribed, often stereotypical, and impersonal expectations. When one chooses that role, one accepts those expectations. When one accepts the role of CEO, one assumes the responsibility for the overall health of that organization. It is part of the job definition. If the organization flounders due to poor management, the CEO is responsible even though he or she may not actually have made the poor decision. Included in the role of CEO is the expectation that he or she will oversee the decisions of subordinates and replace ones who are incompetent before the death of the organization. Thus, one accepts the responsibility not only for what one does personally and directly, but for the behavior of others when supervision of their behavior is included in a role one has chosen to accept. (The range of role responsibility seems to be culturally defined. The responsibility of the CEO appears to be more comprehensive outside of the United States. David Broder (1985) contrasts Yasumoto Takagi's resignation as chair of Japan Airlines following the August 1985 crash and Lord Carrington's resignation as British Foreign Secretary the day after the Argentines occupied the Falkland Islands with counterparts in the United States who did not accept responsibility.)

3. Felt Responsibility. As mentioned earlier, the state of *cognitive and emotional acceptance of responsibility* is a concept distinct from responsibility. We labeled it *felt responsibility.* It is important to distinguish it from responsibility. One is objective, while the other is subjective. Responsibility is observable, while felt responsibility is a matter of individual perception and can be inferred from the external manifestation.

Whereas responsibility determines the area of one's felt responsibility, felt responsibility does not determine responsibility. It is not a reciprocal relationship. One is responsible when there exists a personal causal influence on an event, whether the individual "feels" that responsibility or not. In an extreme example, hardened criminals or social deviants can go through life without ever feeling responsible or without ever accepting responsibility, yet as long as they remain capable of rational choice, society still holds them both responsible and accountable for their behavior, its outcomes, and their consequences (see Figure 10.4).

On the other hand, felt responsibility cannot normally exist without responsibility of some type. There are different ranges of human activity for which one "feels responsible." Felt responsibility can be very broad, based on our common heritage as members of the human race. In John Donne's words (in Coffin, 1948, p. 440): "No man is an island, entire of itself; every man is a piece of the continent, a part of the main." And Christian scripture contends that we are responsible for our neighbor, who is defined as anyone, even a stranger, who is in need (Luke 10:25ff.) Carnevale (1985, p. 230) notes that "people even feel accountable [responsible] to unborn generations when concerned about how 'history' will treat them."

Although the constructs of responsibility and felt responsibility are distinct, they are commonly used interchangeably because in a person of maturity and integrity, the two are identical—that is, the mature person feels responsible or *accepts* responsibility for events for which one *is* responsible. Society terms a person whose felt responsibility does not correspond to his responsibility as "irresponsible."

While one is judged on responsibility, one acts on felt responsibility. Cognitive dissonance or self-justification processes

Figure 10.4. Relationship Between Responsibility and Felt Responsibility.

RESPONSIBILITY ←——//——— FELT RESPONSIBILITY

Feeling responsible does not determine responsibility.

RESPONSIBILITY ——————→ FELT RESPONSIBILITY

Responsibility is necessary for felt responsibility.

are mediators between felt responsibility and behavior. Cooper (1971, p. 354) showed that "a person will experience cognitive dissonance *only* to the extent that he *feels responsible* for his discrepant behavior and the consequences of that behavior" (emphasis added). Thus the necessary internal sequence is Responsibility→Felt Responsibility→Dissonance→Behavior. The high correlation between responsibility and felt responsibility is important. The psychological process of reflection and the social processes of socialization encourage the identity of responsibility and felt responsibility. Existential philosopher Max Scheler (1973, p. 487) writes that "in the execution of acts, the person experiences himself as 'responsible' [that is, feels responsible] for his actions in his reflection on his having done the action himself."

Here, one can see the necessity of our prior assumption of the reflectivity of the person. If the person merely lived from behavior to behavior, never reflecting on past behavior or anticipating future behavior, it would be impossible for him or her to claim or accept ownership of any event. Reflectivity is the basic process uniting responsibility and felt responsibility.

Reflectivity also addresses other issues about responsibility. Because reflectivity transcends time, one can be responsible for more than immediate, at-hand events. It can be *ex post or retrospective*, looking back over past events one has caused, or *ex ante or prospective*, foreseeing future events one may or may not cause, or behavior one may or may not entertain.

4. *Accountability.* Our model incorporates the basic assumption that a person does not live in an isolated context. Essential to being human is being social. Thus responsibility does not lead to behavior only when one feels personally responsible internally. It is because of this social context that one also is called to answer to others for one's actions. This calling to give reasons or accounts is a construct separate from felt responsibility. It is *accountability.*

It is not unusual for social scientists to note two distinct constructs, felt responsibility and accountability. In his review of the literature, Maclagan (1983, p. 414) finds both external and internal definitions of responsibility. His "internal" construct we interpret as felt responsibility and the "external" we label accountability. He finds that external responsibility indicates "performance criteria and accountability in respect of which rewards and punishments will be administered." It has "no reference to individuals' feelings," and leads to control and regulation. "By contrast, a person's internally defined conceptualization refers to his own beliefs and reactions to a situation." It is internally imposed and leads to development and revelation.

Staw and associates (Fox and Staw, 1979; Staw, 1981) find commitment to be affected by both internal and external justification. As Staw (1981, p. 580) says, "when justification is considered primarily as an intra-individual process, individuals are posited to attend to events and to act in ways to protect their own self-image (Aronson, 1976). But with most social settings, justification may also be directly externally. . . . [The] force for such external justification could well be stronger than the protection of self-esteem."

It is this second, external dynamic that we contend is the construct of accountability. We define accountability as the calling to give accounts (excuses or justifications) to another (or others) for deviation between the event for which one is responsible and the relevant expectations or norms, and, when necessary, to bear the consequences for that deviation. We recognize that one can bear good consequences as well as bad, that is, be rewarded for deviation above the expectations as well as punished for deviations below the expectations.

Unlike felt responsibility, accountability requires a public component; it is necessarily an external event. It is *the others* treating one as responsible, calling one to give answers or reasons that we have termed accountability. This is supported from both a psychological and a philosophical perspective. Shotter (1981, p. 279) contends that one only qualifies for the right to be autonomous and responsible "if it is possible for others to treat one as responsible, that is, as able to 'answer for' one's reasons for acting as one did." From a philosophical viewpoint, Scheler (1973, p. 487) writes that "accountability and unaccountability are formed from the outside, from visibly executed action." He notes that not being able to hold one accountable (unaccountability) "does not deny responsibility but simply the determination of responsibility" by others than the actor.

It presumes (1) *responsibility* for a specific event, either by choice, group membership, or assumed responsibility by role; (2) certain *mediators* (discussed later); and (3) personally or socially accepted *expectations*. Two elements can be distinguished relating to these expectations: What is the nature of the expectations? Who is imposing the expectations?

First, the expectations vary in type or nature of expectation. By that we mean that they can be objective, public goals or standards one is expected to meet. This could be contractual obligations, job description requirements, or financial bottom lines. They can also be widely held societal norms that one is expected to observe. This would include social roles and professional norms. They are not necessarily written down. Part of one's socialization process is learning that one "just doesn't do that." It is the notion in law of "what the reasonable person would do." Finally, these expectations can be expectations about the attributions made by others based on the observation of one's behavior.

Tetlock (1985, p. 307) notes that "although a powerful case can be made for the trans-historical and cross-cultural invariance of accountability . . . (Semin and Manstead, 1983) the specific norms, values, and ideologies to which people are held accountable differ dramatically from one situation to the next."

Second, expectations are often imposed by external sources. That source can be an individual, a group, an organization, or society. One's family and friends have certain norms and standards; a boss has goals to be met; an organization has rules to be maintained; society has norms that everyone is expected to meet.

Expectations also can be self-imposed even though they are to be judged by another. "In the words of cultural anthropologist Linton (1945, p. 9), 'The need for eliciting favorable responses from others is an almost constant component of personality'" (Tetlock, 1985, p. 308). Thus issues of impression or image management are directly relevant. The acting person also has a self-concept that he or she expects him or herself to live up to. One has certain self-expectations of which one is both imposer and judge. These expectations are based on beliefs and values that are likely to be products of socialization in both organizations and professional education (Maclagan, 1983). It is a matter of *integrity,* being true to oneself. Integrity affects felt responsibility rather than accountability.

Connections Between the Constructs. We have contended that people engage in behavior consistent with standards because they feel responsible for an event and/or because they are accountable for an event. We also contend that there are mediators and moderators between these constructs. It is possible for a leader or a manager to manipulate the degree of felt responsibility and/or the effect of accountability to achieve socially desirable behavior. In addition, by knowing the moderators, one can guard against a situation with counteracting manipulations.

5. Moderators Between Responsibility and Felt Responsibility. We said earlier that one is judged on responsibility yet one acts on felt responsibility. We also said that through the processes of reflection and of socialization and education, a person learns to feel responsible for what he or she is in fact responsible for. The correspondence between responsibility and felt responsibility is critical.

In experiments involving responsibility, scholars have suggested several moderators that could increase or decrease felt responsibility. Several of these moderators and their interactions remain untested. The moderators are illustrated in Figure 10.5.

Situation, mentioned earlier as a moderator between the event and responsibility, also has an effect here. The more one perceives other conditions or external events—real or imagined—affecting the event for which one is responsible, the less one feels responsible for that event. The difference between "situation" here and above is that as a moderator between event and responsibility, it must be real. Here it is a matter of perception. It can be real and not perceived and thus not affect felt responsibility or not real but perceived and thus affect felt responsibility.

Dimensions of Accountability

The *clearer the expectations and the role,* the more one will feel responsible. Maclagan (1983, p. 415) argues this point: "The use of an objective definition of his responsibilities, external to the individual, in management theory, itself tends to ensure that theory's usefulness as an aid to managerial control because it results in influence over people's attitudes as to what they ought to feel responsible for."

The more one acts against others' advice, or fights the environment, or "goes against the flow," the more one attributes the outcome to one's behavior and the greater the responsibility one feels for the event. In other words, there is a correlation between *resistance* and commitment.

Fox and Staw (1979, pp. 457-458) found empirical evidence for this phenomenon. They operationalized resistance by giving the subjects a memo that read: " . . . I can tell you first hand that several Board members were very dissatisfied and critical of your recommendation." These subjects were subsequently given a confirming memo reading: "The Board members were highly skeptical and critical of your recommendation and were firmly convinced you had recommended the wrong course of action." In the second group—the low-resistance group—

Figure 10.5. Moderators Between Responsibility and Felt Responsibility.

members were told that the Board was highly satisfied and supportive. Results showed that members of the high-resistance group felt more need for internal justification or, in our terms, felt more responsible, which resulted in increased commitment.

Similarly, we hypothesize that the more *unique* the behavior—that is, the less it is standard operating procedure and the more it is one's own creation—the more one will feel responsible for the behavior.

The more *significant* the event the more intensely one perceives the responsibility. Two illustrative studies support the reasoning.

McAllister, Mitchell, and Beach (1979) operationalized the significance of an event by informing subjects that their decisions involved investing 80 percent of the company's funds (high significance) or only 10 percent (low significance). In the experiments involving felt responsibility, they found analytic strategies used more often in the significant decision cases than in the insignificant cases.

Collins and Hoyt (1972, p. 573) increased significance by telling subjects (dorm residents) that the essays they write are "going to be used by administrators in deciding whether or not to make open visitation a permanent dorm policy" or they "will merely be used in a historical report and in no way will it be used by administrators or policy-makers." They found that when a subject was personally responsible and the consequences were significant, there was increased change to have behavior and attitude consistent. It is important to note that Collins and Hoyt examined forced compliance. With both significance (or high consequences) and feeling of responsibility, one tends to adjust behavior and attitude to conform to one another. In their studies, since behavior was fixed (forced), the result of the adjustment was attitude change.

The sixth moderator of responsibility is the *irreversibility* of the event. In the preceding experiment, McAllister, Mitchell, and Beach (1979) operationalized irreversibility by informing the subject that his or her decision is a temporary one only and can be reflected on and reviewed later (reversible condition) or that the company has to live with the choice made (irreversible condition). The results here were similar to those above.

In situations where responsibility is a group phenomenon, the *size of the group* affects responsibility. Schlenker (1980, p. 142) states that when people share responsibility they "thereby claim minimal responsibility for any negative consequences."

Empirical tests have shown that group size affects effort. Latane and associates (Harkins, Latane, and Williams, 1980; Latane, 1981; Latane, Williams, and Harkins, 1979) showed this on a variety of tasks, and Petty, Harkins, and Williams (1980) extended it to cognitive tasks. In a pair of studies, Weldon and Gargano (1989) used shared responsibility as an explanation for cognitive social loafing effects. They found that subjects who shared responsibility with fifteen others exerted less cognitive effort in judgment tasks than subjects who were told "you alone are responsible." This finding is reinforced by the conclusions of Weldon and Mustari (1988).

6. *Mediators Between Felt Responsibility and Socially Desirable Behavior.* There is, we believe, a *psychologically mediating process between felt responsibility and socially desirable behavior.* It is the process of cognitive dissonance (Cooper, 1971; Festinger, 1957; Festinger and Carlsmith, 1959) and/or self-justification (Fox and Staw, 1979; Staw, 1980). Collins and Hoyt (1972, p. 578) reported "statistically clear and theoretically conclusive" data to show that forced compliance only resulted in attitudinal change under conditions of felt responsibility. Cognitive dissonance occurs and one subsequently adjusts either behavior or attitude only when one feels responsible for events.

Cognitive dissonance theory would hold that one corrects a logical inconsistency. One would adjust behavior to be consistent with one's accepted or felt responsibility. In the self-justification theory, the factor of self-concept is added. Rather than cognitive inconsistency arousing dissonance, it is "the inconsistency between behavior or attitude and one's own self-concept that is dissonance-arousing" (Staw, 1980, p. 256). One thinks "I am a responsible person" and a responsible person behaves in ways consistent with what one feels is one's responsibility.

7. *Mediators Between Responsibility and Accountability.* Thus far we have suggested the intervening variables between responsibility and behavior consistent with standards, considering the

internal process of felt responsibility. But felt responsibility is not the *only* way one can move between responsibility and behavior. There is also the public, external, social process of accountability.

We are not accountable for all the actions for which we are responsible. But we can be "held responsible" (that is, be accountable) even when we do not "feel responsible."

In this case, we posit that there are three necessary intervening states that must be present before one is held accountable. These intervening states are illustrated in Figure 10.6.

As seen in the figure, the three mediators between responsibility and accountability are (1) capacity for rational behavior, (2) foreseeability of the consequence, and (3) deviation from expectations. All three are necessary. We assume that they act contemporaneously.

First, one must have the *capacity for rational behavior*. The law calls this *mens rea,* which "refers to the mental or psychological state of the defendant and is concerned with whether or not the state of the person at the time of the incident in question departed from that of a 'normal adult'" (Semin and Manstead, 1983, p. 131). One who is mentally impaired either temporarily or permanently and is therefore not capable of rational behavior is not accountable. One does not have to give account of the reasons behind one's behavior if one is not capable of doing so.

Figure 10.6. Mediators Between Responsibility and Accountability.

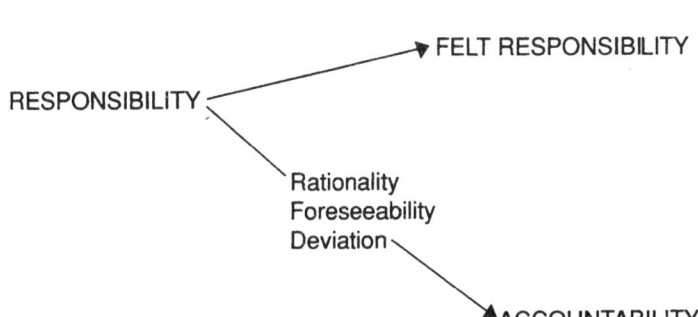

Note: Rationality, foreseeability, and deviation are all necessary.

Dimensions of Accountability 275

Second, the outcome and consequence must be *foreseeable* in order for one to be accountable. This is not to be confused with *foreseen*. One can still be held accountable for outcomes and events that one did not foresee. "How was I to know that hiring someone who had no knowledge of finance as corporate comptroller would make such a mess of things?" would hardly get a CEO off the hook with her or his board of directors. There are some things that one does not foresee, and other things that are not foreseeable by any rational person. It is the latter that one does not have to account for.

There have been empirical studies in the forced compliance literature on foreseeability that are applicable here. The results were conflicting as to whether dissonance occurs only for the consequences of a decision that were foreseen at the time the decision was made (Cooper, 1971), or whether one also feels dissonance for decision consequences that become known only after the decision was made (Goethals and Cooper, 1972).

Goethals and Cooper (1972) analyzed this conflicting literature and found the key to be not foreseen or unforeseen but in the foreseeability of the event. By foreseeable consequences they mean those results that any reasonable person could have anticipated in light of the information they were given (see Goethals and Cooper, 1972, p. 1180).

Third, there must be some *deviation* from the expected for one to be called to account. "It is the problematic contexts, i.e., when routine expectations are violated," write Semin and Manstead (1983, p. 144) that one's actions are called into account, "for it is here that questions about conduct are implicitly or explicitly raised. What is it that triggers such questions? The simple answer is that such questions are posed when there is a mismatch between expectation and action, that is, there is some disjunction between conduct, on the one hand, and routine expectations or moral standards, on the other." It is the violation of expectations that provides the occasion for the questions to be asked legitimately about the reasons for one's conduct.

8. *Moderators Between Accountability and Socially Desirable Behavior.* Here we make a major shift in our development. Responsibility has been posited to lead to felt responsibility and/or accountability. Up until this point felt responsibility and

accountability have been the dependent variables. Now they will be considered the independent variables and we will introduce a new dependent variable: socially desirable behavior, that is, behavior consistent with a normative standard or public expectations.

Although both felt responsibility and accountability will remain our interest, we will center our attention from this point forward on accountability. In the case of felt responsibility affecting behavior, the manipulation is to be done by increasing the felt responsibility. (One could argue more manipulation is possible by influencing one's self-concept. But such manipulation is outside the boundary of this model.) In the case of accountability, more manipulation is possible.

We contend that accountability has a major effect on behavior. It motivates and constrains and can change the course of behavior. But before looking directly at the resultant behavioral effects of accountability, we will introduce possible moderators between accountability and behavior (see Figure 10.7).

Figure 10.7. Moderators Between Accountability and Behavior.

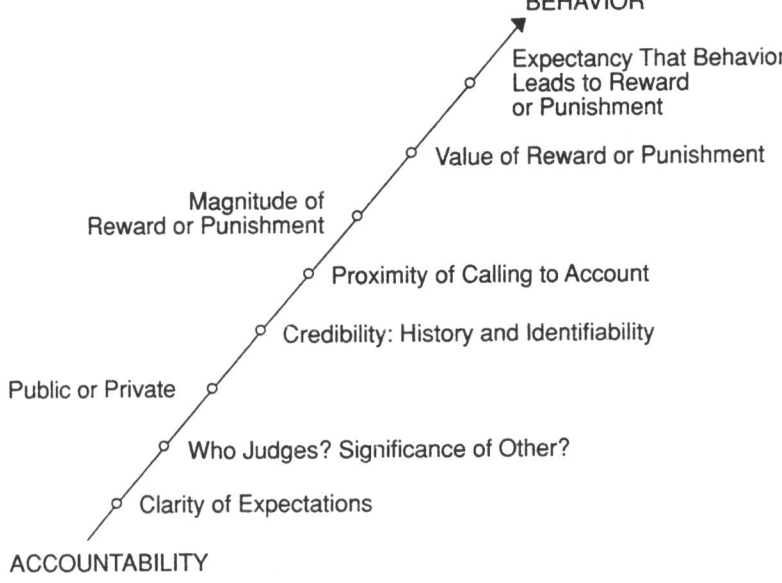

First, we suggest that the degree to which behavior is affected by accountability will be moderated by the *clarity of the expectations*. If one is unsure of one's role or if one is unclear what socially acceptable behavior is, then one will be less likely to adjust behavior.

Second, the degree that behavior is affected by accountability is moderated by the *person to whom one is accountable*. Tetlock (1985) speculates that people are motivated by a general desire to sustain the respect and positive regard of those to whom they are accountable. The more significant the person to whom one is accountable the more one will be concerned with the approval of that person.

Another factor that may moderate behavior is the *circumstance of the accountability* (whether it is public or private). The more public the accountability, the more it will affect behavior.

For accountability to have an effect on behavior, one must believe that one will be called to account. If one thinks that the system is so large or indifferent that it is impossible to identify an individual and call him/her to account, one would be less likely to adjust behavior. The *credibility* of holding one responsible is determined by (1) past performance — that is, have others been called to account in the past or have they "gotten away with" certain behaviors? It is also determined by (2) the possibility of identification or detection. Weldon (1986, personal communication) found that "accountability reduced loafing only when students were also identifiable." She operationalized identifiability by asking subjects to write their name and phone number so the experimenter could identify their response.

Carnevale (1985, p. 233) noted that in negotiation studies identifiability had to be distinguished from surveillance: "Surveillance produces a greater concern for the behavior that constituents want, whereas accountability produces a greater concern for pleasing constituents in the final decision." (There would be no difference, one would think, in those cases where certain behavior is the final goal of the constituency — for example, more vigilant information processing.)

The closer the calling to account becomes, the more accountability will affect behavior. If one has to face one's boss tomorrow to account for a certain behavior, accountability will affect behavior more than if the accounting is not to take place until the end of the fiscal year. *Proximity* is very important, therefore.

The same is true of the *expectancy, value, and magnitude of the reward or punishment*. There is substantial evidence suggesting that the more one expects a certain behavior to lead to a certain reward or punishment, the more one values that reward, and the greater the magnitude of the reward or punishment expected, the more accountability is expected to affect behavior.

If a manager says that ethical behavior is of great importance to a certain corporation, and a new system of accountability on ethical standards is being initiated, yet the employees do not expect their ethical rating to make a difference in some valued records, then the accountability will have little effect on the employees' behavior.

There has been some empirical work on the magnitude of the reward. Fox and Staw (1979) increased the magnitude of reward or punishment in their commitment experiment. They operationalized the construct by making one's position clearly dependent on the results of the specific decision under deliberation. In one group they told the acting financial vice president that "your job will become permanent or you will be demoted, depending on your performance." The other group was told that "you can expect support and assistance from your peers, especially if you do not perform well immediately" (Fox and Staw, 1979, p. 457). The group whose position was dependent on the immediate decision felt more need for external justification and made a greater commitment to previous decisions.

Finally, there will be an "error factor" or the effect of individual differences: "Personality variables such as social anxiety, public self-consciousness, and need for approval are like predictors of how motivated people will be to gain the approval and respect of those to whom they are accountable" (Tetlock, 1985, p. 325).

All of the preceding factors moderate the behavior that results for holding one accountable.

We have now introduced and elaborated all of the components of the model. The complete structure is shown in Figure 10.8.

Dimensions of Accountability 279

This model suggests the enhancement of socially desirable behavior or expected outcomes by providing two alternatives to manipulate (felt responsibility and accountability) and several levers on each alternative. The model is comprehensive, manageable, and parsimonious.

Figure 10.8. The Structural Elements of the Model of Responsibility and Accountability.

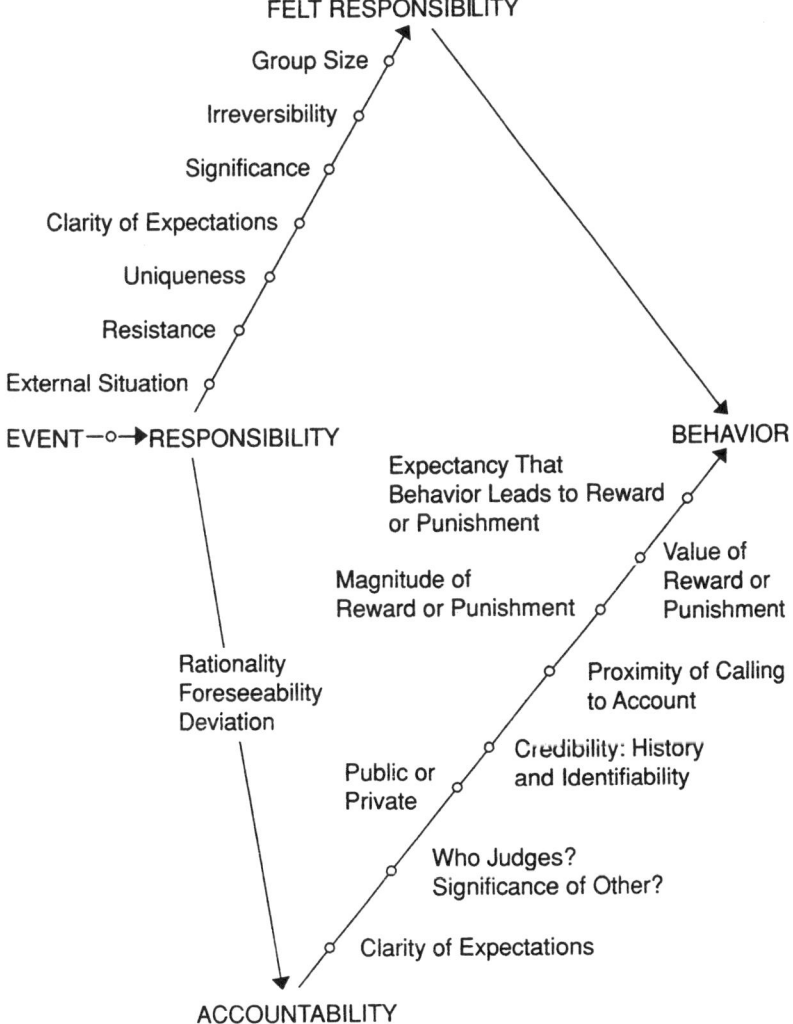

The Appreciative Dimensions of Accountability

Equally important as the logical structure are matters of affect and appreciation that inform the implementation of the model. Affective and appreciative dimensions can be viewed from two perspectives, the perspective of the principal or the perspective of the agent.

The Perspective of the Principal. When viewed from the perspective of the principal, three aspects of the principal's appreciation are likely to significantly influence the accountability exchange. These are the principal's appreciation of (1) human personhood, (2) the individual agent, and (3) work itself.

First, the principal's *appreciation of the human person* affects the implementation of the model. Does the principal view the agent as an organizational positionholder or as another unique human being worthy of the dignity and respect of a person? In similar fields, as performance review, the social justice literature contends that whether the principal treats the agent with politeness, with respect, and with dignity influences the perception and the response of the agent to the process itself. Bies and Moag (1986) found that the principal's respect for the agent was a key factor in the agent's reaction. Tyler and associates (Tyler, 1987, 1988; Tyler and Bies, 1988; Tyler and Folger, 1980) also found that "people react quite strongly to the quality of interpersonal treatment they receive during the enactment of the procedure" (Tyler and Bies, 1988, p. 9). Specifically, "whether the arena involved is business, law or politics, people feel that they are entitled to dignity of treatment by those in positions of authority," and "particularly important is that those affected by decisions have rights as people that third parties cannot appropriately ignore" (Tyler and Bies, 1988, p. 10).

The response of an agent to being called to account is not merely dependent on the logical and mechanistic accountability process itself. We believe that whether or not the principal values and appreciates those involved in the exchanges as persons entitled to dignity and with rights that must be respected influences the logical structure.

Dimensions of Accountability 281

Second, several bodies of literature (performance review, attitude change, trust) suggest that the principal's *appreciation of a specific agent* also affects the process. One not only values people in general but often one identifies with or is familiar with specific agents more than others. The literature indicates that the principal allows a wider zone of indifference and more latitude of discretion to the extent that familiarity discovers similarity between the two parties. How much one will bend the boundaries of the structure is influenced by this appreciation.

Third, the principal's own *appreciation of work* influences the accountability model toward either a monitoring process or a mentoring process.

There are radically different values one can have toward the nature and purpose of work itself. If one sees work as purely functional and aimed solely at greater productivity, then the structure of accountability becomes instrumental; it is solely at the service of the end product. Here, the accountability process becomes one of monitoring and control. It is a calling to account for how much one has produced or failed to produce.

There is, however, another conception of work. In his popular study *Habits of the Heart* (1985, p. 66) sociologist Robert Bellah speaks of work as a *calling* that "makes a person's work morally inseparable from his or her life. It subsumes the self into a community of disciplined practice and sound judgment whose activity has meaning and value in itself, not just in the output or profit that results from it." Barta (1984, p. 166) talks of work as a *vocation* that "demands that we search out our unique gifts; it demands self-knowledge and at the same time calls for an effort to convert our gifts into a service for others, for the community. There is a certain intimacy in the way our concept of vocation links us to our work." Gillett (1985) develops this notion of the intimacy of work, speaking of work as having both intrinsic and extrinsic meaning. Work is appreciated and valued for more than what it produces externally. It is a calling or a vocation that has intrinsic meaning for the worker. Soelle (1984) defines work as having three dimensions: (1) the individual's self-expression (self-creation, developing one's identity and personality), (2) social relatedness (building community), and (3) reconciliation with nature (developing the earth, continuing creation).

We believe that if one has an appreciation for this more integrated conception of work, one can envision the accountability structure in a radically different fashion. The principal calls the agent to account not only for what the agent produces but also for the agent's personal development. The accountability structure becomes one of nurturing and mentoring.

Perspective of the Agent. To recapitulate, we have thus far suggested that the logical model of accountability developed previously is significantly influenced by three appreciations of the principal: (1) the appreciation for the dignity of the human person, (2) the appreciation of the individual agent, and (3) the appreciation for different concepts of work.

There also exist several important emotional and affective dimensions of accountability when viewed from the perspective of the agent. We will explicate and develop three: (1) appreciation of exchange fairness, (2) appreciation of the principal's motive, and (3) appreciation of established psychological contract.

First, the agent will evaluate the accountability exchange (both its definition and its execution) with reference to the *fairness or justice of the interaction.*

Organizational researchers exploring judgments of fairness found that procedural criteria are more influential than actual outcomes in one's perceptions of the fairness of an evaluation or allocation structure (Folger and Greenberg, 1979; Greenberg, 1986a, 1986b; Landy, Barnes-Farrell, and Cleveland, 1980). One is willing to take a lesser outcome if one thinks the *process* leading to that outcome was fair. In the implementation of the logical structure of accountability, do openness, trust, and caring characterize the episode?

Of particular importance is a chance to have a "voice" in the process and to feel that one is heard (Bies, 1987b; Bies and Shapiro, 1988; Bies, Shapiro, and Cummings (1988); Folger, 1977; Folger and Greenberg, 1979; Lind and others, 1980; Tyler, 1988; Tyler, Rasinski, and Spodick, 1985). In the implementation of the logical structure, does the agent have a

Dimensions of Accountability

chance to contribute to the process, to have a voice, to state his or her side, and to introduce information and reasons? Or do deception and secrecy prevail as accountability is implemented?

We believe that the accountability process will receive support and cooperation or will be undermined and fought to the extent that the agent perceives the individual episodes between principal and agent as just.

Second, not only does the perceived fairness of the implementation of the procedure affect the accountability exchange, but the perceived motives of the individual principal will also affect the exchange. The agent will respond to efforts to hold him or her accountable in accordance with the agent's *appreciation of the perceived motives of the principal*. Is the principal perceived to have the best interests of the organization in mind? Or is the act of being held accountable perceived by the agent as mostly the pursuit of self-interest by the principal? Is the purpose of this interaction the achievement of organizational, public, mutually agreed-on goals or to further the career, prestige, or power of the principal? "Impropriety," write Tyler and Bies (1988, pp. 16, 19), "implies that the decision-maker is not shaping the procedure to achieve its intended goals. Instead they are subverting those goals to achieve private objectives. . . . The research we have examined makes clear that impropriety in procedural enactment can lessen and even eliminate the positive effects of using a procedure otherwise regarded as fair. If people view the implementation process as subverting the true goals of the procedure, then their reaction to it, and to the authorities implementing it, will be quite negative."

In addition to adhering to the true goals of the organization, the principal must be unbiased. Does the principal execute the process consistently across persons and over time and prevent personal self-interest at all points in the process? Or does the agent see the principal as one who plays favorites for personal reasons? Such perceived bias might result in frustration on the part of the agent (Folger, 1977) and make the decision procedure suspect.

Research by Bies (1987a) found that in addition to avoiding bias and impropriety, perceived decision-maker sincerity had a significant and positive association with procedural fairness judgments.

We hold that the success of the accountability structure is influenced by this judgment of the principal as either one who acts impartially and sincerely on behalf of the ideology, group, or organization, or who acts in the pursuit of personal self-interest.

Third, judgments of procedural fairness and the principal's motives in the accountability exchange do not occur in a vacuum. They will be interpreted by the agent in the *context of the history of exchanges between the principal and the agent.* It is likely that this history has yielded a psychological contract between the parties.

Any organization is a set of elaborate relationships, only a few of which are discrete and/or explicit. Macneil (1985, pp. 492-493) argues that "the corporation itself is one of the greatest relational contracts ever. . . . Corporations have always been exchange relations writ large." Within such a relational system an appreciation has developed within the last decade or so for the psychological contract between an employer and employee, principal and agent in our terms. Dunahee and Wangler (1974, p. 520) argue that a psychological contract involves a "whole pattern of rights, privileges, and obligations." They find such a contract to be dynamic and evolutionary: "The relationships between the manager and managed are interactive, unfolding through mutual influence and mutual bargaining. . . . It is an evolving set of mutual expectations. Thus, neither party to the transaction, since the transaction is such a continuing one, knows fully what he wants over the length of the psychological contract, although each acts as if there were a stable frame of reference which defines the relationship."

Such contracts can either developed over time through patterns of interaction or implied through various more objective behaviors such as oral promises and company manuals (see Rousseau, 1987, for conceptual distinctions, and Koys, Briggs, and Grenig, 1987, for legal distinctions). Empirical research has shown that both the time one has spent on a job and the pattern of evolving, unwritten commitments between parties significantly influence judgments of both obligations and fairness in the relationship (Rousseau and Anton, 1988a, 1988b).

Dimensions of Accountability

This psychological contract, we suggest, is yet another appreciative dimension that will likely impact the interpretation of the substance of the accountability episode and the affective evaluation of the process of implementation as well as the perceived outcomes of the exchange.

We argued that accountability is an important issue in organizational behavior and deserves increasing attention. To assist in that discussion, we developed a logical structure of accountability. However, we believe that the logical structure cannot stand alone. Like many logical structures, it must be supplemented by its affective, appreciative, value dimensions to be properly understood. As examples, we have suggested several appreciative factors from the perspectives of the principal and the agent respectively.

Future Research and Conclusions

Finally, we list several research areas that are implied by our model and that invite future research as the field of organizational behavior increases its understanding of the role of responsibility and accountability.

Research is needed on the relationship between the various determinants of responsibility (direct, group, role). If one is a member of a task force responsible for the implementation of a project and one is also the person within the group who is responsible for the chosen specific implementation strategy, is responsibility increased?

The various moderators between responsibility and felt responsibility need to be empirically tested. In particular, the relationship between them should be investigated. Is there a ceiling effect? Is there an interaction between the moderators?

What is the role of self-concept in the psychological processes connecting felt responsibility and behavior? Do different self-images have a bearing on felt responsibility? Are they identifiable?

The moderators between accountability and behavior also need empirical testing for main effects, interactions, and ceiling effects.

Perhaps the most interesting area for future research is the relationship between felt responsibility and accountability. Is there an interaction? Are they additive? Do they counteract each other under certain circumstances; if so, when? Does the relationship differ under different conditions? Is there a ceiling?

Among the seven points of interaction where one can make an excuse or justification, are some interaction points more effective than others?

Finally, while the role of responsibility and accountability has been researched in the areas of negotiations, problem solving, and information processing, the effect of responsibility and accountability can be tested against the whole range of behavior in organizations. Of particular interest to the authors is the role of responsibility and accountability in producing ethical behavior in organizations.

We have stated the need to return the concepts of responsibility and accountability to the forefront of organizational behavior scholarship. We have stated the philosophical assumptions on which we built our model, which necessitates considering both concepts together—that is, the person is both reflective and social. We have developed the model by defining the constructs, suggesting important mediators and moderators, and have incorporated an affective element into the structure. Finally, we have suggested a few of the many areas of research that this model elicits and for which this model could be a foundation.

PART THREE

Processes of Appreciative Action

11

Appreciating Executive Action

Peter J. Frost
Carolyn P. Egri

This is success. To live well. To laugh often. To love much. To gain the respect of intelligent men. To win the love of little children. To fill one's niche and accomplish one's task. To leave the world better than one finds it, whether by an improved flower, a perfect poem, or another life ennobled. Never to lack appreciation of earth's beauty or fail to express it. Always to look for the best in others. To give the best one has. To make one's life an inspiration and one's memory a benediction.

—Anonymous

These evocative phrases have been variously attributed to many authors, among others, Ralph Waldo Emerson, Robert Louis Stevenson, and one Bessie Anderson Stomley (verified by her son, Arthur J. Stomley, Jr.). It is a definition of success that seems to reside in our collective consciousness.

As in life in general, this definition can also be applied to organizational life. And within organizations, we find ex-

---

Note: We would like to express our sincere appreciation to Larry Cummings, Diana Cawood, Thomas Cummings, Diane Cyr, Dafna Eylon, Mary Ann Hazen, Devereaux Jennings, Nancy Langton, Cecelia McMillen, Philip Mirvis, Walter Nord, Larry Shetzer, and Roy Staveley for their thoughtful contributions to the preparation of this chapter.

ecutives to be in unique positions to channel the course not only of their own lives but of those of other organizational members. The crux of enduring appreciative action is that executives can create enduring change that should be for the betterment of others as well as for themselves.

What exactly is meant by the term *appreciative action*? First of all, appreciative action is guided by an individual's intention to produce constructive outcomes for the actor and others in the organization. These constructive outcomes incorporate both objective and subjective life goals and achievements.

Appreciative action is also a healing force in situations where harm has been done in organizations. It is healing that is focused on alleviating the potentially destructive effects of organizational life on its members' personal well-being. Appreciative action also encompasses the expression of an individual's own creativity in ways that not only recognize the veracity of others' creativity but that also cherish and nurture it for the benefit of all.

Finally, appreciative action is that which is guided by and contributes to a new vision and practice for the collective good of the organization and society. It is action that integrates individual fulfillment with that of others.

Appreciative action embraces a holistic approach to an organizational life in which one does not deny the diverse claims on one's life from the personal and work arenas. Instead, such action integrates and builds on the potentialities within all organizational members. It is an approach that runs counter to many traditional views of people's roles and relations within their working lives—views that deem one's personal life, values, and goals to be separate from (or much less valued than) those of the organization.

Hazards Blocking Appreciative Action

However, in reaching for this vision of appreciative action, there are a number of hazards or roadblocks. In this respect, the executive must not only be cognizant of the real world of organizations but also skillful in balancing the demands and restraints that world may impose on individual behavior.

Executive appreciative action involves finding balances between and among the technical, practical, strategic, and moral issues confronting today's managers while avoiding or negotiating the personal and organizational traps that constrain appreciative action.

Foremost among the organizational traps is a social system that demands that executives focus exclusively on their work to the detriment of their personal and spiritual fulfillment. The outcomes of a unidimensional paradigm of executive success and effectiveness can be both positive and negative. On the positive side, we witness the objective productivity of executives blindly committed to the Protestant work ethic. For those who have internalized this value system (and as part of the organization's dominant coalition, this is a likely possibility), the personal psychic and material rewards can be substantial. However, it is legitimate to ask, At what price? For the executive driven by the external demands of organizational life, these hazards are only too real.

The Protestant work ethic with its sole emphasis on organizationally defined achievement and success (to the exclusion of personal accomplishment) can be addictive in a destructive way. Schaef and Fassel (1988) trace how organizations structure and pattern addictive behavior in their employees. It is an addiction encouraged by a society imbued with the Protestant work ethic ideology in all its social institutions—family, schools, churches, and so forth (Maier, 1988).

On an individual level, there may be a loss of control over the course of one's life such that "many individuals are so fully indoctrinated with work values and routines that, psychologically, they are not free to make reasonable choices about how much work to do, how hard to work, and how central a role to let work play in their lives" (Frost, Mitchell, and Nord, 1986, p. 245). Research evidence on the personal and social consequences of such addictive behavior is not very encouraging (Kofodimos, 1986; Schaef and Fassel, 1988). Workaholism often leads to family problems (marital and parental) and health problems (stress-related illness and behaviors), as do other types of addictive behavior.

What then is our vision of the future of appreciative executive action? The key may lie in a reconceptualization of the role of executives within organizational life. Modern industrial society is built on a model that is essentially hierarchical and authoritarian. It is one that reflects a societal worldview of the power of domination and control. It is also one where, all too often, "'you see all round you people engaged in making others live lives which are not their own, while they themselves care nothing for their own real lives'" (William Morris, *News from Nowhere* (1891), in Berman, 1981, p. 15). As Morris observes, a life without vision, without appreciation of self and of others, can be a destructive one. For organizational executives, the challenge is to enhance both their own and others' lives, to nurture and give meaning to life.

A Script for Appreciative Action

For executives embarking on a course of appreciative action, the organizational framework within and on which this action takes place is important. This framework is composed of three basic arenas of activity—Action in Principle, Strategic Action, and Action in Practice (these are diagrammed in Figure 11.1). While such triads are often interpreted in a linear way (for example, Strategy→Principle→Action), we intend the flow to be circular with the matter of sequence being a function of where executives and their organizations are at a given time and in a particular context.

Additionally, effective executive action involves asking a set of questions at each point in the framework, the most crucial question being, "What is right?" Further, such action involves understanding the processes through which executives are able to access, master, and integrate the diverse requirements of each arena of organizational activity as they ask and answer the critical questions of executive action. These essential processes of executive action involve an awareness of self and others, political astuteness, and an alignment of individual values and needs with those of the organization. Although we present these processes last in this sequence, they are in effect the primary point of focus for executive action. We will attempt to make this argument clear later in the chapter.

Appreciating Executive Action 293

As we will elaborate, these three arenas of organizational activity and three processes of executive functioning constitute the basic framework for organizational action. We will also explore how the interplay of these processes can facilitate appreciative action within organizations. A number of examples will illustrate the means by which executives can enhance their ability to function in appreciative ways. To delve into the underlying dynamics of the roles prescribed for and assumed by executives in our society, we will examine the archetypes of Warriors, Healers, and Magicians. Each archetype represents a distinct constellation of unconscious beliefs and assumptions about one's life role that powerfully inform executives' thoughts, goals, and actions in organizational settings.

Within a wider context, we will then focus on the forces in society and within organizations that are providing the impetus for a reconceptualization of the role of executives and their organizations in a changing world. This is a world where the mindset of individualistic nationalism may be giving way to a global worldview; where hierarchical mechanistic control of people and material things is yielding to the pressures of an almost

Figure 11.1. Appreciative Executive Action.

instantaneous transfer of knowledge in a world of systems and networks; where the logical empirical conception of science is being challenged by a sociorationalistic approach which recognizes the integral part that subjective consciousness plays in human understanding and knowledge (Ackoff, 1980; Harman, 1988; Bohm and Peat, 1987; Naisbitt, 1984; Cooperrider and Srivastva, 1987). We will explore how engaging in appreciative action is not only a desirable but also a necessary condition for modern executives operating in this new world.

The Trinity of Executive Action

The dictionary defines a trinity as "any union of three parts or elements in one; a trio; triad." At the organizational level we envision a trinity of *Action in Principle, Strategic Action,* and *Action in Practice* with each of these elements emphasizing a different realm or arena of organizational action. The triadic conceptualization of organizational and executive action has a precedent in the organizational behavior literature. For example, in 1955, Robert Katz asserted that effective and successful executive administration "rests" on three basic skills: technical skill, conceptual skill, and human skill. More recently, Harold Leavitt (1986) used a similar triad (pathfinding, problem solving, and implementing) in his model of the management process.

Action in Principle is the realm of *technique,* of the systems, models, theories, and routines that have been developed by the organization or imported into it. They are rational prescriptions that can be fitted, unmodified, into the static and ideal world of laboratories and closed systems. Examples include, in human resources, the ideal or the academically validated selection test, performance appraisal procedure, or compensation system. Examples in production include the latest planning models (for example, PERT and Just in Time Scheduling); and in administration, the currently touted management information systems for fiscal accounting and budgeting control.

The defining characteristic of the realm of technique is that it deals with ideas and tools designed "in the abstract," which are then expected to generalize unmodified to a variety of situa-

Appreciating Executive Action

tions. Strong adherents of the realm of technique frequently see systems, models, standardized tools, and so forth as the *right* (or correct) way, the efficient way to accomplish organizational objectives. At the extreme, this adherence will take the form of insisting that technique, action in principle is the only way, the one best way to reach organizational goals. This operational assumption of universality compromises appreciative action in that it denies the inherent diversity of people and the equifinality of many human endeavors. For those enamored solely of organizational Action in Principle, the practical contingencies of implementation are often viewed as nuisance factors that sully the purity and integrity of scientifically derived plans and systems. In the event of a system failure or suboptimal performance, these actors often revert to external attributions of blame rather than consider the failure to be the fault of a universal system to accommodate situational contingencies.

To these extremely principled actors, the future is seen as a linear continuation of the past with future uncertainties treated in terms of current variables given probability assignments. Discontinuous change is perceived as a threat to their probability models and is thus ignored or at the very least, treated as irrelevant for consideration. These actors will be suspicious of attempts to raise and explore strategic questions except as they are amenable to a technical formulation and modeling exercise (for example, a technically ordered MBO system). Discussion of values and open-ended discussions and explorations are resisted and create discomfort.

Action in Practice is the realm of *implementation*, of what is feasible given the circumstances in which executives and other organizational actors find themselves at a particular point in time. Here, the executive must cope primarily with the dynamics, the flow, the interplay between the demands of the task, the needs of individuals and groups engaged in the task, and such contingencies as arise in and around the task. Whereas the emphasis in the realm of technique was on "ideal" systems, the emphasis here is on doing the right thing given the circumstances of the moment. Thus, Action in Practice drops the technically rational assumption of universality. For example, managers using a performance appraisal system might choose to adapt and modify it considerably to suit what they perceive to be the requirements they face in getting a job done. Rather than using the performance review to appraise subordinates in an objective, comparative way, some managers report they variously use it to motivate individuals who have tried hard but had a difficult year; to put a troublesome subordinate in his or her place; to force adherence to a particular set of company objectives; and so on (Longnecker, Gioia, and Sims, 1987).

Managers may adapt or work around an "ideal" production system because they see it as unworkable in their oganizations without such modifications. Administrators may give only lip service to bureaucratic systems while pressing ahead to do what "really" needs to be done in the "real" world of practice. Adherents to the realm of implementation frequently emphasize bootstrapping, tinkering, and improvising to get the technical side of the task accomplished. They will often resort to manipulation, negotiation, brokering, and compromise to ensure that people carry out the task as the managers believe it should be done to accomplish organizational objectives. At the extreme, adherents will see only the world of practice and see those "abstract, ivory towered" techniques as a hindrance and a waste of time. They will see strategic issues as too long term and fuzzy to be worth worrying about. Their emphasis will be exclusively tactical in meeting the immediate demands of a situation in an expedient manner (Culbert and McDonough, 1985).

Strategic Action is in the realm of *envisioning* and *planning* for a future state—societal, economic, and/or organizational—thereby providing a sense of purpose or mission for the organization. Strategic Action is the motivating factor that guides organizational functioning and direction. In its outward focus on the interaction between an organization and its external environment, Strategic Action necessitates an evaluation of external contingencies, problems *and* opportunities that may impact on the organization's ability to survive and function as an entity. Concurrently, Strategic Action involves an inward focus to envision and evaluate alternate paths by which the organization can adapt to and/or change future realities. Thus, the organiza-

Appreciating Executive Action

tion is simultaneously a passive recipient of changes and an active change agent in molding the course of the future. For example, the record of organizational innovations demonstrates how organizations have responded to externally generated opportunities as well as altering societal lifestyles and the nature of competition through the introduction of revolutionary new products.

But like the extremists in the principle and practitioner camps, narrowly focused strategists cut off the options and realities of the other action spheres. They tend to be disinterested in the technical and/or practical elements that flow into and out of the Stategic Action process. The dream is the focus. Grounding it in systems and politics is neglected or repressed. Thus, development of strategic plans in isolation from Action in Principle or Action in Practice can lead to a rarefied existence concerned with dreams of a utopian future where future possibilities dominate with little regard for the realities of current limitations of both technical and practical natures. Assembled together, this trinity of Action in Principle, Action in Practice, and Strategic Action provides the basis for an "envisioned game plan" for organizational action with the plan being the technology and the game being implemented through organizational political activity. Taken together with strategic vision, a game plan is simultaneously vision in action and in a technically informed direction.

Many of the challenges and opportunities executives face revolve around the tensions that are set up by the impact these realms have on organizational processes and outcomes. These three realms of organizational action cannot be taken in isolation. Within different organizations and within the same organization at different times, the relative emphasis on one facet over others may vary; however, they constitute an intertwined system of functioning (Tichy, 1982). Thus we see this model of organizational functioning as essentially holonomic with all parts being "enfolded" or contained within the others. At any point in time, the focus of immediate attention may be directed toward one part; however, it cannot be to the exclusion of the others. The other parts need consideration during the executive decision-making process.

Consider the plight of many human resource executives as an illustration of some of the tensions that occur when the three action facets are not incorporated into organizational operation. Given the low status frequently accorded the human resource function in many organizations, a personnel executive may not be included in a policy decision that has subsequent implications for the organization's human resources (Legge, 1978). Thus the policy may be narrowly addressed as a marketing, financial, or engineering problem. However, as the policy is implemented, human resource problems invariably emerge, whereupon the human resource executive is assigned the task of "fixing" the problem. Placed in the role of problem solver without an understanding of the overall strategic context from which the problem previously arose, the human resource executive is limited to dealing in a fragmented and symptomatic way, drawing on techniques not shaped or chosen in anticipation of the strategic context. Using existing techniques while operating in a crisis mode of "fighting fires," the prognosis for effective problem resolution is bleak for the human resource executive and thus for the organization. The resulting mistakes and lowered credibility of the human resource function lead, in turn, to a vicious cycle of the exclusion of the human resource function from future strategic planning activities and a relegation to the realm of implementation and ill-informed technical choices (Legge, 1978). For the organization, the opportunity to avoid future human resource problems in regard to policy implementation is a thing of the past. Attention to the way strategy, technique, and implementation interact would serve to throw such problems into relief before they occur. The fact that these problems occur when they need not, turns on how successful executive action is. We focus our attention next on the key processes that take place in support of this triad.

The Underpinnings of Executive Action—Asking the Right Questions. As executives grapple with each realm and with the interaction of these realms, we believe they are required to ask a number of important questions of the who, what, why, how, and when variety. In his 1965 State of the Union Speech, Lyndon

Appreciating Executive Action

Baines Johnson stated that "a president's hardest task is not to do what is right but to know what is right." We concur with President Johnson's belief that the most fundamental and penetrating question is "What is right?"

Asked in the realm of strategy, it deals with what is the right vision, direction, stance, and approach for the individual and the organization. A crucial component of strategic action stems from the visions that inform that action. As Tichy and Devanna (1983, p. 126) note, "The vision is the ideal to strive for. It releases the energy needed to motivate the organization to action. It provides an overarching framework to guide day-to-day decisions and priorities and provides the parameters for planful opportunism." Vision is what separates leaders from managers (Bennis and Nanus, 1985). Of course, there frequently are competing visions of where the organization ought to go, thereby giving intensity to deciding what is right strategically. (For the purpose of clarity, we have focused here on the concept of visioning as prospective goal setting. However, this does not deny the process of retrospective sense making of goals as argued by Weick (1969). Instead, this latter process is incorporated into the process of reflective awareness to be discussed in the next section of this chapter.)

The force of what is right in terms of the direction the organization will embark on is demonstrated in the case of Apple Computer during the early 1980s (Hafner, 1987; Uttal, 1985). The two main protagonists were founder Steven Jobs and the recently recruited CEO John Sculley. Confronted with what were ostensibly the same environmental cues (a change in the competitive market with IBM's entry into the personal computer market, a general slump in the personal computer business, and sales problems in the Macintosh division), each person arrived at a conflicting answer to the strategic "What is right?" question. For Jobs, the answer lay in a continuation of past strategy, a product-driven strategy focusing on the development of innovative products. In contrast, Sculley's answer lay in the development of a market orientation with more stable operating systems and processes—an administrative response to cope with a turbulent environment. Eventually, Sculley's answer prevailed and

Jobs left Apple to form a new corporation (NeXT Inc.) in which he could pursue his vision of a personal computer that would transform the market.

Within the Strategic Action realm, the question "What is right?" also triggers consideration of the underlying values of the organization. This raises the issue of whether the direction taken will be congruent with the values of a societal culture. It is not enough that executives ask "What is right?" for themselves and for their organizations; consideration must also be given to what is right for external constituencies (customers and others). If not, we witness the ethnical dilemma posed by the case of the Beech Nut apple juice scandal, where corporate executives condoned and facilitated the sale of baby "apple juice" (which contained no apple juice whatsoever) to unsuspecting consumers over an eight-year period (Traub, 1988). In this case, the answer to the Strategic Action question of what is right was synonymous for both executives and their organization; however, their combined value of "profit by any means" violated a more fundamental societal ethic of honesty and integrity.

Applied to the realm of technique, the question "What is right?" has to do with the correctness of a model, or of choices among competing models—what is right given available technology and the current resources of the organization. For the executive, "knowing what is right" primarily involves problem solving and analysis. The feedback mechanisms for the organization and executives as to the rightness of action are typically in the form of quantitative performance measures—production, sales, and so forth. Negative deviations from predetermined and accepted standards and norms are signals for action.

Here again, the issue of ethics arises in arriving at the technical answer to this question. For example, even though a particular technological innovation may be the most efficient one possible in the interests of corporate profits, productivity, and efficiency, it may also be one that produces noxious or toxic by-products. How then does the engineer reconcile the issue of productive efficiency with the larger issue of environmental pollution? Is it right to use a technical system that in turn may endanger or harm the lives of those who come in contact with it, both inside and outside the workplace?

In another vein, what is right within the technical realm cannot be divorced from the psychological effects of a model of technological production. If the process reduces workers to the level of mere automatons or unthinking adjuncts to the production process, can this be considered "right"? As Nord, Brief, Atieh, and Doherty (1988) elaborate, this has been one destructive element of modern capitalism that denies the validity of individual worker choice within the context of a class conflict between the interests of ownership and labor. By focusing solely on technical rationality, Action in Principle can become merely a reinforcement of a capitalistic ideology of work values.

Asked in the realm of implementation, "What is right?" is the question of what is the feasible, practical thing to do under the circumstances. The answer to what is right in this arena is often a decision as to *whose* interests will be served. What is right also plays a part in the selection of the processes by which implementation is enacted. What is right influences the means by which one gains the cooperation and commitment of organizational members to new strategic directions. Are there tradeoffs between the speed and nature of implementation that need to be considered? Is the right way one that involves adversarial power plays or is it one of compromise and negotiation? At this juncture, there is a requirement that the choice of the means of implementation be one that is both right for the executive (in terms of preferences and values) and right for the organization (in terms of objectives and fairness). When dealing with others, there are no easy answers to the ethical nuances of the "What is right?" question, for as Sir Adrian Cadbury (1987, p. 69) admonishes, "There is no simple universal formula for solving ethical problems. We have to choose from our codes of conduct whichever rules are appropriate to the case in hand; the outcome of those choices makes us who we are."

Focusing on rightness tends to energize each realm—it can also intensify and narrow the focus so that commitment is made to what is right in only one arena—at the expense of the others. Returning to our earlier assertion, the key for executive action is to realize that the three realms mesh and are enfolded in one another. What is right becomes a matter of tradeoffs, of balancing rightness across strategy, technique, and practice.

It is the fundamental question "What is right?" that motivates the executive's and his or her organization's search for purpose and meaning. The answer for appreciative executive action must be couched within the technological requirements of the organization while recognizing the social diversity of organizational members. An organization's code of ethical and moral behavior contains not only the executive's sense of what is right but also that which is shared with others. In order to gain acceptance and commitment, it needs to be developed in an evolutionary manner with other organizational members.

It is all very well to talk of frameworks and what activates action in and on the framework; however, what are the processes of executive action that enables an executive to arrive at an appreciative answer? We see three interacting processes as primary for appreciative executive action, given the context we have just sketched.

The Processes of Appreciative Action

The means by which the executive answers the question of "What is right?" for himself or herself and for the organization involves the processes of awareness, astuteness, and alignment (see Figure 11.2). These processes operate in a continuous spiraling cycle of appreciative action within each of the three realms of organizational action.

In the fascinating account of his own personal and professional journey, physicist Fritjof Capra (1988) describes a turning point in his life—a moment in which he became aware of the connection between his spiritual and his professional life. He reports a meeting in 1968 with a famous Eastern mystic, J. Krishnamurti, who was giving a series of lectures at University of California at Santa Cruz. At that time, Capra was wrestling with the issue of whether he could pursue spiritual faith and a scientific career at the same time in that he saw the two as being mutually exclusive. Putting this question to Krishnamurti, the answer came back: "*First* you are a human being, *then* you are a scientist" (Capra, 1988, p. 29). Krishnamurti went on to suggest that discovering one's humanity came from medita-

Appreciating Executive Action

tion intended to foster self-awareness. Gaining this awareness would facilitate Capra's ability to work effectively as a scientist. Capra reports this meeting and the advice he received as decisive in helping him orient both his life and his work.

We think this anecdote captures the sense and importance we attach to the processes of awareness and alignment in executive action. We see them as at the center of such action as the executive works in and on an organizational framework. We have added one additional process—that of *astuteness*. Given the competing values, self interests, and goals of the actors who comprise an organization and its environment, we believe that it is not possible to get things done in organizations without attending to political matters. As a means of understanding the essential elements of each process, it is instructive to identify each process and to trace out how we believe they operate within each arena.

Figure 11.2. Processes of Appreciative Action.

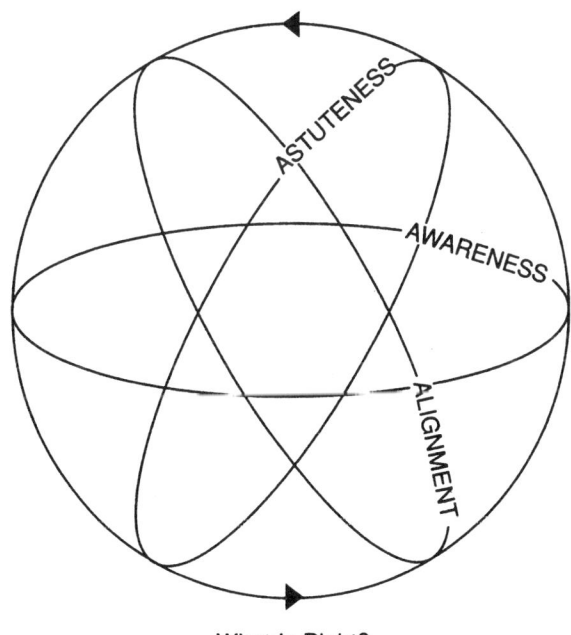

What Is Right?

Awareness. Awareness is essentially an amalgam of vision, intuition, and creativity in the quest for information and knowledge of oneself, of others, and of the material world. Often it is attending to the subjective and sometimes subconscious elements of life—the past, present, and future. It involves recognition of the values held, the morality, the spiritual essence of "being," and the inner drives that lead to action (Owen, 1987). The path toward enhanced awareness therefore is multidimensional, starting with first being cognizant of one's own self before one can fruitfully guide others, since "we understand another person in the same way as we understand, or seek to understand, ourselves. What we do not understand in ourselves we do not understand in the other person either" (C. G. Jung, in Jacobi and Hull (eds.), 1978, p. 222). As Jung asserts, the first step to awareness is often through personal introspection. For the executive, this is particularly cogent in that one's self-image determines one's interactions and regard of others. Executive awareness needs to be on two levels, of one's self and of others. Others may be the relevant group, organization, or society—the deep structure within which the executive operates.

Outside of the self, it is an awareness of others' vision of reality and their underlying values and morality that guide action and missions. Part of heightened subjective awareness involves learning to trust one's intuition—that internal sounding board of judgment. It involves being able to access the intuitive sphere of abstract ideas, complexity, uncertainty, relationships—all qualities espoused as necessary in the executive role. Awareness is also a key to practicing the "art" of managing, which combines both intuitive judgment and skill with "reflection-in-action" (the "on-the-spot surfacing, criticizing, restructuring, and testing of intuitive understandings of experienced phenomena" (Schön, 1983, p. 291)). Awareness enables one to adopt an intuitive management style that, when compared to the rational style, avoids early commitment (planning); plays with unknowns (conducts an orderly search for information); has holistic simultaneous processing of alternative (sequential consideration and refinement of alternatives); and is unsystematic (systematic).

Appreciating Executive Action

One example of a successful executive who operates on a heightened level of awareness is John Sculley, CEO of Apple Computer. Following his recruitment from PepsiCo, he had demonstrated considerable political acumen in his struggle with founder Steven Jobs for control over the nature of the corporate vision. However, as a self-proclaimed "intuitive leader," he recognized that "you can only be intuitive about something you understand. When I first came to Apple, I didn't know enough to be intuitive [about personal computers]" (Labich, 1988, p. 62). Astutely focusing on the one facet of organizational activity in which he was deficient (and which was also a source of concern among other corporate stakeholders), Sculley set out and became technically knowledgeable.

Awareness is not only concerned with what *is* but also with what *might be*. The executive needs to utilize his or her knowledge of current states in order to unleash his or her imagination in creative ways to "envision alternative futures" (Leavitt, 1986). This awareness can also be that of the body of technical knowledge that is enacted through organizational models and systems. Such an awareness can serve as the creative springboard for future technological and social innovations.

An absence of creative vision limits the executive to mimicking lower-level management in organizations, where the tension is solely between the technical and pragmatic organizational requirements. For the executive trapped at this level of activity, there is no frame of reference, no sense of direction, no sense of what is right and what is wrong, what is valuable and what is valueless. The frame of reference is based on the past with feedback only relevant to the historically set systems and formulas. John W. Gardner (1978, p. 135) summarizes this quandary well in his observation that "all too often, on the long road up, young leaders become 'servants of what is rather than shapers of what might be.' In the long process of learning how the system works, they are rewarded for playing within the intricate structure of existing rules. By the time they reach the top, they are very likely to be trained prisoners of the structure. This is not all bad; every vital system re-affirms itself. But no system can stay vital for long unless some of its leaders remain sufficiently independent to help it to change and grow." Thus, one of the consequences of overemphasizing plans and systems can be the demise of organizational vision, strategy, and direction. In the flurry of perfecting technical and human resource systems and techniques, the external realities of the organization's environment can easily be forgotten. Consequently, an excessive emphasis on internal short-term day-to-day activities can prevent the executive from seeing the "big picture" and interpreting external environmental changes.

This image of executive as technician and implementor is one described by Mintzberg (1973) in his study of five chief executive officers. Mintzberg discovered that the bulk of senior managers' working lives is spent working at high speed on fragmented activities. Communicating to subordinates and outsiders takes up the bulk of their days. They also tend to dwell on concrete immediate issues — to the detriment of any reflective planning. Similar findings are reported by Luthans, Hodgetts, and Rosenkrantz (1988). These and other studies of managers depict a world in which time for reflection is at a premium, if not virtually impossible.

How can an executive enhance his or her level of awareness? Carl Rogers (1961) identified a number of conditions that would enhance constructive creativity. These include inner conditions of openness to experience, an internal locus of evaluation, and the ability to play with elements and concepts. External conditions include, first, psychological safety (absence of external evaluation and presence of empathic understanding) and, second, psychological freedom to explore.

Research on creativity indicates that to a certain extent, creativity can be a talent and a skill (Harman and Rheingold, 1984). Creative visualization and imagery techniques of the kind provided by Shakti Gawain (1978) are suggested as ways to tap into one's creative unconscious for new insights and awareness. Others have shown how the creative process can be facilitated by the use of Janusian theory (the simultaneous acceptance of two seemingly contradictory thoughts) and metaphorical thinking (use of analogy and imagery such as metaphors) followed by a logical consideration of alternative explanations (McCaskey, 1982; Bohm and Peat, 1987).

As a leader, the executive can also foster creativity among others in the organization. The executive can, first of all, create a climate in which employees are able to take risks. They then can facilitate the creation of a vision of the future by collaboratively developing organizational and leadership agendas based on the projections of employees (Tichy and Devanna, 1983). Similarly, there is research evidence that intuition can be enhanced through techniques of meditation, self-hypnosis, and training exercises (Agor, 1984).

In reviewing the literature on awareness, there is a basic irony in prescribing or expecting its development in executives in that management is in a world of action (Mintzberg, 1983; Kotter, 1982) and political power in action (politics) (Culbert and McDonough, 1985). How then can the executive take or risk the time for reflection? Given the centrality we and others have given to vision and the importance of reflection to fuel awareness (and to check morality), what is the path to reflection in the active, political organizational world?

Astuteness. Astuteness is the process of interpreting, organizing, and pragmatically utilizing the information emerging from awareness in all arenas. Operating from a recipe for implementation, executive action strives to interpret the feedback from the organization. Dealing with on-line information provided by interactions with people and situations, executives develop contingency plans to accommodate resistance and uncertainty. It is the realm of "sensation," of material things—an aspect of the executive's working life that is time consuming and demands a considerable degree of attention (Kotter, 1982) as the astute executive continually adapts to the uncertain flux of environmental and technological change and implementation politics.

It is also the realm of "transformative leadership" espoused by Bennis and Nanus (1985, p. 217), which "is collective, there is a symbiotic relationship between leaders and followers, and what makes it collective is the subtle interplay between the followers' needs and wants and the leader's capacity to understand . . . these collective aspirations." Executive leadership, in this context, is the invention and creation of institutions that empower subordinates to fulfill the organizational mission.

When political power is not used in an empowering way, the net result can be one of unfulfilled expectations. This is illustrated by Roger Smith's chairmanship of General Motors into economic decline during the early 1980s. In his review of Smith's efforts to transform GM production into computer- and robotics-driven "lights-out" factories, Thorsell (1988, p. 33) notes that "Roger Smith emerges as a naive visionary who fundamentally misdiagnosed the dynamics of a new industrial age. He thought it was solely about technology. He didn't see that it's about people in a new technical environment." By treating GM workers as merely adjuncts to machines, rather than partners in a cooperative venture, and by neglecting the political aspects of implementation, Smith's tenure has been one fraught with dissension and turmoil.

The executive's astuteness or political will and skill determines how he or she will influence others in the implementation of his or her strategic vision. If employed in a constructive manner, executive political action can lead simultaneously to the empowerment of others and the betterment of the organization. Empowerment entails respect for the subjective element of organizational functioning, the giving and/or sharing of power with others. Conversely, executive political action can be a negative force when power is used to abuse and control. The denial and taking of power from others to assert one's own agenda and self-interest to the detriment of others is a destructive element in organizations (Culbert and McDonough, 1985; Kanter, 1988).

At the helm of the organization, executives have access to both formal (hierarchical, resource control, network centrality) and informal (personal) sources of power (Astley and Sachdeva, 1984; Mintzberg, 1983). Power is defined as the potential capacity to effect outcomes deemed to be desirable. Power can be both on the surface (overt and direct) or in the deep structure (covert and subtle) of organizations (Frost, 1989). Power as a covert form is in the deep structure of the organization, where it informs the interpretive frames and cognitive maps of organizational members. For this reason, deep structure power is very difficult to identify without a careful tracing of the sociohistorical origins of these frames and the rules of the current organizational game (Ranson, Hinings, and Greenwood, 1980; Conrad, 1983).

At the level of the deep structure, astute executive political activity focuses on the power to create frames within which organizational activity takes place and on the systematic distortion of perceived reality to influence others. Executive action in the deep structure involves an awareness of the historical past that determines the present structure of reality within the organization and society. It may include a political strategy of "small wins" to achieve a deep structural change (Weick, 1984).

At the surface level of political activity, executives exercise power and influence over others in order to implement their goals. Surface politics are a relational dynamic that may be either competitive or collaborative, empowering or controlling. When used in constructive and creative ways (as in empowering) political action is

- A way of envisioning inspirational and/or meaningful goals (Bennis and Nanus, 1985)
- A means of developing and promoting organizational policies, structures, programs, and processes that empower other organizational members to contribute to the executive and organizational visions (Kanter, 1983; Conger and Kanungo, 1988; Bradford and Cohen, 1984; Beck and Hillmar, 1986)
- "A process of enhancing feelings of self-efficacy among organizational members through the identification of conditions that foster powerlessness and through their removal by both formal organizational practices and informal techniques of providing efficacy information" (Conger and Kanungo, 1988, p. 474)

Developing political astuteness in an empowering manner relies heavily on an initial awareness of the sometimes irrational realm of organizational power and politics. Such an awareness permits an accurate interpretation of the formal power inherent in organizational structures and processes and an understanding how these are influenced by informal interactions. This capacity for discernment is largely a learned skill that can be only partially acquired through the formal learning experiences offered by books or in classrooms.

Given the unique dimensions of political games within different organizations, the executive's political learning is largely founded on his or her personal experience. Learning to become politically astute derives from observing and learning from the political activity of others in the organization. It is "action learning" (Argyris, 1982a) in that there are no hard-and-fast rules for political activity—what works and what does not. The executive needs to be willing to experiment with various avenues of political action, evaluate their outcomes (on both the surface and deep structure levels), and then continue on with this enlarged knowledge base. The politically astute executive is continually adapting to the uncertain flux of implementation politics.

The necessity for astuteness is particularly evident when one examines the interplay of power and politics in organizational and product innovation within both the visionary and implementation arenas (Frost and Egri, 1988). Whether in the pursuit of a technological product or a social administrative innovation, innovation success or failure often hinges on the political skills of the innovator. Visualizing a new order or a new product is not enough to ensure the eventual adoption and diffusion of an innovation. We also find that the framing of contexts and self-interests at the deep structure level proves to be fundamental to the acceptance or rejection of any proposed change (Pettigrew, 1985; Noble, 1984; Kanter, 1983).

The duality of politics at both levels is illustrated by the political activity engaged in by both innovators and those opposed to an innovation. For successful innovations, the political activities of networking and coalition building are critical in the organizational implementation of any change or innovation. Furthermore, the role of the executive (as a sponsor or champion of change) has proved to be essential in facilitating the process of change (Pinchot, 1985; Kelley, 1976; Hage and Dewar, 1973). As part of the organizational dominant coalition, the executive emerges as the key player who makes things happen.

For example, in the case of "Chipco," Kanter (1983) relates how a manager was able to successfully implement a social innovation by framing it as part of the company's integrationist culture. Combined with the surface political games of networking, building consensus, managing committees, and so forth, this manager was able to use the deep structure games of socialization and legitimation to advantage.

However, the choice of political strategies in implementation is not a value-free choice. The executive's sense of moral and ethical conduct guides his or her selection of implementation tactics. Similarly, the technical plans and systems of production determine both the objectives and effects of political activity. For example, technologically determined operating systems define the likely sources of organizational power. In a manufacturing facility, the primary political arena may be the technical core, whereas in a professional organization (for instance, universities), the political arena may be the determination of the ideology and values of the organization.

Alignment. Alignment is the congruence of individual balance with that of the organization and the wider society. Culbert and McDonough (1985, p. 129) define alignment as follows: "An alignment represents an internal structure for putting one's every action into personally meaningful terms. It explains how individuals orient to organizational events and what they are trying to accomplish both personally and organizationally. In short, the term alignment is a way of understanding an individual's personal relationship with the job." When there is an effective alignment, there is synergy between personal and organizational needs. Successful alignments are those that elicit the organizational context, when "others understand and publicly acknowledge the value of the individual using it" (Culbert and McDonough, 1985, p. 130). The tension between the executive trinity and his or her organization's trinity lies in the *alignment* of each. It is a dynamic interaction in that the push of individuals and organizations is toward congruence while the realities of the world serve to pull it astray.

Perhaps nowhere is the concept of alignment more critical than in the case of strategic vision. Within Strategic Action, it is the process of finding a synchronous balance between the individual's direction, the organization's direction, and that of society that does not impair or violate goals or values at any level. An alignment between an executive's strategic vision and that of his or her organization is an especially contentious one, as illustrated in the Jobs-Sculley struggle over control of Apple Computer.

Fundamentally, the keys to the alignment process are awareness of personal and organizational values, mission, and strategy coupled with a proactive approach to achieving a balance among them. As Culbert and McDonough (1985) assert, the route toward productive alignments is one that encompasses, first, an awareness and recognition of the subjective reality of organizational relationships and, second, involves adopting a collaborative strategic orientation that constructively integrates (rather than a narrow tactical orientation that suppresses) divergent interests. Essentially, it is the exercise of political strategies and tactics in a constructive and empowering manner.

Revisiting Executive Appreciation. Thus far, we have sketched a perspective on appreciative executive action that posits a framework of interdependent realms (strategy, techniques and practice) that are activated when the key question—"What is right?"—is asked. We have asserted that answering this question appreciatively requires that three processes (awareness, astuteness, and alignment) are successfully engaged within the executive function. These processes, spiraling across and through the framework, throw into relief the network and the nuances of the problems and opportunities that executives encounter in their actions, thereby enabling them to deal with them.

How executives enact these processes will dictate the appreciativeness of their performance. We think that there are a few predominant archetypes that strongly influence this, thus mediating the degree to which executive action is appreciative.

In the next section we discuss three such archetypes, the Warrior, the Healer, and the Magician.

Appreciative Executive Action in Archetypes

Within our Western culture there are two basic archetypes of executive leaders, the *Warrior* and the *Healer,* and an emerging one, the *Magician*. The Warrior archetype is the one that has the longest tradition within our society (Pearson, 1986). This archetype depicts the highly competitive and achievement-oriented executive who is motivated by the acquisition of power and its material rewards in his or her quest up the corporate ladder. Obstacles encountered in the Warrior's path are regarded as challenges to be mastered and overcome. The Warrior is most comfortable when dealing with objective realities and observable behaviors and has little patience, interest in, or feel for the softer subjective nuances of organizational functioning. This is reflected in the Warrior's predilection for self-interested political games, which often force competitive responses when collaborative ones may be called for.

A contrasting leader archetype is that of the Healer. Derived from the humanistic tradition of organization theory, the Healer is one who focuses more on the subjective element of organizational functioning. He or she is devoted to helping others in a collaborative and empowering manner. Most often we see executives as Healers working in the helping professions, nonprofit agencies, and religious organizations.

The motivating factor for the Healer is to help and empower others to achieve their full potential in life. At the extreme, the Healer is willing to sacrifice his or her personal wellbeing or interests in order that others may benefit. Unlike the Warrior, the Healer is externally directed and considers his or her reward to be the goodwill, friendship, and well-being of others. Under duress and in its extreme form, the Healer archetype can easily become that of the Martyr (Pearson, 1986) who sacrifices himself or herself for the sake of others. The Healer is also one who avoids negative adversarial confrontations when facing issues where it is warranted.

Both of these archetypes denote a narrow partial approach to the executive's role in organizations. Each can survive and flourish within restrictive (albeit dissimilar) circumstances. To go beyond a linear perspective, the leadership archetype of the Magician offers the most promise for appreciative executive action. The Magician's goal is one of authenticity, wholeness, and balance between the harsh realities of a competitive world and the need for individual well-being and empowerment (Pearson, 1986). It is an approach that incorporates the drive and energy of the Warrior with the helping care of the Healer. The Magician operates from a heightened level of awareness of both the objective and subjective elements of organizational functioning. It is this awareness that enables the executive Magician to see creative linkages that others have overlooked. He or she is not locked into a singular mode of action but rather is comfortable with acting in either mode as required by the situation.

The Magician is particularly skillful at the process of alignment, of balancing the needs and values of the organization with his or her own needs and values and those of other organizational members. If anything, the Magician is one who is extremely flexible, but in a purposeful way. These individuals are masters at accommodating diverse interests and coordinating them in unique and creative ways — somewhat like the modern day Lech Walesa, leader of Poland's Solidarity movement, who is able to transcend almost insurmountable political obstacles to see linkages and opportunities for conflict resolution that have eluded others (Tagliabue, 1988). These leaders work simultaneously as political brokers and healers in making future realities accessible.

We find numerous descriptions of such executives in the literature. They are the *strategists* who operate within a holistic duality in a managerial style that is aware of paradoxes and contradictions; are process and goal oriented; value individuals and relationships; and are able to creatively resolve conflict (Torbert, 1987).

They are the *effective managers* who are masters in balancing the needs of a diverse set of managerial roles — managers who have transcended (through a sometimes painful process) the dualistic rational logic of the "novice" to "see their world in more dynamic, holistic, and intuitive ways" (Quinn, 1988, p. 161).

And they are also the corporate *pathfinders* who are unique in that "they are men and women of *vision;* their *value* systems are clear, and strongly held; and they are *determined* to turn their visions into realities" (Leavitt, 1986, p. 61).

In that the Magician's goals are authenticity, wholeness, and balance within himself or herself and in personal relationships, interactions with others are not competitive but rather cooperative engagements. The subjective side of life is allowed to emerge as "synchronicity." For the Magician, life is a process of acausal connections and not the result of rational cause and effect. This is in contrast to the current societal ideal of the executive as a Warrior who is motivated to win the test through personal sacrifice and the control of others. Rather than being locked into this dichotomous approach, the Magician has learned the goals and tasks of the Warrior (strength and courage) and integrated them with those of other archetypal heroes along life's journey.

In a real world that has dualities — a world where executive action is the balancing of formality and informality, technology and humanity — the executive is one who transcends into the magical realm. To bring the Magician into the light and to let the empowering process flow, the executive must coordinate all these facets in a balance. To fulfill the vision of what is right, the executive must transcend the restrictions of the "either/or" modality to a new level that emphasizes the unity of "both/and." The executive needs to mesh the vision and knowledge of the Magician with the political skill of the Warrior. He or she is one who has the ability to see linkages that those around them are unable to see. This executive practices vision, which "is the art of seeing things invisible" (Jonathan Swift, *Thoughts on Various Subjects,* in Rawson and Miner, 1986, p. 399).

Taken all together, this image of an appreciative executive is one that can appear to be an unattainable ideal. We think that the Magicians are able to accomplish much of the intricate balancing we are talking about without burning out — at least not in the short run. For "the leaders we most admire have a sense of balance in their lives. They know when to close the door and go home" (Labich, 1988, p. 66). Nevertheless, there are very real pressures that are system induced which make it difficult to sustain (and attain) the Magician role. To answer the question of why Magicians are such a rarity in our organizations and why in the long run we expect they do burn out like other executive types, we now turn to a discussion of the larger context within which executive action takes place.

Appreciative Action in a Sociohistorical Context

Do the processes of appreciative inquiry require special circumstances? Perhaps foremost is the necessary acknowledgment that it is the subjective rather than objective reality which has primacy in organizational life. This assertion is echoed in Cooperrider and Srivastva's (1987, p. 133) observation that "never before in history have ideas, information, and beliefs—on theory—been so central in the formulation of reality itself. . . . Today, the very fact that society continues to exist at all is experienced not so much mechanistically (an extension of machines) or even naturalistically (a by-product of fateful nature) but more and more humanistically as a social construction of interacting minds."

The processes of appreciative action—awareness, astuteness, and alignment—describe how this interaction can be channeled in productive and meaningful ways. Denial or ignorance of these processes constrain their potential benefits.

One characteristic of appreciative inquiry is a value premise of egalitarianism that respects the integrity of others. For the process of alignment to function effectively, one must first respect the validity and merit of opposing sets of values and needs. Appreciative action involves the recognition of this fact in a positive manner by working with these differences rather than overpowering or denying their expression. The egalitarian ethic also underlies the process of empowerment that seeks to enhance the potential of others rather than to exploit them for one's own needs.

Adopting a holistic approach to organizational life is also a prerequisite for appreciative action. It is a rejection of the

Appreciating Executive Action

"either/or" mentality of hierarchies in favor of the integrative "both/and." This approach to organizing is one of collaborative rather than competitive structures and systems. Organizations based on nonhierarchical principles are becoming increasingly necessary in an era of turbulent environments, instantaneous information flows, and scarce resources. In his prediction of the "imminent" demise of bureaucratic structures two decades ago, Bennis (1967) was one of the first to identify the need for integration, collaboration, and adaptation in a rapidly changing world. This theme continues to the present day in the writings of others, such as Harman (1988), Naisbitt (1984), and Ackoff (1980).

However, bureaucratic structures have proved to be resilient and remain the current context of Western society and its organizations, thereby serving to prevent the processes of appreciative inquiry from reaching their full potential. The fundamental dynamics of society continue to be driven by divisive competitive forces that counteract an executive's ability to operate appreciatively. This intimation is elaborated on in a historical analysis of societal work values conducted by Nord, Brief, Atieh, and Doherty (1988, p. 2). They adopt "a radical perspective — one that views the assumed harmonious relations between work and the rest of life as a pre-lapsarian myth, not as accurate history." They note that the conventional ideology of work values (one that is based on Max Weber's description of the Protestant ethic) holds that work is central to individual self-fulfillment and societal economic success. This view of work has proved to be vital to the development of modern capitalism and is now contained within the deep structure of our society. What is not often explicitly elucidated is the "dark side" of the Protestant work ethic—namely, how it promotes a content-free view of work, advances individual isolation (to the detriment of collective class differences), and contradicts a number of "ethical and historical views about the nature of work and its relationship to individuals and society" (Nord, Brief, Atieh, and Doherty, 1988, p. 12).

Alternative views of the development of work values highlight the coercive aspects of this worldview. Promoted by self-interested capitalistic and middle classes, the Protestant work ethic has served well to deny the "harsh realities of work." As the cornerstones of modern society, hierarchical structures legitimate the centralization of power into the hands of the few at the tops of hierarchical pyramids. Hierarchical structures limit the autonomy of those at the base of these pyramids. Hierarchical structures endorse the "right" of those at their apexes to exercise power and control as they see fit. Fundamentally, hierarchies are premised on the notion of the power of domination in a dichotomous world (French, 1985; Eisler, 1987). Carrying out appreciative executive action in such a setting is a formidable (though as we have argued, not impossible) task.

However, there are cracks in the armor of the hierarchical model. Some of these can be traced to the increasingly destructive by-products of an ideological paradigm based on the domination of nature and of others. The short-term fragmented perspective of this hierarchical ideology has led to an era where the threat of global extinction due to nuclear arms proliferation and environmental pollution are regarded in terms of probabilities rather than possibilities (Harman, 1988; French, 1985). Given these predictions, one is led to query whether such a future is inevitable or whether a fundamental change in our society, its organizations, and its leadership can be affected to avert such an outcome.

One clue that a significant shift is possible is found by looking into the distant past. Our current model of complex society has not been the *only* successful one in human history. In her historical analysis of the prehistory of human society, Eisler (1987) presents evidence of an earlier epoch (around 4000 B.C.E.) in which human society was based on what she terms a *partnership model,* founded on nonhierarchical, egalitarian principles. Recent significant archaeological findings have revealed an Old European Culture that flourished from 7000 to 3500 B.C.E. In this period, an egalitarian social system prevailed within a sophisticated agricultural economy. Archaeological excavations in Middle Eastern Neolithic sites (about 7000 B.C.E.) reveal an advanced lifestyle where people lived in plastered brick houses (some with chimneys) and pioneered early irrigation farming. Vestiges of a peaceful and art-loving culture are found in the remains of Neolithic pottery, copper and gold ornaments, and tools. (See Eisler, 1987, for a detailed and richly informative discussion of the political history of this era.)

The "fatal flaw" of this culture was its inability (or perhaps a lack of political astuteness, will, or skill) to withstand the invasions of the warlike Indo-European (Kurgan) tribes, which spread outward from a North Central Asian homeland. This Kurgan era is the foundation of our current *dominator* model of social organization, which exemplifies the familiar Warrior archetype. By 2800 B.C.E., the Kurgan culture had supplanted the earlier Neolithic era and was brutally effective in destroying many of the remnants (physical and ideological) of the Neolithic. Since that time, there have been isolated reemergences of the partnership model—most notably during early Christianity, as was revealed in the Gnostic Gospels discovered in Egypt in 1945. As documented by theological historian Elaine Pagels (1981), the forces of the dominator type of culture effectively transformed or obliterated themes of egalitarianism contained in the initial teachings of Jesus Christ and the Gnostic Apostles.

What then might we learn from such historical accounts of cultural prehistory? We learn that

1. Egalitarian models of complex society have occurred in the past; therefore the current hierarchical model is *not* necessarily the *only* model available to us. That is enlightening—a point of awareness.
2. Egalitarian models have not survived well-orchestrated and sustained attacks by protagonists of dominator models. To attain and maintain an egalitarian model requires substantial political will and skill—astuteness buttressed by awareness (staying in touch with the vision) and alignment (maintaining balance).

In our modern era, we must recognize both the contributions and drawbacks of a particular societal form and work toward creating and facilitating those aspects that best meet new emerging challenges. As Ackoff (1980), Eisler (1987), and Harman (1988)—among others—argue, we are at a choosing point in our history. This is a time when holistic, egalitarian alternatives or complements to the existing dominator model are needed if we are to avoid widespread destruction on this planet. We would expect, given the philosophy of egalitarianism, that if this is one of the new societal models to emerge, it will do so slowly, proceeding by small wins and by evolutionary means. Nevertheless, dramatic shifts in the environment may hasten the transition. While not suggesting that the current Soviet transition necessarily reflects an egalitarian model, the relative shift from domination to sharing occasioned by Perestroika is certainly the most dramatic experiment of its kind at present (Gorbachev, 1987). We suspect that, in time, there will be much in that experiment that will be relevant to the concepts and models we have developed and surfaced in this chapter.

Many factors will contribute to a shift toward egalitarianism—one critical factor being appreciative executive action. In our judgment, the path to an egalitarian model requires strategy, technique, and practice in the hands of "master" managers (Quinn, 1988). If we are right in our proposals regarding the framework, processes, and ingredients for appreciative action, then the incumbents of the executive function should be able to meet the challenges of this new era. These executives are pioneers in their own right and would need to be special in their characteristics and talents. In many ways they might appear to be "Magicians" to those who are locked into old modalities.

The appreciative executive is one who is also able to apply the processes of appreciative action to his or her organizational and personal life in order to protect against the negative effects of a hierarchical society. Whereas these processes enable an executive to achieve a harmonious and productive relationship with his or her organization, they can also be used to the same effect in the personal arena. One needs to engage in the process of awareness to understand the interplay between one's work life and personal life. One needs to use his or her intuition and creativity to develop a lifestyle that originates within oneself rather than following the dictates of external demands. One needs to be astute in integrating the diverse requirements of the roles of corporate executive, spouse, parent, and community

Appreciating Executive Action 321

member. One also needs to bring about an effective alignment between one's personal frame of reference of needs and values with those of significant others.

It is these individuals who have achieved the necessary level of integration within themselves and with the world. This is a state of functioning where "integration of the self means using all one's capacities, talents, and abilities valued in the public and the private domains" and where "integration of the self and the world means involving oneself in a community of some sort—whether a set of friends, neighbors, colleagues, or family—and participating in the public world" (French, 1985, pp. 543-544).

Toward a New Vision of Executive Action

In reflecting on our trinity of executive appreciation, the executive in action emerges as a critical force at the levels of organizational vision and implementation. At the apex of the organizational structure, the executive as pathfinder influences and directs the organizational vision. In developing this vision, the executive must harness the technology and knowledge of the organizational process and reflect on his or her vision of the future direction of the organization. Translating this vision into reality necessitates the will and skill of working through people and managing the socially constructed reality of the organization.

While our treatment of appreciative executive action incorporates the idea that in its fullest form, it is embodied in the style and behavior of the Magician, we believe that it is also within the executive function that such concepts apply. Thus one might expect to find attention to strategy, technique, and action, and facility with the processes of alignment, awareness, and astuteness in an executive *team* that produces appreciative outcomes. Our hunch, nevertheless, is that within that assemblage, one would find one or more individuals who fit the Magician archetype.

It is a common mistake to think solely in terms of a utopian future without regard for the existing context. Any transition toward a new order brings new challenges, opportunities, and problems. In some ways the egalitarian model may appear to be better purely by comparison to the current model, which may have outlived its benefits and inhibits, very drastically, the kind of executive action we offer.

In a tough competitive world where survival is at issue, executive action is often one of compromises. Executives need to be realistic visionaries—creative and rational in vision, supportive and directive in implementation leadership. In this chapter, we have identified a number of tension points around and within appreciative executive action. However, unlike others, we have depicted these tensions as part of a dynamic interchange within the individual and between his or her organization and society. We have also postulated three key processes by which an executive can manage these tensions. In this manner, we have gone beyond the limitations of dichotomies and linear solutions. For when we do look at dichotomies—which we do in the sociohistorical contest between hierarchical and nonhierarchical systems—we see the negative consequences of a linear approach. This reinforces our assertion that the appreciative executive needs to transcend dichotomies and work with both as a Magician to integrate and build on the positive contributions of each perspective.

We expect any new transformed world would contain contradictory, paradoxical, and political elements that will challenge the executive of the future. We think that efforts of executives to act appreciatively may help tilt the balance to the side of light, while recognizing that the shadow is inevitable as well. As in life in general, there is always light and shadow in the life of executives for whom " 'Nirvana occurs when you match your own shadow, not what other people think . . . when you are nicely in synch with your own strengths' " (executive quoted by Morgan, 1987, p. 81). However, as we initially proposed, the journey toward appreciative action is one worthy of commitment. For organizations and for society, the promise of a constructive and creative new paradigm is intoxicating. In the meantime, we believe that the current, daily actions of the appreciative executive constitute small but important wins along the way to that alternative!

12

Executive Development as Spiritual Development

Peter B. Vaill

In the film *Lawrence of Arabia,* Lawrence (Peter O'Toole) has been sent into the desert to find the headquarters of Sherif Faisal (Alec Guinness). He meets Colonel Brighton (Anthony Quayle), who has come out from Faisal's camp to find Lawrence. Brighton is very skeptical of Lawrence's qualifications to be visiting Faisal and at one point during their ride through the desert he asks Lawrence just what the British government's Arab Bureau back in Cairo expects him to do. Lawrence's answer is a perfect introduction to the issue this chapter is concerned with. He says his job is rather vague, but that he is supposed to "appreciate the situation."

Lawrence does not yet know what leadership he personally will exert in the coming years with the Arabs. The Arabs for their part have little idea of how they will respond to Lawrence, or what they are truly capable of against the Turks. A deep process of the *discovery of spirit* goes on between Lawrence and his Arab compatriots. As such it is an archetype for a similar process that needs to go on between executives and the organizations they lead. Or, rather, it *should* be an archetype, but often it is not. Instead, the primary emphasis among contemporary writers seems to be *exhortation* of executives about the sense of mission, the new vision, vitality, and spirit they are supposed to impart to their organizations. I see very little attention being given to the question of where this vision, vitality, and spirit are going to come from in the leader who is imparting them.

This then is the question addressed in this essay: *What are the implications for the spiritual condition and the spiritual growth of individual executives of the need for them to foster vision, vitality, and spirit in the organizations they lead?* Stated not as a question but as a hypothesis, the idea that to a large extent *executive development for leadership of modern organizations* is *spiritual development* is the subject of this chapter.

There are a number of parts to the overall question, I must first summarize the significance for the *organization* of these ideas about vision, vitality, and spirit. This section will be relatively brief because there has been a great deal of discussion of these qualities already; I will assume that readers are generally aware of the emphasis that has been placed recently on them. The second question is, What about the spiritual condition, present and future, of the men and women who are organizational leaders? This is a difficult question and will only be addressed in a speculative and preliminary fashion here. It is also a subject on which we are all about equally informed and/or opinionated, and it is with considerable diffidence that I undertake a discussion of it at all.

The final section will then discuss the process of spiritual development. It will raise some questions and offer some possibilities about how this might be done by those who are concerned with the spiritual condition of modern executives, including those executives themselves.

As one final word of introduction, I wish to say that I think the problems I am talking about here are the most important contemporary problems in management. I think it is a scandal that there should be so little discussion of them in the mainstream of management education and development. At best, we tend to treat the subject as primarily a matter of ethics. The practice of any system of ethics, though, makes all kinds of assumptions about the spiritual condition of those who are going to do the practicing. I am genuinely embarrassed for myself and my colleagues that we should, by and large, be leaving these deep questions of executive character unaddressed, all the while calling for new vision, vitality, and spirit in Western organizations. The book for which this essay has been prepared can

Executive Development as Spiritual Development

only be described as an act of intellectual heroism — one that I fervently hope will have a lasting impact on the profession and be the first of a new genre.

Vision, Vitality, and Spirit

At the present time, the broadest topics that organizational leaders are being encouraged to inject into their organizations are *mission* and *vision*. These at least are the two terms one hears over and over in executive seminars, in the opening chapters of books on strategic management, and in admiring accounts of how one executive or another achieved a dramatic turnaround. Among consultants and seminar leaders, the hottest subject these days is the vision workshop, and countless organization members are going through fairly carefully thought out programs whose object is to produce a vision or mission for the organization around which more detailed planning and organizing can take place.

I do not intend to discuss these processes at any great length in this chapter. I do think they are the right thing to be focusing on in this period in history when so many organizations have lost their way in the midst of all the turbulence, change, paradox, and contradiction that there is abroad. I have tried to describe elsewhere just why it is that organizations have trouble getting clear and staying clear on their mission (Vaill, 1982). I have named the process for doing it *purposing* and have argued that it is the essential leadership quality for achieving high performance. I define (Vaill, 1982, p. 29) purposing as "that continuous stream of actions by an organization's formal leadership that has the effect of inducing clarity, consensus, and commitment regarding the organization's basic purposes." It is my perception that many other writers on leadership have similarly identified this capacity to state the basic direction, chart the course, articulate the vision, as the key quality of the organization leader.

Such statements, though, are of the outer nature of purposing. What we have not been paying enough attention to is the inner side — the personal qualities that make it possible for an individual to engage in these actions called purposing. These qualities are partly matters of sheer intellect. They are partly matters of having had enough experience with the organization and its environment to see clearly what is needed and what is possible. A way with words, or a speechwriter with a way with words, certainly helps, and an understanding of the psychology of those who have to hear and understand seems to be a crucial element. Knowledge of the technical role a statement of mission or a vision is going to play in the organization's strategic guidance system is important, because otherwise it will not be understood how important follow through is. The leader has to care about implementation—that is, translating vision into concrete steps.

Millions of training dollars are being spent annually to develop these skills I have named—intellect, experience, verbal charm, insight into others, knowledge of strategic management process—and they are key qualities, there is no question about it. But in my judgment, they are not enough. What is still missing are the core values of the person who would do this thing I am calling purposing. What is it the person *cares* about? What is it that *matters?* What does the person have genuine, spontaneous, unrehearsed, unmodulated, and unhomogenized energy for? What is at the core of the person's *being?*

To the extent that attempts to state vision and mission and introduce vitality are conducted *apart* from these basic qualities of the executive's character, to that extent the mission will not take hold, the vision will just be an abstract and impersonal dream, and there will not be the vitality that is needed to set a complex organizational process in motion. Instead, fear will be the main engine of vitality. People will do their jobs well enough to avoid getting fired even though they do not know the broader mission and purpose. The implementation process will run on the rails of habit, "the way we did it last year" . . . and the year before that . . . and the year before that.

It is up to the leadership to state with intelligence and conviction the value groundings on which the work of the organization should rest. These value groundings may be a wide variety of different things. For example, they may be such things,

Executive Development as Spiritual Development

singly or in combination, as the following: (1) financial goals, (2) quality demands of the task, (3) what is good for the customer or for other stakeholders, (4) what conformity with the law and other ethical standards requires, (5) consistency with past decisions and actions, (6) attainment of the kind of organizational climate members want, (7) obedience to legitimate higher authority, and so on. In other words, one or a combination of the preceding grounds (or others) must be offered persuasively in response to the question, "Why are we doing things the way we are?"

The trouble is, *all* of the above kinds of value groundings can be undercut by change, whether change in personnel, change in technology, or change in markets and other contextual forces. When the grounds of values are undercut, the meaning goes out of the activity. When values are chronically in doubt and adrift in the organization, its operations begin to become literally and profoundly absurd. And when positive reasons cannot be discovered and agreed on for going about things in any particular way, the most basic value of all in the organization has come into question: This is that the organization's mission is meaningful and valuable, and that the organization should exist to pursue it.

There are millions of executives who *do* care about their organizations, for whom some things *do* matter more than others. It is not an argument about spiritual emptiness I am primarily making, although for some spiritual emptiness is an issue and has to be considered further. No, it is more often a problem of a *discontinuity* between what the executive is feeling and what kind of person the organization apparently needs as a leader and what kind of contribution that person needs to make. We have so thoroughly technicalized and intellectualized the job of the organizational leader that there is no place for the real passions and pains that men and women in these jobs feel. In my experience, more and more of these executives are becoming thoroughly "other-directed," that is, preoccupied with how some action on their part will "play" to the many constituencies who will receive it. It is understandable, but it is tragic because it directs the executive's attention *away* from the very inner qualities that most need to be developed and expressed.

Here for example are two mission statements, the first of which was fashioned over a two-day off-site meeting by the top team of a data processing division in a major, global financial institution:

> To provide responsive automation expertise and cost-effective automated services and facilities to the organization and its clients.
>
> To excel in providing responsive automation leadership, expertise, and cost-effective automated services and facilities to the organization and its clients.

The first statement was hammered out over two days, and the second emerged in about an hour after the first one was finally crystallized and the team was getting ready to move on. The change was caused by the boss, who was a senior vice president in the parent institution. He had been playing a relatively peerlike role during the workshop. No one had any reason to suspect he was dissatisfied, but he finally popped. He said he just could not accept the first statement. It had no juice for him, no challenge. He said he had been playing what he called a "participative" role because he did not want to dominate the discussion and he had hoped that an ambitious statement would emerge from the group. But it had not, he said, so he would just have to insist on it himself. He went on to talk intensely about doing the data services job really well, which is what led to the insertion of the term *excel*. Even more important to him was the *leadership* role because, he said, users had little idea what these systems could do. They needed help; they needed education. That was the true function of the group, he insisted, not just reliable number crunching.

It was an impassioned speech by him, not a group discussion. He apologized continually for "dominating." There was no resistance to his ideas, but some grumbling about why he had not spoken up sooner—to which he only repeated his fears of "dominating."

Executive Development as Spiritual Development

What impresses me about this situation is how this man's theory about his role, as well as probably considerable personal shyness and diffidence about expressing strong feelings, almost led him to let his group produce a mission statement that he found boring and not consistent with his own values and aspirations. I have been in other meetings where it is only learned after the session is all over that one or more key people are not at all enthused with what was achieved.

What I think is going on in such cases is what Carl Rogers called "incongruence," and it is on a massive scale. Rogers (1961, p. 339) was concerned with the degree of match/mismatch between three things: a person's total experience of a situation, the parts of it which are allowed into awareness, and what is actually overtly communicated to others. I think we are possibly in a situation where the real feelings top managers have about themselves, their organizations, and their stakeholders are being systematically suppressed and distorted and ignored in favor of maintaining a front called "Executive." Considerable amounts of personal and organizational energy are going into the creation and maintenance of these fronts. It is evident to me, after having sat in many meetings where the boss needs to try to say clearly what he or she really wants the organization to be, that for many executives the only way to do that is to drop the front and be more real. And it is also evident to me that a considerable number of executives are either not letting themselves entertain the possibility of dropping the front, or if they are thinking about it they are feeling a lot of anxiety and confusion about it.

It also needs to be said that dropping the front and being more real often makes those around the executive quite anxious themselves. It puts *them* into an environment of novelty and unpredictability that can be very stressful. One senior executive I know in a Fortune 500 firm tried to initiate a series of shirt-sleeve, anything-is-fair-game discussions with cohorts of junior managers going through the company's management development program. Only the first two or three meetings were at all candid. A few questions were asked at which the top man became quite testy and even embarrassed. The word quickly went out that these meetings were being held and that there were certain subjects that the boss probably did not want to discuss. Junior managers rehearsed with each other before attending. The bosses of these junior managers gave them questions they (the bosses) wanted asked, and named topics that the juniors were not to raise with the top man. In short, what started out as an honest atttempt by a senior person to be more real with up-and-coming junior managers turned into a charade. The troops could not handle his testiness and undertook to protect themselves from it.

Hard as it is to be more honest, and complex as the psychology of the process is, we are in a situation from which there is no turning back. All organizations in Western society, public and private, profit and nonprofit, either are now deep in a process of search for new mission and purpose, or soon will be; and as long as the pace of change continues its chaotic course, the capacity to search and research for basic direction will be the prime element in an organization's survival. It is not an exaggeration to say, therefore, that the deeper springs of leadership energy and commitment are involved in an organization's survival. We have known for decades, even centuries, that the best leaders are able to reach deeply into themselves for inspiration and courage and toughness. This capacity is not "just another element" on the leadership list, though. Given what is happening in the world, I think if we are not talking about these capacities, we are not talking about leadership.

Executive Values and the Statesman Myth

The executive's values are the key thing. This is the basic thrust of the previous section—that to the extent the person's values are suppressed or politicized or outright altered to fit some presumed organizational need, to that extent the person will not be able to bring wholehearted energy and commitment to the task of purposing the organization. I suppose we could try to finesse the problem by arguing that an executive's personal values *should be* those that are appropriate for the organization. If they are not, the person should not be in the job. But that is a static and mechanistic way of talking. It is mechanistic be-

Executive Development as Spiritual Development

cause it treats values as *things* that can somehow exist in some degree of clear match versus mismatch with each other. While this may be true for such simple questions as whether one likes one kind of pie better than another kind, the world of organizational values and value conflicts is a much grayer one where choices are rarely clearly "either this or that." Thus statements about the degree of fit between a person's values and what an organization needs are not so much matters of geometry as they are matters of, in the currently popular metaphor, chemistry.

Furthermore, to say an executive's values *should* fit the organization's need is static because it assumes that neither the organization nor the person are growing and changing, whereas in fact each is. In fact, the problem of fit is created just *because* organizations are trying to stay adaptive in a turbulent environment. The organization finds itself possibly needing to go off in directions its leadership is not interested in; or conversely, the leadership perceives needs and opportunities it values and wants to pursue that the organization structure, technology, and culture are not ready for.

By contrast in a more tranquil and stable world, leaders could become thoroughly acculturated to their organizations and industries and settle in for lifelong leadership and service without any thought of encountering a crisis of organizational mission, role, and indeed survival; and they could contemplate tenures of thirty, forty, and even fifty years of accumulating wisdom and leadership skill in pursuing the basic purposes of the organization using essentially the qualities of mind, body, and spirit that they had acquired by their late twenties. I call this complex of ideas and experiences the *Statesman Myth*. It is wonderfully captured in the novels of such writers as J. P. Marquand, C. P. Snow, James Gould Cozzens, and Louis Auchincloss.

That is all now passed, even though the myth lives on in the philosophy underlying most executive development programs. The presumption of these programs is that *self*-knowledge, *self*-discovery, and personal growth are not properly part of senior executive education. With very few exceptions, we are tending to treat senior management development as a primarily intellectual process, a matter essentially of knowledge acquisition.

We are doing very little to help these men and women take off their masks. We are acting as though the executive position exists secure and ready-made for them, and the only real question is whether they can acquire enough information to govern wisely once they are in place.

The reality today is that we have a much more tenuous relation between leaders and organizations. We have rapid turnover in the top jobs. We have leaders and organizations getting in and out of phase with each other on basic values and missions. We have organizations having to reinvent themselves, and leaders correspondingly going through profound personal transformations, not the least of which involve their physical and mental health and their family relationships. No one ever told the men and women who are living through this period that this is what life at the top levels was going to be like. What they grew up with was the Statesman Myth, and I suspect that many yearn for a return to that way of being an executive leader.

The most painful part of the collapse of the Statesman Myth is that it forces reexamination of values. The capacity to *re*think and *re*examine basic values is not, to my knowledge, on anyone's present list of key executive abilities. Everybody is talking about paradigm shifts and moving from the Industrial to the Information Age, but few are talking about the qualities of mind, body, and spirit that are involved in executing such shifts, to say nothing of leading others in making the shift. And few are talking about the creation of settings in which the men and women we expect to lead organizations can really engage themselves, each other, and the issues at a deep level, at a level that brings their spiritual condition into the conversation and provides them with the opportunity to learn and grow spiritually.

The Spiritual Condition of Leaders

It is possibly quite presumptuous to undertake a discussion of the spiritual condition of the men and women who occupy positions of organizational leadership in our society. This topic has not been part of the mainstream of management and leadership theory and research. In a real sense, it is no one's

Executive Development as Spiritual Development

business but the person himself or herself what sort of spiritual condition they are in; or at least that is what the norms of Western society say. To talk of another person's spiritual condition easily can become "fightin' words," and Americans tend to believe it is better not to try.

The only response I can make to this norm is that we cannot afford the luxury of silence about the spiritual condition of our leaders. They themselves are experiencing stresses at a deep personal level that many of them cannot cope with; and they are taking actions in their organizations that in many cases reflect their fragile and embattled spiritual condition, and thus others are being affected by their spiritual condition. The challenge is to see if we can conduct a discussion of the leader's spiritual condition and spiritual development without being either judging or condemning. Both of these are easy modes to fall into, and they probably account for why Americans can be so touchy about the subject of spirituality.

With the phrase *spiritual condition* I am talking about the feeling a person has about the fundamental meaning of who they are, of what they are doing, and of the contributions they are making. I invite the reader to reflect on this phrase, too. It is one that seems intuitively to mean something significant, but that is difficult to pin down very exactly. Behind the phrase is of course the fact that the term *spirit* itself is difficult to define exactly, even though again many of us would find uses for the word in everyday conversation, and feel when we use it that we mean something which no other word captures quite as well. A moment's reflection will show that we routinely use many phrases with the word *spirit* in them, and that for most of these phrases, no other word is quite right for what is intended.

To talk about a spiritual *condition* is to imply that this condition can change, that it is not a fixed characteristic of a person, even though we may not always be able to change our spiritual condition consciously and planfully. Conscious control remains an open question, notwithstanding the enormous literature and body of practice that exists regarding how to improve one's spiritual condition.

Spiritual is the really difficult term to be very clear about.

Why not use *psychological* or some other word that does not have all the potential for various meanings that *spirit* does? I use *spirit* because I think we have to, and here is why.

There are two ways in which a leader is propelled inexorably into the realm of the spiritual. One is in the leader's own desire to act rightly and responsibly. This desire, I suggest, goes beyond the sheer technical correctness of one's actions. As a matter of empirical truth, leaders tend not to be satisfied with being merely technically correct. They want to be correct consistent with their deeper beliefs about what is important and about what the meaning of their life is. I am not saying a given leader applies this test with equal intensity to all actions. Nor am I saying all leaders exhibit the need to be more than technically correct with equal fervor. I *am* saying that to one degree or another, leaders tend to want to be correct in relation to their values. In this sense, then, *spiritual condition* refers to the degree to which the person acts on values that transcend the sheer material conditions and events of the world, that is, on values that are not contingent for their validity on these conditions and events.

The other way that leaders are propelled into the realm of the spiritual is that their actions are scrutinized by others in terms of these others' values. The leader's spirit and spirituality are seen through the eyes of others. If the leader is only being technical and materialistic, he or she will be experienced by at least *some* as insufficiently in touch with the deeper things in life. One cannot touch the spirit of others very deeply without coming from the deeper parts of oneself. In this sense, *spiritual condition* refers to the extent to which one is experienced by others as concerned with more than superficial and transitory things.

The one thing I am *not* claiming is that *spiritual condition* refers to one's degree of closeness to and contact with something otherworldly and *divine*. For many, spirituality does point in this direction and indeed is specifically concerned with one's experience of the divine. But spirit does not have to mean this, and I am willing to let it mean whatever the reader wants in terms of the degree to which it is natural versus supernatural, sacred versus secular. In other words, human beings have found meaningful spirit in all kinds of different places. Where one finds spirit

Executive Development as Spiritual Development 335

and how one experiences it and is *inspired* by it varies widely. These differences are part of and reflect one's spiritual condition.

Just as we find inspiring phenomena widely in human experience, so too are there *dispiriting* phenomena—forces and events that seem to take spirit out or that inhibit the experience of it or the apparent action of it. Modern organizations can be very dispiriting places, and sadly, there are dispiriting leaders—leaders whose impact blocks the spirit of others, setting people against each other and souring the climate of the organization.

The presence of dispiriting forces is another reason why we can leave the natural versus supernatural question open. We do not have to decide it, *because it does not make any difference whether spirit and spirituality deal with the divine or not.* Human experience shows that the dispiriting forces can eat away at spirit whether one has been seeking it in sacred or secular places. Religious faith is no more immune to temptation and despair than secular faith. The difference between them is not in their degree of immunity, but in the explanations they offer for the source and meaning of spirit. Those *within* religious faith will insist that their faith is stronger and better grounded than those who are trying to sustain a secular faith; but it also has to be said that religious faith can be sorely tested. Dispiriting events and experiences do not melt away once religious faith is acquired. In short, whatever modes of spirit one is trying to have faith in and stay in touch with, whether sacred or secular, will be challenged by the dispiriting evils of the world.

The question, then, is not which is right: a sacred faith or a secular faith. The question is what one is able to *do,* and how one is able to *move* and *develop* in one's awareness and spiritual condition when the dispiriting experiences occur. The opportunity is to grow in one's faith, to develop in it both as one experiences the positive fruits of spirit as one understands it *and* as one is challenged by dispiriting evil. In other words, I am framing the question of spiritual condition and spiritual growth in *process* terms rather than in terms of finally discovering something fixed that one can believe in. Nothing is fixed. The meaning of everything is under assault in this chaotic world. Any equilibrium one achieves will be temporary and dynamic.

The spiritual challenge of leadership is to be able to adapt to all these changes without becoming dispirited, for if that happens the danger is that others in the organization will become dispirited, too. The need is to create, maintain, and develop one's spiritual condition, and this is why executive development is spiritual development.

Avenues of Spiritual Development

One may ask what is to be worked on as dispiriting experiences are confronted and a deeper sense of spirit is sought. There can be no exact answer to this, since it will vary with the person and with the circumstances. It will also depend heavily on the modes of spirituality one is particularly attuned to. The spirit of altruistic service to the poor, the spirit of artistic creativity, and the spirit as one finds it in the worship of one's God may imply quite different experiences and opportunities as one's spiritual condition unfolds.

However, given that we are talking about men and women who are leaders of organizations, and given that values and human relationships play such an important part, perhaps it is possible to suggest tentatively what some avenues of spiritual development might be for leaders. Furthermore, since leaders are *initiators* of thought and action toward others, the avenues of spiritual development should be matters that can themselves be fostered in the organization. If possible, it would be preferable that we not have the leader developing in one direction spiritually while job opportunities and demands are tugging in another direction, because that is a recipe for anger and cynicism.

In much of what I say from now on, readers will recognize things that have been said before about what leaders need to be doing. That is as it should be, for I think we have been all around the subject of spirituality in much of leadership theory for some time.

Here are seven fields or modes or contexts of spiritual growth. They overlap and interrelate; they are to be thought of as a system, not a list. They are suggestive rather than definitive, and readers are urged to help fill in the picture for each of the seven as well as to critique them and to think of whole new categories. I have not listed the seven in any particular order of importance, except that the one mentioned last is in my mind the most important and in some sense integrates all the others.

1. *Toward Embracing New Values and the Possibilities They Imply, and the Relativity of Values to Each Other.* Some might call this the evolving ability to see shades of gray rather than only blacks and whites. It might also be called the ability to experience the world hypothetically in "as-if" terms — that is, to imagine other states of affairs than those before one, or toward which one has been devoting energy. The behavioral sciences have been calling this process one of moving out of a win/lose frame of mind and toward a win/win mentality.

To some who have not moved out of the either/or mode of judging things, multivalued thinking may look wishy-washy, that is, ready to cave in and accept some atrocious notion at the slightest sign of conflict and pain. The truly democratic spirit that is determined to hear all sides is of course anything but weak; in fact it is usually tougher than the simplistic single-valued posture. It has to be tougher: It has more complexity to handle, more disparate imperatives to juggle, more pressure and more stress because it is letting its own values interact with others, more reason to throw up its hands and retreat into the black-and-white frame of mind. This is why development of the capacity to practice a democratic style *is* spiritual growth, for a more flexible and resilient spirit is needed to be democratic.

An organization is a place where everybody is right and everybody is wrong. Each person has hold of a piece of the truth; no person has all the truth. Life for the leader in an organization is a process of ongoing discovery of all the ways that various organization members have their truths. Thus, all the talk about a participative style of leadership is superficial to the extent that it does not recognize the spiritual growth which this style entails. In fact, to call this way of being in relation to others a *style* indicates that we have not understood the spiritual demands it places on the person. It is more than a style. Participative management is a way of being, and not something one just adopts after reading a book or sitting through a two-day workshop. "Largeness of spirit" is the quality I am talking about here. The largeness is this capacity to embrace the shades of gray and the many facets of any human situation.

2. *Toward a Passionate Reason.* Spirituality is wholehearted and wholeheaded, and the more profound it is, the less it resides in any one faculty of the human being, the less it is either mental or emotional, either reasonable or passionate. Spiritual growth is toward a feeling of and a practice of the wholeness of oneself and cannot entail the suppression of one part in favor of another.

I do not think the great philosopher of science Karl Popper (1965) was intending to be spiritual when he settled on the phrase "conjectures and refutations" as the most thorough expression of his philosophy of inquiry and the growth of knowledge. But I think it is a spiritual proposition to say that human beings can proceed only by making the most passionate and daring guesses, hypotheses, and conjectures possible and then by attempting to refute them with all the force of their intellectual powers of criticism. To practice either while ignoring the other is to operate at a less than fully human level. *Both* conjectures and refutations partake of the spiritual, but to grasp that and practice it involves a more profound spiritual condition than to be simply good at either one or the other.

Three qualities that are much desired in organizational life these days are creativity, courage, and leadership. A little reflection will show, I think, that each of these qualities is an example of passionate reason. Creativity is both a primal energy for what is new and different and a cool understanding of what is indeed new and different. Courage blends the knowledge of the danger one is in with the determination not to be conquered by fear. "Determination" and "resolve" are much more matters of emotion, I believe, than they are logical conclusions. But courage would not be courage if it did not blend rational understanding of the situation with emotional commitment to hold to a particular course no matter what. And leadership is neither just knowledge of what is needed nor just the desire and willingness to provide what is needed; it is both, bound inextricably together such that neither makes much sense without the other.

Executive Development as Spiritual Development

We *try* to teach leadership as if its essence can be communicated in theories and research findings, but without the feeling that accompanies the intellectual appreciation of situations, there can be no real leadership. Of course, you can err on the other side, too. If we overemphasize the raw energy of leadership at the expense of stressing how very smart and insightful most effective leaders are, we miss the mark again.

Doubtless many of the qualities we most admire in people are examples of what I am calling "passionate reason." One more in particular deserves some further comment. That is the ability to have faith, the ability in the currently popular (but originally biblical) phrase to "keep the faith." It is hard for many of us to have faith, to acquire it and to grow in it. The dispiriting forces I was just discussing cut directly into our faith and make us feel wrong or silly or naive or sorrowful. The best defense we have against these assaults lies in the conjoining of head and heart, of intellect and feeling. Faith grounded more in passionate feeling than reason is vulnerable to surprise, to embarrassment, to discrediting. The loss of faith whose basis was emotion in the first place is agony and despair. In the extreme, it is death. Faith grounded more in reason than passionate feeling (which we then call "having reasons") is untested and somewhat oblivious to the intensity of the tests that can be put to it. Faith that is just mainly *reasons* is curiously dual: The faith is in the correctness of the reasons, but the faith is also in the *adequacy* of the reasons. Reasons for believing what one believes may be quite correct, but they may be quite inadequate relative to the intensity and relentlessness of challenges that can arise. Intellectual reasons for not sinning are rarely enough, for opportunities to sin can be too tempting. The determination has to go deeper than merely having reasons not to indulge oneself.

The deepening faith that accompanies an improving spiritual condition has to be more and more thoroughly this thing I am calling a passionate reason. The process of spiritual growth presents continuing opportunities to err too far into one kind of faith or the other, that is, into a mindless ecstasy or an intellectual labyrinth of nuances and distinctions. Yet, if one's spirituality is going to remain in the world and engaged with the world's people, its problems, and its objectives, it seems to me that the balance captured in the notion of passionate reason is the best approach.

3. *Toward the Development of an Open Value System.* Value *system* is such a common phrase that it is virtually a cliché. However, what it truly means for a set of values to constitute a *system* is a relatively unexplored notion.

The creation of a value *system* has to be viewed as an *achievement,* since it would mean that a person had undertaken a searching comparison of the content of the various values in the system and worked through—both speculatively, but more importantly in lived experience—the relationships that exist among the values not just as concepts but in concrete action. It would mean that the various elements of values were understood not in isolation but as a whole taken together, and that no subsets of values in the value system could be substituted for the whole system without altering its character. Value *systems* are not lists of values that coexist in the mind of a person, and from which individual values, principles, or guidelines are selected to fit an occasion.

Viewed this way, fewer of us than might be thought possess truly genuine *value systems.* Possession of a value system is truly a concomitant of spiritual growth and development.

The *openness* of a value system also deserves comment, because the first two avenues I have already discussed will surely bring new elements into one's value system and cause substantial changes in it. One of the key aspects of openness is the discovery of values deep in another's psyche that one can barely comprehend as values. Openness takes us out of our own value system and into the value systems of others. One of the clearest examples of this is in cross-cultural relationships where another's values can be so alien and mysterious that they are not even recognized as positive values. I am thinking of common everyday things like differences in eating habits, differences in uses of time, differences in the significance of material possessions, or differences in the significance of family relationships. The differences can be so great that one cannot believe that the other

Executive Development as Spiritual Development 341

person's behavior is basically an expression of a different value system; at least one cannot believe it if one is not sufficiently far along in spiritual development. Capacity to experience the *spirit* of another across the cultural gulf is a prerequisite to true intercultural understanding and valuing.

Another type of gulf exists between the various technical specialties that one finds in modern organizations. It is common for a specialist in one technology to feel that the spirit of his or her specialty is being denied by the way the other specialties are intruding—in terms of budget, space, influence on broader objectives, attention of key personnel, and so forth. Many, many professionals are throwing up their hands daily because they feel the organization is crushing the spirit of their specialty or profession. At one level of spiritual awareness and development, spirit may seem to be a win/lose game. This type of "spiritual warfare" cannot continue, though, for the modern organization needs the spirited practice of all its various special fields of technical competence. Spiritual empowerment is one of the most important kinds of empowerment there can be.

These problems are usually discussed under the rubric of *boundary management,* but without the notion of spirit and spiritual development, boundary management can hardly mean more than merely keeping people out of each other's way. This may be enough in some cases, but most organizations are more than loose coalitions of high-energy teams whose spiritual values and energy are for the most part imploded on their own specific mission.

The various parts of the organization *are* a value system in addition to a system in structure and in communication. You do not hear it put this way very often—that an organization *is* a value system—but the more one perceives the action of spirit in an organization, the clearer this becomes. What this says to leaders, therefore, is this: "You are a living value system yourself and you are leading a living value system (that is, your organization). The nature of each of these as well as their relationship will become clearer and clearer to you as your own spirit develops and deepens." Without this avenue of spiritual development, the leader is likely to experience little more than a cacophony of competing priorities and constraints, both inside the self as well as outside in the organization and the wider environment.

4. *Toward Spiritual Development That Is Shared with Others.* The discussion of boundaries and of others' value systems in the previous section suggests another avenue of spiritual development, namely, the growing ability to work on matters of spiritual development *with* others. The *fellowship* aspect of spiritual development is a very old quality of spiritual growth in many of the world's great religions. One can guess that its significance stems partly from the conviction that humanity *is* a family, and partly from the more practical realization that we may be able to develop more richly and creatively if we have the presence and the support of others who are engaged in spiritual search with us.

Perhaps there is no more significant avenue of spiritual development for organizational leaders than this one, because it involves leading organization members into a fuller realization of their interdependence and of their common feelings, common loyalties, common opportunities, and common strengths. It involves confronting the loneliness, disappointment, and pain of the modern organization, and deciding that these conditions should not continue to rot the spirit of the organization and the people in it.

There is relatively little discussion of organizations *as spiritual families,* although the data that have been accumulating on excellent organizations makes it very clear that this is what these organizations are: spiritual brotherhoods and sisterhoods. What it takes in leadership and membership to move toward spiritual kinship is not well understood in contemporary Western organizations. The literature is small, which makes the appearance of books that do confront the spiritual horror of organizational life all the more significant. Some recent examples are Scott and Hart (1979), Kelly (1988), and Harvey (1988). Harvey in particular makes it crystal clear that spiritual horror coexists with the potential for spiritual kinship in the modern organization.

It is ironic, even tragic, that we already know in precise detail how to help people move toward a deeply felt conviction of their membership in a spiritual family. The methodology is that of the encounter group, the sensitivity training group, or the T group—I take all these phrases to mean virtually the same thing. By just asking a group of ten or a dozen people to focus on what is happening right there in the group, it is possible to help group members experience feelings in themselves and in others that are not as easy to attend to and learn from in everyday life. *Discovery* of things in oneself and in others that one never knew were there is the hallmark experience of these groups. The discovery is sometimes of dark and frightening things, but much more often it is of tender and beautiful and positive things. I do not think there is any question that these groups produce these experiences, even though they have now become largely passé and tend to be dismissed as one of the kooky things we played with in the 1960s (Vaill, 1985).

To some extent, we misinterpreted what these groups were all about when they were in their heydey, and as a result they did not achieve the objectives we thought they should be capable of achieving, and so they passed from prominence in adult learning and development. It is a great tragedy that this happened. What we did not understand, I believe, was that we had invented a fairly modest and nonthreatening setting in which people could experience their *spiritual kinship* more thoroughly and deeply than many of them ever had before. We tended to downplay this aspect, though, in favor of interpreting these groups as places where technical learning about oneself and others could go on; where we could learn about communicating effectively; where we could get feedback from others about ourselves in little packets of information that we could then use to improve ourselves. It is as if we thought these groups were primarily places where one could gather a lot of *facts* about what people are really like and how to work effectively with them.

At the same time that we were treating them as vehicles for technical learning, we were *evaluating* these groups, using very technical behavioral science methods, to see where the technical learning we thought was going on was actually paying off in increased personal effectiveness with people at work. We tried to follow the effects of these groups through to the bottom line. In general, the net of all attempts to prove effectiveness and payoff is about zero. T groups did not prove out as tools for making people and organizations more effective and efficient. As a result, Corporate America tended to lose interest.

There was one research finding that emerged repeatedly in these groups, but not much importance was attached to it per se. In fact, many did not even interpret this constant occurrence as a "research finding" at all. The occurrence I refer to was that in these groups people talked about things that for the most part they could not and did not talk about anywhere else; and they felt things about themselves and others that for the most part they could not let themselves feel in quite as full and healthy a way in any other place. These groups affected people's spiritual condition, and the effect I think was overwhelmingly positive. Possibly now, twenty years after they peaked in popularity, we are in a better position to see what these groups were really about. And perhaps if it is spiritual development we are interested in, some of these methods of facilitating human encounter warrant another look.

5. *Toward a New Vocabulary and Grammar of Spirituality.* We have to talk with ourselves and others if we are going to understand and improve our spiritual condition. The adequacy of the language we have for conducting this talk is itself a matter of growth and change. The vocabulary of Sunday School, augmented by the wisdom of greeting cards, bumper stickers, and T shirts, may not be quite enough for leaders to conduct the personal and organizational processes I am talking about.

The two aspects of this issue that I think deserve special attention are the problem of self-consciousness and the problem of prayer.

For some, the use of language that deals with spirituality sounds artificial, stilted, and preachy. It is not "cool" in some circles to interpret experience in spiritual terms, and many will err on the side of keeping silent or of rephrasing their ideas in right-sounding psychologistic language rather than risk being perceived as having "got religion." This of course is not true of everyone, and indeed in the late 1980s there are millions of people who *are* exploring the new vocabularies of spirituality, whether from the inside or outside of an established religion. Still, I think hesitancy to let one's vocabulary become infused (and inspired?) with spiritual language is real and has to be worked through even as the ideas and spiritual feelings behind the words have to be worked through.

One of the interesting things that happens along this avenue is the rediscovery of genuine, here-and-now meaning in words and phrases one has been hearing all one's life but not really comprehending. I am referring to phrases that are used at invocations and benedictions, weddings and funerals, the verses of songs and the mottoes and even mission statements that organizations chisel across their facades but then do not look up at often enough.

Along this avenue, the things people say about their basic beliefs take on a deeper meaning. Their personal credos become virtually a call of their spirit. For example, leadership theorist Harlan Cleveland (personal communication, 1987) reports hearing the explorer Thor Heyerdahl say that his personal credo is "translating ideas into events to serve people." Or again, there is Churchill's (1948, p. 667) profound portrayal of himself on becoming prime minister in 1940: "I felt as if I were walking with Destiny, and that all my past life had been but a preparation for this hour and for this trial."

The further one goes into the spirituality in and of language, the more that tried and true words like *faith, soul, sin, tragedy, redemption,* and *spirit* itself are heard and felt afresh. It is not too much to say that the rediscovery of the spiritual meaning in these words we have been hearing all our lives can powerfully enrich one's own spiritual growth.

The spirituality in music and art and other creative forms also comes forth as one reflects on why particular works were created or what the words in a musical work mean. These nonverbal "vocabularies" are limitless sources of spiritual insight if one simply assumes that the artist's spirit is present in the work. In my experience, the encounter with an artist's spirit through the work can be a powerful factor in one's own development. The occasions on which one feels personally touched by an artist's spirit should be cherished.

The question of prayer is also intimately bound up with the condition of our spiritual vocabulary. While there is no one vocabulary for prayer, our capacity to engage in prayerful action is heavily influenced by the ease with which we can express our spiritual feelings to ourselves and others. The more our vocabulary does not get in the way, the more richly and fully we can engage in what is called prayer.

So much has been written about what prayer is and about how to do it that I am very hesitant even to raise the subject. But if we are talking about improving one's spiritual condition, I think we are talking about prayer among other things. *What if prayer were simply defined as the attempt to improve our conscious contact with the spiritual?* If prayer is just a word for that, then maybe much of what makes so many of us nervous about the word (and the theology within it that we half-consciously think the word will force on us) falls away. Perhaps "prayer" is nothing more than focusing deliberately on this spiritual stuff I have been talking about, with possibly just one additional qualifier: Somehow it seems to me that in prayer we are not standing back and "checking out" the spiritual, but rather we are immersing our awareness in whatever form of the spiritual is before us. We try to feel *with* Albinoni in his *Adagio,* for example, rather than eye detachedly the sweet sadness he conveys. We listen passionately to a speaker rather than skeptically, seeking to merge our awareness with the other's rather than standing back to critique it. We try to look *into* the feeling of the writer rather than just stay on the surface of the words.

Spirit is where you find it and spirit-*uality* is finding it and embracing it in prayer, I think. William Barrett (1978, p. 281) anticipates our protest that we cannot lead our lives in this mode by quoting Isaac Bashevis Singer: " 'Whenever I am in trouble, I pray. And since I'm always in trouble, I pray a lot. Even when you see me eat and drink, while I do this, I pray.' "

Following this reasoning out to its logical conclusion, the exploration by leaders of these various avenues of spiritual development is *prayer!* It would then be prayer to try to sense more fully the capacity and the potential organization members have for commitment to the mission. It would be prayer to try to understand another person's spirit. It would be prayer to seek to express oneself as clearly and persuasively as possible. It would

Executive Development as Spiritual Development

be prayer to seek to develop a value *system* that is honest to one's own spirit and responsive to the spirit of others.

The negative form would be this: Actions that avoid or are indifferent to spirit are at least potentially antiprayer. They may diminish conscious contact with spirit. Defined this way, there can be nothing automatic or ritualistic about prayer, even though one may have *forms* of prayer one uses repeatedly. Each occasion becomes a new opportunity to develop contact with the spirit in whatever the action is about.

This approach also throws light on why prayer is hard for so many of us. If you think about it, there really should not be anything hard about prayer. It is a private activity with relatively few rules and no apparent costs of failure. Furthermore, prayer by the definition I have given should be quite easy, since what one is doing is dwelling on one's contact with the spirit in something. As one experiences the spirit in something, the feelings are joy, eagerness, curiosity, wonder, comfort, relief. These are not feelings that one normally avoids or suffers from, so why then should prayer be difficult?

I am afraid the answer is inescapable: Too many of us, too much of the time, have committed ourselves to actions that are indifferent to or that outright deny the spirit in us which propels the action and the spirit in the people and things toward which we are acting. It is as if we cannot afford to seek the spirit, because this will bring us face to face with the wastefulness, emptiness, or destructiveness of much that we do. In the presence of the spirit of the forest, you do not trash the ground. Feeling the spirit in a person's loyalty, we would not then preemptively fire him or her. Sensing our own yearning for more authentic contact with those around us, we would not schedule ourselves so tightly that we can engage in no more than superficial pleasantries with any of them. Perceiving the spirit of a person's cherished innovation, one would not tell them that it will not work. Feeling a sense of comradeship with an attractive colleague beginning to replace the selfish lust we first felt toward them, we would not then go ahead and "hit" on them anyway.

Yes, I think prayer is hard because of the shift it requires within us. This perhaps is the deepest mode of leadership we can speak of — the decision by a leader to turn toward the spirit in self and in others and begin to try to experience it more fully in prayer. Will this result in greater profits? more efficient attainment of objectives? better adaptation to the environment? We have no way of knowing. It *will* result in more spiritually grounded action, whatever that turns out to be.

6. *Toward Appreciation of the Spirit in Larger and Larger Wholes.* Thinking holistically and appreciating the "big picture" are routinely mentioned as key qualities of the executive leader. What we do not know as much about is just *how* one manages to see the big picture, unless it is just by accumulating more and more data and more and more experience and hoping that in rolling these around in one's mind a larger synthesis will emerge. Data and experience, however, do not automatically yield a synthesizing vision.

The reason it is hard to see the big picture in any collection of people and things is that they are just too miscellaneous and various, there is just too much change and confusion and too much clamor from the various parts for attention. Since the person who would grasp the big picture is part of the system, the big picture to be seen is what *we* have in common, what *we* are involved in, what the meaning is of what *we* are doing. One has to include oneself in the big picture. It is not an abstract intellectual exercise, but instead an act of taking the lead in interpreting for oneself and others the broader meaning of the group or organization.

Perhaps it is the spirit of the enterprise, whatever it is, that transcends all the miscellany. Perhaps the spirit can first be felt in oneself and then felt in reverberation from others. Feeling it and articulating the feeling to onself and others is the task. It will be faint and equivocal at first and may remain so. But it may not. Possibly as one works to experience it more fully it becomes clearer and stronger and one becomes more sure of the meaning and value of the activity, and more able, indeed eager, to communicate it to others in acts of spiritual leadership.

The appreciation of the whole is not a once and for all act, because every whole exists within a larger whole. There is no reason why the process I have just described cannot go on indefinitely. Seeing the big picture then becomes instead a progressive process, *a process of progressive transcendence of the limits of one's understanding and appreciation of what one is involved in.* This progressive transcendence is, I think, the spiritual growth I have been talking about all along. By definition, the spiritual dimension is unlimited in scope. The "higher consciousness" that has been intuited so often over the centuries may be just this attainment of a scope and richness of appreciation that goes beyond the ordinary.

An organizational leader with the usual everyday pressures and responsibilities might well view this process as departing into abstract and ethereal visions of the organization, so far removed from getting work done as to be of no use at all. I think the exact opposite might be the case, and my reason concerns what "feeling the spirit" of something really amounts to. The experience of the spirit in things brings us into closer touch with the *concrete*. It is grasping the spirit of a factory, for example, that would permit one to walk through it attending to myriad details, holding multiple simultaneous conversations, asking and answering questions, pausing to be briefed on particular problems, making promises and juggling conflicts, and so on, all the while staying engaged and cheerful about the place. *The sense of the spirit of it all is what makes creative immersion in the details possible!* Really effective leaders are legendary for their attention to detail and for their tireless involvement with specifics. It is not because their view is narrow and compulsive, I am convinced, but just the opposite: Their view is infused with the spirit running through all the specifics.

So, once again, we come upon spiritual development as indispensable to what we already agree needs to be done—in this case to help leaders grasp the whole or the big picture of the activities and organizations they are involved in.

7. *Toward Centering in the Present.* Back at the beginning of this discussion of avenues of spiritual development, I said that this last avenue was the most important one to me and that in many ways it integrates all the others. My main reason is that organizational leadership is so much a matter of one's capacity to be effective in the moment of action; and organizational life is so full of distractions that pull one out of the present moment.

Roethlisberger (1954, pp. 3-29) gave an extraordinary account of how effective action in organizations is an ongoing process of balancing in the here-and-now the many conflicting pressures that any manager feels. Genuine skill, for him, could be found in the way the healthy personality is able to pay attention simultaneously to what is going on outside and inside oneself. Thoughts and feelings are inside; other people and the events they cause are outside. "Attention" is the meeting of the two, and "experience" is the cumulative effect through time of paying attention. When inside and outside are meeting and affecting each other freely, effectiveness results. When inner is suppressed in favor of outer or vice versa, or when one stops paying attention and relies on a preprogrammed formula or otherwise disengages one's attention, the danger is that inappropriate action will result.

At about the same time the Harvard point of view was evolving in the 1930s and 1940s, Gestalt psychology was developing its own notions about being centered in the present and was actually defining anxiety as primarily a disorder of attention: a depressive preoccupation with the past or obsession about the future.

I am taking a minute to link Roethlisberger and other forerunners to the discussion because I do not want the spiritual possibilities of the present to be thought of as just a piece of New Age trendiness. The ability of a leader to have a lasting effect is an old notion, not just the teaching of the latest guru.

Among modern executive leaders, one of the biggest barriers to experiencing spirit in the present is *workaholism,* or "hurry sickness," as it is also known. This subject is too large to be explored here, but we have to consider the likelihood that the compulsive action patterns the workaholic develops, and all the rationalistic explanations the workaholic develops to defend these patterns, stand squarely between the person and spiritual growth. In terms of Roethlisberger's ideas about balanced attention, my hypothesis is that workaholism is a disorder of attention: It interprets cues indiscriminately as signals that one must work more hours and more intensely and that everything depends on one's willingness to make a superhuman effort. The self-exploration

Executive Development as Spiritual Development 351

that spiritual growth entails is hard for the workaholic to undertake, since such exploration will reveal the extent to which one is addicted to the compulsive workaholic patterns.

If we can agree that expressions of human spirit are constantly running through the thoughts, feelings, and actions of human beings, that means that wherever the leader is, and whatever the leader is doing, the *present moment* is full of spirit. Even when things feel very flat and humdrum, it is unwise to assume there is no spirit anywhere in the situation or that the other people in the situation are feeling no stirrings of spirit within. *The present is the place where spirit is most naturally found—that is the main point.* There may be set, ceremonial occasions when a more intense and visible outpouring of spirit occurs, but relative to everyday life these ceremonies are artificial and misleading. We have all walked, full of hope, out of some extravagant ceremony where there has been much excitement and expressions of new commitment, only to find a few days later that things have settled back into a business-as-usual mode. The spirit of the ceremony seems to have evaporated entirely. Not surprisingly, over a period of time we become cynical about the value of ceremonies.

But the artificiality of the ceremony is the wrong place to look for spiritual energy. We must look in the normal expressions of the present, because it is from those normal expressions that a more focused and visible outpouring is going to occur if it is going to occur at all.

There is another curious thing about the present, if this is not too mystical an idea. The present is the only door through which the eternal can enter our awareness. "When mating with Heaven," says my favorite translation of the *Tao Te Ching*, "can you take the female part?" (Bynner, 1980, p. 30). We are counseled to open ourselves, to be willing to *receive* the larger truths of life, rather than to believe that we can *wrest* these truths from experience through intense, sustained effort. The Big Idea, the New Vision, the Breakthrough—these kinds of experiences can only come to us in the present. If some management team is so locked on the rails of its plan or the anxieties of its present crisis or is exhausted and without energy to engage the situation in which it finds itself, the New Vision for the organization is simply not going to come.

Therefore, all the other avenues of spiritual development come together in this last one. *All the things I have talked about are going to be felt and done in the present, or they are not going to be done at all.*

Summary

The main point of this discussion is that it makes no sense to talk about a leader inspiring an organization if the leader's own spiritual condition and spiritual development are not also considered. Such consideration then takes us into the whole subject of spirituality as it applies to men and women in positions of leadership responsibility, and in the process a variety of difficulties and complexities are discovered, not the least of which is the somewhat taboo nature of the subject. It is not necessary to take a position on religion in discussing spirituality, because problems of spiritual growth and development arise whether one's interest in spirit is this-worldly or otherworldly. In the final section of the chapter, seven avenues of spiritual development have been discussed. While these seven paths are by no means the only ones, taken together they involve many important aspects of spiritual growth.

13

The Illusion and Disillusion of Appreciative Management

Max Pagès

I feel stimulated as well as anxious at the prospect of dialoguing with my American colleagues on the topic of executive appreciation. Some personal remarks may be relevant to provide the reader with an understanding of my intellectual approach.

The first concerns the differences in intellectual backgrounds between Europe, particularly France, and the United States. In France, our background in the social sciences has been deeply marked over the years by the influence of Marxism and psychoanalysis, the latter having taken precedence over the former. I personally have always resisted the hegemonic tendencies of these two systems of thought; I believe they are in need of a critical analysis leading to considerable revision. However, I still feel they constitute priceless intellectual reservoirs that a serious scholar cannot disregard.

This leads me to view analysis, be it sociological or psychological, as an essential and distinct step, separate from evaluation and action. Within this analytical frame of reference, I

Note: I want to express here my gratitude to Asbjörn Osland and my full appreciation of his work in helping me to prepare the final version of this paper. He not only corrected my English but also, thanks to his thorough understanding of my thinking, often helped me clarify it and, I hope, find ways of communicating better to the American reader.

value the recognition of the negative (for example, anxiety, conflicts, unconscious or covert phenomena, and so forth) as much as the positive. I thus share the suspiciousness of many European scholars regarding some trends in American research in the social sciences, particularly those that fail to recognize the role of conflict in analysis. Examples of such lines of thought include mysticism and idealism on the one hand, and functionalism, with its emphasis on objective empirical measurement, on the other. Both appear to me as two symmetrical ways of escaping the recognition of conflict between values and reality.

My initial discomfort with executive appreciation relates to my perception of it as an idealistic way to avoid conflict due to its focus on the positive dimensions of organizational life. I fear it may be used to create an illusion so distinct from reality that one could view it as a defense mechanism rather than a visioning process grounded in reality. Such a coping mechanism may overlay profound conflict; it may prove ephemeral and damaging in the long run. The references to spirituality in relation to executive appreciation also disturb me, as having nothing to do with scientific research. The current fashionable rapprochement between science and religion, excluding magic, is a cultural trait of our era that I regard as regressive rather than progressive. The social constructionist argument, used to support executive appreciation, if taken to its logical end leads to nihilism.

Hence I entered the symposium that gave rise to this volume in a state of discomfort with executive appreciation. The following pages can be considered as a counterpoint. I will resume the argument at the end of the chapter on the basis of the experience at the symposium.

Yet my debt to the American tradition is equally great. I was deeply influenced by my postdoctoral work with Carl Rogers. My stay in Cleveland and study at Case Western Reserve University, in 1951, are sources of fond memory. My involvement with NTL at Bethel had a lasting impact on my work. These influences have helped me, fundamentally, to fight dogmatism, to recognize the importance of intermediate areas—such as the group and the organization—and to emphasize the commitment of the change agent as a major part of the change process. I am not trying now to distribute marks to my various spiritual predecessors and mentors, but simply to identify some of the biases that they helped me recognize and that I believe we all have to fight. May the American reader be reminded of this when my argument sounds obsolete or paranoid!

Finally, years ago, I have left a practice in action research in organizations and training and moved to individual and group psychotherapy. My experience of the former has led me to serious doubts as to the possibility of reconciling the role of management consultant with the professional ethics of a social scientist. But I have continued to investigate organizations, in a purely research role.

All this has led me to study the relationship between the organization and the individual and the genesis of professional pathology, of which I will speak in this chapter. In it, I discuss the following themes:

- *Dialectical Approach.* Here, social reality is interpreted as being made up of dynamic systems of conflicts and of responses to conflicts, focusing on the interaction between intrapsychic and outer (that is, social) systems.
- *Research on Organizational Power.* The central hypothesis here concerns the evolution of the interaction between sociological mediation processes and psychological unconscious defense mechanisms in the "hypermodern" organization as a means of avoiding conflict.
- *Mediation Processes.* This term refers to the ambiguous, unobtrusive processes used to prevent "contradictions" from turning into overt conflicts, such as ideology, double discourse, indirect control, and so on.
- *Hypermodern Organization.* This represents technologically and managerially sophisticated organizations where the change in the process of production leads to a qualitative change in the system of control—from economic pressure and authoritarian coercion toward more refined means of control, such as the use of economic and political advantages, and moreover of ideological and psychological seduction.

- *Unconscious Processes.* In the hypermodern firm, the organization replaces the boss as the object of unconscious investment, fantasy, and conflict. Furthermore, one observes a regression toward archaic, maternal rather than oedipal, types of conflicts. Separation anxiety is the core here, leading to idealizing the organization on the basis of identifying with the aggressor.
- *Professionalization.* I use this term to mean the sociomental processes that govern the construction of professional values. These processes are at the center of psychological and social conflicts and interact with one another.
- *Professional Stress.* Ideologization, through the vehicle of the hypermodern organization's grip on the individual's commitment and quest for meaning, exacerbates the individual's vulnerability to depression and disillusion when the organization fails to fulfill its promise.

On the basis of the preceding concepts, some components of a theoretical model of professional stress will be developed.

Dialectical Approach

Out of the empirical research and practice of a group of colleagues is emerging the epistemological framework of a dialectical approach in the social sciences. This dialectical approach can be summarily characterized in two ways.

First, it interprets social reality in *dynamic* rather than functional terms. Social reality is seen as made up of meaningful systems of conflicts with their ensuing responses. For example, behavior at work is not viewed as the mechanical result of the balance between task constraints imposed by the organization and individual needs for affirmation and safety. Rather, it is seen as the product of managing intrapsychic conflicts and outer, interpersonal and organizational, conflicts. The emphasis is on behavior as a meaningful human event, even when it is destructive, rather than as a purely utilitarian or economically driven one.

Second, I assume that fruitful scientific models in the human sciences rely on the *interaction between inner and outer struc-*

Illusion and Disillusion of Appreciative Management   357

tures and processes. They describe a dialectic between the social (societal, organizational, interpersonal) and the psychological (unconcious-conscious) levels.

Psychoanalysis and Marxism—the most powerful systems of dynamic interpretation—and other important schools of thought in the human sciences raise a dilemma for the theoretician. They are at the same time necessary, and impossible to use in conjunction, since they contradict themselves on basic issues (refer for example to the endless polemics between Freudians and Marxists, or Freudians and Reichians). One is then tempted to reject them all, with the risk of throwing out the baby with the bathwater.

The contradiction between such systems of thought (for example, Marxism and psychoanalysis) is due to these systems intimately mixing metatheoretical explanations of the universe with intermediate process theories, in which reside their real scientific contributions. Metatheories are guided by ultimate principles (the libido for Freudians, class struggle for Marxists, sexual energy for Reichians . . .), earthly manifestations of an ultimate source of energy, which can be seen as so many figures of God. This is responsible for the philosophical hegemony of each system of thought. Researchers who share such beliefs are able to operate within their particular philosophy, but have difficulty establishing a dialogue with others who are tied to another ultimate principle.

A critical analysis of these systems of thought is necessary in order to overcome their hegemonic tendencies and to use them, more modestly, at the intermediate level of process theory. One could then work, horizontally, across areas and disciplines, establishing links between social, psychological, and biological phenomena, discovering the ways and knots of an *interprocessual network,* without any more pretending that it is ruled by a central all-explaining principle.

Research on Organizational Power

This dialectical method developed out of research on power conducted within the European subsidiary of a multinational firm, hereafter referred to as TLTX. This was chosen because we saw it as an example of a "hypermodern" organization—that is, a firm that was at the apex of economic success as well as technological and managerial sophistication. It was our desire to study the new forms of power developed within this type of organization and particularly the relationship between the social and psychological aspects. This study confirmed the usefulness of the dialectical approach and shed some light on the interaction between social and psychological dimensions.

On the social side, sophisticated decision-making procedures, personnel policies, and organizational ideologies appear to function as mediating processes against collective conflicts. For instance, the political (that is, decision-making) system of the firm studied had evolved to a system based on *rules* internalized by the employees. This was in contrast to the standard order-prohibition system of decision making.

A system of rules such as that present in TLTX is consistent with the sophisticated technology and the competent, well-educated, and highly motivated employees required in such a company. Contrary to an order or a prohibition, a rule needs to be interpreted. It is to be understood, accepted, and ultimately, internalized.

Just as rules are part of the ideology of the firm, externally so to speak, they become a part of the individual, through internalization, of his or her conscious and unconscious motivations (that is, ego ideal, superego). Paradoxically, the system of rules simultaneously fosters the autonomy of the individual and his or her dependency on the organization. The employee becomes more autonomous, given his or her role as an interpreter of rules and even a generator of ideas for rules, or their modifications. However, rules' coherence and logic can only be referred to the organization. Dependency on the organization is evident in comments such as the following: "TLTX is always right; no one can oppose it," or, "The more decentralized we are, the more centralized."

To complete the system of rules, there is a strict hierarchy of priorities: For example, research takes precedence over production and the latter over sales.. There is a vast armada of specialized staff who permeate the fabric of the organization and "help" interpret (that is, control) the rules.

In this way, the typical conflicts between research, production, and sales are averted and each actor's autonomy is encouraged. Sales managers of national subsidiaries must develop their own policy, but production is determined at the local level. Since one can only sell what is produced, the level of control at the sales level is obviously limited, with the sales manager required to be autonomous while at the same time dependent. In addition, no one European country produces the whole array of products necessary for assembling the complex TLTX material. Thus, all continental subsidiaries are interdependent in production, even though independent in sales, but dependent on the United States for research. Furthermore, each manager is "helped" by rules and staff to decide in the right way. This combination of various means of control—a clear hierarchy of political priorities, the rule system enforced by staff having internalized them—precludes secession, the ultimate consequence of unresolved conflict, by a renegade subsidiary. Only in the United States is independence evident in that all the functions of sales, production, and research are entirely performed there.

Other potential sources of conflicts (for example, ethnic, linguistic, political, or national) are also suppressed or averted in the same way. For example, during one visit, a president of one subsidiary proudly proclaimed, "You can investigate! There are no Americans in our backrooms." This often heard joke is quite literally true: A strictly observed personnel policy precludes Americans from appearing on the local payroll, with their employment limited to the continental or world headquarters. Even there, their numbers are declining. TLTX wants its rules to be recognized as international rather than American. Moreover, TLTX need not exert direct personal control, especially by foreigners, which would represent an obsolete form of power in the hypermodern organization and lead to the familiar antagonisms (for example, labor strife or resentment of imperialist rule). The preferred enforcement of TLTX international rule is to develop "TLTXians"—that is, employees with TLTX internalized rules—out of any ethnic or national stock who would be capable of applying the rules "freely," or so they would consciously perceive it, to their own context.

This system of controlled, or limited, autonomy, based on internalized rules, was reinforced by the firm's ideology. While the classical firm relies on established ideology (for example, the Church, the School, or the State), the hypermodern organization generates its own ideology in the form of mission statements and manuals. TLTXians referred to these as the *gospels,* and continued the religious metaphor with terms such as *rituals, cult, priests,* and the like, when referring to their most solemn staff meetings.

Such social construction of intellectual meaning is also evident in the mix of the ethical with the technical, resulting in humanistic values such as excellence and service. These appeal to the altruistic needs of employees and add meaning to their work and lives, all serving to reinforce their allegiance to the organizational philosophy.

The preceding may appear to the reader as simply a strong corporate culture where the organization has succeeded in unifying a varied group of people, in far-flung operations, around a common goal and vision. This reading of the data neglects the means of pressure, which we have just indicated, exerted by the organization to obtain conformity of thought, the functions of social conformity for avoiding social conflict and negotiation, as well as its psychological cost for individuals, as will become apparent further on in this discussion.

The personnel policies are strictly consistent with the ideology described. They are planned to comfort the believers' beliefs. "These are not mere words; the policies are applied," as one TLTXian reports. And they truly are. Their applicability strengthens their symbolic value as tests of the veracity of the organizational discourse. Although of no practical bearing for loyal TLTXians, a rule such as the right of appeal, to one's boss and on up the hierarchy, has a symbolic meaning because one knows it would be observed if set into motion.

Ambiguity is embedded in all personnel policies, which always present a dual face, one which is controlling-demanding while also being a benevolent-helping one. The evaluation-counseling interview, a fundamental personnel practice, exemplifies this uncertainty. The psychodramas that we organized, with the TLTX staff acting out some of these procedures in their ambiguous portrayal of the manager, unchained the uncontrollable laughter of the participants as a result of underlying contradictions and conflicts being brought to the fore through the play.

The consequences of such personnel policies overflow to the personal relationships of the employees. For example, an executive had made a long monologue describing his fear of his most dangerous rival. In response to my question, "On what terms are you with him?" he told me, "He is my best friend; we go on vacation together." For the TLTXian, the frontiers between friend and enemy, public and private life, trust and distrust, truth and lie, reality and illusion, inner and outer reality, have all become blurred. TLTXians have been obligated to learn, as Orwell envisioned, double or triple discourse, thereby confusing themselves regarding their loyalties.

Mediation Processes

The concept of *mediation*, which I developed in the research, proved useful to interpret these various social phenomena. It designates the processes used to prevent contradictions from turning into overt conflicts. The term *contradiction* is used here in the Marxist sense of the word to refer to class and status struggles, as well as other struggles, like national ones, which may bear a relationship with the former.

The basic logic of mediation is to *mix* the demands exerted by the organization on the individual with a whole gamut of advantages, both material (for example, salary, security, upward mobility, and so on) and psychosocial (status, meaning, power, initiative, and so forth). This is different from the classical relationship of the old capitalistic firm where the advantages, the "pleasant" things, are there on one side, and clearly distinct from the "unpleasant" ones, such as the duration of work, fatigue, and submission to superiors. In this utilitarian arrangement, individuals can balance the two and choose to remain or exit. Obviously, some people are freer than others in this utilitarian exchange, as has often been said. However, it is true that in this functioning individuals are more or less able to maintain their psychological integrity.

This is much less true in the hypermodern organization, where mediation processes are at their peak. Here the unpleasant takes on a pleasant look, and one can hardly separate one from the other. One works harder than in most places, but for a high salary. One must follow innumerable rules, but one is expected to interpret them and even to create new ones. One is oppressed but one has the right to speak up to anyone in the firm. One is little and insignificant alone but one belongs to one of the largest organizations in the world. When I asked the TLTXians, who participated in our group laboratory research experience, what they liked best in their work, a maintenance engineer replied that it was being called one Sunday morning for an urgent repair job. He said, "You must understand. I'm the only one working in the neighborhood, the only one who can do the job. I'm the TLTX man." His was by no means an isolated view. "We're all masochists," said another TLTXian.

The Hypermodern Organization

The concept of mediation is an important addition to Marxist theory. Through it we can better understand the change in the system of control. There has been a shift from the readily observable economic utilitarian pressure and authoritarian coercion of the classical capitalist firm to more refined and subtle means in the *hypermodern organization*.

These hypermodern means are more sophisticated and rely on economic, political, and ideological mediation processes, as well as on psychological seduction. I have just described the former in the preceding sections of this chapter, and I will come to psychological aspects in the following section. The general meaning of all these changes is a shift from direct to indirect control.

These changes in the system of control, which in the Marxist theory would be referred to as referring to the *productive relationships*, accompany fundamental changes in the technology and personnel, the *productive forces* in Marxist terms. Technology is complex; it implies the cooperation of thousands of workers and hundreds of professions; it is ever-changing. It

Illusion and Disillusion of Appreciative Management

requires highly skilled personnel, motivated by their work, capable of initiative and cooperation. The changes in the system of control are made necessary by these qualitative changes of technology and personnel. A system of government of vast multitudes of people must be invented, which enhances their capacity of producing "freely," indispensable under the new conditions of production, and at the same time maintains an overall control of their action within the objectives of capitalistic development (for example, profit and market expansion).

Thus our hypothesis on the hypermodern can be reformulated as stating that, in present times, significant and qualitative changes in the productive forces (technology, personnel) are leading to qualitative changes of the productive relationships—that is, means of controlling and governing organizations. It is this set of interacting changes that mark the entry into the *hypermodern era*. This term means that a revolution is shaking the capitalistic world, which affects simultaneously the various segments of economic, social, and psychological life.

While we focus on organizations, we should also recognize that organizational phenomena are fused with broader, larger-scale social phenomena, such as changes in the political and communication systems, in social values, and the like. The hypermodern organization overlaps with the hypermodern era. These terms should not be reified, however, and taken to describe pure types, to be observed as such in society. They are Ideal types in the Weberian sense, to be used as tools of scientific analysis of modern society. They point to trends of evolution. Real organizations can be more or less hypermodern, and they often present various states of compromise between hypermodernism and more traditional capitalism.

If we follow this reasoning, the contradictions are not directly observable phenomena, as was the case in the classical exploitation of the working class by nineteenth-century firms, for example. In the hypermodern organization, the contradictions are hypothetical constructs, with the observable consequences being mediation. But then, why do we keep speaking of contradictions? Why not simply acknowledge and accept the dissolution of such "classical" conflicts in modern organizations?

Are we merely paying our respects to an obsolete system of Marxist thought?

I think not. I believe the hypermodern organization, by creating such elaborate means of mediation, demonstrates that its basic concern is the elimination of conflict. It is thus legitimate to maintain underlying conflict—that is, contradiction—as a basic concept for the analysis of organizations.

As evidence that avoidance of conflict is of critical importance to the hypermodern organization, I cite the following example that was reported to me. In a staff training conference in Sweden, a participant raised a minor question concerning one of TLTX's policies, to which the trainer was unable to respond. The president of the subsidiary, who was also present, returned home and reflected on the matter after the conference. Although he was not responsible for Sweden nor the issue discussed, he thought it was important, and he wrote to the European headquarters. He entered into a dialogue with them concerning the probability of such a question being asked by executives of the age and profession of the individual who originally asked the question. After very extensive correspondence, a rule was issued as an addition to the training manual providing the appropriate answer to the type of question originally raised during the conference in Sweden. Apparently, nobody thought to directly contact the Swedish engineer, nor to provide a list of competent people to whom future questions could be directed. This incident, although it may seem to have been a caricature, did in fact take place and is illustrative of the *anticipatory* character of the hypermodern organization's avoidance of conflict. Direct conflict, overt opposition and negotiation, are the abhorred Evils, and are not even to be mentioned but rather anticipated so that they can be avoided. Defense against conflicts of all kinds is a hallmark of the hypermodern organization. This could be called a *society of solicitude,* where the claimed and often practiced attention to people's needs masks a profound discomfort and fear of differences and conflicts.

Organization and mediation are related concepts. The old capitalistic world—of frontal opposition between capitalists wearing top hats and workers in work clothes—knows no organizations, only firms. The organization emerges out of this world as a huge system of interconnected mediations of all kinds, aimed at preventing and attenuating all sorts of conflicts.

Further, the executives themselves can be viewed as agents of mediation. Their functions can be interpreted as basically mediating internal and external conflicts. When the process is completed, the executives have absorbed both ends of the continuum: the workers and the capitalists. Thus, once the logic of mediation has permeated the entire firm, what evolves is this smooth, round object—the seemingly conflict-free hypermodern organization—where all are cared for and controlled, consciously and unconsciously, devoid of class, ethnic, and other meaningful group struggles. What was simply a firm has then truly become an Organization.

Unconscious Processes

The central hypothesis of this research concerns the evolution of the interaction between these sociological mediation processes and psychological unconscious processes in the hypermodern organization. For example, superiors traditionally are the object of both conscious and unconscious concerns of employees. Yet, bosses seem to be of very minor importance in the minds of TLTX employees. This decreased psychological importance given to superiors by subordinates is a reflection of the reality of the work milieu. The potentatelike bosses of yesterday have been supplanted by more modest TLTX rule interpreters. At the psychological conscious-unconscious levels *the organization seems to have replaced the boss as the major invested object* of TLTXians. For many TLTXians, the organization has become the target of passionate and ambivalent love-hate, as shown in the following remarks, chosen among many others: "I can say I love TLTX as much as I hate it," or "I'm a part of TLTX as it is a part of me," or finally, "TLTX is a sort of drug I cannot do without."

Such comments were interesting. While much of the accepted organizational discourse and theory would lead us to expect a rise in rationality, following the now obsolete world of paternalistic dependency on bosses, we were confronted with new unconscious phenomena. Underneath rational arguments regarding the advantages offered by the organization, such as power, benefits, and so forth, it became clear to us that an unconscious imaginary figure was at work. It was described as an omnipotent entity, capable of giving and destroying life. Some participants at the research seminar made a drawing on the theme, "me and the organization," which depicted a tiny person standing on an endless stairway. When the group was asked to creatively represent the organization with symbols, they chose images of death, masks of corpses, Nazi slogans, and the like (the reader is reminded that this was a group of "normal" executives, by no means revolutionary!). In an interview, a person compared TLTX to a school of fish where "when a small fish strays, it dies."

In contrast to the boss, in psychoanalytic terms the previously expected focus of one's transference among professionals, the new image is (1) *impersonal* versus personal; it is an entity (that is, the organization or its philosophy) and no longer a person; and (2) it evokes *maternal* rather than paternal conflicts. This new unconscious figure mobilizes more conflicts linked with archaic mother-child relationships than Oedipal ones. The latter stimulates ambivalent relationships with bosses as substitute fathers, identification wishes to them, rivalries with peers, and so on. The basic anxiety at work underneath is castration anxiety. In contrast, in the hypermodern world the basic anxiety is separation anxiety from an entity that is contradictorily felt as life-giving, nourishing, on the one hand, and destroying, suffocating, on the other. One feels a permanent wish to be separated from it, as well as the impossibility of this separation since, once separated, one dies. This accounts for the permanent "dream" expressed by many TLTXians to leave TLTX. TLTXians feel a profound longing for the security of being part of something omnipotent, yet they feel imprisoned by it and want to be separated. But it is an impossible wish since it implies their metaphorical "death" in terms of status, benefits, and above all psychological identity. The dream reflects the dilemma of these irreconcilable conflicts lived by people who feel psychically and

Illusion and Disillusion of Appreciative Management   367

materially imprisoned by TLTX. This pattern looks very much like a "Kleinian" mother-baby relationship, albeit with the expected differences between individuals in the intensity experienced of such a relationship.

It is interesting to note the contrast between the regressive character of the maternal image in the unconscious pattern just mentioned and the sophisticated rationality of the organization and of the conscious functioning and efficacy of its members. Had our primary concern in our research been rationality and efficacy leading to strong economic performance, we might have arrived at conclusions different than the sociopsychic mechanisms described thus far. We might have used terms such as *strong corporate culture* or *high-performing organization,* but what we saw, heard, and experienced in our interviews, and in the psychodrama and laboratory experience, was sociopsychic oppression of a subtle nature that caused TLTXians to suffer psychologically.

This psychological suffering was masked by unconscious defenses against aggression and anxiety used to construct this unconscious object: TLTX as the substitute of an archaic love object. The TLTXian defense system was characterized by repression and denial of aggression and anxiety, idealization, and above all projective identification with the felt aggressor, TLTX. The main defense against fear and aggression provoked by working in TLTX resided in idealizing the organization and identifying with it, with its "good" values of service, excellence, and care for TLTXians, and with its power.

Thus, the system of the hypermodern organization is reinforced externally and internally. Externally, the real organization exerting its power and dominance over the individual provokes fear and aggression. This precipitates the internal defense systems of individuals and the construction of the idealized object (that is, TLTX), with which the TLTXians identify, thereby subsuming their identity in that of the organization. But this object also finds strong and constant support in the real organization itself, which mediates its internal conflicts in producing an image of itself as a seductive and lovable object.

The imaginary *ideal organization* is, so to speak, sociomentally constructed, in terms of the social functioning and the intrapsychic processes of TLTXians. Mediation processes against social conflicts are extended and linked to individual processes of defense against unconscious conflicts.

Thus the organization reproduces itself by producing individuals capable of producing it, dialectically. This process is one example of what I have labeled a sociomental system:

Real Organization   *Ideal Organization*
Mediation processes ⟷ Defense processes
Social contradictions ⟷ Psychological conflict
Dialectical Relationship

The Process of Professionalization

It is this notion of *sociomental systems* that the preceding reflections have led me to propose. It expands Eric Trist's famous notion of the sociotechnical system. The sociomental systems approach to organizational analysis spans the technological, economic, political, ideological, and psychological dimensions of a given system and analyzes the linkages between these varied components. This method of analysis places heavy emphasis on the horizontal linkages between the components to better understand creation and change within the system. The hypermodern organization in this sense is understood as a particular sociomental system, a new organizational form, defined by related major changes occurring along the various dimensions listed above.

One of the important changes is the shift of emphasis from the technical-economic to the political-ideological-psychological aspects of work. Work then becomes more and more a matter of ideas, desires, self— and group—realization, a process I call *professionalization*. But this in turn shifts conflicts within the organization toward these spheres. *The main battles within modern organizations are fought over professionalization itself. They concern not so much salary, conditions of work, or material needs, as ideas, plans, dreams, and wishes. They also use these as main weapons. Direct exploitation and alienation tend to be replaced by ideological and psychological struggle and manipulation.*

In this perspective, management theory, including organizational science, is seen as part of the hypermodern organizational system. Its contributions reflect the changes described earlier. But its authors may be seen more as inner agents of the system—among its most powerful ones—than as external analysts. They have internalized the methods by which the hypermodern organizations mask their own functioning, which they help shape and rationalize, providing the structure of a new discourse of and in organizations. I would submit that this discourse accept a critical analysis following a dialectical approach of the sort I have suggested.

Professional Stress

It was with this background of study of the hypermodern organization and "professionalization" that I joined a group of colleagues in a preliminary investigation of professional stress conducted in various organizations in France. We attempted to complement the American studies in terms of "factors" of stress, which already showed the interaction of social, organizational, and individual dimensions, to create an expanded dynamic model. Our research showed the central role played by professional *illusion* and *disillusion* in the genesis of stress, and how they resulted from a complex of interrelated social and psychological processes. I will describe these briefly, beginning with a case history of Mr. L.

The Case of Mr. L. As in all cases, the case of Mr. L. is difficult to summarize. At first glance, it appears to be a straightforward case of depression as a result of job dequalification.

Mr. L. works for a training and consulting association (that is, the Association). It was founded as a support organization to an employer's federation of banks (that is, the Federation). Then, three years prior to our seeing Mr. L., the Association was deemed as no longer necessary, due to a change in policy of the Federation. Consequently, its employees were progressively reintegrated into the Federation, with the legal status of the Association, as a separate entity, being maintained during the transition period.

Mr. L. is the last one to appear on the Association payroll. His job as a technician in visual aids, including films, has deteriorated in status from the "noble" (his word) task of helping directors make films to merely administrative ones.

During this time, Mr. L. starts having severe anxiety crises, usually during holidays. After a medical examination and hospitalization, it is determined that there is no discernible physical disorder. He has been receiving psychiatric help, in the form of medication and regular interviews, since then but has not recovered. Furthermore, he is skeptical about his ability to ever recover. His job-related performance has declined and his prospects outside of his present employment are poor. Beyond this rather dry résumé, I will now attempt a sociomental analysis of the case, bringing in relevant data on the organizational environment of Mr. L. and of its individual history.

Taking the social side first, we learned, through interviews with Mr. L. and his colleagues at the Association, about the conditions of the creation and subsequent closing of the Association.

The Association was created by a top executive of the Federation who initially staffed it with Federation volunteers, from both the executive and nonexecutive, but salaried, levels. The legal structure of the Association provided for significant policy making participation by the Association's clients, the individual banks of the Federation, with these banks having representation on the Association's board. (The 1901 French law, on which the Federation based its creation of the Association, is to be used to structure educational, cultural, religious, and other noneconomic, nonprofit, socially responsive activities. However, these associations are often used to camouflage situations which may actually be profit oriented. In that case the socially responsive structure and goals of the Association function as an ideological cover for other goals, such as profit, power, and so on.) This related to a desire of the Federation to rejuvenate the cooperative spirit present when it was created and to help member banks rise above the prevailing commercial perception they maintained of it. Association employees enthusiastically adopted this renewed spirit of collaboration, describing themselves as "militants," and developed a strong feeling of ownership and pride in their jobs.

Illusion and Disillusion of Appreciative Management 371

Given the zeal of the employees, the Federation's decision to phase out the Association was met with violent anger, bitterness, and/or despair. Their unanimously held view of the reasons leading to the Association's closure was one of rivalry between the directors, with the director of the Association losing to his counterpart at the Federation. Yet, they saw the apparent rivalry as camouflaged by the organization under the guise of a policy change. The audit, which the Federation ordered of the Association, was seen by the Association personnel as predetermined in advance. Mr. L. revealed in his interview that it was at this time that he had his first crisis.

Moreover, as a result of this phaseout, the Association personnel came to discover the emptiness and meaninglessness of their work in this organization. They claimed serious policies were abandoned for no apparent motive with new ones imposed on the spot. They saw the espoused professionalism, the motto of the Federation, as a mere facade. The real objective was merely pleasing: pleasing the hierarchy, which wants to please the president, who wants to please political or other influential authorities. Internally, "hype" became the currency, in the form of trendy, fashionable ideas. The star employees were doted on. The respondents described the organization and its stakeholders in the environment as a vast and complex network where good (and bad!) self-images were reflected and exchanged in mirrors. The organization had become a *large market of social recognition*. Production of services, the official work of the Federation and Association, had vanished as a real target, or rather was used as a smokescreen for the real terms of exchange.

These comments reminded me of Baudrillard's (1972) ideas of economics undergoing transformation from production of goods and services into a market of signs. The term *narcissistic exploitation* came to my mind. The system described by the interviewees was not one of traditional exploitation of the energy and skills with which employees serve but rather, directed at the very essence and core of their professional lives, exploitation of one's commitment to values and beliefs. This commitment, at the ideological level of values and beliefs, was not used for economic gain or for power, but rather for the magnification of the self-image of others, "other-aggrandizement" if you will. It is as though each worker were used as a narcissistic mirror for the others in a collusive manner.

The preceding remarks point to the central role of ideology in the hypermodern organization. Professional values are used as ideological traps to obfuscate the social contradictions permeating the organization. Various mechanisms of denial reinforce these ideological traps such as the following: ambiguity of the power structure; double discourse, with its variance between real and espoused meaning; nonauthoritarian leadership used as a means of protecting the leader, and so forth. I have labeled all this—the ideological content and the denial mechanisms—as the sociological process of "ideologization."

Ideologization, a social process, results in mobilizing the individual's *Ideals,* as they were built in his or her psychological inner life. It encourages idealization, a mechanism through which Ideals cleave themselves from reality. It thus has momentous repercussions for the person's level of commitment to his or her task, or pleasure, professional and personal relationships, and so on. It exacerbates the person's vulnerability.

Symmetrically we could name *de-ideologization* the processes through which the organization loses momentarily or durably its capacity to cover its contradictions, which then appear nakedly revealed. De-ideologization leads to de-idealization and disillusion. The case of the Association is clearly a case of brutal de-ideologization.

But what about the role of the individual in this process? Among the personnel of the Association, only the director and Mr. L. went through depression. The others, including one of Mr. L.'s brothers, were very upset, but they demonstrated no specific pathology and were able to adjust to the new work conditions. Some clarification lies in Mr. L.'s interview.

His is a long history of conflict with an authoritarian father (the mother being described as a weak figure), complete with a background of submission, impotent revolt, and humiliation. The child repeatedly enacts behaviors of failure through a humiliation-provocation-punishment-humiliation cycle. For example, feeling humiliated by bad grades at school, he tears up the

Illusion and Disillusion of Appreciative Management 373

report card, which he is obligated to show to his parents, but hides it where it can be found. After the inevitable punishment by his father, he then responds by being truant from school for eight days, in perfect ecstasy during the day, but torn by anxiety while back home. Finally, the whole thing explodes and he is deprived of his holidays.

Mr. L.'s dreams and fantasies play an important role, but not on the creative side because they do not lead to sustained action. Instead, they function as defenses against inner and outer threats and conflicts, as well as expressions of impotent revolt.

As a young man, Mr. L. wants to go to art school to study that which appeals to him. However, his father blocks his application and instead compels him to enter the Federation, where he himself is a senior executive, specializing in computerized information systems. Mr. L. experiences his first job as tension provoking with ensuing fatigue.

When the Association is founded, he voluntarily applies, attracted by its "noble" (that is, noncommercial, professional, democratic) values, and, moreover, by the position's artistic side, also seen as "noble." He fully invests himself in his job and the Association and, prior to the Association's crisis, seems to be reasonably happy and successful, in spite of conflicts with the director, whom he admires, fears, and fights, in an ambivalent relationship, repetitious of the one with his father.

Without indulging in gratuitous or superficial psychoanalytic interpretation, one could advance the hypothesis of a fragile sublimation process. Castration fears have not been adequately coped with, resulting in his aggression being incorporated into social goals. The "noble" ideals, divorced from reality, entertain to some extent the permanent struggle with authority. Failure to self-actualize through these ideals results in Mr. L. feeling persecuted. This revives his fantasies of castration-destruction-death that had never been worked through, of which there are numerous indications in his descriptions of his crises, but which are too lengthy to report here.

The loss of the privileged relationship with his boss, even though it had been difficult and conflictual, probably acted as a determining element in Mr. L.'s pathology. Conflict and punishment by authority figures, in like manner as his relationship with his father, functioned as a defense against Mr. L.'s deeper anxieties. The actual experience of punishment protects Mr. L. against unconscious fantasies of castration.

His illness renders Mr. L. dependent in many ways: on his psychiatrist (a woman), on the firm, on social security, all figures more or less associated with the mother image. He feels humiliated by having regressed to a childlike dependency. Unconsciously, he lives his illness as enacted castration. This is a new motive for grief against authority and the organization. Admitting that he is sick and in need of help is felt as capitulation to the enemy. Furthermore, in his present state, Mr. L. encounters another, more archaic, stratum of conflicts relating to the mother figure in the form of deep feelings of abandonment, distrust, and anger. Thus, his illness, as is often the case, is completely incorporated into his neurosis, which results in strong resistance to healing.

This history and personality structure help explain both Mr. L.'s initial excitement in, and commitment to, the Association and his job, as well as his subsequent breakdown. It is a story of illusion and disillusion, of the mobilization in the workplace of inner idealized structures, and of their incapacity to sustain reality when the environment changed. But the role of the environment is equally important as a stimulus of both illusion and disillusion. It is this dialectic that I will now explore.

A Tentative Model of Professional Stress

On the basis of the preceding, let us now develop some of the components of a theoretical model of professional stress, which I believe will be useful for the analysis of professional stress and the field of psychopathology. These components are the following:

1. Symmetry of social and individual processes
2. Use of idealization and ideologization to block awareness and expression of conflict
3. Two "moments," illusion and disillusion, of the process of stress

Illusion and Disillusion of Appreciative Management 375

4. Professionalization as the set of social and psychological processes used to create workplace ideals
5. The multidimensional causes of pathology

Discussion of each follows.

1. *Symmetry of Social and Individual Processes.* One is struck by how idealization, as a defense mechanism against inner conflicts, corresponds to ideologization as avoidance of social conflicts. One process activates the other which then impacts the first to create a set of interacting processes, as is schematically shown below.

Social level   *Individual level*
Ideologization   ⟵⟶   Idealization

The same relationship applies to the opposite processes:

Social level   *Individual level*
De-ideologization   ⟵⟶   De-idealization

2. *Use of Idealization and Ideologization to Block Awareness and Expression of Conflict.* Conflict avoidance is common to both social and individual level processes. Conflict itself is not pathological per se; rather, it is the impossibility to become aware of, express, and manage it that precipitates pathology. This refers to all levels of conflict: intrapsychic, interpersonal, organizational, and social.

Ideals and illusion are normal and necessary phenomena. They are the foundation for social and individual creativity. My use of the terms *idealization* and *ideologization* refers to defensive and aggressive means by which individuals and social systems use ideals and ideology to indirectly perpetuate unresolved conflict. The result is rigidity and a cleavage from reality, an impossibility to test ideals against reality, other ideals, or destructive fantasies. This is not to say that I offer precise criteria to distinguish between the creative and pathological uses of ideals and illusion. Rather, at this point I simply put it forth as a useful construct in analysis.

Appreciative Management and Leadership

3. Two "Moments," Illusion and Disillusion, of the Process of Stress. In analyzing the process of stress, it is useful to distinguish between the two moments. Herein, the term moment refers to two qualitatively different dimensions of stress and not chronological time.

The moment of *illusion* corresponds to the building up of professional ideals that perform inner and outer defensive functions as a result of the ideologization-idealization mechanisms. The ultimate outcome, fortunately seldom attained, is suppression of any distance between the imaginary and real organization. This is where individuals attribute to the organization the ability to fulfill their fantasies, while the organizational policies and functioning aim at stimulating a fantasy life for individuals adapted for its organizational purpose, as I have shown previously in describing the hypermodern organization. This moment of illusion corresponds to "slight" stress, well contained within the limits of mild pathology, resulting from a typical combination such as the following:

hard work
    + excitement
        + insomnia
            + tranquilizers
                + fatigue . . .

Present in the moment of *disillusion* is "heavy" stress, as manifested in temporary or permanent cessation of work, episodes requiring psychiatric attention, hospitalization, and so forth.

The underlying processes are brutal de-ideologization–de-idealization, here again interacting with one another. A loss of confidence in the organizational ideology following an organizational crisis can have dramatic consequences for those individuals whose inner ideal structures are too fragile to tolerate confrontation with reality. Unconscious fantasies of castration and destruction, which never ceased to loom in the background as a threat, have now unconsciously occurred.

The organization is still seen as a vehicle for the fulfillment of individuals' fantasies but in the moment of disillusion it becomes a threatening source of persecution. Again, the organization is seen as mutually responsible for this state, due to its inability to face conflict, its double discourse, and denial mechanisms.

4. Professionalization as the Set of Social and Psychological Processes Used to Create Workplace Ideals. I define *professsionalization* as the confluence of the whole set of social and psychological processes used to build up people's ideals concerning their work. This is a broader use of the term than the current one, confined to work qualification.

I have defended the thesis that professionalization is becoming one of the central issues in organizations. The more developed are variables such as technology, economic factors, educational level of employees, managerial science and practice, the more crucial professionalization becomes.

Professionalization functions concurrently as a universal objective for modern workers, and as a focus of conflict for each of them and social groups. It is a locus of inner and outer conflicts, the ideological and psychological weapons that are themselves borrowed from professional values (for example, commitment to higher calling, excellence, and so on). Modern or hypermodern conflicts concerning work tend to move from the technological-economic to the ideological-psychological sphere.

A stereotypical model of the "normal" individual, generally accepted by psychologists and psychoanalysts, is a person who has more or less worked through the neurotic conflicts, attained a satisfactory relationship with society and its laws, and built up stable sublimated structures and ideals, thereby becoming capable of social adjustment, as seen in a stable and satisfactory commitment to work. This model is based on the hypothesis of a harmonious, nonconflictual social world.

But conflict is very apparent in the battle for professional achievement that continues on the social scene, following the preliminary fight for self-worth in the family and at the intrapsychic level. Forming professional ideals and practices by no means constitutes a right, a natural condition of any normally socialized individual. Rather, it is a stake in new conflicts, the more or less open social conflicts through which the individual must pass. The process of "professionalization" thus has to be analyzed as a multidimensional one, integrating social and individual dimensions.

5. *The Multidimensional Causes of Pathology.* In this perspective, pathology is viewed as a complex set of phenomena in that it is seen as multidimensional. It cannot be reduced to social or individual determinants, not even to a combination of varying amounts of each. Rather, it must be viewed holistically as the result of interaction of both processes. As we have seen, the ways in which the organization promotes ideals, in order to deny its contradictions, confirm and stimulate the individual idealization process. The organization then becomes a part of the individual's system of defense.

But the corollary and inverse proposition is equally true. Individual projections, idealized images of the organization, as well as negative ones, all constitute essential parts of organizational functioning. They feed the mechanisms through which the organization defends itself against social conflicts. Thus, we become mired in a sociomental system with loops from within and without.

However, this liaison between the social and individual systems is by no means obligatory. Each subsystem, social, organizational, interpersonal, and individual, enjoys what can be termed relative autonomy. Though influenced by the other subsystems, it has its own laws of variation and its own area of autonomy. Each of us knows of isolated examples of health within a poorly functioning organization, due to, for example, a particular group microclimate or the personality of the leader. Sometimes the reverse is true with the organization appearing reasonably healthy, with some of its parts being pathological.

We are not accustomed to thinking in dialectical terms, in terms of interaction or multicausation, which forces us to venture out from the security of hegemonic thought. It is still more difficult to act on a world perceived as a system of interacting, multidimensional factors.

The ideas presented here flow from pure research, with no pretensions being made to offer practical conclusions or treatment of professional stress. And I am not prepared to hastily improvise some. But I am convinced that this perspective could open new forms of action, be they for the manager or personnel director, not to mention the physicians and psychotherapists treating cases of professional stress.

Many of these professions suffer from a linear conception of their work, dominated by one hegemonic theory, one set of criteria. But in practice they often have to articulate and integrate various heterogeneous dimensions, without adequate theoretical resources to do so. A reconsideration of practices, taking into account the complexity of the object and its articulations, may be useful.

Implications for Executive Appreciation

I have been pressed by my colleagues at the symposium to make more explicit my position about executive appreciation. I hesitate to do so because of my lack of practical experience with that approach. I feel some reluctance to express myself on a purely ideological stand. However, my experience of the symposium itself as an appreciative experience has somewhat modified my original attitude.

At the beginning of the chapter I formulated my initial reservations about executive appreciation. I hope the basis for these has become clearer for the reader. I could now reformulate my questioning of executive appreciation in the following way: This approach appears to me clearly as a part of hypermodern functioning. As such it is likely to be used as a means of indirect control of individuals, through avoiding social and individual conflicts. The result is reinforcing organizational and social goals the individuals cannot basically influence.

But hypermodern functioning is not bad or good per se. It reflects the ways struggles and conflicts are taking in contemporaneous life. *In that sense the very weapons that are used by hypermodern organizations to limit individual and group autonomy are the same ones that can be used to enlarge it.* After all, TLTX, a hypermodern organization, was the only one that accepted a study of the kind

I have reported (although it has subsequently tried to hinder me from publishing the results!). More traditional firms were not interested.

I should like to end with a series of questions and a challenge to executive appreciation. How can spaces of trust, free expression, and appreciation be created and expanded within organizations, which would

- augment, rather than limit, expression of individual and group differences and conflicts within the organization?
- strengthen the mutual understanding of these differences and action on the basis of this understanding, including separation from the organization?
- augment, rather than limit, awareness and analysis of the organizational functioning in its social setting?

I was informed of a standard joke in British psychoanalytic circles saying that paranoia is a mental disease very much to be deplored were it not so often objectively justified. Perhaps we should find out the exact amount of paranoia we should maintain as regards executive appreciation.

14

Appreciative Organizing: Implications for Executive Functioning

Suresh Srivastva
Frank J. Barrett

The major premise of this volume is that executive appreciation is what makes good organizing possible. The word *appreciate* originates from the Latin *ad + pretium*, which means to "place a value on." When we place a value on something, we make a statement of preference in regard to its significance, its status within a horizon of objects to which we compare it in order to determine its importance. The implication here is that when one "appreciates," one is engaged both in an active comparison and an active selection. Something is chosen as worthy of notice from a myriad of other objects competing for attention.

There is also an *anticipatory element to the appreciative process*. Because I anticipate something of future value, I am ready to see the relevant details, the exquisite features in the present. The story that I imagine myself participating in—that is, the future I anticipate—determines what I see in the present, what I know about a given object now.

In this sense there is a strong connection between what I value and what I know. Further, all understanding involves the dialogical interaction between the person and the cultural setting. This is the spirit Gadamer (1975) was after when he wrote of the dialogical nature of knowledge embodied in his metaphor of knowledge as the encounter of subject + artwork. Imagine if one were to enter an art museum and encounter a painting with the name *van Gogh* on it. One would no doubt immediately *anticipate* an unusual degree of beauty, coherence, and precision. One would take time to notice the exquisite details, the expressions of passionate vision. However, if the same painting had the name *J. B. Smith* printed beneath it, one would most likely not approach the painting with the same anticipation and wonder and would not notice as much detail in the work. Anticipating, expecting, projecting, and believing make knowledge and understanding possible. I *know* more about the painting (the world) if I anticipate that it can reveal something meaningful. Conversely, if I approach this object with no sense of anticipatory awe or wonder and instead stay on "automatic pilot," perceiving and processing information, projecting meaning in the same automatic mode in which I ate my breakfast, filled my car with gas, cut the lawn, and kissed my spouse, I am unlikely to see anything new or significant in this painting, to achieve any new awareness. Or to use Heidegger's (1962) language, in such a mental mode the world will not "reveal itself" to me unless I anticipate its meaningfulness.

Where do these anticipatory musings originate? Where do I learn to approach this painting marked *van Gogh* with a sense of awe and anticipatory beauty? Surely I was not born with this awareness. It is through interaction within the wider culture that I learn to expect, project, and value. Within the horizon of the current culture, *van Gogh* has many prestigious connotations and reverberations. The society in which I live has led me to associate beautiful, ingenious creations with the name *van Gogh*. The group's horizon of possible scripts primes its members' expectations.

If we begin to think of the appreciative process this way, we begin to widen our scope to notice how prevalent this active (although largely nonconscious) selection is in the course of human affairs, how cultural contexts trigger us to notice and select certain objects, people, events as having value. This is the sense in which Sir Geoffrey Vickers (1968) referred to "appreciative systems." The appreciative system of a culture refers to the group's system of values, beliefs, and expectations that guides the culture's perception and actions. It "resides not in

Appreciative Organizing 383

a particular set of images, but in a *readiness* to see and value and respond to its situation in a certain way" (Vickers, 1968, p. 50). The appreciative system of a culture is usually latent, but it is manifest in the tendency to make judgments about selective aspects of the world and evaluate them in terms of selected values. It depends on the appreciator's current state of readiness to perceive situations, and again this involves the way we approach the event with the anticipation of something meaningful about to happen: "In any field in which men function, the relevant facts and forces include not only what is happening but also what men think is going to happen; not only what they are doing to each other, but also what they expect, hope, fear, from each other and themselves" (Vickers, 1968, p. 56). Thus a culture's linguistic categories and evaluations are related to what is anticipated in the future.

Expansive, optimistic cultural scripts have a contagious, creative effect also. Consider, for example, President Kennedy's 1961 speech to Congress in which he announced that the United States would have a person on the moon by the end of the decade (Erhard, 1982). It is difficult now to imagine the outrageous nature of such an intention. Many cynics and skeptics were convinced of the impossibility of such a plan. As scientists and technologists argued about the proper kind of metal or energy necessary to accomplish this, this fictional script was being implanted in people's minds. The idea and the anticipation that it is possible to put a person on the moon in ten years was contagious and within this context, research and development progressed. President Kennedy's initiative helped to create an entirely new social and intellectual context that ignited the conversations and debates which made technological and intellectual breakthroughs possible. He held out a possibility that based on all past achievements up to that point was highly improbable if not impossible. As scientists debated the prospect of the idea, they were beginning to *unfreeze the existing language and expectations concerning what was deemed possible.* Even those who disagreed were participating in conversations about "humans on the moon" and had to hold the image up in their minds in order to debate it. They were expanding the horizon of possible knowledge by considering mental trials, playing out imaginative scenarios, creating a new language that became a context for action. It was within this metaphorical domain of what a moon landing might look like if it could ever really happen that scientists began to form the calculus for action, the technological and metallurgical experiments that would eventually work.

The idea of "person on the moon" formed an anticipatory script, began to expand the range of possible action for many participants. A new collective appreciative schema emerged that unfroze existing language and habits. An old script called "it is impossible to do" began to thaw. A new series of "scientific actions" began to have value. Different experiments and different qualities of metals and energy that once seemed irrelevant were now noticed and valued. Further, this script became the opportunity for people to invest the best of their life energy. Scientists were called on to think beyond their previous accomplishments, to stretch outward for a larger purpose. For many who participated, this period was a peak experience: engineers "overcoming insurmountable odds" to fight for and realize technological visions (Murray and Cox, 1989). If the old script of impossibility had been kept in place, countless scientists and engineers would never have had the opportunity to experience their brilliance and creativity.

The philosopher's task is really the task of every human being—to notice and admire the wonders, to marvel at the ineffable mysteries on this planet. The ancient Greeks probably knew this better than we. Their sense of the "good life" was held up as an ideal for much of their activity in everyday affairs. The "good life" was the life of active wonderment—one in which humans stop to wonder, to marvel in awe at the world's beauty, to appreciate the miracles of the Greek sky, to discuss the beauty and harmony of the just society, and to stand in fearful dread of the unpredictable power of the immortals who could seemingly wreak havoc among mortals at whim. They knew, as every poet knows, that to stand in wonder toward the world is to open oneself, to make oneself defenseless and vulnerable before the world, to experience both fascination and dread, admiration and puzzlement, mobilization and paralysis. They were suspicious

Appreciative Organizing

of the seductions of furious activity and high velocity that, in the absence of a watchful internal eye, could draw the protagonist off center and indulge him or her in excess. The fall of most tragic figures in Greek literature was related to just that—a failure to stop to contemplate, to withdraw from the field of activity in search of something meaningful and larger than self.

This capacity to ponder in this way, to leave the world of appearances in search of something more, is not only a uniquely human endeavor but a human imperative. The human animal has no choice but to bring a conviction of meaning to the world. This is the sense in which Hannah Arendt (1969) saw the process of thinking as synonymous with living fully. Arendt's study of fascism and totalitarianism left her puzzled about how humans could render such evil in the world. Her conclusion is that no human *wants* to do evil. The real culprit is nonthinking behavior, people's willingness to "hold fast to prescribed rules of conduct." The failure to awarely (thinkingly) adopt a meaningful and life-enhancing concept, dream, or fiction is at the root of all mindless, alienated, and ultimately evil human activity.

What we see, know, and experience in the world is largely a manifestation of a future script that we imagine. We are cognitively attuned to the present world depending on the values, beliefs, and cultural fictions we hold. Put simply, if one imagines a future of gloom and doom, one's life in the present will be gloomy. If one approaches the future with optimism and hope, the present appears more promising. If one's range of action is the present, one's possible actions for attaining worth and meaning are limited by the scope of the latent guiding fiction one has inherited and enacts, then the more expansive the horizon of the anticipated future script, the greater the range of creative, meaningful action at one's disposal. If we can consciously change the script we imagine for the future, then if we anticipate a positive, fulfilling future, we will begin to live that script now. These scripts are to a great extent a social-cultural accomplishment. This latent, nonconscious element of a culture can become conscious. Within organizations, members can deliberately create values, fictional scripts, and anticipations. The more that organization members become aware of its value-creation potential and fiction-making powers, the more open members become for life-enhancing judgments and creative action. This is why perhaps the most important task of a leader is to become attuned to the future scripts members have in their heads and perhaps the most potent creative act is to alter the collective anticipatory fiction perpetuated by the organization's culture; to expand members' vision of their future to become optimistic, holistic, and facilitative, to help people reframe scripts and see possibilities where they once foresaw hindrances.

The Appreciative Organization

What this volume is calling for is a transformation that leads to the creation of a fiction of sorts, the continual proposal and reproposal of a set of expectations that allow us to experience new possibilities in the world and in ourselves. *We need to enable a script to emerge that enhances the potential for creative, fresh human action toward a life-enhancing purpose. This is a call to enliven the unconstricted capacity to make expansive choices and to relate to objects and persons in the world fully and meaningfully rather than on the basis of habitual and shallow, automatic patterns, the fleeting sensations that so easily operate in nonreflective managerial cultures.* Such expansive cultural movements begin with small, vulnerable mental gestures that operate like time bombs in the future. This notion that we can *consciously choose* the appreciative schema, the context that guides human knowledge, the breakthroughs that make creative action possible, is one of the most powerful and underacknowledged capacities at our disposal. We can decide what we will know. We can decide what we will experience. We can decide how we want to live. What if organizations become aware of this metacognitive, appreciative capacity to create the world that is then experienced as real? If such an organization were to emerge, what would it look like? We contend that it is possible to design organizations with this in mind—that we can consciously create life-enhancing anticipatory scripts that bring out the best in members. We would like to set out a few of the dimensions of what such an appreciative organization would look like.

Mission of Purpose. The human animal, as Paul Tillich (1952) knew so well, needs to know that in some way his or her life makes a difference, that he or she is making a positive contribution toward some higher purpose. Humans need a higher purpose and sense of unity that calls on their best energies. In the course of human history, having an enemy has usually served to galvanize groups into feeling they are contributing to a higher purpose. Despite the travesties of war, veterans sometimes refer to their war experience as "the best time of my life," a time when they felt unswerving commitment to a worthy, meaningful cause that made them call on that latent, inner reserve. These are commitments based on painful emotion channeled toward targeting some enemy. Often the battlefield language of strategic planning reflects a similar danger of siege mentality. Members of teams often have fondest memories of moments when they were in a crisis, meeting a deadline, competing with an opponent. Organizational structures and task forces reflect this thinking, often organized around imagined battle lines. These examples serve to illustrate the innate human readiness to *belong* to a group dedicated to a meaningful cause.

Most humans are asking for the opportunity to participate in creating a better world, in contributing to a higher purpose, to invest their personal power in a way that brings out the best that is in them. All employees at Disneyland, for example, are told that their purpose is to make people happy (Peters and Waterman, 1982). Extensive training time is taken to demonstrate to those doing seemingly trivial and demeaning jobs like running rides or cleaning up trash that they are contributing to *making people happy*. In this sense, their jobs really are not trivial. They are encouraged by the surrounding culture to see that their small, micro acts are, in fact, contributions to a large overarching purpose—to enhance the quality of human life. There is a playfulness in their acts, a sense of suspended animation in which they are liberated from all rational constrictions and "play out" a fantasy script of "never-never land" and "tomorrow land" in order to bring others enjoyment. Again, when one feels one's acts are contributing to a worthy purpose, it is natural to bring conviction and meaning to one's gestures.

There is an innate readiness in us to collectively bond to make a contribution to something and to contribute our highest selves. Humans are waiting for the opportunity to contribute to something meaningful and purposeful, to participate in a drama of contribution, seeing and playing out the unfolding of collective creation. Humans are yearning to belong to a collective cause worth investing the best of their energy.

The appreciative organization continually holds up the authentic, essential purpose of members' acts. A sanitation worker does not clean floors because some cranky, irate boss might get angry if he or she does not do so. Floors need to be cleaned in order to create a safe, healthy environment. In this sense every task assumes significance.

Creating Generative Distinctions. In the appreciative organization, members remain aware of the *power of words,* the capacity for conversations to create categories and distinctions that have consequences for the way members experience the world. Especially those expressions that have become automatic and taken for granted receive the scrutiny of the appreciative eye. Through generative conversations, members become aware that distinctions once made commit speakers to a whole series of implications. The distinction employer-employee, for example, begins to unconsciously limit the range of action members can enact in relation to one another. By labeling another member *subordinate,* I begin to limit the range of competent behaviors I allow myself to see. I may unconsciously impose a whole series of limiting assumptions—that supervisors "have" better qualities, that subordinates "have" less learning capacity, and so on. One who learns to think of himself or herself as a "subordinate" may feel the urge to act "subordinatelike" and leave the thinking and planning to those called leaders. Similarly, those labeled *bosses* may feel a pull to act "bosslike," perhaps adapt a sense that it is appropriate to be more detached and authoritative in relation to subordinates. They may feel the urge to look and act like they are in charge even though they feel vulnerable and uncertain. The appreciative organization is aware that these seemingly innocuous labels cue well-ingrained scripts in this culture and have unintended and potentially insidious consequences.

Appreciative Organizing

Referring to developing countries as the "Third World," for example, is a form of status degradation and again, this label can have insidious consequences. Unconsciously one begins to see "Third World citizens" as less capable, less gifted, less intelligent than the progressive nations who by implication are members of a superior "First World" or "Second World." The appreciative organization deliberately creates language that enhances the capacity to see the fullness and integrity of the other. Labels that assign subordinate status or leave one feeling helpless and unable or unwilling to act are replaced with more generative language.

One organization we work with had been having trouble with employee morale and turnover. After extensive scrutiny, they realized that their performance appraisal process was creating unintended consequences—members were being evaluated, promoted, and granted raises based on an antiquated inventory of characteristics. Further, many members were feeling it was a punishing process. Managers had been avoiding and sometimes ignoring the performance appraisal mechanism. The leaders of the organization needed to create a more generative script for the process. First, they changed the title to *performance development* to emphasize the goal of ongoing learning and development. Rather than the manager evaluating the subordinate, rather than evaluations, associates use the process to send performance "messages," informing each other of work areas that are going well or that need to be changed. Associates are asked to give each other feedback around specific categories that call attention not to isolated and obedient behavior, but to independent thinking, cooperation, and leaderlike behavior. The previous form asked managers to give employees feedback around categories like attendance, neatness, appearance, and so on. They realized that these categories of evaluation had a subordinating and punishing effect. After spending ten months in planning sessions, they devised a form that called for more generative distinctions—that is, they highlighted, and therefore furthered the potential for, expansive and growthful behavior. The word *employee* was eliminated and members were now encouraged to give reciprocal performance messages. The new form included elements such as the following:

- Member conveys a positive outlook when discussing problems. Does not focus on blaming others when searching for solutions.
- Courage to experiment. Member is willing to try new tasks and new behaviors even if they do not feel comfortable. Behavior is not controlled by fear (for example, fear of making mistakes), but by a desire to grow and develop.

Expansive Promises. So often work life is spent inside small, unimaginative spaces reworking old issues that were not interesting the first time they were addressed. Members often decide to choose to address only those problems that are familiar and that they know they can solve because they have done so in the past. This is reminiscent of the story of the drunkard searching under a street lamp for his house key that he had dropped some distance away. When he was asked why he doesn't look where he had dropped it, he replied, "The light is better here!" Too many human initiatives in the workplace are similar to the drunkard's search.

The appreciative organization consciously and carefully empowers members' expansive potential to venture into the strange and unfamiliar, to initiate previously unforeseen action, organized around the belief that members' capacity is beyond even what they themselves can sometimes imagine. This pull to enhance each member's highest ideal self is reinforced by the *social promise*. Members are encouraged to make promises that stretch them beyond the comfortable and familiar and into the realm of the possible. The promise is the embodiment of the creative act in words. The capacity to make promises separates humans from all other animals. It is a testimony to the human faculty to start new and unending processes, to interrupt automatic, unthinking processes of daily life and begin something anew.

This promise to do what is uncomfortably challenging is not seen as something confirming but as a liberation into action, an *opportunity* to go beyond what one would have, had one not imagined and articulated a promise. A distinction needs to be made here between promise and prediction. Predictions involve foretelling the future based on knowledge of some past. Promises involve the creation of something new, not predicated on any past event. President Kennedy's 1961 speech was not a prediction, but a *promise* to put a person on the moon, a courageous statement given the limited knowledge and technological achievements of the day. Once made, however, this expansive promise formed the skeleton of a script that then drew others to act in new and courageous ways.

Promising is not a solo act, however. Expansive, creative acts require the support of an other. Further, once articulated, they inspire others to consider their own capacity to live at a higher level. The appreciative organization acts as a supportive *holding environment* for members' ventures into difficult and unpredictable spaces. Members *hold* their promises to one another as part of a larger commitment to support each other to achieve potential. Members support each other to aim to the edge and beyond of what is currently possible.

Not only are promises important in expanding one's self, they also are necessary for upholding the social bond. Expansive promises are islands of security that allow continuity and durability in relations between people. Without the fulfillment of promises we would never be able to keep our identities. Further, these promises depend on the presence of others. One cannot feel bound to a promise only to oneself. Recognizing that promises are the first step in the creation process, Hannah Arendt (1958, p. 145) attests to the miraculous power of expansive promises: "The sovereignty of a body of people bound and kept together, not by an identical will which somehow magically inspires them all, but by an agreed purpose for which alone the promises are valid and binding, shows itself quite clearly in its unquestioned superiority over those who are completely free, unbowed by any promises and unkept by any purpose. This superiority derives from the capacity to dispose of the future as though it were the present, that is, the enormous and truly miraculous enlargement of the very dimension in which power can be effective."

In one management group we work with, many executives had been hearing reports about the difficulties managers were having with one particular account manager who had been a company employee for twenty years. In a moment of disclosure and honesty, the executive responsible for this manager's area openly admitted having a difficult time confronting this manager:

KARL: All right, I admit he's had an attitude problem the last six months. It's very frustrating to talk to him. I admit I avoid him. It's not easy to confront him . . . but I will.

TIM: We understand it's tough. He's been loyal to this group for years and he's tough to deal with. But it has to be done. When will you do it?

KARL: I'll try to do it by the end of the month. No. I will do it by the end of the month.

TIM: All right. We're going to hold you to it.

KARL: Good. I need that.

Continuous Creativity and Openness to "Breakthrough." As Berger and Luckmann (1967) point out, social relationships *become* organizations when interaction patterns are repeated and become automatic and habitual. The advantage of this automaticity is that new choices do not have to be made for every act. Members of the appreciative organization, however, have a respectful irreverence for the past.

As poets and artists have always known, creativity, intuition, and insight sometimes seem to come in flashes from unexpected sources outside of self. Beethoven and Mozart, among others, reported having creative leaps come like lightning-flash insights during unsuspecting moments when their attention was directed elsewhere. These artists probably were not born with creative genius but learned to develop the capacity for creative breakthroughs, the secrets of inner listening.

Members of the appreciative organization also learn to take these playful illuminations seriously. The appreciative organization heightens the conditions for constructive creativity. There exists a spirit of openness to experience, a tolerance for ambiguity, the ability to process conflicting information without the press for closure. Also, members are encouraged to engage in serious *play* with ideas and concepts, to juggle impossible juxtapositions, to consider wild hypotheses, to express the ridiculous, to take spontaneous hunches as serious prospects. To foster such transformational experiences, *the appreciative organization seeks to ensure a sense of psychological safety, a sense that each individual has inherent worth and boundless potential.* Therefore, individual members are given complete freedom, permission to express the impermissible, permission to experiment, permission to fail, and permission to feel uncertain and confused. Under such conditions, members feel free to reevaluate their own thoughts and actions without defensiveness or pretense. The appreciative organization is suspicious of automaticity and habit; members are willing to destroy habitual practices to eliminate anything that gets in the way of creative responsiveness and imaginative acts. One executive director of a global volunteer organization demonstrated this principle: "You have to be willing to look at everything with fresh eyes and not be seduced by yesterday's success. Last month I had this great idea for how to draw on our volunteer base and we did it last week, and it felt great. Then I woke up two days ago and realized, 'How could we be so stupid?' It took us away from our mission. I wanted to do damage to it. I felt terrible. We spent a whole meeting the next day talking about why it was stupid. It was a very important meeting. It was a breakthrough." *In the appreciative organization, members do not become overly attached to established practices; rather they eliminate anything that hinders the capacity to create something new.* Overinvestment and excessive pride in past successes are discouraged as members continually take stands for possible futures.

Responsibility for the Whole. Traditional bureaucratic organizations limit the span of responsibility of members (Weber, 1953). With the reinforcement of boundaries of responsibility, there is a subtle psychological encouragement to issue disclaimers and accounts of responsibility avoidance to oneself as well as to others. Such blaming and counterblaming are psychological efforts to withdraw from action because it puts action under the control of others. Thus, even attributions that the people on top are ineffective are forms of self-invalidation because they allow one to avoid responsibility, and therefore capability, for transforming problems. A major dilemma, therefore, for executives of such organizations is that by seeking to delimit and embrace their own area of responsibility, they set in motion a process that results in others acting irresponsibly (Jonas, Fry, and Srivastva, 1989).

In the appreciative organization, all members from CEO to secretary take responsibility for the whole organization. All social activity is coauthored; members assume accountability for every organizational activity. One CEO of a large organization told this story: "If I come in someday and see the office a mess, or papers left unfinished, I stop and reflect and wonder, 'What's wrong with me? How did I let myself and my accountability slip that I didn't see this coming? It's not others' fault, it's my fault. *It's as if I did it.* How did I not notice they were not living at their highest self?' And should they do the same for me? In fact, they have. Each person here is 100 percent responsible for the whole organization all of the time."

Commitment to Valuing. So often meetings and conversations within organizations focus on identifying and solving problems. Members tend to achieve awareness through immersion in concrete, troublesome details. In a sense, managers become taxonomists of the deficient, citing numerous examples of problems as evidence that they are competent, involved, and have superiority in some area. The problematic, concrete world is the world many managers come to know confidently as specialists.

In the appreciative organization, members reawaken their innate capacity to appreciate value and see in wholes rather than exclusively focusing on particulars and each person's innate capacity to come up with sound ideals for a good future for oneself and one's world. Members learn to perceive organizations as creative constructions that are alive, vital, and dynamically emergent. As participants in a living, human system, they adopt the assumption that the world (or the organization or the person) *has* fundamental value.

Considerable time is spent giving voice to members' highest aspirations and values, to keep alive visionary images of possibilities. The mere act of valuing creates new ways to approach organizational life. Deliberate efforts are made to keep members' attention on the emergent, the new, and the evocative. At least as much time is spent in meetings discussing the *ideal future state* as is spent discussing present and past issues. Groups develop a capacity to discuss not only "what is" but "what ought to be." In the same spirit, members develop awareness not through immersion in concrete details, but *through conscious awareness* itself. That is, members pay attention to the cognitive ecology, the intellectual environment that directs attention. Meeting time is spent discussing what conditions "draw out" others' authentic voices and contribute to positive discussions.

Commitment to Listening. As Milan Kundera (1980, p. 80) notes, "All men's life among men is nothing more than a battle for the ears of others." Tamina, a character in one of Kundera's novels, is a bartender who spends most of her time listening to customers' stories. One day a customer asks her about *her life* and looks genuinely interested. From that moment on, her life is transformed. No one had ever before asked her about herself and genuinely listened. "Love," Kundera writes, "is a constant interrogation," a continuing curiosity about and inquiry of the other.

Perhaps the most empowering as well as powerful gesture we can offer one another is to truly *listen* to one another. All dysfunctional and neurotic behavior is a result of accumulated emotions from the experience of *not being heard*. Bad feelings and distress accumulate and keep us from being entirely clear and present. The only antidote is the experience of releasing distress, while another is truly listening to the real person beneath the real stress. *Committed listening means listening to the other complain, whine, and express distress without blame, judgment, or reproach. Listened to well enough, people will climb out of their cluttered thinking and reveal their brilliance.* The appreciative organization is dedicated to this principle of committed listening.

It is only through the experience of being heard that members' true authentic voices can find full expression. One organization has adopted this "technology" and encourages each member to choose at least one committed listener. When the individual feels the weight of daily distress hindering his or her contributions to the organizational purpose, they have the responsibility to *talk through these distractions,* to discharge the bad feelings that feel burdensome.

Attention to Affective Bonds as the Foundation for Consensus. Often groups and organizations that experiment with consensus decision making experience frustration and boredom that lead to dissolution of the experiment. What seems to be overlooked is that a positive, affective ethos is necessary for consensus to operate. A positive, affective *holding environment* that engenders a sense of hope and optimism is what makes possible members' patience and the energy necessary to search for consent.

Conclusion

Now that we have considered a few of the dimensions of the consciously appreciative organization, the question lurks: Is it really possible to recapture the living sense of wonderment, curiosity, affection, and joy described here? Surely this is not the real world. Surely the day-to-day stressful demands of organizational life keep us from realizing these ideals. The necessary compulsive activity, the velocity of managerial life, the drive for profit, all keep managers from living such a utopian existence. We have two responses to these objections, both of which challenge us to *reconsider exactly what the real situation is.* First, compulsive, furious activity that managers so often engage in is really an expression of a need to feel complete, unconditional love. There is no other rational reason to engage in such furious activity repeatedly. Also, all gestures of withdrawal, avoidance, and disruption are a yearning for unqualified acceptance and appreciation. Once we see what people often call "the real demands of real business" as a manifestation of this human need, we can recognize that appreciative processes lie at the heart of many of our activities. Second, on a collective level, all of these dimensions explored here must exist in every organization at least to some degree in order for social arrangements to persist

Appreciative Organizing

at all. There must be some agreement in regards to purpose, some degree of expansive language creation to grasp novelty, some degree of listening, and so on in order for any relationship to exist. What we are calling for in this chapter is the need to *deliberately cue these appreciative processes* so as to enhance our capacity to create more potent organizational forms. We would like to cite one fairly common and recognizable scenario that occurred between a group of executives to illustrate the pervasive, although largely tacit, workings of the appreciative processes and the capacity for humans (even male executives) to open themselves to wonderment, to unfreeze old language and structures, to create new anticipatory scripts.

Consider the following scenario that occurred at a high-tech organization. Smith, Director of Research, and Roberts, Director of Engineering, have just returned from a meeting with the Vice President of Finance where they have spent several hours comparing their high costs to the competitors' and the threat of a hostile takeover. Smith and Roberts have been in turf battles before. Importantly, Smith has never spoken comfortably and honestly with Roberts so it is unusual for them to sit across from each other and look at each other directly. Smith has rarely openly shared important information with Roberts, for fear that it could be used to his disadvantage. Smith begins for the first time to share his ideas about possible restructuring and new research developments. As they fly back to the office, for the first time they tell each other stories about their families and their mutual love for golf. When they arrive at the office the next day, one of the General Managers in Roberts' division informs him that once again there has been a delay on the part of one of Smith's managers to disclose the plans and schedule for a new equipment project. As gently as possible, Smith asks the managers for the schedule, also for the first time. Surprised, the manager does not protest as usual. Smith knows that to produce such estimates will be difficult and time consuming, and feels the familiar urge to deny Roberts's request. He glances at Roberts and offers to call his group together to offer computer support and "anything else" Roberts needs. Smith searches for the phone, smiling slightly, as Roberts shows him where it is kept. A dialogue of gestures of significance is quietly shared by them. This is a moment of an epiphany of the ordinary, seeing the inherent nature of each other rather than the competitive, distressful patterns that each has so often defensively engaged in in order to survive.

Smith was learning firsthand the difficulties that Roberts and others are facing. He also is able to experience tenderness within himself. Roberts, too, can see this for the first time and talks to him more comfortably during a routine activity in which they are usually separated. Further, between members of both groups, an expansion of the appreciative process has begun. Members now begin to imagine different future possibilities and act on a new knowledge that up to this point could not have been predicted, testimony to the contagion effect of appreciative expansion. By the time Smith begins reorganizing his department, he already "knows" that he can count on Roberts to participate and cooperate even though he has never done so before. The silent acknowledgment of this transformation comes in smiles they exchange as they search for the phone. The anticipated hindrances that once preoccupied Smith when making plans that called for interaction with Roberts's department slowly begin to melt away. Roberts also "knows" he will be able to successfully cooperate in Smith's reorganization, an experience that has revealed for him his openness and willingness to risk cooperation. Smith's subordinate also gets in on this knowledge game. He knows now that Roberts will be more approachable. He imagines loosening his rigid gestures and begins to joke with Roberts, occasionally teasing him. For the first time he defends Roberts when he overhears him being talked about in luncheon conversation, a conversation similar to ones he himself has initiated.

In this scenario, ancient habit patterns are subtly thawed, and new knowledge emerges as members begin to see the inherent brilliance in one another that had been occluded. How can we maximize such stripping away of the ordinary, such moments of "breakthroughs," that allow us to see what is missing in our perception of the world? What then needs to happen in order for organizations to enhance their appreciative capacity?

Appreciative Organizing

What processes need to be transformed in organizational life to create the expansive, optimistic script that characterizes the appreciative organization?

In order for organizations to adopt a mission of purpose, leaders need to move away from a problem, deficiency orientation focused on past task behavior and adopt a generative capacity to notice and explore "the best" of what exists. Leaders and members need to pay attention to the *real purpose* behind human acts and attend to the innate human yearning to make a purposeful contribution to the world. Under such conditions, no act is trivial. Executives need to free themselves from becoming prisoners of their own language by attending to the generative power of words, the capacity to create generative distinctions that enhance rather than constrict the range of meaningful action. This is a call to abandon the exclusive individual-competency view of organizations and acknowledge the social construction of the world. Members need to abandon the familiarity and comfort of habitual behavior and appreciate the power of the *expansive social promise*. When the social group can act as a *holding environment,* simultaneously supporting the present state of the individual and the individual's future capacity to transcend present limitations and live at a higher, more authentic level, a safe environment is created wherein members can imagine and create new scenarios that pull for a higher, more ideal self. In such a safe holding environment dedicated to a meaningful purpose, members are free to go beyond habits and not overinvest in past successes so that they are free to pay attention to intuitive hunches and remain open to creative breakthroughs. Members need to abandon the learned tendency to focus on problems and to feel efficacy and competency based on the capacity to create taxonomies of the deficient and demonstrate superiority over some inferior part of the world. Instead, members need to develop the capacity to notice *the value and beauty already inherent* in the world. In this sense, it would make sense to create "organizational time-outs" in which members do nothing except notice and articulate unqualified appreciation of self and world. Perhaps most important, members need to escape from the prison of self-indulgent speaking and become committed listeners to one another, to notice the rich inherent nature of every human being.

This chapter is a call for exploring what is inherent and given as part of human nature, our innate capacity for unconditional love, curiosity, wonder, playfulness, joy. That so many of these qualities become constrained and constricted, submerged and repressed as we become adults and learn to behave "properly," does not alter our inherent nature. By acknowledging the appreciative tendencies in organizational life, we can rediscover what is already there.

Expanded Edition

APPRECIATIVE INQUIRY IN ORGANIZATIONAL LIFE

David L. Cooperrider and Suresh Srivastva

ABSTRACT

This chapter presents a conceptual refiguration of action-research based on a "sociorationalist" view of science. The position that is developed can be summarized as follows: For action-research to reach its potential as a vehicle for social innovation it needs to begin advancing theoretical knowledge of consequence; that good theory may be one of the best means human beings have for affecting change in a postindustrial world; that the discipline's steadfast commitment to a problem-solving view of the world acts as a primary constraint on its imagination and contribution to knowledge; that *appreciative inquiry* represents a viable complement to conventional forms of action-research; and finally, that through our assumptions and choice of method we largely create the world we later discover.

> We are sometime truly to see our life as positive, not negative, as made up of continuous willing, not of constraints and prohibition.
>
> Mary Parker Follett
>
> We are steadily forgetting how to dream: in historical terms, the mathematicist and technicist dimensions of Platonism have conquered the poetical, mythical, and rhetorical context of analysis. We are forgetting how to be reasonable in nonmathematical dialects.
>
> Stanley Rosen

INTRODUCTION

This chapter presents a conceptual reconfiguration of action research.[1] In it we shall argue for a multidimensional view of action-research which seeks to both generate theory and develop organizations. The chapter begins with the observation that action-research has become increasingly rationalized and enculturated to the point where it risks becoming little more than a crude empiricism imprisoned in a deficiency mode of thought. In its conventional *unidimensional* form action-research has largely failed as an instrument for advancing social knowledge of consequence and has not, therefore, achieved its potential as a vehicle for human development and social-organizational transformation. While the literature consistently signals the worth of action-research as a managerial tool for problem solving ("first-order" incremental change), it is conspicuously quiet concerning reports of discontinuous change of the "second order" where organizational paradigms, norms, ideologies, or values are transformed in fundamental ways (Watzlawick, et al., 1974).

In the course of this chapter we shall touch broadly upon a number of interrelated concerns—scientific, metaphysical, normative, and pragmatic. Linking these streams is an underlying conviction that action-research has the potential to be to the postindustrial era what "scientific management" was to the industrial. Just as scientific management provided the philosophical and methodological legitimacy required to support the bureaucratic organizational form (Clegg & Dunkerly, 1980; Braverman, 1974), action-research may yet provide the intellectual rationale and reflexive methodology required to support the emergence of a more egalitarian "postbureaucratic" form of organization. Unlike scientific management however, which provided the means for a technorational science of administration, action-research holds unique and essential promise in the sociorational realm of human affairs. It has the potential to become the paradigmatic basis of a truly significant—a humanly significant—generative science of administration.

In the first part of the essay it is suggested that the primary barrier limiting the potential of action-research has been its romance with "action" at the expense of "theory." This tendency has led many in the discipline to seriously underestimate the power of theory as a means for social-organizational reconstruction. Drawing largely on the work of Kenneth Gergen (1978; 1982), we re-examine the character of theoretical knowledge and its role in social transformation, and then appeal for a redefinition of the scientific aims of action-research that will dynamically reunite theory and practice. The aim of science is not the detached discovery and verification of social laws allowing for prediction and control. Highlighted here instead, is an alternative understanding that defines social and behavioral science in terms of its "generative capacity," that is, its "capacity to challenge the guiding assumptions of the culture, to raise fundamental questions regarding contemporary social life, to foster reconsideration of that which is 'taken for granted' and thereby furnish new alternatives for social actions" (Gergen, 1978, p. 1346).

Assuming that generative theory is a legitimate product of scientific work and is, in fact, capable of provoking debate, stimulating normative dialogue, and furnishing conceptual alternatives needed for social transformation, then why has action-research till now so largely downplayed creative theorizing in its work with organizations? Here we will move to the heart of the chapter and argue that the generative incapacity of contemporary action-research derives from the discipline's unquestioned commitment to a secularized problem-oriented view of the world and thus to the subsequent loss of our capacity as researchers and participants to marvel, and in marvelling to embrace, the miracle and mystery of social organization. If we acknowledge Abraham Maslow's (1968) admonition that true science begins and ends in wonder, then we immediately shed light on why action-research has failed to produce innovative theory capable of inspiring the imagination, commitment, and passionate dialogue required for the consensual re-ordering of social conduct.

Appreciative inquiry is presented here as a mode of action-research that meets the criteria of science as spelled out in generative-theoretical terms. Going beyond questions of epistemology, appreciative inquiry has as its basis a metaphysical concern: it posits that social existence as such is a miracle that can never be fully comprehended (Quinney, 1982; Marcel, 1963). Proceeding from this level of understanding we begin to explore the uniqueness of the appreciative mode. More than a method or technique, the appreciative mode of inquiry is a way of living with, being with, and directly paticipating in the varieties of social organization we are compelled to study. Serious consideration and reflection on the ultimate mystery of being engenders a reverence for life that draws the researcher to inquire beyond superficial appearances to deeper levels of the life-generating essentials and potentials of social existence. That is, the action-researcher is drawn to affirm, and thereby illuminate, the factors and forces involved in organizing that serve to nourish the human spirit. Thus, this chapter seeks to enrich our conception of administrative behavior by introducing a "second dimension" of action-research that goes beyond merely a secularized problem-solving frame.

The proposal that appreciative inquiry represents a distinctive complement to traditional action-research will be unfolded in the following way: First, the role of theory as an enabling agent of social transformation will be considered; such consideration can help to eliminate the artificial dualism separating theory from practice. Second, we will challenge the problem-oriented view of organizing inherent in traditional definitions of action-research, and describe an affirmative form of inquiry uniquely suited for discovering generative theory. Finally, these insights will be brought together in a general model of the conceptual underpinnings of appreciative inquiry.

TOWARD GENERATIVE THEORY IN ACTION-RESEARCH

The current decade has witnessed a confluence of thinking concerning the paradigmatic refiguration of social thought. As Geertz (1980) notes, there is now even a "blurring of genres" as many social scientists have abandoned—without apology—the misdirected quest to mimic the "more mature" physical sciences. Turning away from a Newtonian laws-and-instances-type explanation rooted in logical empiricist philosophy, many social theorists have instead opted for an interpretive form of inquiry that connects organized action to its contextually embedded set of meanings, "looking less for the sorts of things that connect planets and pendulums and more for the sorts that connect chrysanthemums and swords" (Geertz, 1980, p. 165).

In the administrative sciences, in particular, this recent development has been translated into observable movement away from mechanistic research designs intended objectively to establish universal causal linkages between variables, such as organizational size and level of centralization, or between technology, environment, and organizational structure. Indeed, prominent researchers in the field have publicly given up the logical positivist idea of "certainty through science" and are now embarking on approaches to research that grant preeminence to the historically situated and ever-changing "interpretive schemes" used by members of a given group to give life and meaning to their actions and decisions (Bartunek, 1984). Indicative of the shift away from the logical positivist frame, researchers are converging around what has been termed the "sociorationalist" metatheory of science (Gergen, 1982). Recognizing the symbolic nature of the human universe, we now find a flurry of innovative work supporting the thesis that there is little about human development or organizational behavior that is "preprogrammed" or stimulus-bound in any direct physical or biological way. In this sense, the social universe is open to indefinite revision, change, and self-propelled development. And, this recognition is crucial because to the extent to which social existence *is* situated in a symbolic realm, beyond deterministic forces, then to that extent the logical positivist foundation of social science is negated and its concept of knowledge rendered illusionary.

Nowhere is this better evidenced than in the variety of works concerned with such topics as organizational paradigms (Brown, 1978; McHugh, 1970); beliefs and master scripts (Sproull, 1981; Beyer, 1981); idea management and the executive mind (Srivastva, 1983; 1985); theories of action and presumptions of logic (Argyris & Schon, 1980; Weick, 1983); consciousness and awareness (Harrison, 1982; Lukes, 1974); and, of course, an array of work associated with the concept of organizational or corporate culture (Ouchi & Johnson, 1978; Schein, 1983; Van Maanen, 1982; Deal & Kennedy, 1982; Sathe, 1983; Hofstede, 1980). As Ellwood prophetically suggested almost half a century ago, "This is the cultural view of human society that is [or will be] revolutionizing the social sciences" (Ellwood, 1938, p. 561).

This developing consensus on the importance of the symbolic realm—on the power of ideas—by such independent sources embracing such diverse objectives reflects the reality of organized life in the modern world. However reluctantly, even the most traditional social thinkers are now recognizing the distinctiveness of the postindustrial world for what truly is—an unfolding drama of human interaction whose potential seems limited or enhanced primarily by our symbolic capacities for constructing meaningful agreements that allow for the committed enactment of collective life.

Never before in history have ideas, information, and beliefs—or theory—been so central in the formulation of reality itself. Social existence, of course, has always depended on some kind of idea system for its meaningful sustenance. The difference now, however, is that what was once background has become foreground. Today, the very fact that society continues to exist at all is experienced not so much mechanistically (an extension of machines) or even naturalistically (a by-product of fateful nature) but more and more humanistically as a social construction of interacting minds—"a game between persons" (Bell, 1973). And under these conditions—as a part of the change from an agrarian society to a goods-producing society at first and then to an information society—ideas and meaning systems take on a whole new life and character. Ideas are thrust center stage as the prime unit of relational exchange governing the creation or obliteration of social existence.

This line of argument applies no less potently to current conceptions of social science. To the extent that the primary product of science is systematically refined idea systems—or theory—science too must be recognized as a powerful agent in the enhancement or destruction of human life. And while this presents an unresolvable dilemma for a logical empiricist conception of science, it spells real opportunity (and responsibility) for a social science that wishes to be of creative significance to society. Put most simply, the theoretical contributions of science may be among the most powerful resources human beings have for contributing to change and development in the groups and organizations in which they live. This is precisely the meaning of Kurt Lewin's early view of action-science when he proposed: "There is nothing so practical as good theory" (1951, p. 169).

Ironically, the discipline of action-research continues to insist on a sharp separation of theory and practice, and to underrate the role of theory in social reconstruction. The irony is that it does so precisely at a time when the cultural view of organizing is reaching toward paradigmatic status. The sad and perhaps tragic commentary on action-research is that it is becoming increasingly inconsequential just as its opportunity to contribute is on the rise (Argyris, 1983).

Observers such as Rappaport (1970) and Bartunek (1983) have lamented the fact that action-researchers have come to subordinate research aims to action interests. Levinson (1972) has gone even further by branding the discipline "atheoretical." And, Friedlander and Brown (1974) have noted that the definition of action-research in classic texts give virtually no mention to theory-building as an integral and necessary component of the research/diagnostic process, or the process of organizational change. Whenever theory is mentioned, it is almost always referred to as a springboard for research or diagnosis, not the other way around. Bartunek (1983, p. 3–4) concludes that "even the most recent papers that describe action-research strategies tend to focus primarily on the process of action-research and only secondarily on the specific theoretical contributions of the outcomes of such research" (e.g., Frohman, Sashkin, & Kavanaugh, 1976; Shani & Pasmore, 1982; Susman and Evered, 1978; see Pasmore and Friedlander, 1982, for an exception). For those of us trained in the field this conclusion is not surprising. Indeed, few educational programs in organizational behavior even consider theory-building as a formal part of their curriculum, and even fewer place a real premium on the development of the theoretical mind and imagination of their students.

According to Argyris (1983), this lack of useful theorizing is attributable to two major factors. On the one hand practice-oriented scholars have tended to become so client-centered that they fail to question their clients' own definition of a problem and thereby to build testable propositions and theories that are embedded in everyday life. Academics, on the other hand, who are trained to be more scientific in their bent, also undercut the development of useful theory by their very insistence on the criteria of "normal" science and research—detachment, rigor, unilateral control, and operational precision. In a word, creative theorizing has literally been assaulted on all fronts by practitioners and academic scientists alike. It must also be noted that implicit in this critique by Argyris (1983), and others (e.g., Friedlander & Brown, 1974), is an underlying assumption that action-research has built into it certain natural conflicts that are likely to lead either to "action" (consulting) or "research" (diagnosis or the development of organizational theory), but not to both.

The situation is summed up by Friedlander and Brown (1974) in their comprehensive review of the field:

Appreciative Inquiry in Organizational Life

> We believe that research will either play a far more crucial role in the advancement of this field, or become an increasingly irrevelant appendage to it . . . . We have generally failed to produce a theory of change which emerges from the change process itself. We need a way of enriching our understanding and action synergistically rather than at one or the other's expense—to become a science in which knowledge-getting and knowledge-giving are an integrated process, and one that is valuable to all parties involved (p. 319).

Friedlander and Brown concluded with a plea for a metatheoretical revision of science that will integrate theory and practice. But in another review over a decade later, Friedlander (1984) observed little progress coming from top scholars in the discipline. He then put words to a mounting frustration over what appears as a recurring problem:

> They pointed to the shortcomings of traditional research and called for emancipation from it; but they did not indicate a destination. There is as yet no new paradigm that integrates research and practice, or even optimizes useful knowledge for organizations . . . . I'm impatient. Let's get on with it. Let's not talk it, write it, analyze it, conceptualize it, research it. Instead let's actively engage and experiment with new designs for producing knowledge that is, in fact, used by organizations (p. 647).

This recurrent problem is the price we pay for continuing to talk about theory and practice in dualistic terms. In a later section in this chapter another hypothesis will be advanced on why there is this lack of creative theorizing, specifically as it relates to action-research. But first we need to look more closely at the claim that social theory and social practice are, indeed, part of a synthetic whole. We need to elaborate on the idea that scientific theory is a means for both understanding *and* improving social practice. We need to examine exactly what it means to merge the idea and the act, the symbolic and the sociobehavioral, into a powerful and integral unity.

The Sociorationalist Alternative

As the end of the twentieth century nears, thinkers in organizational behavior are beginning to see, without hesitation, why an administrative science based on a physical science model is simply not adequate as a means for understanding or contributing in relevant ways to the workings of complex, organized human systems (see, for example, Susman and Evered, 1978; Beyer & Trice, 1982). Kurt Lewin had understood this almost half a century earlier but his progressive vision of an action science fell short of offering a clear metatheoretical alternative to conventional conceptions of science (Peters & Robinson, 1984). Indeed, the epistemological ambiguity inherent in Lewin's writing has been cited as perhaps the critical shortcoming of all his work. And yet, in hindsight, it can be argued that the ambiguity was intentional and perhaps part of Lewin's social sensitivity and genius. As Gergen (1982) suggests, the metatheoretical ambiguity in Lewin's work might well have been a protective measure, an attempt to shield his fresh vision of an action science from the fully dominant logical positivist temper of his time. In any event, whether planned or not, Lewin walked a tightrope between two fundamentally opposed views of science and never did make clear how theory could be used as both an interpretive and a creative element. This achievement, as we might guess, would have to wait for a change in the intellectual ethos of social science.

That change, as we earlier indicated, is now taking place. Increasingly the literature signals a disenchantment with theories of science that grant priority to the external world in the generation of human knowledge. Instead there is growing movement toward granting preeminence to the cognitive processes of mind and the symbolic processes of social construction. In *Toward Transformation in Social Knowledge* (1982), Kenneth Gergen synthesizes the essential whole of this movement and takes it one crucial step beyond disenchantment to a bold, yet workable conception of science that firmly unites theory with practice—and thereby elevates the status of theoretical-scientific work. From a historical perspective there is no question that this is a major achievement; it brings to completion the work abruptly halted by Lewin's untimely death. But more than that, what Gergen offers, albeit indirectly, is a desperately needed clue to how we can revitalize an action-research discipline that has never reached its potential. While a complete statement of the emerging sociorationalist metatheory is beyond the scope of this chapter, it is important at least to outline the general logic of the perspective, including its basic assumptions.

At the heart of sociorationalism is the assumption of impermanence—the fundamental instability of social order. No matter what the durability to date, virtually any pattern of social action is open to infinite revision. Accepting for a moment the argument of the social constructionists that social reality, at any given point, is a product of broad social agreement (shared meanings), and further granting a linkage between the conceptual schemes of a culture and its other patterns of action, we must seriously consider the idea that alterations in conceptual practices, in ways of symbolizing the world, hold tremendous potential for guiding changes in the social order. To understand the importance of these assumptions and their meaning for social science, let us quote Gergen (1982) at length:

> Is not the range of cognitive heuristics that may be employed in solving problems of adaptation limited only by the human imagination?
>
> One must finally consider the possibility that human biology not only presents to the scientist an organism whose actions may vary in an infinity of ways, but it may ensure as well that novel patterns are continuously emerging . . . variations in human activity may importantly be traced to the capacities of the organism for symbolic restructuring. As it is commonly said, one's actions appear to be vitally linked to the manner in which one understands or construes the world of experience. The stimulus world does not elicit behavior in an automatic, reflex-like fashion. Rather, the symbolic translation of one's experiences virtually

transforms their implications and thereby alters the range of one's potential reactions. Interestingly, while formulations of this variety are widely shared within the scientific community, very little attention has been paid to their ramifications for a theory of science. As is clear, without such regularities the prediction of behavior is largely obviated . . . to the extent that the individual is capable of transforming the meaning of stimulus conditions in an indeterminate number of ways, existing regularities must be considered historically contingent—dependent on the prevailing meaning systems of conceptual structure of the times. In effect, from this perspective the scientist's capacity to locate predictable patterns of interaction depends importantly on the extent to which the population is both homogeneous and stable in its conceptual constructions (pp. 16-17).

While this type of reasoning is consistent with the thinking of many social scientists, the ramifications are rarely taken to their logical conclusion: "Virtually unexamined by the field is the potential of science to shape the meaning systems of the society and thus the common activities of the culture" (Gergen, 1978, p. 1349). Virtually unexamined is the important role that science can—and does—play in the scientific construction of social reality.

One implication of this line of thought is that to the extent the social science conceives its role in the logical positivist sense, with its goals being prediction and control, it not only serves the interests of the status quo (you can't have "good science" without stable replication and verification of hypotheses) but it also seriously underestimates the power and usefulness of its most important product, namely theory; it underestimates the constructive role science can have in the *development* of the groups and organizations that make up our cultural world. According to Gergen, realization of this fact furnishes the opportunity to refashion a social science of vital significance to society. To do this, we need a bold shift in attention whereby theoretical accounts are no longer judged in terms of their predictive capacity, but instead are judged in terms of their generative capacity—their ability to foster dialogue about that which is taken for granted and their capacity for generating fresh alternatives for social action. Instead of asking, "Does this theory correspond with the observable facts?" the emphasis for evaluating good theory becomes, "To what extent does this theory present provocative new possibilities for social action, and to what extent does it stimulate normative dialogue about how we can and should organize ourselves?" The complete logic for such a proposal may be summarized in the following ten points:

1. The social order at any given point is viewed as the product of broad social agreement, whether tacit or explicit.
2. Patterns of social-organizational action are not fixed by nature in any direct biological or physical way; the vast share of social conduct is potentially stimulus-free, capable of infinite conceptual variation.
3. From an observational point of view, all social action is open to multiple interpretations, no one of which is superior in any objective sense. The in-

terpretations (for example, "whites are superior to blacks") favored in one historical setting may be replaced in the next.

4. Historically embedded conventions govern what is taken to be true or valid, and to a large extent govern what we, as scientists and lay persons, are able to see. All observation, therefore, is theory-laden and filtered through conventional belief systems and theoretical lenses.[2]

5. To the extent that action is predicated on ideas, beliefs, meanings, intentions, or theory, people are free to seek transformations in conventional conduct by changing conventional codes (idea systems).

6. The most powerful vehicle communities have for transforming their conventions—their agreements on norms, values, policies, purposes, and ideologies—is through the act of dialogue made possible by language. Alterations in linguistic practices, therefore, hold profound implications for changes in social practice.

7. Social theory can be viewed as a highly refined language with a specialized grammar all its own. As a powerful linguistic tool created by trained linguistic experts (scientists), theory may enter the conceptual meaning system of culture and in doing so alter patterns of social action.

8. Whether intended or not, all theory is normative and has the potential to influence the social order—even if reactions to it are simply boredom, rebellion, laughter, or full acceptance.

9. Because of this, all social theory is morally relevant; it has the potential to affect the way people live their ordinary lives in relation to one another. This point is a critical one because there is no such thing as a detached/technical/scientific mode for judging the ultimate worth of value claims.

10. Valid knowledge or social theory is therefore a communal creation. Social knowledge is not "out there" in nature to be discovered through detached, value-free, observational methods (logical empiricism); nor can it be relegated to the subjective minds of isolated individuals (solipism). Social knowledge resides in the interactive collectivity; it is created, maintained, and put to use by the human group. Dialogue, free from constraint or distortion, is necessary to determine the "nature of things" (sociorationalism).

In Table 1 the metatheory of sociorationalism is both summarized and contrasted to the commonly held assumptions of the logical empiricist view of science. Especially important to note is the transformed role of the scientist when social inquiry is viewed from the perspective of sociorationalism. Instead of attempting to present oneself as an impartial bystander or dispassionate spectator of the inevitable, the social scientist conceives of himself or herself as an active agent, an invested participant whose work might well become a powerful source of change in the way people see and enact their worlds. Driven by a desire to "break the hammerlock" of what appears as given in human nature, the scientist attempts to build theories that can expand the realm of what is conventionally

Table 1. Comparison of Logical Empiricist and Socio-Rationalist Conceptions of Social Science

Dimension for Comparison	Logical Empiricism	Socio-Rationalism
1. Primary Function of Science	Enhance goals of understanding, prediction, and control by discerning general laws or principles governing the relationship among units of observable phenomena.	Enhance understanding in the sense of assigning meaning to something, thus creating its status through the use of concepts. Science is a means for expanding flexibility and choice in cultural evolution.
2. Theory of Knowledge and Mind	Exogenic—grants priority to the external world in the generation of human knowledge (i.e., the preeminence of objective fact). Mind is a mirror.	Endogenic—holds the processes of mind and symbolic interaction as preeminent source of human knowledge. Mind is both a mirror and a lamp.
3. Perspective on Time	Assumption of temporal irrelevance: searches for transhistorical principles.	Assumption of historically and contextually relevant meanings; existing regularities in social order are contingent on prevailing meaning systems.
4. Assuming Stability of Social Patterns	Social phenomena are sufficiently stable, enduring, reliable and replicable to allow for lawful principles.	Social order is fundamentally unstable. Social phenomena are guided by cognitive heuristics, limited only by the human imagination; the social order is a subject matter capable of infinite variation through the linkage of ideas and action
5. Value Stance	Separation of fact and values. Possibility of objective knowledge through behavioral observation.	Social sciences are fundamentally nonobjective. Any behavioral event is open to virtually any interpretative explanation. All interpretation is filtered through prevailing values of a culture. "There is no description without prescription."

(continued)

Table 1. (Cont.)

Dimension for Comparison	Logical Empiricism	Socio-Rationalism
6. Features of "Good" Theory	Discovery of transhistorically valid principles; a theory's correspondence with fact.	Degree to which theory furnishes alternatives for social innovation and thereby opens vistas for action; expansion of "the realm of the possible."
7. Criteria for Confirmation or Verification (Life of a Theory)	Logical consistency and empirical prediction; subject to falsification.	Persuasive appeal, impact, and overall generative capacity; subject to community agreement; truth is a product of a community of truth makers.
8. Role of Scientist	Impartial bystander and dispassionate spectator of the inevitable; content to accept that which seems given.	Active agent and co-participant who is primarily a source of linguistic activity (theoretial language) which serves as input into common meaning systems. Interested in "breaking the hammerlock" of what appears as given in human nature.
9. Chief Product of Research	Cumulation of objective knowledge through the production of empirically disconfirmable hypothesis.	Continued improvement in theory building capacity; improvement in the capacity to create generative-theoretical language.
10. Emphasis in the Education of Future Social Science Professionals	Rigorous experimental methods and statistical analysis; a premium is placed on method (training in theory construction is a rarity).	Hermenuetic interpretation and catalytic theorizing; a premium is placed on the theoretical imagination. Sociorationalism invites the student toward *intellectual expression* in the service of his or her vision of the good.

understood as possible. In this sense the core impact of sociorationalist metatheory is that it invites, encourages, and requires that students of social life rigorously exercise their theoretical imagination in the service of their vision of the good. Instead of denial it is an invitation to fully accept and exercise those qualities of mind and action that make us uniquely human.

Now we turn to a question raised earlier: How does theory achieve its capacity to affect social practice, and what are some of the specific characteristics of generative theory?

The Power of Theory in Understanding Organizational Life

The sociorationalist vision of science is of such far-reaching importance that no student, organizational scientist, manager, educator, or *action-researcher* can afford to ignore it. Good theory, as we have suggested, is one of the most powerful means we have for helping social systems evolve, adapt, and creatively alter their patterns over time. Building further on this metatheoretical perspective we can talk about five ways by which theory achieves its exceptional potency:

1. Establishing a conceptual and contextual frame;
2. Providing presumptions of logic;
3. Transmitting a system of values;
4. Creating a group-building language;
5. Extending visions of possibility or constraint.

1. *Establishing a Perceptual and Contextual Frame*

To the extent that theory is the conceptual imposition of order upon an otherwise "booming, bustling, confusion that is the realm of experience" (Dubin, 1978), the theorist's first order of business is to specify what is there to be seen, to provide an "ontological education" (Gergen, 1982). The very act of theoretical articulation, therefore, highlights not only the parameters of the topic or subject matter, but becomes an active agent as a cueing device, a device that subtly focuses attention on particular phenomena or meanings while obscuring others. In the manner of a telescope or lens, a new theory allows one to see the world in a way perhaps never before imagined.

For example, when American eugenicists used the lens of biological determinism to attribute diseases of poverty to the inferior genetic construction of poor people, they literally could see no systematic remedy other than sterilization of the poor. In contrast, when Joseph Goldberg theorized that pellegra was not genetically determined but culturally caused (as a result of vitamin deficiency and the eating habits of the poor), he could discover a way to cure it (Gould, 1981). Similarly, theories about the "survival of the fittest" might well help executives locate "predators," "hostile enrivonments," and a world where self-interest reigns, where it is a case of "eat or be eaten." Likewise, theories of leadership have been known quickly to facilitate the discovery of Theory X and Theory Y interaction. Whatever the theory, it provides a potential means for members of a culture to navigate in an otherwise neutral, meaningless, or chaotic sea of people, interactions and events. By providing an "ontological education" with respect to what is there, a theory furnishes an important cultural input that affects people's cognitive set. In this sense "the world is not so constituted until the lens is employed. With each new distinction the groundwork is laid for alterations in existing patterns of conduct" (Gergen, 1982, p. 23).

As the reader may already surmise, an important moral issue begins to emerge here. Part of the reason that theory is, in fact, powerful is that it shapes perceptions, cognitions, and preferences often at a preconscious level, much like subliminal communications or even hypnosis. Haley (1973) talks about how Milton Erickson has made this a central feature of this psycho-therapeutic work. But Lukes (1974) cautions that such thought control may be "the supreme and most insidious exercise of power," especially when it prevents people from challenging their role in the existing order of things and when it operates contrary to their real interests.

2. Providing Presumptions of Logic

Theories are also powerful to the extent to which they help shape common expectations of causality, sequence, and relational importance of phenomena within a theoretical equation. Consider, for example, the simple logic underlying almost every formal performance-appraisal system. Stripped to essentials, the theoretical underpinnings run something like this: "If you want to evaluate performance (P), then you must evaluate the individual employee (E); in other words, '$P = E$'." Armed with this theory, many managers have entered the performance-appraisal meeting shaking with the thought of having to pass godlike judgment on some employee. Similarly, the employee arrives at the meeting with an arsenal of defenses, designed to protect his or her hard-won self-esteem. Little genuine communication occurs during the meeting and virtually no problem-solving takes place. The paperwork is mechanically completed, then filed away in the personnel office until the next year. So powerful is this subtle $P = E$ equation that any alternative goes virtually unnoticed, for example the Lewinian theory that behavior (performance) is a function of the person *and* the environment (in this case the organizational situation, the "OS" in which the employee works). Following this Lewinian line, the theory underlying performance appraisal would now have to be expanded to read $P = E \times OS$. That is, $P \neq E$. To adequately assess performance there must be an assessment of the individual *in relation to* the organizational setting in which he or she works and vice-versa. What would happen to the performance-appraisal process if this more complete theory were used as a basis for re-designing appraisal systems in organizations throughout the corporate world? Isn't it possible that such a theory could help shift the attribution process away from the person-blame to systems analysis?[3]

By attributing causality, theories have the potential to create the very phenomena they propose to explain. Karl Weick, in a recent article examining managerial thought in the context of action, contends that thought and action are part and parcel of one another; thinking is best viewed as a kind of activity, and activity as the ground of thought. For him, managerial theories gain their power by helping people overlook disorder and presume orderlinesss. Theory *energizes* action by providing a *presumption of logic* that enables people to act with certainty, attention, care, and control. Even where it is originally inadequate as a description of current reality, a forceful theory may provoke action that brings into the world a new reality that then confirms the original theory. Weick (1983) explains:

> Once the action is linked with an explanation, it becomes more forceful, and the situation is thereby transformed into something that supports the presumed underlying pattern. Presumptions [theories] enable actions to be tied to specific explanations that consolidate those actions into deterministic events. . . .
>
> The underlying explanation need *not* be objectively "correct." In a crude sense any old explanation will due. This is so because explanation serves mostly to organize and focus the action. The focused action then modifies the situation in ways that confirm the explanation, whatever it is.
>
> Thus, the adequacy of any explanation is determined by the intensity and structure it adds to potentially self-validating actions. More forcefulness leads to more validation and more perceived adequacy. Accuracy is subordinate to intensity. Since situations can support a variety of meanings, their actual content and meaning are dependent on the degree to which they are arranged in sensible, coherent configurations. More forcefulness imposes more coherence. Thus, those explanations that induce greater forcefulness become more valid, not because they are more accurate, but because they have a higher potential for self-validation . . . the underlying explanations they unfold (for example, "This is war") have great potential to intensify whatever action is underway (1983, pp. 230–232).

Thus, theories are generative to the extent that they are forceful (e.g., Marx), logically coherent (e.g., Piaget), and bold in their assertions and consistency (e.g., Freud, Weber). By providing a basis for focused action, a logic for attributing causality, and a sequence specification that grounds expectations for action and reaction, a theory goes a long way toward forming the common expectations for the future. "And with the alteration of expectation, the stage is set for modification of action" (Gergen, 1982, p. 24).

3. Transmitting a System of Values

Beyond abstract logic, it is often the affective core of social theory that provides its true force and appeal, allowing it to direct perception and guide behavior. From the tradition of logical positivism, good "objective" theory is to be value-free, yet upon closer inspection we find that social theory is infused with values and domain assumptions throughout. As Gouldner (1970) so aptly put it, "Every social theory facilitates the pursuit of some, but not all, courses of action and thus, encourages us to change or accept the world as it is, to say yea or nay to it. In a way, every theory is a discrete obituary or celebration of some social system."

Nowhere is this better exemplified—negatively—than in the role scientific theory played in the arguments for slavery, colonialism, and belief in the genetic superiority of certain races. The scientific theory in this case was, again, the theory of biological determinism, the belief that social and economic differences between human beings and groups—differences in rank, status, political privilege, education privilege—arise from inherited natural endowments, and that existing social arrangements accurately reflect biological limits. So powerful was this theory during the 1800s that it led a number of America's highest-ranking scientific researchers unconsciously to miscalculate "objective" data in what has been brilliantly described by naturalist Steven Jay Gould (1981, p. 54) as a "patchwork of fudging and finagling in the clear interest of controlling a priori convictions". Before dismissing this harsh judgment as simple rhetoric, we need to look closely at how it was determined. One example will suffice.

When Samual Morton, a scientist with two medical degrees, died in 1851, the *New York Tribune* paid tribute saying, "Probably no scientific man in America enjoyed a higher reputation among scholars throughout the world than Dr. Morton" (in Gould, 1981, p. 51). Morton gained this reputation as a scientist who set out to rank racial groups by "objectively" measuring the size of the cranial cavity of the human skull which he regarded as a measure of brain size. He had a beautiful collection of skulls from races throughout the world, probably the largest such collection in existence. His hypothesis was a simple one: The mental and moral worth of human races can be arrived at objectively by measuring physical characteristics of the brain; by filling skull cavities with mustard seed or lead shot, accurate measurement of brain size is possible. Morton published three major works which were reprinted repeatedly as providing objective, "hard" data on the mental worth of races. Gould comments:

> Needless to say, they matched every good Yankee's prejudices—whites on top, Indians in the middle, and blacks on the bottom; and among whites, Tuetons and Anglo-Saxons on top, Jews in the middle, and Hindus on the bottom. . . . Status and access to power in Morton's America faithfully reflected biological merit (p. 54).

Morton's work was undoubtedly influential. When he died, the South's leading medical journal proclaimed: "We of the South should consider him as our benefactor, for aiding most materially in giving the Negro his true position as an inferior race" (in Gould, 1981, p. 69). Indeed Morton did much more than only give "the Negro his true position," as the following remarks by Morton himself convey:

> Negroes were numerous in Egypt, but their social position in ancient times was the same as it is now, that of servants and slaves.

> The benevolent mind may regret the inaptitude of the Indian civilization . . . [but values must not yield to fact]. The structure of his mind appears to be different from that of the white man, or can the two harmonize in social relations except on the most limited scale. [Indians] are not only averse to restraints of education, but for the most part are incapable of a continued process of reasoning on abstract subjects (in Gould, 1981, p. 53).

Appreciative Inquiry in Organizational Life

The problem with these conclusions—as well as the numerical data which supported them—was that they were based not on "fact" but purely and simply on cultural fiction, on Morton's belief in biological determinism. As Gould meticulously shows, all of Morton's data was wrong. Having reworked it completely, Gould concludes:

> Morton's summaries are a patchwork of fudging and finagling in the clear interst of controlling a priori convictions. Yet—and this is the most intriguing aspect of the case—I find no evidence of conscious fraud: indeed, had Morton been a conscious fudger, he would not have published his data so openly.
>
> Conscious fraud is probably rare in science. . . . The prevalence of *unconscious* finagling, on the other hand, suggests the general conclusion about the social context of science . . . prior prejudice may be found anywhere, even in the basics of measuring bones and totaling sums (pp. 55–56).

Morton represents a telling example of the power of theory. Theory is not only a shaper of expectations and perceptions. Under the guise of "dispassionate inquiry" it can also be a peddler of values, typecasting arbitrary value as scientific "fact." Along with Gould, we believe that we would be better off to abandon the myth of "value-free" science and that theoretical work "must be understood as a social phenomenon, a gutsy, human enterprise, not the work of robots programmed to collect pure information" (Gould, 1981, p. 21). Even if Morton's data were correct, his work still could not be counted as value-free. His data and theories were not only shaped by the setting in which he worked; they were also used to support broad social policy. This is akin to making nature the source of cultural values, which of course it never can be ("What is" does not equal "what should be").

4. Creating a Group-Building Language

The sociorationalist perspective is more than a pessimistic epitaph for a strictly logical positivist philosophy. It is an invitation to inquiry that raises the status of theory from mere appendage of scientific method to an actual shaper of society. Once we acknowledge that a primary product of science—theory—is a key resource for the creation of groups, the stage is set for theory building activity intended for the use and development of human society, for the creation of human options.

Students of human behavior have been aware of the group as the foundation of society since the earliest periods of classical thought. Aristotle, for example, discussed the importance of bands and families. But it was not until the middle of the present century that scientific interest in the subject exploded in a flurry of general inquiry and systematic interdisciplinary research (for a sample review of this literature see Hare, 1976). Among the conclusions of this recent work is the crucial insight that:

> The face-to-face group working on a problem is the meeting ground of individual personality and society. It is in the group that personality is modified and socialized; and it is through the workings of groups that society is changed and adapted to its times (Thelen, 1954, p. vi).

Similarly, in the field of organization development, Srivastva, Obert, and Neilsen (1977) have shown that the historical development of the discipline has paralleled advances in group theory. And this, they contend, is no accident because:

> Emphasis on the small group is responsive to the realities of social change in large complex organizations. It is through group life that individuals learn, practice, develop, and modify their roles in the larger organization. To enter programmatically at the group level is both to confront and potentially co-opt an important natural source of change and development in these systems (p. 83).

It is well established that groups are formed around common ideas that are expressed in and through some kind of shared language which makes communicative interaction possible. What is less clear, though, is the exact role that science plays in shaping group life through the medium of language. However, the fact that science frequently does have an impact is rarely questioned. Andre Gorz (1973) offers an explosive example of this point.

In the early 1960s a British professor of sociology by the name of Goldthorpe was brought in from a nearby university to make a study of the Vauxhall automobile workers in Luton, England. At the time, management at the factory was worried because workers in other organizations throughout the United Kingdom were showing great unrest over working conditions, pay, and management. Many strikes were being waged, most of them wildcat strikes called by the factory stewards, not by the unions themselves. Goldthorpe was called in to study the situation at Vauxhall, to find out for management if there was anything to worry about at their factory. At the time of the study there were at Vauxhall no strikes, no disruptions, and no challenges by workers. Management wanted to know why. What were the chances that acute conflict would break out in the "well-managed" and "advanced" big factory?

After two full years of research, the professor drew his conclusions. Management, he said, had little to worry about. According to the study, the workers were completely socialized into the system, they were satisfied with their wages and neither liked or disliked their work—in fact, they were indifferent to it, viewing it as boring but inevitable. Because their job was not intrinsically rewarding, most people did it just to be done with it—so they could go home and work on other more worthwhile projects and be with their family. Work was marginal and instrumental. It was a means to support other interests outside the factory, where "real life" began. Based then on his observations, Goldthorpe theorized that management had nothing to worry about: Workers were passively apathetic and well integrated into the system. They behaved according to middle-class patterns and showed no signs of strength as a group (no class-consciousness). Furthermore, most conflict with management belonged to the past.

The sociologist's report was still at the printer's when some employees got hold of a summary of his findings. They had the conclusions copied and distributed reports to hundreds of co-workers. Also at around this time, a report of Vauxhall's profits was being circulated, profits that were not shared with the employees. The next day something happened. It was reported by the *London Times* in detail:

> Wild rioting has broken out at the Vauxhall car factories in Luton. Thousands of workers streamed out of the shops and gathered in the factory yard. They besieged the management offices, calling for managers to come out, singing the 'Red Flag,' and shouting, 'String them up!' Groups attempted to storm the offices and battled police which had been called to protect them (quoted in Gorz, 1973).

The rioting lasted for two days.

All of this happened, then, in an advanced factory where systematic research showed workers to be apathetic, weak as a group, and resigned to accept the system. What does it all mean? Had the researchers simply misread the data? To the contrary. Goldthorpe knew his data well. He articulated the conclusions accurately, concisely, and with force. In fact, what happened was that the report gave the workers a *language* with which to begin talking to one another about their plight. It brought them into interaction and, as they discussed things, they discovered that Goldthorpe was right. They felt alike, apathetic but frustrated; and they were apathetic because they felt as individuals working in isolated jobs, that no one could do anything to change things. But the report gave them a way to discuss the situation. As they talked, things changed. People were no longer alone in their feelings, and they did not want things to continue as they were. As an emergent group, they now had a means to convert apathy into action, noninvolvement into involvement, and individual powerlessness into collective strength. "In other words," analyzes Gorz, "the very investigation of Mr. Goldthorpe about the lack of class-consciousness helped tear down the barriers of silence and isolation that rendered the workers apathetic" (p. 334).

The Vauxhall case is an important one for a number of reasons. At a general level it demonstrates that knowledge in the social sciences differs in quality and kind from knowledge generated in the physical sciences. For instance, our knowledge of the periodic chart does not change the elements, and our knowledge of the moon's orbit does not change its path. But our knowledge of a social system is different. It can be used by the system to change itself, thus invalidating or disconfirming the findings immediately or at some later time. Thus the human group differs from objects in an important way: Human beings have the capacity for symbolic interaction and, through language, they have the ability to collaborate in the investigation of their own world. Because of our human capacity for symbolic interaction, the introduction of new knowledge concerning aspects of our world carries with it the strong likelihood of changing that world itself.

Gergen (1982) refers to this as the "enlightenment effect" of scientifc work, meaning that once the formulations of scientific work are made public, human beings may act autonomously either to disconfirm or to validate the propositions. According to logical positivist philosophy, potential enlightenment effects must be reduced or—ideally-eliminated through experimental controls. In social psychology, for example, deception plays a crucial role in doing research; enlightenment effects are viewed as contaminants to good scientific work. Yet there is an alternative way to look at the reactive nature of social research: it is precisely because of the enlightenment effect that theory can and does play an important role in the positive construction of society. In this sense, the enlightenment effect—which is made possible through language—is an essential ingredient making scientific work worthwhile, meaningful, and applicable. It constitutes an invitation to each and every theorist to actively participate in the creation of his or her world by generating compelling theories of what is good, and just, and desirable in social existence.

5. Extending Visions of Possibility

The position taken by the sociorationalist philosophy of science is that the conduct of inquiry cannot be separated from the everyday negotiation of reality. Social-organizational research is, therefore, a continuing moral concern, a concern of social reconstruction and direction. The choice of what to study, how to study it, and what to report each implies some degree of responsibility. Science, therefore, instead of being considered an endpoint, is viewed as one means of helping humanity create itself. Science in this sense exists for one singular overarching purpose. As Albion Small (1905) proposed almost a century ago, a generative science must aim at "the most thorough, intense, persistent, and systematic effort to make human life all that it is capable of becoming" (pp. 36–37).

Theories gain their generative capacity by extending visions that expand to the realm of the possible. As a general proposition it might be said that theories designed to empower organized social systems will tend to have a greater enlightenment effect than theories of human constraint. This proposition is grounded in a simple but important consideration which we should like to raise as it relates to the unity of theory and practice: Is it not possible that scientific theory gains its capacity to affect cultural practices in very much the same way that powerful leaders inspire people to new heights? Recent research on the functioning of the executive mind (Srivastva, 1983; 1985) raises a set of intriguing parallels between the possibilities of a generative science and the workings of the executive mind.

The essential parallel is seen in the primary role that ideas or ideals play in the mobilization of diverse groups in the common construction of a desired future. Three major themes from the research stand out in this regard:

a. *Vision:* The executive mind works largely from the present and extends itself out to the longer-term future. It is powerful to the extent that it is able to envision a desired future state which challenges perceptions of what is possible and what can be realized. The executive mind operates beyond the frontier of conventional practice without losing sight of either necessity or possibility.

b. *Passion:* The executive mind is simultaneously rational and intuitive, which allows it to tap into the sentiments, values, and dreams of the social collectivity. Executive vision becomes "common vision" to the extent that it ignites the imaginations, hopes, and passions of others—and it does so through the articulation of self-transcending ideals which lend meaning and significance to everyday life.

c. *Integrity:* The executive mind is the mental muscle that moves a system from the present state to a new and different future. As such, this muscle gains strength to the extent that it is founded upon an integrity able to withstand contrary pressures. There are three dimensions to executive integrity. The first, *system integrity*, refers to the fact that the executive mind perceives the world (the organization, group, or society) as a unified whole, not as a collection of individual parts. The second type of integrity is *moral integrity*. Common-vision leadership is largely an act of caring. It follows the "path of the heart," which is the source of moral and ethical standards. Finally, *integrity of vision* refers to consistency, coherence, and focus. Executive vision—to the extent to which it is compelling—is focused and unwavering, even in the midst of obstacles, critics, and conflicting alternatives.

Interestingly, these thematic dimensions of the executive mind have their counterparts in recent observations concerning the utilization of organizational research. According to Beyer and Trice (1982), the "affective bonding" that takes place during the research largely determines the attractiveness of its results and generates commitment to utilize their implications. For example, Henshel (1975) suggests that research containing predictions of an appealing future will be utilized and preferred over research that points to a negative or repelling future: "People will work for predicted states they approve of and against those they detest" (p. 103). Similarly, Weiss and Bucavalas (1980) report that results which challenge the status quo are most attractive to high-level executives because they are the persons expected to make new things happen, at least on the level of policy. And, with respect to passion and integrity, Mitroff (1980) urges social scientists to become caring advocates of their ideas, not only to diffuse their theories but also to challenge others to prove them wrong and thus pursue those ideas which have integrity in action.

This section has explored a number of ways in which social theory becomes a powerful resource for change and development in social practice. The argument is simple. Theory is agential in character and has unbounded potential to affect patterns of social action—whether desired or not. As we have seen, theories are not mere explanations of an external world lying "out there" waiting to be objectively recorded. Theories, like powerful ideas, are formative. By establishing perceptual cues and frames, by providing presumptions of logic, by transmitting subtle values, by creating new language, and by extending compelling visions of possibility or constraint—in all these ways social theory becomes a powerful means whereby norms, beliefs, and cultural practices may be altered.

REAWAKENING THE SPIRIT OF ACTION-RESEARCH

The key point is this: Instinctively, intuitively, and tacitly we all know that important ideas can, in a flash, profoundly alter the way we see ourselves, view reality, and conduct our lives. Experience shows that a simple economic forecast, political poll, or technical discovery (like the atomic bomb) can forever change the course of human history. Thus one cannot help but be disturbed and puzzled by the discipline of action-research in its wide-ranging indifference to theory. Not only does it continue to underrate the role of theory as a means for organizational development (Friedlander & Brown, 1974; Bartunek, 1983; Argyris, 1983) but it appears also to have become locked within an assumptive base that systematically distorts our view of organizational reality and inadvertantly helps reinforce and perfect the status quo (Brimm, 1972).

Why is there this lack of generative theorizing in action-research? And, more importantly, what can be done to rekindle the spirit, excitement and passion required of a science that wishes to be of vital significance to organizations? Earlier we talked about a philosophy of science congenial to the task. Sociorationalism, it was argued, represents an epistemological point of view conducive to catalytic theorizing. Ironically though, it can be argued that most action-researchers *already do* subscribe to this or a similar view of science (Susman & Evered, 1978). Assuming this to be the case, it becomes an even greater puzzle why contemporary action-research continues to disregard theory-building as an integral and necessary component of the craft. In this section we shall broaden our discussion by taking a look at some of the metaphysical assumptions embedded in our conventional definitions of action-research—assumptions that can be shown to govern our thought and work in ways inimical to present interests.

Paradigm I: Organizing As A Problem to be Solved

The intellectual and spiritual origins of action-research can be traced to Kurt Lewin, a social psychologist of German origin who coined the term *action-research* in 1944. The thrust of Lewin's work cenetered on the need to bridge the gap between science and the realm of practical affairs. Science, he said, should be used to inform and educate social practice, and subsequent action would then inform science: "We should consider action, research, and training as a triangle that should be kept together" (Lewin, 1948, p. 211). The twofold promise of an action science, according to Lewin, was to simultaneously contribute to the development of scientific knowledge (propositions of an if/then variety) and use such knowledge for bettering the human condition.

The immense influence of Lewin is a complete puzzle if we look only to his writings. The fact of the matter is that Lewin published only 2 papers—a mere 22 pages—concerned directly with the idea of action-research (Peters & Robinson, 1984). Indeed, it has been argued that his enduring influence is attributable not to these writings but to the sheer force and presence of the man himself. According to biographer Alfred Marrow (1968), Lewin was a passionate and creative thinker, continuously knocking at the door of the unknown, studying "topics that had been believed to be psychologically unapproachable." Lewin's character was marked by a spirit of inquiry that burned incessantly and affected all who came in contact with him, especially his students. The intensity of his presence was fueled further by the belief that inquiry itself could be used to construct a more democratic and dignified future. At least this was his hope and dream, for Lewin had *not* forgotten his experience as a refugee from facism in the late 1930s. Understanding this background, then, it is clear why he revolted so strongly against a detached ivory-tower view of science, a science that is immersed in trivial matters, tranquilized by its standardized methods, and limited in its field of inquiry. Thus, the picture we have of Lewin shows him to have been a committed social scientist pioneering uncharted territory for the purpose of creating new knowledge about groups and societies that might advance the democratic ideal (see, for example, Lewin, 1952). It was this spirit—a relentless curiosity coupled with a conviction of the need for knowledge-guided societal development—that marked Lewin's creative impact on both his students and the field.

Much of this spirit is now gone from action-research. What is left is a series of assumptions about the world which exhibits little, if any, resemblance to the process of inquiry as Lewin lived it. While many of the words are the same, they have been taken too literally and in their translation over the years have been bloated into a set of metaphysical principles—assumptions about the essence of social existence—that directly undermine the intellectual and speculative spirit. Put bluntly, under current norms, action-research has largely failed as an instrument for advancing social knowledge of consequence and now risks being (mis)understood as little more than a crude empiricism imprisoned in a deficiency mode of thought. A quick sketch of six sets of assumptions embedded in the conventional view of action-research will show exactly what we are talking about while also answering our question about the discipline's lack of contribution to generative theory:

Research equals problem-solving; to do good research is to solve "real problems." So ingrained is this assumption that it scarcely needs documentation. Virtually every definition found in leading texts and articles equates action-research with problem solving—as if "real" problem solving is virtually the essence of the discipline. For example, as French and Bell (1978) define it, "Action-research is both *an approach to problem solving*—a model or paradigm, and a *problem-solving process*—a series of activities and events" (p. 88)[4] Or in terms of the Bradford, Gibb, and Benne (1964) definition, "It is an application of scientific methodology in *the clarification* and *solution of practical problems*" (p. 33). Similarly, Frohman, Sashkin, and Kavanaugh (1976) state: "Action researach describes a particular process model whereby behavioral science knowledge is applied to help a client (usually a group or social system) *solve real problems and not incidentally learn the process involved in problem solving*" (p. 203). Echoing this theme, that research equals problem solving, researchers at the University of Michigan's Institute in Social Research state,

> "Three factors need to be taken into account in an organization development [action-research] effort: The behaviors that are problematic, the conditions that create those behaviors, and the interventions or activities that will correct the conditions creating the problems. What is it that people are doing or not doing, that is a problem? Why are they doing or not doing these particular things? Which of a large number of possible interventions or activities would be most likely to solve the problems by focusing on why problems exist?" (Hausser, Pecorella & Wissler, 1977, p. 2).

Here it is unmistakeably clear that the primary focus of the action-research approach to organizational analysis is the ongoing array of concrete problems an organization faces. Of course, there are a number of differences in the discipline as to the overall definition and meaning of the emerging action-research paradigm. But this basic assumption—that research equals problem solving—is not one of them. In a recent review intended to discover elements of metatheoretical agreement within the discipline, Peters and Robinson (1984) discovered that out of 15 different dimensions of action-research studied, only 2 had unanimous support among leaders in the field. What were these two elements of agreement? Exactly as the definitions above suggest: Social science should be "action-oriented" and "problem focused."

Inquiry, in action-research terms, is a matter of following the standardized rules of problem solving; knowledge is the result of good method. "In essence," write Blake and Mouton (1976), "it is a method of empirical data gathering that *is comprised of a set of rather standardized steps:* diagnosis, information gathering, feedback, and action planning" (pp. 101–102). By following this ritual list, they contend that virtually any organization can be studied in a manner that will lead to usable knowledge. As Chiles (1983) puts it, "The virtue of the model lies in the sequential process. . . . Any other sequence renders the model meaningless" (p. 318). The basic idea behind the model is that "in management, events proceed as planned unless some force, not provided against by the plan, acts upon events to produce an outcome not contemplated in the plan" (Kepner & Tregoe, 1973, p. 3). Thus, a problem is a deviation from some standard, and without precise diagnosis (step one) any attempt to resolve the problem will likely fail as a result of not penetrating the surface symptoms to discover the true causes. Hence, like a liturgical refrain which is seldom questioned or thought about, Cohen, Fink et al. (1984) tell the new student that *knowledge is the offspring of processing information through a distinct series of problem-solving stages:*

> Action-research begins with an identified problem. Data are then gathered in a way that allows a diagnosis which can produce a tentative solution, which is then implemented with the assumption that it is likely to cause new or unforeseen problems that will, in turn, need to be evaluated, diagnosed, and so forth. *This action-research method assumes a constantly evolving interplay between solutions, results, and new solutions. . . . This model is a general one applicable to solving any kind of problem in an ongoing organization* (pp. 359-360).

Action-research is utilitarian or technical; that is, it should be initiated and designed to meet a need in an area specified by the organization, usually by "top management." The search is controlled by the "felt need" or object of inquiry; everything that is not related to this object should be dismissed as irrelevant. As we are beginning to see, action-research conventionally understood does not really refer to research per se but rather to a highly focused and defined type of research called problem solving. Taken almost directly from the medical model, the disease orientation guides the process of inquiry in a highly programmed way. According to Levinson (1972), diagnostic action-research, "like a therapeutic or teaching relationship should be an alliance of both parties to discover and resolve these problems. . . . [The researcher] *should look for experiences which appear stressful to people. What kinds of occurrences disrupt or disorganize people*" (p. 37). Hence in a systematically limiting fashion, the general topic of research is largely prescribed—before inquiry even begins. As we would guess:

> Typical questions in [action-research] data gathering or "problem sensing" would include: *What problems* do you see in your group, including problems between people that are interfering with getting the job done the way you would like to see it done? And *what problems* do you see in the broader organization? Such open-ended questions provide latitude on the part of respondents and encourage a *reporting of problems* as the individual sees them (French, 1969, pp. 183-185).

In problem solving it is assumed that something is broken, fragmented, not whole, and that it needs to be fixed. Thus the function of problem solving is to integrate, stabilize, and help raise to its full potential the workings of the status quo. By definition, a problem implies that one already has knowledge of what "should be"; thus one's *research* is guided by an instrumental purpose tied to what is already known. In this sense, problem solving tends to be inherently conservative; as a form of research it tends to produce and reproduce a universe of knowledge that remains sealed. As Staw (1984) points out in his review of the field, most organizational research is biased to serve managerial interests rather than exploring broader human and/or social purposes. But even more important, he argues, the field has not even served managerial interests well since research has taken a short-term problem focus rather than having formulated logics of new forms of organization that do not exist. It is as if the discipline's *concept of social-system development* means only clearing up distortions in current functioning (horizontal development) and does not include any conception of a stage-based movement toward an altogether new or transformed reality (vertical development or second-order change).

Action-research should not inquire into phenomena that transcend the competence of human reason. Questions that cannot be answered should not be asked and issues that cannot be acted upon should not be explored (i.e., action-research is not a branch of political philosophy, poetry, or theology). This proposition is a "smuggled-in" corollary to the preceding assumptions. It would appear that once one agrees with the ground rules of a pragmatic problem-solving science, the universe for inquiry is largely predetermined, defined, and delimited in scope. Specifically, what one agrees to a secularized view of a human universe that is predictable, controllable, and rational, one that is sequentially ordered into a series of causes and effects. As both a credit and a weakness, the problem-solving mode narrows our gaze in much the same manner that a blinder over one eye narrows the field of vision and distorts one's perception of depth. As a part of a long-term movement evidenced in social sciences, contemporary action-research embodies the trend toward metaphysical skepticism and denial (Quinney, 1982). That is, it operates out of a sacred void that cuts off virtually any inquiry into the vital forces of life. Indeed, the whole promise of modern science was that it would finally banish illusion, mystery, and uncertainty from the world. An inquiry process of immediate utility (problem solving), therefore, requires an anti-religious, secular spirit that will limit the realm of study to the sphere of the known. And because of the recognition that the formulation of a problem depends largely on one's views of what constitutes a solution, it is not surprising to find that *research on the utilization of research* shows a propensity for social scientists and organizations to agree on studying only those variables that can be manipulated (Beyer & Trice, 1982). As one might imagine, such a view has crippling implications for generative theorizing. For example, as typically practiced, action-research does little in the way of theorizing about or bringing beauty into organizational life. Does this mean that there is no beauty in organizing? Does this mean that the realm of the esthetic has little or nothing to do with organizational dynamics?

The tidy imagery of the problem-solving view is related to what Sigmund Koch (1981) has called, in his presidential address to the APA, the syndrome of "ameaningful thinking." One element of this syndrome is the perpetuation of the scientistic myth which uses the rhetoric of prediction and control to reassure people that their lives are not that complex, their situations not all that uncertain—and that their problems are indeed manageable through causal analysis. In the process, however, science tends to trivialize, and even evade, a whole class of

Appreciative Inquiry in Organizational Life

issues that "transcend the competence of human reason" yet are clearly meaningful in the course of human experience. One way in which the field of inquiry is restricted, according to Koch, has to do with one's choice of methodology:

> There are times and circumstances in which able individuals, committed to inquiry, tend almost obsessively to frustrate the objectives of inquiry. It is as if uncertainty, nootness, ambiguity, cognitive infinitude were the most unbearable of the existential anguishes.... A meaningful thought or inquiry regards knowledge as the result of "processing" rather than discovery. It presumes that knowledge is an almost automatic result of a gimmickry, an assembly line, a "methology".... So strongly does it see knowledge under such aspects that it sometimes seems to suppose the object of inquiry to be an ungainly and annoying irrevelance (1981, p. 259).

To be sure, this is not to argue that all action-research is "ameaningful" or automatically tied to a standardized problem-solving method. Likewise, much of the success achieved by action-research until now may be attributed to its restricted focus on that which is "solvable." However, it is important to recognize that the problem-solving method of organizational inquiry quite systematically paints a picture of organizational life in which a whole series of colors are considered untouchable. In this way the totality of being is obviously obscured, leading to a narrowed conception of human nature and cultural possibility.

Problems are "out there" to be studied and solved. The ideal product of action-research is a mirror-like reflection of the organization's problems and causes. As "objective third party," there is little role for passion and speculation. The action-researcher should be neither a passionate advocate nor an inspired dreamer (utopian thinker). One of the laudable and indeed significant values associated with action-research has been its insistence upon a collaborative form of inquiry. But unfortunately, from a generative-theory perspective, the term *collaboration* has become virtually synonymous with an idealized image of the researcher as a facilitator and mirror, rather than an active and fully engaged social participant. As facilitator of the problem-solving process, the action-researcher has three generally agreed-upon "primary intervention tasks": to help generate valid organizational data; to enable others to make free and informed choices on the basis of the data; and to help the organization generate internal commitment to their choices. Elaborating further, Argyris (1970) states:

> One condition that seems so basic as to be defined as axiomatic is the generation of *valid information*.... Valid information is that which describes the factors, plus their interrelationships, that create the problem (pp. 16-17).

Furthermore, it is also assumed that for data to be useful there must be a claim to neutrality. The data should represent an accurate reflection of the observed facts. As French and Bell (1978) describe it, it is important for the action-researcher to stress the objective, fact-finding features: "A key value inculcated in organizational members is a belief in the validity, desirability, and usefulness of the data" (p. 79). Then through feedback that "refers to activities and processes that 'reflect' or 'mirror' an objective picture of the real world" (p. 111), the action-researcher facilitates the process of prioritizing problems and helps others make choices for action. And because the overarching objective is to help the organization develop its own internal resources, the action-researcher should not play an active role or take an advocate stance that might in the long run foster an unhealthy dependency. As French and Bell (1978) again explain, an active role "tends to negate a collaborative, developmental approach to improving organizational processes" (p. 203).

As must be evident, every one of these injunctions associated with the problem-solving view of action-research serves directly to diminish the likelihood of imaginative, passionate, creative theory. To the extent that generative theory represents an inspired theoretical articulation of a new and different future, it appears that action-research would have nothing to do with it. According to French and Bell (1978) "Even the presenting of options can be overdone. If the [action-researcher's] ideas become the focal point for prolonged discussion and debate, the consultant has clearly shifted away from the facilitator role" (p. 206).

At issue here is something even more important. The fundamental attitude embodied in the problem-solving view is separationist. It views the world as something external to our consciousness of it, something "out there." As such it tends to identify problems not here but "over there": Problems are not ours, but yours; not a condition common to all, but a condition belonging to this person, their group, or that nation (witness the acid-rain issue). Thus, the action-researcher is content to facilitate *their problem solving* because he or she is not part of that world. To this extent, the problem-solving view dissects reality and parcels it out into fragmented groups, families, tribes, or countries. In both form and substance it denies the wholeness of a dynamic and interconnected social universe. And once the unity of the world is broken, passionless, mindless, mirror-like inquiry comes to make logical sense precisely because the inquirer has no ownership or stake in a world that is not his or hers to begin with.

Organizational life is problematic. Organizing is best understood as a historically situated sequence of problems, causes, and solutions among people, events, and things. Thus, the ultimate aim and product of action-research is the production of institutions that have a high capacity to perceive, formulate, and solve an endless stream of problems.

The way we conceive of the social world is of consequence to the kind of world we discover and even, through our reconstructions, helps to create it. Action-researchers, like scientists in other areas, approach their work from a framework based on taken-for-granted assumptions. To the extent that these assumptions are found useful, and are affirmed by colleagues, they remain unquestioned as a habitual springboard for one's work. In time the conventional view becomes so solidly embedded that it assumes the status of being "real," without alternative (Morgan, 1980; Mennhiem, 1936). As human beings we are constantly in symbolic interaction, attempting to develop conceptions that will allow us to make sense of and give meaning to experience through the use of language, ideas, signs, theories, and names. As many have recently shown, the use of metaphor is a basic mode under which symbolism works and exerts an influence on the development of language, science, and cognitive growth (Morgan, 1980; Ortony, 1979; Black, 1962; Keely, 1980). Metaphor works by asserting that A equals B or is very much like B. We use metaphors constantly to open our eyes and sensitize us to phenomenal realities that otherwise might go unnoticed. Pepper (1942) argues that all science proceeds from specifiable "world hypotheses" and behind every world hypothesis rests the boldest of "root metaphors."

Within what we are calling Paradigm I action-research, there lies a guiding metaphor which has a power impact on the theory-building activity of the discipline. When organizations are approached from the deficiency perspective of Paradigm I, all the properties and modes of organizing are scrutinized for their dysfunctional but potentially solvable problems. It is all too clear then that the root metaphor of the conventional view is that *organizing is a problem.* This image focuses the researcher's eye on a visible but narrow realm of reality that resides "out there" and is causally determined, deficient by some preexisting standard—on problems that are probably both understandable and solvable. Through analysis, diagnosis, treatment, and follow-up evaluation the sequential world of organizing can be kept on its steady and productive course. And because social existence is at its base a problem to be solved, real living equals problem solving, and living better is an adaptive learning process whereby we acquire new and more effective means for tackling tough problems. The good life, this image informs, depends on solving problems in such a way that problems of utility are identified and solutions of high quality are found and carried out with full commitment. As one leading theorist describes:

> For many scholars who study organizations and management, the central characteristic of organizations is that they *are* problem-solving systems whose success is measured by how efficiently they solve problems associated with accomplishing their primary mission and how effectively they respond to emergent problems. Kilmann's approach (1979, pp. 214-215) is representative of this perspective: "One might even define the essence of management as problem defining and problem solving, whether the problems are well-structured, ill-structured, technical, human, or environmental. . . . " In this view, the core task of the executive is problem management. Although experience, personality, and specific technical expertise are important, the primary skill of the successful executive is the ability to manage the problem-solving process in such a way that important problems are identified and solutions of high quality are found and carried out with the full commitment of organizational members (Kolb, 1983, pp. 109-110).

From here it is just a short conceptual jump to the idealized aim of Paradigm I research:

Action-research tends to build into the client system an institutionalized pattern for continuously collecting data and examining the system's processes, as well as for the continuous review of *known* problem areas. *Problem solving becomes very much a way of organizational life* (Marguiles and Raia, 1972, p. 29).

I have tried in these few pages to highlight the almost obvious point that the deficiency/problem orientation is pervasive and holds a subtle but powerful grasp on the discipline's imagination and focus. It can be argued that the generative incapacity of contemporary action-research is securely linked with the discipline's guiding metaphor of social-organizational existence. As noted by many scholars, the theoretical output of the discipline is virtually nonexistent, and what theory there is is largely problem-focused (theories of turnover, intergroup conflict, processes of dehumanization. See Staw, 1984 for an excellent review). Thus, our theories, like windsocks, continue to blow steadily onward in the direction of our conventional gaze. Seeing the world as a problem has become "very much a way of organizational life."

It is our feeling that the discipline has reached a level of fatigue arising from repetitious use of its standardized model. Fatigue, as Whitehead (1929) so aptly surmised, arises from an act of excluding the impulse toward novelty which is the antithesis of the life of the mind and of speculative reason. To be sure, there can be great adventure in the process of inquiry. Yet not many action-researchers today return from their explorations refreshed and revitalized, like pioneers returning home, with news of lands unknown but most certainly there. Perhaps there is a different root metaphor from which to work.

Proposal for a Second Dimension

Our effort here is but one in a small yet growing attempt to generate new perspectives on the conduct of organizational research, perspectives that can yield the kind of knowledge necessary for both understanding and transforming complex social-organizational systems (Torbert, 1983; Van Maanen et al., 1982; Mitroff & Kilmann, 1978; Smirchich, 1983; Forester, 1983; Argyris, 1970; Friedlander, 1977). It is apparent that among the diverse views currently emerging there is frequently great tension. Often the differences become the battleground for fierce debate about theories of truth, the meaning of "facts," political agendas, and personal assertions of will. But, more fruitfully, what can be seen emerging is a heightened sensitivity to and interdisciplinary recognition of the fact that, based on "the structure of knowledge" (Kolb, 1984), there may be multiple ways of knowing, each of them valid in its own realm when judged according to its own set of essential assumptions and purposes. In this sense there are many different ways of studying the same phenomenon, and the insights generated by one approach are, at best, partial and incomplete. According to Jürgen Habermas (1971) different perspectives can be evaluated only in terms of their specified "human interests," which can broadly be differentiated into the realm of practical rationality and the realm of technical rationality. In more straightforward language Morgan (1983) states:

> The selection of method implies some view of the situation being studied, for any decision on how to study a phenomenon carries with it certain assumptions or explicit answers to the question, "*What is being studied?*" Just as we select a tennis racquet rather than a golf club to play tennis because we have a prior conception as to what the game of tennis involves, so too, in relation to the process of social research, we select or favor particular kinds of methodology because we have implicit or explicit conceptions as to what we are trying to do with our research (p. 19).

Thus, in adopting one mode over another the researcher directly influences what he or she will finally discover and accomplish.

It is the contention of this chapter that advances in generative theorizing will come about for action-research when the discipline decides to expand its universe of exploration, seeks to discover new questions, and rekindles a fresh perception of the extra ordinary in everyday organizational life. In this final section we now describe the assumptions and philosophy of an applied administrative science that seeks to embody these suggestions in a form of organization study we call appreciative inquiry. In distinction to conventional action-research, the knowledge-interest of appreciative inquiry lies not so much in problem solving as in social innovation. Appreciative inquiry refers to a research perspective that is uniquely intended for discovering, understanding, and fostering innovations in social-organizational arrangements and processes.[5] Its purpose is to contribute to the generative-theoretical aims of social science and to use such knowledge to promote egalitarian dialogue leading to social-system effectiveness and integrity. Whatever else it may be, social-system effectiveness is defined here quite specifically as a congruence between social-organizational values (the ever-changing normative set of values, ideas, or interests that system members hold concerning the question, "How should we organize ourselves?") and everyday social-organizational practices (cf. Torbert, 1983). Thus, appreciative inquiry refers to both a search for knowledge and a theory of intentional collective action which are designed to help evolve the normative vision and will of a group, organization, or society as a whole. It is an inquiry process that affirms our symbolic capacities of imagination and mind as well as our social capacity for conscious choice and cultural evolution. As a holistic form of inquiry, it asks a series of questions not found in either a logical-positivist conception of science or a strictly pragmatic, problem-solving mode of action-research. Yet as shown in Figure 1, its aims are both scientific (in a sociorationalist sense) and pragmatic (in a social-innovation sense) as well as metaphysical and normative (in the sense of attempting ethically to affirm all that social existence really is and should become). As a way of talking about the framework as it is actually practiced, we shall first examine four guiding principles that have directed our work in the area to date:

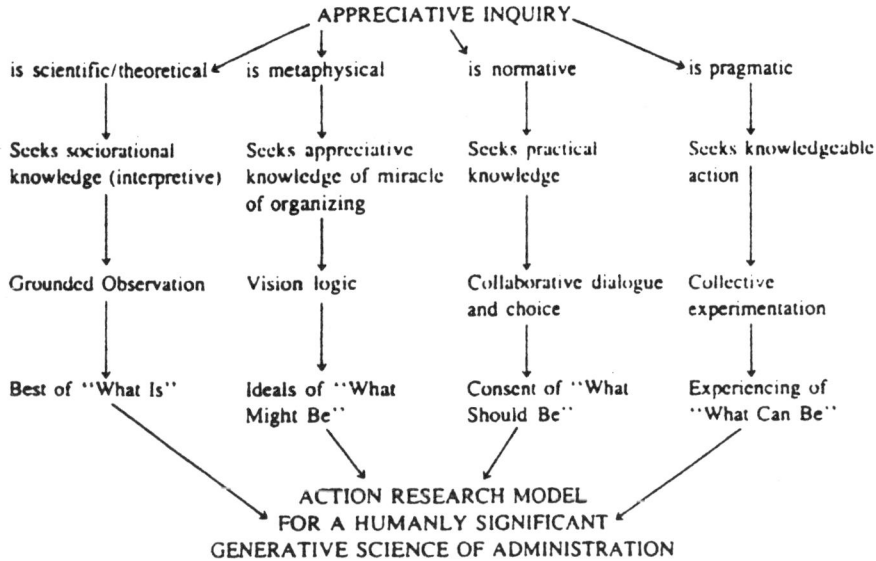

Figure 1. Dimensions of Appreciative Inquiry

Principle 1: Research into the social (innovation) potential of organizational life should begin with appreciation. This basic principle assumes that every social system "works" to some degree—that it is not in a complete state of entropy—and that a primary task of research is to discover, describe, and explain those social innovations, however small, which serve to give "life" to the system and activate members' competencies and energies as more fully functioning participants in the formation and transformation of organizational realities. That is, the appreciative approach takes its inspiration from the current state of "what is" and seeks a comprehensive understanding of the factors and forces of organizing (ideological, techno-structural, cultural) that serve to heighten the total potential of an organization in ideal-type human and social terms.

Principle 2: Research into the social potential of organizational life should be applicable. To be significant in a human sense, an applied science of administration should lead to the generation of theoretical knowledge that can be used, applied, and thereby validated in action. Thus, an applicable inquiry process is neither utopian in the sense of generating knowledge about "no place" (Sargent, 1982) nor should it be confined to academic circles and presented in ways that have little relevance to the everyday language and symbolism of those for whom the findings might be applicable.

Principle 3: Research into the social potential of organizational life should be provocative. Here it is considered axiomatic that an organization is, in fact, an open-ended indeterminate system capable of (1) becoming more than it is at any given moment, and (2) learning how to actively take part in guiding its own evolution. Hence, appreciative knowledge of *what is* (in terms of "peak" social innovations in organizing) is suggestive of what *might be* and such knowledge can be used to generate images of realistic developmental opportunities that can be experimented with on a wider scale. In this sense, appreciative inquiry can be both pragmatic and visionary. It becomes provocative to the extent that the abstracted findings of a study take on normative value for members of an organization, and this can happen only through their own critical deliberation and choice ("We feel that this particular finding is [or not] important for us to envision as an ideal to be striving for in practice on a wider scale"). It is in this way then, that appreciative inquiry allows us to put intuitive, visionary logic on a firm empirical footing and to use systematic research to help the organization's members shape the social world according to their own imaginative and moral purposes.

Principle 4: Research into the social potential of organizational life should be collaborative. This overarching principle points to the assumed existence of an inseparable relationship between the process of inquiry and its content. A collaborative relationship between the researcher and members of an organization is, therefore, deemed essential on the basis of both epistemological (Susman & Evered, 1978) and practical/ethical grounds (Habermas, 1971; Argyris, 1970). Simply put, a unilateral approach to the study of social innovation (bringing something new into the social world) is a direct negation of the phenomenon itself.

The spirit behind each of these four principles of appreciative inquiry is to be found in one of the most ancient archetypes or metaphorical symbols of hope and inspiration that humankind has ever known—the miracle and mystery of being. Throughout history, people have recognized the intimate relationship between being seized by the unfathomable and the process of appreciative knowing or thought (Marcel, 1963; Quinney, 1982; Jung, 1933; Maslow, 1968; Ghandi, 1958). According to Albert Schweitzer (1969), for example, it is recognition of the ultimate mystery that elevates our perception beyond the world of ordinary objects, igniting the life of the mind and a "reverence for life":

> In all respects the universe remains mysterious to man.... As soon as man does not take his existence for granted, but beholds it as something unfathomably mysterious, thought begins. This phenomenon has been repeated time and time again in the history of the human race. Ethical affirmation of life is the intellectual act by which man ceases simply to live at random.... [Such] thought has a dual task to accomplish: to lead us out of a naive and into a profounder affirmation of life and the universe; and to help us progress from ethical impulses to a rational system of ethics (p. 33).

For those of us breastfed by an industrial giant that stripped the world of its wonder and awe, it feels, to put it bluntly, like an irrelevant, absurd, and even distracting interruption to pause, reflect deeply, and then humbly accept the depth of what we can never know—and to consider the ultimate reality of living for which there are no coordinates or certainties, only questions. Medicine cannot tell me, for example, what it means that my newborn son has life and motion and soul, anymore than the modern physicist can tell me what "nothingness" is, which, they say, makes up over 99 percent of the universe. In fact, if there is anything we have learned from a great physicist of our time is that the promise of certainty is a lie (Hiesenberg, 1958), and by living this lie as scientistic doctrine, we short-circuit the gift of complementarity—the capacity for dialectically opposed modes of knowing, which adds richness, depth, and beauty to our lives (Bohr, 1958). Drugged by the products of our industrial machine we lose sight of and connection with the invisible mystery at the heart of creation, an ultimate power beyond rational understanding.

In the same way that birth of a living, breathing, loving, thinking human being is an inexplicable mystery, so too it can be said in no uncertain terms that *organizing is a miracle* of cooperative human interaction, of which there can never be final explanation. In fact, to the extent that organizations are indeed born and re-created through dialogue, they truly are unknowable as long as such creative dialogue remains. At this point in time there simply are no organizational theories that can account for the life-giving essence of cooperative existence, especially if one delves deeply enough. But, somehow we forget all this. We become lulled by our simplistic diagnostic boxes. The dilemma faced by our discipline in terms of its creative contribution to knowledge is summed up perfectly in the title of a well known article by one of the major advocates of action-research. The title by Marv Wiesbord (1976), has proven prophetic: "Organizational diagnosis: six places to look for trouble, with or without a theory." Content to transfer our conceptual curiosity over to "experts" who finally must know, our creative instincts lie pitifully dormant. Instead of explorers we become mechanics.

This, according to Koch (1981), is the source of "ameaningful" thinking. As Kierkegaard (1954) suggests, it is the essence of a certain dull-minded routine called "philistinism":

> Devoid of imagination, as the Philistine always is, he lives in a certain trivial province of experience as to how things go, what is possible. . . . Philistinism tranquilizes itself in the trivial (pp. 174–175).

As we know, a miracle is something that is beyond all possible verification, yet is experienced as real. As a symbol, the word *miracle* represents unification of the sacred and secular into a realm of totality that is at once terrifying and beautiful, inspiring and threatening. Quinney (1982) has suggested with respect to the rejuvenation of social theory, that such a unified viewpoint is altogether necessary, that it can have a powerful impact on the discipline precisely because in a world that is at once sacred and secular there is no place, knowledge, or phenomenon that is without mystery. The "miracle" then is pragmatic in its effect when sincerely apprehended by a mind that has chosen not to become "tranquilized in the trivial." In this sense, the metaphor "life is a miracle" is not so much an idea as it is—or can be—a central feature of experience enveloping (1) our perceptual consciousness; (2) our way of relation to others, the world, and our own research; and (3) our way of knowing. Each of these points can be highlighted by a diverse literature.

In terms of the first, scholars have suggested that the power of what we call the miracle lies in its capacity to advance one's perceptual capacity what Maslow (1968) has called a B-cognition or a growth-vs-deficiency orientation, or what Kolb (1984) has termed integrative consciousness. Kolb writes:

> The transcendental quality of integrative consciousness is precisely that, a "climbing out of".... This state of consciousness is not reserved for the monastary, but it is a necessary ingredient for creativity in any field. Albert Einstein once said, "The most beautiful and profound emotion one can feel is a sense of the mystical.... It is the dower of all true science" (p. 158).

Second, as Gabriel Marcel (1963) explained in his William James lectures at Harvard on *The Mystery of Being*, the central conviction of life as a mystery creates for us a distinctly different relationship to the world than the conviction of life as a problem to be solved:

> A problem is something met which bars my passage. It is before me in its entirety. A mystery on the other hand is something I find *myself* caught up in, and whose essence is therefore not before me in its entirety. It is though in this province the distinction between "in me" and "before me" loses its meaning (p. 80).

Berman's (1981) recent analysis comes to a similar conclusion. The re-enchantment of the world gives rise to a "participatory consciousness" where there is a sense of personal stake, ownership, and partnership with the universe:

> The view of nature which predominated the West down to the eve of the Scientific Revolution was that of an enchanted world. Rocks, trees, rivers, and clouds were all seen as wondrous, alive, and human beings felt at home in this environment. The cosmos, in short, was a place of *belonging*. A member of this cosmos was not an alienated observer of it but a direct participant in its drama. His personal destiny was bound up with its destiny, and this relationship gave meaning to his life.

Third, as so many artists and poets have shown, there is a relationship between what the Greeks called *thaumazein*—an experience which lies on the borderline between wonderment and admiration—and a type of intuitive apprehension or knowing that we call appreciative. For Keats, the purpose of his work was:

> to accept things as I saw them, to enjoy the beauty I perceived for its own sake, without regard to ultimate truth or falsity, and to make a description of it the end and purpose of my appreciations.

Similarly for Shelley:

> Poetry thus makes immortal all that is best and most beautiful in the world . . . it exalts the beauty of that which is most beautiful . . . it strips the veil of familiarity from the world, and lays bare the naked and sleeping beauty, which is in the spirit of its forms.

And in strikingly similar words, learning theorist David Kolb (1984) analyzes the structure of the knowing mind and reports:

> Finally, appreciation is a process of affirmation. Unlike criticism, which is based on skepticism and doubt (compare Polanyi, 1968, pp. 269ff.), appreciation is based on belief, trust, and conviction. And from this affirmative embrace flows a deeper fullness and richness of experience. This act of affirmation forms the foundation from which vital comprehension can develop. . . . Appreciative apprehension and critical comprehension are thus fundamentally different processes of knowing. Appreciation of immediate experience is an act of attention, valuing, and affirmation, whereas critical comprehension of symbols is based on objectivity (which involves a priori controls of attention, as in double-blind controlled experiments), dispassionate analysis, and skepticism (pp. 104–105).

We have cited these various thinkers in detail for several reasons: first, to underscore the fact that the powerful images of problem and miracle (in)form qualitatively distinct modes of inquiry which then shape our awareness, relations, and knowledge; and second, to highlight the conviction that the renewal of generative theory requires that we enter into the realm of the metaphysical. The chief characteristic of the modern mind has been the banishment of mystery from the world, and along with it an ethical affirmation of life that has served history as a leading source of values, hope, and normative bonding among people. In historical terms, we have steadily forgotten how to dream.

In contrast to a type of research that is lived without a sense of mystery, the appreciative mode awakens the desire to create and discover new social possibilities that can enrich our existence and give it meaning. In this sense, appreciative inquiry seeks an imaginative and fresh perception of organizations as "ordinary magic," as if seen for the first time—or perhaps the last time (Hayward, 1984). The appreciative mode, in exploration of ordinary magic, is an inquiry process that takes nothing for granted, searching to apprehend the basis of organizational life and working to articulate those possibilities giving witness to a better existence.

The metaphysical dimension of appreciative inquiry is important not so much as a way of finding answers but is important insofar as it heightens the living experience of awe and wonder which leads us to the wellspring of new questions—much like a wide-eyed explorer without final destination. Only by raising innovative questions will innovations in theory and practice be found. As far as action-research is concerned, this appears to have been the source of Lewin's original and catalytic genius. We too can re-awaken this spirit. Because the questions we ask largely determine what we find, we should place a premium on that which informs our curiosity and thought. The metaphysical question of what makes social existence possible will never go away. The generative-theoretical question of compelling new possibilities will never go away. The normative question of what kind of social-organizational order is best, most dignified, and just, will never go away, nor will the pragmatic question of how to move closer to the ideal.

In its pragmatic form appreciative inquiry represents a data-based theory-building methodology for evolving and putting into practice the collective will of a group or organization. It has one and only one aim—to provide a generative-theoretical springboard for normative dialogue that is conducive to self-directed experimentation in social innovation. It must be noted, however, that the conceptual world which appreciative inquiry creates remains—despite its empirical content—an illusion. This is important to recognize because it is precisely because of its visionary content, placed in juxtaposition to grounded examples of the extraordinary, that appreciative inquiry opens the status quo to possible transformations in collective action. It appreciates the best of "what is" to ignite intuition of the possible and then firmly unites the two logically, caringly, and passionately into a theoretical hypothesis of an envisioned future. By raising ever new questions of an appreciative, applicable, and provocative nature, the researcher collaborates in the scientific construction of his or her world.[6]

CONCLUSION

What we have tried to do with this chapter is present conceptual refiguration of action-research; to present a proposal arguing for an enriched multidimensional view of action-research which seeks to be both theoretically generative and progressive in a broad human sense. In short, the argument is a simple one stating that there is a need to re-awaken the imaginative spirit of action-research and that to do this we need a fundamentally different perspective toward our organizational world, one that admits to its uncertainties, ambiguities, mysteries, and unexplicable, miraculous nature. But now we must admit, with a certain sense of limited capability and failure, that the viewpoint articulated here is simply not possible to define and is very difficult to speak of in technological, step-by-step terms. From the perspective of rational thought, the miraculous is impossible. From that of problem solving it is nonsense. And from that of empirical science, it is categorically denied (Reeves, 1984). Just as we cannot prove the proposition that organizing is a problem to be solved, so, too, we cannot prove in any rational, analytical, or empirical way that organizing is a miracle to be embraced. Each stance represents a commitment—a core conviction so to speak—which is given to each of us as a choice. We do, however, think that through discipline and training the appreciative eye can be developed to see the ordinary magic, beauty, and real possibilitiy in organizational life; but we are not sure we can so easily transform our central convictions.

In sum, the position we have been developing here is that for action-research to reach its potential as a vehicle for social innovation, it needs to begin advancing theoretical knowledge of consequence; that good theory may be one of the most powerful means human beings have for producing change in a post-industrial world; that the discipline's steadfast commitment to a problem-solving view of the world is a primary restraint on its imagination, passion, and positive contribution; that appreciative inquiry represents a viable complement to conventional forms of action-research, one uniquely suited for social innovation instead of problem solving; and that through our assumptions and choice of method we largely create the world we later discover.

NOTES

1. While we draw most of our examples from the Organization Development (OD) school of action-research, the argument presented here should be relevant to other applications as well. As noted by Peters and Robinson (1984), the discipline of action-research has been prevalent in the literature of community action, education and educational system change, and organization change, as well as discussions of the social sciences in general.

2. As physicist Jeremy Hayward (1984) has put it, "I'll see it when I believe it," or oppositely, "I won't see it because I don't believe it." The point is that all observation is filtered through belief systems which act as our personal theories of the world. Thus, what *counts* as "fact" depends largely on beliefs associated with theory and therefore, on the community of scientists espousing this belief system.

3. A group of colleagues and we are engaged in a two-year study of a major industrial plant where introduction of this simple theory has led to changes in job design, work relations, training programs, motivational climate, and hierarchical ideology. For an introduction to this work see Pasmore, Cooperrider, Kaplan and Morris, 1983.

4. Emphasis in this and the following definitions are ours, intended to underscore the points being made. Earlier we noted the importance of language as a subtle cueing device. Keeping this in mind, the reader is asked to pay special attention to the language of problem solving, and perhaps even count the sheer number of times the word problem is used in relation to definitions of action research.

5. Following Whyte (1982), a social innovation will be defined as: (1) a new element in organizational structure or interorganizational relations; (2) innovative sets of procedures, reward systems, or interaction and activity and the relations of human beings to the natural and social environment; (3) a new administrative policy in actual use; (4) new role or sets of roles; and (5) new belief systems of ideologies transforming basic modes of relating.

6. For an example of the type of theory generated through appreciative inquiry, see "The Emergence of the Egalitarian Organization" (Srivastva and Cooperrider, 1986).

REFERENCES

Argyris, C. (1973). Action science and intervention. *The Journal of Applied Behavioral Science, 19,* 115–140.

Argyris, C. (1970). *Intervention theory and methods.* Reading, MA: Addison-Wesley.

Argyris, C. & Schon, D. (1978). *Organizational learning: A theory of action perspective.* Reading, MA: Addison-Wesley.

Bartunek, J. (1983). How organization development can develop organizational theory. *Group and Organization Studies, 8,* 303-318.
Bartunek, J. (1984). Changing interpretive schemes and organizational restructuring: The example of a religious order. *Administrative Science Quarterly, 27,* 355-372.
Bell, D. (1973). *The coming of the post-industrial society.* New York: Basic Books.
Beyer, J. (1981). Ideologies, values and decision making in organizations. In P. C. Nystrom and W. H. Starbuck (Eds.), *Handbook of organizational design, Vol. 2.* Oxford University Press.
Beyer, J. & Trice, H. (1982). Utilization process: Conceptual framework and synthesis of findings. *Administrative Science Quarterly, 22,* 591-622.
Blake, R. & Mouton, J. (1976). *Consultation.* Reading, MA: Addison-Wesley.
Bohr, N. (1958). *Atomic theory and human knowledge.* New York: John Wiley.
Bradford, L. P., Gibb, J. R., & Benne, K. (1964). *T-group theory and laboratory method.* New York: John Wiley.
Braverman, H. (1974). *Labor and monopoly capital.* New York: Monthly Review Press.
Brimm, M. (1972). When is change not a change? *Journal of Applied Behavioral Science, 1,* 102-107.
Brown, R. H. (1978). *Leadership.* New York: Harper & Row.
Chiles, C. (1983). Comments on "design guidelines for social problem solving interventions." *The Journal of Applied Behavioral Science, 19,* 189-191.
Clegg, S. & Dunkerley, D. (1980). *Organization, class, and control.* Boston: Routledge and Kegan Paul.
Cohen, A. R., Fink, S. L., Gadon, H., & Willits, R. D. (1984). *Effective behavior in organizations.* Homewood, IL: Irwin.
Cooperrider, D. (1986). *Appreciative inquiry: Toward a methodology for understanding and enhancing organizational innovation.* Unpublished Ph.D. dissertation, Case Western Reserve University, Cleveland, OH.
Deal, T. E. & Kennedy, A. A. (1982). *Corporate cultures.* Reading, Mass.: Addison-Wesley.
Dubin, R. (1978). *Theory building.* New York: The Free Press.
Ellwood, C. (1938). *A history of social philosophy.* New York: Prentice-Hall.
Forester, John (1983). Critical theory and organizational analysis. In G. Morgan (Ed.), *Beyond method.* Beverly Hills, CA: Sage Publications.
French, W. L. (1969). Organization development objectives, assumptions, and strategies. *California Management Review, 12*(2), 23-34.
French, W. L. & Bell, C. H. (1978). *Organization development.* New Jersey: Prentice-Hall.
Friedlander, F. (1984). Producing useful knowledge for organizations. *Administrative Science Quarterly, 29,* 646-648.
Friedlander, F. (1977). Alternative modes of inquiry. Presented at APA Convention, San Francisco, Ca.
Friedlander, F. & Brown, L. D. (1974). Organization development. *Annual Review of Psychology, 25,* 313-341.
Frohman, M., Sashkin, M., and Kavanaugh, M. (1976). Action-research as applied to organization development. *Organization and Administrative Sciences, 1,* 129-161.
Geertz, C. (1980). Blurred genres: The refiguration of social thought. *American Scholar, 49,* 165-179.
Gergen, K. (1982). *Toward transformation in social knowledge.* New York: Springer-Verlag.
Gergen, K. (1978). Toward generative theory. *Journal of Personality and Social Psychology, 36,* 1344-1360.
Ghandi, M. (1958). *All men are brothers.* New York: Columbia University Press.
Gorz, A. (1973). Workers' control is more than just that. In Hunnius, Garson, and Case (Eds.), *Workers control.* New York: Vintage Books.
Gould, S. J. (1981). *The mismeasure of man.* New York: Norton and Company.
Gouldner, A. (1970). *The coming crisis of Western sociology.* New York: Basic Books.

Habermas, J. (1971). *Knowledge and human interests*. Boston: Beacon Press.
Haley, J. *Uncommon therapy*. New York: W. W. Norton, 1973.
Hare, P. H. (1976). *Handbook of small group research*. New York: The Free Press.
Harrison, R. (1982). *Leadership and strategy for a new age: Lessons from "conscious evolution."* Menlo Park, CA: Values and Lifestyles Program.
Hausser, D., Pecorella, P., & Wissler, A. (1977). *Survey-guided development II*. LaJolla, Calif.: University Associates.
Hayward, J. (1984). *Perceiving ordinary magic*. Gouldner: New Science Library.
Hiesenberg, W. (1958). *Physics and philosophy: The revolution in modern science*. London: Allen and Urwig.
Henshel, R. (1975). Effects of disciplinary prestige on predictive accuracy. *Futures, 7*, 92–106.
Hofsteede, G. (1980). *Culture's consequences*. Beverly Hills, CA: Sage.
Jung, C. (1933). *Modern man in search of a soul*. New York: Harcourt, Brace & Company.
Keeley, M. (1980). Organizational analogy: Comparison of orgasmic and social contract models. *Administrative Science Quarterly, 25*, 337–362.
Kepner, C. & Trego, B. (1973). *Executive problem analysis and decision making*. Princeton, NJ.
Kierkegaard, S. (1954). *The sickness unto death*. New York: Anchor Books. Translated by Walter Lowrie.
Kilmann, R. (1979). Problem management: A behavioral science approach. In G. Zaltman (Ed.), *Management principles for non-profit agencies and organizations*. New York: American Management Association.
Koch, S. (1981). The nature and limits of psychological knowledge. *American Psychologist, 36*, 257–269.
Kolb, D. A. (1984). *Experiential learning*. Englewood Cliffs, NJ: Prentice-Hall.
Kolb, D. A. (1983). Problem management: Learning from experience. In S. Srivastva (Ed.), *The executive mind*. San Francisco: Jossey-Bass.
Levinson, H. (1972) The clinical psychologist as organizational diagnostician. *Professional Psychology, 10*, 485–502.
Levinson, H. (1972). *Organizational diagnosis*. Cambridge, MA: Harvard University Press.
Lewin, K. (1948). Action research and minority problems. In G. W. Lewin (Ed.), *Resolving social conflicts*. New York: Harper & Row.
Lewin, K. (1951). *Field theory in social science*. New York: Harper & Row.
Lukes, S. (1974). *Power: A radical view*. London: Macmillan.
Mannheim, K. (1936). *Ideology and utopia*. New York: Harcourt, Brace & World.
Marcel, G. (1963). *The existential background of human dignity*. Cambridge: Harvard University Press.
Margulies, N. & Raia, A. P. (1972). *Organization development: Values, process and technology*. New York: McGraw Hill.
Marrow, A. (1968). *The practical theorist*. New York: Basic Books.
Maslow, A. (1968). *Toward a psychology of being*. New York: Van Nostrand Reinhold Co.
McHugh, P. (1970). On the failure of positivism. In J. Douglas (Ed.), *Understanding everyday life*. Chicago: Aldine.
Mitroff, I. (1980). Reality as a scientific strategy: Revising our concepts of science. *Academy of Management Review, 5*, 513–515.
Mitroff, I. & Kilmann, R. (1978). *Methodological approaches to social sciences*. San Francisco: Jossey-Bass.
Morgan, G. (1983). *Beyond method*. Beverly Hills: Sage Publications.
Morgan, G. (1980). Paradigms, metaphors, and puzzle solving in organization theory. *Administrative Science Quarterly, 24*, 605–622.
Ortony, A. (Ed.) (1979). *Metaphor and thought*. Cambridge: Cambridge University Press.
Ouchi, W. G. & Johnson, J. B. (1978). Types of organizational control and their relationship to emotional well-being. *Administrative Science Quarterly, 23*, 293–317.

Pasmore, W., Cooperrider, D., Kaplan, M. & Morris, B. (1983). Introducing managers to performance development. In *The ecology of work*. Proceedings of the Sixth NTL Ecology of Work Conference, Cleveland, Ohio.
Pasmore, W. & Friedlander, F. (1982). An action-research program for increasing employee involvement in problem solving. *Administrative Science Quarterly, 27*, 343-362.
Pepper, S. C. (1942). *World hypothesis*. Berkeley, CA: University of California Press.
Peters, M. & Robinson, V. (1984). The origins and status of action research. *Journal of Applied Behavioral Science, 20*, 113-124.
Quinney, R. (1982). *Social existence: Metaphysics, Marxism, and the social sciences*. Beverly Hills, CA: Sage Publications.
Rappaport, R. W. (1970). Three dilemmas of action-research. *Human Relations, 23*, 499-513.
Reeves, G. (1984). The idea of mystery in the philosophy of Gabriel Marcel. In J. Schlipp, & L. Hahn, (Eds.), *The philosophy of Gabriel Marcel*. LaSalle, IL: Open Court.
Sargent, L. T. (1982). Authority and utopia: Utopianisms in political thought. *Polity, 4*, 565-584.
Sathe, V. J. (1983). Implications of corporate culture. *Organizational Dynamics*, Autumn, 5-23.
Schein, E. (1983). The role of the founder in creating organizational culture. *Organizational Dynamics*, Summer, 12-28.
Schweitzer, A. (1969). *The teaching of reverence for life*. New York: Holt, Rinehart and Winston.
Small, A. (1905). *General sociology: An exposition of the main development in sociological theory from Spencer to Ratzenhofer*. Chicago: University of Chicago Press.
Smirchich, L. (1983). Studying organizations as cultures. In G. Morgan (Ed.), *Beyond method*. Beverly Hills, CA: Sage Publications.
Sproull, L. S. (1981). Beliefs in organizations. In P. C. Nystrom & W. H. Starbuck (Eds.), *Handbook of organizational design*, Vol. 2. New York: Oxford University Press.
Srivastva, S. (1985). *Executive power*. San Francisco: Jossey-Bass Publishers.
Srivastva, S. (1983). *The executive mind*. San Francisco: Jossey-Bass Publishers.
Srivastva, S. & Cooperrider, D. (1986). The emergence of the egalitarian organization. *Human Relations*. London: Tavistock.
Srivastva, S., Obert, S. & Neilsen, E. (1977). Organizational analysis through group process: A theoretical perspective for organization development. In C. Cooper (Ed.) *Organization development in the U.K. and U.S.A.* New York: The Macmillan Press.
Staw, B. (1984). Organizational behavior: A review and reformulation of the field's outcome variables. *Annual Review of Psychology, 35*, 626-666.
Susman, G. & Evered, R. (1978). An assessment of the scientific merits of action-research. *Administrative Science Quarterly, 23*, 582-603.
Thelen, H. (1954). *Dynamics of groups at work*. Chicago: University of Chicago Press.
Torbert, W. (1983). Initiating collaborative inquiry. In G. Morgan (Ed.), *Beyond method*. Beverly Hills, CA: Sage Publications.
Van Maanen, J., Dabbs, J. M., & Faulkner, R. R. (1982). *Varieties of qualitative research*. Beverly Hills, Calif.: Sage Publications.
Watzlawick, P., Weakland, J., & Fish, R. (1974). *Change: Principles of problem formation and problem resolution*. New York: Horton.
Weick, K. E. (1983). Managerial thought in the context of action. In S. Srivastva (Ed.), *The executive mind*. San Francisco: Jossey-Bass.
Wiesbord, M. (1976). Organization diagnosis: Six places to look for trouble with or without a theory. *Group and Organization Studies, 1*, 430-447.
Weiss, C. H. & Bucuvalas, M. (1980). The challenge of social research to decision making. In C. H. Weiss (Ed.), *Using social research in public policy making*. Lexington, MA: Lexington Books.
Whitehead, A. N. (1929). *The function of reason*. Boston: Beacon Press.
Whyte, W. F. (1982). Social inventions for solving human problems. *American Sociological Review, 47*, 1-13.

The Emergence of the Egalitarian Organization

Suresh Srivastva[1] and David L. Cooperrider[1,2]

This paper develops an egalitarian theory of organizing, a theory which is premised on the emergence of an interhuman logic *that transcends instrumental or techno-economic rationality as a basis for collective action. An interhuman logic, it is proposed, is one that seeks to create and maintain social-organizational arrangements that heighten or maximize the* ideal membership situation *for all members of a given organization. Through an "appreciative" analysis of field data collected from a world-reknowned medical group practice, propositions are developed which seek to explain and extend the implications of an interhuman logic for understanding the potential of participatory systems.*

> *The loss of possibility signifies: either that everything has become necessary to man or that everything has become trivial.*
>
> *Kierkegaard*

INTRODUCTION

Participation: The Central Feature of Organizing

Since the 1950's, we have witnessed an explosion in the emergence of organizational forms, interventions, and concepts that seek, either explicitly or implicitly, to enhance the participatory involvement of organizational members. American participative forms of management, European industrial democracy, quality of worklife experiments, worker-owned cooperatives,

---

[1]The authors are grateful to Dr. William S. Kiser, Chairman of the Board of Governors of the Cleveland Clinic Foundation, and his colleagues, for their contribution, participation, and thoughtful collaboration in this research.
[2]Requests for reprints should sent to David L. Cooperrider, Department of Organizational Behavior, Case Western Reserve University, Cleveland, Ohio 44106.

Japanese management, and the post-industrial rise in professionalism represent a few of the disparate streams of thought and action converging around the notion of participation. Observers throughout the world and from a variety of perspectives—in universities and factory plants, in hospitals and government agencies, as well as in corporate and religious institutions—have voiced agreement that the widespread effort to extend the sphere of authentic participation in the workplace will continue to be one of the most pronounced and visible phenomenon of our time (Bell, 1976; Cordova, 1982; Vanek, 1971; Toffler, 1980; Ferguson, 1980; Bennis & Slater, 1968; Kanter and Zurcher, 1973; Trist, 1968; Laidlaw, 1980; Baxter, 1982; Ouchi & Johnson, 1978).

The development of this focus on participation by such independent sources with such diversity in objectives is responsive to the realities of organized life in the modern world. In perceptual terms, the social system of participation is entering the foreground of consciousness in a post-industrializing society, a society that is most aptly characterized as a symbolic interhuman phenomenon, "a game between persons" (Bell, 1973; Trist, 1968; Bennis & Slater, 1968).

However, in spite of the well-intended developments in knowledge and application, there continues to be a lack of firm identity, direction, and meaningful advance for the field as a whole. We continue in our attempts to solve new puzzles about participatory phenomenon within the framework of older industrial paradigms (Scholl, 1976), reflecting a deeper concern that Gouldner (1955) disparagingly refers to as the "metaphysical pathos" of bureaucratic theory. As it relates specifically to the burgeoning literature on participation, Dachler and Wilpert (1978) have concluded:

> No clear set of questions, . . . which begin to define the nature of participatory phenomenon are discernable. Participation literature includes a plethora of undefined terms and characteristically lacks explicitly stated theoretical frameworks.

While the authors optimistically propose that the divergence in views, inherent contradictions, and heterogeneity of approaches could indicate an active, healthy, and rapidly developing area of administrative thought, it could also be symptomatic that something is very wrong with our science in this area.

In his *Adventure of Ideas*, Whitehead (1933) notes that profound flashes of insight frequently remain ineffective for decades or even centuries, not because they are unknown, but by reason of dominant interests which inhibit direct response to that type of generality. In this connection, there appears to lie at the core of our dialogue about participation a crippling contradiction, a broad-based cultural denial of the essential character of the participatory process and the nature of organizational reality. Put simply, the contradiction is this: The language so powerfully used in the popular doctrine of our day holds that people *should be allowed to participate* in the determination of realities that affect their lives, yet the most advanced twentieth century philosophies and scholarly studies into the intrinsic nature of social and cultural realities *show that they already do*. People participate in the construction of social reality even through the act of "nonparticipation." "Nonparticipation" itself must be recognized as a form of participation; it is one particular form in the continuous process of taking part in the creation, maintenance, and transformation of personal as well as organizational realities. Looked at from this perspective, organizations (as holistic structures of interlocked activities and meanings) are brought into being, sustained, and developed in and through the vital act of participation; this is an occasion which is not a thing but a process, not so much a quantity but a quality.

This has a number of important implications for the study of participation and its relevance to the development of a humanly significant applied science of administration. Most important, it casts the fierce and costly debate concerning the merits of more or less participation into serious question. Basically, if all organizations are, in essence, participatory systems and that "organizing," to use Weick's (1979) terminology is ". . . a consensually validated grammar for reducing equivocality by means of sensible interlocked behaviors," then it follows that what we are talking about is *not whether* to have participation, but what kind and how. More than a subtle semantic difficulty, we are challenged by a qualitatively different kind of study when we begin to view the participatory process as the central feature of organizing. For instance, it is instructive to imagine the implications of large-scale programs of study that move: (1) away from a "treatment" view of participation as a thing to be given or taken away to a view where the participatory process is seen as an essential consequence of organizational life, (2) away from arguments seeking to establish a predestined state of affairs (Weber, 1968; Bennis & Slater, 1968) to a view of participatory social arrangements as conditional, where moral responsibility is possible and conscious choice is infinite (Rothschild-Whitt, 1979), and (3) away from a problem centered or deficiency-oriented research, toward a "being"-oriented approach pointing the way toward authentic possibilities for the construction of qualitatively advanced forms of participatory social arrangements.

Inquiry into the Potential of Participatory Work Systems

The present study is an effort to build on this line of thought. To date there have been very few empirically grounded studies of the potential of participatory work systems which take a comprehensive and systemic approach to the social system of participation as *the central feature of organizing*. Dachler and Wilpert's (1978) critical review of the topic suggests a number of reasons why.

First, our conceptualizations of participation too often have a narrow focus guided by a singular disciplinary view when, in fact, an understanding of participation potential as a complex social phenomenon requires a multifaceted interdisciplinary approach. Thus, our understandings of participation have been confined by the restricted and often competing sets of questions asked about it. Second, research in this area, while obviously dealing with a social process, has primarily emphasized individualistic or psychological qualities and has not grappled with the question of integrating the social-phenomenological and structural-functional considerations that unite participation potential into a coherent system of psychosocial and contextual factors. Third, the traditional scientific view which maintains that value judgments and scientific inquiry are basically incompatible "makes it difficult if not impossible to adequately research the potential of participatory systems" (Dachler & Wilpert, 1978) because the very word "potential" requires the research to take on a moral burden of discussing what is meant by potential or improvement. Fourth, much of the organizational research (particularly in America) is politically conservative and frequently has a focus on pathology rooted in an economically utilitarian cultural matrix. The deficiency orientation is inherently conservative because: (1) the pathology is usually defined by those who hire the researchers, and (2) the statement of deficiency implies an *a priori* set of assumptions about what is "normal" which generally typifies the status quo (Gouldner, 1970). Finally, by modeling the physical sciences, our positivistic research methods too often concern themselves with such things as sample size and efficient technique. These frequently have the effect of defining the subject as a passive object of inquiry and thereby limit our understanding of participation potential beginning with the very act of doing nondialogical or interactive research.

This paper responds to these insights by approaching the study of participation potential using a rich array of field data analyzed inductively and mediated through a mode of "appreciative inquiry."[2]

After a description of our data collection methods, a specific case is presented of a world-reknowned professional-medical organization that has made a commitment to an open participatory process as a central feature of organizing. A thematic analysis of field data is undertaken which focuses on three major areas that were most clearly associated with the potential of the organization in this realm: the ideology and general ethos, the formal structures of interaction such as the sociotechnical and sociopolitical spheres,

---

[2]The "Appreciative Inquiry" model (Cooperrider, 1985; Cooperrider & Srivastva, 1986) is based on an assumption that *organizing is a miracle* to be understood rather than a *problem to be solved*. It seeks to uncover the forces which give organizational life its vitality and self-generative capacity. It seeks to contribute knowledge about organizations-in-action which is: (1) appreciative, (2) applicable, (3) provocative, and (4) collaborative.

and the predominant social paradigms such as assumptions about organizational knowledge and people. Finally, concepts inductively derived from each of these areas are linked together toward the construction of an egalitarian theory of organizing, a theory premised on a consensual nature of social arrangements and the emergence of an interhuman administrative logic which transcends instrumental rationality as a basis for collective action.

BACKGROUND OF THE STUDY

The primary source of data for the analytical points developed in this paper was the physician group practice of the Cleveland Clinic (CC), a private, nonprofit, tertiary care center located in Northeastern Ohio.

In contrast to the typical image associated with the word "clinic," the CC is one of the largest medical centers in the world. Beginning in 1921 as a small group practice engaged in patient care, medical research, and postgraduate medical education, the CC has evolved into a multifaceted institution with a technical complex of over 38 specialties and 67 areas of subspecialization. The physician group practice itself is made up of more than 300 members (the second largest in existence), and is complemented by an employee population of about 7000 personnel. Presently, the CC records some 30,000 annual admissions to its hospital and, by 1987, it anticipates yearly service in the form of ambulatory care to more than 450,000 outpatients. Thus, the CC represents a large, viable, and rapidly developing organization with all the issues of transformation and growth.

The tremendous growth of the organization has been due, in part, to its reputation as a "cutting edge" professional organization capable of providing high quality patient care in the treatment of the most complicated of diseases. Recognized nationally, the United States Congress has formally awarded the CC the title of "National Health Resource" because of its "pioneering advances in basic clinical research, the responsible development and integration of new technology into patient care, and the education of future generations of physicians and those physicians already in practice" (*Cleveland Press*, 1980).

Beyond its medical contribution, however, the group practice of the CC is of theoretical interest as a "social invention" (Whyte, 1982) for the study of participation potential. Even as a professional bureaucracy, the CC has a number of unique features (Jensen, 1982). Perhaps most notable is that, from the perspective of the physician group practice, the CC is wholly managed and governed by the productive workers themselves (see Fig. 1). CC physicians have taken total responsibility for the operation of their organization. While all physicians, including those in leadership positions,

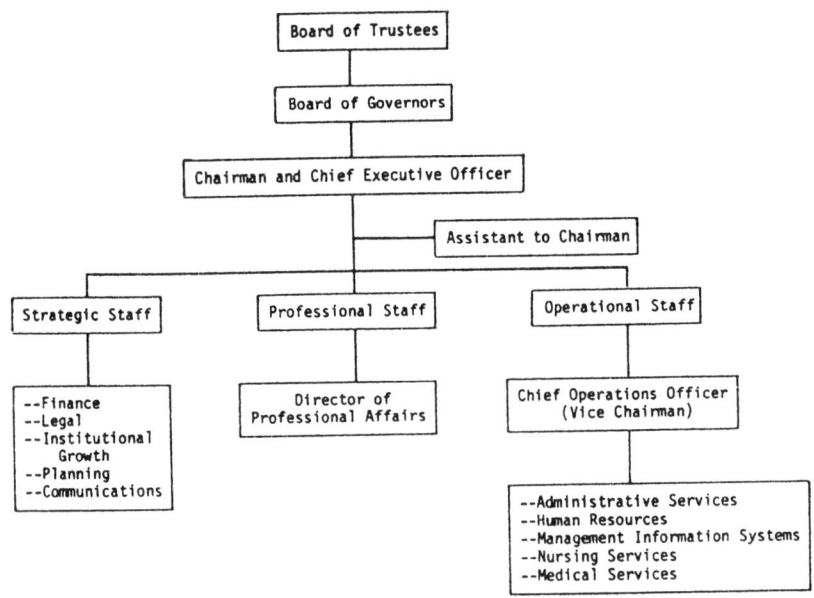

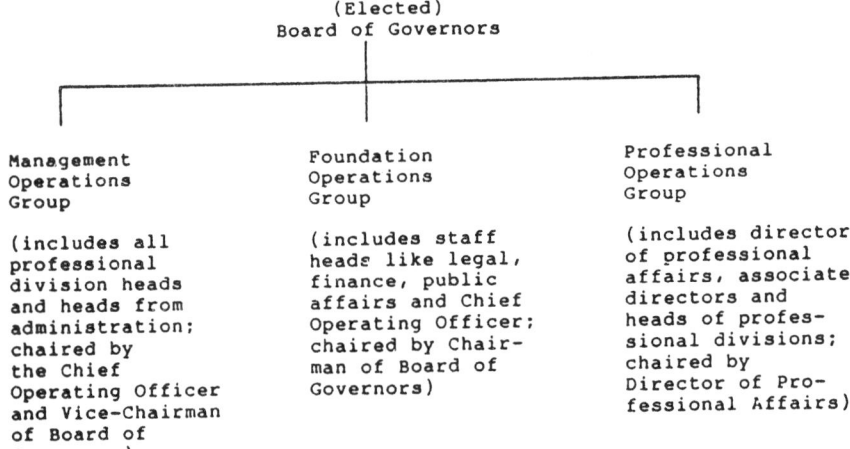

Fig. 1. Cleveland clinic organizational chart, committee structure, and functional concept of organization.

The Emergence of the Egalitarian Organization

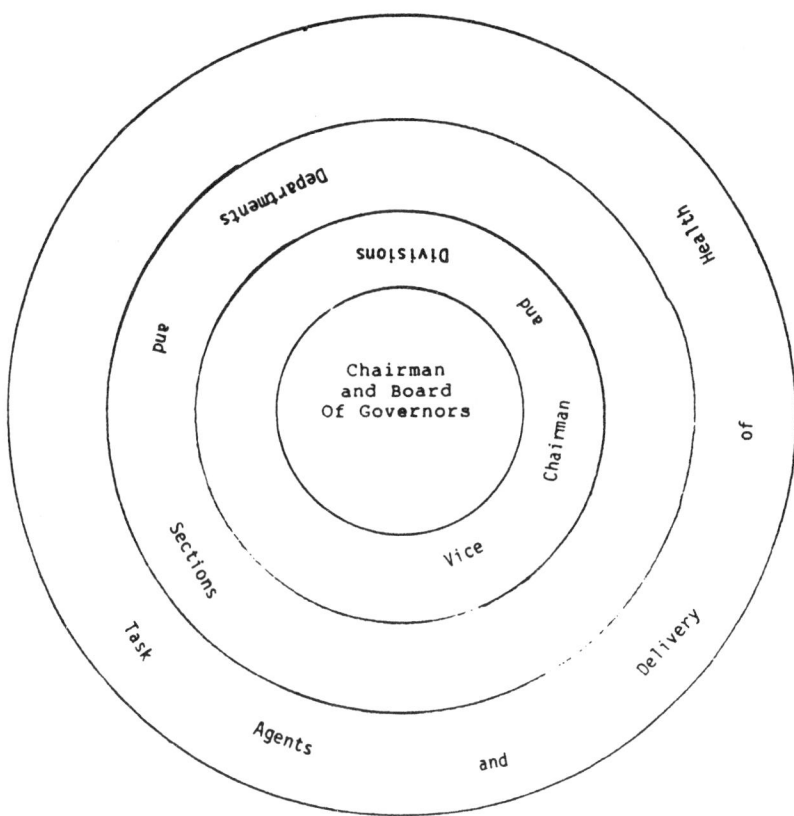

continue to practice medicine, a dynamic self-regulating system of cooperative governance has been established whereby the traditional distinction between management and labor has effectively been eliminated. Those who do the specialized work of the organization also control all aspects of the organization—medical and administrative—through a collective authority structure encompassing decision making at the operational, tactical, and stragetic levels. As one member described it:

> This is a unique organization because all the doctors feel that they are a vice-president. That is, everyone has responsibility and say in place. Everyone is considered on an equal basis . . . .

The excitement for this paper was ignited during a dissertation study in 1981 concerned with the question of how professionally trained individuals translate or apply their "professional instincts" to the management of organizational activities (Jensen, 1982; Srivastva, Jensen, & Cooperrider, 1981). During this research at the CC, it became readily apparent that the general spirit and guiding logic behind the organization's growth was qualitatively different than predominant bureaucratic rationality of efficiency and effectiveness (Thompson, 1967). Consensus about the primary task of organizing went beyond the economizing functional one (to make profits or fulfill a market demand) and centered around a broader, open-ended psychosocial one. The efficiency logic of instrumental rationality was by no means inoperable or rejected; it was simply circumscribed by the professionals' practical concern for the ongoing development of an active, responsive, and cooperative social system in an organization committed to a democratic/participatory process.

For example, it was no accident that the dominant theme dramatizing the clinic's history in a recent book was the theme, *"To Think and Act as a Unit."* Primary concern for the health of the social system was at the focal point early on in the awareness of each member of the group practice; yet, the full implication of this for a coherent theory of administration was admittedly fraught with ambiguity, myth, and mystery:

> It is like Ezekiel's vision of the wheels, in which the big wheel moved by faith and the little wheel moved by the grace of God. The keys to success are the participants' desire to do what is best for the Clinic and their confidence in one another's integrity. Businessmen looking at this "unhierarchical" organization feel as mystified as Ezekiel did about what made the wheels work. But they do and the reason why can best be summarized in the expression of "esprit de corps"! (Crile and Bunts, 1971).

Our effort began as an attempt to understand this phenomenon in terms of participation potential and soon progressed into a broader exploration seeking to generate grounded theory of the defining dimensions, categories, and dynamic properties of the emerging egalitarian organization (Glaser & Strauss, 1967).

Collection and Analysis of Data

Data were collected throughout a 4-year period (1979–1983) using a number of common social science methods including:

1. *Interviews.* Open-ended formal interviews were conducted with 55 members of the CC group practice including all members of the Board of Governors, all division and department chairpersons, the Director of Professional Affairs, and all members of the Medical Division Council. Each interview lasted from 1–2 hours covering a range of general questions about their involvement in organizational affairs, their work, relationships within and between departments, decision processes, rewards, reasons for the institution's "cooperative spirit," factors associated with success, and perceptions about the future.

2. *Historical Documents.* Newspaper articles, books, unpublished papers and minutes of the governing board were reviewed and content analyzed. The most prominent historical document used in the analysis was the book, *To Act as a Unit: The Story of the Cleveland Clinic Foundation* (Crile & Bunts, 1971; Hartwell, 1985).

3. *Observations.* Numerous board, committee, and departmental meetings were attended providing a direct experiential basis for understanding and complementing the interview data.

4. *Surveys and Group Discussion of Data.* Following each interview, a survey was given asking the interviewee to rate their peers on measures of professional and organizational effectiveness. The purpose of this survey was to provide convergent validation around norms of successful membership with the system.

In a second phase of our research, another survey was developed to again provide convergent validity to the interview data. The survey summarized 30 themes from our interviews and, for each theme, asked members to rate the extent to which they felt the statement represented an important "ideal" to continue to be pursued by the organization. For example, people were asked how important it is that "all members have an equal opportunity to become involved in the affairs of the organization and to help it become what it can potentially become." In a larger sample of 130, including physicians at all levels, the median score for the 30 ideal-type themes was 6.15 ("very great" importance) on a 7-point Likert scale, providing a high level of cross-validation for our thematic analysis. Also, in an effort to check whether participants in the survey interpreted the themes in a similar way, more than 20 face-to-face "feedback" sessions were conducted which allowed for dialogue concerning each item (see Cooperrider, 1985 for details on the processes used for "consensual validation" of normative theory).

Analysis of Data

The qualitative data were handled in two ways. All interviews were taped or transcribed verbatim. An initial reading of the data provided a set of 30 general themes used in constructing our survey and became the basis for an organizational report and discussion with the Board of Governors. From these early activities emerged a preliminary description of a set of characteristics loosely organized around a concept of "the potential of participatory social systems." Taken together, this set of characteristics pointed to what a number of members referred to as the "common ground" between the person and the organization. Viewed as a substantive and dynamic ideal type, this common ground was later termed the *ideal membership situation* (see Table I). Representing a sphere which Kanter (1968, p. 499) notes "arises at the intersection of organizational requisites and personal experience," the notion of the ideal

Table 1. Dimensions of the Ideal Membership Situation[a]

1. *Commitment/conviction.* This refers to an internally regulated willingness to engage with others to address the inevitable problems, conflicts, and opportunities arising on the basis of the developmental nature of organizing. It represents a belief that there is something serious, meaningful, and purposefully significant about one's existence as an organizational participant. One is convinced about the need to "willingly engage with others."
2. *Critical control/ownership.* Critical control refers to the experience of being an integral coparticipant in the creation, maintenance, and transformation of organizational realities. Based on a self-confident belief that one has the authority to offer up ideas for effectual action, the experience of having critical control is realized when organizational members feel that the organizational world about them reflects the unique expression of their own creative powers. Having selectively (critically) tapped the system's balance of forces in a way that builds on feelings of efficacy, empowerment, and responsibility, the processes of organizing become infused with members' own special contributions and meanings. Hence, members take possession of the organization. They are not "owned" by it, rather it becomes their "own."
3. *Normative consciousness.* One of the prerequisites and outcomes of existing critical control is the experiencing of increased levels of practical (normative) awareness. This dimension refers to the experience of having the capacity and opportunity to bring one's thinking, sensing, feeling, and intuiting to bear on normative questions of organizing. It relates to a capacity to participate in strategic dialogue around common organizational issues of what is, what isn't, what could be, and how it might become so. Hence, it represents a radical spirit of inquiry whose aim is to bring the best available knowledge to bear on public questions of what is possible and what ought to be.
4. *Community of competence.* This dimension is related to the desire to increase one's feelings of self-worth, learning and discovery, and productive contribution through an intimate task involvement with a community of "competent" others. Fueled by a deep desire to believe that one can count on the competence, challenge, and support of one's colleagues, this factor rests upon the assumption that the collegial group is more than the sum of its individual parts, and that the individual becomes more as a result of an active participatory association with the whole. The colleagueship ideal refers to a profound faith in others, a belief that the self and others in the organization can find within their own collegial setting the support, affirmation, challenge, and diverse talent for setting in motion generative interactions leading to the ongoing discovery and achievement of selected values.

[a]The use of the word "ideal" is used to indicate a state where the structures and processes of organizing maximize each of these dimensions for all members throughout an organization.

membership situation provided an important analytic tool for linking phenomenological (subject world) and structural–functional (object world) considerations.

Guided by the theoretical heuristic of the ideal membership situation, the data were then re-analyzed, *appreciatively,* looking specifically at factors of organizing (social arrangements and unique cultural meanings) associated with the intensity, breadth, and duration of the ideal-type situation. Thus, the coding process was a *highly* selective one, attending more to the centrality and importance of certain features of organizing rather than a summative quantitative assessment.

This point of *selective focus* is an important one because it differentiates the appreciative methodology from other more ethnographic or cultural mappings. In the appreciative mode, the researcher examines the best of "what is" to ignite the imagination of the possible and then seeks to unite practice and possibility into a theoretical articulation of a positively envisioned future. The aim is to construct "generative theory," a theory which helps foster dialogue about that which is taken for granted and has the capacity for generating fresh alternatives for social action (Gergen, 1978).[3]

Emergent Themes

Figure 2 presents the major descriptive themes of our analysis. While each point can be highlighted by numerous instances of data, we have chosen only those exmples most relevant for building a sense of clarity around the thematic framework. As Rothschild-Whitt (1979) has pointed out, no number of examples ever constitute a proof. Therefore, it is hoped that this work is judged in terms of its appreciative, applicable, and provocative qualities as well as its capacity to be used as a basis for collaborative experimentation and future research.

Following Fig. 2 as a thematic outline, the rest of the paper is organized into three sections: (1) "The Organizational Ethos", (2) "The Formal Structures of Interaction," and (3) "The Predominant Social Paradigms." Each section carefully builds upon the other through a presentation of complexly interwoven themes. Data are presented to bring life and specificity to the themes. Then at the end of each section, the themes are taken to a higher level of generality through a propositional logic building on key theoretical points.

THE ORGANIZATIONAL ETHOS

Any meaningful analysis of the participatory transformations occurring in modern organizational life must attempt to identify the deep underly-

---

[3]This aim also helps explain our selective sample of institutional leaders or "activists" in the system. It was in this group that ideal membership situation was most visibly expressed and, therefore, provided the clearest data for building our theory. Subsequent research is now underway to explore the importance of the theory for all members of the institution (Cooperrider, 1985).

	EGALITARIAN ETHOS/IDEOLOGY		
I. Organizational Ethos	Inclusion	Consent	Excellence
	SOCIO-POLITICAL STRUCTURE		SOCIOTECHNICAL STRUCTURE
II. Developing Catalytic Structures of Interaction	Shared Governance		Catalytic Primary Task
	EPISTEMIC STRUCTURE		RELATIONAL STRUCTURE
II. Predominant Social Paradigms	Co-Inquiry-in-Action		Community of Competence

Fig. 2. Themes related to the generative membership situation and the emergence of the egalitarian organization.

ing aspirations, sentiments, and ideological forces shaping the newer, more cooperative forms of organizing. We refer to this complex of forces as the organizational ethos: the general human spirit serving to characterize the disposition of an organization as a dynamically formulated living social system. Drawing on symbolism and metaphor used by one of the clinic members, ethos can be likened to a powerful oceanic tide:

> On the ocean it is easy to see the crest of wave or to feel the surge of the ground swell, but the full flood of the tide may be almost imperceptible even to those who are borne upward on it . . . [the organizational ethos] may be like a tide . . . .

Central to the concept of the "egalitarian ethos" is a threefold ideal that is viewed as a self-reinforcing system of ideas: inclusion, consent, and excellence. These themes, taken together, form an indispensible visionary scheme for building an understanding of the *processual logic* of the egalitarian organization. Most important, this reinforcing system of ideas helps explain the birth and ascendency of a social system logic as articulated in the concept of the ideal membership situation; it is a core set of ideas which constitute the ideological basis for a theory of organizing that is relatively free of arbitrary forms of hierarchical domination.

The Spirit of Inclusion

This theme can be summarized as follows: Based on inclusion as an organizational member, every person should share in the right and responsibility for *actively* taking part in the creation, maintenance, and transformation of the organization's operating realities. Similarly, and perhaps more congruent with the spirit of the term, inclusion refers to an organizing impulse that seeks a quality of membership that is summed up by the word *partnership:* a cooperative relational stance whereby each participant accepted into an organization has, by sheer definition of membership, an inalienable obligation to take part in the security, well being and determination of the various patterns of individual and organizational development. It represents, as one respondent in our study put it, "a very high concept of group":

> There is another thing that is important for you to understand. It is not only the concept of the group practice that is important in understanding the CC, but it is a very high concept of group. We deal with each other as professionals here and have to consider one another equal potentials. Dealing with each other goes back to life's first lesson: We have to learn to trust our colleagues and trust them implicitly. It means that anyone who comes into this group and is absorbed into it, has to sense the serious level of commitment required.

How serious is the commitment? Another member talked about the inclusive spirit and described it as having a distinctive marriage-like quality:

> At the CC we bring together, under one roof top, specialists in every area of medical care. We are a partnership of physicians. And like any marriage it continues to require continual interchange, work, tolerant attitudes and trust. But the relationship is non-negotiable. It is not about to be put off, put asunder, or be divorced. We see the same patients, work in the same system, use the same tools, we share space — and we take care of patients together. No matter what our difficulties, they will never amount to a breach . . . . Do we see eye to eye on every issue? No. But we work things through.

In functional terms, it can be hypothesized that the inclusionary ideal is one whose integrative aim is to draw upon the totality of member energies and to bring those energies to bear on organizational activities of all kinds. That is, inclusion represents a desire to open the process of organizing up to the latent and existing powers inherent in a collective body of active participants. It represents an explicit desire to cooperate with human energy rather than to control it and, as Baxter (1982) has cogently discussed, the theme of inclusion speaks to the "ontological" basis of an authentic social construction. More concretely, a member of the CC characterized the premise of inclusion as the defining feature of a "real" organization:

> What you have to infuse in an institute is that it is a unified, developmental, growth situation.... That's the real secret of an institution. And, if you can corral the forces, then you will have a charging animal on your back. Now the CC is still not a real institute in this sense, but it is getting to be one ... as you can see, there is a tremendous amount of energy flowing through this place.

Ideologically, the theme of inclusion has an important paradoxical quality. On the one hand, it is viewed as a journey, a process of bringing in, not closing out. In this sense, it points to the continuing pursuit of a largely mythical state of wholeness, integrity, shared meaning, coordination, and balance, e.g., in the CC founder's words, "to think and act as a unit." On the other hand, however, inclusion does not imply some distant aim at all. It gains its ideological potency through a simple acknowledgment of "what is"; one which recognizes the *a priori* of *relationships* between participants who *share* the same social space, time, and resources. Inclusion, in this sense, is viewed less as a distant aim and more as an original and powerful force that refuses to give itself over to arbitrary barriers of differentiation and stratification making members impervious to one another and their common interests (Cooper, 1983). So, more than a mere economic or legal arrangement, the notion of inclusion bespeaks of a subtle yet profound systemic "recognition that we are partners" in an interdependent social life world. In a kind of *declaration of interdependence,* Dr. Will Mayo spoke to this issue at the CC's opening day ceremonies more than 60 years ago:

> The critical feature of medicine of the immediate future will be the development of medical cooperation ... properly considered, group medicine is not a financial arrangement, except for minor details, but is scientific cooperation for the welfare of the sick.

Later, in another ceremonial speech, elaborating on this ideal, one of the CC founders talked about what he called the "spirit of collective work":

> With the rapid advance of medicine to its present day status in which it invokes the aid of all the natural sciences, an individual is no more able to understand the intricate problems alone. Our institution is designed to meet what we believe to be a public need in a more flexible organization.... The result of such an organization will be that the entire staff—the bacteriologist, the pathologist, the biochemist, the physicist, the physiologist, the radiologist, no less the internist and general surgeon— each, we hope and believe we will maintain the spirit of collective work, and each of us will accept as our reward for work done, our respective part in the contribution of the group, however small, to the comfort, and usefulness, and the prolongation of human life.

The spirit of inclusion, of partnership, continues to pervade the culture of the CC's group practice. Some argue that its ideological overtones are clearly communal or collectivistic. But it is more than that. The inclusive spirit is a powerful ideological commitment that affirms both the individual *and* the group by affirming the inevitable interdependence between the two. This affirmation has been translated into the construction of

The Emergence of the Egalitarian Organization

organizational arrangements that dramatically depart from the divisive and exclusionary dynamic of more traditional bureaucratic arrangements. Thus, the sentiment and spirit of the inclusionary theme will resonate throughout the rest of this paper, just as it has been felt throughout the more than 60-year history of the CC.

The Spirit of Consent

Amplifying the theme of inclusion, the consensus ideal premises that: (1) organizational decisions, plans, or rules become morally binding to the extent that they emerge from a process where all relevant stakeholders have access to full, active, and mutual involvement in their determination, (2) the ultimate basis of authority does not rest with any one individual (or set of individuals) based on ownership, formal position, *or* expertise; rather, it is based on the dynamic consent of the group, and (3) there is not authority that can unilaterally command obedience nor any tradition that can demand conformity without seeking to elicit voluntary agreement on the basis of dialogue, persuasion, or negotiation, i.e., use of logic, facts, or appeal to values. As an ideology, Gouldner (1976, p. 33) observes that the consensus ethic has a deep rooted structure. It is one that:

> ... encompasses and refers to the inner rather than the external, to the chosen rather than the imposed, to the indigenous rather than the alien, to the natural rather than the artificial. It refers to that which is capable of self-movement and self-direction, rather than to that which is externally driven.

Commenting directly on both the self-governing and group-centered essence of this ideal, a number of members of the CC explained:

> Let me tell you something about this group. When dealing with any major issue we have to resolve it through consensus because we know that the Board of Governors, although it is made up of elected representatives, will not be able to make its dictates stick by trying to force something on the rest of the group. The issue will keep bubbling to the top . . . . In this kind of (inclusive) environment *where we agree up front to function as a group, it is the only way you can function!*

Echoing this philosophy, another member described the institutional decision-making process in consensual terms:

> In other organizations when an order is given, it goes right down the pecking order and gets carried out. But here, if the Chairman of the Board gives a directive and I don't agree, I may go through channels and dispute it. And I have every right to do that. The Chairman operates here on a year-by-year basis at the pleasure of the Board which is elected by all the staff members. If the members were mobilized around a basic issue, they would have the final say.

Needless to say, the consensus mode, as described here, is not an outcome or even a logical extension of an economizing system of technical-rational thought. Nor, however, can it simply be viewed as a rejection of organized activity or the use of power. Instead, it can only be fully appreciated as it reflects an alternative, perhaps higher order logic. Later in the paper, we describe this logic as a relational one, an "interhuman logic." But for now, it is only important to highlight the point that the egalitarian ideology carries within it the seeds of an alternative administrative logic. For example, consider the logic-in-use enbedded in the following quotes:

> Through ongoing discussions we all become aware of the problems. Being part of the process we are not being dictated to. And as a result we learn more about the process and this leads to a higher level of intelligent action among all who work here.

> One disadvantage of our system is that decision making isn't that easy . . . . But when finally a decision is made, a consensus is reached, it is probably a far better decision and one which can be embraced by a great number of people . . . . It means that you will have good morale and good relations.

> The great opportunity here is one of being involved in the information flow, the dialogue, and the negotiation of decisions . . . . Here each and every one of the full time staff is responsible for and allowed to have an impact on the work environment. This is an extremely important asset, opportunity and perhaps, for some, a liability. But as for me, I love the opportunity.

In each of these quotes, one is hard-pressed to find traces of a traditional bureaucratic rationality. And, unlike bureaucracy which Weber (1968, p. 975) has argued "advances the more it dehumanized," the consensus ideal stipulates that a system of collective action is likely to advance the more it calls for the voluntary energies and contributions its members have to offer. *Perhaps more than anything else, it is the consensual spirit that most clearly differentiates the egalitarian ethos from other normative systems, especially that of bureaucracy.* This point cannot be overemphasized.

To cite just one example, we can look at a recent 2-day planning meeting with 60 leaders of the CC. Six strategic action items were on the agenda. The aim of the meeting was to build agreement so that organizational action could be taken around each item. At one point in the meeting, subgroups were formed and asked to write a letter to the Chairman of the Board "telling the Chairman what your group gives its full consent to." At the end of the 2-day meeting, after agreements were forged around each strategic issue, the Chairman closed the meeting saying something like the following:

> This, I believe, will be considered a historic meeting for the CC. We have dealt thoroughly with some very complex issues as a group, but we have not balked. We have agreed to action, and we will act swiftly. I want to thank *each of you for empowering me, for giving me the authority* to now move ahead with certainty to make our agreements happen.

The consensus ideal means that ultimate authority rests with the group. It is an ideal that demands an ecology of participants who have the freedom to propose or oppose. It places a high premium on the *face-to-face* meeting between thought and action. And it presupposes that member-generated normative controls are socially and developmentally more effective than coercive, formal-hierarchical, or strictly remunerative controls. Thus, throughout our study, there was little surprise when finding open resentment toward the more traditional bureaucratic ethic emphasizing "compliance," "obedience," "discipline," "rule," and "authoritarian power of command" (Antonio, 1979). For example, when asked to comment on the possibility of having a more traditional form of management, one member of the CC forcefully claimed:

> A person trained in management is just an administrator. That type of person hasn't a feel for this kind of organization or our field. They don't know how I think or what motivates someone like me. They only know what motivates them. They want to get to the top of the pyramid and jockey people around. Therefore, they will keep memos on everything and everybody. They just want efficiency. If we ran our department like that, it would be sterile and static.

The Spirit of Excellence

To remain static is antithetical to the egalitarian ideal. In his landmark study of equality, de Tocqueville (1969, pp. 452-456) observed that an egalitarian system:

> ... puts many ideas into the human mind which would not have come there without it and it changes almost all the ideas that were before ... [members of such a system] discover that nothing can confine them, hold them, or force them to be content with their present lot. They are all, therefore, conscious of the idea of bettering themselves.

Furthermore, observed de Tocqueville, as increased levels of interaction between people are set in motion through the widening of inclusionary boundaries, then new facts and truths would be discovered, and changes continuously witnessed. "Then," writes de Tocqueville, under these conditions, "... the human mind images the possibility of an ideal but always fugitive perfection."

Similarly, one of the more striking features of the CC's egalitarian system is an almost insatiable appetite for the new, an optimism toward an uncertain future, and feelings of relatively unlimited opportunities for ongoing development. The egalitarian ethos at the CC is marked by an espoused belief in the infinite perfectability of self and organization. When asked about this optimistic perspective, a member of the CC reflected on perhaps the most widely shared sentiments discovered throughout our study:

> I see *tremendous potential here*. There are almost no limits if you have ideas . . . . There are very few obstacles here. In fact, my greatest obstacle is myself. I always have to have everything accomplished yesterday.

And echoing this belief, other members explained (using almost identical words):

> Everyone here has the same opportunity to broaden their perspective and realize their full potential. The main thing is to recognize what the potential is and then go after it. The common goal among all of us is to *have an outstanding medical group* here .... We are an idealistic group devoted to becoming the best we can become.

The word "excellence" itself is an indefinite. It has no stable empirical referent and, therefore, refuses precise definition as an administrative science construct (Peters & Waterman, 1982). But as an ideal, and ideology, the symbolism of excellence holds a romantic and imaginative quality that is expressed in a style of organizational life built around commitment to what members in our study continually referred to as "the frontier," and to staying at the "cutting edge" of their own capacities. It was referred to as "a goal without design," marked by an intensity of becoming more, achieving more, learning more, and directly experiencing more. In sociological terms, the theme of excellence can be translated as the corporate version of society's *modernist spirit:* "The self-willed effort of a style and sensibility to remain in the forefront of advancing consciousness" (Bell, 1976, p. 46). Excellence, as a word symbol, is perhaps the corporate representation of the modernist "self-infinitizing spirit."

For example, on his eightieth birthday, one of the retired founders of the CC spoke out and asserted, "We must forever remain flexible and open to the newer and better things that come along." And more recently, the organization's Board of Governors discussed and agreed with an agenda item that stated: "The Cleveland Clinic is structured for adaptability and rapid change and is predictably unstable—it is in the process of becoming." In fact, members argued that it was precisely because of the devotion to growth and excellence that attracted many of them to the institution:

> I think those of us here seek out this kind of organizational setting. And we deserve the opportunities that exist here—the possibilities of developing our skills and being on the cutting edge. Long ago we had a business manager running this place who told people what to do and how .... But not any more. Our greatest growth as an organization has come in the last decade, ever since we were allowed more participation and have become directly involved in the governance of this institution.

This quote is especially important in that it touches directly on an ideological implication of the spirit of excellence. The words from the quote can be translated into a simple equation of associated ideas: excellence = the desire for the cutting edge = the need for active involvement and participation. There is a simple political logic in this equation of ideas which is often overlooked.

The quest for excellence is accompanied by a public recognition of the dynamically emergent nature of organizing. Thus, in a changing organizational setting, how can *a priori* exclusion from the opportunity for active participation in organizational affairs be legitimized? In a transforming system reaching toward higher levels of innovation and development, it becomes empirically and logically impossible to calculate on an *a priori* basis whose contribution, noncontribution or countercontribution will have the greatest impact on the welfare of the whole. When organizing is realized as an unfolding social enactment, then the multiple definitions of an organization's welfare will necessarily be in flux; and, as some have argued, these definitions can only be understood in retrospect (Weick, 1979; Pfeffer, 1978). Furthermore, as definitions of an organization's welfare change, such as particular objectives, values, policies, and procedures, differences inevitably arise in terms of who, what, and how various members will participate. In other words, organizational excellence requires, and perhaps even equals, active member involvement. Building on this logic, one of the CC's leaders summarized:

> We are often faced with trying to solve problems and make decisions without having all the data. But in an environment like this there are highly intelligent and capable people. So you must always keep your eyes and ears open. Through involvement on various committees and groups we try and get as much participation as we can, and usually, the right course of action will be defined by someone or another.

While active participation in organizational affairs is conventionally viewed as a barrier to organizational efficiency, it is perhaps the keystone of a system ideologically committed to long-term excellence. Again, equating excellence and member participation, one of the CC's leaders summarized the whole matter this way:

> The CC expects excellence from all members . . . . To be successful here you have to be willing to fully participate in the organization. In my experience those who are most successful are those that truly love the CC and make the organization an avocation just as much as their professional life . . . . They function as if the very survival of the system was dependent on their actions.

Ideologies Have Social Force

The egalitarian spirit, as thematically presented above, is not to be mistaken as a doctrine of natural rights or specified set of legal property arrangements (Jones, 1983), but is to be understood as a compelling set of social expectations that have as their essential thrust the enactment of organizational conditions supporting a consensual relational stance between partners in a human enterprise devoted to excellence. The word "egalitarian" is used, therefore, to signify an expressive, responsive, reciprocating quality of face-to-face interaction between "colleagues" that is relatively free of reified and arbitrary barriers inhibiting active participation in the management of common organizational affairs. These ideas can be summarized in the following propositions:

Proposition 1. All organizing is ideological. There is no such thing as an ethically neutral, totally dispassionate or apolitical form of management that does not favor certain forms of social activity over others, certain social arrangements over others, and certain values over others.

Proposition 2. All ideologies are their own ethical advocate, they all have social force. Not only will ideology tend to specify the general rights and obligations of organizational "membership" but, more subtly, ideology: (1) focuses attention in some areas more than others providing a primitive set of "selection mechanisms" through which members enact events (Weick, 1979; Sproull, 1981), (2) generates a consistency drive for the unification between ideals and practice (Heider, 1944; Gouldner, 1976), (3) focuses attention on the types of questions to ask and problems to solve (Weber, 1968; Gergen, 1978; Barnard, 1938), and (4) treats the organizational world as directly and deliberately transformable and susceptible to rational discourse (Gouldner, 1976).

Proposition 3. The egalitarian spirit of inclusion, consent, and excellence emphasizes member attention on the qualitative functioning of the social system — on the nature and quality of interaction *between* participants — and treats this part of the organizational world as deliberately transformable *and* susceptible to rational action.

Proposition 4. The egalitarian ideal gives rise to an emerging *interhuman logic* that supercedes and circumscribes the technical mode as a legitimate basis for organizing, unlike bureaucracy which deflects our focus away from the sphere of interaction and represents the application of an economizing, atomizing, technical rationality to social activity.

Proposition 5. The primary aim of an interhuman administrative logic is to activate the potential of a work system as cooperative human social system and it accomplishes this aim *dialogically* through: (1) reducing or eliminating arbitrary barriers to active participation which tend to inevitably arise in organizations, and (2) creating arenas of interaction that are catalytic; interactive forums that cultivate, reinforce, and rely upon the ideal membership situation.

In sum, it is proposed that an interhuman logic is one that is activated by egalitarian ideals of inclusion, consent, and excellence. As a system of *sociological* thought, it represents a rational administrative orientation that places active participatory contribution at the leading edge of any consideration having to do with the design or development of the organization itself. It means putting conscious effort into keeping an organization "as free as possible of arbitrary barriers to cooperation" so that members can regulate their organizational lives in accordance with publicly agreed upon values, aspirations, and needs.

The Emergence of the Egalitarian Organization   463

In an especially clear articulation of this point of view, an account of the CC's research division highlights the centrality of an interhuman logic as it relates to their own theory of administration:

> If problems of human beings are to be solved, the solutions must originate with people. In the Division of Research, a *determined effort has been made to ensure the cooperative effort* of scientists in a variety of disciplines . . . . Every effort has been made to keep the Division as *free as possible of arbitrary barriers to cooperation* . . . . This has allowed everyone to participate actively . . . . Odd as it may seem, much effort was required to maintain such a seemingly structureless organization because of the inherent tendency of people to organize and give titles or assume roles (Crile & Bunts, 1971).

It is interesting to note that from an outsider's perspective, the interhuman logic operative at the CC has often appeared mysterious, counterintuitive, nonlogical, or even irrational. For example, we might revisit a quote use earlier in the paper:

> Businessmen looking at this "unhierarchical" organization feel as mystified as Ezekiel did about what made the wheels work. But they do and the reason why can best be summarized in the expression of "esprit de corps"! (Crile & Bunts, 1971).

We have shown in this section that what "makes the wheels work" is not so much a result of mysterious forces or nonlogical managerial perspectives; it is a result of a different kind of administrative logic which goes beyond traditional technical-rational thinking. As we will continue to elaborate, the interhuman logic is, above all else, a relational logic. It is an administrative perspective founded upon a belief that the basic problem of organizing is a problem of human/social organization. "Develop a group where there is a high degree of commitment to excellence, professional opportunity, belief in service to the public, and a strong sense of ownership," argued one of the CC's leaders, "and the economic success factors will take care of themselves." In the next section, we will take a closer look at how such an ideology is being put into practice.

DEVELOPING CATALYTIC STRUCTURES OF INTERACTION

Much of the history of the group practice at Cleveland Clinic can be read as the emerging application of an interhuman theory of administration. The perennial challenge has been one that asks: Given this time and place, what organizational arrangements can we experiment with to optimize the ideal membership situation and thereby ensure that the cooperative capacity of our system will be reached? How can we continue to heighten, throughout our organization, the experiencing of high levels of commitment, critical control and ownership, normative consciousness, and a community of competence? How can we maintain the "unique esprit de corps" that continues to breathe *life* into the institution and make it what it is?

In this section, these questions are addressed by viewing the organization as an ensemble of structurally patterned *arenas* of social interaction (Bowles & Gintis, 1981; Giddens, 1979). Specifically, we examine the analytically distinct arenas of work and politics. While we take the viewpoint that structural arrangements such as definitions, cues, rules, patterned relationships, and resources people use in interaction are both a medium and product of interaction, we are primarily concerned here with how they mediate interaction. We are concerned thematically with the exploration of those structural characteristics that support, reinforce, and rely on an active–cooperative relational stance among participants. Organizational arrangements that heighten the potential for such interaction, that enhance the ideal membership situation, are termed *catalytic*.

The Political Arena: Shared Governance

In 1954, voices of rebellion echoed throughout the hallways of the CC. There was mounting concern over "the gradual hardening of the lines of authority." About 10 years earlier, a plan of organization had been implemented placing final authority for policy and administration in the hands of the Board of Trustees. A fundamental condition of the plan called for policy proposals to emerge through committees, while authority for decision making would be vested in individual administrative offices according to a clearly defined hierarchical chain of command.

For the next few years, the institution grew and prospered economically under this conventional form of management. However, in the Spring of 1954, staff members voiced their distaste over being "treated as employees" and reacted actively against the fact there were no open forums whereby they could register either their protests or preferences. Revolted by the "exploitive" character inherent in the monocratic feature of bureaucracy, and frustrated by numerous barriers of red tape and secrecy inhibiting their direct participatory involvement in the shaping of policy and goals, members began demanding changes. To justify their critical sentiment, they called upon principles of medical ethics laid down by the American Medical Association, one of which stated:

> . . . physician[s] should not dispose of their professional attainments or services to a hospital body, or organization, group or individual by whatever name called or however organized under terms or conditions which permit exploitation of the physician . . . (Crile & Bunts, 1971).

Debate over the emotion-filled issues continued for months. To channel the energy, an assessment was conducted involving direct consultation with every member of the staff. A report was then issued which set the stage for a search for a more effective governing process, a quest which continues today. The underlying theory behind the report reflected the theme of an interhuman logic: that an organization's governing process can be considered to be a healthy one to the extent that it is: (1) open and responsive to its membership, and (2) is designed in such a way that it enhances, throughout the group, the experiences of commitment, responsibility, and ownership. The leading conclusion of the study captures the matter succinctly:

> The government of the Cleveland Clinic must become more democratic so that every member of the staff will feel greater responsibility for the welfare of the institution and have a more definite stake in the future (Crile & Bunts, 1971).

It is now conventional wisdom that organizations are not the "ideal" administrative entities as described in classical Weberian theory. The notion, perpetuated by bureaucratic thought, that organizations are pure technical-administrative systems devoid of passion and politics has been widely challenged and exposed as myth (Brown, 1978; Weinstein, 1979; Antonio, 1979; Pfeffer, 1978). In fact, as Brown (1978) has demonstrated, the very conception of an instrumentally rational form of administration is itself an achievement of a political form of interaction. It is a symbolic product of noncalculable human interaction resulting in the formation of a shared set of governing beliefs or understandings. Thus, if we take the word political to refer to that sphere of interaction dealing with uncertainty, equivocality, or non-agreement concerning means and ends in organizational affairs, then it is the political that might well represent the cutting edge of organizing. No doubt, this point is one that would be hotly contested by a great number of organizational theorists. In fact, many continue to argue that organizations are "economic entities" and should not be treated as if they contain a political sphere. However, while the scholarly debate over this issue will, of course, continue, the essential question raised by members of our study was not whether an organization has a political dimension, but rather "what kind"? What form of governance should the organization choose to enact?

Reacting against the monological system of hierarchical authority, members of the CC set out to establish a system of *shared governance.* While the espoused logic legitimizing the chain-of-command bureaucratic form is conventionally understood as an economizing one of least cost and instrumental rationality (Bell, 1976), the principal passion associated with shared governance is hypothesized as a drive to heighten the ideal membership situation throughout an organization, especially the total level experiencing of *critical control and ownership.* In this sense, *shared* governance represents a search for an effective political process that substitutes the processual criteria of participatory efficacy for hierarchical efficiency and, in so doing, challenges the basic assumption that organizations can only achieve their purposes through hierarchical interactions between those structurally classified as "superiors" and those defined as "subordinates."[4]

What then is the role of the leader in such a system? Using the criteria of participatory efficacy, one member of our study defined the leadership task in highly catalytic terms:

> I have one firm belief as a chairperson. The chairperson serves only one basic and good purpose. It is to utilize their knowledge and skill and political acumen to incite and charge other younger members with political and professional growth and development. I use every ounce of my energy to see to it that they develop . . . . If a department chairperson doesn't have this goal in mind, then they shouldn't be the chairperson.

Without going into details, it was not until the late 1960's that clinic members realized their aim of becoming the governors (the working managers) of their own group practice. Accounts of the events culminating in the elimination of the system as hierarchical authority remain clouded, but the period is clearly remembered by many as one of "new birth" and major transformation. In was described as a period of "ideological confrontation . . . the revolution of 1968":

> Up until 1968 there was no real group practice democracy except in the limited sense of our being responsible for the hiring of medical staff and the overseeing of the quality of professional practice. There was nothing in the way of the total institution as a democratic system. There was mounting unrest over this fact which then resulted in an ideological confrontation with the Trustees. I can remember very distinctly 30 of us (leading members of the staff) going to the trustees and saying, "We want this place restructured or else we go." We said that we could run it better ourselves as a group . . . so they agreed to let us do it. Since then there has been the gradual evolution of our own Board of Governors (elected members of the staff) assuming responsibility for the total operation of the institution. The concept of physician-as-manager and CEO was born soon after the ideological confrontation.

Since that time, with the "group in command," an ongoing process of experimentation has been enacted in order to discover and rediscover more effective means of bringing people's talents and energies to bear on the persistent challenge of shared governance within the corporate setting. For members of the CC, the inclusionary ideal of "thinking and acting as a unit" had, in fact, become a realistic concern. There were many who predicted that the "unprecedented" experiment in physician management would fail. But it has not failed. And based on our observations, there are five thematic characteristics that are essential to an understanding of the *catalytic* features of this egalitarian system of organizational governance:

---

[4]In a provocative analysis, Thayer (1981) reviews the history of the productive value of hierarchy and suggests that as an assumption it carries little truth value. He concludes, in agreement with our observations, that anything of major significance that is achieved in organizational life is achieved because of a cooperative rather than hierarchical relational stance. He then raises an important question, "Is it possible that the effective conduct of social business occurs *in spite of hierarchy,* not because of it?"

1. *Power Equals the Formation of Group Will.* Power in the shared governing system is viewed as a function of the participatory process leading to the formation of collective public opinion. It is the "growing together" of a unified group will. Power is not, therefore, a person-centered nor position-centered phenomenon; it is a situational and interactive phenomenon that can be measured by a group's capacity for evolving a synthesizing collective vision in response to specific challenges and aspirations. The greater the capacity for mobilizing an integrated collective will, the greater the organizational power. As one person put it, "I rule by consensus . . . . To be successful here you must be able to mobilize the consent of the group and this happens through discussion, negotiation and just plain persistence."

2. *Classlessness in Social Authority Arrangements.* In a system of shared governance, there is no such thing as a formal hierarchy of authority in which "subordinates" are expected to surrender their own judgment and opportunity to make decisions to the commands of a "superior."[5] The class distinction between the governing and governed is eliminated not only because it is just or moral, but because it is the only practical means of securing the widest possible cooperative ownership and involvement. While hierarchy remains, it is not hierarchy in the sense of chain-of-command. Instead, it is best depicted as a "chain-of-consent." The focus is not on ruling, commanding, or even power sharing; the primary focus is on power expansion (advancement of the group will). It is a system where the concept of potential is more important than what is and where the mobilizing *power of ideas* is more important than the idea of power itself. Thus, it is an internally responsible system where politics is more a matter of the advancement of the whole rather than a mere balance of interests or control over different groups.

3. *Driven by Dialogical Substance and Temporal Group Forms.* The substance of shared governance is the *ongoing process of dialogue* in which guiding values are created through the active interplay of relevant individuals, groups, or intergroups. This dialogical core is translated into a consensus system of high political intensity which can be roughly measured as the ratio of organizational activities that are guided by publicly derived ideals and policies vs. those that are unilaterally or privately determined and imposed. All major governance decisions having to do with new policy, allocation of resources, performance review, membership selection, budgeting, and strategic planning emerge through collegial group forums made up of those

---

[5] A good example of this was in a training session on Victor Vroom's decision-charting model. In brief, this well-known model helps a "superior" determine when to include a "subordinate" in decision making. During our training session with members at the CC, one of the physicians came up to one of the authors and asserted, quite angrily, "This training is bullshit, you know!" He then went on to explain: "I bet if you count how many times you or Vroom's article used the word subordinate, it would be close to 50 times . . . . I resent what this training is trying to do to us! I'm not a subordinate . . . I'm a partner."

who do the work of the organization. The political forums include a wide array of intra- and interdepartmental groups, committees, and councils which are designed to have rotating leadership and membership, and are open to any member who has something to add to the development of consensus. While the committee structure itself is too complex to be discussed in detail, it is important to point out that, in this 300-member group practice, there were over 100 committees in operation during the time of our research. When asked about this myriad of groups, one member reported:

> The network of committees is very complex and difficult to understand. In fact, we recently formed one more committee to study the committees, to determine if all were needed. Our findings were intriguing. We discovered the only committee we could afford to get rid of was our own!

4. *Requires the Learning of Group and Political Skills.* An egalitarian system of shared governance does not mean a leveling of differences, but implies a face-to-face meeting of differences. In terms of the participatory process, members are treated equally simply because they are "members" and are assumed to possess unique and valid resources that can potentially empower or disempower the whole. Everyone is considered an "executive" in that each is expected to help the organization become what it can possibly become. The price of membership is, therefore, demanding, and requires the ongoing learning of those capacities needed for effective participation in a relatively structureless group setting. The ultimate test of a shared governing system is not past or current performance, but the preparedness of its members for cooperatively managing their common affairs of the future.

5. *Nobody is Exempt from the Law of Common Consent.* A shared governing system is not a system without rules, but is a system where the rules are governed by common consent and are binding on all. There is no such thing as a pyramid of privilege where those at the top are exempt from the consensus of the group. "Management prerogative" as a working concept does not exist. It is a governance process where all are equal in the eyes of the normative "law." It is a system where "if the group were mobilized around a basic issue, it would have the final say."

Each of these five themes is essential in understanding the catalytic nature of shared governance. But the overarching characteristic of such a governing process is its *emergent quality*. It is viewed as a permeable form whose open involvement, fluid structure, and intensive interaction are most responsive to the natural rhythms of organizational construction and reconstruction. An account of the clinic's history puts the matter pragmatically, recognizing the inevitability of change:

> At the present time the form of the Clinic's organization seems close to ideal, but past experience indicated that with time comes change . . . . The plasticity of the Clinic's organization, based as it is on the democratic method, will continue to enable it to meet the challenges of the future (Crile & Bunts, 1971).

Commitment and the Catalytic Task Arena

The egalitarian organization is a complex and dynamic product of human interaction. And while the ideal of open participation emerges as a consequence of many diverse and often incidental forces, there are concrete factors that are amenable to analysis and purposive action. Here we consider one of the most potent of these, the interactive arena of work. The proposition to be advanced is that under norms of an interhuman administrative logic, an organization will define and structure its primary task in such a way that it serves as a highly democratizing and group-building force. That is, the work of an organization will be socially constructed in ways that catalyze committed interaction, thereby heightening the participation potential of the total system.

What are the catalytic factors? Five thematic characteristics stand out as most important: (1) the *work frontier* is actively pursued in all jobs and is used as a group-building force, (2) intensive *task interdependencies* are developed and contractually prescribed where possible, (3) *systemic rewards* and peer appraisal mechanisms are used to link members promotively to one another, (4) the design of work advances not just technically but progresses in *moral significance* as well, and finally, (5) responsibility for task design is a group-centered, *inclusive design process* where the discretionary elements of work, e.g., goals, roles, and procedures, are given meaning and form through the creative interplay of all relevant participants.

The observation that the first theme, the frontier, effectively functions as a unifying and democratizing force is not a new one (de Tocqueville, 1969; Bennis & Slater, 1968; Festinger, 1957). In a recent field study, for example, Blau and Alba (1982) report that the introduction of sheer complexity and uncertainty into an organization can undermine inequalities among bureaucratic units and that a more egalitarian system emerges as complex role relations promote extensive inter-unit communications. Such findings are generally quite consistent in the literature and raise an interesting question for organizational theory. Is it not possible that when people in organizations choose to move along the path of the frontier, in all its uncertainty and possible complexity, that they do so not so much as a reactive response to "objective" environmental stimuli, but do so more as a self-creative means of constructing interactive structures worthy of their committed involvement? Clearly, there appears to be a positive correlation between environmental turbulence and participation potential. Could it be that a turbulent context is largely a social construction, a construction associated with the ideological drive toward more egalitarian social arrangements and relations?

Our observations lend support to this often neglected point of view. Consistent with the egalitarian ideology of inclusion, consent, and excellence, the group practice of the CC has "enacted" (Weick, 1979) a complex task environment which, in turn, has made it imperative upon members to perform effectively as a group. The organization itself has largely built its own stimulating external world through defining its technical identity in terms of the frontier. In fact, the CC did what virtually any organization could choose to do. Together, members continue to agree that an essential feature of their work system would be to "forever remain open to the newer and better things that come along." In other words, the work sphere of the clinic was defined in terms of impermanence, signifying an openness to continuous learning, discovery, and diversity. To remain at the "cutting edge" of their own capacities meant the system of work would have to be viewed in highly temporary terms, in a relatively endless state of formation and transformation. Furthermore, it can be argued that the decision to enter or not enter into the foreground of change was largely an ideological decision. To enter the frontier is essentially a commitment to operate as a group; it required opening the system to the strengthening contributions each participant may have to offer. As one member at the clinic clearly explained, the ability to "pounce on new modalities . . ." was directly associated with their ability to bring a cohesive force together:

> Our strength comes from belonging to a group . . . . Part of the excuse of the CC's existence is its ability to respond to new developments in a timely manner and to get things on board before anyone else. The Clinic has the capacity for rapid change. It has the ability for alteration of configuration, the ability to pounce on new modalities, and the ability to bring a cohesive force together.

The second catalytic element, the intensification of task-based interdependencies, is also viewed as a powerful group development agent. Here, the task arena is marked by a belief that all members control critical resources for organizational success (Neilsen, 1984), and that the system's total capacity for achievement and innovation will be higher to the extent that "key" performance interdependencies are clearly agreed upon (Pasmore & Sherwood, 1978). Task interdependence can be said to exist when members perceive one another as essential for the accomplishment of their operative goals and it becomes more intensive when the tasks grow in difficulty, variability, novelty, and knowledge content, and when the resources to perform the tasks are distributed among members. The egalitarian organization we hypothesize moves in the direction of a growing intensity of interdependence and, at least the clinic, has shown that the more fully developed and integrated the network of task-based interaction, the more the system is able to become. It is in this sense then that we can understand the elegant simplicity in the management logic concisely proposed by one of the clinic's successful leaders:

> I would envision myself as a catalyst who gets people (diverse specialists) working well together toward making this the best department of its kind in the world.

The Emergence of the Egalitarian Organization

Much like Durkheim's theory of solidarity, realization of technical interdependence gives people cause to act in ways that benefit the whole (Collins & Makowsky, 1978). In the form of a practical theory, another clinic member put it this way, "Along with ultraspecialization comes the need for ultracooperation." Committed action becomes essential. When summarizing this view and why it works, others said:

> There is little trouble relating because they want something and you want something. We relate technically, share experiences, consult with each other, operate together, and educate each other through meetings and the sharing of interests. I think it all boils down to the nature of the CC.

> The type of work we're doing here requires us to work together. My whole career has been to work collaboratively—and it has been successful. To make this work there must be enthusiasm for the excellence of results without striving for personal recognition. It takes a certain kind of person to work here. It takes people who can say, "We did this, the CC group did this."

The third catalytic factor, the systemic approach to rewarding and appraising performance, reinforces the partnership contract. It involves the consideration that all members should benefit through the elevation of the organization as a whole, and that the best source of appraisal is a combination of self-appraisal and peer review. It also means creating collective reward structures so that one member's advance is not contingent upon another's failure. Speaking to this theme, one member describes:

> . . . it (the compensation program) is a positive thing because then, in a group practice such as this, it means I no longer have to build an empire. And that automatically means there is much more interaction between departments . . . . What we do is for the good of the whole Clinic and we all benefit from the good of the Clinic. For example, everyone knows that our cardiac surgery department generates a tremendous amount of revenue for the institution and that those in that department are not paid what they generate. What they generate is shared by the whole Clinic. Similarly, we have a Department of Pediatrics that doesn't generate much, yet is considered valuable. When you look at the median pay scale between the two, they are very close together. But that is one of the benefits here: We are all in this together.

The fourth catalytic task factor, the moral progression of the work of the organization, is perhaps the most critical thematic element necessary to explaining the maintenance of commitment required to sustain the egalitarian form. What the clinic has called "ultracooperation" was shown to be dependent on the progressive realization of a morally relevant primary task; this is a mission which, in essence, calls forth the conviction that there is something serious, meaningful, and humanly significant about one's existence as an organizational participant. One member, for example, touched on this feeling when he traced his commitment to a sense of larger destiny concerning the institution:

> There is a sense in an institution like this of tithing to the organization. We feel that the CC will go on forever, even after we're gone. So, psychologically, you say that

you are part of it all and you buy in. Many organizations don't have that sense of significant mission, but it is very strong here.

The theme of moral progression points to the idea that whatever separate interests members might hold, they can potentially be synthesized in the pursuit of higher order end-values of their own making (Burns, 1978). Thus, when referring to moral progression, we are not speaking of a specific moral code or even specific level of morality (Kohlberg, 1964); instead, we are talking about the process of surfacing normative differences concerning the work of the organization and seeking to exploit those differences by seeking a synthesis of value at a higher, more inclusive level, a level where a growing consensus emerges that "Yes, we agree *in principle* that this is a direction or task we should pursue."

Two factors have been found to be especially instrumental in promoting this process of moral progression. The first, as described earlier, is simply that the potential for exploiting multiple perspectives is encouraged through a *primary task definition* emphasizing the ubiquity of incompletion, i.e., "We must forever remain open . . . ." The second factor builds on this open transitory orientation by providing a backdrop of stability through which dynamic and conflicting membership interests can progressively be dealt with. This stabilizing or "centering" factor has been well defined in another detailed study of the clinic as the "syntonic" leadership type (Srivastva et al., 1981). Briefly this type has exhibited itself as a quality of leadership that promotes among institution participants: (1) a sense of timeless *destiny* about the institution,[6] its role in its own field as well as its larger role in its service to society, (2) a *holistic* view of the organization through appreciation and acceptance of all positions, (3) a climate where people can picture and debate the *polar opposite* of what has been declared in order to keep alive the possibilities of mobility and progression, and (4) a process of decision making where value relevant matters are not permanently decided but rather are *permanently in dialogue* in order to work through the extremes of dualisms.

Against this backdrop of stability, i.e., sense of destiny, wholeness, acceptance of polar realities, and the role of perpetual dialogue, the institution has enabled itself to enter into the foreground of change thereby allowing for, or more accurately yielding to, the progression of the system's highest values as translated into its day-to-day work. In this sense, it can be said that one of the more important managerial tasks in an egalitarian system

---

[6]Even the word "institution," which was used repeatedly by members in reference to the organization, conjures up a certain sense of destiny, stability, and purpose of a higher order. Sociologically, the term institution has been used to describe well-established patterns of behavior, such as the institution of marriage. And theologically, "to institute" has meant to assign or invest with spiritual power.

is to find ways to rejuvenate, on an ongoing basis, a shared sense of conviction that the difficult process of direct participation in organizational affairs is indeed worth members' voluntary effort.

The last factor, an inclusive task design process, is based on the idea that the designers and implementers of a given work system should be co-designers, or one and the same (Weick, 1977). It is an idea that is directly linked and coterminous with the political arena of shared governance. In fact, being an acknoweldged partner in the determination of new goals, roles, procedures, or work relations *is* shared governance, distinguishable at the level of the local work process.

So integral is the inclusive task design process as a group-building force that it can be said, perhaps too bluntly, that the task arena will never be catalytic, no matter how much in the frontier, intensively interdependent, collectively rewarding, or morally significant, if members are successfully barred from making their creative energies felt in the construction of their own work. Unless people take part in constituting the technical arrangements which shape their lives, they will never view each other as partners. Partnership in this sense is not a thing given or imposed; it is an achievement of the creative collective act. It is a realization that one is a part of an authentic negotiated order, or, as one member of the CC aptly put it:

> We are a partnership of physicians and function as a group which means that if you have a good idea and take the time to educate and sell it to others, then it will go. There is no suppression from the top. I think this evolves from the fact that we govern ourselves.

Summing up this theme, a division chairperson described the primary executive task as the task of building a self-designing system:

> My aim and goal is to contribute to the creation of an atmosphere where each department is strong, has strong leadership, strong performance and to enable it to go as far as it wants to go . . . . We are setting up an organization that can pretty much run itself.

Organizing is Based on an Interhuman Logic

We can now state more clearly, in summary propositional form, the themes that have emerged from our inquiry into the interactional arenas of work and politics. The following additional propositions provide a summary of the interhuman logic of organizing:

Proposition 6. Under norms of an interhuman administrative logic, an organization will open the boundaries of its governance process and seek to create political structures that are increasingly catalytic.

6.1. Members will discover more effective means of authentic consensus formation, for building and mobilizing a dynamic group will.
6.2. Members will develop processes of shared governance which eliminate formal hierarchical distinctions between the governing and the governed.
6.3. Members will establish a system of group organization that is highly politicized, i.e., where publicly relevant governance decisions emerge through collegial group forums.
6.4. The system of organizing will foster the learning of group and political skills; everyone will be viewed as an "executive" in the sense that all will be expected to help the organization become what it can potentially become.
6.5. Members will develop a system of self-regulating rules or sanctions. It will become a system where nobody is exempt from the authority of common consent.

Proposition 7. Under norms of an interhuman administrative logic, an organization will construct work arenas that catalyze cooperative group action.

7.1. Members will define their mission in open-ended terms and support a system where the work frontier is pursued by participants in all jobs.
7.2. Members will build a system of increasingly intensive task-based interdependence.
7.3. The organization will seek to link members promotively to one another through the use of systemic rewards and peer appraisal or feedback mechanisms.
7.4. As the work advances technically, there will be corresponding developments in its moral significance as a normatively synthesizing force.
7.5. Members will continuously seek to establish an inclusive design process where the discretionary elements of work are actively constituted through their own direct and active involvement.

PREDOMINANT SOCIAL PARADIGMS

In the preceding sections, we have presented an appreciative analysis of both the ideological spirit and set of political and work arrangements that heighten the potential of a work organization as an open, egalitarian system. The egalitarian organization emerges, we have argued, as a result of spirited commitment to a group-based organization of inclusion, consent, and excellence which by its very nature, focuses member attention on the nature and quality of interaction between participants in a shared social life world. It is this level of cooperative consciousness which, in turn, gives rise to what has been called an interhuman logic of administration; a system of sociological thought that places the participatory process and elements of the ideal membership situation at the fore of most any consideration having to do with the creation, maintenance, or transformation of the organization itself. We now move to our final thematic discussion which is introduced in the following additional proposition:

Proposition 8. Direct experience in catalytic structures of interaction will reinforce the egalitarian spirit by having an educative effect on members (Pateman, 1970; Elden, 1983; Torbert & Rogers, 1972). It socializes members in the direction of a cultural paradigm that is characterized by: (1) an "open" view concerning the nature of organizational reality, and (2) a "semi-autonomous" ontological relational stance between self and other. The potential of an *open participatory* system is largely a function of these two paradigmatic dimensions (see Fig. 3).

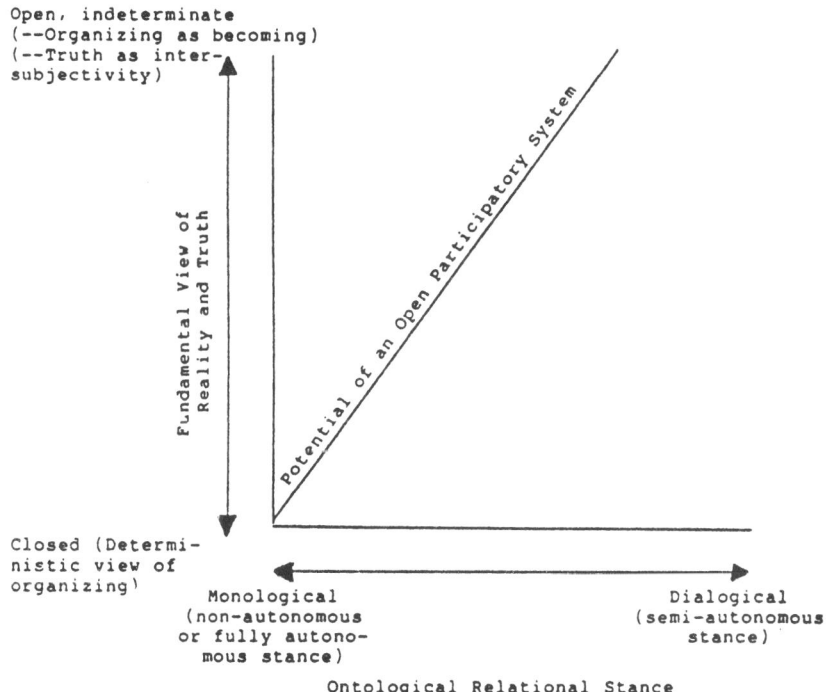

Fig. 3. Participation potential as a function of assumptions about knowing and relating to the world.

This final proposition is grounded in a set of themes that have been infused throughout this paper. Any sense of repetition that may exist reflects the profuse difficulty in analytically separating factors that in practice are complexly interwoven.

By cultural or social paradigm "we refer to those sets of assumptions usually implicit, about what sorts of things make up the social world, how they act, how they hang together, and how they may be known" (Brown, 1978, p. 373; Schein, 1983, p. 16). As a powerful set of presuppositions, used to guide inquiry and action in organized social settings, a social paradigm represents a product of socialization built deeply into one's character structure. It can be argued that *organizations* develop and encourage distinctive social paradigms (Brown, 1978) which then become the taken-for-granted foundation on which sustained collective action is made possible.

Two conceptual dimensions of an organization's social paradigm have surfaced in our study as most important: (1) participant's view of organizational reality, the epistemic structure, and (2) the underlying participatory schema or "ontological relational stance" (Baxter, 1982) informing members' interactions with one another, the relational structure (Fig. 3).

The *epistemic* structure of the egalitarian system is thematically summarized as *co-inquiry-in-action*.[7] As a way of knowing, co-inquiry is to be understood as an "open" nondeterministic view of an organizational reality which is forever perceived in a dynamic state of flux. And while change is apparent, it is viewed as a certain type of change. In the egalitarian system, organizational change is conceived largely as a social construction based on participant agreement. Co-inquiry, therefore, fuels a strong faith in, and belief in the need for, an intellectually demanding *inquiry-in-action* which is public in nature, open to the scrutiny of the group. As such, the stance of co-inquiry assumes, that for most problems of organizing, the guarantors of valid information are the members themselves. What is valid, true, or right for the organization emerges through a collegial inquiry process resulting in intersubject agreement. People "know" through consensual validation.

Is this the same as pointing out, more simply, that the organization relies on *consensus* as the primary mode of decision making? We don't think so. This section is intended to highlight something more.

What our data imply is that the consensus mode itself depends on a set of deeply structured background assumptions for its effective operation. It depends on an epistemology that is crudely portrayed by the following subthemes of co-inquiry (along with sample corresponding quotes):

1. *Reality is Always Changing, It Is a Verb.*

> Our mission is changing. The whole ball game is changing; the things that are going to happen in the next 20 years are going to boggle the mind.

---

[7]For brevity, we will refer simply to co-inquiry from now on.

The Emergence of the Egalitarian Organization

> ... It is through areas of uncertainty that opportunities arise. They should not be erased. The alternative is a very rigid system.

2. Truth is Intersubjectivity.

> If problems of human beings are to be solved, the solutions must originate with people.

> Knowledge is for everyone to share. The physician is trained to share not only locally but worldwide. This is their reason for being . . . . If we find an answer to something, we broadcast it.

3. Need for Experimentation-in-Action.

> Excellence is so strongly expected that from the moment you join the organization you are continuously questioning, seeking to find better ways.

> I found that management builds on the training we get in professional fields...you live in an assessment mode all day in the world of medicine.

4. Creator-of-History-Attitude.

> You must create your own way and not become reactionary. To be successful here you need to set the expectations.

> ...most people want to be involved in building and determining their future. In fact, that is why many people come here.

The life of the Cleveland Clinic revolves around its capacity to reproduce a collective belief system supportive of co-inquiry-in-action. Without an open view of reality, and without a questioning, learning, experimenting membership willing to enter into relationships of *joint* inquiry, the Cleveland Clinic would likely lose the self-generative capacity essential for sustaining its form.

While this is a possibility, we don't view it as very likely. For centuries, the physician has been the working model of the pragmatic scientist. As Plato saw it, medicine was the embodiment of a profession founded upon a code rigorous enough to be held up as an ideal-type image of the competent relation between knowledge and its use in practical affairs, a system of inquiry-in-action devoted to enhancing the quality of human life (Ford et al., 1967). Bound by a system of high ethics, the best-known antidote to incomplete knowledge for physicians has been an experimental and systematic approach to inquiry while in the act of doing. The simultaneity of thought and action and reflection and experimentation so critical to a holistic form of learning (Kolb, 1984; Dewey, 1933) has never been institutionalized anywhere quite so profoundly as in the world of medicine. Physicians have shown that when the need for answers is demanded, yet the world in question will not stand still, the best known response continues to be an open, intellectually thorough stance of inquiry in the course of direct treatment of problems. Interestingly, Weick (1983) has recently written about the importance of this orientation as the essence of the executive mind.

In many respects, this study can be conceived of as a look into what happens when the epistemology of the physician is translated into the day-to-day affairs of managing an organization. Through the political system of shared governance, CC physicians, as workers-managers, have made their viewpoint on the nature of organizational reality felt.

The importance of this cannot be overstated. In contrast to the orientation of co-inquiry stands the epistemic mentality of "scientific management." Introduced in the 1920's, the Taylorist philosophy has become firmly entrenched in the minds, structures, and operations of the bureaucratic organizational world. The scientific management approach promulgated the positivist belief that there is one ultimate reality to be found "out there" (one best solution to production problems), that the best way to understand something or generate knowledge is to separate thinking (conception) from doing (execution), that unilateral measurement technique should override personal experience as the source of valid data, and that the worker should bow obediently to hierarchically positioned sources of "true" knowledge (Braverman, 1974; Jenkins, 1973; Clegg & Dunkerley, 1980). As we have described, co-inquiry is based on an alternative set of assumptions which link thinking and acting, and thereby link executives and workers. In the egalitarian system, all members, by definition, are called to function as executives. All executives are called upon as workers. And in terms of significant planning and decision making, *the consensual mode is the only logical extension of the beliefs embedded in co-inquiry*. While the scientific management paradigm exhibits a strong ideological affinity to bureaucratic hierarchy, co-inquiry is uniquely suited for that form of organization committed to the ideals of inclusion, consent, and excellence.

The final theme of our study is largely a summarizing one. Throughout this appreciative assessment, one factor has stood out among all others: The egalitarian organization is one that rationally fuels and depends on the quality of cooperative interhuman experience. To single out the last paradigmatic dimension as the organization's basic *relational structure* may then appear unnecessary, but there are several things that need to be said, especially as it relates to possible ways of understanding the participatory transformations taking place in the modern workplace.

The relational structure of the Cleveland Clinic is thematically characterized by a profound commitment to a form of colleagueship that fuels what we have called a *community of competence*. This theme refers first of all to a profound faith in all those accepted into the organization, a belief that people can find within their organization the support, competence, affirmation, challenge, and diversity of talent required for the continuing discovery and achievement of selected values. The foundation of the community-of-competence was shown to be a commitment to a *semi-*

autonomous world view where Self and Other are oriented together reciprocally, and where actions are jointly attempted based on collegial respect, trust, and/or friendship. Elaborations on this concept together with descriptive data are presented in the following subthemes:

1. *Semi-Autonomous Relational Stance.*

> You can't be an individual and not care about the group at all. So long as you can see what is going on from the group mentality that you can work from it.
>
> We are a federation of semi-independent states.
>
> I manage my interdependence and achieve a certain amount of independence. You have to cooperate with others but there is a lot of room for negotiation.
>
> I rule by consensus.

2. *Basic Assumption Respect of Trust.*

> Even if I haven't worked with them yet, I know they are good because they are a part of the CC.
>
> This if not a normal group of people. Most everyone in this group is competent and interested in doing a good job.
>
> . . . Working with a group like this you have confidence in group decisions.
>
> The CC, as it is set up now, is a remarkable collection of human beings.

3. *The Group as Vehicle for Achievement.*

> To be successful, we need to find people who want to work together, who realize the strength of putting groups together, and realize that a number of minds are better than individual efforts.
>
> The concept of group practice revolves around the concept of working with one another. We build and maintain the CC through our support of one another.
>
> Our strength comes from belonging to a group.
>
> . . . somebody has to decide how we are going to make allocations of physical space, and this is best done through discussion and negotiation among colleagues.

4. *Learning and Discovery through Colleagueship.*

> To be successful here you must have the ability to give and take with other professional colleagues and to join up, teach, and investigate with others.
>
> Recognizing my weaknesses (as a new manager), I formed an advisory group of colleagues . . . I would toss ideas off me. It was a challenge because we were all changing. I'm still learning.

The theoretical importance of this theme has been spelled out brilliantly in the recent work of Brian Baxter (1982). In this scholarly work, Baxter

Category	Nature of Activity	Relationship to the Other
1. The Self in <u>non-autonomous</u> existence with the Other	Actions are Other directed	Adoration
2. The Self in <u>semi-autonomous</u> existence with the Other	Actions are jointly attempted or Other supported	Respect or love
3. The Self in <u>full</u> <u>autonomous</u> existence with the Other	Actions are for the Self's own ends and/or "playful"	Indifference or hostility

Fig. 4. Forms of ontological life (Baxter, 1982).

proposes a model of "forms of ontological life" (see Fig. 4). It is a framework addressing the questions of a person's (the Self) "being-in-the-world" in relation to all nonself factors (the Other). Accordingly, there are three basic forms the Self-Other relationship can take: the non-autonomous, semi-autonomous, and fully autonomous modes of relatedness. Viewing God as the most complex Other, Baxter builds a description of the three archetypal forms of ontological life. The key point is that the Other, "Whether it is as venerable as Horus the Egyptian god of heaven or as modern as capitalism," confronts each person as a living presence that is co-extensive to the Self. Thus, the ontological choice of how one relates to the Other permeates all of one's belief and actions in the world, including the world of work.

Possible choices are raised in reference to the work context such as: Do people relate to the workplace as an all powerful Other, providing ultimate direction and strength to one's life, a non-autonomous stance? Is it perceived as a supportive presence in which people enter into reciprocal relationships where actions are jointly attempted based on respect or love, a semi-autonomous stance? Or is it conceived as a barrier to one's full existence, an ever-present obstacle that must be defiantly overcome, a fully autonomous stance?

The tacit theme in the conclusion of Baxter's important work is that we are at a crossroad in the evolution of organizational theory. Today, as we enter the post-industrial era, we, as scientists, need to acknowledge the fact that we literally have no more idea of what kind of organization is possible than did the earliest capitalists paving the way for the Industrial Revolution (Srivastva & Cooperrider, 1983). Seemingly immutable ideas about people and organizations are being directly challenged and transformed on an unprecedented scale. Social inventions as wide ranging as the Mondragon industrial system in Spain (Whyte, 1982), to the emerging egalitarian partnership found in professional organizations such as the Cleveland Clinic, represent a glimpse of the possibilities at hand. Other significant developments include the global workplace democracy movement, new understandings of Japanese management and organizational excellence, and thousands of dispersed quality of worklife and organization development experiments designed to transform the quality of participatory processes in organizations of all types. Developments as broad as these are important, not only because they encourage an overdue involvement of the worker in traditionally isolated management areas, but because they represent the possibility of a paradigmatic shift in the ontological relationship of the Self to the organizational Other (Baxter, 1982). A spiritual and cultural shift from a largely non-autonomous perspective (hierarchical) to a reciprocal semi-autonomous (egalitarian) world view may indeed usher in a new era in organizational theory, an era where students of organizational life not only seek to understand such trends, but also, through their inquiry, seek to advance the possibilities inherent in the more cooperative forms of organizing.

What we have found at the Cleveland Clinic are examples of a system that we believe is successfully responding to a shift from a largely non-autonomus perspective (hierarchical) to a reciprocal semi-autonomous (egalitarian) world view, on an organization-wide basis. Its success to-date stems largely from its capacity to create and re-create structures of interaction which continue to catalyze a cooperative approach to organizational action. As a post-industrial social invention, the CC might well be a prototype of the knowledge-based professional organization of our future. But this is only speculation. At the very least, this case presents important considerations for all those interested in more cooperative organizational forms. It is hoped that the theory generated from the case helps widen the scope of what we consider to be within the realm of possibility.

SUMMARY

In this article, we have used an "appreciative inquiry" process to build grounded theory concerning the potential of work systems as sites of qualitatively advancing participatory involvement. The usefulness of the approach was illustrated by examining a social invention in the health care industry, a large professional medical group practice that has made a commitment to an open participatory/egalitarian form of organizing. An analysis of field data collected over several years suggests that the potential of participatory work systems is coterminously affected by: (1) an egalitarian ideology of inclusion, consent, and excellence, (2) catalytic structures of technical and political interaction, and (3) egalitarian social paradigms relating to organizational thought and action. Concepts in each of these areas were linked toward an initial construction of an egalitarian theory of organizing, a theory premised on the emergence of an *interhuman* administrative rationality which transcends (does not replace) technical rationality as a basis for collective action.

REFERENCES

ANTONIO, R. J. The contradiction of domination and production in bureaucracy: The contribution of organizational efficiency to the decline of the Roman Empire. *American Sociological Review,* 1979, *44,* 895-212.
BARNARD, C. *The functions of the executive.* Cambridge, Massachusetts: Harvard University Press, 1938.
BAXTER, B. *Alienation and authenticity.* London: Tavistock Publications, 1982.
BELL, D. *The coming of the post-industrial society.* New York: Basic Books, 1976.
BENNIS, W., & SLATER, P. *The temporary society.* New York: Harper and Row, 1968.
BLAU, J., & ALBA, R. Empowering nets of participation. *Administrative Science Quarterly,* 1982, *27,* 363-379.
BOWLES, S., & GINTIS, H. Education as a site of contradictions in the reproduction of the capital-labor relationship. *Economic and Industrial Democracy,* 1981, *2,* 223-242.
BRAVERMAN, H. *Labor and monopoly capital.* New York: Monthly Review Press, 1974.
BROWN, R. H. Bureaucracy as praxis: Toward a political phenomenology of formal organizations. *Administrative Science Quarterly,* 1978, *23,* 365-382.
BURNS, J. M. *Leadership.* New York: Harper & Row, 1978.
CLEGG, S., & DUNKERLEY. *Organization, class and control.* Boston: Routledge and Kegan Paul, 1980.
COLLINS, R., & MAKOWSKY, M. *The discovery of society* (2nd ed.). New York: Random House, 1978.
COOPER, R. Some remarks on theoretical individualism, alienation and work. *Human Relations,* 1983, *36,* 717-724.
COOPERRIDER, D. *Appreciative inquiry: Towards a methodology for understanding and contributing to organizational innovation.* Ann Arbor, Michigan: University Microfilms International, 1985.
COOPERRIDER, D., & SRIVASTVA, S. Appreciative inquiry. In W. Pasmore & R. Woodman (Eds.), *Research in organizational change and development.* Greenwich, Connecticut: JAI Press, 1986. In press.
CORDOVA, E. Workers participation in decisions within enterprises: Recent trends and problems. *International Labor Review,* 1982, *121,* 125-140.
CRILE, G., & BUNTS., F. *To act as a unit: The story of the Cleveland Clinic.* Cleveland, Ohio: Cleveland Clinic Foundation, 1971.
DACHLER, P. H., & WILPERT, B. Conceptual dimensions and boundaries of participation in organizations: A critical evaluation. *Administrative Science Quarterly,* 1978, 23, 1-39.
DEWEY, J. *Freedom and culture.* New York: Capricorn Books, 1939.
ELDEN, M. *Democracy at work for a more participatory politics.* Ann Arbor, Michigan: University Microfilms International, 1983.
FERGUSON, M. *The aquarian conspiracy: Personal and social transformation in the 1980's.* Los Angeles: Houghton Mifflin, 1980.
FESTINGER, L. A theory of cognitive dissonance. Standord: Stanford University Press, 1957.
FORD, A., ORT, T., LISKE, R., & DENTON, J. *The doctors perspective.* Cleveland: Case Western Reserve University, 1967.
GERGEN, K. J. Toward generative theory. *Journal of Personality and Social Psychology,* 1978, *36,* 1344-1360.

GIDDENS, A. *Central problems in social theory.* Berkeley, California: University of California Press, 1979.
GLASER, B. G., & STRAUSS, A. L. *The discovery of grounded theory.* Chicago: Aldine, 1967.
GOULDNER, A. Metaphysical pathos and the theory of bureaucracy. *American Political Science Review,* 1955, 49, 496-507.
GOULDNER, A. *The coming crisis of western sociology.* New York: Basic Books, 1970.
GOULDNER, A. *The dialectic of ideology and technology: The origins, grammar, and future of ideology.* New York: Seabury Press, 1976.
HARTWELL, S. W., M.D. *To act as a Unit: The story of the Cleveland Clinic.* Philadelphia: W. B. Saunders Co., 1985.
HIEDER, F. *The psychology of interpersonal relationships.* New York: Wiley, 1944.
JENKINS, W. *Job power: Toward blue and white collar democracy.* New York: Wiley, 1944.
JENSEN, A. Professional approaches to organizational life. Unpublished doctoral dissertation, Case Western Reserve University, Cleveland, Ohio, 1982.
JONES, G. R. Transaction costs, property rights and organizational culture: An exchange perspective. *Administrative Science Quarterly,* 1983, 28, 454-467.
KANTER, R. Commitment and social organization: A study of commitment mechanisms in utopian communities. *American Sociological Review,* 1968, 33, 499-517.
KANTER, R., & ZURCHER, L., JR. Editorial introduction: Alternative institutions. *The Journal of Applied Behavioral Science,* 1973, 9, 137-143.
KOHLBERG, L. Development of moral character and ideology. *Review of Child Development Research.* New York: Russell Sage, 1964.
KOLB, D. A. *Experiential learning.* Englewood Cliffs, New Jersey: Prentice-Hall, 1984.
LAIDLAW, A. F. *Cooperatives in the year 2000.* Paper presented at the 27th Congress of the International Cooperative Alliance, 1980.
NEILSEN, E. *Becoming an OD practitioner.* Englewood Cliffs. New Jersey: Prentice-Hall, 1984.
OUCHI, W. G., & JOHNSON, J. B. Types of organizational control and their relationship to emotional well-being. *Administrative Science Quarterly,* 1978, 23, 293-317.
PASMORE, W. A., & SHERWOOD, J. J. *Sociotechnical systems: A sourcebook.* LaJolla, California: University Associates, 1978.
PATEMAN, C. *Participation and democratic theory.* New York: Cambridge University Press, 1970.
PETERS, T. J., & WATERMAN, R. H. *In search of excellence.* New York: Harper and Row, 1982.
PFEFFER, J. *Organizational design.* Arlington Heights, Illinois: AHAM, 1978.
ROTHSCHILD-WHITT, J. The collectivist organization: An alternative to rational—bureaucratic models. *American Sociological Review,* 1979, 44, 509-527.
SCHEIN, E. The role of the founder in creating organizational culture. *Organizational Dynamics,* Summer, 1983, 13-28.
SCHOLL, W. *Theoretical reflections on influence, power and its alienating effects and participation.* Paper presented at the EGOS Symposium on Power, University of Bradford, Great Britain, 1976.
SPROULL, L. S. Beliefs in organizations. In P. C. Nystrom & W. H. Starbuck (Eds.), *Handbook of organizational design* (Vol. II). New York: Oxford University Press, 1981.
SRIVASTVA, S. & COOPERRIDER, D. Transcending the question of alienation. *Contemporary Psychology,* 1983, 28, 22-24.
SRIVASTVA, S., JENSEN, A., & COOPERRIDER, D. The transfer of professional instincts into organizational activities. Technical report, Cleveland Clinic Foundation, 1981.
THAYER, F. C. *An end to hierarchy and competition: Administration in a post-affluent world.* New York: New Viewpoints, 1981.
THOMPSON, J. D. *Organizations in action.* New York: McGraw-Hill, 1967.
DE TOCQUEVILLE, A. *Democracy in America* (translated by George Lawrence). New York: Anchor Books, 1969.
TOFFLER, A. *The third wave.* New York: Bantam Books, 1980.
TORBERT, W. C., & ROGERS, M. *Being for the most part puppets.* Cambridge, Massachusetts: Schenkman Publishing, 1972.

TRIST, E. *Urban North America: The challenge of the next thirty years.* Paper presented at the Toron Planning Institute of Canada, Minski, Ontario, 1968.
VANEK, J. *The participatory economy.* Ithaca, New York: Cornell University Press, 1971.
WEBER, M. In G. Roth & C. Wittick (Eds.), *Economy and society: An outline of interpretive sociology.* New York: Bedminister Press, 1968.
WEICK, K. E. (1977). Organization design: Organizations as self-designing systems. *Organizational Dynamics,* 1977, *2*, 293-317.
WEICK, K. E. (1979). *The social psychology of organizing.* Reading, Massachusetts: Addison-Wesley, 1979.
WEICK, K. E. Managerial thought in the context of action. In S. Srivastva (Ed.), *The executive mind.* San Francisco: Jossey Bass, 1983.
WEINSTEIN, D. *Bureaucratic opposition.* New York: Pergamon Press, 1979.
WHITEHEAD, A. N. *Adventure of ideas.* New York: Mentor Books, 1933.
WHYTE, W. Social inventions for solving human problems. *American Sociological Review,* 1982, *47*, 1-18.

BIOGRAPHICAL NOTES

SURESH SRIVASTVA has been Professor of Organizational Behavior in the Department of Organizational Behavior since 1970, serving as Chairman of that Department from 1970-1984 at Case Western Reserve University. Before coming to CWRU he was a Senior Professor (1962-1969) at the Indian Institute of Management in Calcutta and was Visiting Professor at the Alfred P. Sloan School of Management at MIT (1966-1967). After receiving his PhD in Social Psychology in 1960 from the University of Michigan and having taught at that University, Professor Srivastva joined the Department of Psychology and the Graduate School of Business Administration at the University of California, Los Angeles (1960-1962), where he taught and did research.

DAVID L. COOPERRIDER, PhD is Assistant Professor of Organizational Behavior in the Weatherhead School of Management, Case Western Reserve University. He received his MS degree in Organizational Behavior from George William College and his PhD from the Department of Organizational Behavior at Case Western Researve University in 1986.

References

Ackoff, R. *Redesigning the Future.* New York: Wiley, 1975.

Ackoff, R. Speech made to the Organization Development Network Board and Bay Area Planning Congress of the Fall 1980 National Organization Development Conference, San Francisco, Jan. 10, 1980.

Adler, A. *The Neurotic Constitution.* New York: Dodd, Mead, 1926.

Agor, W. *Intuitive Management: Integrating Left and Right Brain Management Skills.* Englewood Cliffs, N.J.: Prentice-Hall, 1984.

Alchian, A., and Demsetz, H. "Production, Information Costs, and Economic Organization." *American Economic Review,* 1975, *65,* 777–795.

Aldrich, H., and Whetten, D. "Organization-Sets, Action-Sets, and Networks: Making the Most of Simplicity." In P. Nystrom and W. Starbuck (eds.), *Handbook of Organization Design.* Vol. 1. London: Oxford University Press, 1981.

Aldrin, B. *Men from Earth.* New York: Bantam Books, 1989.

Alexander, F. *Psychosomatic Medicine: Its Principles and Applications.* New York: Norton, 1950.

Allen, R., Hitt, M., and Greer, C. "Occupational Stress and Perceived Organizational Effectiveness in Formal Groups: An Examination of Stress Level and Stress Type." *Personnel Psychology,* 1982, *35,* 359–370.

Amiel, R. *Entreprise santé, manuel de psychopathologie du travail et de psychiatrie sociale.* Paris: Malonine, 1985.

Antonovsky, A. *Health, Stress, and Coping: New Perspectives on Mental and Physical Well-Being.* San Francisco: Jossey-Bass, 1979.

Arendt, H. *The Human Condition.* Chicago: University of Chicago Press, 1958.

Arendt, H. *On Revolution.* New York: Viking Press, 1963.

Arendt, H. *The Life of the Mind.* New York: Harcourt Brace Jovanovich, 1971.

Argyris, C. *Integrating the Individual and the Organization.* New York: Wiley, 1964.

Argyris, C. "The Executive Mind and Double-Loop Learning." *Organizational Dynamics,* 1982a, *11,* 5-22.

Argyris, C. *Reasoning, Learning, and Action: Individual and Organizational.* San Francisco: Jossey-Bass, 1982b.

Argyris, C., and Schön, D. *Theory in Practice: Increasing Professional Effectiveness.* San Francisco: Jossey-Bass, 1974.

Arnheim, R. *Visual Thinking.* Berkeley: University of California Press, 1969.

Aries, E. "Interaction Patterns and Themes of Male, Female, and Mixed Groups." *Small Group Behavior,* 1976, *6,* 7-18.

Aries, E. "Verbal and Nonverbal Behavior in Single-Sex and Mixed-Sex Groups: Are Traditional Sex Roles Changing?" *Psychological Reports,* 1982, *51,* 127-134.

Aries, E. "Gender and Communication." In P. Shaver and C. Hendrick (eds.), *Sex and Gender: Review of Personality and Social Psychology,* 1987, *7,* 149-176.

Aronson, E. *The Social Animal.* San Francisco: Freeman, 1976.

Ashen, A. "Eidetics: An Overview." *Journal of Mental Imagery,* 1977, *1,* 5-38.

Astley, W., and Sachdeva, P. "Structural Sources of Interorganizational Power: A Theoretical Synthesis." *Academy of Management Review,* 1984, *9* (1), 104-113.

Aubert, N. *Le Pouvoir usurpé? Femmes et hommes dans l'entreprise.* Paris: Laffont, 1982.

Averill, J. *Anger and Aggression.* New York: Springer-Verlag, 1982.

Axelrod, R. *The Evolution of Cooperation,* New York: Basic Books, 1984.

Badinter, E. *Mother Love: Myth and Reality.* New York: Macmillan, 1980.
Bailey, J., and Guenther, R. "Top Bankers Received Healthy Bonuses, Despite Firms' Record Losses in 1987." *Wall Street Journal,* Mar. 29, 1988, p. 28.
Bakan, D. *The Duality of Human Existence.* Chicago: Rand McNally, 1966.
Bales, R. *Personality and Interpersonal Behavior.* New York: Holt, Rinehart & Winston, 1970.
Bandura, A. *Social Foundations of Thought and Action: A Social Cognitive View.* Englewood Cliffs, N.J.: Prentice-Hall, 1986.
Barfield, O. *Saving the Appearances: A Study in Idolatry.* New York: Harcourt Brace Jovanovich, 1957.
Barnard, C. *The Functions of the Executive.* Cambridge, Mass.: Harvard University Press, 1938.
Barrett, W. *Irrational Man.* Garden City, N.Y.: Doubleday Anchor, 1962.
Barrett, W. *Time of Need: Forms of Imagination in the Twentieth Century.* Middletown, Conn.: Wesleyan University Press, 1972.
Barrett, W. *The Illusion of Technique.* Garden City, N.Y.: Doubleday Anchor, 1978.
Barrett, W. *Death of the Soul.* Garden City, N.Y.: Doubleday Anchor, 1986.
Barta, R. "Work: In Search of New Meanings." *Chicago Studies,* 1984, *23* (2), 155-168.
Basowitz, H., Persky, H., Korchin, S., and Grinker, R. *Anxiety and Stress.* New York: McGraw-Hill, 1955.
Bateman, T., and Organ, D. "Job Satisfaction and the Good Soldier: The Relationship Between Affect and Employee 'Citizenship.'" *Academy of Management Journal,* 1983, *26,* 587-595.
Bateson, G. *Steps to an Ecology of the Mind.* New York: Ballantine, 1972.
Batson, C., and others. "Influence of Self-Reported Distress and Empathy on Egotistic Versus Altruistic Motivation to Help." *Journal of Personality and Social Psychology,* 1983, *45,* 706-718.
Baudrillard, J. *Pour une Critique de l'économie politique du signe.* Paris: Gallimard, 1972.

Baumeister, R. "How the Self Became a Problem: A Psychological Review of Historical Research." *Journal of Personality and Social Psychology*, 1987, *52*, 163-176.

Baumhart, R. *Ethics in Business.* New York: Holt, Rinehart & Winston, 1968.

Beck, A. *Depression: Causes and Treatment.* Philadelphia: University of Pennsylvania Press, 1967.

Beck, A., and Hillmar, E. *Positive Management Practices: Bringing Out the Best in Organizations and People.* San Francisco: Jossey-Bass, 1986.

Becker, E. *The Birth and Death of Meaning.* New York: Free Press, 1971.

Becker, M. "Factors Affecting Diffusion of Innovations Among Health Professionals." *American Journal of Public Health*, 1970, *60*, 294-304.

Beckhard, R. *Organization Development.* Reading, Mass.: Addison-Wesley, 1969.

Beecher, H. "The Powerful Placebo." *Journal of the American Medical Association*, 1955, *159*, 1602-1606.

Beehr, T., and Newman, J. "Job Stress, Employee Health, and Organizational Effectiveness: A Facet Analysis." *Personal Psychology*, 1978, *31*, 665-699.

Beehr, T., Walsh, J., and Taber, T. "Relationship of Stress to Individually and Organizationally Valued States: Higher Order Needs as a Moderator." *Journal of Applied Psychology*, 1976, *61* (1), 41-47.

Behn, R., and Vaupel, J. *Quick Analysis for Busy Decision Makers.* New York: Basic Books, 1982.

Bellah, R. *Habits of the Heart: Individualism and Commitment in American Life.* Berkeley: University of California Press, 1985.

Bennett, A. "Corporate Chiefs' Pay Far Outpaces Inflation and the Gains of Staffs." *Wall Street Journal*, Mar. 28, 1988, pp. 1, 6.

Bennis, W. "Organizations of the Future." *Personnel Administration*, 1967, *8*, 5-18.

Bennis, W., and Nanus, B. *Leaders: The Strategies for Taking Charge.* New York: Harper & Row, 1985.

Bennis, W., and Slater, P. *The Temporary Society.* New York: Harper & Row, 1968.

Benson, H., and Allen, R. "How Much Stress Is Too Much?" *Harvard Business Review*, 1980, *58*, 86-92.

Benson, K. "The Interorganizational Network as a Political Economy." *Administrative Science Quarterly*, 1975, *20*, 229-249.

Berg, D., and Smith, K. *The Self in Social Inquiry.* Beverly Hills, Calif.: Sage, 1988.

Berger, P., and Luckmann, T. *The Social Construction of Reality.* Garden City, N.Y.: Doubleday Anchor, 1967.

Berkowitz, L. "Social Norms, Feelings, and Other Factors Affecting Helping and Altruism." In L. Berkowitz (ed.), *Advances in Experimental Social Psychology.* New York: Academic Press, 1972.

Berlew, D. "Leadership and Organizational Excitement." *California Management Review*, Winter 1974, *17*, 21-30.

Berlin, I. *Personal Impressions.* New York: Viking Press, 1980.

Berman, M. *The Re-enchantment of the World.* Ithaca, N.Y.: Cornell University Press, 1981.

Berscheid, E., and Walster, E. *Interpersonal Attraction.* Reading, Mass.: Addison-Wesley, 1969.

Beyer, J., and Trice, H. "Studying Organizational Cultures Through Rites and Ceremonials." *Academy of Management Review*, 1984, *9*, 653-690.

Bhagat, R. "Intellectual Performance and Utilization in a Two-Paradigm Administrative and Organizational Science: A Philosophy of Science-Based Assessment." In R. Kilmann, K. Thomas, and Associates, *Producing Useful Knowledge for Organizations.* New York: Praeger, 1983.

Bies, R. "Beyond 'Voice': The Influence of Decision Maker Justification and Sincerity on Procedural Fairness Judgments." *Representative Research in Social Psychology*, 1987a, *17*(1), 3-14.

Bies, R. "The Predicament of Injustice: The Management of Moral Outrage." In L. Cummings and B. Staw (eds.), *Research in Organizational Behavior.* Greenwich, Conn.: JAI Press, 1987b.

Bies, R., and Moag, J. "Interactional Justice: Communication Criteria of Fairness." In R. Lewicki, B. Sheppard, and M. Bazerman (eds.), *Research on Negotiating in Organizations.* Greenwich, Conn.: JAI Press, 1986.

Bies, R., and Shapiro, D. "Voice and Justification: Their Influence on Procedural Fairness Judgments." *Academy of Management Journal,* 1988, *31* (3), 676-685.

Bies, R., Shapiro, D., and Cummings, L. "Causal Accounts and Managing Organizational Conflict: Is It Enough to Say It's Not My Fault?" *Communication Research,* 1988, *15* (4), 381-399.

Block, J. "Conception of Sex Roles: Some Cross-Cultural and Longitudinal Perspectives." *American Psychologist,* 1973, *28,* 512-526.

Block, N. *Imagery.* Cambridge, Mass.: MIT Press, 1981.

Bohm, D., and Peat, F. *Science, Order, and Creativity.* New York: Bantam Books, 1987.

Boje, D. "Towards a Theory and Praxis of Transorganizational Development: Stakeholder Networks and Their Habitats." Working paper 79-6. Behavioral and Organizational Science Study Center, Graduate School of Management, University of California at Los Angeles, Feb. 1982.

Bolman, L., and Deal, T. *Modern Approaches to Understanding and Managing Organizations.* San Francisco: Jossey-Bass, 1984.

Boulding, K. *The Image.* Ann Arbor: University of Michigan Press, 1966.

Bourdieu, P., *La Distinction, critique sociale du jugement.* Paris: Editions de Minuit, 1979.

Bower, G. "Mood and Memory." *American Psychologist,* 1981, *36,* 129-148.

Braden, W. *The Age of Aquarius.* Chicago: Quadrangle Books, 1970.

Bradford, D., and Cohen, A. *Managing for Excellence: The Guide to Developing High Performance in Contemporary Organizations.* New York: Wiley, 1984.

Brewin, C. "Depression and Causal Attributions: What Is Their Relation?" *Psychological Bulletin,* 1985, *98,* 297-309.

Brief, A., and Motowildo, S. "Prosocial Organizational Behaviors." *Academy of Management Review,* 1986, *11,* 710-725.

Broder, D. "Takagi's Lesson for Leaders." *Washington Post,* Aug. 25, 1985, p. B7.

Broms, H., and Gahmberg, H. "Communication to Self in Organizations and Cultures." *Administrative Science Quarterly,* 1983, *28,* 482-495.

References

Brophy, D., and Good, T. *Teacher-Student Relationships: Causes and Consequences.* New York: Holt, Rinehart & Winston, 1974.

Broverman, I. K., and others. "Sex Role Stereotypes and Clinical Judgments of Mental Health." *Journal of Consulting and Clinical Psychology,* 1970, *34,* 1-7.

Brown, L. "Planned Change in Underorganized Systems." In T. Cummings (ed.), *Systems Theory for Organization Development.* New York: Wiley, 1980.

Bruner, J. *Actual Minds, Possible Worlds.* Cambridge, Mass.: Harvard University Press, 1986.

Buck, W. *Ramayana.* New York: New American Library, 1978.

Bunker, B., and Bender, L. "How Women Compete: A Guide for Managers." *Management Review,* 1980, *3,* 15-23.

Burke, W. "Leadership as Empowering Others." In S. Srivastva and Associates, *Executive Power: How Executives Influence People and Organizations.* San Francisco: Jossey-Bass, 1986.

Burns, J. *Leadership.* New York: Harper & Row, 1978.

Bynner, W. (trans.). *The Way of Life According to Lao Tzu.* New York: Putnam, 1980. (Original from about sixth century B.C.)

Byrne, D. "Interpersonal Attraction and Attitude Similarity." *Journal of Abnormal and Social Psychology,* 1961, *62,* 713-715.

Cadbury, A. "Ethical Managers Make Their Own Rules." *Harvard Business Review,* 1987, *65,* 69-73.

Caldwell, D., and O'Reilly, C., III. "Responses to Failure: The Effects of Choice and Responsibility on Impression Management." *Academy of Management Journal,* 1982, *25,* 121-136.

Cannon, W. *The Wisdom of the Body.* New York: Norton, 1939.

Caplan, R. "Person-Environment Fit: Past, Present, and Future." In C. Cooper (ed.), *Stress Research.* New York: Wiley, 1983.

Capra, F. *Uncommon Wisdom: Conversations with Remarkable People.* New York: Bantam Books, 1988.

Carnevale, P. "Accountability of Group Representatives and Intergroup Relations." In E. Lawler (ed.), *Advances in Group Processes.* Greenwich, Conn.: JAI Press, 1985.

Caroff, P. "A Study of School-Agency Collaboration in Social Work in Health Curriculum Building." *Social Work in Health Care,* 1977, *2,* 337.

Cash, J. "Interorganizational Systems: An Information Society Opportunity or Threat?" *Information Society,* 1985, *3,* 199-228.

Castoriadis, C. *L'Institution imaginaire de la société.* Paris: Seuil, 1975.

Catalyst. *Female Management Style: Myth or Reality?* New York: Catalyst, April 1986.

Chandler, A. *The Visible Hand: The Managerial Revolution in American Business.* Cambridge, Mass.: Harvard University Press, 1977.

Chasseguet-Smirgel, J. *L'Idéal du moi, essai psychanalytique sur la maladie d'idéalité.* Paris: T'chou, 1975.

Chevalier, M. "Stimulation of Needed Social Science Research for Canadian Water Resource Problems." Ottawa, Canada: Privy Council Science Secretariat, 1967.

Churchill, W. *The Gathering Storm.* Boston: Houghton Mifflin, 1948.

Clark, M. S., and Isen, A. M. "Toward Understanding the Relationship Between Feeling States and Social Behavior." In A. H. Hastorf and A. M. Isen (eds.), *Cognitive Social Psychology.* New York: Elsevier, 1982.

Cohen, S., and Syme, S. (eds.). *Social Support and Health.* Orlando, Fla.: Academic Press, 1985.

Collins, B., and Hoyt, M. "Personal Responsibility for Consequences: An Integration and Extension of the 'Forced Compliance' Literature." *Journal of Experimental Social Psychology,* 1972, *8,* 558–593.

Conger, J., and Kanungo, R. "The Empowerment Process: Integrating Theory and Practice." *Academy of Management Review,* 1988, *13* (3), 471–482.

Conrad, D. "Organizational Power: Faces and Symbolic Forms." In L. Putnam and M. Pacanowsky (eds.), *Communication and Organizations: An Interpretive Approach.* Newbury Park, Calif.: Sage, 1983.

Cooper, H. "Pygmalion Grows Up: A Model for Teacher Expectation, Communication, and Performance Influence." *Review of Educational Research,* 1979, *49,* 389–410.

Cooper, H., and Good, T. *Pygmalion Grows Up: Studies in the Expectation Communication Process.* New York: Longman, 1983.

Cooper, J. "Personal Responsibility and Dissonance: The Role of Foreseen Consequences." *Journal of Personality and Social Psychology,* 1971, *18,* 354–363.

Cooperrider, D. *Appreciative Inquiry: A Methodology for Understanding and Enhancing Organizational Innovation.* Ann Arbor, Mich.: University Microfilms International, 1986.
Cooperrider, D., and Srivastva, S. "Appreciative Inquiry in Organizational Life." *Research in Organizational Change and Development,* 1987, *1,* 129-169.
Coulter, J. *The Social Construction of Mind.* New York: St. Martin's Press, 1979.
Cousins, N. *Human Options.* New York: Berkeley Books, 1981.
Cousins, N. *The Healing Heart.* New York: Avon Books, 1983.
Crano, W., and Mellon, P. "Causal Influence of Teacher's Expectations on Children's Academic Performance: A Cross-Lagged Panel Analysis." *Journal of Educational Psychology,* 1978, *70,* 39-49.
Crocq, L. "Stress et névrose traumatique." *Psychologie médicale,* 1974, *6-8,* 1493-1531.
Crozier, M. *Le Phénomène bureaucratique.* Paris: Seuil, 1963.
Crozier, M., and Friedberg, E. *L'Acteur et le système.* Paris: Seuil, 1977.
Culbert, S., and McDonough, J. *Radical Management: Power Politics and the Pursuit of Trust.* New York: Free Press, 1985.
Cummings, T. "Designing Effective Work Groups." In P. Nystrom and W. Starbuck (eds.), *Handbook of Organizational Design.* Oxford: Oxford University Press, 1981.
Cummings, T. "Transorganizational Development." In B. Staw and L. Cummings (eds.), *Research in Organizational Behavior.* Greenwich, Conn.: JAI Press, 1984.
Cunningham, M., Steinberg, J., and Grev, R. "Wanting to and Having to Help: Separate Motivations for Positive Mood and Guilt Inducing Helping." *Journal of Personality and Social Psychology,* 1980, *38,* 181-192.
Darley, J., and Gross, P. "A Hypothesis Confirming Bias in Labeling Effects." *Journal of Personality and Social Psychology,* 1983, *44,* 20-33.
Dawes, R. "Formal Models of Dilemmas in Social-Decision Making." In M. Kaplan and S. Schwarts (eds.), *Human Judgment and Decision Processes.* New York: Academic Press, 1975.
Deal, T., and Kennedy, A. *Corporate Cultures.* Reading, Mass.: Addison-Wesley, 1985.

Deaux, K., and Emswiller, T. "Explanations of Successful Performance on Sex Limited Tasks." *Journal of Personality and Social Psychology,* 1974, *24,* 80-85.

Debord, G. *La Société du spectacle.* Paris: Buchet-Chastel, 1967.

Dejours, C. *Travail, usure mentale.* Paris: Editions Le Centurion, 1980.

DeRopp, R. *The Master Game: Pathways to Higher Consciousness Beyond the Drug Experience.* New York: Delta Books, 1968.

Derrida, J. *Of Grammatology.* Baltimore: Johns Hopkins University Press, 1976.

Deutsch, M. *The Resolution of Conflict: Constructive and Destructive Processes.* New Haven, Conn.: Yale University Press, 1973.

Devos, G. "Achievement and Innovation in Culture and Personality." In E. Norbeck, D. Price-Williams, and W. McCord (eds.), *Personality: An Interdisciplinary Approach.* New York: Holt, Rinehart & Winston, 1973.

Dimancescu, D., and Botkin, J. *The New Alliance: America's R&D Consortia.* Cambridge, Mass.: Ballinger, 1986.

Dohrenwend, B. "Social Status and Stressful Life Events." *Journal of Personality and Social Psychology,* 1973, *9,* 203-214.

Doi, T. *The Anatomy of Dependence.* Tokyo: Kokansha International, 1973.

Donne, J. "Meditations Roman XVII." In C. Coffin (ed.), *The Complete Poetry and Select Prose of John Donne.* New York: Random House, 1948.

Douglas, M. *Thinking in Institutions.* London: Routledge & Kegan Paul, 1987.

Dozier, J., and Miceli, M. "Potential Predictors of Whistle-Blowing: A Prosocial Behavior Perspective." *Academy of Management Review,* 1985, *10,* 823-836.

Dunahee, M., and Wangler, L. "The Psychological Contract: A Conceptual Structure for Management/Employee Relations." *Personnel Journal,* 1974, *53* (7), 518-526.

Dunbar, H. *Mind and Body.* New York: Random House, 1947.

Dyer, W. *Team Building.* Reading, Mass.: Addison-Wesley, 1977.

Eagley, A. *Sex Differences in Social Behavior: A Social-Role Interpretation.* Hillsdale, N.J.: Erlbaum, 1987.

Eccles, J. *The Wonder of Being Human.* New York: Free Press, 1984.

Eden, D., and Shani, A. "Pygmalion Goes to Boot Camp: Expectancy, Leadership, and Trainee Performance." *Journal of Applied Psychology,* 1982, *67,* 194-199.

Eisler, R. *The Chalice and the Blade: Our History, Our Future.* San Francisco: Harper & Row, 1987.

Emery, F. *Futures We Are In.* Leiden: Nijhoff, 1977.

Emery, F., and Trist, E. "The Causal Texture of Organizational Environments." *Human Relations,* 1965, *18,* 21-32.

Emery, F., and Trist, E. *Towards a Social Ecology.* London: Plenum, 1973.

Enscoe, G. *Eros and the Romantics: Sexual Love as a Theme in Coleridge, Shelley, and Keats.* The Hague: Mouton, 1967.

Epstein, R. *Takings.* Cambridge, Mass.: Harvard University Press, 1985.

Erhard, W. *The End of Starvation: Creating an Idea Whose Time Has Come.* San Francisco: Hunger Project, 1982.

Erikson, E. *Identity, Youth, and Crisis.* New York: Norton, 1968.

"The Executive as Social Activist." *Time,* July 20, 1987, p. 50.

Fénichel, O. *La Théorie psychanalytique des névroses.* Paris: PUF, 1953.

Festinger, L. *A Theory of Cognitive Dissonance.* Stanford, Calif.: Stanford University Press, 1957.

Festinger, L., and J. Carlsmith. "Cognitive Consequences of Forced Compliance." *Journal of Abnormal and Social Psychology,* 1959, *58,* 203-210.

Fink, S., Beak, J., and Taddeo, K. "Organizational Crisis and Change." *Administrative Science Quarterly,* 1971, *7,* 15-37.

Fisher, V., and Brown, F. "Interjurisdictional Policy Makers Workshop." Storrs: Institute of Public Service, University of Connecticut, Aug. 1977.

Folger, R. "Distributive Justice and Procedural Justice: Combined Impact of 'Voice' and Improvement on Experienced Equity." *Journal of Personality and Social Psychology,* 1977, *35,* 108-119.

Folger, R., and Greenberg, J. "Procedural Justice: An Interpretive Analysis of Personnel Systems." In K. Rowland and G. Ferris (eds.), *Research in Personnel and Human Resources Management.* Vol. 3. Greenwich, Conn.: JAI Press, 1979.

Folkman, S., and Lazarus, R. "An Analysis of Coping in a

Middle-Aged Community Sample." *Journal of Health and Social Behavior,* 1980, *21,* 219-239.

Follett, M. *Dynamic Administration.* London: Management Publications Trust, 1949. (Reprinted as *Freedom and Co-ordination.* New York: Garland, 1987.)

Fosler, R., and Berger, R. *Public-Private Partnerships in American Cities: Seven Case Studies.* Lexington, Mass.: Lexington Books, 1982.

Foucault, M. *Les Mots et les choses.* Paris: Gallimard, 1966.

Fox, F., and Staw, B. "The Trapped Administrator: Effects of Job Insecurity and Policy Resistance upon Commitment to a Course of Action." *Administrative Science Quarterly,* 1979, *24,* 449-471.

French, J., Rogers, W., and Cobb, S. "Adjustment as a Person-Environment Fit." In G. Coelho, D. Hamburg, and J. Adams (eds.), *Coping and Adaptation: Interdisciplinary Perspective.* New York: Basic Books, 1974.

French, M. *Beyond Power: On Women, Men, and Morals.* New York: Ballantine Books, 1985.

Friedman, M. *Capitalism and Freedom.* Chicago: University of Chicago Press, 1963.

Friedman, M., and Rosenamn, R. *Type A Behavior and Your Heart.* New York: Knopf, 1974.

Friend, J., Power, J., and Yewlett, C. *Public Planning: The Intercorporate Dimension.* London: Tavistock, 1974.

Fritz, R. *The Path of Least Resistance.* Salem, Mass.: DMA, 1984.

Frost, P. "Power, Politics, and Influence." In F. Jablin, L. Putnam, K. Roberts, and L. Porter (eds.), *Handbook of Organizational Communication.* Newbury Park, Calif.: Sage, 1987.

Frost, P. "The Role of Organizational Power and Politics in Human Resource Management." In G. Ferris and K. Rowland (eds.), *International Human Resources Management, Supplement 1.* Greenwich, Conn.: JAI Press, 1989.

Frost, P., and Egri, C. "Is It Better to Ask for Forgiveness Than to Seek Permission? The Influence of Current and Past Political Action on Innovation in Organizations." Paper presented at Academy of Management national meeting, Anaheim, Calif., Aug. 1988.

Frost, P., Mitchell, V., and Nord, W. (eds.). *Organizational Reality: Reports from the Firing Line.* (3rd ed.) Glenview, Ill.: Scott, Foresman, 1986.
Gadamer, H. *Truth and Method.* New York: Seabury Press, 1975.
Galbraith, J. *The New Industrial State.* Boston: Houghton Mifflin, 1967.
Galbraith, J., and Kazanjian, R. *Strategy Implementation: Structure, Systems, and Process.* (2nd ed.) St. Paul, Minn.: West, 1986.
Gardner, J. *Morale.* New York: Norton, 1978.
Gardner, M. *The Whys of a Philosophical Scrivener.* New York: Quill Books, 1983.
Garment, S. "U.S. Sanctions Just a Sideshow in African Drama." *Wall Street Journal,* Aug. 18, 1985, p. 18.
Garreau, J. *The Nine Nations of North America.* New York: Avon, 1981.
Gawain, S. *Creative Visualization.* New York: Bantam Books, 1978.
Geertz, C. *The Interpretation of Cultures.* New York: Basic Books, 1973.
Gergen, K. *Toward Transformation in Social Knowledge.* New York: Springer-Verlag, 1982.
Gergen, K. "The Social Constructionist Movement in Modern Psychology." *American Psychologist,* 1985, 40 (3), 266-275.
Gergen, K., and Davis, K. (eds.). *The Social Construction of the Person.* New York: Springer-Verlag, 1985.
Gergen, K., and Gergen, M. "Narrative and the Self as Relationship." In L. Berkowitz (ed.), *Advances in Experimental Social Psychology.* New York: Academic Press, 1988.
Gerlach, M. "Business Alliances and the Strategy of the Japanese Firm." *California Management Review,* 1987, 30, 126-142.
Gillett, R. *The Human Enterprise: A Christian Perspective on Work.* Kansas City, Mo.: Leaven Press, 1985.
Gilligan, C. *In a Different Voice.* Cambridge, Mass.: Harvard University Press, 1982.
"The Glass Ceiling." *Wall Street Journal,* Mar. 24, 1986.
Goethals, G., and Cooper, J. "Role of Intention and Post-Behavioral Consequences in the Arousal of Cognitive Dis-

sonance." *Journal of Personality and Social Psychology*, 1972, *23*, 293-301.

Goldberger, L., and Breznitz, S. (eds.). *Handbook of Stress: Theoretical and Clinical Aspects.* London: Free Press, 1985.

Goleman, D. "Research Affirms Power of Positive Thinking." *New York Times*, Feb. 3, 1987, pp. 15-19.

Gorbachev, M. *Perestroika: New Thinking for Our Country and the World.* New York: Harper & Row, 1987.

Gouldner, A. "The Norm of Reciprocity: A Preliminary Statement." *American Sociological Review*, 1960, *25*, 161-178.

Gricar, B. "Fostering Collaboration Among Organizations." In H. Meltzer and W. Nord (eds.), *Making Organizations Humane and Productive.* New York: Wiley, 1981.

Gricar, B., and Brown, L. "Conflict, Power, and Organization in a Changing Community." *Human Relations*, 1981, *34*, 877-893.

Greenberg, J. "Determinants of Perceived Fairness of Performance Evaluations." *Journal of Applied Psychology*, 1986a, *71*, 340-342.

Greenberg, J. "Organizational Performance Appraisal Procedures: What Makes Them Fair?" In R. Lewicki, B. Sheppard, and M. Bazerman (eds.), *Research on Negotiating in Organizations.* Greenwich, Conn.: JAI Press, 1986b.

Grinker, R., and Spiegel, J. *Men Under Stress.* Philadelphia: Blakiston, 1945.

Growald, E., and Luks, A. "Beyond Self." *American Health*, 1988, *7*, 51-53.

Hackman, R. "Group Influences on Individuals." In M. Dunnette (ed.), *Handbook of Industrial and Organizational Psychology.* Chicago: Rand McNally, 1976.

Hackman, R., and Morris, C. "Group Tasks, Group Interaction Process, and Group Performance Effectiveness." In L. Berkowitz (ed.), *Advances in Experimental Social Psychology.* New York: Academic Press, 1975.

Hafner, K. "The World According to John Sculley." *Business Week*, Sept. 28, 1987, pp. 71-72.

Hage, J., and Dewar, R. "Elite Values Versus Organizational Structure in Predicting Innovation." *Administrative Science Quarterly*, 1973, *18*, 279-290.

Hall, R., and others. "Patterns of Interorganizational Relations." *Administrative Science Quarterly,* 1977, *22,* 457-474.

Hardin, G. "The Tragedy of the Commons." *Science,* 1968, *162,* 1243-1248.

Hardin, G. *Filters Against Folly: How to Survive Despite Economists, Ecologists, and the Merely Eloquent.* New York: Viking, 1985.

Harkins, S., Latane, B., and Williams, K. "Social Loafing: Allocating Effort or Taking It Easy?" *Journal of Experimental and Social Psychology,* 1980, *16,* 457-465.

Harlan, A., and Weiss, C. *Moving Up: Women in Managerial Careers.* Working Paper, no. 86. Wellesley, Mass.: Center for Research on Women, Wellesley College, 1981.

Harman, W. *Global Mind Change.* Indianapolis, Ind.: Knowledge Systems, 1988.

Harman, W., and Rheingold, H. *Higher Creativity: Liberating the Unconscious for Breakthrough Insights.* Los Angeles: Tarcher, 1984.

Harré, R. "Psychological Variety." In P. Heelas and A. Lock (eds.), *Indigenous Psychologies: The Anthropology of the Self.* London: Academic Press, 1981.

Harrigan, K. *Managing for Joint Venture Success.* Lexington, Mass.: Lexington Books, 1986.

Harris, M., and Rosenthal, R. "Mediation of Interpersonal Expectancy Effects: Thirty-One Meta-Analyses." *Psychological Bulletin,* 1985, *97,* 363-386.

Harrison, R. "Strategies for a New Age." *Human Resource Management,* 1983, *22,* 209-235.

Harvey, J. *The Abilene Paradox and Beyond: Meditations on Management.* Lexington, Mass.: Heath, 1988.

Hastie, R., and Kumar, P. "Person Memory: Personality Traits as Organizing Principles in Memory for Behaviors." *Journal of Personality and Social Psychology,* 1979, *37,* 27-38.

Heidegger, M. *Being and Time.* New York: Harper & Row, 1962. (Originally published 1927.)

Hemp, P. "Britain's 'Intransigent' Rubber Workers Bow to Japanese Management Practices." *Wall Street Journal,* Mar. 29, 1988, p. 26.

Hermann, C. "Some Consequences of Crisis Which Limit the Viability of Organizations." *Administrative Science Quarterly,* 1963, *8,* 61-82.

Hinkle, L., Whitney, L., and Lehman, W. "Occupation, Education, and Coronary Heart Disease." *Science,* 1968, *161,* 238–246.

Hirsch, P., and Andrews, J. "Ambushes, Shootouts, and Knights of the Roundtable: The Language of Corporate Take-Overs." In R. Pondy and others (eds.), *Organizational Symbolism.* Greenwich, Conn.: JAI Press, 1983.

Ho, D. "Cultural Values and Professional Issues in Clinical Psychology: Implications from Hong Kong Experience." *American Psychologist,* 1985, *40,* 1212–1218.

Holmes, J., and Rahe, R. "The Social Readjustment Rating Scale." *Journal of Psychosomatic Research,* 1967, *11,* 213–218.

Holt, R. "Occupational Stress." In Leo Goldberger and S. Breznitz (eds.), *Handbook of Stress: Theoretical and Clinical Aspects.* London: Free Press, 1985.

Homans, G. *Social Behavior: Its Elementary Forms.* New York: Harcourt Brace Jovanovich, 1974.

House, R., and Rizzo, J. "Role Conflict and Ambiguity as Critical Variables in a Model of Organization." *Organizational Behavior and Human Performance,* 1972, *7,* 467–505.

House, R., and Singh, J. "Organizational Behavior: Some New Directions for I/O Psychology." *Annual Review of Psychology,* 1987, *38,* 669–718.

Hudson, W., and van Reijen, W. (eds.) *Modern Versus Postmodern.* Utrecht: Hes Vitgerers, 1986.

Humphreys, L., and Stubbs, J. "A Longitudinal Analysis of Teacher Expectation, Student Expectation, and Student Achievement." *Journal of Educational Measurement,* 1977, *14,* 261–270.

Huxley, A. *The Perennial Philosophy.* New York: Harper & Row, 1945.

Isen, A. "The Influence of Positive Affect on Decision Making and Cognitive Organization." In T. Kinnear (ed.), *Advances in Consumer Behavior.* Ann Arbor, Mich.: Association for Consumer Research, 1984.

Isen, A., and Levin, A. "Effect of Feeling Good on Helping: Cookies and Kindness." *Journal of Personality and Social Psychology,* 1972, *21,* 384–388.

References

Isen, A., and Means, B. "The Influence of Positive Affect on Decision Making Strategy." *Social Cognition*, 1983, *2*, 18-31.

Isen, A., and Patrick, R. "The Effect of Positive Feelings on Risk Taking: When the Chips Are Down." *Organizational Behavior and Human Performance*, 1983, *31*, 194-202.

Isen, A., and Shalker, T. "The Influence of Mood State on Evaluation of Positive, Neutral, and Negative Stimuli." *Social Psychology Quarterly*, 1982, *45*, 58-63.

Isen, A., Shalker, T., Clark, M., and Karp, L. "Affect, Accessibility of Material in Memory, and Behavior: A Cognitive Coop?" *Journal of Personality and Social Psychology*, 1978, *36*, 1-12.

Jackson, D. *Personality Research Form Manual.* Goshen, N.Y.: Research Psychologists Press, 1967.

Jacobi, J., and Hull, R. (eds.) *C. G. Jung: Psychological Reflections, A New Anthology of His Writings, 1905-1961.* Princeton, N.J.: Princeton University Press, 1978.

Jaffe, D., and Bresler, D. "Guided Imagery: Healing Through the Mind's Eye." In J. Schorr and others (eds.), *Proceedings of the First Annual Conference of the American Association for the Study of Mental Imagery.* New York: Plenum, 1980.

James, W. "Is Life Worth Living?" In W. James (ed.), *The Will to Believe.* New York: Dover, 1956. (Originally published 1895.)

James, W. *The Varieties of Religious Experience.* New York: Modern Library, 1929. (Originally published 1902.)

Janis, I. "Problems of Theory in the Analysis of Stress Behavior." *Journal of Social Issues*, 1954, *10*, 12-25.

Jantsch, E. *The Self-Organizing Universe.* Elmsford, N.Y.: Pergamon Press, 1980.

Jemison, D., and Sitkin, S. "Acquisitions: The Process Can Be a Problem." *Harvard Business Review*, 1986, *64*, 107-116.

Jenkins, C., Rosenman, R., and Zyzanski, S. "Prediction of Clinical Coronary Heart Disease by a Test for the Coronary-Prone Behavior Pattern." *New England Journal of Medicine*, 1974, *23*, 1271-1275.

Jensen, M., and Meckling, W. "Theory of the Firm: Managerial Behavior, Agency Costs, and Ownership Structure." *Journal of Financial Economics*, 1976, *3*, 305-360.

Johnston, R., and Lawrence, P. "Beyond Vertical Integration: The Rise of the Value-Adding Partnership." *Harvard Business Review,* 1988, *66,* 94-101.

Johnston-O'Connor, E., and Kirschenbaum, D. "Something Succeeds Like Success." *Cognitive Therapy and Research,* 1986, *10,* 123-136.

Jonas, H., Fry, R., and Srivastva, S. "The Functioning of the CEO: Understanding the Executive Experience." *Academy of Management Executive,* 1989, *3,* 205-215.

Jung, C. G. *Psychological Types.* London: Routledge & Kegan Paul, 1923.

Jussim, C. "Self-Fulfilling Prophecies: A Theoretical and Integrative Review." *Psychological Review,* 1986, *93* (4), 429-445.

Kahn, R., and others. *Organizational Stress: Studies in Role Conflict and Ambiguity.* New York: Wiley, 1964.

Kanter, R. *Men and Women of the Corporation.* New York: Basic Books, 1977.

Kanter, R. *A Tale of "O": On Being Different in an Organization.* Cambridge, Mass.: Goodmeasure, 1980.

Kanter, R. *The Change Masters.* New York: Simon & Schuster, 1983.

Kanter, R. "When a Thousand Flowers Bloom: Structural, Collective, and Social Conditions for Innovation in Organizations." *Research in Organizational Behavior,* 1988, *10,* 169-211.

Katz, R. "Skills of an Effective Administrator." *Harvard Business Review,* 1955, *33,* 33-42.

Kavanaugh, J. *Search.* San Francisco: Harper & Row, 1985.

Kegan, R. *The Evolving Self: Problem and Process in Human Development.* Cambridge, Mass.: Harvard University Press, 1982.

Keller, E. F. *Reflections on Gender and Science.* New Haven, Conn.: Yale University Press, 1985.

Kelley, G. "Seducing the Elites: The Politics of Decision Making and Innovation in Organizational Networks." *Academy of Management Review,* 1976, *1* (3), 66-74.

Kelly, C. *The Destructive Achiever.* Reading, Mass.: Addison-Wesley, 1988.

Kerckhoff, A., and Davis, K. "Value Consensus and Need Complementarity in Mate Selection." *American Sociological Review,* 1962, *27,* 295-303.

Kets, M. "Organizational Stress: A Call for Management Action." *Sloan Management Review*, 1979, *21*, 3-14.

Kets, M., and Miller, D. *The Neurotic Organization*. New York: McGraw-Hill, 1985.

Kilmann, R., Covin, T., and Associates. *Corporate Transformation: Revitalizing Organizations for a Competitive World*. San Francisco: Jossey-Bass, 1987.

King, A. "Self-Fulfilling Prophecies in Training the Hard-Core: Supervisors' Expectations and the Underprivileged Workers' Performance." *Social Science Quarterly*, 1971, *52*, 369-378.

Kirschenbaum, D. "Self-Regulation and Sport Psychology: Nurturing an Emerging Symbiosis." *Journal of Sport Psychology*, 1984, *8*, 26-34.

Kitching, J. "Why Do Mergers Miscarry?" *Harvard Business Review*, 1967, *45*, 84-101.

Klass, P. "Are Women Better Doctors?" *New York Times Magazine*, Apr. 10, 1988, pp. 32-97.

Klonglan, G., Mulford, C., Warren, R., and Winklepleck, J. "Creating Interorganizational Coordination: Project Report." Sociology Report, no. 122A. Ames: Department of Sociology, Iowa State University, 1975.

Kobasa, S., Maddi, S., and Courington, S. "Personality and Constitution as Mediators in the Stress-Illness Relationship." *Journal of Health and Social Behavior*, 1981, *22* (4), 368-378.

Koestenbaum, P. *The Heart of Business: Change, Power, and Philosophy*. Dallas, Tex.: Saybrook, 1987.

Kofodimos, J. "To Love or to Work: Must We Choose?" *Issues and Observations*, 1986, *6* (2), 1-7.

Kohlberg, L. "Stage and Sequence: A Cognitive-Developmental Approach to Socialization." In D. Goslin (ed.), *Handbook of Socialization Theory*. Chicago: Rand McNally, 1969.

Kolb, D., and Boyatzis, R. "On the Dynamics of the Helping Relationship." In D. Kolb, I. Rubin, and J. McIntyre (eds.), *Organizational Psychology*. (4th ed.) Englewood Cliffs, N.J.: Prentice-Hall, 1974.

Kosslyn, S. *Image and Mind*. Cambridge, Mass.: Harvard University Press, 1980.

Kotter, J. *The General Managers*. New York: Free Press, 1982.

Koys, D., Briggs, S., and Grenig, J. "State Courts, Disparity on Employment at Will." *Personnel Psychology,* 1987, *40* (3), 565–577.

Krebs, D. "Altruism: A Rational Approach." In H. Eisenberg (ed.), *The Development of Prosocial Behavior.* New York: Academic Press, 1982.

Kuhnert, K., and Lewis, P. "Transactional and Transformational Leadership: A Constructive/Developmental Analysis." *Academy of Management Review,* 1987, *12,* 648–657.

Kundera, M. *The Book of Laughter and Forgetting.* New York: Penguin Books, 1980.

Labich, K. "The Seven Keys to Business Leadership." *Fortune,* Oct. 24, 1988, pp. 58–66.

Landy, F., Barnes-Farrell, J., and Cleveland, J. "Perceived Fairness and Accuracy of Performance Evaluation: A Follow-Up." *Journal of Applied Psychology,* 1980, *65,* 355–356.

Latane, B. "The Psychology of Social Impact." *American Psychologist,* 1981, *36* (4), 343–356.

Latane, B., and Darley, J. *The Unresponsive Bystander: Why Does He Not Help?* New York: Appleton-Century-Crofts, 1970.

Latane, B., Williams, K., and Harkins, S. "Many Hands Make Light the Work: The Causes and Consequences of Social Loafing." *Journal of Personality and Social Psychology,* 1979, *37,* 822–832.

Lauffer, A. *Social Planning at the Community Level.* Englewood Cliffs, N.J.: Prentice-Hall, 1978.

Lawless, M. "Directed Interorganizational Systems: Network Strategy Making in Public Service Delivery." Unpublished paper, Department of Management, California State University, Northridge, 1982.

Lawson, H. *Reflexivity: The Post-Modern Predicament.* London: Hutchinson, 1985.

Leavitt, H. "Beyond the Analytic Manager." *California Management Review,* 1975a, *27* (4), 5–12.

Leavitt, H. "Beyond the Analytic Manager, Part II." *California Management Review,* 1975b, *27* (5), 11–21.

Leavitt, H. *Corporate Pathfinders: Building Vision and Values into Organizations.* New York: Penguin Books, 1986.

Lebra, T. *Japanese Women: Constraint and Fulfillment.* Honolulu: University of Hawaii Press, 1984.

Legge, K. *Power, Innovation, and Problem Solving in Personnel Management.* London: McGraw-Hill, 1978.
Levinson, H. "A Psychologist Diagnoses Merger Failures." *Harvard Business Review,* 1970, *48,* 138-147.
Levinson, H. *Psychological Man.* Cambridge, Mass.: Levinson Institute, 1976.
Levitt, T. "The Dangers of Social Responsibility." *Harvard Business Review,* 1958, *36* (5), 41-50.
Lewin, K. *Psychologie dynamique.* Paris: PUF, 1959.
Ley, R., and Freeman, R. "Imagery, Cerebral Laterality, and the Healing Process." In A. Sheikh (ed.), *Imagination and Healing.* New York: Baywood, 1984.
Lind, E., and others. "Procedure and Outcome Effect on Reactions to Adjudicated Resolution of Conflict of Interest." *Journal of Personality and Social Psychology,* 1980, *39,* 643-653.
Lippitt, G. *Organization Renewal.* Englewood Cliffs, N.J.: Prentice-Hall, 1982.
Litwak, E., and Hylton, L. "Interorganizational Analysis: A Hypothesis on Coordinating Agencies." *Administrative Science Quarterly,* 1962, *6,* 395-420.
Loevinger, J. *Ego Development: Conceptions and Theories.* San Francisco: Jossey-Bass, 1976.
Logeay, P., and Gadbois, C. "L'Agression psychique de la mort dans le travail infirmier." In C. Dejours, C. Veil, and A. Wisner (eds.), *Psychologie du travail.* Paris: Enterprise Moderne d'Edition, 1985.
Longnecker, C., Gioia, D., and Sims, H. "Behind the Mask: The Politics of Employee Appraisal." *Academy of Management Executive,* 1987, *1* (3), 183-193.
Lorenz, K. *L'Agression.* Paris: Flammarion, 1969.
Luhmann, N. *Love as Passion: The Codification of Intimacy.* Cambridge, Mass.: Harvard University Press, 1986.
Luthans, F., Hodgetts, R., and Rosenkrantz, S. *Real Managers.* Cambridge, Mass.: Ballinger, 1988.
Lyotard, J. *The Post-Modern Condition: A Report on Knowledge.* Minneapolis: University of Minnesota Press, 1984.
McAllister, D., Mitchell, T., and Beach, L. "The Contingency Model for the Selection in Decision Strategies: An Empirical Test of the Effects of Significance, Accountability, and Revers-

ibility." *Organizational Behavior and Human Performance,* 1979, *24,* 228-244.

Macaulay, J., and Berkowitz, L. "Overview." In J. Macaulay and L. Berkowitz (eds.), *Altruism and Helping Behavior.* New York: Academic Press, 1970.

McCann, J. "Design Guidelines for Social Problem Solving Interventions." *Journal of Applied Behavioral Science,* 1983, *19,* 177-192.

McCaskey, M. *The Executive Challenge: Managing Change and Ambiguity.* Boston: Pitman, 1982.

McClelland, D. *The Achieving Society.* Princeton, N.J.: Van Nostrand, 1961.

McClelland, D. *Power: The Inner Experience.* New York: Wiley, 1975.

Maccoby, M. *The Gamesman: The New Corporate Leader.* New York: Simon & Schuster, 1976.

MacGrawth, J. "Stress and Behavior in Organizations." In M. Dunnette (ed.), *Handbook of Industrial and Organizational Psychology.* Chicago: Rand McNally, 1976.

McGregor, D. *The Human Side of Enterprise.* New York: McGraw-Hill, 1960.

Maclagan, P. "The Concept of Responsibility: Some Implications for Organizational Behavior and Development." *Journal of Management Studies,* 1983, *20* (4), 411-423.

MacLean, A. "Job Stress and the Psychosocial Pressures of Change." *Personnel,* 1976, *53,* 40-49.

Macneil, I. "Relational Contract: What We Do and Do Not Know." *Wisconsin Law Review,* 1985, *23,* 483-525.

Maier, M. "The Compulsion to Perform: Achievement and Success Addiction in the American Family." Workshop at the 50th annual conference of the National Council on Family Relations, Philadelphia, Nov. 13-18, 1988.

Margolies, B., Kroes, W., and Quinn, R. "Job Stress: An Unlisted Occupational Hazard." *Journal of Occupational Medicine, 16,* 1974, 97-110.

Markley, D. "Human Consciousness in Transformation." In E. Jantsch and C. Waddington (eds.), *Evolution and Consciousness: Human Systems in Transition.* Menlo Park, Calif.: Addison-Wesley, 1976.

Marks, M., and Mirvis, P. "The Merger Syndrome: When Corporate Cultures Clash." *Psychology Today,* Oct. 1986, pp. 36-42.

Marrett, C. "On the Specification of Interorganizational Dimensions." *Sociology and Social Review,* 1971, *56,* 83-89.

Marty, P. *Les Mouvements individuels de vie et de mort.* Paris: Petite Biblothèque Payot, 1969.

Maslow, A. *Motivation and Personality.* New York: Harper & Row, 1954.

Maslow, A. *Eupsychian Management.* Homewood, Ill.: Irwin, 1965.

Maslow, A. "A Theory of Metamotivation: The Biological Rootings of the Value Life." *Journal of Humanistic Psychology,* 1967, *7,* 108-109.

Mayo, E. *Some Notes on the Psychology of Pierre Janet.* Cambridge, Mass.: Harvard University Press, 1948.

Mechanic, D. *Students Under Stress: A Study in the Social Psychology of Adaptation.* New York: Free Press, 1962.

Michael, D. *On Learning to Plan and Planning to Learn.* San Francisco: Jossey-Bass, 1973.

Michael, D., and Mirvis, P. "Changing, Erring, and Learning." In P. Mirvis and D. Berg (eds.), *Failures in Organization Development and Change.* New York: Wiley Interscience, 1977.

Miles, R., and Snow, C. "Network Organizations: New Concepts for New Forms." *California Management Review,* 1986, *27,* 62-73.

Miller, D. (ed.). *Popper Selections.* Princeton, N.J.: Princeton University Press, 1985.

Mintzberg, H. *The Nature of Managerial Work.* New York: Harper & Row, 1973.

Mintzberg, H. "A Note on that Dirty Word, 'Efficiency.'" *Interfaces,* 1982, *12* (5), 101-105.

Mintzberg, H. *Power in and Around Organizations.* Englewood Cliffs, N.J.: Prentice-Hall, 1983.

Mirvis, P. "The Art of Assessing the Quality of Work Life." In E. Lawler, D. Nadler, and C. Camman (eds.), *Organizational Assessment.* New York: Wiley Interscience, 1980.

Mirvis, P. "Negotiations After the Sale: The Roots and Ramifications of Conflict in an Acquisition." *Journal of Occupational Behavior,* 1985, *6,* 65-84.

Mirvis, P., and Louis, M. "Self-Full Research: Working Through the Self as Instrument in Organizational Research." In D. Berg and K. Smith (eds.), *Exploring Clinical Methods for Social Research.* Newbury Park, Calif.: Sage, 1985.

Mitchell, T., Rediker, K., and Beach, L. "Image Theory and Organizational Decision Making." In H. Sims, Jr., D. Gioia, and Associates, *The Thinking Organization: Dynamics of Organizational Social Cognition.* San Francisco: Jossey-Bass, 1986.

Mitroff, I. *Stakeholders of the Organizational Mind: Toward a New View of Organizational Policy Making.* San Francisco: Jossey-Bass, 1983.

Moch, M. "Toward a Theory of Administrative Practice: For What? For Whom? and For How Long?" Unpublished manuscript, Department of Management, University of Texas, 1982.

Mook, D. *Motivation: The Organization of Action.* New York: Norton, 1987.

Morgan, G. *Images of Organization.* Newbury Park, Calif.: Sage, 1987a.

Morgan, G. "Riding the Cutting-Edge of Change: A Study of Emerging Managerial Competencies." Working Paper, Faculty of Administrative Studies, York University, Toronto, 1987b.

Morris, C. *The Discovery of the Individual: 1050-1200.* London: Camelot Press, 1972.

Morrison, A., White, R., Van Velsor, E., and Center for Creative Leadership (eds.). *Breaking the Glass Ceiling: Can Women Reach the Top of America's Largest Corporations?* Reading, Mass.: Addison-Wesley, 1987.

Murray, C., and Cox, C. *Apollo: Race to the Moon.* New York: Simon & Schuster, 1989.

Murray, E. *Imaginative Thinking and Human Existence.* Pittsburgh, Pa.: Duquesne University Press, 1986.

Murray, H. *Explorations in Personality.* New York: Oxford University Press, 1938.

Nadler, D. "The Effective Management of Organizational Change." In J. Lorsch (ed.), *Handbook of Organizational Behavior.* Englewood Cliffs, N.J.: Prentice-Hall, 1987.

Naisbitt, J. *Megatrends.* New York: Warner Books, 1984.

Nathan, M., and Cummings, T. "Collective Strategies for Technological Innovation: The Case of University-Industry R&D Consortia." Paper delivered at the Conference on American Competitiveness, University of Pittsburgh, Oct. 1988.
Neilsen, E. "Empowerment Strategies: Balancing Authority and Responsibility." In S. Srivastva and Associates, *Executive Power: How Executives Influence People and Organizations*. San Francisco: Jossey-Bass, 1986.
Nicklaus, J. *Golf My Way*. New York: Simon & Schuster, 1974.
Noble, D. *Forces of Production*. New York: Knopf, 1984.
Nord, W., Brief, A., Atieh, J., and Doherty, E. "Work Values and the Conduct of Organizational Behavior." *Research in Organizational Behavior*, 1988, *10*, 1-42.
Olson, M., Jr. *The Logic of Collective Action*. Cambridge, Mass.: Harvard University Press, 1965.
Olson, M., Jr. *The Rise and Decline of Nations: Economic Growth, Stagflation, and Social Rigidities*. New Haven, Conn.: Yale University Press, 1982.
O'Regan, B. "Psychoneuroimmunology: The Birth of a New Field." *Investigations: A Bulletin of the Institute of Noetic Sciences*, 1983, *1*, 1-11.
Ornstein, R., and Sobel, D. *The Healing Brain*. New York: Simon & Schuster, 1987.
Ostrander, S. *Superlearning*. New York: Delacorte, 1979.
Ouchi, W. *Theory Z: How American Business Can Meet the Japanese Challenge*. Reading, Mass.: Addison-Wesley, 1981.
Ouchi, W. *The M-Form Society: How American Teamwork Can Recapture the Competitive Edge*. Reading, Mass.: Addison-Wesley, 1984.
Ouchi, W., and Bolton, M. "The Logic of Joint Research and Development." *California Management Review*, 1988, *30*, 9-33.
Owen, H. *SPIRIT: Transformation and Development in Organizations*. Potomac, Md.: Abbott, 1987.
Pagels, E. *The Gnostic Gospels*. New York: Vintage Books, 1981.
Parsons, J. E., Kaczola, C. M., and Meece, J. L. "Socialization of Achievement Attitudes and Beliefs: Classroom Influences." *Child Development*, 1982, *53*, 322-339.
Pascale, R., and Athos, A. *The Art of Japanese Management*. New York: Simon & Schuster, 1981.

Pavio, A. *Imagery and Verbal Processes.* New York: Holt, Rinehart & Winston, 1971.

Pearlin, L., and Schooler, C. "The Structure of Coping." *Journal of Health and Social Behavior,* 1978, *19,* 2-21.

Pearson, C. *The Hero Within: Six Archetypes We Live By.* San Francisco: Harper & Row, 1986.

Personnel Decisions, Inc. "Data from the Management Skills Profile, 1982-1986." In A. Morrison, R. White, E. Van Velsor, and Center for Creative Leadership (eds.). *Breaking the Glass Ceiling: Can Women Reach the Top of America's Largest Corporations?* Reading, Mass.: Addison-Wesley, 1987.

Peters, T., and Waterman, R. *In Search of Excellence.* New York: Harper & Row, 1982.

Peterson, C., and Seligman, M. "Causal Explanations as a Risk Factor for Depression: Theory and Evidence." *Psychological Review,* 1984, *91,* 347-374.

Pettigrew, A. *The Awakening Giant.* Oxford: Blackwell, 1985.

Petty, R., Harkins, S., and Williams, K. "The Effects of Diffusion of Cognitive Effort on Attitudes: An Information Procession View." *Journal of Personality and Social Psychology,* 1980, *38,* 81-92.

Pfeffer, J. *Power in Organizations.* Boston: Pitman, 1981.

Pfeffer, J., and Salancik, G. *The External Control of Organizations: A Resource Dependence Perspective.* New York: Harper & Row, 1978.

Piaget, J. *The Moral Judgment of the Child.* New York: Free Press, 1948.

Piliavin, I., Piliavin, J., and Rodin, J. "Costs, Diffusion, and the Stigmatized Victim." *Journal of Personality and Social Psychology,* 1975, *32,* 429-438.

Pinchot, J., III. *Intrapreneuring.* New York: Harper & Row, 1985.

Polak, F. *The Image of the Future.* New York: Elsevier, 1973.

Polanyi, M. *Personal Knowledge.* London: Routledge & Kegan Paul, 1958.

Polanyi, M. *The Tacit Dimension.* New York: Doubleday, 1966.

Popper, K. *Conjectures and Refutations: The Growth of Scientific Knowledge.* New York: Harper & Row, 1968.

Popper, K., and Eccles, J. *The Self and Its Brain.* Springer-Verlag, 1981.

Porras, J., and Berg, P. "The Impact of Organization Development." *Academy of Management Review*, 1978, *3*, 249-266.

Powell, W. "Hybrid Organizational Arrangements." *California Management Review*, 1987, *30*, 67-87.

Price, F., and Bergen, B. "The Relationship to Death as a Source of Stress for Nurses on a Coronary Care Unit." *Omega*, 1999, *8* (3), 229-237.

Pylyshyn, Z. "What the Mind's Eye Tells the Mind's Brain: A Critique of Mental Imagery." *Psychological Bulletin*, 1973, *80*, 1-24.

Quick, J., and Quick, J. *Organizational Stress and Preventative Management*. New York: McGraw-Hill, 1984.

Quinn, R. *Beyond Rational Management: Mastering the Paradoxes and Competing Demands of High Performance*. San Francisco: Jossey-Bass, 1988.

Rader, M. *A Modern Book of Esthetics: An Anthology*. New York: Holt, 1973.

Ranson, S., Hinings, B., and Greenwood, R. "The Structuring of Organizational Structures." *Administrative Science Quarterly*, 1980, *25*, 1-17.

Ravenswaaij, I. "Novelty-Detecting Capabilities." Paper presented to the Strategies of Change Conference, World Federation of Mental Health, Amsterdam, The Netherlands, 1972.

Rawson, H., and Miner, M. (eds.). *The New International Dictionary of Quotations*. Toronto: Fitzhenry & Whiteside, 1986.

Reich, C. *The Greening of America: How the Youth Revolution Is Trying to Make America Livable*. New York: Bantam Books, 1971.

Richardson, A. *Mental Imagery*. London: Routledge & Kegan Paul, 1969.

Richardson, A. "Imagery: Definition and Types." In A. Skeikh (ed.), *Imagery: Current Theory, Research, and Application*. New York: Wiley, 1983.

Rist, R. "Student Social Class and Teacher Expectations: The Self-Fulfilling Prophecy in Ghetto Education." *Harvard Educational Review*, 1970, *40*, 411-451.

Roethlisberger, F., and others. *Training for Human Relations*. Boston: Harvard Business School Division Research, 1954.

Rogers, C. *On Becoming a Person*. Boston: Houghton Mifflin, 1961.

Rogers, D., and Glick, E. "Planning for Interagency Cooperation in Rural Development." *Card Report US.* Ames: Center for Agriculture and Rural Development, Iowa State University, 1973.

Rogers, D., and Molnar, J. "Organizational Antecedents of Role Conflict and Ambiguity in Top Level Administrators." *Administrative Science Quarterly,* 1976, *21,* 598-610.

Rogers, D., and Whetten, D. *Interorganizational Coordination: Theory, Research, and Implementation.* Ames: Iowa State University Press, 1982.

Romo, M., Siltany, T., and Rahe, R. "Work Behavior, Time Urgency, and Life Satisfactions in Subjects with Myocardinal Infarction: A Cross-Cultural Study." *Journal of Psychosomatic Research,* 1974, *18,* 1-8.

Rosenhan, D., Salovey, P., and Hargis, K. "The Joys of Helping: Focus of Attention Mediates the Impact of Positive Affect on Altruism." *Journal of Personality and Social Psychology,* 1981, *40,* 899-905.

Rosenthal, R., and Rubin, D. "Interpersonal Expectancy Effects: The First 345 Studies." *Behavioral and Brain Sciences,* 1978, *3,* 377-415.

Rotter, J., and Stein, D. "Public Attitudes Toward the Trustworthiness, Competence, and Altruism of Twenty Selected Occupations." *Journal of Applied Social Psychology,* 1971, *1,* 334-343.

Rousseau, D. "Psychological and Implied Contracts in Organizations." Unpublished working paper, Department of Organizational Behavior, Northwestern University, 1987.

Rousseau, D., and Anton, R. "Fairness and Implied Contract Obligations in Job Terminations: A Policy Capturing Study." *Human Performance,* 1988a, *1,* 273-299.

Rousseau, D., and Anton, R. "Fairness and Implied Contract Obligations in Job Terminations: The Role of Contributions, Promises, and Performance." Unpublished manuscript, 1988b.

Rubovitz, R., and Maehr, M. "Pygmalion Black and White." *Journal of Personality and Social Psychology,* 1973, *25,* 210-218.

Runciman, W. *Weber: Selections in Translation.* Cambridge, Mass.: Harvard University Press, 1978.

Rushton, J. *Altruism, Socialization, and Society.* Englewood Cliffs, N.J.: Prentice-Hall, 1980.
Ryle, G. *The Concept of Mind.* New York: Harper & Row, 1949.
Saleh, S. "Relational Orientations and Organizational Functioning: A Cross-Cultural Perspective." *Canadian Journal of Administrative Science,* 1987, *4* (3), 276-293.
Sales, A., and Mirvis, P. "When Cultures Collide: Issues in Acquisition." In J. Kimberly and R. Quinn (eds.), *Managing Organization Transitions.* Homewood, Ill.: Irwin, 1984.
Salk, J. *The Survival of the Wisest.* New York: Harper & Row, 1973.
Sampson, E. "The Debate on Individualism: Indigenous Psychologies of the Individual and Their Role in Personal and Societal Functioning." *American Psychologist,* 1988, *43,* 15-22.
Sarason, S. *The Creation of Settings and the Future Societies.* San Francisco: Jossey-Bass, 1972.
Sarason, S., and Lorentz, E. *The Challenge of the Resource Exchange Network.* San Francisco: Jossey-Bass, 1979.
Schaef, A. *When Society Becomes an Addict.* San Francisco: Harper & Row, 1987.
Schaef, A., and Fassel, D. *The Addictive Organization.* New York: Harper & Row, 1988.
Schein, E. *Organizational Psychology.* Englewood Cliffs, N.J.: Prentice-Hall, 1980.
Schein, E. *Organizational Culture and Leadership: A Dynamic View.* San Francisco: Jossey-Bass, 1985.
Scheler, M. *Formalism in Ethics and Non-Formal Ethics of Values.* Evanston, Ill.: Northwestern University Press, 1973.
Schermerhorn, J., Hunt, J., and Osborn, R. *Managing Organizational Behavior.* New York: Wiley, 1988.
Schlenker, B. *Impression Management: The Self-Concept, Social Identity, and Interpersonal Relations.* Monterey, Calif.: Brooks/Cole, 1980.
Schmidt, W. (ed.). *Organizational Frontiers and Human Values.* Belmont, Calif.: Wadsworth, 1970.
Schmidt, W., and Posner, B. *Managerial Values in Perspective.* New York: Membership Publication Division, American Management Association, 1983.

Schön, D. *The Reflective Practitioner: How Professionals Think in Action.* New York: Basic Books, 1983.

Schuler, R. *Definition and Conceptualization of Stress in Organization.* New York: Academic Press, 1980.

Schultz, A. *The Phenomenology of the Social World.* Chicago: Northwestern University Press, 1967.

Schultz, D. "The Use of Imagery in Alleviating Depression." In A. Sheikh (ed.), *Imagination and Healing.* New York: Baywood, 1984.

Schwartz, R. "The Internal Dialogue: On the Assymetry Between Positive and Negative Coping Thoughts." *Cognitive Therapy and Research,* 1986, *10,* 591-605.

Schwartz, S. "The Justice of Need and the Activation of Humanitarian Norms." *Journal of Social Issues,* 1975, *31* (3), 111-136.

Scott, W., and Hart, D. *Organizational America.* Boston: Houghton Mifflin, 1979.

Seligman, M. *Helplessness: On Depression, Development, and Death.* San Francisco: Freeman, 1975.

Selye, H. *The Stress of Life.* New York: McGraw-Hill, 1986.

Selznick, P. *Law, Society, and Industrial Justice.* New York: Russell Sage Foundation, 1969.

Semin, G., and Manstead, A. *The Accountability of Conduct: A Social Psychological Analysis.* London: Academic Press, 1983.

Sheane, D. "Ulster: The Leading Edge." Informal discussion paper, Central Personnel Department, Imperial Chemical House, Milbank, London, England, 1977.

Sheikh, A. *Imagery: Current Theory, Research, and Application.* New York: Wiley, 1983.

Sheikh, A. *Imagination and Healing.* New York: Baywood, 1984.

Sheikh, A., and Panagiotou, N. "The Use of Mental Imagery in Psychotherapy: A Critical Review." *Perceptual and Motor Skills,* 1975, *41,* 555-585.

Shideler, M. *In Search of the Spirit: A Primer.* New York: Ballantine Books, 1985.

Shotter, J. "Vico, Moral Worlds, Accountability, and Personhood." In P. Heelas and A. Lock (eds.), *Indigenous Psychologies: The Anthropology of the Self.* London: Academic Press, 1981.

Shotter, J. "Remembering and Forgetting as Social Institutions." In D. Middleton (ed.), *Collective Memory.* London: Sage, 1988.

Siegan, B. *Economic Liberties and the Constitution.* Chicago: University of Chicago Press, 1980.
Siegel, B. *Medicine and Miracles.* New York: Harper & Row, 1986.
Siu, R. *The Portable Dragon: The Western Man's Guide to the I Ching.* Cambridge, Mass.: MIT Press, 1968.
Siu, R. *The Way to Executive Serenity.* New York: Beech Tree Books, 1985.
Skinner, B. *About Behaviorism.* New York: Knopf, 1974.
Skolimowski, H. "The Methodology of Participation and Its Consequences." Unpublished manuscript, Institute for Social Research, University of Michigan, 1988.
Slater, P. *The Pursuit of Loneliness: American Culture at the Breaking Point.* Boston: Beacon Press, 1970.
Sloterdijk, P. *Critique of Cynical Reason.* Minneapolis: University of Minnesota Press, 1987.
Smart, C., and Vertinsky, I. "Designs of Crisis Decision Units." *Administrative Science Quarterly,* 1977, *22,* 640-657.
Smith, A. *An Inquiry into the Nature and Wealth of Nations.* New York: Modern Library, 1936. (Originally published 1776.)
Soelle, D. *To Work and to Love: A Theology of Creation.* Philadelphia: Fortress Press, 1984.
Soinsaulieu, R. *L'Identité au travail.* Paris: Presses de la Fondation Nationale des Sciences Politiques, 1977.
Sommers, A. "Of Markets and Ethics: The Future of the Mixed Economy." *Executive,* 1977, *4* (11).
Sorokin, P. *A Long Journey: The Autobiography of Pitirim A. Sorokin.* New Haven, Conn.: College and University Press, 1963.
Spence, J. "Achievement American Style: The Rewards and Costs of Individualism." *American Psychologist,* 1985, *40,* 1285-1295.
Spence, J., and Helmreich, R. "Achievement-Related Motives and Behavior." In J. Spence (ed.), *Achievement and Achievement Motives: Psychological and Sociological Approaches.* San Francisco: Freeman, 1983.
Spengler, O. *The Decline of the West.* New York: Knopf, 1926.
Sperry, R. "Changing Priorities." *Annual Review of Neurosciences,* 1981, *6,* 1-10.
Sperry, R. "Structure and Significance of the Consciousness Revolution." *Journal of Mind and Behavior,* 1987, *8* (1), 37-66.

Sperry, R. "Psychology's Mentalist Paradigm and the Religion/Science Tension," *American Psychologist,* 1988, *43,* 607-613.

Srivastva, S., and Associates. *The Executive Mind: New Insights on Managerial Thought and Action.* San Francisco: Jossey-Bass, 1983.

Srivastva, S., and Associates. *Executive Power: How Executives Influence People and Organizations.* San Francisco: Jossey-Bass, 1986.

Srivastva, S., and Associates. *Executive Integrity: The Search for High Human Values in Organizational Life.* San Francisco: Jossey-Bass, 1988.

Srivastva, S., and Cooperrider, D. "The Emergence of the Egalitarian Organization." *Human Relations,* 1986, *39,* 683-724.

Staw, B. "Knee-Deep in the Big Muddy: A Study of Escalating Commitment to a Chosen Course of Action." *Organizational Behavior and Human Performance,* 1976, *16,* 27-44.

Staw, B. "Rationality and Justification in Organizational Life." In B. Staw and L. Cummings (eds.), *Research in Organizational Behavior.* Greenwich, Conn.: JAI Press, 1980.

Staw, B. "The Escalation of Commitment to a Course of Action." *Academy of Management Review,* 1981, *6,* 577-587.

Staw, B., and Fox, F. "Escalation: Some Determinants of Commitment to a Previously Chosen Course of Action." *Human Relations,* 1977, *30,* 431-450.

Staw, B., and Ross, J. "Commitment to a Policy Decision: A Multi-Theoretical Perspective." *Administrative Science Quarterly,* 1978, *23,* 40-64.

Staw, B., and Ross, J. "Behavior in Escalation Situations: Antecedents, Prototypes, and Solutions." In L. Cummings and B. Staw (eds.), *Research in Organizational Behavior.* Greenwich, Conn.: JAI Press, 1987.

Steers, R. *Introduction to Organizational Behavior.* Glenview, Ill.: Scott, Foresman, 1988.

Sullivan, H. *Conceptions of Modern Psychiatry.* Washington, D.C.: White Psychiatric Foundation, 1947.

Swann, W., and Snyder, M. "On Translating Beliefs into Action: Theories of Ability and Their Application in an Instructional Setting." *Journal of Personality and Social Psychology,* 1980, *38,* 879-888.

Taber, T., Walsh, J., and Cooke, R. "Developing a Community-Based Program for Reducing the Social Impact of a Plant Closing." *Journal of Applied Behavioral Science,* 1979, *15,* 133-155.

Tagliabue, J. "Lech! Lech! Lech!" *New York Times Magazine,* Oct. 23, 1988, 37-46.

Tannenbaum, R., Margulies, N., Massarik, F., and Associates. *Human Systems Development: New Perspectives on People and Organizations.* San Francisco: Jossey-Bass, 1985.

Tetlock, P. "Accountability and the Complexity of Thought." *Journal of Personality and Social Psychology,* 1983, *45* (1), 74-83.

Tetlock, P. "Accountability: The Neglected Social Context of Judgment and Choice." In L. Cummings and B. Staw (eds.), *Research in Organizational Behavior,* Greenwich, Conn.: JAI Press, 1985.

Thorsell, W. "GM's Big Mistake." *Report on Business Magazine,* Oct. 1988, pp. 33-36.

Tichy, N. "Managing Change Strategically: The Technical, Political, and Cultural Keys." *Organizational Dynamics,* 1982, *11* (2), 59-80.

Tichy, N., and Devanna, M. *The Transformational Leader.* New York: Wiley, 1983.

Tillich, P. *Shaking the Foundations.* New York: Scribner, 1948.

Tillich, P. *The Courage to Be.* New Haven, Conn.: Yale University Press, 1952.

Tillich, P. *The New Being.* New York: Scribner, 1955.

Tillich, P. *The Eternal Now.* New York: Scribner, 1963.

Toffler, B. *Tough Choices: Managers Talk Ethics.* New York: Wiley, 1986.

Torbert, W. *Creating a Community of Inquiry.* London: Wiley, 1976.

Torbert, W. "Executive Mind, Timely Action." In S. Srivastva and Associates, *The Executive Mind: New Insights on Managerial Thought and Action.* San Francisco: Jossey-Bass, 1983.

Torbert, W. *Managing the Corporate Dream: Restructuring for Long-Term Success.* Homewood, Ill.: Dow Jones-Irwin, 1987.

Toynbee, A. *A Study of History.* New York: American Heritage Press, 1972.

Traub, J. "Into the Mouths of Babes." *New York Times Magazine,* July 24, 1988, p. 18.

Trist, E. "New Directions of Hope." John Madge Memorial Lecture, Glasgow University, Glasgow, Scotland, Nov. 1978.

Trist, E. "Referent Organizations and the Development of Interorganizational Domains." *Human Relations,* 1983, *36,* 269–284.

Trist, E. "Quality of Working Life and Community Development: Some Reflections on the Jamestown Experience." *Journal of Behavioral Science,* 1986, *22,* 223–237.

Tuan, Y. *Segmented Worlds and Self.* Minneapolis: University of Minnesota Press.

Tuchman, B. *The March of Folly: From Troy to Vietnam.* New York: Ballantine Books, 1984.

Tyler, T. "Conditions Leading to Value-Expressive Effects in Judgment of Procedural Justice: A Test of Four Models." *Journal of Personality and Social Psychology,* 1987, *52,* 333–344.

Tyler, T. *Why People Obey the Law: Procedural Justice, Legitimacy, and Compliance.* New Haven, Conn.: Yale University Press, 1988.

Tyler, T., and Bies, R. "Beyond Formal Procedures: The Interpersonal Context of Procedural Justice." In J. Carroll (ed.), *Advances in Applied Social Psychology: Business Settings.* Hillsdale, N.J.: Erlbaum, 1988.

Tyler, T., and Folger, R. "Distributional and Procedural Aspects of Satisfaction with Citizen-Police Encounters." *Basic and Applied Social Psychology,* 1980, *1,* 281–292.

Tyler, T., Rasinski, K., and Spodick, N. "The Influence of Voice on Satisfaction with Leaders: Exploring the Meaning of Process Control." *Journal of Personality and Social Psychology,* 1985, *48,* 7281.

Unamuno, M. de. *The Tragic Sense of Life.* New York: Dover Publications, 1954. (Originally published 1921.)

Unger, R. *Social Theory: Its Situation and Its Task.* New York: Cambridge University Press, 1987.

Uttal, B. "The Fall of Steve Jobs: Behind the Scenes at Apple Computer." *Fortune,* 1985, *112* (3), 20–24.

References

Vaill, P. "The Purposing of High Performing Systems." *Organizational Dynamics*, 1982, *11*, 23-39.

Vaill, P. "Integrating the Diverse Directions of the Behavioral Sciences." In R. Tannenbaum, N. Margulies, F. Massarik, and Associates, *Human Systems Development: New Perspectives on People and Organizations.* San Francisco: Jossey-Bass, 1985.

Vaill, P. *Managing as a Performing Art: New Ideas for a World of Chaotic Change.* San Francisco: Jossey-Bass, 1989.

Van de Ven, A. "On the Nature, Formation, and Maintenance of Relations Among Organizations." *Academy of Management Review*, 1976, *4*, 24-36.

Vickers, G. *The Art of Judgment: A Study of Policy Making.* New York: Basic Books, 1965.

Vickers, G. *Towards a Sociology of Management.* New York: Basic Books, 1967.

Vickers, G. *Value Systems and Social Process.* New York: Basic Books, 1968.

Vickers, G. *Freedom in a Rocking Boat.* New York: Penguin, 1972.

Wald, G. "Cosmology of Life and Mind." *Los Alamos Science*, 1988, *16*, 21-29.

Warren, R. "The Interorganizational Field as a Focus for Investigation." *Administrative Science Quarterly*, 1967, *12*, 396-419.

Watson, D., and Clark, L. "Negative Affectivity: The Disposition to Experience Aversive Emotional States." *Psychological Bulletin*, 1984, *96*, 465-490.

Watzlawick, P., Helmick-Beavin, J., and Jackson, D. *Une Logique de la communication.* Paris: Seuil, 1972.

Weber, M. *From Max Weber: Essays in Sociology.* New York: Oxford University Press, 1953.

Weber, M. *The Protestant Work Ethic and the Spirit of Capitalism.* New York: Academic Press, 1958.

Weick, K. *The Social Psychology of Organizing.* Reading, Mass.: Addison-Wesley, 1969.

Weick, K. "Managerial Thought in the Context of Action." In S. Srivastva and Associates, *The Executive Mind: New Insights on Managerial Thought and Action.* San Francisco: Jossey-Bass, 1983.

Weick, K. "Small Wins: Redefining the Scale of Social Problems." *American Psychologist*, 1984, *39* (1), 40-49.

Weinstein, R. "Reading Group Membership in First Grade: Teacher Behaviors and Pupil Experience Over Time." *Journal of Educational Psychology,* 1976, *68,* 103–116.

Weldon, E., and Gargano, G. "Cognitive Effort in Additive Task Groups: The Effects of Shared Responsibility on the Quality of Multi-Attribute Judgments." *Organizational Behavior and Human Performance,* 1989.

Weldon, E., and Mustari, E. "Felt Dispensability in Groups of Co-Actors: The Effects of Shared Responsibility and Explicit Anonymity on Cognitive Effort." *Organizational Behavior and Human Decision Processes,* 1988, *41* (3), 330–351.

Whetten, D. "Towards a Contingency Model for Designing Interorganizational Service Delivery Systems." *Organization and Administrative Sciences,* 1977, *8,* 77–96.

White, L., Tursky, B., and Schwartz, G. (eds.). *Placebos: Theory, Research, and Mechanisms.* New York: Guilford Books, 1985.

Whitehead, A. *Science and the Modern World.* New York: Free Press, 1967. (Originally published 1925.)

Whitehead, A., and Russell, B. *Principia Mathematica.* Vol. 3. Cambridge, England: Cambridge University Press, 1910.

Wieman, H. *Religious Experience and Scientific Method.* Carbondale: Southern Illinois University Press, 1926.

Wilbur, K. *No Boundary: Eastern and Western Approaches to Personal Growth.* Boston: Shambhala, 1979.

Williams, M. *The Velveteen Rabbit.* New York: Holt, Rinehart & Winston, 1983.

Williams, T. "The Search Conference in Active Adaptive Planning." *Journal of Applied Behavioral Science,* 1980, *16,* 470–483.

Williamson, O. *Markets and Hierarchies: Analysis and Antitrust Implications.* New York: Free Press, 1975.

Williamson, O. *The Economic Institutions of Capitalism: Firms, Markets, Relational Contracting.* New York: Free Press, 1985.

Wilson, E. *On Human Nature.* Cambridge, Mass.: Harvard University Press, 1978.

Winter, D. *The Power Motive.* New York: Free Press, 1973.

Wise, P. "Penny Wise Column." *Vancouver Sun,* Dec. 12, 1973, p. 81.

Wittgenstein, L. *Philosophical Investigations.* New York: Macmillan, 1963.

References

Wolman, C., and Frank, H. "The Saleswoman in a Professional Peer Group." *American Journal of Orthopsychiatry*, 1975, *45*, 171–174.

Worchel, S., Cooper, J., and Goethals, G. *Understanding Social Psychology.* Chicago: Dorsey Press, 1988.

Wright, B. (ed.). *The Federalist.* Cambridge, Mass.: Harvard University Press, 1961.

Zaleznik, A., Kets de Vries, M., and Howard, J. "Stress Reactions in Organizations: Syndromes, Causes, and Consequences." *Behavioral Science*, 1977, *22*.

Index

A

Accountability, 22-23, 257-286
  appreciative dimensions of, 280-285
  in appreciative organization, 394
  defined, 258, 267, 268
  issues and processes concerned with, 257-258
  responsibility vs., 267-268
  socially desirable behavior and, 275-278
Accountability model constructs, 258, 260-279
  accountability, 267-270, 273-278
  connections between, 270-279
  event, 261-262
  felt responsibility, 265-267, 270-273
  responsibility, 262-265, 270-275
Acquisitions. *See* Takeovers, corporate
Action
  orientation to, 83, 87-88
  positive, and positive imagery, 93-94, 97-114
  in Practice, 295-296, 301
  in Principle, 294-295, 300-301
  Strategic, 296-297, 299-300, 312
  See also Appreciative action
Action-sets. *See* Transorganizational systems
Adler, A., 159
Affect, 153-174
  modernism and, 159-168
  postmodernism and, 168-174
  romanticism and, 156-159, 162-168
Affirmative theory of organization, 114-125
Alignment
  as internal regulating process, 87-88
  as process of appreciative action, 311-312
Alliances. *See* Transorganizational systems
Alpha Corporation, 56-57, 63, 64, 65-67, 71-74, 78-80
Altruism, 21, 106-107, 158, 164, 228-256
  in daily life, 229-230
  egotism vs., 245-247
  examples of, 228-229, 248-250
  in management research, 230
  meaning in organizational contexts, 241-247
  moral, 246-247
  mutual, 246
  need for, 230, 238-241
  predisposing conditions and, 250-252
  promotion of, 250-254
  reasons for existing attitudes toward, 231-238
  situational conditions and, 252-254
  utilitarian, 246
Antitrust laws, 208
Anton, Ronald J., 22-23, 257-286
Apathetic egotism, 245-246
Apple Computer, 299-300, 305, 312
Appraisal, in appreciative leadership, 59, 60

523

Appreciation
  cultural, stages of, 127-129
  romanticism and, 156-159, 162-168
  transorganizational, 210-214
  See also Executive appreciation
Appreciative action, 23-29, 289-322
  in archetypes, 313-316
  dimensions of, 25
  hazards blocking, 290-292
  meaning of, 290
  in Practice, 295-296, 301
  in Principle, 294-295, 300-301
  processes of, 302-313
    alignment, 311-312
    astuteness, 307-311
    awareness, 304-307
  script for, 292-294
  in sociohistorical context, 316-321
  Strategic, 296-297, 299-300, 312
  trinity of, 294-302
  values and, 300-302
Appreciative capability, 58-60, 89-90
Appreciative inquiry, 45
Appreciative interchange, 15-23, 175-204
  development of cooperation and, 188-192
  inclusive vs. exclusive decision making and, 192-196
  management education and, 199-202
  prisoner's dilemma and, 182-185
  salaries and, 189-190
  traditional employer-employee relations and, 176-182
  "yes/and" perspective and, 19, 185-187
Appreciative knowing, 10-15
Appreciative management, 353-380
  dialectical approach and, 355, 356-357
  hypermodern organization and, 362-365
  mediation processes and, 355, 361-362
  professionalization and, 356, 368-369
  professional stress and, 356, 369-379
  research on organizational power and, 355, 357-361
  unconscious processes and, 356, 365-368
Appreciative organizing, 29, 381-400
Appreciative setting, 61-63
Appreciative system, origin of, 39
Aram, John D., 18-19, 175-204
Archetypes, of executive leaders, 313-316
Arendt, Hannah, 179-180, 385, 391

Aries, E., 130, 133, 137
Aristotle, 94
Association habit, 223
Astuteness, as process of appreciative action, 307-311
Attention
  in appreciative leadership, 59-60
  in corporate takeovers, 63-65
Attunement, 87-88
Autonomy, and rules, 358, 360
Awareness, as process of appreciative action, 304-307
Axelrod, Robert, 188-191, 203

B

Bakan, David, 239
Barrett, Frank J., 29, 381-400
Barrett, William, 346
Becker, Ernest, 112
Beech Nut apple juice scandal, 300
Behavior
  accountability and, 275-278
  altruistic vs. egotistical, 245-247
  constructionism and, 155-156
  executive
    context for, 37-54
    in crises, 57-58, 64-88
  felt responsibility and, 273
  organizational
    affect and, 167-168
    values and, 26-28
  rational, capacity for, 274
  of women executives, 142-146
Bellah, Robert, 23, 281
Bentham, Jeremy, 233
Berlin, Isaiah, 121-122
Berman, Morris, 44
Blacks
  exclusivity and, 193
  in organizational culture, 144-146
Boulding, Kenneth, 95
Boundary management, 341
Bronfman, Samuel, 228
Bunker, Barbara Benedict, 10, 14-15, 126-149
Bureaucracy, vs. transorganizational systems, 209, 212
Burlingame, Martin, 56-57, 63, 64, 65-67, 71-74, 78-80, 82-84, 85-86, 87
Business alliances. *See* Transorganizational systems

Index

C

Cadbury, Adrian, 301
Cambridge meeting, 74-77
Capability, appreciative, 58-60
Capra, Fritjof, 302
Carter, John, 133, 148
Case history, of professional stress, 369-374
Centering, in present moment, 349-352
Children, labor laws concerning, 177-178
Chile, privileged class in, 193
Christianity, partnership model of society in, 319
Churchill, Winston, 121-122, 345
Cleveland, Harlan, 345
Climate, organizational, 253-254
Coase, Ronald, 200
Cognitive dissonance, 273
Collaboration
 in organizational culture, 131-132, 133, 148
 transorganizational systems and, 212-213
 See also Transorganizational systems
Committed listening, 395-396
"Commons Dilemma," 239
Compassionate consciousness, 12, 43
Competition
 altruism vs., 231-232
 in female group culture, 138-139
 in male group culture, 131-132
 in mixed-sex culture, 148
 transorganizational systems and, 212-213
Conflict, avoidance of, 354, 355, 359, 364, 375
Conger, Jay A., 21-22, 228-256
Consciousness
 brain model of, 92-93
 as causal reality, 46-47
 compassionate, 12, 43
 scientific understanding of, 49-51, 53
Consciousness revolution, 92
Consortia. *See* Transorganizational systems
Constructionism, 154-156
Contract, freedom of, 177
Cooperation, development of, 188-192
Cooperrider, David L., 1-33, 61, 91-125
Coppage v. *Kansas,* 177
Corporate takeovers. *See* Takeovers, corporate

Cousins, Norman, 98-99
Creativity
 appreciative organizing and, 392-393
 executive fostering of, 307
Crisis management, 55-90
 creating structure in, 71-77
 examples of leadership in, 65-88
 executive appreciation and, 82-90
 executive conduct in crisis, 57-58, 64-65
Critique of Cynical Reason (Sloterdijk), 108, 110
Culture
 altruism and, 237-238, 255-256
 assumptions underlying, 126-127
 clash in takeovers, 77-78
 concept of self and, 237-238
 new, appreciation of, 127-129
 organizational, 129-149
  collaboration in, 131-132, 133, 148
  competition in, 131-132, 138-139, 148
  executive appreciation and, 139-146
  female, 133-136
  formation of, 129-130
  male, 130-133
  mixed sex, 136-149
  race and, 144-146
 positive image and, 110-112
 process of enculturation, 40-41
 worldviews and, 83
Cummings, Larry L., 22-23, 257-286
Cummings, Thomas G., 19-21, 205-227
Cynicism, 7-8

D

Darwin, Charles, 179
DC Corporation, 55-56, 63, 64, 67-70, 74-77, 78, 80-82, 84-85, 86, 88
Decision making
 in corporate takeovers, 70-71
 inclusive vs. exclusive, 192-196
Defection option, 200
De-ideologization, 372, 376
Dialectical approach to social reality, 355, 356-357
Dialogue, internal, 107-110
Disease, and negative affect, 104-106
Disillusion, 376-377
Douglas, Mary, 165
Duality of Human Existence, The (Bakan), 239

Due process, economic, 178
Dukes, Nancy, 178
Dunlop Holdings, 195
DuPont Canada, 228

E

Economic due process, 178
Eddy, Janice, 144
Education, of management, 199-202, 230
Egalitarianism
 appreciative inquiry and, 316
 in female group culture, 133-134
 in prehistory, 318-320
Egotism, 245-246
Egri, Carolyn P., 24, 25-26, 289-322
Einstein, Albert, 95
Eisler, R., 318-319
Emotional scenarios, 166, 174
Emotions. *See* Affect
Employees
 monitoring of, 200-201
 payoffs of, 189-190
 personnel policies and, 361
 shirking by, 200-201
 spiritual development of. *See* Spiritual development
 traditional relations with employers, 176-182
Employer-employee relations
 salaries and, 189-190
 terminology and, 388-390
 traditional, 176-182
Enculturation, 40-41
End values, 250-251
Esoteric religion, 50
Ethics
 executive action and, 300-302
 training in, 230
Evaluation, in appreciative leadership, 59, 60
Exclusivity, 192-196
Executive action. *See* Appreciative action
Executive appreciation
 bases for understanding, 30-33
 importance of, 11-12
 as language of understanding, 17-18
 postmodernism and, 171-174
Executive behavior
 context for, 37-54
 in crises, 57-58, 64-88
Executives
 appreciative capability of, 58-60, 89-90
 archetypes of, 313-316
 astuteness of, 307-311
 awareness level of, 304-307
 effects of takeovers on, 55-57, 64-65
 function in creating transorganizational systems, 214-221
 personal characteristics of, 223-225, 226
 role in fostering creativity, 307
 salaries of, 189-190
 skills of, 222-223, 226
 Statesman Myth and, 330-332
 technical knowledge of, 305-306
 transorganizational systems, 221-225, 226
 values of, 330-332
 See also Management
Experience, orientation to, 83, 86-87

F

Faith, 335-336, 339
Families, spiritual, 342-343
Federalist, The, 178
Feedback, 300, 307
Fellowship, in spiritual development, 342-344
Felt responsibility, 258, 265-267, 270-273
Follett, Mary Parker, 114, 202
Forestructures, anticipatory, 14
Freedom of contract doctrine, 177-178
"Free fall" concept, 24
Friedman, Milton, 233
Friendship, 158, 173
Frost, Peter J., 24, 25-26, 289-322
Fry, Ronald E., 1-33

G

Gardner, John W., 305
Garment, Suzanne, 193
Garreau, J., 126
Gawain, Shakti, 306
Gender differences, and organizational culture, 130-139, 147-149
 See also Women
General Motors Corp., 308
Gergen, Kenneth J., 16-18, 153-174
Gergen, Mary, 165-166
Gestalt psychology, 350
Gilligan, Carol, 159

Index

"Glass ceiling," 139-146
Global mind change
   executive appreciation and, 11
   as postmodern theme, 5-6
Gnostic Gospels, 319
Golf My Way (Nicklaus), 113-114
GrandCo, 55-56, 63, 64, 67-70, 74-77, 80-82, 85, 86, 88
Grieving meeting, 67-68
Groupthink, 70, 179

H

Habits of the Heart (Bellah), 281
Hammer v. *Dagenhart*, 177-178
Hardin, Garrett, 184, 194
Harman, Willis W., 10, 11-12, 37-54, 95, 119
Healer archetype of executive leader, 313
Hedonistic egotism, 245
Heidegger, M., 97, 382
Heliotropic movement, 117-118
Helplessness, learned, 104-107
Heresy, new, 53
Heyerdahl, Thor, 345
Historical perspectives
   appreciative action in sociohistorical context, 316-321
   historic peculiarity of Western science, 40-49
Holding environment, 391, 396
Holism, 43-44, 45-46, 348-349
Human beings
   environment and, 161
   interaction between social and psychological levels of, 355, 356-357
   mechanical view of, 160-162
   moral development of, 250-252
   predictability of, 161-162
   Pygmalion dynamic in, 100-104
   social construction of, 154-156
   socialization of, 161
   unconscious processes and, 356, 365-368
   view of, 83, 84-86
   See also Self
Human Options (Cousins), 99
Human resources, and executive action technique, 294
"Hurry sickness," 350-351
   See also Workaholism
Huxley, Aldoux, 50
Hypermodern era, 363

Hypermodern organization, 28-29
   appreciative management and, 355, 362-365
   mediation processes in, 362

I

Idealization, 375
Ideologization, 372, 375
Illusion, 376
Imagery, positive, 94-114
   culture and, 110-112
   internal dialogue and, 107-110
   learned helplessness and, 104-107
   in medicine, 98-100
   metacognition and, 113-114
   physiological effects of, 96-97
   positive action and, 93-94, 97-114
   Pygmalion dynamic and, 100-104
Immune functioning, and positive imagery, 106-107
Incongruence, 329
Individualism, 21-22, 234-236, 238-240
   self-contained, 21-22
   social and economic freedom and, 179-180
Information economics, 200-201
Inquiry, appreciative, 45
Institutional life, managerial implications of, 187-196
Integrity, 270
Interchange. *See* Appreciative interchange
Interconnection, ecology of, 3-4
Interdependency
   autonomy vs., 211-212
   management of, 175-176
   among organizations, 211-212
   prisoner's dilemma and, 182-185
Internal dialogue, 107-110
Interorganizational domains. *See* Transorganizational systems
Interorganizational systems. *See* Transorganizational systems
Isen, Alice, 106

J

James, William, 18, 91, 107, 119
Jantsch, Erich, 95
Japanese business practices
   appreciative interchange and, 190, 195
   concept of self and, 237
Jobs, Steven, 299-300, 305, 312

Johnson, Lyndon Baines, 298-299
Joint ventures. *See* Transorganizational systems
Joyce, James, 124
Jung, C. G., 304
Just in Time Scheduling, 294

K

Kanungo, Rabindra N., 21-22, 228-256
Katz, Robert, 294
Keats, John, 158
Kennedy, John F., 383, 391
King, Martin Luther, Jr., 96
Krishnamurti, J., 302-303
Kundera, Milan, 395
Kurgan culture, 319

L

Labor laws, traditional, 177-178
Lamilie Associates, 55
Language of appreciation, 16-18
Lawrence of Arabia, 323
Leader-coordinators, 222
Leadership
  appreciative, 58-60, 65-67
  archetypes of, 313-316
  examples of, in takeovers, 65-88
  spiritual condition and, 332-336
  transformative, 307-308
  of transorganizational systems, 220-221, 226
Learned helplessness, 104-107
Leavitt, Harold, 294
Levitt, Theodore, 232
Listening, commitment to, 395-396
Living value system, 6, 27-28
Lochner v. New York, 177
Love, 155, 157-159, 162, 395

M

McClelland, David, 106-107, 240
McClintock, Barbara, 44
Maccoby, Eleanor, 135
McGill University, 228
McGregor, Douglas, 196
Macrodeterminism, 92
Madison, James, 178, 192
Magician archetype of executive leader, 313, 314-316, 321-322
Management
  definitions of, 37
  education of, 199-202, 230
  salaries of, 189-190
  women in, 139-149
  See also Appreciative management; Executives
Management by Objectives (MBO), 295
Marks, Mitchell, 63, 66-67, 78
Marxism, 357, 362
Maslow, Abraham, 230
Mechanical self, 160-162
Mediation process, 355, 361-362
Medicine
  negative imagery and, 104-106
  positive imagery and, 98-100, 106-107
Medieval view of reality, 51-52
Megacities, 3-4
Men
  group culture of, 130-133
  in mixed-sex culture, 136-149
Mens rea, 274
Mentalist paradigm, 92
Merger Coordination Council, 71, 73
Mergers. *See* Takeovers, corporate
Metacognition, 113-114
Metaphysics, 45, 47-54
Mintzberg, H., 306
Mirvis, Philip H., 10, 12-13, 55-90
Mission, 325-330
Mission statements, 328
Mitroff, I., 159
Models
  brain model of consciousness, 92-93
  partnership model of human society, 318-319
  production planning, 294
  of professional stress, 374-379
Modernism, and appreciation, 159-168
Moral altruism, 246-247
Moral development, and altruism, 250-252
More, Thomas, 112
Morris, William, 292
Multiplicity of perspectives, 4-5, 168-170
Murray, Edward, 95
Mutual adjustment, in transorganizational systems, 212
Mutual altruism, 246

N

"Narcissistic exploitation," 371-372
National Collaborative Research Act (1984), 208-209

Negative affect, and disease, 104-106
Networkers, 222
Network organizations. *See* Transorganizational systems
Newco, 71-74, 86-88
NeXt Inc., 300
Nicklaus, Jack, 113-114
Nine Nations of North America (Garreau), 126

O

Objectivist assumption, of Western science, 41, 43-45
Oceana (Harrington), 112
Olson, Mancur, 191-192
Omega Corporation, 56-57, 63, 64, 65-67, 71-74, 78-80
Openness, 392-393
Open value system, 340-342
Optimism, vs. cynicism, 7-8
Orange, Richard, 144
O'Regan, Brendan, 107
Organization
  affirmative theory of, 114-125
  hypermodern, 355, 362-365
  view of, 82-84
Organizational climate, and altruism, 253-254
Organizational culture, 129-149
  collaboration in, 131-132, 133, 148
  competition in, 131-132, 138-139, 148
  executive appreciation and, 139-146
  female, 133-136
  formation of, 129-130
  male, 130-133
  mixed sex, 136-149
  race and, 144-146
Organizational power, research on, 355, 357-361
Organizing, appreciative, 29, 381-400

P

Pagès, Max, 10, 24, 28-29, 353-380
Paranormal, and science, 42
Participation, vs. objectivism in science, 43-45, 48
Partnership model of human society, 318-319
Passionate reason, 338-340
Pathology, multidimensional causes of, 378-379
Payoffs, employees vs. management, 189-190

Perennial Philosophy, The (Huxley), 50
Perennial wisdom, 50, 53
Performance development, 389
Personal characteristics, of transorganizational systems executives, 223-225, 226
Personnel policies, 360-361
Perspectives, multiplicity of, 4-5, 168-170
PERT, 294
Petersdorf, Robert, 238
Physiology
  negative imagery and, 104-106
  positive imagery and, 96-97, 106-107
Placebo response, 98-100
Planetization, 3-4
Plato, 91, 107, 112
Play, serious, 173-174
Polak, Fred, 111-112
Politeia (Plato), 112
Political activity, 308-311
Popper, Karl, 45, 47, 338
Positive imagery. *See* Imagery, positive
Positivist assumption, of Western science, 41, 46-47
Postmodernism, 168-174
  executive appreciation and, 171-174
  themes of, 3-9
Power
  executive astuteness and, 308-311
  organizational, research on, 355, 357-361
  of words, 388-390
Prayer, 345-348
Present moment, centering in, 349-352
Prisoner's dilemma, 182-185, 191
Problem finding and problem solving, 70-71
Production planning models, 294
Professionalization, 356, 368-369, 377-378
Professional stress, 356, 369-379
Promises, expansive, 390-392
Protestant work ethic, 291, 317-318
Psychoanalysis, 357
Purpose, need for, 387-388
Purposing, 325-326
Pygmalion dynamic, 100-104

R

Race
  exclusivity and, 193
  organizational culture and, 144-146

Radhakrishnan, Sarvepalli, 50
Reality
  conflicting pictures of, 38-39
  modern vs. medieval view of, 51-52
  social, dialectical approach to, 355, 356-357
Reason, passionate, 338-340
Reductionist assumption, of Western science, 41, 45-46
Reflectivity, 267
Religion, 50
Religous Experience and Scientific Method (Wieman), 119-120
Research, on organizational power, 355, 357-361
Responsibility
  acceptance of, 264-265, 266
  in accountability model, 262-265, 270-275
  in appreciative organization, 393-394
  defined, 258, 262-263
  felt, 258, 265-267, 270-273
Reticulists, 222
Richardson, A., 96-97
Richardson, Lester, 55-56, 63, 66-70, 74-77, 78, 80-82, 84-85, 86
Ritz-Carlton Hotel, 228
Roethlisberger, F., 350
Rogers, Carl, 159, 306, 329, 354
Role acceptance, 264-265
Romanticism, and appreciation, 156-159, 162-168
Roosevelt, Franklin, 178
Rules, system of, 358-361

S

Salaries, of employees vs. management, 189-190
Sampson, Edward, 234
Scheler, Max, 267
Schwartz, Robert, 107-108, 109
Science
  as definer of reality, 38-39, 51-54
  human, 45, 46
  life, 45, 46
  physical, 45, 46
  spiritual, 45, 47-54
  Western. *See* Western science
Sculley, John, 299, 305, 312
Seagram Corp., 228
Search conferences, 218

Self
  concept in various cultures, 237-238
  mechanical, 160-162
  as relationships, 163-167
  virtual, 170
Self-contained individualism, 21-22, 234-236
Self-destructive egotism, 246
Self-image, and Pygmalion dynamic, 100-104
Selfishness, in business, 231-238
Separation anxiety, 356, 366
Serious play, 173-174
Setting, appreciative, 61-63
Shirking, 200-201
Shotter, John, 165, 262, 268
Siegan, B., 178-179
Sieyès, Abbé, 112
Singer, Isaac Bashevis, 346
Skills, of transorganizational systems executives, 222-223, 226
Skolimowski, Henryk, 43
Sloterdijk, Peter, 108, 110
Smith, Adam, 233
Smith, Roger, 308
Social action systems. *See* Transorganizational systems
Social construction
  of organizational reality, 196-198
  of person, 154-156
Social Darwinism, 178
Social helpfulness, 106
Socialization
  altruism and, 229-230
  mechanical self and, 161
Social promise, 390
Social theory, postmodern, 6-7
Society, possible transfiguration of, 51-54
"Society of solicitude," 364
Socrates, 107
Sommers, Albert, 199
South Africa, exclusivity in, 193
Spence, J., 234, 235, 236
Sperry, Roger, 11, 47, 92
Spirit, defining, 333-334
Spiritual condition
  dispiriting phenomena and, 335-336
  of leaders, 332-336
Spiritual development, 27-28, 323-352
  avenues of, 336-352
  centering in present moment, 349-352

Index

fellowship, 342-344
holism, 348-349
new values, 337-338
new vocabulary and grammar of spirituality, 344-348
open value system, 340-342
passionate reason, 338-340
mission and, 325-330
prayer and, 345-348
Statesman Myth and, 330-332
vision and, 325-330
Spiritual families, 342-343
Spirituality, new vocabulary and grammar of, 344-348
Spiritual kinship, 343
Spiritual sciences, 45, 47-54
Spiritual traditions, esoteric vs. exoteric, 50
Srivastva, Suresh, 1-33, 61, 381-400
Stakeholders of the Organizational Mind (Mitroff), 159
Statesman Myth, 330-332
Strategic Action, 296-297, 299-300, 312
Stress, professional, 356, 369-379
case history of, 369-374
disillusion and, 376-377
illusion and, 376
tentative model of, 374-379
Sullivan, Harry Stack, 97
Sumitomo Rubber Industries, 195
Superego, 251
Superlearning (Ostrander), 113
Swift, Jonathan, 315
Sympathy, 158

T

Takeovers, corporate, 12-13, 55-90
clash of cultures in, 77-78
creating structure during, 71-77
decision making in, 70-71
effect on executives, 55-57, 64-65
examples of leadership in, 65-88
grieving meetings during, 67-68
task forces in, 72
Tao Te Ching, 351
Task force, in corporate takeover, 72
Technique, of executive action, 294-295, 300-301
Technological imperative, 52
Teleological questions, and science, 48
Terminology, effect of, 388-390

Thoughts on Various Subjects (Swift), 315
Tillich, Paul, 387
Toynbee, Arnold, 2, 10
"Tragedy of commons," 239
Transaction cost, 200
Transformative leadership, 307-308
Transorganizational appreciations, 210-214, 226
collaboration vs. competition, 212-213
interdependence vs. autonomy, 211-212
mutual adjustment vs. hierarchical control, 212
Transorganizational systems (TSs), 19-21, 205-227
advantages of, 208
barriers to, 208-209
bureaucracy and, 209, 212
cost vs. benefits of, 218-219
defined, 206
executives in
functions in development, 214-221
skills and characteristics of, 221-225, 226
interdependence vs. autonomy and, 211-212
leadership of, 220-221, 226
purpose of, 217-218
stages in development of, 215-221
convening members, 217-219
identifying potential members, 215-217
organizing members, 219-221
Trinity of executive action, 294-302
Trust, in male group culture, 133
TSs. *See* Transorganizational systems
Tuchman, Barbara, 186, 198

U

Unconscious processes, 356, 365-368
Unger, Roberto, 6-7
Unico, 63, 78-80, 85, 88
Unions, 177
U.S. Supreme Court, 176-179
Utilitarian altruism, 246
Utopia (More), 112

V

Vaill, Peter D., 10, 24, 26-28, 323-352
Value groundings, 326-327

Values
  changes in, 5-6
  end, 250-251
  executive action and, 300-302
  of executives, 330-332
  new, 337-338
  organizational behavior and, 26-28
  Protestant work ethic, 291, 317-318
  revaluation and, 11
  Statesman Myth and, 330-332
  See also Spiritual development
Value system
  living, 6, 27-28
  open, 340-342
Valuing
  appreciation and, 14
  commitment to, 394
van Gogh, Vincent, 122-123
Velveteen Rabbit, The (Williams), 128
Vickers, Geoffrey, 20, 23-24, 58, 61-62, 69, 382-383
Vindictive egotism, 246
Virtual self, 170
Vision, 299, 325-330
Vitality, 326
Vivekananda, Swami, 50
Vocabulary of understanding, 16-18

W

Wald, George, 49
Walesa, Lech, 25, 314
Warrior archetype of executive leader, 313
Weber, Max, 317
Western science, 40-54
  assumptions of, 41, 43-49
  consciousness as causal reality, 46-47
  holism, 45-46
  objectivism, 41, 43-45
  participation, 43-45, 48
  positivism, 41, 46-47
  reductionism, 41, 45-46
  historic peculiarity of, 40-49
  paranormal and, 42
  restructuring of, 41-49
Wieman, Henry, 119-120
Williams, M., 128
Williamson, Oliver, 200
Women
  "glass ceiling" and, 139-146
  group culture of, 133-136
  in mixed-sex culture, 136-149
  in postmodern corporations, 5
Women's movement, 136
Words, power of, 388-390
Workaholism, 291, 350-351
Work ethic, 291, 317-318
Worldviews
  comparison of, 83
  crisis management and, 89

Y

"Yes/and" perspective, 19, 185-187, 317